This is a clear and comprehensive approach to crime prevention. The focus of the book is applied and practical, which makes it ideal for the classroom. The new edition provides an excellent in-depth coverage of what works in crime prevention, and how prevention programs are evaluated to assess their impact on crime and fear of victimization. It is an essential resource for both students and practitioners.

Jonathan Kremser,
Kutztown University

This book, in comparison to others I have seen, offers the widest coverage regarding the different possible approaches to crime prevention—it addresses strategies as diverse as environmental design, block-watch initiatives, media-driven public service announcements, community-oriented policing, correctional rehabilitation, and many, many more. As such, it provides students with the foundation for an impressive breadth of knowledge regarding crime prevention.

Pamela Wilcox,
University of Cincinnati

I have used Professor Lab's text on crime prevention and found that his crime prevention typology is great for the classroom. Grouping tactics by primary, secondary, and tertiary prevention allows students to really think about some of the underlying factors driving these crimes and gives them some basis for critiquing the initial efficacy of a program. This text is great for students and professionals alike.

Eric Martin,
George Washington University

CRIME PREVENTION

Crime Prevention: Approaches, Practices, and Evaluations, Ninth Edition, meets the needs of students and instructors for engaging, evidence-based, impartial coverage of the origins of crime, as well as of public policy that can reduce or prevent deviance. The book examines a range of approaches to preventing crime and elucidates their respective goals. Strategies include primary prevention measures designed to prevent conditions that foster deviance; secondary prevention measures directed toward persons or conditions with a high potential for deviance; and tertiary prevention measures to deal with persons who have already committed crimes.

This edition provides research and information on all aspects of crime prevention, including the physical environment and crime, neighborhood crime prevention programs, community policing, crime in schools, and electronic monitoring and home confinement. Lab offers a thorough and well-rounded discussion of the many sides of the crime prevention debate, in clear and accessible language.

Steven P. Lab is Professor of Criminal Justice and Chair of the Department of Human Services. He holds a Ph.D. in Criminology from the Florida State University School of Criminology and Criminal Justice. Dr. Lab is the author or coauthor of five books, the editor/coeditor of two readers, and coeditor of one encyclopedia. He is the author of more than 50 articles or book chapters and has presented more than 70 papers to academic or professional societies. He is a past editor of the *Journal of Crime and Justice* and has been an assistant editor or on the editorial boards of several additional journals. Dr. Lab has been a Visiting Professor at the Jill Dando Institute of Crime Science of University College London and at Keele University in Staffordshire, England, as well as a Visiting Fellow at Loughborough University (England) and a Research Consultant with the Perpetuity Research Group at Leicester University (England). Dr. Lab has received grant funding for several large research projects from the National Institute of Justice, and has served as a consultant to the Ohio Attorney General's Office, the Arizona Governor's Office, and various offices of the U.S. Department of Justice. Dr. Lab is also a past-president of the Academy of Criminal Justice Sciences.

A range of further resources for this book are available on the Companion Website:
www.routledge.com/cw/lab

CRIME PREVENTION

Approaches, Practices, and Evaluations

NINTH EDITION

STEVEN P. LAB

Routledge
Taylor & Francis Group

NEW YORK AND LONDON

First published 2016
by Routledge
711 Third Avenue, New York, NY 10017

and by Routledge
2 Park Square, Milton Park, Abingdon, Oxon, OX14 4RN

Routledge is an imprint of the Taylor & Francis Group, an informa business

Library of Congress Cataloging in Publication Data
Lab, Steven P.
    Crime prevention : approaches, practices, and evaluations/
Steven P. Lab. -- Ninth Edition.
    pages cm
    Revised edition of the author's Crime prevention, 2014.
    Includes bibliographical references and index.
    ISBN 978-1-138-94693-4 (hardback : alk. paper) --
    ISBN 978-0-323-35772-2 (pbk. : alk. paper) 1. Crime prevention--
United States. 2. Crime prevention--United States--Evaluation. I. Title.
    HV7431.L33 2016
    364.40973--dc23
    2015030160

ISBN: 978-1-138-94693-4 (hbk)
ISBN: 978-0-323-35772-2 (pbk)
ISBN: 978-1-315-71276-5 (ebk)

Typeset in Adobe Garamond Pro
by Servis Filmsetting Ltd, Stockport, Cheshire

Printed and bound in the United States of America by Sheridan

To Danielle

CONTENTS

PREFACE TO THE NINTH EDITION

This ninth edition of *Crime Prevention: Approaches, Practices, and Evaluations* carries forth the successful format developed over the previous eight editions. While there are many different ways to approach the field of crime prevention, the feedback I have received over the years from a wide range of individuals has consistently pointed out that the format of the text lays a nice pedagogical outline for the academic study of crime prevention. Consequently, I have endeavored to stay true to the approach in the book while simultaneously adding emerging new ideas and prevention initiatives to the discussion. The general organization of the book remains the same following the public health prevention model of primary, secondary, and tertiary prevention. Adding more recent materials does not always result in a clean, clear division of prevention into the basic public health model. Many of the topics bridge across the three components. Two easy examples are in discussion of physical design and prevention aimed at high-risk individuals/situations. Physical design is a cornerstone of primary prevention, particularly Crime Prevention Through Environmental Design, and also appears in many situational prevention activities, most notably product design for high-emerging items. Prevention that seeks to target high-risk individuals/situations fits both in secondary prevention activities (that by definition target risk) and tertiary prevention where deterrence, incapacitation, and rehabilitation may target high-risk offenders. These facts do not detract from the presentation in the book; rather they point out the growing interest in and focus on emerging prevention techniques.

The field of academic crime prevention continues to see major advances. These changes cover the entire gamut of prevention, from physical design to developmental prevention to identifying high-risk individuals to situational initiatives to partnerships and beyond. Across almost all topics it has become necessary over the years to expand the discussions to cover the many emerging programs and approaches in crime prevention, while preserving the more classic bases of crime prevention. This current edition has been modified in the following ways:

- Data on crime and crime prevention have been updated throughout the book.

- Chapter 1 has updated crime/victimization data and expanded discussion of identity theft and forms of victimization not found in official measures.

- Chapter 4 offers a new discussion of CPTED that places territoriality at the apex of initiatives for prevention activities, with surveillance, activity support, image, and other elements as components in the building of territoriality; expanded discussions of the use of CCTV; a new Third-Generation CPTED for consideration; and shifts the topic of product design to another point in the book.

- Chapter 5 offers a new logic model for neighborhood crime prevention, adds a more in-depth discussion on guardianship, and enhances the material on leveraging guardianship.

- In Chapter 6 the presentation on crime pattern theory has been reworked for clarity, and more research on displacement has been added.

- The material on mass media and prevention (Chapter 7) now includes a discussion of the use of social media both in terms of crime and crime prevention.

- Chapter 8 has added more examples of effective developmental prevention programs, including a new section on Mentoring Programs.

- The discussion on risk factors (Chapter 10) now includes materials on risk assessment instruments used at various points in criminal justice system processing.

- The Situational Prevention chapter (11) has added material on how to make prevention techniques more useful for practitioners (the 11Ds), has added a revised discussion of product design, and eliminated sections on Organized Crime and Crowd Violence (these topics can be found on the book web site).

- Chapter 12 has a new section on Hot Spot Policing, has added Civil Injunctions to the discussion of abatement, eliminated sections on Weed and Seed and Business Improvement Districts, and expanded on the discussions of PSN and gang suppression.

- Chapter 13 has a reworked discussion on drug use by offenders, including a new section on ADAM II, and presents information on the most recent incarnation of D.A.R.E.

- The schools chapter (14) has updated information on the G.R.E.A.T. program and police in schools.

- The final chapters on specific deterrence/incapacitation and rehabilitation have been updated but are largely unchanged.

ACKNOWLEDGMENTS

Over the various iterations of this book, there are many people who deserve mention and thanks for helping me along the way. First and foremost I need to thank my friends and colleagues who have supported me in numerous ways and prompted me to look at things in different ways. This group includes Bob Langworthy and John Whitehead, who have remained good friends and colleagues. Since entering the crime prevention arena, I have had the great pleasure and honor to get to know many people who have provided insight, material, and friendship—Paul and Pat Brantingham, Ron Clarke, Ralph Taylor, George Rengert, Paul Cromwell, Tim Hope, Graham Farrell, Shane Johnson, Kate Bowers, Marcus Felson, Gloria Laycock, Martin Gil, Nick Tilley, Jim LeBeau, David Farrington, Brandon Welsh, Dennis Rosenbaum, and Wes Skogan. Finally, I have to thank my editor, Ellen Boyne, who has endured the changes in publisher and continues to watch my back and make sure I don't look foolish in print. I am certain that I have missed some people who deserve to be mentioned. The fact that they know me means that they are probably aware of my penchant for forgetting names and will forgive me for the oversight. I thank you all for helping make this book a success. The errors and omissions, of course, are mine alone.

Hopefully you will find this edition helpful in your individual pursuits. Please do not hesitate to let me know what you think. It has been the feedback of many people over the years that has helped make this book a success.

S.P.L.

CHAPTER 1 Crime and the Fear of Crime

CHAPTER OUTLINE

LEARNING OBJECTIVES

After reading this chapter you should be able to:

- Identify and discuss two different measures of crime and victimization.
- Discuss the changing crime rates in the United States.
- Identify shortcomings with the UCR.
- Explain how a panel survey works.
- Discuss the NCVS and what it shows about victimization.
- Provide information on the costs of crime/victimization.
- Give a definition of fear and discuss how it manifests itself.
- Explain the differences between fear, worry, and assessments of crime.
- Discuss the levels of fear in society and how fear relates to crime and victimization.
- Define vicarious victimization.
- Provide reasons for the reported levels of fear.
- Define incivility and show how it relates to fear.

Crime remains an indisputable fact of life for many, if not most, members of modern society. This is true despite the frequent declarations that crime continues to fall and is reaching levels not seen in years. While the overall level of crime has fallen in recent years, large numbers of citizens are still victimized every year and the impact of crime on everyone in society is substantial. Beyond those who are actually victimized, many individuals are fearful of crime and victimization. That fear has consequences of its own for both individuals and our communities. Crime and fear lead most individuals to turn to the criminal justice system for help. The ability of the criminal justice system to single-handedly alleviate crime and fear in society has been seriously questioned by both proponents and opponents. Despite the claims by some that the reductions in crime since the early 1990s are due to concerted police actions, there is little reason to believe that actions of the criminal justice system are the primary (or sole) cause of the reductions. At the same time, crime and fear still impact the lives of many individuals. Society clearly needs to continue to pursue means of preventing crime and fear.

This first chapter attempts to show how crime and fear have changed over time and remain problems that need to be addressed. It is this information that forms the basis for continued calls for crime prevention actions. After examining the level and change in actual crime in society, this chapter will examine the impact of crime on victims and society. It will also examine the companion issue of fear of crime. Indeed, the "fear of crime" poses a greater, more far reaching problem for society and its members. Demonstrating a need for crime prevention is not difficult to accomplish when you consider the levels of crime and fear in society.

The Problem of Crime in Society

The magnitude of the crime problem can be evaluated using both official and victimization measures of crime. The use of official crime statistics, such as the Federal Bureau of Investigation's *Uniform Crime Reports*, provides a view of crime from the standpoint of what the formal criminal justice system must handle. Many critics argue that this provides an inaccurate and incomplete analysis of the true levels of crime in society. These individuals point to the results of victimization surveys as a basis for their argument. While each presents a different absolute level of crime, both tend to reveal similar patterns in criminal activity over time.

Official Measures of Crime

The FBI **Uniform Crime Reports (UCR)** are the most widely used and cited official measures of crime in the United States. The UCR represents the number of criminal offenses known to the police. The reported crime rate reflects only those offenses known as **Part I crimes** (violent crimes: murder, rape, robbery, and assault; property crimes: burglary, larceny, auto theft, and arson). A host of other offenses (i.e., fraud, kidnapping, and drug offenses), known as **Part II crimes**, are not included in the computations and reported crime rates. The resulting crime rates, therefore, reflect only a portion of the offenses with which the formal criminal justice system comes into contact.

According to the UCR, there were more than 9.75 million index crimes committed in 2013. Of that number, almost 1.2 million were personal crimes (murder, rape, robbery, and aggravated assault) and 8.6 million were property offenses (Federal Bureau of Investigation, 2014). This translates into 3,099 index crimes for every 100,000 people in the United States (also known as the "crime rate"). The corresponding crime rates for personal and property crime are 367.9 and 2,730.7, respectively. Conklin (2003) notes that many individuals compare these figures to those from the mid-1980s and early 1990s and trumpet the great decreases in crime. Even further, these figures are used by various groups to take credit for the decreases: police leaders claim that aggressive police tactics caused the decline, mayors have pointed to wider ranging community policies as the cause, and politicians claim that mandatory sentencing laws caused the changes (Conklin, 2003). While determining the cause of the reductions is important, it is beyond the scope of this book to attempt that task. What is more important is to place the "great reductions" in crime into context.

> ┌─ ON THE WEB ─────────────────────────
> *Detailed information on official crime numbers*
> *and rates from the UCR can be found at the FBI*
> *UCR site at http://www.fbi.gov/about-us/cjis/ucr/*
> *crime-in-the.us/2013/crime-in-the.u.s.-2013*

The trend in violent and property crime since 1962 is shown in Figures 1.1 and 1.2. Figure 1.1 illustrates that the 2013 violent crime rate has fallen almost to the levels in 1970. Thus, it is a true claim that violent crime is lower today than any time in almost 45 years. Similar claims can be made about property crime, although the reference point would be roughly 1968 (see Figure 1.2). Interestingly, all of the levels in these two figures are significantly higher than they were in the 1960s when the President's Commission on Law Enforcement and the Administration of Justice lamented the great growth in crime and the need to do something about it.

The crime rates today are significantly higher than throughout the 1960s. This is especially problematic if you consider the data for violent crimes, which are those crimes that most concern people. Figure 1.1 shows that the violent crime rate in 1962 was 162 offenses for every 100,000 persons. This was less than one-third of the rate in 1977 and roughly one-third of the rate in 1992. Similarly, the property crime rate in 1962 (1,858) was less than half of the 1971 rate and only about one-third of the 1980 property crime rate (Figure 1.2). In both cases, the recent figures are still significantly higher than those of 40 years ago when society was lamenting the high crime it was facing. The property crime rate in 2013 is 126 percent higher than the rate in 1962, while the personal crime rate is

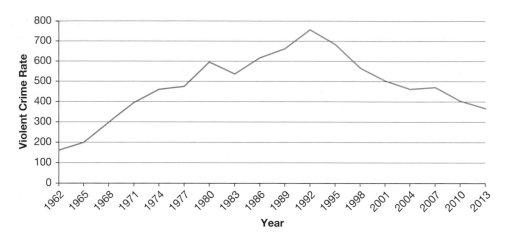

Figure 1.1

Change in Violent Crime Rate (per 100,000 population)

Source: Constructed by author from UCR data.

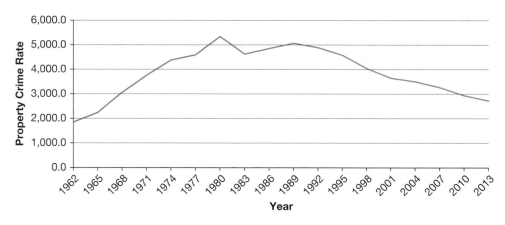

Figure 1.2

Change in Property Crime Rate (per 100,000 population)

Source: Constructed by author from UCR data.

roughly 46 percent higher. This suggests that those who point to the great strides made combating crime should be careful not to congratulate themselves too much.

While the UCR shows a large number of crimes are committed in the United States, it still comes under fire from a variety of sources for underreporting the actual level of crime in the country. O'Brien (1985) points out that concerns over the way the data is collected and how the police learn about crime lead many to question the validity of the results. Foremost among the concerns is the question of whether the police records and reports provide an unbiased, complete view of crime in society. Popular wisdom would answer this question with a resounding "No!" Examination of the UCR reveals three major points at which the UCR can be inaccurately adjusted.

First, the UCR is a voluntary system of data collection. It is possible for police departments to adjust their figures in order to enhance the image of their operation and/or their jurisdiction. Police funding is based on service delivery and productivity is often measured by the crime figures they report (O'Brien, 1985). As a result, it may be in the best interests of the department to alter its collection and reporting practices in order to make itself look better. Interestingly, this may be accomplished through both increasing and decreasing the level of crime. For example, an increase in the reported crime rate may be touted as an indication of better police work and improved police effectiveness. This would be especially true if the police had previously announced a "crackdown" on a selected crime and then wished to demonstrate their success. Similarly, a decrease in the level of crime may be pointed to as deterrence brought on by improved police performance.

A second major problem with the UCR involves the ability of individual police officers to adjust the crime rate. Any officer can refrain from making an arrest or a formal report on an incident. Such activity may allow the officer to deflect minor or unimportant events away from an already overburdened criminal justice system. More importantly, however, such discretion factors into a distorted and underrepresented crime rate. Departmental policies may also contribute to this shift in reported crimes. Administrative procedures concerning the handling of crimes may alter the level of reported offenses. McCleary et al. (1982) found that, by requiring all reported cases of burglary to be investigated by detectives, the number of officially recorded burglaries showed an immediate drop. This was attributable to the detectives reclassifying offenses that were not burglaries (i.e., thefts) to their correct UCR categories. Less experienced officers who used to handle these offenses elevated many instances to the burglary category. It is clear that the UCR crime rates are subject to unintentional, as well as intentional, manipulation.

The third criticism of the UCR revolves around the claim that many offenses are not brought to the attention of the police. The police are a reactive force. This means that they primarily respond to calls for service. Despite their patrol function, little crime is encountered directly by the police. They must rely on victims and witnesses to call them for help. The absence of such calls when offenses do occur translates into crimes that are not known to the police and that do not become part of official crime figures. The fact that there is much unreported crime, along with the potential problems of data collection, has prompted many individuals to rely on victimization surveys in order to assess the extent of the crime problem.

A fourth concern is that most UCR data is restricted to Part I offenses and ignores the Part II crimes. While the UCR does collect some information on Part II offenses, it is related almost exclusively to data on the number of persons arrested for various categories of crimes. Included here are other assaults (besides aggravated assault), forgery and counterfeiting, fraud, vandalism, sex offenses (besides forcible rape and prostitution), drunkenness, and disorderly conduct. Assuming that greater attention is paid to the Part I offenses and the clearance (arrest rate) for those crimes is roughly 20 percent, it can be assumed that the arrest data for Part II offenses are serious underreports of the number of such offenses. Nevertheless, the arrest rate for other assaults is 360.5 (per 100,000 population), fraud is 46.2, vandalism is 66.0, drunkenness is 145.7, and disorderly conduct is 152.7 (FBI, 2014). Looking solely at the known Part I offenses, therefore, presents a limited picture of crime, even given limitations with UCR figures.

Limitations of the UCR suggest that other means of measuring crime are needed. Perhaps the main alternative source of data involves surveys of the public.

Measuring Victimization

Victimization surveys are surveys of the population carried out to measure the level of criminal victimization in society. This form of crime measurement was prompted by the 1967 President's Commission on Law Enforcement and the Administration of Justice, which commissioned surveys to assess the accuracy (or lack thereof) of the UCR. The results of those early surveys suggested that the police data reflected only half of the crime in society (see, for example, Ennis, 1967). Based on those early investigations, victim surveys became a common method for measuring crime by the late 1970s, with the federal government institutionalizing the National Crime Victimization Survey (originally the National Crime Survey) in 1972. These surveys typically inquire about the victimization experiences of a subject and/or his household over a specified period of time (usually the preceding six months or year). Such surveys have been lauded as a more accurate reading of crime in society because they circumvent the problems of official records and they uncover crimes that are not reported to the police.

The **National Crime Victimization Survey (NCVS)** is the best known of the victimization surveys. It is a **panel survey** of households drawn from across the United States, in which a panel of subjects (in this case addresses) are surveyed repeatedly over a specified period. The NCVS contacts the same households every six months for a period of three years, with one sixth of the sample dropping out and being replaced every six months.

┌─ ON THE WEB ─────────
In-depth discussion of the NCVS can be found at http://bjs.ojp.usdoj.gov/index.cfm?ty=dcdetail&iid=245 and http://bjs.ojp.usdoj.gov/index.cfm?ty=pbdetail&iid=2173

Interviewers attempt to talk with every household member aged 12 and older. While the NCVS has undergone considerable change in data collection methods in recent years, including the use of computer-aided interviewing and changes in preliminary screen questions, the findings relative to official statistics have remained fairly stable. The success of the NCVS has prompted similar victim surveys in other countries, most notably the British Crime Survey (BCS).

According to the 2013 NCVS, there were almost 23 million victimizations in the United States against persons aged 12 or older (Truman and Langton, 2014). Of that number, 6.1 million were violent crimes and almost 17 million were property crimes. These raw figures translate into victimization rates of 2,380 violent crimes (per 100,000 population) and 13,140 property crimes (per 100,000 households). These figures, both the raw numbers and the crime rates, are significantly higher than the UCR data. Indeed, the NCVS violent crime rate is almost 6.5 times as high as the UCR violent crime rate. While the NCVS property crime rate is considered for households instead of individuals as in the UCR, the fact that the rate is almost five times as high as the UCR rate is indicative of the fact that property crime is larger than reported in police data. The claim that the UCR underreports crime, therefore, is supported in these figures.

> **ON THE WEB**
>
> *Detailed information on the 2010 NCVS can be viewed in Truman and Langton's (2014) report that can be found on the textbook's web site.*

Consistent with UCR figures, the NCVS reveals decreasing victimization levels, with great reductions in violent crime over the past decade. The NCVS estimates that there were 35,646,755 offenses in 1973. This number rose to 41,267,496 in 1981. Since 1981 there has been a relatively steady decline in property victimizations (Rand et al., 1997; Rand, 2009). Conversely, the violent crime rate held fairly steady throughout the 1970s, decreased in the early 1980s, increased from about 1986 until 1994, and has steadily declined since that time (Rand, 2009; Rennison and Rand, 2003). This trend varies somewhat for individual crimes (motor vehicle theft, for example, increased steadily between 1985 and 1991) but the overall trend is consistent with the findings from the UCR. See Table 1.1.

Victimization surveys have the ability to uncover crime and victimization not typically seen in official measures or the traditional NCVS data. Identity theft is one growing area of concern, particularly due to the growth of the Internet and electronic records. As society has moved toward paperless records and the storage of information on computers, offenders no longer have to have physical access to the records. Instead, they can access the information over the Internet by either having lawful access to the files, or illegally gaining entry to the records by hacking into a computer system. Electronic methods can be used for theft from next door or from around the world. Based on findings from a national survey of almost 5,000 adults conducted in 2006, most victims did not even know they were victimized or how it was done (56 percent) (Synovate, 2007).

Identity theft can take a variety of forms. The NCVS has included questions on identity theft since 2004 (Baum, 2007). The Federal Trade Commission (FTC) has surveyed the public on identity theft since 2003 (Synovate, 2007). According to the NCVS, roughly 7.9 million households were the victims of identity theft in 2012 (see Table 1.2).

TABLE 1.1 Criminal Victimization, 2013 (number and rates per 100,000)

Type of Victimization	Number	Rate
Total violent crimes	6,126,420	2,320
Rape/sexual assault	300,170	110
Robbery	645,650	240
Aggravated assault	994,220	380
Simple assault	4,186,390	1,580
Total property crimes	16,774,090	13,140
Household burglary	3,286,210	2,570
Motor vehicle theft	661,250	520
Theft	12,826,620	10,050

Source: Adapted by author from J.L. Truman and L. Langton (2014). *Criminal Victimization, 2013*. Washington, DC: Bureau of Justice Statistics.

TABLE 1.2 Types and Extent of Identity Theft

Type	Number
Existing Credit Cards	7,698,500
Existing Bank Accounts	7,470,700
Other Accounts	1,696,400
New Account	1,125,100
Personal Information	883,600
Total	7,928,500

Source: Constructed by author from E. Harrell and L. Langton (2013). *Victims of Identity Theft, 2012*. Washington, DC: Bureau of Justice Statistics.

Theft involving existing credit cards or other existing accounts is the most common form of identity theft. The establishment of new accounts and the theft of personal information are also prevalent forms of theft.

Information on identity theft offers a wealth of additional information. The NCVS data show that most victims of identity theft are from households with incomes of $75,000 and more (Harrell and Langton, 2013). Information from the NCVS suggests that this form of crime has been on the increase since the first survey was completed in

2003. Many victims fail to realize that a theft has occurred until long after the event. The most common means by which victims discovered the theft was being contacted by a financial institution about account activity (Harrell and Langton, 2013).

Another form of theft not typically found in data involves mass-marketing fraud. This can occur through schemes that seek to obtain relatively small amounts of money from a large number of victims or through maximizing the return on a smaller number of wealthier victims. Again, this type of fraud can target victims virtually anywhere in the world. The use of mail, telephones, the Internet, and the mass media makes borders, whether physical or symbolic, almost meaningless. While there are a number of different mass-marketing fraud schemes, there are several commonalities in the approaches. First is the use of some form of mass communication to reach a wide range of potential victims spread over a large geographic area (often internationally). A second common feature is the attempt to convince victims to provide funds or access to funds in return for a promised service or benefit. Some of these schemes can appear very similar to those seen earlier under identity theft.

> ┌─ **ON THE WEB** ─────────────
> *Read more about mass-marketing fraud and responses for victims and society at http://www.justice.gov/criminal/fraud/internet/*

Gauging the extent of mass-market fraud schemes is not an easy task. Three main reasons can be offered for the lack of definitive data on these offenses. First, many of these offenses are relatively new crime forms, and both the public and the criminal justice system are playing catch-up in identifying and addressing them. Second, there is no systematic method for collecting and disseminating information on mass-market crimes. While the FBI and other agencies are working to gather such data, the work is still in its infancy. Third, many individuals either do not know they have been victimized or do not report the event to the authorities due to embarrassment and shame. Despite these facts, we can glean some information on the extent and impact of mass-marketing fraud.

Most of the information that is available is from victim surveys or complaints filed by victims. The U.K. Office of Fair Trading (2006) reports that almost half of its survey respondents had been approached by a scammer in some way over their lifetimes. Of those individuals, 8 percent had been the victim of some form of scam, with most of the events taking place in the past year. The survey report estimates that more than 3.2 million people (6.5 percent of the U.K. adult population) are victimized every year. In the United States, a Federal Trade Commission survey on consumer fraud claims that 10.8 percent of the U.S. adult population was victimized in 2011, with a total of almost 38 million fraud incidents (Anderson, 2013). An alternative source of data comes from the Internet Crime Complaint Center. In 2012, the Center received 289,874 complaints (Internet Crime Complaint Center, 2013). It is important to note that these data reflect only those incidents reported to that office and not victimizations reported to any other agency.

Victimization studies are not without their critics and shortcomings. Among the many problems inherent in the surveys are the lack of knowledge of what constitutes various crimes on the part of respondents, problems of respondent recall, and issues of question wording. These issues are well documented elsewhere (see O'Brien, 1985) and will not be considered here. The magnitude of the difference between official and victimization figures, however, is too large to be offset solely by the problems of victim surveys. There is little question that victim surveys uncover more crime than official measures.

Summary

Clearly, no single measure of crime/victimization is perfect. Each measure taps something different. The exact nature and level of crime in society is unknown. Official UCR figures reveal a staggering amount of crime. More than doubling those numbers to account for unreported offenses, as victimization figures would suggest, compounds the problem. Measures of new and emerging forms of crime further exacerbate the crime problem. Even with the recent reductions in crime, the number of offenses is staggering.

The level of crime, whether at its peak or more moderate numbers, exceeds the limits of what the criminal justice system can hope to handle. The system is already overburdened and often simply processes people through the maze of legal requirements while having a questionable impact on the level of crime (Conklin, 2003). Even if the criminal justice system could claim credit for the recent reductions, there is still a lot of work to do. Compounding the situation is the fact that the bulk of criminal justice system activity (e.g., arrests, convictions, incarceration, and corrections) reflects an after-the-fact approach to crime. The system deals primarily with crimes which have already been committed. There is little, if any, evidence to show that the criminal justice system actually stops crime *before* it occurs.

The Costs of Crime/Victimization

The problem of crime and victimization goes beyond simple counts of the number of offenses. Crime has a number of different impacts on both the victims and society, and in many ways these impacts surpass the size and scope of the UCR and NVCS figures. Economic loss, injuries, the need for medical care, and lost time from work are additional measures of crime's impact.

Information on the impact of crime is routinely collected each year by both the UCR and victimization surveys. Data on direct economic loss from various crimes according to both the UCR and NCVS appear in Table 1.3. According to the UCR figures, victims experienced more than $17 billion in direct loss from crimes. This ranges from $7.5 billion for theft, with an average loss of $1,259 per incident, to $20 million for bank

TABLE 1.3 Economic Loss for Specific Crimes

Offense	Avg. Loss		Total Loss	
	UCR	NCVS	UCR	NCVS
Burglary	$2,322	$1,539	$4.5B	$4.9B
Theft	1,259	524	7.5B	6.4B
Motor Vehicle Theft	5,872	6,077	4.1B	4.8B
Robbery	1,170	1,482	404M	885M
Bank Robbery	3,542		20M	
Assault		236		1B
Arson	14,390		645M	

Source: Constructed by author from FBI (2014). *Crime in the United States, 2013*. https://www.fbi.gov/about-us/cjis/ucr/crime-in-the-u.s/2013/crime-in-the-u.s.-2013; Bureau of Justice Statistics (2010). *Criminal Victimization in the United States, 2007, Statistical Tables.* Washington, DC: Bureau of Justice Statistics.

robbery, at an average loss of $3,542. NCVS data report similar losses at just under a total of $18 billion. Theft is again the most costly overall ($6.4 billion) but has the lowest per crime costs ($524), while robbery experiences the lowest total loss ($885 million). The differences are largely due to variation between the two data sources. What is important to note beyond these dollar figures is that, despite the reductions in the number and rates of crime in recent years, the economic loss per event has steadily increased at a rate greater than inflation.

Beyond measures of monetary loss, the NCVS provides information on the impact of physical injuries and lost time due to victimization. In 2008, 36 percent of robbery victims and 23 percent of assault victims sustained a physical injury, with 17 percent of the robbery victims and 10 percent of the assault victims requiring medical care (Bureau of Justice Statistics, 2010). Roughly 10 percent of the robbery, assault, and burglary victims reported losing time from work, with the related loss of income. Of those who lost time from work, almost 26 percent of assault victims and 12 percent of robbery victims lost more than 10 days.

While the above information paints a serious picture of the impact of crime, the actual impact extends beyond the direct financial loss due to the crime or the time lost by victims as reflected in the UCR or the NCVS. Indeed, crime exacts a wide range of additional costs on the individual and society. Among these are the criminal justice system costs

┌─ ON THE WEB ─────────────────────
│ *NCVS and UCR cost figures and the Miller et al.*
│ *(1996) report can be found on the textbook web site.*
└──────────────────────────────────

of investigating, arresting, prosecuting, adjudicating, and incarcerating/punishing the offender. Besides the direct crime losses suffered by the victims, there are the medical costs related to injuries and lost income, as well as intangible costs which include pain and suffering, psychological impacts, and reduced quality of life.

In a recent analysis, McCollister et al. (2010) provide a detailed discussion of the data and computations on the costs of crime to society. The authors draw data from the UCR, National Incident-based Reporting System (NIBRS), the NCVS, the Federal Emergency Management Agency, the U.S. Fire Administration (for arsons), the Bureau of Justice Assistance (for jail and prison data, criminal justice system employment data, and expenditures), and the Bureau of Labor Statistics (income and earnings). They also rely on data and input from other analyses, including the work of Miller et al. (1996) and Aos (2003b). Table 1.4 presents the tangible and intangible costs for 13 crime types in 2008 dollars. The total costs range from a high of almost $9 million for each murder to a low of $3,532 for each larceny/theft. While these per-crime figures are themselves staggering, multiplying the costs of homicides by the number of homicides in 2010 reveals a total cost of more than $132 billion just for this one offense category. Carrying out this same computation for all 13 crime categories reveals a total costs of more than $295 trillion in 2010!

TABLE 1.4 Tangible and Intangible Costs of Crime

Offense	Victim Costs	Criminal Justice System Cost	Crime Career Cost	Total Tangible Costs	Pain and Suffering Costs
Murder	$737,517	$392,352	$148,555	$1,278,424	$8,442,000
Rape/Sex Assault	5,556	26,479	9,212	41,247	198,212
Aggravated Assault	8,700	8,641	2,126	19,537	13,435
Robbery	3,299	13,827	4,272	21,398	4,976
Motor Vehicle Theft	6,114	3,867	533	10,534	262
Arson	11,452	4,392	584	16,428	5,133
Household Burglary	1,362	4,127	681	6,170	321
Larceny/Theft	480	2,879	163	3,523	10
Stolen Property	n/a	6,842	1,132	7,974	0
Vandalism	n/a	4,160	701	4,860	0
Forgery/Counterfeiting	n/a	4,605	660	5,265	0
Embezzlement	n/a	4,820	660	5,480	0
Fraud	n/a	4,372	660	5,032	0

Source: Constructed by author from K.E. McCollister et al. (2010). "The cost of crime to society: New crime-specific estimates for policy and program evaluation." *Drug and Alcohol Dependence* 108:98–109.

The economic impact of crime on the individual and society is huge. Simply looking at the immediate loss due to the victimization itself is short-sighted. To these losses you need to add the costs of the criminal justice system, other costs to the victim and his family, pain and suffering, and lost productivity by the offender. While the actual level of crime has fallen in recent years, the staggering economic costs to the individual victims and to society cannot be ignored.

The Fear of Crime

To further compound the problem of the levels of "actual crime" and the economic and physical impact of crime in society, one needs only to examine the perceived levels of crime and the resultant fear held by many members of society. The "fear of crime" presents a view of criminal victimization that, although not necessarily real, forms the basis for daily "inactivity" and anxiety. Because fear reduction is an important component of many crime prevention programs, it is important to understand the extent of fear and issues related to measuring and understanding fear.

Fear of crime emerged as a social issue in the mid-1960s and soon became a permanent part of criminological research. Lee (2007) argues that fear was "invented" in the 1960s through a convergence of various factors. Among these were the development of victimization surveys as a part of the 1967 President's Commission on Law Enforcement and the Administration of Justice (and subsequently in other countries), the growth of professional/academic interest in crime and its causes, the use of crime and fear as political capital, and the feminist movement (Lee, 2007). The newly discovered "fear of crime" became an integral part of national and local government policymaking.

Defining Fear

What exactly is **fear**? Despite the growth of interest in "fear of crime," there remains a lack of consensus on exactly what the term means. Perhaps the most recognized work on this issue is that of Kenneth Ferraro and his associates. Ferraro defines *fear* as:

> an emotional response of dread or anxiety to crime or symbols that a person associates with crime. This definition of fear implies that some recognition of potential danger, what we may call perceived risk, is necessary to evoke fear.
>
> (1995, p. 8)

While this definition requires an emotional response, the fear may manifest itself in various ways depending on the person involved and the basis for his anxiety. Some individuals fear walking on the streets in their neighborhood while others fear physical attack within their own home. As a result, there may be a shift in physical functioning such as high blood pressure and rapid heartbeat. Alternatively, the individual may similarly alter his attitudes about walking alone in certain places or avoiding various activities. To a great extent, the source of the fear for the individual will determine the response to the fear. Regardless of the source of this fear, it is real for the individual.

Measuring Fear

Ferraro (1995) points out that researchers have attempted to measure fear in a variety of ways. Some surveys question respondents about how much they worry about being a victim. Others ask about perceptions of the crime problem in their community. Still other surveys have respondents rate their chances of becoming a victim. These various approaches do not provide the same information.

In an attempt to show the differences between various fear measures, Ferraro and LaGrange (1988) provide a classification scheme that considers the perceptions of the respondent being tapped and the degree to which the method addresses the individual or others (see Figure 1.3). This classification taps judgments of risk— how safe the respondent or others are, values—how concerned the person is about crime or victimization, and emotions—how much the individual is afraid or worried about becoming a victim. Personal fear of crime appears in the lower right hand cell (F). This measure would ask respondents directly about how afraid they are of being the victim of specific crimes, often without reference to any specific place or time. These questions directly tap the "emotions

Level of Reference	Level of Perception		
	Cognitive Judgments	Values	Affective Emotions
General	A Risk to others; crime or safety assessments	B Concern about crime to others	C Fear for others' victimization
Personal	D Risk to self; safety of self; personal intolerance	E Concern about crime to self	F Fear for self-victimization

Figure 1.3

Classification and Examples of Crime Perceptions

Source: K.F. Ferraro and R.L. LaGrange (1988). "Are older people afraid of crime?" *Journal of Aging Studies* 2:277–287. Reprinted with permission from Elsevier Science.

of dread or anxiety" of the individual. At the other extreme (cell A), respondents assess the general safety of other people, quite possibly without even mentioning crime.

Interestingly, while discussions of "fear of crime" are common, many researchers utilize measures that reflect risk or assessments of crime levels, rather than the emotional response of the individual (Ferraro, 1995). This diversity is seen in many of the common and large-scale surveys. Table 1.5 presents a sample of "fear" questions used in past surveys

---

TABLE 1.5 Common "Fear" Questions

National Crime Victimization Survey:
How safe do you feel or would you feel being out alone in your neighborhood at night?

General Social Survey:
Is there any area right around here—that is, within a mile—where you would be afraid to walk alone at night?

Taking a Bite out of Crime Campaign Evaluation:
How likely do you think it is that your home will be broken into or burglarized during the next year?
Is having your home burglarized or broken into something that you worry about?

National Opinion Survey on Criminal Justice:
Do you worry very frequently, somewhat frequently, seldom or never about:
 − Yourself or someone in your family getting sexually assaulted
 − Being attacked while driving your car
 − Getting mugged
 − Getting beaten up, knifed or shot
 − Getting murdered
 − Your home being burglarized while someone is at home
 − Your home being burglarized while no one is at home

Gallup Poll:
 − Is there more crime in your area than there was a year ago, or less?
 − Is there more crime in the U.S. than there was a year ago, or less?
 − Overall, how would you describe the problem of crime in the U.S.? Is it extremely serious, very serious, moderately serious, not too serious, or not serious at all?

Fear of Crime in America Survey:
Rate your fear of: (1 = not afraid at all; 10 = very afraid)
 − being approached on the street by a beggar or panhandler
 − being raped or sexually assaulted
 − being murdered
 − being attacked by someone with a weapon
 − having your car stolen
 − having your property damaged by vandals

and research. Note that the questions vary from asking about perceptions on changes in crime (Gallup Poll), to feeling safe outside at night with no mention of crime (NCVS), to rating fear of specific criminal actions (Fear of Crime in America Survey). These differing measures all tap some aspect of the fear definition presented earlier.

The Level of Fear

Trying to delineate the actual level of fear is like trying to hit a moving target. No two studies provide the same results. This may be due largely to the use of varying measures of fear. Despite this fact, it is possible to offer some insight and "ballpark" figures for fear.

Many researchers report that 40 to 50 percent of the population express a fear of crime (Hindelang, 1975; Maguire and Pastore, 1995; Skogan and Maxfield, 1981; Toseland, 1982). In 2011, 38 percent of respondents report that there are areas near their home where they would be afraid to walk alone at night (Maguire, 2011). Questions asking about perceived changes in crime in the United States or a respondent's area often result in greater fear levels with 66 percent or more reporting that there is "more" crime than in the past (Jones, 2010).

Table 1.6 presents data on the level of "worry" about being a victim of specific crimes. Maguire (2011) reports that one out of five respondents worries frequently or occasionally about being murdered, almost half worry about having their home burglarized when they are not home, 30 percent worry about a burglary when they are home, 44 percent worry about having their car stolen or broken into, and one out of three

TABLE 1.6 Percentage of Respondents who Frequently or Occasionally Worry About Different Forms of Victimization

	Male	Female	White	Non-white	Total
Home being burglarized when not home	47	52	48	49	47
Car stolen or burglarized	39	50	45	43	44
Being mugged	27	47	33	37	34
Home being burglarized when home	24	36	29	33	30
Being sexually assaulted	6	37	21	26	22
Getting murdered	14	24	17	28	20
Being attacked while driving	15	23	17	24	19

Source: K. Maguire, (2011). *Sourcebook of Criminal Justice Statistics.* Washington, DC: Bureau of Justice Statistics. Retrieved from http://www.albany.edu/sourcebook/toc_2.html

worries about being mugged. Interestingly, few respondents report ever being a victim of any of these crimes.

Fear and Crime

One very important fact to keep in mind is that the level of fear exceeds the actual levels of crime. Skogan and Maxfield (1981) illustrate the lack of a connection between crime and fear by showing that, in terms of robbery, approximately 48 percent of the non-victims report feeling somewhat or very unsafe, while 54 percent of the victims report the same fear. The expectation was that victims should express significantly more fear than non-victims. Similarly, both official and victimization measures show that less than 10 percent of the population is victimized, despite fear of 40 percent or more. Perhaps more interesting is the fact that, despite the reductions in crime found in both official and victimization figures, 66 percent of the respondents to a Gallup Poll in 2002 believe there was more crime in the United States than in the previous year (Jones, 2010).

Another way of looking at fear and crime is to examine the link between fear and past victimization of respondents. Some studies offer empirical support of a positive relationship between victimization and fear of crime (Bachman et al., 2011; Ferguson and Mindel, 2007; Keane, 1995; Lumb et al., 1993; McCoy et al., 1996; Roundtree, 1998; Skogan, 1987; Will and McGrath, 1995; Zhao et al., 2015). Other studies, however, fail to find any relationship between victimization and fear (Ferraro, 1995; Garofalo, 1979; Gates and Rohe, 1987; Liska et al., 1982; McGarrell et al., 1997; Perkins and Taylor, 1996; Rifai, 1982). Yet another group of researchers argue that the relationship depends on the definitions and measures of fear and/or victimization (Baumer, 1985; Bennett and Flavin, 1994; Ferraro and LaGrange, 1987; Garofalo, 1981; Gomme, 1988).

Fear and Demographics

Besides the diversity in the fear–victimization relationship, the level of fear is not consistent across all demographic groups in the population. It is principally an urban problem and affects the elderly and women to a greater extent than other groups. Greater than 60 percent of those persons living in urban areas express fear of crime. Conversely, only 30 percent of rural residents voice the same fears. A wide range of studies reveal that the elderly and women are the most fearful groups in society (Baumer, 1985; Bennett and Flavin, 1994; Ferraro, 1995; Hindelang et al., 1978; McGarrell et al., 1997; Perkins and Taylor, 1996; Riger et al., 1978; Skogan and Maxfield, 1981; Will and McGrath, 1995). This persists despite the fact that the elderly and women are the least victimized groups. Some researchers argue these fear results are an artifact of how fear is measured and that the young are actually the most fearful (Chiricos et al., 1997; Ferraro, 1995; Lumb et al., 1993).

Fear also varies along other demographic lines. Numerous studies report that fearful people tend to be black (Biderman et al., 1967; Chiricos et al., 1997; Lab, 1990; Smith and Lab, 1991; Parker, 1988; Parker and Ray, 1990; Skogan and Maxfield, 1981), lower socioeconomic status (Bennett and Flavin, 1994; Biderman et al., 1967; Gomme, 1986; Greenberg et al., 1985; Riger et al., 1978; Will and McGrath, 1995), and live in large communities (Baumer, 1985; Biderman et al., 1967; Boggs, 1971; Kennedy and Silverman, 1985; Liska et al., 1982; Will and McGrath, 1995). Other studies, however, note the lack of a relationship or a reverse relationship between some of these demographic factors and fear (Gomme, 1986; Gomme, 1988; Kennedy and Krahn, 1984; Kennedy and Silverman, 1985; Lab, 1990; Smith and Lab, 1991; Menard and Covey, 1987; Ortega and Myles, 1987; Toseland, 1982).

Explaining the Divergent Findings

Two basic questions arise from an inspection of past research on fear of crime. First, how do you justify the levels of fear in light of the actual levels and chances of victimization? Second, why do different studies find divergent sets of characteristics among fearful individuals? There is no clear answer to these questions. Instead, there may be many contributing factors.

Vicarious Victimization

Hough (1995) argues that fear is related to measures of vicarious victimization. **Vicarious victimization** refers to knowing someone or hearing about others who have been the victim of a crime. This information may elicit a sympathetic reaction and empathetic fear of crime. Grohe et al. (2012), using a phone survey of residents in one southeastern U.S. city, report that fear of burglary is significantly related to actual burglary in the city. Analyzing fear among Houston residents, Zhao et al. (2015) note that local crime is related to fear of violent, property, and disorder offenses independent of actual victimization. Vicarious fear can also come from real or dramatic depictions of crime in the media, particularly television. Both fictional police dramas and the reporting of crime and violence in the news inundate the populace with a view that crime is a constant threat to every individual. It is also noteworthy that most depictions are not of everyday "street crimes." Instead, they focus on more heinous and frightening offenses such as murder, rape, and home burglary. Several studies (Chiricos et al., 1996; Lane and Meeker, 2003a; Weitzer and Kubrin, 2004) report that exposure to crime in the media is related to higher reported fear.

Perceived Risk and Harm

A second possible explanation for inordinate levels of fear centers on the potential harm one encounters when victimized (Riger et al., 1978; Skogan and Maxfield, 1981; Warr, 1984). That is, victimization has a greater impact on some individuals than others. The elderly, for example, are largely on fixed incomes and any loss due to theft, property damage, or medical expenses cannot always be accommodated within their budgets. A minor dollar loss can translate into a major hardship. Similarly, physical injuries to elderly victims can result in lengthy, painful recuperation beyond that needed by younger individuals. The elderly and females also have a great physical disadvantage when faced with young male offenders who hold an edge in strength and physical prowess. The perceived potential for physical harm is greatly enhanced when the victim and offender represent opposite positions in physical and social power. McCoy et al. (1996) and Smith and Torstensson (1997) find that perceived vulnerability is a strong predictor of fear among women and the elderly.

Vulnerability also appears in the form of social isolation (Akers et al., 1987; Bursik and Grasmick, 1993; Kennedy and Silverman, 1985; Riger et al., 1978). Many elderly live alone and have few family members or close friends living nearby. These individuals may feel they have no one to call on for assistance in the aftermath of a crime. They are socially isolated from support networks that are more common among younger members of the population.

Incivility

A third possible explanation for the lack of a direct victimization–fear connection involves area incivility. **Incivility** refers to physical and social factors involved in disorder and community decline. Physical signs of incivility include the deterioration of buildings, litter, graffiti, vandalism, and abandoned buildings and cars. Among the social signs of incivility are public drunkenness, vagrancy, loitering youths, harassment (such as begging or panhandling), and visible drug sales and use. Both residents and potential offenders may see signs of incivility as indicative of a lack of social cohesion, high transiency, a lack of resources, and/or an uncaring attitude (Lewis and Salem, 1986; Skogan, 1990). Residents may feel a lack of control in the neighborhood that in turn may generate a greater fear of crime. Conversely, areas that display collective efficacy and strong social integration should have lower levels of fear (Doran and Burgess, 2012; Jackson and Gray, 2010; Zhao et al., 2015).

Several studies have analyzed the contribution of incivilities to the level of fear. McGarrell et al. (1997) report that neighborhood disorder/incivility contributes significantly to variation in respondents' fear of crime. Roundtree (1998) finds similar results when analyzing survey data from 5,302 Seattle residents. Residents' perceptions of disorder significantly increased fear of both violent and burglary victimizations. Lane and colleagues (Lane, 2002; Lane and Fox, 2012; Lane and Meeker, 2000, 2005, 2011) have demonstrated that neighborhood conditions and signs of disorder are related to levels of fear. Finally, McCoy et al. (1996) note that dissatisfaction with one's neighborhood (a possible indicator of incivilities) is a key to residents' fear.

Methodological Factors

Differing methodologies in the studies may also influence the results. As noted earlier, varying "fear" measures can contribute to divergent findings. It is not improbable that the same respondents could provide two different views of fear when asked different questions. For example, survey respondents may give "fearful" responses when asked about walking alone after dark anywhere "within a mile," but few "fear" responses to the likelihood of being raped. Similarly, respondents may feel that crime is a greater problem today than a year ago, but still not worry much about being mugged. The extent of fear also may vary depending on who is answering which questions. Females, for example, worry more about sexual assault than do males. Ferraro (1995) notes that general fear among women is better understood as an extension of the fear of rape. Operationalizing fear in different ways, therefore, produces greatly different results. Variation in fear also may reflect the locale of the study. For example, Chiricos et al. (1997) point out that their results on fear differ from those of Covington and Taylor (1991), despite the similar concerns addressed in the two studies. They speculate that the variation is due to differences between Tallahassee, Florida and Baltimore, Maryland. The setting of the analysis, therefore, can influence the results.

Crime and Fear

Yet another factor influencing the levels of fear involves the actual level of crime. While the fear of crime varies independently from actual victimization and crime, it would be naive to claim that changes in the crime rate have no influence on reported fear. Media reports of increasing crime and spectacular offenses undoubtedly hold some sway over perceptions of safety in the community. Unfortunately, lower crime rates probably do not bring about lower fear as easily. The media does not promote good news to the same extent as bad news. Feelings of fear and worry, once formed, would be difficult to reverse.

Benefits of Fear

Throughout this discussion, fear has been presented primarily as a negative concept. That is, fear is a bad thing that has negative consequences for the individual. Among these negatives are changes in behavior, retreating behind closed doors, not trusting other people, anxiety, and/or depression, to name a few. The logical conclusion to draw is that we need to reduce, and hopefully eliminate, fear. It is possible, however, to view fear as a positive thing.

Jackson and Gray (2009) note that there is such a thing as **functional fear**. In essence, fear can be a good thing, provided the individual uses it as motivation to take precautions. These precautions may range from avoiding certain risky places or times, to utilizing safety devices at home, to pairing up with others for safety when outdoors. A similar proposition is offered by Lee (2007) when he discusses the **fearing subject**. This person is someone who becomes responsible for the safety of himself and his property. Jackson and Gray (2010), using the Safer Neighborhoods Survey in London, report that fear actually promotes precautions, which reduce subsequent fear for a significant number of respondents.

Based on these arguments, it would be ill-advised to try to completely eliminate fear. Rather, fear can be healthy for people. The key would be to determine what that "healthy level" is and how to limit a person's fear at that optimal level. Under this approach, eliminating fear would result in people taking unnecessary chances and ignoring risky situations.

Fear Summary

Despite the issues and concerns inherent in measuring fear of crime, one fact remains unchanged. That is, people report being fearful to a much greater extent than they report (either officially or unofficially) being a victim of crime. Because of fear, people respond in a variety of ways. Some individuals will avoid certain places at certain times, or stop going somewhere altogether. Others may install locks and security devices and stay inside their fortress. The public may demand greater police presence. Funds may be expended on self-defense classes, dogs, guns, or other items in an attempt to protect one's self and reduce the feelings of fear. Whatever the response, it is indicative of fear's impact on the individual and society.

Summary

The extent of the crime problem is hard to accurately gauge and is multifaceted. Attempts to measure the level of crime present a variety of findings and anomalies. While these various counting procedures may not agree on the numerical magnitude of crime and victimization, there is consensus that crime remains a major social problem. Crime may be on the decrease, but it remains far higher today than in the 1960s when the President's Commission proclaimed that major changes were needed to stem the problem of crime and victimization. Beyond the enumeration of criminal acts, the economic, impact of crime on the individual and society is substantial. Psychological and time losses due to crime are also significant. Also problematic are the inordinate levels of fear of crime. Fear far exceeds the actual amount of crime and affects many individuals who never have been, and may never be, crime victims. Crime prevention must be cognizant of both the real and perceived levels of crime and must be prepared to attack crime in all its aspects.

KEY TERMS

- fear
- fearing subject
- functional fear
- incivility
- National Crime Victimization Survey (NCVS)
- panel survey
- Part I crimes
- Part II crimes
- Uniform Crime Reports (UCR)
- vicarious victimization
- victimization surveys

CHAPTER 2 Crime Prevention

LEARNING OBJECTIVES

After reading this chapter you should be able to:

- Discuss the historic methods used by individuals and communities to respond to and prevent crime.
- Provide a definition of crime prevention.
- Contrast crime prevention and crime control.
- Outline the crime prevention model based on the public health model.
- Define primary, secondary, and tertiary crime prevention.
- Provide examples of prevention activities for each part of the crime prevention model.
- Offer examples of other crime prevention models.
- Identify the difference between micro-, meso-, and macro-level prevention.
- Define and discuss crime science.

Crime prevention is not a new idea. Indeed, for as long as people have been victimized there have been attempts to protect oneself and one's family. The term "crime prevention," however, has only recently come to signify a set of ideas for combating crime. Many people suggest that crime prevention today is new and unique, particularly in terms of citizen participation. In reality, many recent activities classified as crime prevention can be seen throughout history. "New" crime prevention ideas and techniques are often little more than reincarnations of past practices or extensions of basic approaches in the (distant) past. It is only in the relatively recent past that the general citizenry has *not* been the primary line of defense against crime and victimization. This chapter will accomplish several things. First, it presents a brief discussion of crime prevention throughout history. Second, a definition for crime prevention will be presented. Third, the chapter presents the general crime prevention model that serves to organize the remainder of the text.

Crime Prevention Through the Ages

In any discussion it is important to set forth the context from which our ideas and thoughts emerge. Perhaps the best place to start is with an understanding of what has happened in the past. The study of crime prevention is no exception.

The earliest responses to crime were left to the individual and his family. Retribution, revenge, and vengeance were the driving forces throughout early history. While such actions would serve to make the victim whole again, it also would eliminate the benefit gained by the offender. It was assumed that potential offenders would see little gain in an offense, thereby *deterring* the individual from taking action. The Code of Hammurabi (approximately 1900 B.C.) outlined retribution by the victim and/or his family as the accepted response to injurious behavior. *Lex talionis*, the principle of "an eye for an eye," was specifically set forth as a driving principle in the Hammurabic law. Such laws and practices provided legitimacy to individual citizen action.

The existence of formal systems of social control is relatively new. Early "policing," such as in the Roman Empire and in France, was concentrated in the cities, conducted by the military, and dealt with issues of the central state and the nobility (i.e., king) (Holden, 1992; Langworthy and Travis, 1994). The general public was left to continue self-help methods.

The Norman conquest of England in 1066 gave rise to a form of citizen policing referred to as **obligatory policing** (Klockars, 1985). Male citizens were required to band together into groups for the purpose of policing each other. If one individual in the group caused harm (to a group or non-group member), the other members were responsible for apprehending and sanctioning the offender. Beyond this obligatory action, a variety of cooperative practices emerged that relied on citizen participation to protect the community and one another. **Watch and ward** rotated the responsibility for keeping watch over the town or area, particularly at night, among the male citizens. Identified threats would cause the watcher to raise the alarm and call for help (**hue and cry**). It was then up to the general citizenry to apprehend and (possibly) punish the offender. Those responding to the call for help were not employees of the state. Rather, they were other common citizens. The "watch and ward" and "hue and cry" ideas were codified in 1285 in the Statutes of Winchester (Klockars, 1985), which also required men to have weapons available for use when called (**assize of arms**), and outlined the role of a **constable**, which was an unpaid position responsible for coordinating the watch and ward system, and overseeing other aspects of the law. It is apparent throughout these actions that crime prevention was a major responsibility of the citizenry.

Similar citizen responsibility was commonplace in the new world colonies and the early United States. The **vigilante movement**, which mirrored early ideas of "hue and cry," was a major component of enforcing law and order in the growing frontier of the young country (Klockars, 1985). Posses of citizens were formed when an offender needed to be apprehended and punished.

The individual, often voluntary, responsibility for crime prevention in England generally persisted until the 1800s. The exceptions to this trend can be seen in the development of paid, private security police for specialized industries or groups (Klockars, 1985; Langworthy and Travis, 1994). The Merchant Police of England, which was established in the sixteenth century to protect the wool industry, is a prime example of an early private police force. The **parochial police**, hired by the wealthy to protect their homes and businesses, is another example.

Entrepreneurial policing appeared with the passage of the Highwayman Act in England in 1692. This law outlined the payment of bounty for the capture of thieves and the recovery of property. The voluntary bounty hunters came to be known as **thief takers** (Klockars, 1985; LaGrange, 1993) who, by the mid-1700s, were organized under the leadership of English magistrates. The thief takers, who were often reformed criminals themselves, were "paid" to protect the public by being able to keep a portion of all recovered property. The evolution of the thief takers from a wholly voluntary activity to a legitimized, organized group under government control was the beginning of a process that ended with the establishment of the Metropolitan Police in London in 1829.

A key to the Metropolitan Police organization was the idea of crime prevention. Sir Robert Peel, who was the driving force behind the Metropolitan Police Act, and Charles Roman, the commissioner of the new organization, both saw crime prevention as the basic principle underlying police work (LaGrange, 1993). Even earlier attempts at formal policing, such as that in seventeenth century Paris, emphasized crime prevention through methods such as preventive patrol, increased lighting, and street cleaning (Stead, 1983). Formal police forces in the United States, mirroring the movement in England, emerged in the mid-1800s and were restricted primarily to the largest cities in the northeast, leaving citizens to continue their efforts at self-protection.

While much of this discussion has emphasized individual action and self-help, it should not be construed as indicative that protective actions were solely a matter of retribution and revenge. There are numerous examples of alternative approaches that would be considered preventive in nature. Easy examples were the use of walls, moats, drawbridges and other physical design features around cities that protected the community from external invasion. Surveillance, as provided by "watch and ward," allowed the identification of problems before they got out of hand. Yet another early prevention approach was the restriction of weapon ownership as a means of eliminating violent behavior (Holden, 1992).

The advent of the twentieth century witnessed a great deal of change in societal response to deviant behavior. Not only was a formal police force becoming the norm, but other forces were emerging to address crime and deviance. The growth of the scientific study of crime and criminal behavior offered new responses to deviant behavior. The emerging fields of psychology and sociology in the late 1800s and early 1900s were beginning to question the causes of deviant behavior. Rather than carry on the dominant tradition of attributing deviance to the battle between good and evil (God and the devil), researchers were starting to note patterns in where and when offenses occurred and who was involved in the offenses, and to relate these facts to changing social structure and personal relationships. The logical result of this growing study was a movement away from simple responses involving repression, vengeance, retribution, and the like to actions that would attack the assumed causes of deviant behavior. The emerging criminal and juvenile justice systems, therefore, responded by incorporating more prevention-oriented functions into their activity.

One prime example of an early "crime prevention" approach was the development of the juvenile court and its efforts to combat the problems of poverty, lack of education, and poor parenting among the lower classes. The preventive nature of the juvenile system can be seen in the *parens patriae* philosophy, which argued that youths needed help and that processing in adult court was geared toward punishment rather than prevention. The expansion of the juvenile court's jurisdiction to cover **status offenses** reflected the belief that curfew violation, smoking, playing in the street, incorrigibility, and other such actions (none of which were proscribed by the criminal code) were indicative of later criminal behavior. Thus, intervening in these status offenses was a means of preventing later crime. The juvenile system, therefore, was clearly an attempt at crime prevention.

Yet another example of early crime preventive action was the Chicago Area Project. Shaw and McKay (1931, 1942) found crime and delinquency concentrating in the central areas of Chicago, where residential transience and an apparent lack of social ties predominated. Shaw and McKay (1942) argued that this constant turnover of residents resulted in an inability of the people to exert any informal social control over the individuals in the area. People were more interested in improving themselves and moving out of these neighborhoods than in improving the area and staying there. Consequently, offenders could act with some degree of impunity in these neighborhoods. The Chicago Area Project, founded in 1931, sought to work with the residents to build a sense of pride and community, thereby prompting people to stay and exert control over the actions of people in the area. Recreation for youths, vigilance and community self-renewal, and mediation were the major components of the project (Schlossman and Sedlak, 1983). In essence, the project sought to build ongoing, thriving communities that could control the behavior of both its residents and those who visited the area.

Modern Crime Prevention

The modern era of crime prevention can be traced to the changes in crime in the 1960s. That decade saw the advent of major increases in crime and delinquency, accompanied by large-scale social unrest in the United States over the Vietnam War and perceived social inequality. The public demanded that something be done to address crime and social unrest. The work of the 1967 President's Commission on Law Enforcement and the Administration of Justice (hereafter the Commission) highlighted the plight of crime victims and the failure of existing criminal justice system actions to curtail problems. The Commission called for new approaches, including educational programs, local crime initiatives, better funding of criminal justice initiatives, and research on the causes of and solution for crime.

Academic interest in the burgeoning crime problem led the way to modern crime prevention activities. One of the first focal areas was on the contribution of the physical design of communities to crime. Jacobs' (1961) *The Death and Life of Great American Cities* focused on urban decay and the natural and social environments, and their impact on crime and deviance. The modern urban environment, as well as many programs to change urban life, were anathema to a vibrant community that protects itself and residents who look out for one another. Jacobs suggested that the physical environment needs to enhance natural surveillance by those in the neighborhood as a means of making streets safe for legitimate users. Similarly, Wood's (1961) evaluation of public housing in Chicago noted that safety is enhanced through resident surveillance and activity in the area.

The 1971 publication of Jeffery's *Crime Prevention Through Environmental Design* took the ideas of Jacobs and Wood further and argued that crime prevention requires environmental engineering. His emphasis was on future offending rather than past behavior (the target of existing systems of social control). Jeffery (1971) argued that criminal behavior, particularly potential future activity, is strongly influenced by the potential future consequences of the individual's actions. It is possible to curtail offending by removing environmental cues that reinforce the offending behavior. The physical and social environments have great potential to determine the levels of pleasure and pain faced by the individual. Jeffery argued that it is possible to make alterations to the environment that will enhance conforming behavior and mitigate offending. Those changes are not limited to physical changes. Rather, Jeffery claimed that increasing citizen involvement in community activities and surveillance, and increased proactive programs by the police and other agents of social control, can hold great potential for the prevention of crime.

While Jacobs, Jeffery, and others were laying out an academic basis for an emerging crime prevention, architects and community planners, along with federal agencies and private corporations, were implementing and testing new initiatives. Newman (1972), in his book *Defensible Space: People and Design in the Violent City*, called on architects to change the physical environment in such a way as to maximize territoriality and natural surveillance by residents and create an image of an area as cared for and protected. He demonstrated the impact of appropriate construction on reduced crime and disorder. Newman's work prompted the U.S. Department of Justice, other government agencies, and private corporations (such as Westinghouse Electric) to fund demonstration projects. The results of these projects led to the development of many different crime prevention efforts, including neighborhood watch, "Take a Bite Out of Crime," citizen patrols, lighting projects, and others.

A final major development in modern crime prevention was the introduction of **situational crime prevention** in 1983. Developed by the British Home Office, situational crime prevention refocused attention from broad social/community change to target-, time- and place-specific efforts that would remove the opportunities for crime. This move took crime prevention from the macro to the micro level of interest.

Summary

This short presentation demonstrates that crime prevention is an idea that has been around for as long as there has been crime. While the form has changed and the term "crime prevention" is relatively new, the concern over safety is age old. Throughout most of history, it was the individual's responsibility, either voluntarily or through obligation, to deal with crime and offenders. In the nineteenth and twentieth centuries, society moved to a system of police, courts, and corrections, which assumed the primary responsibility for crime.

Since the 1960s there has been a growing movement toward bringing the citizenry back as active participants in crime prevention. While many see this type of community action as "new," in reality it is more a movement back to age-old traditions of individual responsibility than it is a revolutionary step forward in crime control. Crime prevention must utilize the wide range of ideas and abilities found throughout society. Community planning, architecture, neighborhood action, juvenile advocacy, security planning, education, and technical training, among many other system and non-system activities, all have a potential impact on the levels of crime and fear of crime. The realm of crime prevention is vast and open for expansion.

Defining Crime Prevention

The definition of crime prevention varies from study to study and program to program. Ekblom (2005, p. 28) states "Crime prevention is intervention in the causes of criminal and disorderly events to reduce the risks of their occurrence and/or the potential seriousness of their consequences." This definition addresses both crime and its impact on individuals and society. As outlined in the last chapter, the consequences of crime are not inconsequential. While most definitions of crime prevention incorporate the ideas of lessening the actual levels of crime or limiting further increases in crime, few deal with the problem of fear of crime and perceived crime and victimization. This book uses a very simple yet encompassing definition:

> *crime prevention* entails any action designed to reduce the actual level of crime and/or the perceived fear of crime.

These actions are not restricted to the efforts of the criminal justice system and include activities by individuals and groups, both public and private. Just as there are many causes of crime, there are many potentially valuable approaches to crime prevention.

This definition differs from Ekblom's in that it does not directly address the consequences of crime. The reason for this is twofold. First, if crime and fear are successfully addressed, the consequences are also affected. Second, it is possible to address the consequences of victimization without ever attacking the underlying crime. This can occur in many ways, including payments to victims through victim compensation, the provision of mental health counselors, actions taken to reduce the time lost from participating with the criminal justice process, and any number of other interventions. While these actions are laudable, they do nothing to address the cause of the problems. Therefore, throughout the discussion in this book, the emphasis is on crime and the fear of crime, with the consequences receiving little direct attention.

Crime prevention and crime control are not synonymous. **Crime prevention** clearly denotes an attempt to eliminate crime either prior to the initial occurrence or before further activity. On the other hand, **crime control** alludes to maintenance of a given or existing level and the management of that amount of behavior. Control also fails to adequately address the problem of fear of crime. Critics of this distinction will fault the author's implicit assumption that society and criminal justice can do something about crime and the fear of crime beyond simple management of an inevitable, inescapable minimal amount of crime. These functionalists would view crime as a social necessity that, regardless of the effort, will always exist. While functionalists may be correct, taking the stance that crime is necessary and all we can do is "control" it leads to a mind-set doomed not to achieve crime "prevention."

Crime Prevention Classifications

Crime prevention can be classified in a number of different ways. Perhaps the earliest attempt to group crime prevention efforts simply borrowed the well-established public health model of disease prevention initiatives (see Brantingham and Faust, 1976; Caplan, 1964; Leavell and Clark, 1965; Shah and Roth, 1974).

Crime Prevention/Public Health Model

The tripartite **public health model** classifies prevention as either primary, secondary or tertiary. Each area attacks the problem at different stages of development. From the public health viewpoint, primary prevention refers to actions taken to avoid the initial development of the disease or problem. This would include vaccinations and sanitary cleanups by public health officials. Secondary prevention moves beyond the point of general societal concerns and focuses on individuals and situations that exhibit early signs of disease. Included at this stage are screening tests such as those for tuberculosis or systematically providing examinations to workers who handle toxic materials. Tertiary prevention rests at the point where the disease or problem has already manifested itself. Activities at this stage involve the elimination of the immediate problem and taking steps designed to inhibit a recurrence in the future. Crime prevention activities are directly analogous to this public health model.

Primary Crime Prevention

Primary prevention within the realm of criminal justice "identifies conditions of the physical and social environment that provide opportunities for or precipitate criminal acts" (Brantingham and Faust, 1976). The types of prevention approaches subsumed here take a variety of forms and are located within a wide range of social organizations (see Table 2.1). Included here are environmental design, neighborhood watch, general deterrence, private security, **developmental prevention** approaches, and education about crime and crime prevention. Environmental design includes a wide range of crime prevention techniques aimed at making crime more difficult for the offender, surveillance easier for residents, and feelings of safety more widespread. The use of building plans conducive to visibility, the addition of lights and locks, and the marking of property for ease of identification fall within the realm of environmental design. Neighborhood watches and citizen patrols increase the ability of residents to exert control over their neighborhood and add risk of observation for potential offenders.

Activities of varied groups/organizations can also play a major role within the realm of primary prevention. The presence of the police may affect the attractiveness of an area

---

TABLE 2.1 Crime Prevention Approaches

Primary prevention:	Secondary prevention:
Environmental design	Identification and prediction
Architectural design	Early ID of problem individuals
Lighting	Crime area analysis
Access control	Situational crime prevention
Property identification	Problem identification
Neighborhood watch	Situation-specific intervention
Surveillance	Community policing
Citizen patrols	Substance abuse
General deterrence	Prevention and treatment
Arrest and conviction	Schools and crime prevention
Sentencing methods	
Public education	**Tertiary prevention:**
Levels of crime	Specific deterrence
Fear	Incapacitation
Self-help	Rehabilitation and treatment
Developmental crime prevention	
Early intervention programs	
Social crime prevention	
Unemployment	
Poverty	
Employment/Job training	

for crime as well as lower the fear of crime. The courts and corrections may influence primary prevention by increasing perceived risk of crime for offenders. Actions of the criminal justice system may also bring about general deterrence. Public education concerning the actual levels of crime and the interaction of the criminal justice system and the public may also affect perceptions of crime and individual choices to violate the law.

Developmental crime prevention approaches focus on risk factors that may lead individuals to deviant behavior. Programs working with parents and children to build parental and social skills, preparation for school, cognitive abilities and more are prime examples of developmental approaches. **Social prevention** activities are those typically aimed at alleviating unemployment, poor education, poverty, and similar social ills that may reduce crime and fear by attending to the root causes underlying deviant behavior. These and many other primary prevention behaviors are implemented with the intent of avoiding initial, as well as continued, crime and victimization and may be instrumental at lowering the fear of crime.

Secondary Crime Prevention

Secondary prevention "engages in early identification of potential offenders and seeks to intervene" (Brantingham and Faust, 1976) prior to commission of illegal activity. Implicit in secondary prevention is the ability to correctly identify and predict problem people and situations. Perhaps the most recognizable form of secondary prevention is the idea of situational crime prevention. *Situational crime prevention* seeks to identify existing problems at the micro level and institute interventions that are developed specifically for the given problem. These solutions may involve physical design changes, altering social behaviors, improving surveillance, or any number of other activities. Closely allied to situational prevention is the emergence of community policing. The community policing approach relies heavily on citizen involvement in a problem-solving approach to neighborhood concerns.

Many secondary prevention efforts resemble activities listed under primary prevention. The distinction rests on whether the programs are aimed more at keeping problems that lead to criminal activity from arising (primary prevention) or if the efforts are focused on factors that already exist and are fostering deviant behavior (secondary prevention). Secondary prevention may deal with predelinquents or deviant behavior which leads to injurious criminal activity. For example, alcohol and other drug use are highly related to other forms of deviance. Targeting drug use as an indicator of criminal propensity is a secondary prevention approach. Schools can play an important role in secondary prevention both in terms of identifying problem youths and in providing a forum for interventions. Clearly, much secondary prevention may rest in the hands of parents, educators, and neighborhood leaders who have daily contact with the individuals and conditions leading to deviance and fear.

Tertiary Crime Prevention

According to Brantingham and Faust (1976), **tertiary prevention** "deals with actual offenders and involves intervention … in such a fashion that they will not commit further offenses." The majority of tertiary prevention rests within the workings of the criminal justice system. The activities of arrest, prosecution, incarceration, treatment, and rehabilitation all fall within the realm of tertiary prevention. Non-justice system input to this process includes private enterprise correctional programs, diversionary justice within the community, and some community corrections. Tertiary prevention is often ignored in discussions of crime prevention due to its traditional place in other texts and the great volume of writing on these topics that already exists.

The types of approaches and interventions within each level of crime prevention are certainly not limited to those mentioned. Within each of the three types of prevention there are many variations and novel ways to approach a given crime problem. Indeed, crime prevention techniques are only limited by the imagination of individuals interested in decreasing the levels of crime and fear of crime.

Alternate Classifications of Crime Prevention

As noted earlier, crime prevention can be classified in other ways than that of a public health model. One is a variation on the tripartite public health model offered by van Dijk and de Waard (1991). Their model adds a second dimension resulting in a 3 × 3 configuration with primary/secondary/tertiary on one axis and victim-oriented/community-neighborhood-oriented/offender-oriented on the other axis. For example, primary prevention techniques can be divided into actions that target victims, the community, or potential offenders. This simply refines the public health-based classification system. Crawford (1998) offers another two-dimensional typology that again uses the primary/secondary/tertiary view as a starting point, and adds a distinction between social and situational approaches within each category. Both of these models offer alternative views of crime prevention and ways of conceptualizing crime prevention interventions.

Hunter (2010) sees crime prevention divided into micro, meso, and macro levels, while maintaining the primary, secondary, and tertiary distinctions. **Micro-level crime prevention** targets individuals, small groups, small areas, or small businesses for intervention. These interventions may be very site-specific and target individual vulnerabilities. **Meso-level crime prevention** looks at larger communities or neighborhoods, or larger groups of individuals or businesses. Examples of this could be entire villages or towns, or possibly a chain of specialty stores. The interventions here will involve larger groups and seek to engender cooperative responses to crime. Finally, **macro-level crime prevention** looks at large communities, society as a whole, or other very large collectives. At this level, responses would involve large scale social changes, major shifts in educational practices, major new employment opportunities, or legislative changes to address crime and disorder (Hunter, 2010).

Tonry and Farrington (1995) divide crime prevention into four categories: (1) developmental, (2) community, (3) situational, and (4) criminal justice. Each of these categories simply parcels out some aspect of the public health model. The criminal justice category, for example, is substantially tertiary prevention, while community is largely primary prevention. Bjørgo (2013) offers a general crime prevention model with nine categories: (1) establishing and monitoring normative barriers, (2) reducing recruitment to criminal activity, (3) deterrence, (4) disrupting acts before they occur, (5) protecting targets, (6) reducing the level of harm from crime, (7) reducing the rewards of crime, (8) incapacitation, and (9) desistence and rehabilitation. Each of these fall somewhere within the public health model.

An emerging area within the realm of crime prevention is that of **crime science**. Laycock (2005) suggests that crime science is a new discipline, or at the very least a new paradigm, for addressing crime by coupling efforts to prevent crime with the detection of and intervention with offenders. This is in contrast to the existing paradigm within criminal justice where "Crime is seen as fundamentally about offenders rather than situations" (Laycock, 2005, p. 21). The emphasis on offenders involves the criminal justice system in the apprehension, adjudication and punishment/treatment of offenders. Little or no concern is paid to prevention of crime. Conversely, "[c]rime science is the application of the methods of science to crime and disorder" (Laycock, 2005, p. 4).

In essence, crime science attacks crime from a wide range of disciplines using a broad array of tools. Among the disciplines included are those traditionally found in discussions of crime and criminality—sociology, psychology, criminology, and criminal justice. Also included, however, are the fields of engineering, biology, physics, architecture, genetics, communications, computer science, education, and many others. Each of these disciplines offers insight to the behavior of individuals, how to control or manipulate the physical and social environment, the development of safety and security devices, or a myriad of other factors that play a role in crime and crime control. A primary goal of crime science is to bring these divergent disciplines together into a functional, coordinated response to crime (Laycock, 2005).

In many ways, crime science fits nicely in the public health prevention model. An examination of the approaches listed in Table 2.1 shows a wide array of actions and interventions that require the knowledge and expertise from disciplines beyond those typically involved in the criminal justice system. At the same time, the criminal justice system is intimately involved in the detection, apprehension and intervention with offenders, as well as the implementation of new prevention initiatives. Many of the prevention approaches and interventions outlined in this book rely on methods and information drawn from disciplines not traditionally involved in crime or its prevention.

Model of Choice

While all of the classifications presented here have merit, this book utilizes the public health framework. Virtually all of the other classifications fit within this model. Primary, secondary, and tertiary crime prevention encompass diverse prevention methods ranging from physical design of homes and communities, to neighborhood watch, to educating the public, to developmental approaches, to situationally unique interventions, to drug prevention, to deterrence, incapacitation, and rehabilitation. Crime prevention is not limited to the work of the criminal justice system. Instead, it relies on the knowledge and abilities of a very diverse set of individuals and groups who work to apply scientific principles to the understanding and prevention of crime. Beyond just presenting a discussion of different prevention approaches, this book attempts to provide insight to the effectiveness of each approach. Evaluating prevention initiatives, however, is not without its problems. It is to the topic of evaluating crime prevention that we now turn.

KEY TERMS

- assize of arms
- Chicago Area Project
- constable
- crime control
- crime prevention
- crime science
- developmental prevention
- hue and cry

- *lex talionis*
- micro-, meso-, and macro-level crime prevention
- obligatory policing
- *parens patriae*
- parochial police
- primary prevention
- public health model

- secondary prevention
- situational crime prevention
- social prevention
- status offenses
- tertiary prevention
- thief takers
- vigilante movement
- watch and ward

CHAPTER 3 Evaluation and Crime Prevention

LEARNING OBJECTIVES

After reading this chapter you should be able to:

- Distinguish between impact and process evaluation.
- Discuss obstacles to undertaking impact evaluations.
- Provide an argument for the value of process evaluations.
- Define cost–benefit evaluation and discuss problems with doing it in crime prevention.
- Give reasons for why programs and evaluation should be based on sound theory.
- Identify measurement problems in evaluating crime prevention programs.
- Explain why the appropriate follow-up period is important.
- Explain what is meant by the "gold standard" in evaluation.
- Discuss the concerns with relying on a single methodological standard for evaluations.
- Discuss both threats to internal and external validity, particularly as they impact crime prevention evaluations.
- Outline the Maryland Scale of Scientific Methods.
- Explain realistic evaluation.

The goal of this book is not just to provide information on crime prevention programs and initiatives. Instead, the intent is to offer insight into what works in crime prevention. To accomplish that task, it is necessary to evaluate prevention programs and efforts. Because this text is a survey of the prevention field, it relies on evaluations conducted by other researchers. At first glance it may seem that reporting on evaluations that have already been conducted would be easy and straightforward. Unfortunately, a good deal of debate has occurred over what constitutes "good" evaluation (see Holcomb and Lab, 2003).

The purpose of this chapter is to discuss the topic of evaluation and lay the groundwork for the evaluation of prevention that appears throughout the chapters. A number of topics will be addressed. First, the different types of evaluations, or as some would argue the different parts of an effective evaluation, are discussed. The second issue to be discussed involves theoretical and measurement problems. The debate about the appropriate methodology for evaluations forms a core topic in the chapter and helps tie together the different threads raised in the earlier sections. The ultimate goal is to lay a foundation for understanding the importance of evaluation in crime prevention.

Types of Evaluation

In general, **evaluation** refers to investigating the usefulness of some exercise or phenomenon. Evaluation of crime prevention, therefore, refers to investigating the impact of a prevention technique or intervention on the level of subsequent crime, fear, or other intended outcome. Making such a determination may require the use of various methodologies. Ekblom and Pease (1995) argue that evaluation research is often viewed as addressing two research goals using diverse methodologies. These goals are generally understanding the implementation of the intervention and the impact of the initiative and are evaluated using two forms of evaluation—process and impact evaluation—respectively. A third form of evaluation—cost-benefit evaluation—is becoming more common.

Impact Evaluation

Impact (outcome) evaluations focus on what changes (e.g., to the crime rate) occur after the introduction of the policy, intervention, or program. There are many examples of impact evaluations in criminal justice. For example, treatment programs used in correctional settings are evaluated on their effectiveness to reduce recidivism or drug use among offenders. Changes in police patrol practices aimed at reducing the level of drug sales in an area are evaluated in terms of subsequent numbers of sales. In-school interventions that teach students how to respond to problems in a non-aggressive fashion are assessed in terms of the type or amount of future physical confrontations in school. Neighborhood watch programs have been evaluated in terms of their impact on crime levels in the neighborhood and the fear of crime reported by residents. Changes in traffic patterns, walkways, building designs, and the layout of residential complexes have been assessed in terms of changes in crime. Evaluations of newsletters and media efforts to promote preventive activity have looked at the ability of such efforts to change not only citizen behavior but also their victimization levels. These are a few of the many evaluations that can be found throughout the crime prevention literature and discussed in later chapters.

Undertaking impact evaluations in crime prevention poses some interesting problems. One major obstacle is the fact that crime prevention initiatives rarely rely on a single intervention or approach. Rather, crime prevention programs often incorporate a menu of different activities at the same time. For example, neighborhood crime prevention typically includes a watch scheme, property identification, neighborhood cleanup, periodic meetings, and some form of prevention newsletter. The problem for evaluators is identifying which of the many prevention activities is responsible for the observed changes (if any). It is possible that the entire package is necessary to bring about the change, it is possible that only one of the elements is responsible for the change, or it is equally plausible that the mix of interventions mitigates any positive impact on crime and fear. It is rare to find that a single prevention activity is undertaken in total isolation from other anti-crime initiatives.

A second set of obstacles for evaluating crime prevention revolves around the fact that the target of the initiatives (and thus the unit of analysis for the evaluation) is a neighborhood or other geographic area. This is not to suggest that implementing a crime prevention program across a neighborhood or community is ill-conceived. Rather, the issue is solely a methodological one, and it is multifaceted. First, neighborhoods cannot be isolated. This means that there are a multitude of other influences on the neighborhood—many of them from the surrounding community or adjacent neighborhoods—that may have an influence on the levels of crime. Second, many interventions are not uniformly applied across an area or adopted by all residents. As a result, it is possible that an intervention appears to have no impact across the area, when in fact those who participate experience a reduction in crime and/or fear. Impact evaluations need to pay special attention to the effectiveness of prevention techniques in cases in which there is not total cooperation or adoption of the intervention.

A third concern with impact evaluations of crime prevention programs involves the competing issues of crime displacement and diffusion of benefits. While both of these will be discussed at length later in the book, they refer to the issue of whether the prevention activity influences the level of crime and fear in areas not involved in the initiative. These obstacles to impact evaluations will receive further consideration later in this chapter.

Process Evaluation

Process evaluations consider the implementation of a program or initiative and involve determining the procedures used to implement a specific program. These evaluations also examine the social context within which the program or initiative operates (Ekblom and Pease, 1995). In general, process evaluations offer a detailed descriptive account of the program and its implementation. Process evaluations look at a wide range of variables and topics starting with the initial goals of the initiative and continuing all the way through the current operations (or closing) of the program. Typical factors considered are the mission/goals of the program, the level and quality of program staff, the funding and other resources of the program, obstacles faced in implementing and sustaining the initiative, the degree to which the project was carried out as planned, the level of support for the program, the degree to which the clients complied with the intervention, the quality of the data gathered, and any changes made in the program over time. All of this information is used in assessing the degree to which the intervention was successfully implemented as planned. Advocates of process evaluations point out that the resulting information is pivotal in answering questions about the context of an intervention and what actually took place in the initiative.

Unfortunately, many evaluations only look only at the process. There is often no attempt to undertake an impact evaluation. Thus, it is possible to know what was attempted and how well it was done, but it is impossible to know whether it had any impact on crime and/or fear of crime. Among the more extensive process evaluations in the United States and the United Kingdom are those examining partnership initiatives, including the Comprehensive Communities Programs, the Strategic Approaches to Community Safety Initiative, the Burglary Reduction Initiative, and the Crime and Disorder Act projects. Almost without exception, the U.S. evaluations have been exclusively process oriented (e.g., Bureau of Justice Assistance, 1997; Kelling, 1998; Rosenbaum and Kaminska-Costello, 1998). Even where impact evaluations were planned, they were often abandoned before they were funded or completed.

Process evaluations of prevention programs or other initiatives often view success in terms other than reaching the outcome goals of the program. Instead, success is often measured in terms of the number of meetings held, participation by different agencies at the meetings, how long the program has been operating, the number of clients handled, the amount of funds expended, or the development of operational plans. What is missing is the assessment of the program's impact on crime, fear, quality of life, or other intended outcome. From the standpoint of having an impact on crime, process evaluations alone offer no insight.

Given the fact that process evaluations do not answer the key question for many programs (i.e., does it reduce crime), why are they so prevalent? Several reasons are apparent. First, doing a process evaluation can set the stage for an outcome study by indicating whether the intervention or initiative has been implemented correctly and whether the target receives the amount of intervention necessary to bring about the intended change. Second, process evaluations can provide insight into the context within which the intervention operates. Knowing the background of the problem, the operations of the program, what took place, problems that arose, and other factors can provide information on whether the intervention can be used in another place at another time. That is, process evaluations provide insight into the potential generalizability of the intervention. In this sense, therefore, a process evaluation becomes an important part of the overall assessment of the program. Finally, process evaluations have the distinct advantage that they cannot fail. Every process evaluation can tell about what happened, how much took place, how many participated, and other factors. Such information can form the basis of a formidable report showing that an initiative is busy doing a lot of things. Thus, a program can point to numerous accomplishments.

In conjunction with an impact evaluation, process evaluations provide information on the different settings, the implementation of the intervention, and other factors that may have an impact on the results (Tilley, 2002). Process evaluations should accompany an impact evaluation. Process evaluations look at how well the intervention was implemented, whether it was maintained at the level needed for success, if the experimental group accepted the intervention, whether there were factors that may have kept the program from succeeding, and similar issues. Clearly, there are unique social, physical, and situational factors that will affect the ability of a prevention program to have an impact (Ekblom, 2002; Tilley, 2002).

Cost–Benefit Evaluations

The third type of evaluation that deserves mentioning here is that of a cost–benefit evaluation. A **cost–benefit evaluation** (or cost–benefit analysis) seeks to assess whether the costs of an intervention are justified by the benefits or outcomes that accrue from it. Aos (2003a) demonstrates that assessing the costs and benefits of a prevention program is an important component of a full evaluation of any program. With limited resources available to it, the criminal justice system (as well as any government or private enterprise) needs to implement programs that can bring about the desired changes for the least cost. Cost–benefit analysis is a form of process evaluation that requires an impact evaluation be completed at the same time. The reason for this is relatively simple: you cannot determine if the costs are justified if you do not measure the ability of the program to bring about the expected change. Thus, a cost–benefit analysis requires both a process and impact evaluation.

Undertaking a cost–benefit analysis in crime prevention and criminal justice poses some problems not always found in other disciplines. The largest problem involves setting monetary values on factors that are not easily enumerated (Tilley, 2009). For example, placing a value on burglaries that do not occur may be accomplished by taking the average dollar lost from past burglaries and assuming that each prevented burglary is a savings at that dollar figure. How do you place a monetary value, however, on things like reduced fear of crime, trauma from victimization, or psychological/emotional loss due to an assault or homicide? How do you account for time loss that may not be related to days off work? The problem of setting values for many factors is pervasive in social science evaluations. A second problem is making certain that all of the costs involved in the program (and related to the program operations) are counted. While counting the number of copies made and office hours spent can be completed, it is harder to enumerate the value of lost time spent on other activities, the level of effort expended, and other factors. These problems do not make it impossible to conduct a cost–benefit analysis, although they do make it more challenging.

Theory and Measurement in Evaluation

The value of any evaluation, as well as the ability to conduct an evaluation, is largely determined by basic factors related to the underlying theory and the measurement of key concepts. It is not uncommon for evaluations to pay little attention to theory and to uncritically use variables that are not appropriate for answering relevant questions. An additional common evaluation shortfall involves the failure to follow up on the project. Each of these issues is addressed in turn.

Theoretical Concerns

Crime prevention programs are often implemented, and evaluations are often undertaken, in a theoretical vacuum (Holcomb and Lab, 2003). This means that those implementing and evaluating the intervention pay no attention to the theoretical assumptions underlying the prevention program. Basic questions, such as why should the redesign of the parking deck have an impact on theft from autos, why should a partnership reduce drug use in the community, and why would an educational program reduce aggressive behavior, are often ignored. This is surprising given their centrality to the evaluation of initiatives. It is not necessary to identify a formal theory for every intervention, but it is necessary to be able to adequately explain why and how the intervention will bring about the desired change.

Despite the argument that evaluations should be guided by the theory underlying the intervention, a great number of successful evaluations are undertaken in a theoretical vacuum. These evaluations may still provide answers to whether or not the program had the intended impact. Why then is the lack of theory a concern for evaluation? One reason is that while these evaluations can tell us if prevention initiatives are successful, they fail to tell us why a program is or is not successful. They also can provide only limited insight to whether the program can be implemented in other places or at other times (Holcomb and Lab, 2003). A second reason for having a solid theoretical basis for the evaluation is that many investigations might not be necessary if the underlying theory for the intervention was examined. There are numerous examples where examination of the underlying theory would have raised questions about the efficacy of the intervention at the outset (Holcomb and Lab, 2003). For example, studies of curfews often fail to recognize that, as they are typically conceived, there is no reason to expect them to have any impact. This is because the underlying argument is that getting youths off the street would make it hard for them to commit offenses. Unfortunately, curfews imposed from late night to early morning (as is typical) will have no impact on the number of crimes during the after school hours when most youths commit their offenses. Clearly, the knowledge of the theory underlying curfews would not only eliminate the need for the evaluation, but also suggest termination of the curfew (Holcomb and Lab, 2003). Basically, evaluations of programs without a theoretical base can be considered as "research in a vacuum." There is no context within which to understand the program, frame the evaluation questions, design the methodological approach, or carry out the evaluation.

If evaluations undertaken with an eye toward theory are preferred, why are so many atheoretical evaluations undertaken? Several reasons are apparent (see Holcomb and Lab, 2003). First, there is an "outcome myopia" that permeates many evaluations. This means that the programs and the evaluators are only interested in whether the program works and not how or why it works. The resulting evaluation simply assumes that a positive outcome is enough to prove the intervention works. While this is a plausible conclusion, it is also possible that other factors are at work and it does not tell anything about why a program does not work when the findings are negative. A second reason for the lack of theory in evaluation is the fact that many program administrators simply "know" that it works. For them, "it is only common sense that it works!" Thus, they are not interested in spending the time, money, and/or effort to prove what they already know. There is no reason to explain exactly how a program works or to undertake an evaluation—it simply does. This blind belief in programs is evident in many initiatives that have the ear of politicians who can provide legislative and funding support. A final explanation for the appearance of atheoretical evaluations of crime prevention initiatives is the fact that many programs are the result of grassroots efforts by small groups. These groups are not always interested in evaluations or how the program works, as long as they are happy with it. Evaluations of these programs, therefore, are undertaken by outside researchers who come to the program long after it was initiated. They have few resources to devote to an evaluation and probably have not been collecting data on the project. The result is evaluations that look only at the outcome and ignore the question of why the program should or does work. The evaluator gets in, completes the evaluation, and gets out in relatively short order.

Truly effective evaluations need to be informed by the underlying theoretical rationale for the program under inspection. Just knowing that a program does or does not work is not enough. It is important to understand why an intervention works or does not work. Of equal value is gaining insight to whether a program can be implemented in another place at another time. The underlying theory provides a great deal of information that is lost in evaluations where theory is missing.

Measurement Issues

Measurement of key concepts is a concern in all forms of research, but nowhere is it more evident than in evaluation research. The types of interventions found in crime prevention present some interesting measurement problems. One problem involves measuring the key outcome variables when the intervention is geographically based. While some studies looking at city-wide crime levels can use police data, many crime prevention programs are based on neighborhoods or other small geographic areas that do not coincide with specific police reporting areas. Thus, a great deal of data manipulation is needed if official crime records are to be used. The advent of geographic information systems that allow for the mapping of crime locations has helped to minimize this problem, but only in those locations where this technology is in use.

One possible solution to the problems with using official data is to rely on victim survey data. Indeed, many prevention evaluations incorporate victim surveys along with official crime data. Victim survey data offer a number of advantages, including the ability to collect data for the exact area under consideration, the ability to capture crimes not reported to the police, and the fact that the survey can collect information on fear and personal perceptions that is not found in official records. Unfortunately, victim data are not always available and the collection of that data can be both time consuming and costly. This lack of data is compounded when an evaluation also needs data from a comparison group or area.

The ability of victim surveys to gather data on key concepts such as fear is not without its own problems. As was seen in Chapter 1, operationalizing fear is not straightforward. Fear has been measured in a number of different ways, making it difficult to compare results across studies. It is also problematic if the measure of fear is inappropriate for the type of intervention. For example, asking questions about perceptions of changing crime may not be germane if the intervention involves lighting the neighborhood so residents go out at night. Instead, asking about whether respondents would walk outside at night on their street would fit the prevention technique. The choice of operationalization is greatly contingent on the prevention initiative and the underlying theory. Thus, the need to use theory to inform the prevention program extends naturally to the choice of variables and how they are measured.

Yet another measurement issue involves finding ways to uncover the competing influences in the project that mask the outcomes. An interesting conundrum in crime prevention initiatives is the fact that the programs often try to simultaneously reduce the level of crime while increasing the reporting of crime to the police. Neighborhood watch programs are a prime example. These programs typically include a number of initiatives such as property identification, surveillance of neighbors' property, and encouraging the reporting of crime to the police. While the intent is to reduce the level of crime in the neighborhood, it is easy to see how an effective program can appear to have no impact. This would occur if, while the program reduces the actual level of offending in the area, the residents report a larger percentage of the crimes that do occur. The official data, therefore, would appear unchanged even though crime is down. Prevention evaluations need to consider this type of problem and utilize methods (such as pre- and post-project victim surveys) that would uncover this complication.

Follow-Up Periods

An issue closely related to how something is measured is the issue of the appropriate length of time to follow up the project. The question of the follow-up period is actually two-sided. First, how long after the implementation of the program or intervention will changes in crime (or other outcome) appear? Second, is there a possibility that over time any initial changes will diminish or disappear? The most common situation is one in which the evaluation considers a relatively short follow-up period, often six months. This occurs because of the immediate desire to know whether the program works and the fact that the costs of an evaluation increase with the follow-up time. A relatively short follow-up time means that any program that requires a lengthy time to have an impact will be seen as ineffective. Alternatively, an initiative with an immediate impact will be declared a success, despite the (unknown) fact that the impact may diminish over time. While there is no rule on the appropriate follow-up time, the evaluation should look to the underlying theory for guidance. The ideal situation would be one where follow-up data are gathered at different intervals, such as three months, six months, 12 months, and 18 months. The use of multiple points in time will illuminate both the speed of an intervention's impact (if any) and any evidence that the impact diminishes over time.

Summary

Evaluations that ignore theory (or evaluations of atheoretical programs) and problems with measurement and follow-up are common in studies of crime prevention programs. Much of this is due to the fact that evaluations are often undertaken late in the life of programs when data is more difficult to gather and the program has undergone several changes since its inception. The evaluation also may be undertaken by individuals or groups connected with the intervention and who "know it works," thus adding a potential source of bias. While solutions to these issues are not always easy or cheap, evaluations need to take whatever steps are possible to avoid these problems.

The Method for Evaluation

An inspection of the crime prevention literature reveals great diversity in the methodologies applied in the search for what works in prevention. A great deal of debate about the appropriate methods to use has ensued over the past 10 years. Where one view argues that true experimental design is the preferred approach, the opposite view suggests that the method should be dictated by the questions being asked and the situation within which the intervention exists.

Experimental Design

A great deal of discussion has centered on the claim that only evaluations using (or approximating) a true experimental design are worthy of consideration. Also known as a *randomized control trial* (Tilley, 2009), experimental design has become the **gold standard** in evaluation. Why is experimental design the preferred approach by many evaluators? From a purely methodological perspective it offers a number of strengths. First, a randomized control trial, which relies on the random assignment of cases into experimental and control groups, increases the likelihood that the two groups being compared are equivalent. Second, there is enough control over the evaluation to make certain that the experimental group receives the treatment or intervention while the control group does not. There is also the expectation that all other possible factors that could influence the outcome are controlled to the extent that they cannot affect either of the two groups. In essence, the experimental design addresses the various **threats to internal validity**—that is, factors that could cause the results to occur besides the measures that were implemented (see Table 3.1). If the project is able to accomplish these things, any changes observed in the experimental group that do not appear in the control group should be attributable to the intervention. The researcher thus feels confident that he "knows" the cause of any observed change.

This "gold standard" has a long history in the hard sciences (e.g. biology and chemistry) and is accepted practice. A great deal of attention has been focused on relying on this approach in criminal justice and crime prevention due to the work of Sherman et al. (1997) which was prepared for the U.S. Congress. In that report, the authors opted to rate the existing literature on prevention initiatives according to how closely a study adhered to the standards of a true experimental design (see Berk and Rossi, 1999; Cook and Campbell, 1979). Using the resulting **Maryland Scale of Scientific Methods** (see Table 3.2), Sherman et al. (1997) conclude that the bulk of the evidence on prevention activities shows there are relatively few effective programs/interventions. Subsequent work using this approach has gone so far as to suggest that policy makers should only consider research that meets the gold standard and that research funds should only be

TABLE 3.1 Selected Threats to Internal Validity

History	Something taking place independently of the experiment causes the change to take place
Maturation	The aging of the study subjects brings about a change independent of the program or stimulus
Testing	The taking of measurements in the study (such as through surveys, observations, or data collection) causes change to occur in place of or beyond the impact of the stimulus
Instrumentation	Changes in the study measures or study procedure that take place during the project bring about changes
Statistical Regression	Implementing a project that focuses on subjects that are at an extreme end of a measurement (such as low or high crime rate) will naturally regress to a statistical average score over time
Selection	Experimental subjects who are not truly representative of the population of interest will influence the results
Mortality	The incidence of study subjects dropping out during the course of the experiment can bias the results if they are different from those who remain in the project

Source: Adapted by author from W. Shadish et al. (2002). *Experimental and Quasi-experimental Designs for Generalized Causal Inference*. Boston: Houghton Mifflin.

expended when an experimental design (or close to it) is possible (Sherman et al., 2002). Unfortunately, applying this standard in crime prevention research (and, more generally, social sciences) is difficult and often not possible.

There are various problems with relying exclusively on experimental designs in crime prevention. Foremost among these is the question of whether the results would be applicable in other places, settings, and times—that is, the **generalizability** of the results. This problem involves what are called **threats to external validity**. Table 3.3 lists a variety of threats to external validity. An inspection of this list reveals the wide range of potential problems inherent in trying to replicate the findings of any program evaluation. One major problem is that many interventions target communities and larger collectives, rather than individuals. It is very difficult, if not impossible, to randomly assign communities to experimental and control groups (Ekblom, 2002; Ekblom and Pease, 1995; Laycock, 2002). In the absence of randomization, the best that can be done is to try and identify neighborhoods or communities for the control group which are matched to the experimental areas on as many characteristics as possible. Matching, however, cannot

TABLE 3.2 Maryland Scale of Scientific Methods

Level 1:	Correlation between a crime prevention program and a measure of crime or crime risk factors at a single point in time.
Level 2:	Temporal sequence between the program and the crime or risk outcome clearly observed, or the presence of a comparison group without demonstrated comparability to the treatment group.
Level 3:	A comparison between two or more comparable units of analysis, one with and one without the program.
Level 4:	Comparison between multiple units with and without the program, controlling for other factors, or using comparison units that evidence only minor differences.
Level 5:	Random assignment and analysis of comparable units to program and comparison groups.

Source: Sherman et al. (1998). "Preventing crime: What works, what doesn't, what's promising." *Research in Brief*. Washington, DC: National Institute of Justice.

guarantee that the areas are comparable. Even if random assignment is possible or good matching is accomplished, there is no way to isolate the experimental and control communities from all other influences. Most importantly, interventions and initiatives implemented in a community cannot be hidden from sight. People in both the experimental community and the control areas will be able to see what is taking place. This can lead individuals and groups in the control areas to adopt the intervention, or to act in such a way as to impede the intervention in the experimental area. There is simply no way to isolate the experimental community from all outside influences as can be done in a laboratory.

> **ON THE WEB**
>
> *The Campbell Collaboration is a leading advocate and supporter of evaluations that rely on the experimental design and the promotion of evidence-based practice in criminal justice. You can learn more about their approach and publications at their web site: http://www.campbellcollaboration.org/*

A number of threats to external validity involve issues related to the implementation of an intervention (Tilley, 2009). The individuals/groups involved in an intervention can vary greatly from place to place. This can affect the quality of the intervention or the degree to which a program is fully implemented/delivered as planned (i.e., the dosage).

The locations, crime, victims, and offenders are rarely (if ever) exactly the same in different places or times, which may affect the outcome of the intervention. The bottom line is, even if an evaluation shows that a crime prevention intervention is effective in one place, there is no guarantee that it will be just as effective in other places.

TABLE 3.3 Threats to External Validity

Threat to External Validity	Explanation
Place attributes	Places are never exactly the same, and the details may be important to the effects brought about
Victim attributes	Patterns of victim attributes will vary from one site to another, and the details may be important to the effects brought about
Offender/likely offender attributes	Patterns of offender/likely offender attributes will vary from one site to another, and the details may be important to the effects brought about
Intervenor attributes	Who is involved in delivering the intervention, in terms of leader, front-line worker, or agency will vary from site to site, and the details may be important to the effects brought about
Community/family/ peer group attributes	The patterns of social relationships in which offenders and victims are embedded will vary from site to site, and the details may be important to the effects brought about
Intervention attributes	What is done can never be duplicated exactly, and the details may be important to the effects brought about
Non-crime options	Other non-crime behaviors available to those who would otherwise commit an offense will vary from site to site, and the details may be important to the effects brought about
Crime options	Different crime possibilities available to those who would otherwise commit some particular type of offense will vary from site to site, and the details may be important to the effects brought about
Dosage	Intensity of intervention in relation to target people, places of crime problems varies from site to site, and the level may be important to the effects brought about

Source: N. Tilley (2009). *Crime Prevention*. Cullompton, Devon, U.K.: Willan. Reprinted with permission.

The underlying problem for external validity is that, too often, experimental designs fail to consider the *context* within which a program or intervention operates. What this means is that the program may be successful in one location at one time while it is a dismal failure at another location or time. There may be something different about the neighborhoods that is not readily apparent from simple demographic, crime, or social information available about the areas. Simple random assignment or matching cannot eliminate these factors. Instead, there is a need for a thorough process evaluation to accompany the impact analysis.

Another flaw in relying too heavily on experimental design is the fact that it is all too easy to jump to a conclusion that something does or does not work. This may occur when no impact emerges in an analysis—the researcher claims it was a failure and suggests abandoning further use of the intervention. The negative findings, however, may be the result of factors such as poor program implementation, misspecification of the appropriate target or causal mechanism underlying the problem, or resistance by the target (Eck, 2002). In these cases, a well constructed experimental design may find no programmatic impact and declare the intervention a failure, when in fact the intervention can and would work in other settings or if it was properly implemented.

Unfortunately, in many evaluations using rigorous experimental designs, the methodology ends up driving the project rather than allowing the underlying theory to dictate the development of the project or its analysis. You can have a good experimental design and find no impact of a project due to the fact that there was no theoretical reason to expect the intervention to work in the first place. One good example of this appears in evaluations of juvenile curfew laws (discussed earlier in this chapter) where the evaluation design meets the level of scientific rigor outlined by Sherman et al. (1997) but ignores the theoretical flaw underlying the approach. There was really no reason to undertake evaluations just because it met some methodological standard when attention to the theory would have suggested that the intervention would not work.

Realistic Evaluation

Overemphasis on the "correct" methodology (i.e., the gold standard) marginalizes the value of other approaches to building knowledge of crime prevention. Basic knowledge essential to crime prevention has come out of a variety of research endeavors, such as ethnographic and qualitative methodologies. A prime example of this is the knowledge we have on burglars and their choice of targets. Extensive ethnographic research has been completed with different groups of burglars, in different settings, across different countries, and using different approaches, such as riding around with them in cars to identify prime targets or having them rate pictures of homes on suitability for burglary. These studies (e.g., Bennett, 1986; Bennett and Wright, 1984; Cromwell et al., 1991; Reppetto, 1974; Wright and Decker, 1994) have provided a great deal of insight on the behaviors of burglars that is consistent across the studies (see Chapter 6 for more information). This information is very helpful for understanding what works to prevent residential burglary. Similar research has been completed targeting robbery and other property crimes and offenders (e.g., Feeney, 1986; Gill and Matthews, 1994; Shover, 1991; Tunnell, 1992). While these projects do not even approximate the experimental design standards, should we simply ignore the information and abandon this line of inquiry? The answer to this question is "No." Indeed, it is important to recognize that the "gold standard" is not appropriate for all investigations.

Pawson and Tilley (1997) call for a more "realistic" approach to evaluation research. In **realistic evaluation**, rather than relying exclusively on experimental approaches, evaluation needs to observe the phenomenon in its entirety. Two key ideas are central to realistic evaluation—mechanism and context. **Mechanism** refers to understanding "what it is about a program which makes it work" (Pawson and Tilley, 1997, p. 66). In other words, by what process does an intervention impact an outcome measure such as crime or fear of crime? While the most rigorous experimental design can indicate whether a program is responsible for any observed changes, it does not tell *why* the program had an impact on the dependent variable. It is vital to understand the mechanism bringing about the change in order to build basic knowledge and to increase the potential success at transplanting a program from one setting to another (Ekblom 2002).

Beyond just examining the mechanism by which something works, Pawson and Tilley (1997, p. 69) note that "the relationship between causal mechanisms and their effects is not fixed, but contingent." By this, they argue that the context in which any intervention is implemented has an impact on its effectiveness. Consequently, the impact of a prevention effort is contingent on the context in which it operates, and subsequently will affect whether the program has a similar impact in different settings (Tilley, 2002). Ekblom and Pease (1995) note that efforts to find a single, best methodological approach to evaluation are short-sighted when they ignore the context of the program being studied. Circumstances unique to one setting and context may directly affect the ability of an intervention to achieve its goals. This requires more than a superficial impact evaluation which meets the "gold standard." It is important to combine knowledge of the mechanism by which change is thought to occur with an understanding of the wider context in which specific crime prevention efforts are implemented.

What is needed is recognition that the problem, the theory, and the context should determine the appropriate methodology for understanding what works. A single standard is not appropriate for all problems or questions. As Laycock (2002, p. 234) has so aptly pointed out, "'the gold standard' should not be any *particular* methodology, but a process of informed decision-making through which the *appropriate* methodology is chosen."

Summary

Based on the above, this book considers the evidence on crime prevention regardless of the methodology used. What is more important is whether the methodology is sound for the problem and the situation in which it is used. While experimental design informed by good theory and attention to the context of the project is preferred, it is not often available. In those cases, the best knowledge available is discussed and used to inform about what appears to work and not work. Even while recognizing that context is important, there is a clear bias in this book toward emphasizing outcome or impact evaluations. Underlying process evaluation materials and information have been considered throughout the chapters but receive little direct presentation due to space concerns.

An Overview of the Book

The balance of this text attempts to expose the reader to some of the predominant crime prevention issues and techniques of the past 40 years. The discussion is, by necessity, limited and does not deal with all of the prevention programs that have been attempted or evaluated. The goal of the book is to present a sampling of prevention approaches, outline the selected programs and issues, present the research and (primary impact) evaluations which have been carried out on the programs (if any have been done), and critically examine the prevention effort and the potential of the approach to affect crime and the fear of crime.

Throughout the text, the key criterion for assessing the effectiveness of various crime prevention methods is lower subsequent offending and/or fear of crime. Subsequent offending could be either initial criminal activity (primary prevention) or recidivism (tertiary prevention). Lowered fear of crime could come from any intervention mechanism, especially primary preventive techniques. Although a variety of other outcome measures have been used in assessing crime prevention programs (e.g., program operation, costs, number of clients served), reductions in crime and fear are the ultimate goals. These other outcomes will receive little attention in the following chapters. This does not mean that they are unimportant considerations. Indeed, from a fiscal standpoint it is important to know the costs of programs. However, this does not indicate the ability of the intervention to alter crime or fear of crime.

KEY TERMS

- context
- cost–benefit evaluation
- evaluation
- generalizability
- gold standard

- impact (outcome) evaluations
- Maryland Scale of Scientific Methods
- mechanism

- process evaluations
- realistic evaluation
- threats to external validity
- threats to internal validity

PART I

Primary Prevention

The words "crime prevention" typically bring to mind programs that are divorced from the formal criminal justice system and are greatly reliant upon the efforts of the citizenry. Such crime prevention efforts typically fall under the rubric of *primary prevention*. Primary prevention deals with eliminating influences in the physical and social environment that engender deviant behavior. Such programs do not target individuals who are already criminal or prone to criminal behavior, except in a most indirect sense. Instead, primary prevention programs work with general physical and societal factors that provide the opportunity for deviance to occur. The following chapters reflect varying methods aimed at removing or mitigating the criminogenic aspects of society.

Chapter 4 focuses directly on physical design components of crime prevention. Crime Prevention Through Environmental Design (CPTED) has been one of the most widely discussed crime prevention approaches of the past 40 years. The idea behind CPTED is making crime harder to commit and making residents feel more secure in their surroundings. This is accomplished by altering the physical environment. Increased lighting, improved locks, stronger doors, use of surveillance equipment, and other physical changes are intended to bring about greater social cohesion, citizen concern and involvement and, ultimately, reduced crime and fear of crime. Chapter 5 moves to a direct analysis of neighborhood crime prevention. The basic focus is on the mechanisms involved in building neighborhood cohesion and concern through crime prevention activities. Block watch and citizen patrols are key elements of many neighborhood efforts. Chapter 6 investigates competing ideas of displacement and diffusion as a result of crime prevention programming. Typically, reduced levels of crime in crime prevention areas serve as an indicator that crime has been eliminated. There is the potential, however, that the crime is simply displaced along some dimension. In displacement, the overall crime rate remains the same while modifications in the type, timing, or placement of crime occur.

One key element in the discussion of crime prevention is the impact of programs on the fear of crime. Mass media crime prevention techniques, outlined in Chapter 7, represent an attempt to deal directly with the fear of crime, as well as actual crime, across a wide range of societal members. Developmental prevention forms the basis of Chapter 8. This chapter discusses the issue of identifying at-risk individuals and situations that can be addressed through early social intervention. Finally, Chapter 9 focuses on the formal criminal justice system. Deterrence is a cornerstone of formal system processing. General deterrence (as opposed to specific deterrence, which is discussed in Chapter 15) seeks to provide disincentives to persons not yet involved in deviant behavior. This is clearly in the realm of primary prevention. While the earlier chapters examine the impact of crime prevention activities on both crime and fear of crime, the chapter on general deterrence looks only at its effect on actual deviant behavior.

CHAPTER 4 The Physical Environment and Crime Prevention

LEARNING OBJECTIVES

After reading this chapter you should be able to:

- Define CPTED.
- Define defensible space.
- List and define Newman's elements of defensible space.
- Explain OTREP and its relation to crime.
- Discuss four intermediate goals of physical design changes.
- List and discuss the core principles of Secure By Design.
- Provide insight on the effectiveness of lighting to prevent crime.
- Define and discuss the ideas of prospect, refuge, and escape as they relate to prevention.
- Discuss the evidence on the effectiveness of CCTV.

- Explain Operation Identification and its impact.
- Demonstrate your knowledge about the impact of street layout on crime prevention.
- Discuss neighborhood-wide environmental design programs and their impact on crime and fear.
- Discuss Merry's analysis of and conclusions on defensible space.
- Explain incivility and its relation to crime and crime prevention.
- Discuss the idea of product design and provide examples for crime prevention.

The advent of modern crime prevention has its roots in architectural design in the 1950s–1970s. At that time, architects and urban designers questioned the impact of the physical layout of cities and urban housing on behavior, particularly criminal actions. Changing the physical design of a community, home, or business could affect crime in a variety of ways.

Physical changes may make it more difficult to carry out a crime. This difficulty can result in lower payoff in relationship to the effort. Another potential impact is that the risk of being seen and caught while committing an offense may be enhanced. Finally, the physical design changes may prompt residents to alter their behavior in ways that make crime more difficult to commit. This chapter introduces and explains various physical design approaches for combating and preventing crime, examines the impact these actions have on crime, and assesses the potential of these approaches.

Crime Prevention Through Environmental Design

Efforts to alter the physical design of an area or location to impact crime are generally referred to as **Crime Prevention Through Environmental Design (CPTED)**. Included in this approach are architectural designs that enhance territoriality and surveillance, target hardening, and the recognition of legitimate users of an area. The basic ideas of CPTED grew out of Newman's (1972) concept of "defensible space."

Defensible space proposes "a model which inhibits crime by creating a physical expression of a social fabric which defends itself" (Newman, 1972). The idea is that the physical characteristics of an area can influence the behavior of both residents and potential offenders. For residents, the appearance and design of the area can engender a more caring attitude, draw the residents into contact with one another, lead to further improvements and use of the area, and build a stake in the control and elimination of crime.

┌─ ON THE WEB ──────────────────

Kushmuk and Whittemore (1981) argue that the effect of physical design changes on crime is indirect and operates through four intermediate goals. The intermediate goals they outline are access control, surveillance, activity support, and motivation reinforcement. Whether they are intermediate goals or parts of CPTED could be debated. The authors illustrate the possible causal sequence in a diagram that can be found on the textbook's web site.

TABLE 4.1 CPTED Elements

Newman's defensible space elements:

Territoriality	A sense of ownership over an area which prompts people to take action when something seems amiss
Natural surveillance	The ability to observe activity, whether inside or outside, without the aid of special devices (such as closed-circuit television)
Image	A neighborhood having the appearance that it is not isolated and is cared for, and that residents will take action
Milieu	The placement of a home, building, or community in a larger area characterized by low crime

Other elements:

Access control	The ability to regulate who comes and goes from an area or building, with the intent of limiting access to legitimate users
Activity support	Functions that assist and enhance interaction between citizens and other legitimate users in the community
Target hardening	Actions that increase the effort by offenders in committing a crime

Source: Compiled by author from O. Newman (1972). *Defensible Space: People and Design in the Violent City*. New York: Macmillan; J. Kushmuk and S.L. Whittemore (1981). *A Reevaluation of the Crime Prevention Through Environmental Design Program in Portland, Oregon*. Washington, DC: National Institute of Justice; Cozens et al. (2005). "Crime prevention through environmental design (CPTED): A review and modern bibliography." *Property Management* 23:328–356.

For potential offenders, an area's appearance can suggest that residents use and care for their surroundings, pay attention to what occurs, and intervene if an offense is seen.

Newman (1972) identifies four elements of defensible space—territoriality, natural surveillance, image, and milieu (see Table 4.1). To these, proponents of CPTED have added several elements—access control, target hardening, and activity support. In some respects there is a great deal of commonality between these elements. At the same time, the elements may conflict with one another. Each of the CPTED factors influences the criminogenic nature of the area.

Territoriality

Territoriality refers to the ability and desire of legitimate users of an area to lay claim to the area. Areal control is based on the establishment of real or perceived boundaries, the recognition of strangers and legitimate users of the area, and a general communal atmosphere among the inhabitants. Territoriality means that an area, building, or property is owned by someone and others have no claim to it. Most important is that the residents/owners/legitimate users (non-offenders), as well as the potential offenders, recognize the "ownership" of the territory and make decisions about actions with that knowledge. Cozens et al. (2005) point out that territoriality takes two distinct forms. These are symbolic and real. **Symbolic territoriality** refers to things such as signs, landscaping, or other items that signal a change in ownership or area. **Real territoriality** is engendered by walls, fences, gates, or other items that place a physical barrier in front of people.

Surveillance

Surveillance involves any action that increases the chance that offenders will be observed. Newman (1972) specifically addresses the idea of **natural surveillance** where residents and legitimate users have the ability to see and observe what is taking place around them without taking special measures (this is what Cozens et al. (2005) would also call *informal surveillance*). Newman suggests placing windows in such a fashion to allow residents to see activity on all sides of their homes. Doors should face the street to allow passersby to view activity taking place inside the entranceways and few families should use the same common entrance so that legitimate users can identify one another. Additionally, pathways in and around the community should leave clear, unobstructed views for residents to see what is awaiting them as they enter and exit their homes (Newman, 1972). Outdoor activity and pedestrian traffic increase the number of "eyes on the street."

Surveillance can be enhanced in a variety of other ways. **Formal or organized surveillance** refers to the use of guards or employees specifically tasked with watching for offending (Cozens et al., 2005). Such formal surveillance may also be done by normal citizens involving themselves in citizen patrols or other organized surveillance activities. Yet another type—**mechanical surveillance**—utilizes cameras or other devices to observe activities, or

> ┌─ **ON THE WEB** ─────
> *Diagrams illustrating the surveillance rationale (natural, formal, and mechanical) can be found on the textbook web site.*

lights to simply increase the ability of people to see what is taking place (Cozens et al., 2005).

Any increase of surveillance activity should have a direct effect on opportunities for crime. The chances of committing a crime and getting away unobserved are diminished as the number of people who are able to see what is taking place increases. Underlying these suggestions is the assumption that, if a crime or suspicious individual is seen, the observer will inform the police or take some other action designed to eliminate crime.

Image and Milieu

Newman's (1972) concept of image is in some ways an extension of territoriality. **Image** is basically the outward appearance of an area or property as cared for by those who belong in the area. This communicates to potential offenders that there are concerned citizens watching over the area who will take actions to protect it. If the residents claim ownership (territoriality) and show that to others, the chances that offenders will take action will be minimized. **Milieu** extends these ideas further by arguing that prevention is enhanced if the surrounding area is also well cared for and maintained, and that there is little crime in those neighboring areas. Thus, building homes, businesses, or new communities within an already low-crime area will protect the new location. Maintaining the image of the area is essential to sending the right message out to both legitimate users and potential offenders (Cozens et al., 2005).

> ┌─ **ON THE WEB**
> *A holistic model illustrating the impact of most CPTED elements on building a community for crime prevention can be seen on the textbook web site.*

Access Control and Target Hardening

Access control seeks to allow only those persons who have legitimate business in an area to enter. This reduces the opportunity for crime by increasing the effort needed to enter and exit a building or area for the purpose of committing crime. Access control is also considered on a larger scale in terms of access to a neighborhood or community. This can be accomplished through gating communities, closing roads, or other means. Neighborhood designs that could make offending more difficult include limiting the flow of traffic through an area by strangers, changes that limit the number of through-streets, establishing cul-de-sacs and dead-end streets, and enhancing the ability of residents to recognize legitimate users. In essence, controlling access and egress to an area limits its **permeability** to those who wish to commit crime.

Target hardening is a closely related element to access control. **Target hardening** efforts are those that make potential criminal targets more difficult to victimize. The use and/or installation of locks, bars on windows, unbreakable glass, intruder alarms, fences, safes, and other devices makes crime more difficult to carry out. Target hardening can also take an indirect approach to crime control through the placement of identifying marks on personal property that makes stolen goods more difficult to fence and easier to identify and return to victims.

Beyond the design of buildings and places, it is possible to design products in ways that make them more difficult targets. While not considered in the early discussions of CPTED, product design to prevent crime has become a major movement. A prime example of this approach in target hardening is the incorporation of steering column locks in automobiles. This has been done for the sole purpose of reducing the incidence of motor vehicle theft. Product design will be discussed again later in this chapter.

It is important to note that access control/target-hardening measures will not eliminate crime. Any form of access control or target hardening can be overcome by a clever and persistent criminal. The hope is that the measures will reduce the absolute level of crime in the community. The actual impact of these approaches on crime is discussed later in this chapter.

Activity Support and Motivation Reinforcement

The ideas of **activity support** and **motivation reinforcement** offered by Kushmuk and Whittemore (1981) relate to the building of a community atmosphere. They are roughly the same thing and involve encouraging law-abiding use of the community and area (Cozens et al., 2005). The ability to recognize neighbors and identify needs of the community should enhance social cohesion among residents and contribute to a communal atmosphere that works to eliminate crime and other common problems. Activity support and motivation reinforcement may occur indirectly through activities such as street fairs, community days, and other social events. It can also be generated by directly recruiting residents for anti-crime activities or other societal/community issues.

The community atmosphere and caring attitude can be built, in part, through the physical appearance and design of an area (Newman, 1972). In a complementary fashion, the impact of access control/target hardening and surveillance relies on the behavior of legitimate users. Windows, better lighting, and clear viewing are important only if someone opts to use these features. In addition, residents need the ability to distinguish legitimate users from strangers in order to assess whether action is needed. This recognition comes from interaction between legitimate users.

Conflicts in CPTED Elements

While the elements of CPTED appear straightforward and have been used and promoted for roughly 40 years, there are potential contradictions between some elements. Cozens et al. (2005), Reynald (2011), and others have pointed out that territoriality, access control, and surveillance have the potential of cancelling out one another. For example, erecting walls, fences, or other structures may demarcate an area but can impede natural surveillance (Reynald, 2011). In a similar fashion, access control and target hardening efforts can lead to the building of fortresses around individuals and areas. These fortresses can keep people from participating in community and neighborhood activities, thus reducing activity support (Cozens et al., 2005). It is important, therefore, to seek a balance between the elements when instituting CPTED.

An important problem for CPTED may be the fact that the key concepts are poorly defined (Ekblom, 2011b). Territoriality has a wide variety of definitions, which makes it hard to apply and evaluate. Surveillance runs the gamut from active measures, such as the use of police and security guards, to passive actions that encourage or enhance citizen action. Implementing activity support through environmental design with a goal of increasing citizen usage of an area is equally difficult to achieve when the terms are not clear (Ekblom, 2011b). Consequently, the implementation and effectiveness of CPTED is compromised.

Johnson et al. (2014) propose a framework for CPTED that places potential interventions/activities in a meaningful configuration for implementation and prevention. Analyzing existing CPTED programs and projects, the authors argue that territoriality should be considered the key concept/mechanism. They base this claim on the fact that all of the other CPTED elements are "preparatory tasks" for enhancing territoriality, as well as "operational tasks" when territoriality is being exercised by residents. Basically, physical design prompts, prepares for, and precedes behavior. Table 4.2 illustrates the relationships in CPTED, with territoriality at the head and other CPTED elements as component parts of territoriality. The framework provides researchers and practitioners guidance for implementing changes. Each of the major concepts (components) have subconcepts. In addition, the implementation of the actions involves both preparatory tasks and operational tasks.

TABLE 4.2 Deconstructed Territoriality

Concept	Components	Example of Tasks (Both Preparatory and Operational)
Surveillance	Formal surveillance	CCTV Lighting Guards Monitoring/Observing Patrols Challenging offenders
	Informal surveillance	Clear sightlines Open streets Use of space Challenging offenders/ strangers Physical design

continued

TABLE 4.2 (continued)

Concept	Components	Example of Tasks (Both Preparatory and Operational)
Positive reinforcement	Image management/ maintenance	Maintaining space Signs of ownership Tackling incivilities Avoiding social stigma Care of public space
	Activity support	Use of public space Design for use Safe areas for activities Legitimate use of space Discouraging offending
Access control	Target hardening	Locks Gates Strong windows Building standards Organized security Entry guards
	Boundary definition	Varied land use Space delineation Physical barriers Users assert area control Identify intruders

Source: Compiled by author from D. Johnson et al. (2014). "Designing *in* crime prevention, designing *out* ambiguity: Practice issues with the CPTED knowledge framework available to professionals in the field and its potentially ambiguous nature." *Crime Prevention and Community Safety* 16:147–168.

Summary

The basis for CPTED rests on the assumption that the physical design influences the behavior of both residents/legitimate users of an areas, as well as potential offenders. For the residents, the expectation is that they will be observant of what is taking place around them and take action if they observe criminal activity. On the other hand, potential offenders should be influenced by the costs and benefits inherent in an action.

Kaplan et al. (1978) illustrate the potential impact on offenders through an idea they refer to as **OTREP**. That is, crime **O**pportunity is the result of **T**arget, **R**isk, **E**ffort, and **P**ayoff. The assumption is that offenses can be avoided when there is a high risk of apprehension with little potential payoff. Crime should be reduced as the potential costs (effort) outweigh the potential benefits (payoff). Manipulating physical design features (reducing the number of targets while increasing the risks of getting caught) may be one way to bring about higher costs relative to benefits.

Implementation of Environmental Design

The implementation of environmental design strategies has not always gone smoothly or followed a clear plan. Much of the reason for this is the fact that most efforts have taken place with little or no long-range planning and only intermittent government organization and support. Many of the initial projects, such as in Hartford, Connecticut, and Portland, Oregon, were demonstration projects backed by the government or a private foundation (such as Westinghouse Electric). This does not mean that environmental design has been ignored or has no organizational support.

It is only since the mid-1990s that we have seen major organized movement toward incorporating environmental design into communities in an ongoing fashion, and most of that movement has taken place outside the United States. In 1989, the Association of Chief Police Officers (ACPO) in England established the **Secured By Design (SBD)** program. This ongoing initiative emphasizes and promotes the inclusion of safety and security measures in new and existing buildings (ACPO, 2009). The SBD project provides architectural and security assistance to any agency requesting its input. At the present time, there are 18 Design Guides available to assist in building safe and secure homes, facilities, and locations (ACPO, 2015). Among these guides are those for new homes, commercial sites, hospitals, and schools. The SBD program includes six Core Principles, which closely align with the ideas of defensible space. These include: (1) an integrated approach, (2) environmental quality and a sense of ownership, (3) natural surveillance, (4) access and footpaths, (5) open space and management, and (6) lighting.

Table 4.3 provides seven attributes of sustainable communities set forth by the British Home Office in 2004 that correspond to the basic SBD principles. These attributes are particularly well suited for crime prevention. Included here are access control, surveillance, ownership (territoriality), and activity (support), all key CPTED concepts.

The passage of the 1998 **Crime and Disorder Act (CDA)** in the United Kingdom is another good example of

---

ON THE WEB

The Secured By Design web site offers a great deal of additional information on the implementation and evaluation of physical design for preventive purposes. You can explore the site at: **http://www.securedbydesign.com/index.aspx**

TABLE 4.3 Attributes of Sustainable Communities

- Access and movement: places with well-defined routes, spaces and entrances that provide for convenient movement without compromising security
- Structure: places that are structured so that different uses do not cause conflict
- Surveillance: places where all publicly accessible spaces are overlooked
- Ownership: places that promote a sense of ownership, respect, territorial responsibility and community
- Physical protection: places that include necessary, well-designed security features
- Activity: places where the level of human activity is appropriate to the location and creates a reduced risk of crime and a sense of safety at all times
- Management and maintenance: places that are designed with management and maintenance in mind, to discourage crime in the present and the future

Source: Home Office (2004) *Safer Places: The Planning System and Crime Prevention*. London: Home Office.

---

governmental adoption of environmental design. The CDA mandated the cooperation of many agencies in addressing crime problems. Included in that mandate were plans to rely on architects and planners in efforts to design out crime (Everson and Woodhouse, 2007).

New Zealand has implemented national guidelines for construction and design that inhibits crime. Table 4.4 lists the elements of the guidelines. The intent of the guidelines is to promote the incorporation of CPTED principles in new developments. Similar guidelines have been adopted throughout Australia. In some instances, such as in Victoria (see Table 4.5) and New South Wales (see Table 4.6), the guidelines have some force of law in as much as the authorities can halt the construction of developments that do not meet the guidelines. An examination of both the Victoria and New South Wales guidelines shows that the elements are direct from CPTED and correspond to the SBD principles in Britain.

ON THE WEB

Download the guidelines and rules for the Victoria (www.dtpli.vic.gov.au/__data/assets/pdf_file/0004/231619/Safer_Design_Guidelines.pdf), New South Wales (http://www.planning.nsw.gov.au/rdaguidelines/documents/duapguide_s79c.pdf), and the State of Virginia (www.dcjs.virginia.gov/cple/documents/cpted.pdf) governments.

Note the adherence to CPTED principles. What new ideas do you see in these that may extend the basic CPTED ideas?

In the U.S. the drive for CPTED is primarily a function of private or professional organizations. Both national and international groups promote environmental design. Among these are the International CPTED Association, CPTED Security, the National Crime Prevention Council, the National Institute of Crime Prevention's CPTED

TABLE 4.4 New Zealand National CPTED Guidelines

1. Access	Safe movement and connections
2. Surveillance and sightlines	See and be seen
3. Layout	Clear and logical orientation
4. Activity mix	Eyes on the street
5. Sense of ownership	Showing a space is cared for
6. Quality environments	Well-designed, managed and maintained environments
7. Physical protection	Using active security measures

Source: Adapted by author from Ministry of Justice (2005). *Crime Prevention Through Environmental Design Principles.* New Zealand Ministry of Justice. http://www.justice.govt.nz/policy/crime-prevention/environmental-design

TABLE 4.5 Victoria Principles for Safer Design

Surveillance	Maximize visibility and surveillance of the public environment
Access, movement, and sightlines	Provide safe movement, good connections and access
Activity	Maximize activity in public places
Ownership	Clearly define private and public space responsibilities
Management and maintenance	Manage public space to ensure that it is attractive and well used

Source: Adapted by author from State of Victoria Department of Sustainability and Environment (2005). *Safe Design Guidelines for Victoria.* East Melbourne: Department of Sustainability and Environment.

Training web site, the Designing Out Crime Association (U.K.), and many others. At the state level, Virginia's Department of Criminal Justice Services has promulgated Safer By Design principles for use in designing communities, housing, and businesses. There has also been a wide range of projects and evaluations that have been attempted to assess the effectiveness of environmental design changes.

The Impact of Physical Design

The impact of CPTED and physical design features on crime and fear has long been a topic for research and evaluation. When Newman (1972) introduced the idea of

---

TABLE 4.6 Safer By Design Elements: New South Wales

Territorial re-enforcement

Actual and symbolic boundary markers to encourage communal responsibility for public areas and facilities and to communicate to people where they should/not be and what activities are appropriate.

Surveillance

Natural surveillance is achieved when normal space users can see and be seen by others.

Technical/mechanical surveillance is achieved through mechanical/electronic measures such as CCTV, help points and mirrored building panels.

Formal (or organised) surveillance is achieved through the tactical positioning of guardians.

Access control

Access control treatments restrict, channel and encourage people and vehicles into, out of and around the development.

Natural access control includes the tactical use of landforms and waterways features, design measures including building configuration, formal and informal pathways, landscaping, fencing and gardens.

Technical/Mechanical access control includes the employment of security hardware.

Formal (or organised) access control includes on-site guardians such as employed security officers.

Space/Activity management

Formal supervision, control and care of the development.

Source: Adapted by author from New South Wales (2015). *Safer By Design*. http://www.police. nsw.gov.au/community_issues/crime_prevention/safer_by_design

---

defensible space, he illustrated the impact of CPTED features by comparing two public housing projects. The first, a high-rise, high-crime project, allowed strangers easy access through unmonitored, multi-user entrances. In addition, the buildings lacked windows and opportunities to observe indoor common areas and outdoor pathways. The size of the project mitigated attempts to recognize legitimate users from strangers due to the great numbers of people in the project. Conversely, the second public housing area consisted of low-rise buildings that experienced lower crime levels. The project limited the number of families using the same entrances. This enhanced the ability of residents to identify strangers. Surveillance was enhanced by entrances that faced public thoroughfares. Additionally, the low-lying structures made casual observation of outdoor activities through windows more feasible and effective.

Newman (1972) argued that defensible space can be accomplished through a variety of physical design actions, including the placement of windows conducive to easy visibility of surrounding areas, the location of entrances that are observable by others, the installation of lights to enhance visibility, and the establishment of common areas that are controllable by residents. All of these features are evident in low-rise housing projects and are either absent or limited in high-rise, high-density projects. Most importantly, these features impact the behavior of both legitimate users and potential offenders (Newman, 1972).

In assessing the impact of physical design, it is important to consider that the impact can be either direct or indirect. Rubenstein et al. (1980) outline three types of changes or effects that appear in analyses of crime prevention (see Figure 4.1). Type 1 effects are those that measure the direct impact of physical design features (such as locks, lights, or fences) on crime. Type 2 effects consider the impact of the physical design on a variety of intervening factors. Possible intervening factors include the attitudes of legitimate users about their community, feelings of territoriality, efforts of community members to combat crime, and an improved community atmosphere. (While territoriality, activity support and motivation reinforcement are considered elements of CPTED by some, the models found on the textbook web site and many discussions view them as intervening or mediating factors.) The physical design features bring about changes in these intervening factors prior to effecting crime. Finally, Type 3 measures deal with the direct effect of the intervening factors on crime and the indirect influence of physical design on crime through the intervening factors.

The following discussion of physical design and its influence on crime is divided into several sections. First, the effect of access control/target hardening and surveillance techniques are

┌─ **ON THE WEB** ─────────────────
│ *The U.S. Office of Justice Programs has initiated a*
│ *valuable source of information on interventions to*
│ *attack crime, including prevention activities. You*
│ *can explore the Crime Solutions site at*
│ *http://crimesolutions.gov/default.aspx*
└──────────────────────────────────

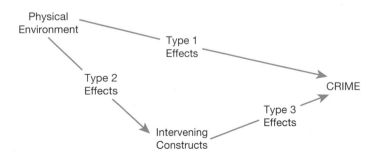

Figure 4.1

Model of Crime Prevention Effects

considered as individual factors. Second, the evaluation moves to studies that examine broad-based uses of defensible space concepts in residential and commercial areas. Finally, altering the physical environment by designing products with prevention in mind is considered.

The Effects of Individual Factors

The ideas of access control/target hardening and surveillance include a wide range of potential interventions for combating crime. Increased street lighting, reduced concealment, installation of locks, use of unbreakable glass, alarms and cameras, marking of property for identification, and security guards are only a few of the available means of prevention. Despite this proliferation of methods, few of these have been subjected to individual evaluation. Most crime prevention programs rely on a range of activities and not just a single approach. Almost without exception, most evaluations look at the direct impact of physical design on crime and/or fear of crime.

Lighting

Efforts to prevent crime by improving the lighting in areas was a major undertaking in the 1970s and remains a common approach in both the United States and the United Kingdom. Pease (1999) suggests that lighting may impact crime through various mechanisms. For example, lighting may lead to increased outdoor activity and, in turn, greater surveillance. Lighting may also enhance the ability to detect a crime in progress or identify an offender. Advocates often point to the deterrent potential of lights, which may make potential offenders choose less well-lit areas for their crimes. Lighting should allow potential victims to see their surroundings and may lead them to avoid less well-lit locations.

Typical research on the impact of lights contrasts criminal activity in an area that has received new lights with areas that do not receive new or improved lighting. In general, studies find a positive impact of lighting. The strongest support for lighting has been offered by Painter and Farrington (1997, 1999a, 1999b) based on a series of analyses conducted in England. Painter and Farrington (1997) report positive effects of lighting in an analysis of experimental and control areas of Dudley (West Midlands). Using victimization survey data, the authors report a 41 percent reduction in crime incidents in the experimental area and only a 15 percent reduction in the control area. In addition, respondents report being more satisfied in the relit areas. A similar analysis of relighting in Stoke-on-Trent (Staffordshire), also revealed significant reductions in crime in the experimental area as compared to the control area (Painter and Farrington, 1999b). They also report some evidence of reduced fear of crime. The crime and fear results, however, are not as dramatic as those found in Dudley. In both studies, the authors report reduced crime in non-relit areas adjacent to the target experimental neighborhoods. They claim that the impact of lighting is diffused into these other areas.

Welsh and Farrington (2009) reviewed the state of the evidence on a number of crime prevention efforts, including lighting. A total of 13 studies from both the United States and the United Kingdom were included in the review. Overall, the studies show a positive impact of lighting, particularly on property crime, with a 21 percent reduction in crime in experimental areas. Studies conducted in the United Kingdom showed the strongest results, possibly due to the fact that they have been completed in more recent years with more rigorous evaluations (Welsh and Farrington, 2009). Overall, lighting has a positive impact on area crime.

> **ON THE WEB**
>
> *The work of Welsh and Farrington is an example of the systematic reviews championed by the Campbell Collaboration. You can find many more reviews of prevention actions at the Collaboration web site: http://www.campbellcollaboration.org/*

Improved lighting schemes remain popular. The reason for this involves the issue of fear. Even if relighting does not always reduce crime, the ability to see better makes people feel safer. Various studies show reductions in fear following improved lighting. In perhaps the earliest review of lighting studies, Tien et al. (1977) found overwhelming reductions in fear of crime. Atkins et al. (1991) report that women and elderly respondents who recognize changes in lighting worry less about crime and feel safer. Finally, Painter and Farrington (1997, 1999b) reveal similar findings on improved area satisfaction and reduced fear of crime. Research on lighting reveals positive impacts on crime, victimization, and fear of crime among citizens.

CCTV

Surveillance is also accomplished by means of mechanical devices, particularly **closed-circuit television (CCTV)**. Research on CCTV has grown tremendously in recent years. While there are no estimates of the number of public CCTV cameras in use in the United States, Norris and McCahill (2006) estimate there are 4.2 million public CCTV cameras in the United Kingdom. The large investment in CCTV has prompted numerous evaluations of its impact on crime and fear.

Brown (1995) and Ditton and Short (1999) report on evaluations of CCTV in five U.K. cities. Each evaluation included experimental and control areas as well as outcome measures both pre- and post-installation of CCTV equipment. Brown (1995) notes that the experimental areas experienced reduced levels of burglary, but thefts, vandalism, and other offenses only declined in some locations. Results in Airdrie, Scotland, show reductions in overall recorded crime, although there are some increases in recorded drug and motor vehicle offenses (Ditton and Short, 1999). The authors note that the increases may be due to increased detection of offenses through the use of CCTV. Results in Glasgow also show that CCTV impacts crime in the target area (Ditton and Short, 1999). Fear also was reduced in areas covered by CCTV (Brown, 1995). Unfortunately, there was also evidence of displacement of crime from areas with CCTV to nearby/surrounding areas (Brown, 1995).

An evaluation of CCTV use in Philadelphia considered its impact on different street crimes. Ratcliffe et al. (2009) examined the effectiveness of two types of cameras (those that could tilt, zoom, and pan and those that were more static but could be relocated) in eight locations. Based on 32 months of police data for the target and surrounding areas, the authors report crime reduction in only four of the eight locations, with greater impact on disorder crimes than serious offenses (Ratcliffe et al., 2009). There was an overall 13 percent reduction in crime. The results also show some evidence of both diffusion and displacement of crime, although this was not uniform and they largely cancelled each other out (Ratcliffe et al., 2009).

CCTV has also been used in businesses and car parks. Tilley (1993) reports that motor vehicle theft, theft from autos, and vandalism were all reduced in areas monitored with CCTV equipment. Reid and Andresen (2012) examined the impact of CCTV at a commuter car park in Surrey, British Columbia. Using victimization survey data, the authors report a significant drop in victimization and improvement in feelings of safety. Theft of motor vehicles fell by 80 percent, and theft from motor vehicles dropped more than 50 percent (Reid and Andresen, 2012). Beck and Willis (1999), examining CCTV in fashion clothing stores, report that stores with extensive CCTV systems experience significant reductions in loss after the installation, compared to other stores. They note that the results, however, diminish over time (Beck and Willis, 1999). Hayes and Downs (2011) compared three different CCTV configurations in retail stores, finding reduced loss after CCTV installation. Winge and Knutsson (2003), studying the use of CCTV in the Oslo (Norway) central railroad station, report increased detection of crime, increased recorded violent crime, reduced theft from autos, and no change in perceptions about crime in the area.

Not all evaluations show positive results. Farrington et al. (2007), looking at both police and victimization data, fail to find any significant positive change in crime in the area covered by CCTV. Waples and Gill (2006) consider the impact of redeployable CCTV, which allows the cameras to be moved from one fixed location to another. Evaluation results show no change in crime or fear for one area, and increased crime in another after deployment of the CCTV initiative (Waples and Gill, 2006). The authors argue that these negative results could be due to various technological problems with the redeployable cameras. McLean et al. (2013), studying CCTV in Schenectady, New York, report reduced crime in the immediate vicinity of the cameras, but the impact varies from location to location in town. Finally, LaVigne et al. (2011) report that CCTV is effective at reducing crime in Baltimore, has varied impact in Chicago, and no impact in Washington, DC. A key finding in the study is that active monitoring of CCTV is essential to bring about an impact (LaVigne et al., 2011).

CCTV has been the subject of several major reviews of evaluation research. Welsh and Farrington (2009) examined 44 CCTV evaluations from 1978 to 2007. Studies fell into categories of city centers, public housing, public transportation, and car parks. The examination of studies in city centers revealed small but insignificant reductions in crime, although the results were better in the U.K. studies (Welsh and Farrington, 2009). Public housing evaluations revealed small, non-significant reductions in crime. Studies of CCTV in public transportation settings found sizable reductions in crime, although they were still statistically insignificant. Finally, CCTV in car parks had the only significant reductions in crime (Welsh and Farrington, 2009). The greatest impact was found in studies from the U.K., prompting the authors to speculate that this is due to the use of longer follow-up times and greater public support for CCTV in the U.K.

Another major review (Gill and Spriggs, 2005) found that crime was reduced in six target areas while it increased in seven areas. However, in the four locations where there was a statistically significant change in crime in the experimental areas relative to the control areas, two changes favored the experimental area and two favored the control areas. At the same time, fear of crime was reducing in CCTV areas. There was also some evidence of displacement of crime from CCTV areas to other locations (Gill and Spriggs, 2005).

The evidence from the studies clearly shows that CCTV can impact crime, although it is not universal and the conditions when it succeeds are not clear. CCTV holds some promise as evidenced by the success of the technique with some crimes in some locations. It is not a universal cure all for crime problems. Future evaluations need to use appropriate methodologies, including control areas and significant follow-up periods. It is also important to try to disentangle the impact of CCTV from other crime prevention techniques that are in simultaneous use (Farrington and Painter, 2003; Welsh and Farrington, 2009).

Surveillability

Lighting is only one factor that can influence the ability to observe an area. Surveillability also is determined by a wide range of other factors. Fisher and Nasar (1992; Nasar and Fisher, 1993) note the physical design impact on prospect, refuge, and escape. **Prospect** refers to the ability of individuals to see an area. Locations that offer greater prospect should engender less fear and victimization than those locations that limit sight lines. **Refuge** deals with the presence or absence of concealment, in which offenders could hide from potential victims. Refuge provides both hiding places and protection for potential offenders. Finally, **escape** addresses the ability of both offenders and victims to escape from an area before and/or after an offense. In essence, physical design features which impact on surveillability should alter both fear and victimization levels.

Fisher and Nasar (1992; Nasar and Fisher, 1993) tested these assumptions using a university site which offered greatly varying degrees of prospect, refuge, and escape. Using both surveys and observations, the authors report strong support for their argument. Areas of increased concealment (refuge), blocked prospect, and limited escape elicit greater fear. Crime figures also show greater victimization accompanying blocked prospect and greater concealment (Nasar and Fisher, 1993). The findings are site specific and suggest that analysis needs to focus on the micro-level. That is, while macro-level analyses may suggest that individuals are fearful in a certain area, that fear is actually more targeted at specific places in the area, not the entire area. Interestingly, lighting has no impact on reported fear once the issues of prospect, refuge and escape are considered (Fisher and Nasar, 1992). While limited to a single site on a university campus, these results suggest that a more general view of surveillability is needed than just an analysis of lighting. The research on prospect, refuge, and escape provides support for the assumption that people make assessments of their surroundings and respond to the potential danger and fear they interpret in different situations.

Surveillance also can be provided through the use of guards or other individuals hired specifically for that function. Hesseling (1995) demonstrates various forms of "functional surveillance" used in The Netherlands. In one instance surveillance was provided by hiring individuals to ride public transportation in order to reduce violence and fare dodging. Similarly, the employment of caretakers in public housing contributed to reductions in vandalism, graffiti, and theft. The use of security guards on city streets to assist the police impacted feelings of safety (Hesseling, 1995). Sorenson (1998) provides similar positive results in an assessment of public housing in three U.S. cities. An evaluation of security guards in car parks finds significant declines in auto thefts (Barclay et al., 1996). In general, assigning surveillance responsibilities and providing the means to contact the authorities impacts the level of calls for police service and the level of arrests. Clearly, surveillability has an impact on both crime and fear of crime.

Property Identification Programs

Property identification programs have a long history in crime prevention, often under the title **Operation Identification**. The basic idea behind property identification is to increase the difficulty for offenders to dispose of marked items. Despite the great proliferation of property identification programs, there is little empirical research on most projects. One early review of 99 projects from across the United States reported that, despite public awareness of the programs, few programs are able to entice more than 10 percent of the population to participate (Heller et al., 1975). Likewise, few programs report significant changes in reported burglary and none find an impact on arrests or convictions for burglary (Heller et al., 1975).

One exemplary evaluation of property marking was undertaken in South Wales (Laycock, 1985; 1990). Three physically proximate villages were targeted for the property marking campaign due to their relative isolation from other residential areas. The choice of isolated villages was made in order to reduce the chance that the program would simply displace crime. The program relied on a high degree of publicity, door-to-door contact, the provision of free equipment to mark property, and window stickers. Project efforts were successful at engendering participation by 72 percent of the homes. More importantly, the evaluation showed a 40 percent drop in burglary for participating homes with little or no displacement to non-participating residences (Laycock, 1985). A follow-up evaluation (Laycock, 1990) revealed greater reductions in burglary in the second year after program implementation. Importantly, both the initial and year two reductions in crime followed heavy publicity of the program. Increases in burglary occurred during times of low publicity (Laycock, 1990). This suggests that the results are more related to the media attention and not the property marking.

A recent trend in property identification has been to tag vehicles with ID numbers to combat motor vehicle theft. Rhodes et al. (1997) report that the marking of vehicle parts has a small impact on theft of cars by professional thieves. Various programs seek to make vehicles that are typically not driven at certain times of the day (particularly early mornings) or in certain areas (such as near borders) more recognizable to law enforcement officers through the use of decals and special license plates (Bureau of Justice Assistance, 1998). These identifying marks alert police that the vehicle is out of place and should be stopped. While the programs have not yet been adequately evaluated, these programs are an interesting extension of property marking at home.

Alarms

Alarms represent another possible deterrent to offending. Silent alarms in various Cedar Rapids, Iowa, schools and businesses increased both the numbers of arrests and the clearance rate in buildings with alarms (Cedar Rapids Police Department, 1975). Break-ins at buildings with alarms revealed entry through places not hooked up to the alarms (Cedar Rapids Police Department, 1975). Buck et al. (1993) examined the impact of alarms and other factors on burglary in three Philadelphia suburbs. Alarms proved to be a strong deterrent to household burglary.

Interviews with offenders also reveal the impact of alarms. Reppetto (1974) found that one-third of the offenders checked on the presence or absence of alarms during the planning stages of the offense. Bennett and Wright (1984) asked burglars to evaluate videotape and photos of potential targets. They found that the presence or absence of alarms was a prime consideration in the choice of their targets. Similarly, Hearnden and Magill (2004) find that 84 percent of active and incarcerated burglars claim that outside alarms are key factors in their decision-making process. Blevins et al. (2012) report that 60 percent of 422 burglars were deterred by alarms. Interviews with burglars in New Zealand reveals that the main deterrent to offending is alarms and security systems (Baker and Gray, 2005).

Locks, Doors, and Related Access Factors

Access control can be improved through the installation of various devices that make entry more difficult. These will not eliminate crime. Rather, a motivated offender will need to work harder and find more effective ways of gaining entrance. The Seattle Law and Justice Planning Office (1975) evaluated the effect of solid case doors, dead bolt locks, pins in sliding glass doors, and construction of short walls aimed at making entry through windows more difficult at four public housing projects. The evaluation found a significant decline in the level of burglary in three of the four target areas. The mode of entry after the improvements were made shifted to the use of open and unlocked windows and doors. This shift was expected due to the increased difficulty posed by the changes (Seattle Law and Justice Planning Office, 1975).

A recent evaluation in Glasgow, Scotland, examined the impact of Secured By Design doors and windows in public housing. Dwellings fitted with both doors and windows in four areas comprised the experimental group and matched control areas were identified for comparison (Teedon et al., 2009). A pre-post-analysis revealed significant drops in housebreaking, attempted housebreaking and theft in experimental dwellings. At the same time, offending increased in the comparison areas (Teedon et al., 2009). The introduction of access control devices, therefore, had a significant positive impact.

Bennett and Wright's (1984) study of burglars also shows support for the use of target-hardening devices. Their subjects list the type of windows and locks as one influence on their decision making. Offenders tend to prefer smaller windows because they are easier to force open. Similarly, the presence of a lock becomes more effective as the difficulty in picking or breaking the lock increases (Bennett and Wright, 1984).

Area Permeability

Efforts to limit access to neighborhoods include the establishment of dead-end streets, cul-de-sacs, one-way streets, alley gating, and closing streets. Such action can project a private atmosphere, cut down on the level of use by strangers, and increase the presence of legitimate users. Often this approach is coupled with broader community planning activities.

In an early study, Newman and Wayne (1974) compared public and private streets in adjacent areas of St. Louis. A private street is one that is owned and maintained by the residents living on the street, is often a cul-de-sac, and is set apart from the connecting streets by means of landscaping, gates, entranceways, or other similar features. The authors found less crime on private streets and the fear of crime was lower among subjects living on those streets (Newman and Wayne, 1974). They also found more interaction between the residents living on these private streets, which should lead to reduced crime.

Unfortunately, the lack of comparability between the experimental and control groups, however, suggests that these results should be viewed with some caution.

Different street layouts have been compared for their effect on crime. Bevis and Nutter (1977) look at the relative effect of dead-end, cul-de-sac, "L" type, "T" type, and through-traffic streets. These are arranged in order of accessibility with the dead-end street being the least accessible. The authors find a clear relationship existing between the type of street layout and burglary. More accessible streets experience higher rates of burglary (Bevis and Nutter, 1977). Johnson and Bowers (2010) note that burglary increases where there is a greater number of roads that intersect with one another.

Newman (1996) reported on the effects of creating mini neighborhoods in Dayton, Ohio, by limiting access to neighborhoods. Each mini-neighborhood was accessible by means of a single entrance. All other streets and alleys were closed to both access and egress. The results of the project were significant reductions in traffic, traffic accidents, overall crime, and violent crime in the mini neighborhoods. Residents also reported fewer victimizations and less fear of crime (Newman, 1996). Operation Cul-de-Sac in Los Angeles set out to curb gang homicides and assaults in a 10-block area by blocking road access in the area. Relying on Part I offense data, Lasley (1998) reports that both homicides and assaults fell significantly during the period of the program and increased after the roadblocks were removed. Donnelly and Kimble (1997) investigate street closures in a 10-square-block area of Dayton characterized by street crime, drugs, and prostitution. After a one-year follow-up, overall crime dropped 25 percent and violent crime fell 40 percent, while there is no evidence of displacement to other areas (Donnelly and Kimble, 1997). These projects clearly show the impact of altering traffic flow in high crime areas. Similar results appear in studies in both the U.S. and U.K. (Armitage et al., 2010, 2011; Johnson and Bowers, 2010; Nubani and Wineman, 2009).

In the United Kingdom, a relatively common attempt to control access is to erect alley gates. **Alley gating** refers to erecting gates on alleys that run behind home and businesses, thereby restricting access to residents or other legitimate users. A key target of this approach is burglary, particularly in areas where the criminals gain access through the rear of the buildings. An evaluation of alley gating in Liverpool reports that roughly 4,000 alley gates had been erected (Home Office, 2001), with a subsequent reduction of 875 burglaries (Bowers et al., 2003). The gates had an impact independent of other crime prevention activities taking place in the target areas. Similarly, an analysis of alley gating in Cadoxton, South Wales, reveals clear decreases in burglary after the installation of the gates (Rogers, 2013). Residents in the gated areas also report reduced perceptions of both crime and disorder in the area. Haywood et al. (2009), examining the impact of alley gating in Oldham (northwest England), find significant reductions in burglary.

The available evidence illustrates the potential of traffic control as a means of combating crime. Streets and areas that are easily accessible to pedestrian and auto traffic tend to experience higher levels of actual crime and fear of crime. The construction of cul-de-sacs, dead-end streets, alley gates, and streets that promote a feeling of ownership will have positive effects for crime prevention.

Summary

As noted earlier, the amount of research aimed at single crime prevention approaches is minimal. Few crime prevention programs are unidimensional in approach. Rather, most plans introduce a variety of techniques to be implemented as parts of a larger prevention package. This makes evaluation of the individual factors problematic and necessitates research focused on entire programs. We now turn to an evaluation of crime prevention efforts that include a range of ideas, including some of those already discussed.

Physical Design of Neighborhoods

Studies of public housing are among the early examinations of area-wide physical design on crime. As noted earlier, Newman (1972) reports that crime varies among public housing with different design features. Various design problems negate attempts to build a sense of community, lay claim to an area (territoriality), present a sense of safety (image), or allow surveillance. Newman and Franck (1980), studying public housing in Newark, St. Louis, and San Francisco, find that accessibility and building size have direct effects on burglary and fear of crime. Building size also affects the use of space and feelings of control over space and indirectly, through control and use of space, on crime and fear. Poyner (1994), reporting on physical design in an English public housing estate, demonstrates that limiting access reduces robbery, but not burglary. The removal of enclosed walkways between buildings effectively limits access, escape and concealment for potential offenders (Poyner, 1994).

Environmental design received one of its biggest tests in the North Asylum Hill area of Hartford, Connecticut. This area implemented a number of crime prevention activities including changes in street patterns, landscaping, neighborhood police patrols, and increased citizen organization. The design elements were primarily the creation of cul-de-sacs, the elimination of through streets, creating one-way streets, and the narrowing of street openings—all geared to making the area appear more private and controlled by residents of the area. An initial evaluation revealed great decreases in both burglary and robbery as compared to neighboring South Asylum Hill and the remainder of Hartford (Fowler et al., 1979). Fear of burglary and potential victimization also declined in the area. In addition, there was a corresponding increase

> ┌─ ON THE WEB ─────────────────
> *You can access and read about the North Asylum Hill project and many others at: https://www.ncjrs. gov/pdffiles1/Digitization/79544-79593NCJRS.pdf*

in the use of the streets and parks by residents. A follow-up evaluation three years later (Fowler and Mangione, 1982) supported the findings of reduced vehicular traffic, increased pedestrian usage, and lower levels of fear, but both burglary and robbery had returned to city-wide levels (Fowler and Mangione, 1982). The effect on crime, therefore, was short-lived.

General characteristics of urban neighborhoods provide further insight into the physical design–crime relationship. Greenberg et al. (1982) compare contiguous low and high crime neighborhoods in Atlanta. Low crime areas are characterized by single-family dwellings, few major through streets, and few vacant lots; are predominantly residential; are bounded by other residential areas; and have characteristics that prohibit easy access. Uniform building setbacks and private parking, which diminish concealment for offenders, are also part of low crime neighborhoods (Greenberg et al., 1982). These results tend to support the argument that physical features can affect criminal behavior.

The use of physical design changes to combat crime in a commercial area was undertaken in the Union Avenue Corridor (UAC) of Portland, Oregon. The UAC was a commercial strip approximately 3.5 miles long and four blocks wide accommodating businesses ranging from light industry to banks to grocery stores and car dealerships. The surrounding area was middle to low income and predominately black, with a crime rate roughly three times that of the remainder of Portland (Kushmuk and Whittemore, 1981). The crime prevention program included improving street lighting, improving street appearance, changing traffic patterns, providing off-street parking, establishing business and neighborhood groups, and using various promotional events, all with the intent of reducing crime and fear and increasing social cohesion and improving the quality of life.

Kushmuk and Whittemore (1981) note that official measures of crime (specifically robbery and commercial burglary) declined as a result of the prevention activities. Victimization surveys, however, revealed no changes in either the number of offenses or perceptions of victimization. In addition, while the overall fear of crime did not change over the study period, customers were *more* fearful at night and the elderly were *more* fearful, in general, after the crime prevention program. Changes in other outcomes also failed to appear. Neither businessmen nor residents reported any increases in social cohesion or cooperation with the police (Kushmuk and Whittemore, 1981). Residents also did not display any changes in communal activity or support of neighbors. While businessmen reported that their sales had increased since the program's implementation, they felt that the UAC was not in as good a condition as before the program (Kushmuk and Whittemore, 1981). In general, the evaluation showed some changes in crime and other social factors but these movements were not much different from those found in the remainder of Portland.

In 1999, the British government began the **Reducing Burglary Initiative (RBI)** by funding 63 projects across the United Kingdom (Kodz and Pease, 2003). The RBI relies on local communities to identify the causes of the burglary problems in their area and to develop appropriate interventions, many of which are physical design changes, such as target hardening, the installation of alley gates, lighting improvements, fencing, and property marking (Kodz and Pease, 2003). Interventions also include neighborhood watch, intensive police crackdowns, and other methods (discussed in later chapters). In 40 out of 55 RBI evaluations, the burglary rates fell relative to the control areas (evaluations using comparison areas were not conducted in eight locations). An evaluation of the Fordbridge (West Midlands) RBI project, which implemented target hardening, alley gates, electronic entry controls for buildings, and improved street lighting, reports a reduction in burglary of 43 percent for the experimental area (Home Office, 2003a).

┌─ ON THE WEB ──────────────────┐
│ *More detail and information on the RBI project is* │
│ *available at: http://webarchive.nationalarchives.* │
│ *gov.uk/20110218135832/rds.homeoffice.gov.uk/rds/* │
│ *pdfs05/hors287.pdf* │
└──────────────────────────────┘

Similarly, the RBI project in Stirchley (West Midlands), relying on alley gates, fences and property marking (along with a crime prevention newsletter), claims a 53 percent drop in burglary, which is twice the reduction seen in the control area (Home Office, 2003b). These results on the effectiveness of the RBI suggest that physical design elements are effective at reducing the burglary problem.

Secure By Design has also received attention for its impact on crime. As noted earlier, SBD seeks to influence the building of new structures or the redesign of existing sites in ways that will mitigate crime and disorder. In one evaluation of SBD in West Yorkshire, Armitage (2000) notes a significant reduction in crime at the sites that were refurbished following the SBD principles. There was a 26 percent drop in the number of dwelling crimes and roughly half as many residents reported being fearful around their homes. An assessment of environmental design features comparing 25 SBD estates with 25 non-SBD estates also shows the effectiveness of physical design for reducing burglary and general crime (Armitage, 2007). Estates conforming to proper design guidelines are at lower risk for crime than estates not using the design features.

In a study of SBD in West Yorkshire, Armitage and Monchuk (2011) report similar positive results. Both burglary and overall crime is significantly lower in SBD developments compared to non-SBD developments and the entire city. They further note that as the concentration of SBD homes increases, the level of overall crime decreases (Armitage and Monchuk, 2011). These results have been maintained over a 10-year period of time. Teedon et al. (2009, 2010) report similar positive results from an analysis of SBD in Glasgow. Compared to non-SBD properties, roughly 60 percent fewer SBD homes experienced burglaries and theft from burglary, and 80 percent fewer attempted burglaries. There was also a drop in crime in a comparison of pre-SBD and post-SBD data (Teedon et al., 2010).

A Challenge to Defensible Space

While it appears that physical design features can impact crime and fear, there is no guarantee that proper design will produce the desired results. Merry (1981) conducted an 18-month participant observation study of a single public housing project that seemed to conform to good defensible space design. The project was composed of low buildings, separate courtyards, few families per entranceway, wide pathways, public space in front of the buildings, and private (fenced) space at the rear of the buildings. Additionally, many of the residents had installed target-hardening devices such as locks and window bars. Using a combination of interviews, observation, and official crime figures, Merry (1981) found that the physical design features failed to have any effect on crime or the residents' feelings of safety. Despite the seeming defensibility of the project, Merry (1981) questioned the design features. First, the stairwells and hallways near doors were not easily observable by residents or passersby. Second, many of the outdoor features, such as fences and enclosed trash collectors, actually provided cover for potential offenders. Finally, the layout of the buildings and outdoor areas, although seemingly conducive to territoriality, confused residents and visitors and produced discomfort and disorientation. Clearly, the physical design did not increase interaction between residents and residents rarely intervened in questionable behavior (Merry, 1981). Residents were unable to distinguish strangers from legitimate users, feared future retaliation, and held an uncaring attitude toward those not identified as friends or relatives. Merry attributed these problems to a lack of social cohesion and community identity among the project's residents.

The general failure of the defensible space concept to bring about clear reductions in crime was placed squarely on the inability of the physical environment to effectively create feelings of territoriality and a sense of community concern and action. Merry (1981) noted that "good defensible space design neither guarantees that a space will appear safe nor that it will become a part of a territory which residents defend effectively." An area may be *defensible but undefended*.

Second-Generation CPTED

These various discussions should not be interpreted as indicating that there is no positive effect of defensible space features on crime and fear of crime. An array of studies have found various design features and crime prevention techniques that affect crime and fear. There are, however, a substantial number of studies that produce negative or equivocal results.

These contradictory findings may stem from the inability to bring about, or lack of attention paid to, changes in intervening factors (see Figure 4.1), such as social cohesion and feelings of territoriality. The basic premise of Newman's argument is that the physical environment engenders feelings of territoriality and citizen control, which then affect crime. Any failure of physical design, therefore, may be due to an inability of the individual implementation program to bring about these intervening factors.

Discussions of CPTED over the past decade have increasingly pointed to the development of a **second-generation CPTED**. Saville and Cleveland (2003), Cozens et al. (2005), and Reynald (2011) all argue that CPTED needs to explicitly look beyond simple physical design and overtly incorporate social factors and activities in prevention. Cozens et al. (2005) note that CPTED needs to consider the social makeup of areas/neighborhoods. Reynald (2011) argues for formal/organized surveillance which is enhanced by focusing on social capital and social cohesion. Saville and Cleveland (2003) outline four components to second-generation CPTED:

1. Social cohesion between residents, businesses, and others.

2. Connectivity of the local area to government agencies, businesses, and others that can contribute to area improvement.

3. Community cultural initiatives that can bring people together.

4. Threshold capacity that builds cohesion among residents and serves to enhance the community and support the needs and efforts of the residents.

In essence, second-generation CPTED seeks to directly enhance the intervening factors needed to prevent crime.

A Third-Generation CPTED

In 2011, the United Nations Interregional Crime and Justice Research Institute (UNICRI) published "Improving Urban Security through Green Environmental Design." This document proposes a **third-generation CPTED** that uses green sustainable design to improve communities and reduce crime (and other social) problems. The key to this is making residents, visitors, and anyone else feel safe in the community (UNICRI, 2011). This is essentially territoriality. Third-generation CPTED "insists on practical measures, physically or cybernetically enhanced, that foster the perception of urban space as safe" (UNICRI, 2011, p. 11). This is done using technologies that transform public space to interactive communal space, which fosters a sense of belonging, ownership, and surveillability.

Third-generation CPTED included four major components: (1) places, (2) people, (3) technology, and (4) networks. This version of CPTED seeks to reprogram urban space to achieve a safer community. Each of the core components promotes efforts that build interaction between users and a sense of ownership that should lead to increased safety (see Table 4.7). A cornerstone to all this is the use of technology and green design for a sustainable community. While the presentation of this approach often reads as very futuristic and utopian (especially when talking about embedded sensors and actuators in

TABLE 4.7 **Third-Generation CPTED: Core Concepts**	
Place	Safe homes; secure employment; activity centers; green space; new developments; healthy environment; natural surveillance; public transportation; public education
People	Ability for people to be heard; communication; sense of belonging; community gatherings
Technology	Energy efficiency; transparency; green energy; surveillance networks; informatics; real time information; interaction; cybernetics
Networks	Physical networks for community; energy; communication; etc.; wireless networks for information transfer; social networking

Source: Adapted by author from UNICRI (2011). *Improving Urban Security Through Green Environmental Design*. Retrieved from http://www.unicri.it/news/files/2011-04-01_110414_CRA_Urban_Security_sm.pdf

buildings throughout the city), it is a very forward-looking, "outside the box" approach that may impact behavior in the future.

Incivility, Disorder, and Crime

A final topic to address is the issue of disorder and incivility. While "crime and disorder" have been addressed throughout this chapter, it is always in terms of action to eliminate these problems. Much of the discussion about physical features deals with the correct design to allow surveillance and feelings of goodwill among legitimate users. It is also important to question the degree to which signs of disorder may actively *promote* criminal activity. This may occur when both signs of physical and social disorder signal that an area or location is not protected and is open to criminal behavior.

Various authors (Hunter, 1978; Skogan, 1990; Taylor and Gottfredson, 1986; Wilson and Kelling, 1982) have presented indicators of physical disorder, including broken windows, abandoned buildings, vacant lots, deteriorating buildings, litter, vandalism, and graffiti. Similarly, they offer social indicators, such as loitering juveniles, public drunkenness, gangs, drug sales and use, harassment (such as begging and panhandling), prostitution, and a lack of interaction among people on the street. Perkins and Taylor (1996), Taylor et al. (1995), and Spelman (1993) suggest that physical disorder can contribute to the growth of social disorder. Examples of such instances would be non-residential property or abandoned structures interrupting a housing block (Taylor, 1988). The physical layout may inhibit social interaction among residents and allow for social incivilities to arise.

These physical and social indicators are typically referred to as signs of disorder or incivility. **Incivility** in a neighborhood has been proposed as evidence that the residents are not concerned, or at least are less concerned, about what is happening around them than people in areas not characterized by incivility (Lewis and Salem, 1986). Signs of disorder may lead residents to withdraw into their homes and abandon cooperative efforts at improving the neighborhood (Skogan, 1990; Taylor, 1988). This would leave the neighborhood open to potential offenders. The idea of incivilities can be viewed as another part of Newman's "image." For the offender, signs of incivility are indicative of lower risk (Taylor and Gottfredson, 1986). Efforts to minimize disorder and incivility through improvement of the physical and social environment, therefore, should increase perceived risk and decrease crime and fear of crime.

Interestingly, incivility has been accepted almost without question as a cause of crime and fear in society, despite the relative lack of research on the subject. This is somewhat easy to understand when one considers the location of crime and fear in communities. Areas exhibiting physical and social signs of incivility are often the same ones experiencing higher levels of crime and fear. Indeed, a number of studies find that crime and fear are higher in areas displaying signs of disorder (Lynch and Cantor, 1992; Perkins and Taylor, 1996; Skogan, 1990; Spelman, 1993).

The logical assumption to draw from the research on incivility is that efforts to reduce physical and social disorder will effectively reduce crime and fear. Taylor (1997), however, questions the extent to which eliminating signs of disorder, particularly physical signs, will have an impact. He points out that the relationship between disorder and fear is highly contingent on how disorder is measured. Specifically, area disorder measured objectively by independent raters is only marginally related to fear and resident behavior. A strong relationship between disorder and fear (and possibly behavior) appears only when *perceived* incivilities are considered, as subjectively reflected in surveys of residents. Consequently, efforts to reduce physical disorder would have only minimal impact on fear (Taylor, 1997). The challenge is to identify methods of altering the *perceptions* of disorder.

While there may be some disagreement about the actual influence of disorder and incivilities on crime, fear, and citizen behavior, many reasons remain for working to reduce signs of incivility. Perhaps the best reason is that no one should have to live in areas with such problems. Additionally, even minimal effects on crime and fear should be considered a success. Unless research finds that efforts to remove disorder increase crime and fear, there is only an upside to their elimination.

Summary

Examination of the existing evidence on physical design shows some promising results along with a number of instances in which the impact of the techniques is inconsistent. Table 4.8 attempts to provide a general summary of the impact of different physical design techniques across different target areas. A great deal of the support for the results in Table 4.8 does not appear in the earlier discussion. Instead, the table rests on evidence presented here and in other analyses.

The left-hand column of the table lists the crime prevention action or technique. The second column lists those instances where the technique has a positive impact, that

TABLE 4.8 Summary of the Evidence on Physical Design Impact on Crimes

Technique	Positive Impact	Unclear Impact	No Impact
Lighting	Burglary Theft Fear	Burglary (business) Theft (business) Robbery (business) Violence	
CCTV	Fear Auto theft	Burglary Theft Robbery Violence	
Traffic patterns/ street layout	Burglary Fear Violence		Theft Robbery
Alarms	Burglary		
Property ID		Burglary Theft	
Informal surveillance	Burglary Theft Robbery Fear		
Building design		Burglary Robbery Theft Fear	
Area improvement	Fear	Burglary Robbery Theft	

is, where the crime or fear has gone down as a result of the crime prevention action. The next column lists those crimes where there is no clear impact of the technique. In these cases, there is conflicting evidence on the technique's impact and a great deal of divergence across studies/contexts. The final column lists those instances where evaluations show the crime prevention techniques have no impact.

An inspection of the table reveals that there are a number of instances in which physical design techniques have been found to be effective. Interestingly, there are also many examples in which the evidence is still uncertain and there are several examples in which the techniques have been found to have no impact (e.g., permeability has no apparent impact on theft or robbery). With so many cases of uncertainty in the findings, how is it possible to have such discrepancies and where does this leave CPTED?

Part of the reason for the discrepancies stems from the nature of social research. First, many of the studies are attempting to investigate the effect of one set of factors on crime. In so doing, the evaluators often fail to consider the vast array of alternative variables that may be contributing to the levels of crime and fear. Second, many studies fail to specify an adequate control group or have no control group. The results of the evaluations, therefore, have no baseline upon which to judge any change or lack of change. The simple use of measures taken prior to and after a change within a single locale or group cannot solve the problem of possible competing influences and factors occurring simultaneously with the intervention of interest. Third, the vast array of study sites makes comparison across studies difficult. It is difficult to compare the various study results in the absence of detailed information on each experimental and control group from each study. The context within which each study is being conducted may greatly influence the results. Evaluations that exhibit positive effects may be taking place in locations that are fundamentally different from those showing negative or no effects. This possibility cannot be assessed from many reports.

The lack of consistent positive results also may be due to the fact that many physical design features contribute to the building of fortresses for protection. Physical design changes, target hardening, and access control serve to isolate people from one another rather than build territoriality. While these efforts may reduce the level of fear of crime, there is a concomitant loss of community. Counter to Newman's assumption that physical design will engender a sense of community, social support, and territoriality, there is little or no evidence that this happens. Crime can be expected to increase where traditional, fortress mentality techniques are employed. As the individual withdraws from the rest of the neighborhood in an attempt to protect himself, the community enters an upward spiral of increased crime, fear, and loss of community.

An alternative is to emphasize second-generation CPTED. Such crime prevention techniques overtly prompt the retention, retrieval, and/or enhancement of the community. Neighborhood/block watch, citizen patrols, community-oriented policing, and similar reactions reflect community-oriented responses to crime and fear. These efforts should reduce crime and fear over time as the community reasserts itself and takes control of the behavior and actions of persons within the community. Rather than assume that alterations in a sense of community, neighborhood cohesion, and similar factors follow physical design changes, a community-oriented model suggests that interventions specifically directed at increasing social interaction, social cohesion, feelings of ownership, territoriality, and reducing fear will be more effective at combating crime and victimization. The next chapter looks at community-oriented crime prevention programs which actively seek to involve the citizens in actions that should engender community/neighborhood cohesion, a sense of control, territoriality, and other factors that will affect both fear and crime. The next chapter focuses on attempts to increase citizen involvement in crime prevention and fill the gap left by simple environmental design approaches.

KEY TERMS

- access control
- activity support
- alley gating
- closed-circuit television (CCTV)
- Crime and Disorder Act (CDA)
- Crime Prevention Through Environmental Design (CPTED)
- defensible space
- escape
- formal or organized surveillance
- image
- incivility
- mechanical surveillance
- milieu
- motivation reinforcement
- natural surveillance
- Operation Identification
- OTREP
- permeability
- prospect
- real territoriality
- Reducing Burglary Initiative (RBI)
- refuge
- second-generation CPTED
- Secured By Design (SBD)
- symbolic territoriality
- target hardening
- territoriality
- third-generation CPTED

CHAPTER 5 Neighborhood Crime Prevention

LEARNING OBJECTIVES

After reading this chapter you should be able to:

- Demonstrate your knowledge of neighborhood watch and the types of activities found in neighborhood watch programs.
- Define community anti-drug programs and discuss their impact.
- Discuss citizen patrols and their crime prevention capabilities.
- Outline routine activities theory.
- Discuss Eck's triplets of guardianship.
- Talk about the impact of neighborhood crime prevention on community cohesion.
- Provide an overview of the impact of neighborhood crime prevention on crime and fear.
- Discuss the Kirkholt Burglary Prevention Project and its impact.
- Explain the Safer Cities program and its impact.

- List problems and issues that hamper the evaluation of neighborhood crime prevention programs.
- Talk about who participates in neighborhood crime prevention.
- Provide reasons for the divergent findings on who participates in crime prevention.
- Discuss research findings on domains of crime prevention.
- Outline the five problematic assumptions underlying neighborhood watch.

The failure of physical, environmental design changes to always impact crime and fear may be directly attributable to the ability of such activities to live up to the assumptions of the basic theory. Few authors claim that changes in physical design alone will have a major impact on crime. By themselves, locks, lights, windows, and the other physical characteristics can only make offending more difficult and lead to alternative means of committing the crimes. The key element that will reduce and prevent crime is the ability of the physical features to enhance active surveillance, engender community cohesion, and promote citizen action against crime.

Crime Prevention Through Environmental Design has faltered because of the inability to motivate residents and legitimate users to become active guardians against crime. As seen in Chapter 4, the evidence in support of a link between physical design features and intervening factors such as increased social cohesion and use of an area is rarely found in the evaluations. This may be due to the lack of attention paid to these factors. Studies that include intervening elements find little support for the connection between physical design and changes in social cohesion, support, and other intervening constructs. In addition, the conflicting evidence concerning the influence of physical features on crime may be due to conflicting levels of social cohesion, community atmosphere, surveillance, and other intervening variables that are unaccounted for in the studies.

Second-generation CPTED seeks to directly build social cohesion, citizen participation, and resident action. The most recognized manifestation of the second-generation goals is neighborhood crime prevention. While predating second-generation CPTED, neighborhood crime prevention seeks to directly influence intervening constructs in the CPTED model and, in turn, build active guardianship and impact levels of crime and fear. Neighborhood crime prevention can take a variety of forms that are broader in scope than just those discussed in connection with physical design. Possible techniques include neighborhood watch, neighborhood advocacy, citizen patrols, physical design, and any actions to engender guardianship. Figure 5.1 illustrates the conceptual framework of neighborhood crime prevention.

The wide array of activities demonstrates the fact that crime prevention relies on a number of approaches and cannot be left to one basic set of ideas, such as physical design. The model in Figure 5.1 proposes that intervening changes must occur before the long-term problems are affected. The model shows that some of the CPTED design characteristics introduced in the last chapter as initial points of intervention

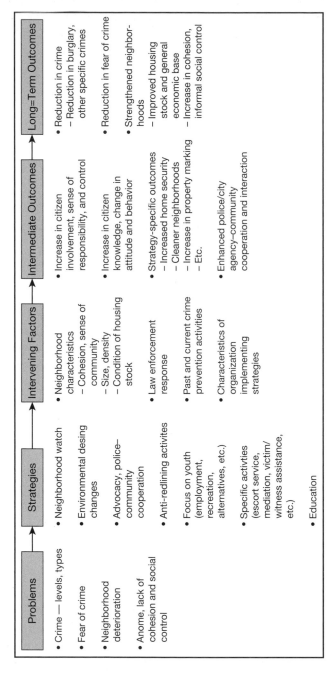

Problems	Strategies	Intervening Factors	Intermediate Outcomes	Long=Term Outcomes
• Crime — levels, types	• Neighborhood watch	• Neighborhood characteristics – Cohesion, sense of community – Size, density – Condition of housing stock	• Increase in citizen involvement, sense of responsibility, and control	• Reduction in crime – Reduction in burglary, other specific crimes
• Fear of crime	• Environmental desing changes			• Reduction in fear of crime
• Neighborhood deterioration	• Advocacy, police–community cooperation	• Law enforcement response	• Increase in citizen knowledge, change in attitude and behavior	• Strengthened neighbor-hoods
• Anome, lack of cohesion and social control	• Anti-redlining activites	• Past and current crime prevention activities	• Strategy-specific outcomes – Increased home security – Cleaner neighborhoods – Increase in property marking – Etc.	– Improved housing stock and general economic base – Increase in cohesion, informal social control
	• Focus on youth (employment, recreation, alternatives, etc.)	• Characteristics of organization implementing strategies		
	• Specific activties (escort service, mediation, victim/witness assistance, etc.)		• Enhanced police/city agency–community cooperation and interaction	
	• Education			

Figure 5.1

Neighborhood-Based Crime Prevention Conceptual Framework

Source: R.F. Cook and J.A. Roehl (1983). *Preventing Crime and Arson: A Review of Community-based Strategies*. Reston, VA: Institute for Social Analysis.

(i.e., property marking and home security) are viewed here as intermediate outcomes of the more general strategies. The most important of these general strategies is citizen involvement. Citizen activity and interest, as we will see, often precede the other factors, including physical design.

Types of Neighborhood Crime Prevention Approaches

A wide variety of neighborhood crime prevention strategies have been proposed and implemented over the years. Since the 1970s, there has been a great proliferation of programs in the United States, United Kingdom, and other countries. While many programs have been instigated and aided by various government agencies or policies, other programs have emerged from the simple realization by citizens that the formal criminal justice system is incapable of solving the crime problem on its own. Regardless of the source of stimulation, neighborhood crime prevention has become a major aspect of crime prevention.

Neighborhood/Block Watch

Neighborhood watch directly seeks to bring neighbors and residents of an area together as a means of enhancing knowledge of one another and their ability to recognize who belongs and who does not in the area. Key activities of neighborhood watch groups include discussions of mutual problems in the neighborhood, actions to increase feelings of community, and the promotion of interventions to address common problems. Neighborhood watch, ideally, is proactive in design. That is, it sets out to identify problems before they occur or, at the very least, as they occur. This requires interaction between citizens and law enforcement, education about crime and prevention efforts, and the implementation of various preventive actions. Figure 5.2 is a logic model by the Bureau of Justice Assistance that outlines activities and expectations for a typical neighborhood watch group. Neighborhood involvement is meant to recognize and circumvent the problems that lead to an area's decline and accompanying increased crime.

In its most effective form, neighborhood watch should provide informal (and possibly formal) social control in the community. Bursik and Grasmick (1993) note that many neighborhoods are socially disorganized and, consequently, are unable to exert any control over residents or visitors to the area. Building on the early work of Shaw and McKay (1931, 1942), the authors argue that neighborhoods need to draw on resources from a variety of sources in an effort to build social control. Friendships, families, local businesses, churches, schools, and interpersonal networks are examples of local resources upon which neighborhoods can draw and build (Bursik and Grasmick, 1993). Neighborhood watch is one incarnation of social control in a neighborhood.

Goal: To help prevent crime in the community

Objectives	Activities	Outputs/ Process Measures	Outcome Measures
1. Increase the community's role in crime prevention 2. Educate the public about crime and crime prevention 3. Reduce incidents of burglary and robbery	Establish a Neighborhood Watch Group Residents hold quarterly Neighborhood Watch meetings Residents conduct nightly Neighborhood Watch patrols Police conduct home security surveys upon request Residents distribute a crime warning and prevention flier to each neighborhood home quarterly	• Number of residents who volunteer to participate in Neighborhood Watch during reporting period • Number of Neighborhood Watch meetings held during reporting period • Number of crime prevention presentations conducted by the police during reporting period • Number of Neighborhood Watch patrols planned for the reporting period • Number of Neighborhood Watch patrols conducted during reporting period • Number of home security surveys requests to police during the reporting period • Number of home security surveys conducted by the police during reporting period • Number of unique crime warning or prevention fliers distributed during reporting period • Total number of crime warning or prevention fliers distributed • Number of residents actually participating (attend meetings, conduct patrols, or distribute fliers) in Neighborhood Watch during reporting period	• Number of crime reports made to the police during the reporting period • Number of crime tips provided to the police during the reporting period • Number of burglary offenses that occurred in the designated area according to police records during the reporting period

Theory

IF community residents look out for suspicious activities (during Neighborhood Watch patrols and other times) and report them to the police and if potential offenders are aware that residents are doing this THEN offenders will be deterred from committing crime in the community because they perceive the risk of getting caught there is greater than it would be in another community.

IF community residents create signs of occupancy at homes when neighbors are away (which they learn how to do at Neighborhood Watch meetings) THEN offenders will be deterred from committing crime in the community because they perceive the risk of getting caught there is greater than it would be in another community.

IF community residents make it more difficult for homes to be burglarized by increasing security at the homes (which occurs following the completion of a home security survey) THEN it will be more difficult for potential burglars to enter the home or increase their risk of getting caught if they do enter the home.

Figure 5.2

BJA Center for Program Evaluation and Performance Measurement: Neighborhood Watch Logic Model

Source: Bureau of Justice Assistance (2015). *Neighborhood Watch Logic Model*. https://www.bja.gov/evaluation/program-crime-prevention/cbcp6.htm

One way that neighborhood watch contributes to social control is through the heavy use of surveillance. Successful surveillance requires the ability to distinguish legitimate from illegitimate users of an area. The absence of such recognition leaves residents unable to identify someone or something that is out of place. Members of neighborhood organizations become eyes and ears for the police. It is impossible for the legal authorities to be everywhere at the same time. It is the responsibility of ordinary citizens, therefore, to assist in the surveillance function of law enforcement.

The exact number of neighborhood or block watches is not known. Many neighborhood watch groups are true grassroots organizations and do not belong to any larger national

ON THE WEB

The National Sheriff's Association, supported by the U.S. Department of Justice, maintains a web site for neighborhood watch that contains a great deal of information. This can be accessed at http://www.nnw.org/ The textbook web site also has a "Neighborhood Watch Manual" from the Bureau of Justice Assistance that you may find helpful.

organization that keeps records on such groups. In the United States, the National Sheriffs' Association sponsors the **National Neighborhood Watch (NNW)** organization. According to NNW (2015), there were more than 25,000 neighborhood watch groups in the United States in 2012, with more than one million volunteers. It is unknown how many other non-affiliated neighborhood watch groups or participants exist. The National Association of Town Watch (2015) claims more than 16,000 communities with 38 million neighbors involved. O'Keefe et al. (1996) note that 31 percent of national survey respondents claimed membership in a neighborhood crime prevention organization. In England and Wales, the Neighborhood and Home Watch Network (2015) claims there are 170,000 neighborhood watch schemes with 3.8 million participating households. According to the 2009–2010 British Crime Survey, roughly 13 percent of the households in England and Wales participate in neighborhood watch schemes. Internationally, neighborhood watch is more common in New World countries (the United States, the United Kingdom, Canada, Australia, and New Zealand) and Asian countries than other areas (see Table 5.1). Beyond a formal neighborhood watch group, greater numbers of people simply call on neighbors to keep an eye on their home when

TABLE 5.1 Cooperative Neighborhood Crime Prevention Participation

Area	Neighborhood Watch	Informal Surveillance
New World	36%	67%
Asia	23	77
Western Europe	18	59
Africa	10	48
Latin America	12	60
Countries in transition	8	49

Source: del Frate (1998). *Preventing Crime: Citizens' Experiences Across the World*. UNICRI Issues and Reports No. 9. New York: United Nations.

they are gone (del Frate, 1998). It is important to remember that any numbers on neighborhood watch participation are only approximations. There is no centralized measure of participation in neighborhood watch, so determining involvement is difficult.

The surveillance goal of neighborhood watch is greatly enhanced by instituting various activities. Garofalo and McLeod (1988), based on a national survey of neighborhood watch programs, reported that the most common activities among groups are Operation Identification (appearing in 81 percent of the programs), followed by security surveys (68 percent), crime hotlines (38 percent), and block parenting (27 percent). Improving street lighting (35 percent) and physical environmental concerns (38 percent) are also common activities adopted by neighborhood watch groups. Among the other activities reported by the neighborhood watch groups are escort services, Whistle Stop, phone chains, court watch, hiring guards, organized surveillance, and victim/witness assistance (Garofalo and McLeod, 1988). One institutionalized neighborhood project is the **National Night Out** program. Started in 1981 and sponsored by the National Association of Town Watch, the program occurs every August and consists of educational programs, neighborhood organizing, social events, and anti-drug and anti-crime activities (natw.org). National Night Out receives a great deal of support from law enforcement and encourages citizens to leave their lights on, come out of their homes, and join together to combat crime and community problems.

Community Anti-Drug Programs

One notable movement in the area of neighborhood anti-crime programs in the 1990s involved the proliferation of community anti-drug (CAD) programs. In response to the surge in drug use, particularly cocaine and crack in inner cities during the early 1990s, residents banded together with each other, the police, and various agencies and organizations to attack drug use, drug sales, and related problems (Davis et al., 1993). Many of the neighborhood efforts mirrored neighborhood watch programs in their use of surveillance tactics, reporting to the police, working with agencies to clean up the area, providing information to residents, instituting anti-drug programs, and participating in citizen patrols.

While no count of CAD programs is available, it is reasonable to assume that they are prevalent, particularly in larger cities and areas with serious, visible drug problems. The Center for Substance Abuse Prevention's Community Partnership Demonstration Program targeted 252 communities for anti-drug activity (Davis and Lurigio, 1996). The White House Office of National Drug Control Policy oversees the Drug Free Communities Support Program. This program offers funding in support of some 2,000 community coalitions

---

ON THE WEB

More information on the Drug Free Communities Support Program is available at http://www.whitehouse.gov/ondcp/Drug-Free-Communities-Support-Program

with 9,000 volunteers in their efforts to combat drug problems on a variety of levels (White House Office of National Drug Control Policy, 2015). Included in the community activities is encouraging citizen participation in prevention activity.

Citizen Patrols

Citizen patrols are often a key element of neighborhood watch and represent an active role in surveillance efforts. The sole purpose of patrols is to put more eyes on the street in order to increase the chances of detecting strangers in the area and discovering crimes in progress. Residents are discouraged from physically intervening in any suspicious activity they may find. While most citizen patrols are on foot, mobile patrols can be found in some communities. Participants can be either volunteers or paid individuals.

As with block watches, no clear number of citizen patrols is available. The **Guardian Angels** is perhaps the most well-known citizen patrol group. Started in 1971, the group is made up primarily of teenagers and young adults, and boasts having over 130 chapters in the United States and 17 other countries. It also provides educational materials on safety, an online, Internet safety component, and works with at-risk youths (www. guardianangels.org). In the United Kingdom, local churches are active in promoting citizen patrols. One group, **Street Pastors**, operates in 250 locations and claims more than 9,000 volunteers. A second group, **Street Angels**, boasts 120 patrols (Bullock, 2014).

Variations on the citizen patrol theme include Whistle Stop, Radio Watch, and similar projects. These surveillance methods use the simple presence of people on the street. Participants in these programs generally do not serve in any formal capacity or follow any set schedules. Instead, they watch for suspicious persons and activity while partaking in normal daily activity. For example, people in **Whistle Stop** blow a whistle if they see something happening out of the ordinary as they are shopping, working, or simply walking out of doors. *Radio Watch* relies on individuals with two-way radios (such as cab drivers and truckers) or cell phones to report questionable behavior when they see it occurring. Once again, the key is to observe, call the authorities, and not take any further action.

> ┌─ **ON THE WEB** ─────────
> *The Guardian Angels support a number of chapters and initiatives. You can explore what they offer at http://www.guardianangels.org/*

Building Guardianship

Throughout all of the different forms of neighborhood crime prevention, the key component is building guardianship. The primary guardians are typically meant to be residents and legitimate users of the areas. Indeed, as discussed in the last chapter, physical design is expected to engender citizen action (guardianship) to stop crime. The failure of CPTED to bring this about led to overt efforts to engender citizen action (as in second-generation CPTED) and neighborhood crime prevention.

The importance of guardianship is demonstrated most effectively in **routine activities theory**. Cohen and Felson (1979) argue that three things must coincide for crime to occur. These are (1) a suitable target, (2) a motivated offender, and (3) an absence of guardians. When these three factors converge in time and place, the opportunity for crime is enhanced. It is important to note that routine activities theory does not posit that crime *will* occur. That is, it is not a cause of criminal activity. Rather, it presents the opportunity for crime and greatly enhances the chances that crime will take place. Addressing crime, therefore, is accomplished by reducing the opportunity.

Neighborhood watch, in particular, and community crime prevention, in general, primarily address the guardianship component of routine activities. Guardianship can take a variety of forms. Eck (1994) proposes triplets of guardianship—*guardians* of targets, *handlers* of offenders, and *managers* of places—which correspond to the elements of routine activities theory. The inner triangle of Figure 5.3 represents the basic components of routine activities—the point at which targets, offenders, and places coincide. The outer triangle indicates the potential guardians or protectors for each of the dimensions. Each type of guardian may be instrumental in determining the level and type of crime that occurs. Guardians, handlers, and managers have the ability to reduce the opportunity for crime by limiting at least one dimension necessary for the commission of an offense. The guardians are typically the owner of the property, a family member or friend, the police or security, or others who provide surveillance and protection to the target.

Figure 5.3

Routine Activities Triangle

Source: R.V. Clarke and J.E. Eck (2005). *Crime Analysis for Problem Solvers in 60 Small Steps.* Washington, DC: Office of Community Oriented Policing Services.

Guardianship requires more than just the existence of a possible guardian. Hollis-Peel et al. (2011) note that guardianship can be either a physical presence to address crime or it can be a symbolic presence that signals higher risk to potential offenders. The guardians themselves do not have to be those tasked with guarding a person or place. Instead, the guardians can be individuals who just happen to be present when a motivated offender is contemplating action. There is also the assumption that the guardian has the physical ability to intervene and the willingness to do so. Reynald (2011) argues that there are three dimensions to actual guardianship. These are (1) the simple availability to observe what is happening around one's self, (2) actually undertaking the task of watching, and (3) acting on what the individual sees. Hollis-Peel et al. (2011) add to this discussion by proposing a hierarchy of guardianship:

4. **Intervening guardians** who are visible, monitoring the area, and take action when something occurs.

3. **Capable guardians** who are visible and actively observing/monitoring.

2. **Available guardians** who are present but are not actively paying attention to what is happening in the area.

1. **Invisible guardians** who are not evident or visible in the area.

This hierarchy suggests that the simple presence of an individual does not guarantee observation or action. Reynald (2011) suggests that, in many instances, guardianship is interrupted at different points, which inhibits successful surveillance and action. These may be an inability to recognize strangers in an area, the absence of personal attachment to the area, a high level of resident turnover that prompts alienation between the residents, or more targets than potential guardians (Reynald, 2011). As a result, Reynald argues that guardianship needs to be conceptualized as Guardianship in Action, which refers to taking steps to ensure that residents and individuals carry out active guardianship. That is, they have the ability to observe, they watch what is happening, and they take action when they see something taking place (Reynald, 2011).

Evaluation of Neighborhood Crime Prevention

Evaluation of neighborhood crime prevention efforts typically involves two distinct measures of effectiveness. The most logical measure is the impact these activities have on crime and the fear of crime. A second measure of effectiveness is the impact of neighborhood organizing on intervening factors such as social cohesion, a sense of territoriality, and neighborliness. Crime rates and fear of crime change to the extent that these

ON THE WEB

CrimeSolutions.gov provides access to a great deal of information on community crime prevention interventions and their effectiveness at http://crimesolutions. gov/ The textbook web site also has a document from the Office of Community-Oriented Policing on "Does NW Reduce Crime?"

intervening factors are enhanced. The following evaluation of neighborhood crime prevention looks at changes in both the intermediate factors as well as crime and fear of crime.

Effects on Community Cohesion

Studies of neighborhood crime prevention often include an evaluation of the effectiveness of the organization effort. The outcome measures range from simple documentation of existing groups and numbers of participants to some statements about the quality of individual involvement. A few studies rely exclusively upon these process evaluation measures and fail to consider the actual impact on crime and fear. The assumption in these later studies is that changes in intermediary factors inevitably lead to crime prevention.

Several analyses of community crime prevention note the extent of citizen participation in terms of number of neighborhood groups and the number of participants in those groups. Garofalo and McLeod (1988) and O'Keefe et al. (1996) demonstrate widespread participation in various crime prevention activities. Bennett (1990) reports that 64 percent of the residents in one London neighborhood and 44 percent in another claim to participate in neighborhood watch. Crawford (1998) notes that more than six million people participate in neighborhood watch organizations in England and Wales.

While these levels of activity may appear to be admirable, it is unknown how many people regularly attend crime prevention meetings, heed the advice they are given, or do more than simply show up at the meetings. How many people show up at more than the initial organizational meeting? How much impact do a few hundred people have when they are spread out among thousands of groups around the country and how much support do they have in the community at large? These key questions are not clearly answered in most analyses.

Crime prevention programs typically report positive results, such as neighborhood improvements, and assume that these are signs of increased community cohesion and territoriality. One of the problems with this evidence is that many times the improvements are funded and undertaken by outside agencies and not residents. While the improvements may be significant, there is little or no evidence that these changes impacted social cohesion or interaction. As noted in the last chapter, crime preventive initiatives may conflict with each other and negate the intended actions. Cozens and Davies (2013), for example, note that the installation of security shutters on homes, a physical design component of neighborhood watch, led to reduced social interaction.

Evaluations of neighborhood watch routinely show that watch participants hold very positive attitudes of the police (Brown and Wycoff, 1987; Laycock and Tilley, 1995b; Shernock, 1986; Skogan and Wycoff, 1986; Williams and Pate, 1987; Wolfer, 2001). Community watch programs bring citizens and officers together in symbiotic, mutual, problem-solving activity. The police serve neighborhood groups as sources of information on crime and crime prevention techniques. The public, in turn, provides information on suspicious persons, crimes in progress, and relevant crime-solving information. This information is routinely used to argue that neighborhood watch leads to improved community cohesion.

Various studies of neighborhood crime prevention efforts attempt to more directly assess changes in community cohesion and communal support. The results, however, are often mixed. Bennett (1987, 1990), studying neighborhood watch in two areas of London, reports that social cohesion increased in one and decreased in the other. Similarly, an analysis of four organized neighborhoods in Chicago (Rosenbaum et al., 1985) reveals no change in community cohesion for three areas and decreased cohesion in the fourth neighborhood. Lewis et al. (1988) analyzed interviews with residents in five neighborhood watch areas of Chicago both before and after the implementation of increased efforts at organization. Unfortunately, the authors find no change in the frequency of informal discussion between residents or in the number of neighbors known by name, both of which indicate that community cohesion appears to be unaffected by the neighborhood watch programs.

Effects on Crime

The primary interest in neighborhood crime prevention is reduced levels of crime and fear of crime. Community crime prevention techniques are aimed primarily at the property offenses of burglary, larceny, and robbery. Little, if any, impact should be found on crimes of interpersonal violence. The reason for this is that many personal crimes occur between individuals who know one another and within the home. Increased surveillance will not alleviate crimes when the offender and victim are co-residents or legitimate users of the area. Neither would appear out of place nor draw attention to themselves. Only crimes that occur between strangers should experience any great reduction from neighborhood watch activities. The following discussion of effects on crime is divided into three primary areas—studies using official data, analysis of victim survey data, and a discussion of two specific prevention initiatives from Great Britain.

Official Records

Official crime records reveal a positive impact of neighborhood watch programs on crime. Most studies report a lower level of crime (particularly property offenses) in the target communities than control areas and/or decreases compared to pre-program levels. An early comparison of Detroit neighborhoods shows a 58 percent reduction in burglary and 61 percent fewer purse snatchings in the crime prevention community (Figgie International, 1983). Perry (1984), investigating citizen crime prevention in 15 Denver neighborhoods, finds that 11 of the 15 neighborhoods had lower crime rates the year following implementation compared to the year prior to the project. Similarly, Latessa and Travis (1987) note significant drops in burglary, larceny, auto theft, and total crime in an organized area of Cincinnati compared to the rest of the city. The efficacy of the neighborhood efforts is supported by the fact that comparable decreases did not appear for personal crimes (aggravated assault and robbery), which are not the typical target of neighborhood actions.

Many of the projects that are a part of the Reducing Burglary Initiative (RBI) in the United Kingdom include neighborhood watch, targeted policing, youth programs, and other interventions, along with physical design changes in their programs (Kodz and Pease, 2003). In early evaluations in Rochdale (Greater Manchester) and Yew Tree, Sandwell (West Midlands), the programs significantly reduced the burglary levels in the experimental areas relative to the control neighborhoods (Home Office, 2003c, 2003d). Millie and Hough (2004) report an average decrease of 21 percent in burglaries in RBI areas, with decreases in 14 of 16 projects. Similar positive results have been reported elsewhere in the United States and the United Kingdom (Anderton, 1985; Jenkins and Latimer, 1987; Kohfeld et al., 1981; Laycock and Tilley, 1995a).

A systematic review of neighborhood watch evaluations reports positive results. Holloway et al. (2008) report on a meta-analysis of existing research on neighborhood watch. The authors were able to locate 18 evaluations primarily from the U.S. and U.K., which provided data for reanalysis. The results of the analyses reveal that neighborhood watch is effective at significantly reducing crime (Holloway et al., 2008). Interestingly, studies from the U.S. and Canada were more likely to uncover positive results than those from the U.K.

These results do not mean that all studies using official records find lower levels of crime in crime prevention communities. An evaluation of neighborhood watch programs in London finds no change in crime for organized areas while there were decreases in control neighborhoods (Bennett, 1990). One possible explanation for mixed results would be pre-program differences in the areas or in offending. Neighborhood watch areas with great reductions in crime are often those with high pre-program offense levels (Henig, 1984). The reductions, therefore, could be due to a regression to the more natural crime levels for these areas.

An important confounding factor in the evaluation of neighborhood watch may be changes in the level of reporting to the police. Successful programs should increase the number of calls to the police. At the same time, there may be a reduction in crime. This is possible if citizens call the police more often but fewer calls reflect criminal activities.

For example, Bolkcom (1981) reports a doubling in calls to police accompanied by a decrease in crime. Similarly, a public housing project in Charlotte, North Carolina, reveals increased reports of crime accompanied by a reduced crime rate (Hayes, 1982). The fact that reporting of crime to the police increases is one indication that the neighborhood watch program is successful.

Victimization Measures

The use of victim survey data avoids the confounding influence of changes in reporting crimes to the police. Studies utilizing victim surveys typically report strong support for neighborhood watch. For example, the Seattle Community Crime Prevention Program noted that community crime prevention areas displayed lower burglary rates after program initiation than did corresponding control areas of Seattle (Cirel et al., 1977). At the same time, reporting to the police increased, thus supporting the view that there was a real reduction in crime. Unfortunately, the lower burglary levels persisted for only 12 to 14 months and then increased to the pre-program levels (Cirel et al., 1977). This finding of time-bounded effects suggests that programs need to be periodically reviewed and promoted in order to prolong their effectiveness. Cook and Roehl's (1983) analysis of Chicago's Northwest Neighborhood Federation also uncovered a 12 percent reduction in the level of criminal victimization. The authors also reported a 26 percent increase in the feeling that residents could do something about crime in their neighborhood. The meta-analysis conducted by Holloway et al. (2008) reveals similar positive results for neighborhood watch in studies using self-report data.

Despite these positive results, a major study of neighborhood watch in London did not find the same positive results using victimization data (Bennett, 1990). Both household and personal crimes showed increases over the course of the program compared to control areas. In fact, some control areas reported reduced crime for the same period of time. It would appear that the neighborhood watch areas did worse than the other areas.

Two Examples—Kirkholt and Safer Cities

Two projects offer a good deal of insight into the effectiveness of community and neighborhood interventions. These are the **Kirkholt Burglary Prevention Project** and the **Safer Cities program**. Kirkholt is a clearly defined residential area comprised of more than 2,200 dwellings near Manchester, England, and owned by the local governmental authority. According to the 1984 British Crime Survey, Kirkholt had a burglary rate more than twice that of other high-risk areas in England (Forrester et al., 1988). The burglary prevention activities included the establishment of "cocoon neighborhood watch" (very small groups of homes banded together for surveillance and support), as well as the removal of pre-payment heating fuel meters in homes, improvements in physical security devices, and the use of community teams to conduct security surveys. While overall security was an issue, the program specifically targeted repeat burglary victims (Forrester et al., 1988).

Evaluation of Kirkholt took place in two phases and involved extensive interviews with residents, agencies, and other program participants. Results from Phase I, which covered the development of the project and the first seven months of operation, showed a large reduction in burglary from 316 offenses in the pre-program period to 147 offenses after program implementation (Forrester et al., 1988). At the same time, there was a small increase in burglary for the surrounding area. Similarly, the project demonstrated a clear impact on repeat burglary victimization (Forrester et al., 1988, 1990). Potential problems for the Phase I results include the short follow-up period (only seven months) and the fact that the pre-program offense levels were unduly high (Forrester et al., 1990). It is possible that the effect was only short term or that the reductions reflect a moderation of unreasonably high offense levels that had nowhere to go but down. The Phase II evaluation, however, provided greater support for the project's impact. Overall, the burglary rate fell roughly 75 percent over the life of the project (over four years), while the remainder of the area only saw a decrease of 24 percent (Forrester et al., 1990). Additional support appeared in the fact that repeat victimization was significantly reduced.

Further evidence of the impact of the Kirkholt project can be seen in the levels of program participation. First, Forrester et al. (1990) report that there were 93 "Home Watch" (cocoon neighborhood watch) groups operating, with 20 to 25 households in each. This represented almost all residents in Kirkholt. Second, various local interventions were initiated by the program, including after-school projects and work with the Probation Service on programs for offenders. Finally, there was a significant increase in the number of victims who took preventive measures after initiation of the program (Forrester et al., 1990). The evaluations concluded that both physical design features (e.g., the removal of the pre-payment meters) and social efforts (e.g., the cocoon neighborhood watch) were essential elements of the successful project.

In the Safer Cities program, the British government provided funds for local initiatives aimed at reducing crime and the fear of crime, and the creation of safer cities. Initial funding was made available to 20 projects in 1988 and was expanded in a second phase in 1993 (Sutton, 1996; Tilley, 1992). Each individual program included a coordinator, police participation, various agency representatives, and a steering committee. Each steering committee was supposed to identify and implement preventive actions according to the unique needs of the community. Many of the interventions initiated under the Safer Cities programs included neighborhood watch, target hardening, property marking, community mobilization, and the use of signs and other media (Tilley and Webb, 1994).

Evaluations of the Safer Cities initiatives reveal generally positive results. Most locations initiated a wide array of prevention initiatives (Sutton, 1996). Evidence shows that the level of burglary was reduced (Ekblom et al., 1996b; Mawby, 2001; Tilley and Webb, 1994), apparently as a result of neighborhood watch, target hardening, and property identification activities. Additionally, publicity concerning an area's activities was seen as an important part of making an impact for the larger community (Tilley and Webb, 1994). At the same time, however, there is some evidence that burglary may have increased in adjacent areas and locations where the program was not adequately or fully instituted (Ekblom et al., 1996a, 1996b). Clearly, greater impacts on crime were evident in areas where more action was undertaken. Despite these positive results, Sutton (1996) points out that many areas in need of assistance were written off by the steering committees as

> ┌─ **ON THE WEB** ─────────────
> *You can read more about both the Kirkholt and Safer Cities initiatives on the British Home Office web site at http://webarchive.nationalarchives. gov.uk/20110220105210/rds.homeoffice.gov.uk/ rds/prgpdfs/fcpu13.pdf and http://webarchive. nationalarchives.gov.uk/20110220105210/http:// rds.homeoffice.gov.uk/rds/pdfs/hors164.pdf*

"lost causes," rather than places to be aggressively targeted. Part of this was due to the fact that some steering committees were much more passive in their activities than others.

Summary

Evaluation of neighborhood crime prevention in both the United States and the United Kingdom shows that preventive actions can impact on the level of crime in the community. This assessment holds true whether the crime rate is measured by official police records or victimization surveys. A few studies, however, suggest that crime can become worse in some targeted neighborhoods (e.g., Bennett, 1990; Latessa and Travis, 1987; Lewis et al., 1988; Pate et al., 1987). Even in those cases where neighborhood watch has an impact, it is far from complete, indicating there is still much to do to prevent crime.

The key to successful crime prevention activities appears to lie in the level of program implementation. Bowers et al. (2003) note that the level of *outcome intensity* (that is, the actual implementation of prevention activities), as opposed to the level of planning, preparation, training, and other factors (i.e., input intensity), is the most important factor in making changes in crime. The greater the outcome intensity, the greater the reduction in crime. Different background characteristics of the target communities, varying types of available data, and varying evaluation designs also impact on the results.

Community Anti-Drug Programs

Community anti-drug (CAD) programs represent a recent incarnation of community crime prevention initiatives. These programs utilize many of the same forms of intervention, including physical design changes, surveillance, group meetings, phone hotlines for anonymous reporting to the police, and citizen patrols, but also add activities directly targeted at drug problems, such as demanding enforcement of zoning and housing codes in order to eliminate drug houses. Many of these programs grew in the late 1980s and early 1990s in response to the growing drug problem in many cities.

The success of CAD programs should be enhanced by increased levels of social cohesion. While there is some evidence that anti-drug programs have a positive impact on social cohesion, the research results are mixed. Lurigio and Davis (1992), reporting on initiatives in Miami, Seattle, Philadelphia and Baltimore, argue that the programs have significantly increased the social cohesion in three of the four sites. Conversely, Roehl et al. (1995) and Davis et al. (1991) note that actual participation by residents is low (often less than 10 percent) and many programs operate with only a small core group of dedicated individuals. Results from an analysis of anti-drug initiatives in Chicago's public housing suggests that change may be hard if the residents actively contribute to the problems and the interventions are being driven by outsiders (Popkin et al., 1999).

The more important issue is whether CAD programs are able to reduce the levels of crime and other problems. Using interviews with residents of four CAD programs, Davis et al. (1991) report overall positive results. Residents report fewer drug problems after initiation of the program. The respondents also point to reduced signs of physical decay, increased feelings of empowerment and social control, and greater satisfaction with the area. Similar results are found in analyses of the Community Responses to Drug Abuse program, the Community Partnership Demonstration Programs, and the Chicago Public Housing Authority's Anti-Drug Initiative (Davis and Lurigio, 1996; Popkin et al., 1999; Rosenbaum et al., 1997). The evaluation of the anti-drug programs in Chicago public housing also reveals reduced victimization. Popkin et al. (1995, 1999) point out that residents of target projects report reduced fighting, shootings, and drug dealing, both inside and outside the buildings. These positive finding from anti-drug programs may reflect the intensity of resident convictions about drugs and drug-related offenses. Where past crime prevention programs dealt mostly with property crime issues, drug problems come with related gangs, violence, and personal crime problems that might cause greater concern and willingness to act by citizens.

Not all CAD initiatives are embraced by or operated by local residents. Popkin et al. (1995, 1999) note that most of the activities in Chicago's public housing initiative were coordinated and implemented by the police and the housing authority. Citizen participation was difficult to engender. The authors report that the program was successful at implementing drug and weapon sweeps, the hiring of security guards, the institution of new security policies, and reducing offending behavior. Despite the positive results, some residents resented the intrusions and methods used by the housing authority. Indeed, successful legal challenges were mounted in reference to some activities, such as sweeps for weapons. The evaluators suggest that greater involvement by the residents is needed in both the planning and implementation of anti-drug activities (Popkin et al., 1999).

Citizen Patrols

Citizen patrols present the most straightforward attempt by neighborhood residents to increase surveillance. Relatively few studies of citizen patrols exist. One examination of citizen patrol studies shows reduced burglary rates on the order of 20 to 50 percent in patrol areas (Titus, 1984). Latessa and Allen (1980), evaluating paid, citizen foot patrol in Columbus, Ohio, report a great drop in crime in the target areas compared to pre-program figures and control areas. In addition, citizens favor the patrols and their activity (Latessa and Allen, 1980). Similarly, Troyer and Wright (1985), assessing the impact of citizen patrols in a middle-class neighborhood and on a university campus, report that residents strongly favored the patrol and report feeling safer since its initiation. Citizen involvement in patrols undertaken on mass transit facilities in The Netherlands appears to have caused a 33 percent increase in feelings of safety and a clear drop in violence (van Andel, 1989). In general, the research suggests that citizen patrols can be effective at reducing both crime and fear.

The Guardian Angels are one example of citizen patrolling that has gained international attention. Despite the large number of Guardian Angel chapters around the world, few methodologically sound evaluations of the program exist. Pennell et al. (1986), evaluating the Guardian Angels in San Diego, report little impact on the level of crime. Indeed, while violent crime fell by 22 percent in the patrolled areas, the control areas exhibited a drop of 42 percent. Additionally, simple assault increased in the patrolled area. These results are not surprising given the fact that the Angels made only two citizen arrests in the course of 672 patrols over six months (Pennell et al., 1986). Kenney (1986) finds the same lack of change in crime when studying Guardian Angel patrols of the New York City subways.

While the impact on crime may not be great, the Guardian Angels have engendered a great deal of goodwill among the citizens in the areas they patrol. Respondents from several cities report a greater feeling of safety when Guardian Angels are around (Pennell et al., 1986). In addition, the organization is able to keep its own members from becoming involved in criminal activity (Pennell et al., 1986). Other positive findings include the fact that the police believe the Guardian Angels help citizens with a variety of concerns. Early concerns about vigilantism held by the public and police, directed at all citizen patrols and not just the Guardian Angels, have not been realized (Latessa and Allen, 1980; Troyer and Wright, 1985; Yin et al., 1977).

Neighborhood Crime Prevention and Fear of Crime

Besides attempting to eliminate or reduce crime, neighborhood crime prevention programs have the potential to impact fear of crime. Many evaluations investigate changes in fear, often through victim surveys that ask residents about their feelings of safety in the community and their perceived risk of future victimization. Research also tests other dimensions discussed by Ferraro (1995), such as impressions of overall crime in the community, feelings about whether citizens can have an effect on crime and neighborhood problems, and general feelings toward components of the criminal justice system.

Reported reductions in fear of crime can be very dramatic. Figgie International (1983) claims 75 percent fewer subjects respond that they are "very fearful" of crime after neighborhood programming. In another study, 95 percent of the senior citizens who participated in crime prevention reported being less fearful in follow-up surveys (Yagerlener, 1980). Cook and Roehl's (1983) evaluation of the Northwest Neighborhood Federation showed decreases in perceptions of rising crime (22 percent), decreased fear of burglary (26 percent), increased feelings that residents could influence crime (26 percent), and an increase in the belief in neighborhood crime control (26 percent). Evidence from the Safer Cities program shows reduced fear and reduced worry about crime, especially in areas where crime prevention activities are well known and intensively implemented (Ekblom et al., 1996a, 1996b; Mawby, 2001; Tilley and Webb, 1994). These findings of reduced fear are replicated in a number of other studies (Bennett, 1990; Cohn et al., 1978; Hayes, 1982; Rasmussen et al., 1979).

Efforts at organizing hard to organize areas or implementing prevention with limited community support also demonstrate the fear-reducing capabilities of such endeavors. Bennett and Lavrakas (1989) report on concerted efforts to organize 10 high-crime, high-fear inner-city neighborhoods in nine cities. Comparing pre-program to post-program periods, and experimental with non-equivalent control groups, the authors find that fear was significantly reduced in six of the 10 neighborhoods. There was no change in three and an increase in one area. Further, overall concern about crime was reduced in five neighborhoods, with no changes in the remaining neighborhoods (Bennett and Lavrakas, 1989). In the analysis of community anti-drug programs in four cities, Davis et al. (1991) report significant reductions in fear, while no changes appear in control areas. Similarly, the Chicago Housing Authority's Anti-Drug Initiative reduced fear, despite the relative lack of resident participation (Popkin et al., 1999). Davis and Lurigio (1996) note that the Community Responses to Drug Abuse program increased resident satisfaction with the area. Finally, Wolfer (2001) reports that elderly respondents who believe there is an active neighborhood watch program nearby are less fearful than those who do not live in a neighborhood watch community.

Not all studies, however, exhibit lower levels of fear nor are the evaluations of fear without problems. Brodie and Sheppard (1977), evaluating crime prevention programs in Denver, uncovered conflicting evidence on fear of crime. While fear of burglary decreased, fear of walking outdoors and feelings of helplessness toward crime increased. Rosenbaum et al. (1986) report increased fear of personal crime, no effect on fear of property crime, and increased perceptions of neighborhood crime. In addition, the programs failed to engender positive attitudes toward the area, had little influence on area deterioration, and did not alter crime prevention efforts of individuals (Rosenbaum et al., 1986). Similarly, the Community Responses to Drug Abuse evaluation reveals no changes in residents' perceptions of crime or fear of crime (Davis and Lurigio, 1996). Other studies also report no change in levels of fear of crime (Bennett, 1987; Latessa and Travis, 1987; Pate et al., 1987).

The failure to find reduced fear in some studies may be due to a variety of problems in the research. First, participation in crime prevention programs and attempts to heighten awareness of crime may engender more, not less, fear and worry. Second, the varying definitions of "fear" makes assessments of program impact difficult. Third, the use of diverse subjects in follow-up surveys (e.g., only those who participate in the crime prevention program, random samples of neighborhoods, or subgroups of the population) makes summarizing the results problematic. Fourth, many programs focus on high crime, high fear areas and prevention efforts face a major challenge for changing attitudes in these locations. Finally, short follow-up times may not be enough to elicit any changes in high crime areas. In general, neighborhood crime prevention appears to successfully reduce fear of crime, particularly where the interventions are appropriately implemented.

Evaluation Issues

Beyond the various problems noted so far in this chapter, there are other issues that hamper the effectiveness and evaluation of neighborhood crime prevention programs. A major concern in any evaluation or discussion of neighborhood watch entails the definition of "neighborhood" and "community." Unfortunately, neighborhood and community are rarely explicitly defined (Tilley, 2009). At one extreme is the use of entire cities, villages, or towns. Research often utilizes census tracts or block groups. Some analyses use mapping techniques to identify high-crime locations and use those as the target "neighborhood." Many studies assume that everyone knows what a neighborhood is and there is no reason to define it. What this means for research and program planning, however, is that everyone involved in the project may be envisioning a (slightly) different area when "neighborhood" is being considered. For example, many cities have areas that can be identified by a name. These names may come from a feature of the area (such as "uptown" or "the park district") or a subdivision name (such as "Shady Acres") or some other identifier. Unfortunately, the simple existence of a name does not mean that the area has set boundaries or that everyone knows the boundaries. Even being able to establish boundaries would not mean that the area is homogeneous. The consequence of organizing and evaluating a heterogeneous community is that the differences can impede success.

Most research takes one of two approaches to handling "neighborhood" in the project evaluation. The first is to allow study participants to interpret "neighborhood" on an individual basis. The second is for the researcher to identify the "neighborhood" and gather information on that area, often without consideration of whether the chosen area is meaningful as a "neighborhood" to the people residing in it. In both cases, what may emerge are very different meanings and views about the "neighborhood."

Crime prevention research is particularly susceptible to variations in the definition of neighborhood. Surveys of crime and fear that reference the respondent's neighborhood will invariably be tapping a range of definitions. Crime prevention programs often operate on very different views of the neighborhood. As noted in Chapter 4, large housing complexes (such as Cabrini-Green), the mixed use Union Avenue Corridor in Portland (which was 3.5 miles long), and North Asylum Hill in Hartford have all been considered as neighborhoods. On the opposite extreme, various studies (e.g., Taylor, 1988, 1997; Weisburd et al., 2012) have considered streetblocks or street segments as the focus. A **streetblock** consists of the homes on either side of a single block (that is, between two cross-streets). Taylor (1988) chooses this bounding based on a belief that it is within this area that social contacts, relationships and interaction are strong. The streetblock may hold more relevance to residents than does the idea of neighborhood. The important point is that "neighborhood" may have many different meanings to different individuals in varied settings.

A second concern revolves around the impact of increased surveillance on levels of crime and fear. Neighborhood watch assumes that areas with higher surveillance will experience less crime. Unfortunately, the time order between surveillance and crime is not clear. High crime can (and should) prompt increased surveillance. At the same time, increased surveillance should uncover more crime, especially as measured by police records, due to increased reports of offending. Actual decreases in the amount of crime may not show up due to elevated levels of reporting. The evaluation of crime prevention efforts, therefore, should consider both the changes in citizen reporting practices and official and victimization levels of crime.

Another key problem in evaluating the impact of neighborhood crime prevention is the fact that most interventions are not implemented in isolation from other prevention activities. A consequence of having simultaneous programs and activities is the difficulty of isolating what component causes the change (Ekblom, 1993; Greenberg et al., 1985). The opposite problem is the expectation that a single intervention will have more than a minimal impact on crime and fear when the causes of the problems are many and varied (Bursik and Grasmick, 1993). A related issue with evaluation research is the failure to adequately assess the program's implementation. Rather than indicate failure, an evaluation showing no or negative impact may reflect the fact that the intervention was not properly implemented, the dosage applied to the problem was not enough, the follow-up time was too short, or there was some other problem (Ekblom, 1993; Laycock and Tilley, 1995a; Pawson and Tilley, 1997). Many of these implementation problems arise from the demands for immediate results, competition for resources, or the lack of adequate funding (Ekblom, 1993; Laycock and Tilley, 1995a).

Citizen Participation and Support

The results of research on neighborhood crime prevention should be qualified in light of information on citizen participation. Many of the results are presented as generalizable to all neighborhoods. The findings, however, may not be applicable to all areas or subgroups of the population. Indeed, some studies find changes only for program participants. Among the questions that must be answered are: Who participates in community crime prevention efforts? Are these individuals representative of the general population? Do crime prevention methods affect all persons in the same, or similar, fashion?

Who Participates?

A demographic analysis of crime prevention participants yields mixed results. Members of community crime prevention and those who take preventive measures more often are males, middle-to-upper income, home owners, more highly educated, white, and live in single family dwellings (Bennett, 1989; Cook and Roehl, 1983; Fisher, 1989; Greenberg et al., 1982, 1985; Lavrakas and Herz, 1982; Lavrakas et al., 1981; Luxenberg et al., 1994; Podolefsky and DuBow, 1980; Roehl and Cook, 1984; Shernock, 1986; Skogan, 1988, 1989; Skogan and Maxfield, 1981). These characteristics suggest a neighborhood that is demographically homogeneous and stable. The residents have built a stake in the neighborhood and are willing to take action to protect their investment.

These findings do not mean that crime prevention measures cannot and do not appear among other demographic groups. While some studies claim that participants tend to be older (Lab, 1990; Menard and Covey, 1987; Shernock, 1986; Shapland, 1988; Skogan and Maxfield, 1981), others find that most participants are middle-aged (Brown et al., 1984; Greenberg et al., 1985; Lavrakas and Herz, 1982) or younger (Smith and Lab, 1991). Some studies report that females participate more often than males (Bennett, 1989; Lab, 1990; Lavrakas et al., 1981). Similarly, there is a good deal of discrepancy about whether whites or blacks are more likely to be involved in community organizations (Lab, 1990; Lavrakas and Herz, 1982; Lavrakas et al., 1981; Shernock, 1986; Skogan and Maxfield, 1981).

Research indicates that participation in crime prevention groups is related to levels of participation in other groups. Various authors note that people involved in crime prevention efforts tend to be "joiners," who have higher feelings of responsibility toward the community than non-participants. Crime prevention is often a secondary extension of other group activities (Greenberg et al., 1982; Lavrakas and Herz, 1982; Lavrakas et al., 1981). This "joining" phenomenon is reflected in the findings that successful organizations tend to have a strong leader who is able to motivate participation, overcome diversity in opinions, set an agenda, and keep residents interested (Ekblom, 1993; Laycock and Tilley, 1995a; Rosenbaum, 1988; Skogan, 1987; Tilley, 1992).

Findings on the relationship between crime/fear and group participation are not as clear. Some evaluations find that higher perceptions of crime, fear, and neighborhood problems are related to crime prevention activity (Bennett, 1989; Lavrakas and Herz, 1982; Menard and Covey, 1987; Pennell, 1978; Skogan, 1987, 1989; Skogan and Lurigio, 1992; Skogan and Maxfield, 1981; Taylor et al., 1987). Conversely, others find little or no connection between perceptions of crime, fear of crime, and prevention participation (Baumer and DuBow, 1977; Bennett, 1989; Lab, 1990; Lavrakas and Herz, 1982; Smith and Lab, 1991).

The divergent findings on participation may be due to a number of factors (Lab, 1990). First, different groups of subjects are used in the analyses. Where one study examines the behavior of young urban residents, another may consider middle-aged suburbanites. Yet another may target older rural residents. It is not surprising, therefore, that different results emerge. Second, studies often measure the key variables in different ways. Victimization surveys and police data may tap different dimensions of prevention behavior. Fear measures vary from study to study. Similarly, crime prevention can take a wide variety of forms ranging from citizen patrols to operation identification and neighborhood watch. This diversity in study methodologies may be the cause of the varied results.

Perhaps the greatest problem in comparing studies on crime prevention involves the dubious assumption that all prevention techniques can be subsumed under the single umbrella of "crime prevention." While various authors have attempted to separate crime prevention actions into groups (Conklin, 1975; Furstenburg, 1972; Lavrakas et al., 1981; Pennell, 1978; Skogan, 1981), there have been few attempts to empirically test the proposed groupings. Lavrakas and Lewis (1980), factor analyzing data from four sources, identify two crime prevention dimensions—avoidance and access control. While these items correspond to theoretically proposed groupings, many crime prevention actions did not fit into either group.

Lab (1990), analyzing the 1983 Victim Risk Supplement (VRS) to the National Crime Survey, finds five dimensions of crime prevention behavior and examines crime prevention participation across the different domains (see Table 5.2). The domains that emerge are surveillance, avoidance, target hardening, personal security, and access control. Lab and Hope (1998) attempted to replicate these results using 1994 British Crime Survey (BCS) data. The authors uncover five different crime prevention domains (also in Table 5.2). These domains include taking evening precautions, neighborhood watch, technological security measures, fortress-type security measures, and self-defense activities. The different results in these two studies may be due to three major factors. First, the BCS data set includes a greater array of crime prevention behaviors for analysis. Second, the two studies are based on respondents from different countries. Third, there is a 10-year time gap between the collection of the two data sets. Despite these issues, the

TABLE 5.2 Crime Prevention Domains and Activities

Lab (1990)	Lab and Hope (1998)

Surveillance
   neighborhood watch activities
	Neighborhood watch
	   neighborhood watch participation, marking property,
	   home insurance

Avoidance	Evening Precautions avoidance, alter habits, go out in groups

Target hardening
   property marking, alarms
	Technological security
	   alarms, light timers, security survey

Personal security
   owning items for protection
	Self-defense
	   carry weapons, alarms, classes

Access control
   locks, door peepholes
	Fortress security
	   deadbolts, locks, bars/grills

Source: Compiled by author from S.P. Lab (1990). "Citizen crime prevention: Domains and participation." *Justice Quarterly* 7:467–492; and S.P. Lab and T. Hope (1998). "Assessing the impact of area context on crime prevention behavior." Paper presented to the Environmental Criminology and Crime Analysis Conference, Barcelona, Spain.

fact remains that distinct domains of crime prevention activities are utilized by respondents. Crime prevention is not unidimensional.

Using these domains to analyze citizen participation, Lab (1990) and Hope and Lab (2001) report clear differences across the various groups of activities in terms of individual demographic characteristics, perceptions of crime and fear, and neighborhood characteristics. Some of the greatest differences in participation across the crime prevention domains are the variations by area characteristics and respondent perceptions, rather than individual demographic characteristics. The results of these two studies suggest that analyses of participation must consider the type of crime prevention being considered. Simply comparing one study to another is prone to comparing different methods and behaviors to one another.

┌─ ON THE WEB ───────────────────────
│ *You can examine the predictors of participa-*
│ *tion in different domains of prevention from*
│ *Lab and Hope on the textbook web site.*
└────────────────────────────────────

Problematic Assumptions in Organizing for Crime Prevention

Participation in crime prevention is clearly a problematic issue for program organizers. Prompting people to become active guardians is the goal of neighborhood watch and community crime prevention. Unfortunately, Rosenbaum (1987) outlines five problematic assumptions underlying neighborhood watch programs (see Table 5.3). The failure of any of the assumptions would hamper both the organization and maintenance of such programs. Many individuals live in areas with few opportunities to participate (counter to Assumption 1). Similarly, it has been shown that many people fail to become involved even when the opportunity to do so exists (Lewis et al., 1988; Pate et al., 1987; Silloway and McPherson, 1985), and participation varies greatly based on demographic, neighborhood, and crime prevention factors (counter to Assumption 2). High-crime areas tend to be very hard to organize. The reason for this failure may be that people in high-crime areas are more fearful of crime and, in turn, are afraid to join others (often strangers) in a

---

TABLE 5.3 Problematic Assumptions Underlying Neighborhood Watch

Assumption 1

Neighborhood watch can be easily implemented on a large scale to provide citizens with an opportunity for participation in crime prevention activities.

Assumption 2

If given the opportunity to participate in neighborhood watch, most citizens would find the program appealing and would become involved regardless of social, demographic, or neighborhood characteristics.

Assumption 3

If and when citizens get together at block watch meetings, the assumption is made that this interaction and discussion will produce a number of immediate effects. These effects include reaching a consensus about problem definition, reducing fear of crime, increasing group cohesion, and increasing participation in both individual and collective crime prevention actions after the meeting.

Assumption 4

Neighborhood watch organizers (both police and community volunteers) invest in this strategy with the belief that such activities, once initiated, will be sustained.

Assumption 5

A final and very fundamental assumption underlying neighborhood watch is that the collective citizen actions implied by this strategy, if set in motion, would reduce the level of criminal activity and disorder in the neighborhood, thereby setting the stage for a reduction in fear of crime and other neighborhood improvements.

Source: Compiled by author from D.P. Rosenbaum (1987). "The theory and research behind neighborhood watch: Is it sound fear and crime reduction strategy?" *Crime & Delinquency* 33:103–134.

similar position. Individuals who have constructed fortresses in and around their homes are fearful of leaving the fortress, even for the purpose of fighting crime and fear.

Assumption 3 cannot be sustained in light of the research showing a failure to increase group cohesion, reduce fear, or increase participation. Counter to Assumption 4 is the fact that maintaining crime prevention activity is a major problem for most organizations. Many programs are initiated because of an existing crime problem, but most flounder once the crime problem subsides. Finally, the assumption that crime prevention is effective at reducing crime and disorder (Assumption 5) finds only qualified support in past research. The failure of neighborhood watch to live up to these five assumptions leads to serious questions about its potential to impact crime and fear.

Leveraging Participation/Guardianship

How then can citizen guardianship be stimulated? Reynald (2011) argues that incentives are needed to get people involved in guardianship. Sampson and Eck (2008) claim that so-called **super controllers** are not doing their job at applying incentives to those who should be more immediately involved in crime prevention. Super controllers are "the people, organizations and institutions that create incentives for controllers to prevent ... crime" (Sampson et al., 2010). An expanded crime triangle illustrates this idea (see Figure 5.4). As depicted in the diagram, the super controllers do not directly impact on any of the key factors that facilitate crime. Rather, the super controllers impact crime by prompting guardians, handlers, and managers to take action.

Figure 5.4

Expanded Crime Triangle

Source: R. Sampson and J.E. Eck (2008). "Super Controllers: Can I be your superman?" Paper presented at the POP Conference. Retrieved from http://www.popcenter.org/conference/conferencepapers/2008/supercontrollers.pdf

Super controllers can influence preventive actions in a variety of ways (Sampson and Eck, 2008; Sampson et al., 2010). Liquor control agencies can threaten to withhold a license if an establishment fails to check the ages of its patrons or if too many assaults take place in and around the bar. Insurance providers can offer incentives to homeowners to get them to install alarms or lights to deter burglars. Cities can file civil suits against property owners who knowingly allow their properties to be used as sites for prostitution or drug sales/use. Newspapers and organizations can spotlight high-crime locations, which may result in patrons avoiding the locations, or publish the names of places or events that take extra preventive precautions, thus attracting more patrons. Finally, the action of parents, clubs, or other groups can put pressure on their neighbors, friends, and acquaintances to take actions that will reduce crime. These are only a few examples of how super controllers can bring both positive and negative incentives to bear on target guardians, offender handlers, and place managers (Sampson and Eck, 2008; Sampson et al., 2010).

ON THE WEB

Sampson and Eck provided a great deal of additional information on guardianship and super controllers in a presentation made to the Problem-Oriented Policing conference in 2008. Their presentation can be accessed at http://www.popcenter.org/conference/conferencepapers/2008/supercontrollers.pdf

Beyond employing super controllers, it is important to integrate different groups and individuals into crime prevention and civic action. Bursik and Grasmick (1993) argue that neighborhood social control requires input from private, parochial, and public sources (see Hunter, 1985). **Private control** is based on interpersonal relationships between family members, friends and close associates. **Parochial control** broadens the sources of control to include neighborhood networks and institutions, such as schools, churches, or businesses. Finally, **public control** reflects the ability to marshal input, support and resources from public agencies. Bursik and Grasmick (1993) suggest that lower-class, transient, high-crime neighborhoods have the greatest problem developing control at any of these levels. Even if the residents can engender the private and parochial control, their ability to tap into the public dimension is hindered by their economic and political position in society.

There is a need to actively link residents and the formal public institutions in ways that will build control and community safety (van Steden et al., 2011). Skogan (1990) notes that some communities are unable to mobilize the resources necessary to deal with disorder. Ramey and Shrider (2014) argue that struggling neighborhoods can bring about change if they are provided outside assistance. They call for a combination of parochial and public control into a **new parochialism**. Ramey and Shrider (2014) demonstrate this approach with the Neighborhood Matching Fund in Seattle, Washington. The fund provides resources to neighborhoods who match funding with other resources, volunteering, local funds, and other commitments that result in a community-building coalition. There is an investment in the community by the local residents, as well as outsiders. Public investment has been shown to impact crime in many communities (Papachristos et al., 2011; Ramey, 2013; Ramey and Shrider, 2014; Velez and Richardson, 2012).

The potential impact of neighborhood watch and community crime prevention is untested in the areas and with the populations where the greatest margin for change exists. It is in high-crime, socially disorganized areas where engendering participation is most challenging, in part because of a vicious cycle between involvement and fear/crime. That is, fear and perceived risk may lead people to retreat into their homes and avoid other people, which in turn mitigates the possibility of group action to address fear and victimization. It takes efforts from various community sources (i.e., sources of control) to break the cycle of non-participation.

Chapter Summary

The evidence tends to support the basic idea of neighborhood crime prevention as a means of combating crime and the fear of crime. Table 5.4 summarizes the evidence from neighborhood initiatives. The results generally present neighborhood watch and its component activities as effective methods to reduce crime, victimization, and fear of crime. The magnitude of the changes, however, often appears to vary from study to study. Some studies show large absolute reductions in crime. Others present little or no change in target areas accompanied by increased crime in control areas. Still other evaluations, although few in number, find small increases in crime. The discrepant results can be attributed to several factors. Foremost among the causes is the fact that the neighborhood

TABLE 5.4 Summary of the Evidence on Neighborhood Prevention Programs

Technique	Positive Impact	Mixed Results
NW Groups	Burglary Theft Robbery Fear	
Community anti-drug programs	Drugs Violence	
Citizen patrols	Fear	Burglary Theft Robbery

initiatives are not always successfully implemented. This means that the failure is not in the crime prevention program itself, but is a failure to mobilize the citizens/guardians, fully implement the intervention, or bring the measures to bear on the problem. The failure of some evaluations to find positive results also may be due to the reliance on short-term follow-up, the absence of control groups for comparison, differing operationalizations of key variables (such as crime and fear), and the inability to identify individual effects of different program components.

One issue often left unaddressed in crime prevention evaluations is the problem of "crime displacement." Crime displacement refers to the movement of crime, usually to another area, as a result of the crime prevention initiative in the target area. The occurrence of crime displacement represents a shift in crime and not an actual decrease in crime. The extent and impact of displacement is the subject of the next chapter.

KEY TERMS

- available guardians
- capable guardians
- citizen patrols
- community anti-drug (CAD) programs
- Guardian Angels
- intervening guardians
- invisible guardians
- Kirkholt Burglary Prevention Project
- National Neighborhood Watch (NNW)
- National Night Out
- neighborhood watch
- new parochialism
- parochial control
- public control
- private control
- routine activities theory
- Safer Cities program
- Street Angels
- streetblocks
- Street Pastors
- super controllers
- Whistle Stop

CHAPTER 6 Displacement and Diffusion

CHAPTER OUTLINE

LEARNING OBJECTIVES

After reading this chapter you should be able to:

- List and define six forms of displacement.
- Discuss the assumptions underlying displacement.
- Provide an explanation of rational choice theory and its relation to displacement.
- Distinguish between benign and malign displacement and discuss each.
- Explain diffusion of benefits.
- Discuss the 10 principles of opportunity and crime.
- Explain the routine activities theory.
- Demonstrate your knowledge of offender decision making.
- Outline CRAVED and how it influences crime activity.
- Outline crime pattern theory and cognitive mapping.
- Discuss the impact of modern technology on the construction of cognitive maps.
- Discuss the evidence on the extent of each type of displacement.
- Provide information on the extent of the diffusion of benefits.

Outcome/impact evaluations of crime prevention focus on changes in the level of the targeted crime, fear of crime, and/or citizen behavior. The fact that most prevention programs are place specific means that evaluations typically focus only on changes within the target, neighborhood, or community. At the same time, crime prevention programs could have an impact beyond that which is intended. The other changes could be either positive or negative. The crime prevention techniques in one area may unintentionally result in increased crime in another area, on other targets, or at different times. In essence, levels of crime or fear may have simply shifted in response to the prevention efforts. This shift in crime is referred to as crime displacement. The opposite may also occur. Crime prevention efforts targeted at a specific problem in one location may have a positive impact on other locations or crimes. That is, there may be a diffusion of benefits.

Unfortunately, evaluations generally fail to consider the possibility of either displacement or diffusion. This is due to the fact that such assessment is a difficult task. Fortunately, there is a growing recognition of the need to examine displacement and diffusion in evaluations. The purpose of this chapter is to outline the concepts of crime displacement and diffusion, discuss the potential of offenders to shift their crime-related activities, and review the literature on displacement and diffusion.

Crime Displacement

Crime displacement represents change in crime due to the preventive actions of the individual or society. Most discussions of displacement focus on the shift of crime from one place to another (often called **crime spillover**). The assumption is that many crime prevention actions simply move the crime around instead of eliminating the overall amount of crime. For example, an increase in police presence in one neighborhood may reduce crime in that area but cause an increase in crime in a contiguous neighborhood. Displacement, however, can take forms other than just the geographical movement of crime.

Types of Displacement

Reppetto (1976) offers five forms of displacement—territorial, temporal, tactical, target, and functional (see Table 6.1). **Territorial (spatial) displacement** is the most frequently discussed and represents movement of crime from one location to another. **Temporal displacement**, the movement of offending to another period while remaining in the same area, may manifest itself through a shift in larcenies from the late evening to the early morning. Under **tactical displacement**, the offender utilizes new means to commit the same offense. A shift in burglary from entering through unlocked doors to breaking windows for entry represents a tactical change in the offense. **Target**

TABLE 6.1 **Forms of Displacement**	
Territorial	Movement of crime from one area to another, typically contiguous, area
Example	A neighborhood watch program is started and the burglars move to another neighborhood
Temporal	A shift in offending from one time to a different time, such as from day to night
Example	A citizen patrol is instituted at night, thus prompting burglars to work during the morning hours
Tactical	Changing the methods used in the commission of a crime
Example	The installation of deadbolt locks on doors results in burglars forcing open windows to gain entry
Target	Choosing a different victim within the same area
Example	A neighborhood watch program is started but only half the homes participate, thereby leading offenders to target non-participating homes
Functional	The offender stops committing one offense and shifts to another
Example	When burglary becomes more difficult due to target hardening devices the offender decides to commit robbery instead
Perpetrator	One offender ceases activity only to be replaced by another offender
Example	While crime prevention actions cause an individual to desist from further offending, another individual sees opportunities and begins offending

displacement involves a choice of different victims within the same area. For example, an increase in the use of weapons by store owners may force robbers to choose elderly pedestrians as victims. Reppetto's final form of displacement, **functional displacement**, suggests that offenders change to a new type of offense, such as shifting from larceny to burglary or burglary to robbery. Each of these forms of displacement represents a change in offense behavior on the part of the offender. Barr and Pease (1990) offer a sixth form of displacement—perpetrator. **Perpetrator displacement** occurs when one offender ceases his deviant behavior, only to be replaced by another offender. Crime prevention techniques are a logical cause of any of these types of displacement.

Assumptions

Displacement makes a number of assumptions about both the potential offender and his target (see Table 6.2). The degree to which these assumptions are accurate will impact the degree to which displacement can and will occur.

TABLE 6.2 Displacement Assumptions

---

1. Crime is inelastic
2. Offenders have mobility
3. Offenders make rational choices
4. Alternative targets and choices are available

Crime Inelasticity

Displacement assumes that crime is **inelastic**. That is, offenders are driven to commit a certain number of offenses over a given period of time (Reppetto, 1976). If crime is inelastic, it is not eliminated by crime prevention activities. Rather, it is simply moved along one of the displacement dimensions. Offenders are motivated to commit crime and will seek out opportunities to offend. One key to displacement, therefore, is available opportunities. Felson and Clarke (1998) argue that opportunities are (or can be) limited, thus having an impact on the possibility of displacement.

Potential Offender Mobility

Displacement assumes mobility on the part of the offender (Reppetto, 1976). The mobility can be across time, place, tactic, or any displacement dimension. Not all potential offenders, however, have the same level of mobility (Brantingham and Brantingham, 1984). For example, youthful offenders may not have access to transportation (limiting territorial displacement) or they may be tied to school and curfews (limiting temporal displacement). Race may inhibit individuals from entering areas populated by other racial or ethnic groups. Some offenders may not be psychologically able to shift from one type of crime to another (functional displacement). While such factors may limit displacement, they will not eliminate it for all potential offenders.

Mobility is not determined solely by characteristics of the potential offenders. It may also be limited by features of the surrounding environment (Brantingham and Brantingham, 2003; Brantingham, 2010). This is primarily true in relation to territorial (spatial) displacement, although it is not limited to the spatial domain. The ability of an offender to shift to another location/time/offense may be limited by the options available to the offender. For example, efforts taken in a small isolated community may not allow for territorial displacement because there are no alternatives for offending nearby. A neighborhood may also be somewhat isolated even within a large city because it has major barriers surrounding it, such as a river on one side and a major interstate highway on another (see Figure 6.1). Individuals who offend in the bounded area of town have

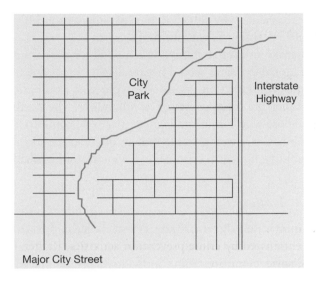

Figure 6.1

Example of a City with a Geographically Bounded Neighborhood

limited options for where to move for future offending, while those on the other side of the river have more options. Boundaries may not make displacement impossible, but they limit the directions any offenders can take if they are to be displaced (Brantingham and Brantingham, 2003).

While mobility may be limited by place, the characteristics of an area may enhance the possibility of offending (Brantingham, 2010). An individual who lives near an area with many targets (such as mixed-use areas with homes, businesses, and entertainment close at hand) may benefit from a wide range of differing opportunities for crime commission. Actions that limit household burglary may simply force the offender to pilfer from stores or rob shoppers in the local commercial strip. In essence, physical location can shut down some opportunities while enhancing others.

Rational Choice of Offenders

A very important third assumption involves the level of volition held by potential offenders. **Rational choice theory** has become a central focus in the study of crime (Clarke and Cornish, 1985; Cornish and Clarke, 1986a). This theory assumes that potential offenders make choices based on various factors in the physical and social environment. Offenders respond to payoff, effort, peer support, risks, and similar factors in making decisions to commit a crime (Cornish and Clarke, 1986b). Displacement views the offender as being a rational individual who is capable of making informed, free-willed choices. He is able to evaluate the costs and benefits inherent in his choice and circumstances, and can make decisions based on those factors.

The ability to make informed choices is required for displacement to occur. The inability to make rational decisions would negate displacement due to crime prevention measures. A seeming contradiction appears between this assumption and the earlier assumption concerning the inelastic nature of offending. The need to commit crime and the ability to choose which crime and where it is to be committed, however, are not exclusive of one another. It is very possible that an offender sees no alternative to crime but is capable of molding his actual criminal behavior around available choices.

Target/Choice Availability

A final assumption is that alternative targets and choices are available to the offender. From a crime prevention perspective, this assumption is easy to accept because program implementation is never complete. Some individuals decide not to participate, some targets are not hardened, some actions fail to have an impact, and some ideas are not well suited to a given problem. More importantly, crime prevention programs generally focus only on limited areas or crimes. This results in alternative choices for potential offenders.

Displacement: Benign or Malign?

The tenor of most discussions of displacement is clearly one of disappointment or dismay at the thought that crime is simply being moved across one of the displacement dimensions. Displacement, however, can be positive. Barr and Pease (1990) divide displacement into two types—"malign" and "benign." **Malign displacement** leads to undesirable outcomes. Efforts aimed at reducing burglary may prompt an increase in robberies and accompanying levels of assault. Another case of malign displacement would be an offender's need to increase the number of crimes in order to offset the reduced payoff garnered from each offense (Gabor, 1990). A third possibility is shifting crime to another area that is unprepared to respond. Such malign displacement may not be tolerable to society.

Benign displacement suggests that changes from displacement may benefit society. For example, the new crime or tactics that are utilized by the offenders may be less serious and offer less danger to the potential victims. Robbery becomes burglary, assault with a deadly weapon becomes simple assault, burglary becomes petty theft, and so on. Displacement may also bring about reduced fear of crime which offsets the problem of actual crime (Barr and Pease, 1990).

Barr and Pease (1990) also propose that displacement can "be used to achieve a spread of crime that can be regarded as equitable." Crime is not evenly spread across the social spectrum, which leads to an unequal burden from crime and fear of crime. Barr and

Pease suggest that society, either consciously or unconsciously, has allowed certain areas or neighborhoods to become what they call **crime fuses**. In the same manner that electrical fuses will carry the dangerous burden and signal a problem by blowing out before the problem spreads to the rest of the system, the crime fuse is an area where crime is allowed to operate without bothering the rest of society until it explodes in the area. The solution is then targeted at the point of the problem before it does major harm to the entire community. Displacement may be benign if crime is moved to a "fuse" location. It would not be benign, however, for those living at the crime fuse. A true benign displacement would be one that provides a more even or equal spread of victimization across the community (Barr and Pease, 1990). For Barr and Pease, the question of displacement deals with redistributing crime and victimization in society.

Diffusion

Another possible effect of crime prevention programming is the **diffusion of benefits**. Clarke and Weisburd (1994, p. 169) define diffusion of benefits as

> the spread of the beneficial influence of an intervention beyond the places which are directly targeted, the individuals who are the subject of control, the crimes which are the focus of intervention or the time periods in which an intervention is brought.

Rather than shifting the crime, diffusion assumes that prevention efforts will benefit people and places other than those targeted. Diffusion is discussed under a variety of names, including "halo effect" (Scherdin, 1986) and "free bonus effect" (Sherman, 1990).

What accounts for diffusion? Clarke and Weisburd (1994) offer two potential sources for diffusion—deterrence and discouragement. Deterrence can have an impact in various ways. While many prevention efforts are short-lived, the impact on crime often outlasts the period of intervention. Similarly, targeting one location or certain merchandise may result in protecting other targets. In each case, there is an assumption that the chances of being apprehended are heightened and potential offenders are deterred by the risk of being caught. Discouragement works by reducing the payoff and increasing the effort needed to commit a crime (Clarke and Weisburd, 1994).

Both displacement and diffusion have received increased attention in recent years and many evaluations now make claims about apparent displacement or diffusion. Unfortunately, the difficulties inherent in assessing displacement and diffusion mean that these issues are not central to many evaluations. In every case, the degree to which displacement or diffusion occur is related to the degree to which offenders can and do make judgments about offending.

Offender Choice and Mobility

Offenders do not commit offenses totally at random. They do not simply walk down the street and attack people, commit robberies, break into homes, or act in other criminal ways with no reason. If offenders acted completely at random, committing crimes with no thought and at any moment, all of our streets would be rife with crimes at any time and nothing anyone could do would have an impact on crime. Thankfully, we know that many places and times are free from crime, and many things can be done to prevent crime. This means that offenders, at least to some degree, make decisions on what to do, when, where, and how. The key for prevention, therefore, is to understand the factors that go into those decisions.

Felson and Clarke (1998) argue that *opportunity* is the cornerstone for all criminal behavior. While opportunity alone is not sufficient for a crime, it is certainly necessary for its commission. In their words, "Individual behavior is a product of an interaction between the person and the setting" (1998, p. 1). Felson and Clarke outline 10 principles of opportunity (see Table 6.3) that attempt to specify how opportunities shape and mold criminal behavior. Many of these principles deal with the variation in opportunities across time, space, and circumstances. They also suggest that reductions in opportunity can reduce crime, with little displacement.

Underlying these 10 principles of opportunity are three primary theoretical orientations—routine activities, rational choice, and crime pattern theory. Felson and Clarke (1998) see each as a form of opportunity theory. The possibility of displacement and

---

TABLE 6.3 Ten Principles of Opportunity and Crime

1. Opportunities play a role in causing all crime.
2. Crime opportunities are highly specific.
3. Crime opportunities are concentrated in time and place.
4. Crime opportunities depend on everyday movements.
5. One crime produces opportunities for another.
6. Some products offer more tempting crime opportunities.
7. Social and technological changes produce new crime opportunities.
8. Opportunities for crime can be reduced.
9. Reducing opportunities does not usually displace crime.
10. Focused opportunity reduction can produce wider declines in crime.

Source: M. Felson and R.V. Clarke (1998). *Opportunity Makes the Thief: Practical Theory for Crime Prevention*. London: Home Office Police and Reducing Crime Unit.

diffusion rely on implicit assumptions about the offenders and decision making that appear in these theoretical perspectives.

Routine Activities

The **routine activities theory** argues that the normal movement and activities of both potential offenders and victims plays a role in the occurrence of crime. Cohen and Felson (1979) outline three criteria that must exist for crime to occur. There must be (1) a suitable target, (2) a motivated offender, and (3) an absence of guardians. The authors believe that much crime is due to opportunity. That does not mean that offenders do not seek out opportunities. Rather, it implies that the actual choice and commission of an offense is determined by the mutual occurrence of the three conditions.

The routine activities of people have greatly changed over the years. Since World War II many households have moved to two-earner incomes, which leaves many homes unoccupied during the day and, therefore, unguarded (Cohen and Felson, 1979). Increased mobility of the population has led to the establishment of "bedroom communities" which are removed from the watchful eyes of workers and pedestrians. Time spent away from home, either at work or in recreation, opens up opportunities for crime.

Another important change involves the increased availability of suitable targets for crime. The risk of a target is directly related to Clarke's (1999) discussion of **hot products**, or items that attract attention and are targeted by offenders. Such products meet the tenets of being **CRAVED** (see Table 6.4). Products that are CRAVED are desired by the offender or others, are visible to potential offenders, and are easier to conceal, transport, and dispose of. What has value today may not be of interest tomorrow. This could be due to the maturation of the offender, the saturation of the item in society, changes in taste, or other factors (Clarke, 1999). The extent to which a target meets the CRAVED criteria will have an impact on the chances of an offense occurring.

TABLE 6.4 The CRAVED Model for Targets of Theft

Concealable	Ability of thief to hide items during the crime
Removable	Size and weight make some items more portable than others
Available	The item must exist and be available to be stolen
Valuable	Items that hold more value will be targeted
Enjoyable	The items must bring enjoyment to the offender
Disposable	There must be a market for the stolen items

Source: Compiled by author from R.V. Clarke (1999). *Hot Products: Understanding, Anticipating and Reducing Demand for Stolen Goods*. London: Home Office Policing and Reducing Crime Unit.

Most tests of the routine activities hypothesis focus on property crimes, although the chances of personal crime also increase through changes in routine activities. Cohen and Felson (1979) find that the amount of time spent away from home is significantly related to the level of property crime. Similarly, Mustaine and Tewksbury (1998) report that theft is influenced by activity outside the home, the number of precautions (guardianship) taken, and the types of outside activities in which victims partake. The same factors related to property crime also apply to enhancing the possibility of physical confrontation between individuals. Personal predatory crimes, such as robbery and sexual assault, are also influenced by routine activities.

Rational Choice

An implicit assumption in routine activities is that offenders make rational choices about when and where to offend. In order for crime prevention activities to have an impact, offenders must be making (somewhat) rational decisions based on their perceptions of needs, risks, payoffs, and other factors. Whether offenders make choices in their offenses can be answered both intuitively and through the literature. On an intuitive level, most people believe that human beings are free-willed. At the same time, however, people recognize that the available choices are limited by time, place, or circumstance. This implies a sort of **soft determinism**. That is, individuals make choices but only within the realm of available opportunities. This is true in all behavior and not just criminal activity. For example, every individual may wish to be comfortable in his daily existence. One person may be independently wealthy while another must work. Further, the choice of work relies upon the physical and mental abilities of the individual, the state of the economy in the area, the competition for jobs, and a host of other factors. The fact that everyone makes choices in life leads to the belief that criminals make similar choices. Additionally, offenders spend the majority of their time participating in normal, socially accepted activities within which they make choices. It would be naive to think that this ability to make choices is removed when criminal behavior is contemplated.

Numerous studies provide evidence that offenders make rational decisions. Studies of both incarcerated and active burglars in England reveal that offenders favor homes with a rear access, cover, isolation from other homes, a lack of nearby surveillance, the absence of alarms and CCTV, and that are unoccupied (Nee and Taylor, 1988; Taylor and Nee, 1988). Research also notes that offenders are attracted by visual signs of wealth, such as well-kept homes and items that can be seen through open windows (Hearnden and Magill, 2004; Nee and Taylor, 1988). Based on interviews with 31 incarcerated burglars in the United States, Rengert and Wasilchick (1985) find that offenders commit their crimes when residents are away from their homes—mainly mid-morning and early afternoon. Importantly, burglars typically rely on an established set of "opportunity cues" to identify appropriate targets. Among the cues are closed-up homes without air conditioning in warm months, an absence of cars at home, the entire family leaving together, available concealment, visual signs of wealth, and easy access to the home (Rengert and Wasilchick, 1985).

Wright and Decker (1994), in a large-scale study of burglars in St. Louis, uncover a mixture of planning and spontaneity in offending. They report that many burglars have a potential target in mind prior to the actual decision to commit the crime. The offenders are always "half looking" for targets, and use various cues for deciding on appropriate targets, such as signs of valuables, the condition of the property, the type of car in the drive, signs of occupancy, and surveillability.

Bennett (1986) notes that burglars make what appear to be quick, uninformed decisions that, in reality, are rational choices based on prior experience and general knowledge. Indeed, Cromwell et al. (1991), asking burglars to "recreate" their past offenses, report that they make rational choices based on surveillability, occupancy, and accessibility. The reconstructions, however, suggest a more "limited rationality" similar to that proposed by Clarke and Cornish (1985). Offenders tend to point out opportunistic features of various targets and react to situations that arise during normal activity. That is, they "happen upon" vulnerable targets as they go about their daily routine (Cromwell et al., 1991). The offenders appear to respond to a set of internalized cues based on past experience and planning rather than specific detailed planning for each event.

While the foregoing discussion focuses on burglary, choice behavior is not restricted to those offenses. Tunnell (1992) reports on the activity of repeat property offenders, which included burglars, robbers, forgers, and others. He notes that criminal activity is a rational response to situations in which the offender finds himself. Research also suggests that more serious persistent offenders undertake more planning and tend to choose targets where the chances of observation are small (Feeney, 1986; Shover, 1991; Tunnell, 1992). Robbery, auto theft, and forgery also show evidence of offender planning and rational decision making (Fleming et al., 1994; Gill and Matthews, 1994; Lacoste and Tremblay, 2003; Morrison and O'Donnell, 1996; Petrosino and Brensilber, 2003).

Various studies portray offenders as rational decision makers who base their actions on the costs and benefits they perceive in the contemplated activity. At the same time, the research suggests that offenders do not necessarily construct detailed plans for each and every offense. Rather, the rational choices and preconceived plans may be set into motion when the offender happens upon a situation or target that fits the general description of an appropriate target. Time, place, target, surveillability, and other factors are all considered in a short-hand version of making a rational choice. Indeed, many daily, non-criminal decisions are made more on the subconscious, rather than the conscious, level.

Crime Pattern Theory

Brantingham and Brantingham's (1993b) **crime pattern theory** proposes that crime and criminal behavior fits patterns that can be identified and understood when viewed in terms of where and when they occur. They argue that crime patterns can be understood because of similarities that emerge when you consider:

> the specific criminal event, the site, the situation, the activity backcloth, the probable crime templates, the triggering events, and the general factors influencing the readiness or willingness of individuals to commit crimes.
>
> (Brantingham and Brantingham, 1993b, pp. 284–285)

Two keys to understanding patterns is to understand the environmental backcloth and the social/crime template of the offender. The **environmental backcloth** refers to the social, economic, cultural, and physical conditions within which people operate. While these dimensions are constantly changing, it is possible to discern patterns from them. The **social/crime template** is the idea that people have templates that outline expectations of what will happen at certain times and places given certain behavior by the individual. In essence, the template tells an offender what should occur in a certain place, time, or situation. Understanding how people learn about the environment and how they construct these templates is an important endeavor for understanding the occurrence of crime.

At the outset, the routine activities of individuals expose them to different times and places. Their normal daily activities as they go to and from work, do their shopping, socialize with others, go to school, and any other routine activities allow them to build knowledge of their environment. Urban communities of today greatly contribute to the routine activities of individuals. Modern cities and urban areas are conglomerations of smaller, specialized land use areas that provide varying needs and activities for residents. The availability of private and mass transportation allows citizens to live, work, shop, and recreate where they choose. People simply commute between the various locations. These locations can be considered **nodes** of activity (see Figure 6.2) (Brantingham and Brantingham, 1993a, 1996). The transit routes between the nodes are referred to as **paths**. The extent to which an individual utilizes each node and takes various routes (paths) between the nodes contributes to his **awareness space**. Andresen (2014) notes that as an individual's knowledge and attachments to different nodes and paths increase, he becomes more comfortable in the area.

Another consideration in how individuals learn about the environment involves cognitive maps. Smith and Patterson (1980) argue that individuals create **cognitive maps** (mental images) of the environment that are used in making behavioral choices. There are four aspects to cognitive mapping: recognition, prediction, evaluation, and action. **Recognition** refers to being able to identify your location and various features in the

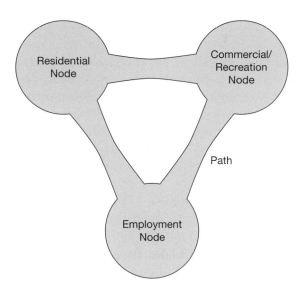

Figure 6.2

Simplified View of a Multinuclei Community with Nodes and Paths

area. Recognition leads to **prediction**, which involves making connections between the identifiable objects in the area and possible lines of behavior. During **evaluation**, the individual uses the information gathered in the earlier stages and determines which options are acceptable modes of behavior. It is based on the information gained in the first three steps that an individual decides on an appropriate **action**. In essence, cognitive mapping entails changing nodes and paths into awareness space. To the extent to which it removes fear and uncertainty about locations, cognitive mapping helps the individual make informed choices and turn the location into an **activity space**.

The further from a node or path an individual moves, the less is known about the area and the individual lacks a meaningful cognitive map. Thus, the chances for action (criminal or legitimate) are diminished. Potential offenders tend to search in the nodes and paths with which they are familiar. Besides the nodes and paths, activity space also includes edges of the areas, which may enhance or hinder deviant behavior. **Edges** can be physical, social, or economic (Brantingham, 2010). Physical edges may limit movement of potential offenders and victims. As such, these edges may limit offending by inhibiting the awareness space. Conversely, social and economic edges can enhance anonymity between strangers. These areas are frequented by diverse users, which brings together potential victims and offenders with limited guardianship (Brantingham, 2010). Greater diversity in people and activity from both sides of the edge enhances the possibility of offenses. (See Brantingham and Brantingham, 1981, 1993a, 1993b, 1996 for more in-depth discussions of these ideas.)

Beyond providing a framework for developing cognitive maps/awareness space/ activity space, nodes can serve to promote crime in other ways (Brantingham and Brantingham, 1996). Some nodes may act as **crime generators** by drawing potential victims to the area. They also may be **crime attractors**. These are areas to which potential offenders and victims are drawn, such as drug markets, sites of street prostitution, and/or adult clubs and bars. Finally, a node may serve as a **hunting ground** for offenders. That is, offenders recognize that potential victims frequent an area, there is a lack of guardians at that location, and, consequently, the offender follows the victims to that place.

An emerging possibility for development of cognitive maps and information on potential targets has been the advent of the Internet and its widespread accessibility. Today, a wealth of information, including visual depictions, can be found online. Programs such as Google Maps, Google Streetview, and government property web sites provide varying levels of detail about different addresses and areas. **Google Streetview**, for example, allows the user to look at an address from the main street, take a 360-degree look into the area, move up and down the street, and zoom in to look at property details. While this information reflects only a single point in time, it provides a basis of information on the area. Publicly accessible government documents also provide details of homes and businesses, including room layouts and sizes. All of this information can be used by potential offenders to build mental maps of a target, the surrounding area, and other useful planning information without ever leaving home and visiting the area. As such, the potential to plan crimes outside the assumptions of routine activities and crime pattern theories is greatly enhanced.

ON THE WEB

Go to Google Maps/Streetview (http://maps. google.com/intl/en/help/maps/streetview/#utm_ campaign=en&utm_medium=van&utm_source= en-van-na-us-gns-svn) and input your home address. Navigate around and observe what you can see about your neighborhood and the houses/businesses.

Although discussions of cognitive mapping usually center on territorial or spatial features of behavior, the extension to other dimensions is straightforward. The same process which provides templates of safe areas can provide information on the most suitable targets, tactics, crimes, and times within a given setting. The prediction and evaluation stages of cognitive mapping suggest that each of these decisions is to be considered in the movement to criminal action.

Summary

Research provides strong evidence that crime is not totally opportunistic. Rather, criminal behavior appears to be a rational decision based on situations in which the offender finds himself. While offenders may not spend a great deal of time planning specific offenses, information gained through normal daily activity or interaction with others can guide the "unconscious" decision making of the offender, just like most people make non-criminal daily choices. These facts suggest that both displacement and diffusion are potential responses to prevention behavior.

Evidence of Displacement and Diffusion

While displacement and diffusion are possible results of prevention activities, they are rarely directly examined in evaluations. Much crime prevention research tends to ignore the issue of displacement and diffusion, or consider them only as an afterthought to the research. Claims that displacement does or does not occur are probably ill-advised. Even in studies that include an analysis of displacement at the outset, basic flaws in the investigations limit the ability to make strong claims.

Displacement Effects

Assessments of displacement need to consider a number of factors. First, all of the forms of displacement should be open to examination. Most analyses only consider territorial displacement and totally ignore the other forms. Second, each crime/problem being targeted by the prevention initiative should be examined in detail to answer a number of questions: Who are the likely offenders? When are the offenses taking place? How are the crimes being committed? Where are they occurring? What purpose does the crime serve (i.e., why does it happen)? and similar concerns. The answers to these questions are crucial for both the selection of the crime prevention measures and the potential for displacement. Interestingly, while most crime prevention programs answer these questions when developing the intervention, they are typically ignored when discussions of displacement occur. This is unfortunate because answers to these questions would inform expectations about the type and extent of possible displacement.

Take for example the development of a crime prevention initiative to attack residential burglary. An examination of crime data shows an increase in residential burglary taking place in mid to late mornings during the work week. The homes are being entered through unlocked doors or by breaking the locks on doors. Items that are taken tend to be jewelry, silverware, and high-end electronics. The police suspect that the offenders are adult professional burglars. Based on this information, a prevention program is initiated that includes the installation of stronger locks, the marking of property, the initiation of increased police patrols during the day, the start of a neighborhood watch group, and midday citizen patrols. The same information provides insight to the possible types of displacement that may emerge. To the extent that the offenders are indeed adult professional thieves, it is wise to assume that territorial displacement is a strong possibility. There may also be temporal displacement to nights or afternoons when the patrols are not as prevalent. The offenders may change targets and focus on the homes without the new locks. Any evaluation of the prevention activities should use this insight to build in an assessment of the different forms of displacement. Unfortunately, most crime prevention evaluators look only for territorial displacement to an immediately adjacent neighborhood. No attention is paid to other forms or areas.

Attempts to assess displacement need to explicitly consider the potential offenders, the type of offense, the location, the victims, and other factors involved in the existing criminal activity (Hamilton-Smith, 2002). In-depth knowledge of the event and actors will allow the crime prevention planner and evaluator to model the potential for displacement, and build in the appropriate intervention or evaluation methods (Brantingham and Brantingham, 2003; Hamilton-Smith, 2002).

There is little reason to ever expect total displacement of crime, regardless of the type of displacement considered. At the same time, assuming that there will be no displacement may be just as naive. Displacement should be considered as a possible confounding factor in every evaluation.

Journey to Crime

The fact that offenders will travel to commit crimes is known as the **journey to crime** and is well established. The distance traveled varies by the type of crime, the physical characteristics of the area, and the demographic characteristics of the individual. The distance traveled can be measured in two ways. First is by **Euclidean distance**, which measures in a straight line from the start to the end point. The problem with this approach is that it ignores the fact that physical features (such as buildings, rivers, and highways) make such travel impossible. Instead, people follow roadways, generally selecting those that reduce both distance and travel time. Measures of distance in this way are called **Manhattan distance**.

Beyond how distance is measured, it is important to note that there is a pattern of **distance decay**. This means that the commission of crime decreases as the distance from the offender's home increases. Individuals have the greatest cognitive maps for the area around their homes, thus is it in this activity space that they commit more offenses. These are short journeys to crime. Elfers et al. (2008) argue that distance decay occurs partly due to the presence of opportunities that exist between the offender's starting point and the intended ending point of travel. Bernasco (2010) adds an interesting dimension to the discussion of crime centering on one's home. He examines crime around the offender's current home as well as around an immediately past residence, using a two-year window around residency. Offenses are 22.5 times more likely around the current or former residence, with the odds of offending around former homes diminishing over time (Bernasco, 2010). This shows that crime is likely in an individual's awareness space, and this awareness shifts over time.

While distance decay is an important factor in distance traveled, opportunities, potential payoff, and ability to travel play a role in long distances. Property offenses, which have a greater chance of being planned, tend to have longer travel averages (Pyle, 1974; Rhodes and Conley, 1981; White, 1932). The expectation and size of offense pay-offs also result in longer journeys (Morselli and Royer, 2008; Snook, 2004; Van Daele and Vander Beken, 2011). Research demonstrates that the distance traveled increases when transportation and road access is more readily available (Bicheler et al., 2012; Snook, 2004; Van Daele and Vander Beken, 2011; Vandeviver et al., 2015). Personal crimes tend to be more spontaneous and occur between family members or friends, thus mitigating long travel distances (Amir, 1971; Bullock, 1955; White, 1932).

The greater distances associated with property crimes are especially important for the discussion of community crime prevention because these programs usually target property offenses. Distance also tends to increase with the offender's age due to the increased mobility that comes with growing older, leaving school, living on one's own, and ownership of some means of transportation (Nichols, 1980; P.P. Phillips, 1980). Additionally, younger individuals probably hold more limited cognitive maps upon which to base offense decisions. Having established the existence of offender mobility, it is reasonable to assume that territorial displacement is a possible consequence of prevention efforts.

Territorial Displacement

The most common form of displacement considered in evaluations is territorial/spatial displacement. Several studies claim evidence of territorial displacement. Fabricant (1979) claims that juvenile arrests cause youthful offenders to move to neighboring locations. Crime prevention programs in Dallas appear to shift some offenders into surrounding suburbs (Dallas Area Criminal Justice Council, 1975). Specifically, changes in Dallas are accompanied by greater increases in six of nine Dallas suburbs. Forrester et al. (1988), investigating the effects of target hardening and social crime prevention measures, claim that the 60 percent decrease in burglary is partially offset by a 25 percent increase in burglary in the surrounding area. Barclay et al. (1996), studying the impact of bicycle patrol on auto theft in one crime hot spot, show large increases in auto theft in two adjacent areas during the project period. The increases also persist after the program ended. Displacement is the best explanation for these findings. Braga et al. (1999), in an analysis of a police crackdown in Jersey City, New Jersey, reports evidence of property crime displacement. In an analysis of CCTV in town centers, Brown (1995) indicates that both robbery and personal theft are displaced to other areas. Territorial displacement is also evident in the Kirkholt and Safer Cities burglary prevention efforts (Ekblom et al., 1996a; Tilley, 1993), in some of the Burglary Reduction Initiative sites (Bowers and Johnson, 2003; Home Office 2003d), in Philadelphia's Operation Safe Streets project (Lawton et al., 2005), and in Rotterdam's efforts to curb thefts from autos (Hesseling, 1995a).

Not all research finds territorial displacement, even when the project actively searches for it. Ditton and Short (1999) and Farrington et al. (2007), examining the impact of

CCTV, report no evidence of displacement. Armitage et al. (1999) also find no territorial displacement as a result of CCTV installations in three police beats. Evaluating the impact of police enforcement of carrying concealed weapons laws in Kansas City, Sherman and Rogan (1995) uncover no evidence of displacement from target areas to a matched control area. Weisburd and Green (1995) report no displacement resulting from police targeting of drug hot spots in Jersey City. Similarly, Braga et al. (1999) find no shift in calls about robbery, assault, drug offenses, street fights, or disorder incidents from the targeted hot spots to the control areas. Weisburd et al. (2006), in a study designed specifically to test for territorial displacement, find no such displacement in either prostitution or drug offending. It is evident that territorial displacement appears in some analyses and not in others. Finally, McLennan and Whitworth (2008) find displacement in only 2 percent of 383 tests of the New Deal for Communities Program in the U.K.

The discrepant results from study to study may be due to the use of different displacement areas in the analyses. Bowers and Johnson (2003) note that the selection of areas into which displacement may occur is critical to the analysis. While most analyses look at an immediately adjacent area, it is not appropriate to assume that the closest neighboring area is the best selection for assessing territorial displacement (Andresen, 2010). It is advisable to identify several buffer zones around the target or experimental area, as well as a central area, and measure changes in zones at different distances from the intervention site (Bowers and Johnson, 2003). In their evaluation of alley gating, Bowers et al. (2003) find no displacement into the areas immediately around the experimental site, but do report displacement to areas further away. One key to uncovering territorial displacement, therefore, may be correctly specifying the potential displacement zone.

Temporal Displacement

Several studies make explicit note about possible offense shifts across time. Two studies claim that, while street lighting reduces the incidence of crime in the relit areas, there is a corresponding increase in daylight crime rates within the same areas (Wright et al., 1974). This suggests the possibility that the offenses simply moved from night to day. Hesseling (1995b) reports finding temporal displacement resulting from increased surveillance in inner city areas. Conversely, in the Barclay et al. (1996) study of auto theft, an explicit attempt to identify temporal changes fails to show any such displacement.

Tactical Displacement

Crime prevention efforts can make the criminal work harder. This is evident through the use of new methods of committing the same crimes on the same targets. One example of this is a shift in burglary from entering through open doors to breaking windows for access. Interviews with burglars indicate that offenders are willing to seek out and utilize different methods when confronted with barriers to committing the crime (Bennett and Wright, 1984; Cromwell et al., 1991; Reppetto, 1974). Crime prevention efforts in Seattle reveal a shift in burglary methods from hardened doors and windows to unlocked entrances (Seattle Law and Justice Planning Office, 1975). Similarly, alley gating has moved the point of entry for burglary from the rear of buildings to the front of homes (Bowers et al., 2003). Allatt (1984) finds that target hardening leads to greater instances of forced locks and broken windows. Finch (2011), looking at the introduction of PIN and chip technology in credit cards, reports increased theft of cards and passwords, as well as other methods, to commit these crimes. Finally, Weisburd et al. (2006) report evidence of tactical displacement based on interviews with offenders.

Target Displacement

Target displacement appears in various studies of crime prevention. Gabor (1981) specifically investigates the shift in offending from one set of victims to another set of potential victims. He finds that the Operation Identification program appears to have shifted offending away from program participants to individuals who have not joined the project. This remains true even after controlling for the pre-program victimization rates of the subjects. Offenders also shift from residential areas to commercial establishments as a result of property marking (Gabor, 1981). There is evidence that offenders target objects that are not as easily marked by the owners. Tilley and Webb (1994) report similar target displacement from property marking efforts. Allatt (1984) finds the unreinforced structures experience higher levels of burglary after the installation of target hardening devices in neighboring buildings. Similarly, Miethe (1991) notes that target hardening devices displace crime to non-hardened targets in the same area of Seattle. Evidence from the Kirkholt burglary project shows that efforts to prevent repeat victimization result in a move to more "new" victims who are not as involved in the program (Forrester et al., 1990). The Reducing Burglary Initiative in Stirchley also reports a shift in burglaries away from homes to non-dwelling structures (Home Office, 2003b).

Functional Displacement

This final form of displacement manifests itself in terms of changes in offenses committed by the offender. The usual way of investigating such displacement is through comparison of different individual crime rates from before and after program implementation. Arthur Young and Co. (1978) report that the crime prevention program at the Cabrini-Green housing project resulted in increased levels of assaults and robbery and decreased numbers of burglaries and thefts. This suggests that the efforts, which deal more with property security, precipitate more personal contact offenses. Allatt (1984) makes similar claims of functional displacement in connection with target hardening efforts in a housing project. Letkemann (1973) shows that bank burglars shift to bank robbery as a response to target hardening undertaken by banks, and Laycock (1984) reveals that efforts to target harden pharmacies results in an increase in the level of pharmacy robberies and other drug offenses. Research on CCTV programs in city centers also shows shifts from motor vehicle theft to theft from motor vehicles (Brown, 1995). Felson et al. (1996) note that improvements in the New York City bus terminal greatly reduced most crime and disorder. There was some evidence, however, of functional displacement to minor property offenses (a form of benign displacement) (Felson et al., 1996). Finally, Finch (2011) reports that property offenders shift from credit card fraud to other forms of theft as a result of introducing PINs and chips to credit cards.

Displacement Summary

This review finds that displacement does appear in various forms. It is important, however, to note that displacement is not an inevitable outcome of prevention initiatives. When displacement does occur, it is *not* 100 percent. Displacement is a viable concern for discussions of crime prevention. Although the list of studies reporting, or not reporting, each type of displacement is limited, this is probably due to the failure of most evaluations to consider displacement. Interestingly, two reviews that claim to find little evidence of displacement and argue that it should not be a major concern (Eck, 1993; Hesseling, 1994) actually uncover a significant level of various forms of displacement. Both Hesseling's (1994) and Eck's (1993) analyses reveal that roughly half of the studies show evidence of displacement, particularly territorial and target forms. The fact that the authors do not find 100 percent displacement, or displacement in all studies, leads them to conclude it is not a major problem. This is an unrealistic criterion and any evidence of displacement should be a concern to be addressed.

Guerette and Bowers (2009) examined 102 studies with a total of 572 tests for displacement or diffusion. As can be seen in Table 6.5, displacement appears in 26 percent of the tests. Temporal displacement is the most common type uncovered (36 percent), with tactical being the least common (22 percent). While not 100 percent, at least one out of five tests for any type of displacement reports positive results. In a meta-analysis of those studies providing enough data for testing, Guerette and Bowers (2009) find that 42 percent of the observations uncover displacement. These findings show that displacement is indeed a common occurrence, although not all programs find displacement, and the displacement does not negate the positive impact of the prevention activities.

It is very important to note that the level of displacement is typically a small proportion of the total decrease in crime

ON THE WEB

You can read more about analyzing for displacement by downloading Guerette's (2009) Analyzing Crime Displacement and Diffusion found on the Center for Problem-Oriented Policing's web site: http://www.popcenter.org/tools/pdfs/displacement.pdf

TABLE 6.5 **Displacement and Diffusion by Type**

Type	N	Displaced	Diffused
Territorial	272	62 (23%)	100 (37%)
Target	80	26 (33%)	19 (24%)
Temporal	31	11 (36%)	5 (16%)
Tactical	49	11 (22%)	6 (12%)
Functional	140	36 (26%)	22 (16%)
Total		146 (26%)	152 (27%)

Source: Adapted by author from R.T. Guerette and K.J. Bowers (2009). "Assessing the extent of crime displacement and diffusion of benefits: A review of situational crime prevention evaluations." *Criminology* 47:1331–1368.

attributed to crime prevention measures. The finding of displacement qualifies the impact of the preventive program, but it certainly does not negate the positive results attributable to the intervention. Indeed, displacement findings show that the prevention programs are capable of altering the behavior of the offenders. The offenders respond to the actions of the legitimate users and limit their criminal behavior in relation to the various targets. The problem is that the only way of truly knowing if crime is displaced is to interview offenders and ask them if the crime prevention measure altered their behavior.

Diffusion Effects

Offsetting displacement may be a diffusion of benefits. As noted earlier, diffusion of benefits means that areas, items, or individuals not targeted by a crime prevention program also benefit from the intervention. For example, if half of the homes in a neighborhood join block watch, mark their property, and take part in surveillance activities, and everyone in the neighborhood experiences reduced victimization and fear, it is probable that the crime prevention of the participants had an impact on the non-participants. This would be a diffusion of benefits. Not unlike displacement, however, measuring diffusion is very difficult.

The typical approach to measuring diffusion is to examine the change in crime and fear in areas contiguous to the target area. Reductions in the contiguous areas could be due to diffusion effects (Clarke, 1995). At the same time, however, the reductions in both the target and control areas could be a result of general decreases in society. Rather than a diffusion effect, the crime prevention intervention has no impact. Determining whether there is no change or if the changes are due to diffusion would require additional comparison areas (or targets) that would not be expected to experience diffusion due to distance or other circumstances (see Bowers and Johnson, 2003).

Another problem with identifying a diffusion effect would appear when both displacement and diffusion occur at the same time, resulting in no apparent change in the non-treatment area (Weisburd and Green, 1995). In this case, the crime prevention program is successful at reducing crime and/or fear in the target area. At the same time, some of the reduction is the result of displacing offenses to another area, which would normally mean that crime and/or fear in the other area increases. A simultaneous diffusion effect of equal magnitude, however, would offset the increase and show no net change in crime and/or fear.

Despite these concerns with identifying diffusion effects, evaluations are beginning to pay more attention to the possibilities of diffusion in their designs and analyses. Green (1995a), analyzing the impact of a program dealing with neighborhood drug problems, reports a diffusion impact in areas surrounding the targeted sites. The two blocks around the target sites show reductions in deviant behavior, although smaller in magnitude to the experimental sites. Miethe (1991) notes that neighborhood watch efforts in Seattle appear to diffuse to non-participating targets in the same area. Painter and Farrington (1999b), in an analysis of street lighting projects, find decreases in daytime offending for the relit areas, thus suggesting temporal diffusion. Diffusion also is apparent in the Safer Cities program, particularly in areas where the prevention efforts are intensively implemented (Ekblom et al., 1996a, 1996b), and in the New Deal for Communities program where 23 percent of 383 comparisons show diffusion of benefits (McLennan and Whitworth, 2008). Guerette and Bowers (2009) also provide evidence of diffusion in their review of situational crime prevention, finding that 27 percent of the tests exhibited diffusion (see Table 6.5). The meta-analytic results also reveal diffusion in 42 percent of the comparisons.

Felson et al. (1996) report that diffusion may actually occur in the opposite direction. That is, changes occurring outside the target area may have an impact on the target, leading to the appearance of program effectiveness. In their study of the New York City bus terminal, Felson et al. (1996) note that reductions in crime outside the terminal, dating from prior to the terminal improvements, may be contributing to the crime reductions inside the terminal. In essence, the external changes in robbery and assault may be diffusing into the terminal. (Felson et al. (1996) note that the reductions are greater in the terminal, thus indicating a programmatic impact beyond any possible diffusion.)

While concerns about displacement have existed for some time in the literature, diffusion is a more recent topic. Diffusion should be considered as a counterbalancing force to displacement (Clarke and Weisburd, 1994). Indeed, in some instances, displacement and diffusion both emerge in studies and, in essence, cancel out one another. Given the fact that both forces could be at work in a project, it is important to design projects that can uncover each of these possible factors. The inability to identify displacement and diffusion would result in an incomplete analysis of program effectiveness.

Implications of Displacement and Diffusion

The possibility of displacement and diffusion is an outcome of crime prevention that should be considered in any program. Studies aptly illustrate that displacement is a plausible outcome of crime prevention programs. At the same time, it would be naive to assume that all crime reduction in an area is due to simple displacement to another place, time, or method, or that programs cannot have a larger impact beyond the immediate target. The amount of displacement is far from 100 percent and typically reflects only a portion of the crime that is prevented in the target area. Diffusion is also a possibility that needs to be considered. Future research needs to pay particular attention to both displacement and diffusion in order to adequately assess their impact on prevention programs.

KEY TERMS

- action (in cognitive mapping)
- activity space
- awareness space
- benign displacement
- cognitive maps
- CRAVED
- crime attractors
- crime displacement
- crime fuses
- crime generators
- crime pattern theory
- crime spillover
- diffusion of benefits
- distance decay
- edges
- environmental backcloth
- Euclidean distance
- evaluation (in cognitive mapping)
- functional displacement
- Google Streetview
- hot products
- hunting ground
- inelastic
- journey to crime
- malign displacement
- Manhattan distance
- nodes
- paths
- perpetrator displacement
- prediction (in cognitive mapping)
- rational choice theory
- recognition (in cognitive mapping)
- routine activities theory
- social/crime template
- soft determinism
- tactical displacement
- target displacement
- temporal displacement
- territorial (spatial) displacement

CHAPTER 7 The Mass Media and Crime Prevention

LEARNING OBJECTIVES

After reading this chapter you should be able to:

- Talk about media accounts of crime and how they relate to actual crime.
- Discuss research on whether the media causes crime.
- Diagram different ways in which the media/publicity can be used in relation to crime prevention.
- Demonstrate your knowledge of the "Take a Bite Out of Crime" campaign and its impact.
- Identify media prevention campaigns and discuss their effectiveness.
- Discuss the use of crime newsletters and evaluations of their effectiveness.
- Explain the use of information lines and their impact.
- Provide examples of "crime-time television" and discuss the pros and cons of these programs.
- Define the term *anticipatory benefit* and discuss its impact.

We have seen that both physical design and neighborhood crime prevention programs have had an impact on crime and fear. At the same time, that impact has been limited in important ways. One shortcoming is that many areas and people are not reached or not involved in the programs. Another potential problem is displacement which may limit the absolute reductions in crime or fear. One response is to utilize programs that reach a wider range of people and engender greater participation. Such efforts would limit the alternatives available to potential offenders. The mass media offers one avenue for creating a more widespread effort.

The impact of the mass media on modern society has been the focus of much research. The great growth of television in the 1950s expanded the potential of the media to influence individual and group behavior. Today, social media has taken mass media beyond the living room into every setting on a constant basis. Inspection of the mass media in relation to crime has predominantly looked at the potential of the various information media to create deviant behavior and fear of crime. Relatively little research has focused on the crime preventive and fear reducing capability of the mass media. Programs such as the "Take a Bite Out of Crime" campaign and Crime Stoppers have used the media as a means of inducing crime prevention activity. Before examining the media and crime prevention, it will be informative to consider the treatment of crime in the media and the effect of the media on deviant behavior and fear.

The Media and Crime

In many respects, one can say that the mass media has an affinity for crime and crime-related activity. This is true whether one looks at the coverage of crime in the news or the content of fictional programming on television. Crime accounts for a major portion of the written and broadcast media. A variety of studies have examined the extent of crime in newspapers and on television.

The Level of Reported Crime

One method for analyzing the reporting of crime is to undertake content analyses of newspapers. In one early study, Deutschmann (1959) finds that between 10 percent and 15 percent of the stories in selected New York and Ohio newspapers focus on crime. Graber (1980) reports greater attention to crime (22 to 28 percent of the stories) in daily newspapers. A wide range of other studies report that crime stories comprise between roughly 5 percent and 30 percent of newspaper space (Cohen, 1975; Deutschmann, 1959; Otto, 1962; Stempl, 1962; Stott, 1967). Chiricos et al. (1997) claim that newspaper coverage of crime has increased more than 400 percent in recent years. Similar results appear in analysis of U.K. newspapers, where the percentage of crime stories has increased from roughly 9 percent from 1945 to 1951, to 21 percent from 1985 to 1991 (Reiner et al., 2000).

Television news also provides crime information. Graber (1977) notes that roughly 20 percent of the local television news and 10 percent of the national news concerns crime. A follow-up study three years later reveals that 12 to 13 percent of television news is devoted to crime (Graber, 1980). Hofstetter (1976), evaluating the extent of crime stories on national network news, reports that between 16 and 19 percent of the news is devoted to crime. Surette (1998) notes that 10 to 13 percent of national news is crime related, while roughly 20 percent of local news deals with crime. Additional evaluations of network newscasts finds that crime represents 10 percent of the stories (Lowry, 1971) and 13 to 18 percent of the broadcast time (Cirino, 1972).

Another way the media provides crime information is through "entertainment" programs. These can take two different forms. The first is fictional programs. The second can be referred to as "reality programs." The number of fictionalized presentations that involve a crime theme has varied over the years. Dominick (1978) notes that the percentage of broadcasting time devoted to crime-related topics has varied from a low of 7 percent in 1953 to a high of 39 percent in 1975. Surette (1998) claims that 20 to 40 percent of prime-time programs focus on law enforcement and the criminal justice system. The number of reality programs has grown since their advent in the late 1980s. They often appear as quasi-news reports on sensational, unsolved crimes, such as *48 Hours, Dateline,* and *20/20.*

Media Accounts and Actual Crime

The correspondence between the media portrayal of crime and the actual extent and types of criminal activity shows a great deal of divergence. Typically, studies report that the media distorts the crime picture by focusing on selected types of crime, overemphasizing the level of crime, and failing to provide accurate or complete information about criminal incidents. There is a disproportionate focus on violence in both news and fictional accounts (Chermak, 1998; Chermak and Chapman, 2007; Dominick, 1978; Ferguson, 2013; Gerbner et al., 1980; Higgins and Ray, 1978; Greer and Reiner, 2012; Jewkes, 2011; Marsh, 1991; Oliver, 1994; Oliver and Armstrong, 1998; Reiner et al., 2000; Robinson, 2011; Surette, 1992). This overemphasis has the potential to raise the fear of crime in society by presenting violent offenses, especially between strangers on the street, as a common occurrence. Potentially violent confrontations elicit the most fear.

The level of crime and specific information about crime also is distorted in the media. Analyzing newspapers from six cities and television news from three, Chermak (1994) reports that roughly half of all crime stories deal with violence, while only 10 percent address property offenses. Further, the seriousness of an offense is significantly related to reporting practices (Chermak, 1998). Research by Lichter et al. (1994) points out that homicides on television occur at a rate more than 1,000 times that found in real life. The media also fails to report on the activity of the criminal justice system or provide much information about the offender and victim (Chermak, 1994; Gordon et al., 1979; Surette, 1992). Skogan and Maxfield (1981) note how the media creates crime images through the skewed presentation of actual crime occurrences. They point out that by drawing together different offenses, committed at different times and places, the media creates an inappropriate image of crime in the community. The various studies show that the media concentrates on the spectacle of the offense and ignores the potential harm, in terms of increased fear of crime, that may arise from incomplete reporting.

Does the Media Cause Crime and Fear?

One potential problem of media presentations of crime is that viewers receive inaccurate images of crime and the criminal justice system. Several studies note that the public image of crime is influenced by media presentations. Gerbner et al. (1977, 1978, 1979) and Barrile (1980) compare the perception of crime and the criminal justice system held by individuals with differing levels of television exposure. The authors consistently find that respondents answer closer to the "television answer" (the answer that is commonly depicted on television) than to the real world information. The images, therefore, are influenced by media presentations. Perhaps of more interest for us is the ability of the media to cause crime or fear.

Media and Crime

Research has investigated the extent to which the mass media can influence the commission of deviant behavior. One early study of high school students relates the level of violence in the subjects' favorite television programs to their self-reported aggressive behavior (Hartnagel et al., 1975). The study finds a weak positive association between the level of media violence and reported violent behavior. More importantly, the students' perception of violence in the programs is related to violent behavior. A similar study of television viewing by youths (Belson, 1978) compares the violent behavior of two groups of boys—those with high exposure to media violence and those with low exposure. Belson (1978) reports that individuals with higher exposure commit more serious violent offenses. This relationship holds true for films that portray violent interpersonal relations, unnecessary violence, realistic violence, and violence presented as acceptable. Sports violence, cartoon, science fiction, and slapstick violence do not elicit the same response in viewers (Belson, 1978).

Two studies by Phillips (1982, 1983) investigate the effect of fictionalized suicides and prize fights on personal violence. One study examines the number of suicides that follow fictionalized suicides on soap operas. Controlling for holidays, non-fictional suicides presented in the media, and season of the year, Phillips (1982) finds that the U.S. suicide rate and attempted suicides significantly increase after soap opera suicides. These increases are true especially for urban females who are most similar to characters presented in daily soap operas. Phillips' second study (1983) reports a significant increase in homicide three to four days after heavyweight prize fights. This finding persists when controlling for day of week, holidays, and season. Indeed, the effect is greater for the more publicized fights. The homicide victims after a fight generally hold the same demographic characteristics as the fight's loser (Phillips, 1983).

Reviewing studies of television violence, Andison (1977) finds that 25 of 67 studies show a moderate positive relationship between viewing violence and subsequent aggression. An additional 27 analyses report a weak positive relationship. Examination of the studies in chronological order reveals increasingly stronger relationships between media presentations and violence. There also appears to be a larger effect on adults. This is possibly due to accumulated exposure over longer time spans (Andison, 1977). Andison's findings rely heavily on laboratory studies that utilize various forms of aggression such as electric shock and self-reported feelings of aggression. The generalizability of these findings to situations outside of the sterile, laboratory environment is highly questionable and Andison (1977) notes more realistic field studies find weaker, but still positive, relationships between television and aggression.

Research also has focused on pornography as a cause of violence, particularly sexual violence against women. The U.S. Attorney General's Commission on Pornography (1986) concludes that there is a direct link between viewing pornography and aggression found primarily in experimental laboratory studies. While laboratory experiments provide the ability to control for many outside influences and, arguably, allow for a closer examination of causality (Huesmann and Malamuth, 1986), there are serious flaws in the methodology that require caution in interpreting the results (Lab, 1987). First, many studies couple exposure to pornography with angering the subject; thus, it is not possible to attribute subsequent aggression to the pornographic stimulus. Second, the method of aggression post pornographic exposure in laboratory studies (such as overinflated blood pressure cuffs, electric shocks, noxious noise, and derogatory evaluations of tasks) is not equivalent to rape, assault, or other forms of violence outside the laboratory setting. Third, the sterile laboratory setting does not provide the same conditions under which the subjects would be viewing pornography and committing aggressive acts in the real world. Finally, the study subjects are typically undergraduate students who are not representative of the general population (Lab, 1987).

Where laboratory research claims a relatively strong media-behavior link, field and natural experiments provide more tentative conclusions (Lab, 1987). In a review of research on media violence, Geen and Thomas (1986) note that field experiments and natural studies show greatly equivocal results. Similarly, Coyne (2007) finds only a tenuous link between television viewing and criminal behavior. Another problem with media studies involves the time order of the assumed causal relationships. Most studies present the results in such a way that exposure to the media causes aggressive behavior. In many analyses, it is equally plausible that people who are already aggressive or are naturally prone to aggression simply choose to view more aggression (Coyne, 2007). Ferguson (2013), reviewing the literature on video games and behavior, finds little support for an exposure-behavior link. Greer and Reiner (2012) note that the impact of media presentations on subsequent behavior is tenuous.

This brief review presents qualified support for a connection between media presentations and viewer behavior. Most studies find weak to moderate relationships between actual behavior and television accounts of crime and aggression. There is also a strong theoretical tradition of modeling, learning, arousal, and cognitive cuing which supports a connection between the mass media and aggression. At the very least, excessive exposure to media violence can influence some viewers to be more aggressive (Huesmann and Malamuth, 1986). The preponderance of data and positive research findings suggest that the media does have some influence on behavior (Surette, 1992).

The Media and Fear

Besides causing deviant behavior, media presentations may also increase people's fear. Several authors note that crime news increases fear (Ditton and Duffy, 1983; Gunter, 1987; Robinson, 2011; Sherizan, 1978; van Dijk, 1978). Heath (1984) and Liska and Baccaglini (1990) report that local crime stories, particularly those dealing with sensational events, tend to raise the level of fear among readers. Examining 10 British daily newspapers and their relationship to fear, Williams and Dickinson (1993) find that fear varies with the saliency of the crime reports. That is, stories that place the offense in a framework familiar to the reader have a greater impact than those more removed from the reader's experiences.

High levels of television viewing also have been found to raise fear (Callanan, 2012; Doob and Macdonald, 1979; Gerbner et al., 1979). Chiricos et al. (1996) report that television and radio news is related to fear, while written news has no relationship with fear levels. Boda and Szabó (2011) note that there is a strong, consistent impact of television violence on increased fear. Callanan (2012) points out that television has a greater impact on levels of fear compared to other media sources.

In is important to note that the media–fear relationship is qualified by demographic factors. Television news is linked to higher fear among victims, women, white, lower-income, and middle-aged respondents (Chiricos et al., 1996). Combining the effects of demographic factors, the news effect is limited primarily to white females. Similarly, Lane and Meeker (2003b) report that television news is related to fear among Latinos, while Weitzer and Kubrin (2004) find a connection between news and fear for blacks. In Great Britain, *Crimewatch U.K.*, a counterpart to *America's Most Wanted*, increased fear in one-third of its viewers (Dobash et al., 1998).

Summary

The preceding discussions show that the media does influence both criminal behavior and fear. Exposure to the media is a daily fact of life for almost every citizen. There is a clear ability for the media to influence the images of crime held by the populace. More importantly, the media appears to be a factor in molding behavior. In the same way that the media may contribute to aggressive behavior and fear, it is possible that exposure to the mass media could bring about more realistic images of crime and prompt people to adopt crime prevention techniques.

Mass Media Crime Prevention Activities

Crime prevention through the mass media can take a variety of forms and has the potential to impact in different ways. Bowers and Johnson (2005) show that the media (publicity) can be used for several purposes: increasing the risk to offenders, increasing the perceived risk to offenders, encouraging safety practices by the public, and reassuring the public (see Figure 7.1). Successful use of the media may result in reduced crime and fear

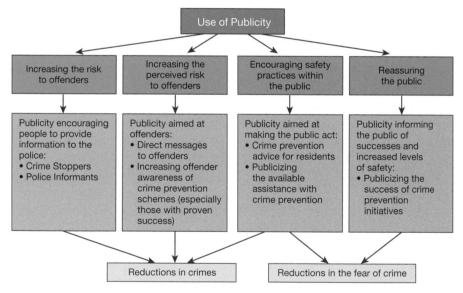

Figure 7.1

Uses of Media/Publicity in Crime Prevention

Source: K.J. Bowers and S.D. Johnson (2005). "Using publicity for preventive purposes." In N. Tilley (ed.), *Handbook of Crime Prevention and Community Safety*. Portland, OR: Willan. Reprinted with permission.

of crime. Examples of the use of media in crime prevention are the McGruff campaigns, crime newsletters, information lines such as Crime Stoppers, the use of social media, and "reality television" programs. Each of these attempts to provide varying amounts of crime education, fear reduction, and crime prevention activity that, hopefully, will translate into lower levels of actual crime.

The McGruff Prevention Campaign

Perhaps the most well-known media crime prevention campaign was instituted in the late 1970s by the Crime Prevention Coalition of America and the Advertising Council. These organizations joined forces to launch the "Take a Bite Out of Crime" program, featuring McGruff the crime dog. In 1982, the National Crime Prevention Council (NCPC) was formed to manage the ongoing McGruff project. The program operates today with the same four basic objectives it had in the beginning. First, it attempts to alter the public's feelings about crime and the criminal justice system. This is clearly an educational component aimed at instilling a realistic view of crime and the role of the legal system in stopping crime. Second, the program attempts to generate feelings of citizen responsibility for crime and crime prevention. Third, it tries to enhance citizen cooperation with the criminal justice system for fighting crime. The final goal is to enhance already existing crime prevention efforts.

Public service announcements on television and radio, print ads, webinars, and podcasts provide the means of realizing these objectives. Many of the announcements feature a cartoon character known as "McGruff" (a dog in a trench coat) who presents simulated crimes and notes the proper actions viewers should take when confronted with similar situations. A number of different themes or issues have appeared over the years (see Table 7.1). The emphasis throughout the campaign is on individual and community ability to take action.

TABLE 7.1 NCPC/McGruff Campaigns

Cyberbullying	Home invasion
Bullying prevention	Burglary
Identity theft	Mortgage fraud
Internet safety	Safe firearms storage
Neighborhood involvement	Hate crime
Senior fraud	Drug abuse
Sexual assault	Cell phone safety
School violence	Work violence

Source: Compiled by author from National Crime Prevention Council (2015). http://www.ncpc.org

The "**Take a Bite Out of Crime**" media campaign is the most recognizable and memorable component of the work of the NCPC. According to the NCPC (2015), more than three-quarters of all youths in the United States recognize McGruff and more than

┌─ **ON THE WEB** ───────────────────────
*You can find out more about the prevention programs
of the National Crime Prevention Council by visiting
their web site at http://www.ncpc.org/programs*

4,000 law enforcement agencies use McGruff in their activities. The "Take a Bite Out of Crime" campaign has relied on a significant amount of monetary support and personnel time from various sources. The NCPC (2015)

notes that advertisers have donated more than $1.4 billion worth of time and space for the program. This does not include production costs or costs of booklets, posters, and other program-related items that have been made available since the program started in 1979. Two large-scale evaluations have been completed on the program.

The First Evaluation

A two-pronged evaluation of this campaign was conducted from 1979 to 1981 (O'Keefe and Mendelsohn, 1984). The first part of the evaluation consisted of surveying 1,200 adults from across the country. The second phase involved a panel survey of adults in Buffalo, Detroit, and Milwaukee. The panel survey took measurements three months prior to the introduction of the campaign and again after more than a year and a half of campaign exposure. Among the issues investigated were the level of exposure to the public service announcements and the impact of the campaign on subsequent attitudes and crime prevention behaviors. The evaluation did not include any measures of actual crime. Self-reported victimization and attitudes served as the dependent variables.

The national survey found that roughly 50 percent of the respondents saw the campaign announcements (O'Keefe and Mendelsohn, 1984). Unfortunately, only 3 percent of this figure were able to recall the advertisements without some prompting by the interviewers. The vast majority (78 percent) saw the advertisements on television. Comparison across demographic groups revealed fairly even exposure in the population. The lone exception to this finding was the low number of older respondents (33 percent) who expressed a familiarity with the McGruff materials. O'Keefe and Mendelsohn (1984) speculated that this could be partly attributable to the fact that the materials typically appear later at night when the advertising time is not as profitable and older respondents are less likely to be watching the television.

The national survey also probed the extent of knowledge retained from the messages and the self-reported behavior of respondents as a result of the information. Almost 90 percent of the respondents were able to describe specific suggestions made and 22 percent said they learned something new (O'Keefe and Mendelsohn, 1984). The evaluators also found that better than 50 percent of the survey subjects felt more responsible for crime prevention because of the advertisements and a full 25 percent reported taking precautions suggested in the announcements. Regrettably, 22 percent of those surveyed reported feeling *more* fearful of criminal victimization. They attributed this feeling directly to the McGruff campaign materials. This increase in fear was opposite to program expectations and directly contradicted the efforts to present scenarios that would not elicit increased fear.

The panel survey component of the evaluation presented more in-depth results. Similar to the national findings, the panel survey revealed wide exposure to the campaign materials (O'Keefe and Mendelsohn, 1984). Interestingly, the level of interest in the materials was higher for those already concerned with crime and crime prevention activities. Exposure to the advertisements had no impact on perceptions of neighborhood crime, perceived changes in the crime rate, or a sense of safety at night. Only minor, and contradictory, changes were found in relation to individual crimes.

Exposure to the public service announcements resulted in changes in crime prevention activities. Specific activities suggested by the announcements (e.g., neighborhood watches, use of lights and locks, reporting suspicious persons to the police) increased after exposure to the materials. Preventive measures not dealt with in the messages (e.g., indoor lighting, stopping mail and paper deliveries, installing alarms) were not affected, as expected. The adoption of the crime prevention measures was not uniform across the panel subjects. While men's attitudes about crime prevention changed more than women's, women and upper-income respondents tended to gravitate more to cooperative crime prevention activities (O'Keefe and Mendelsohn, 1984). Lower-income respondents chose individual alternatives like increased lighting and more outdoor activities.

The Second Evaluation

A second evaluation was conducted in 1992 and involved interviewing a national sample of adults, as well as law enforcement and media representatives. Compared to the earlier evaluation, 80 percent of the citizen respondents reported having seen the announcements, an increase of 30 percent (O'Keefe et al., 1996). Exposure was greatest among younger respondents, males (by 6 percent over females), those with at least a high school education, and victims. The impact of the announcements was uniformly in the expected direction. Respondents reported feeling more competent about crime prevention participation, taking more action, and becoming more concerned about crime (O'Keefe et al., 1996). Interestingly, the evaluation did not uncover demographic differences between those learning from the announcements and those reporting no impact.

Similar positive results appear in the media and law enforcement responses. More than two-thirds of the media respondents reported using the materials in the past, with 75 percent of the television stations having aired announcements during the past year (O'Keefe et al., 1996). Both the media and law enforcement respondents noted that the materials were valuable in both crime and drug prevention efforts. Of particular note was the introduction of "WE PREVENT" announcements in the early 1990s which asked viewers to call a toll free telephone number and request information on how to deal with problems such as random violence. Media respondents rated these announcements high in terms of quality, appropriateness, and interest compared to other public service materials (O'Keefe et al., 1996).

Summary

In general, the "Take a Bite Out of Crime" campaign facilitates attitudinal changes in the groups that traditionally are the least vulnerable to crime and those already interested in crime prevention issues. This mirrors the findings of who joins neighborhood watch and other crime prevention programs. O'Keefe and Mendelsohn (1984) also note that behavioral changes do not always correspond to attitudinal adjustments. That is, many individuals try out various crime prevention measures without reporting any attitudinal shifts about crime or fear. Based on both evaluations, O'Keefe et al. (1996) suggest that the program keep its main themes and continue to find ways to reach vulnerable groups in society. In addition, the campaign should attempt to identify distinct needs of different audience groups and target announcements to their situations.

Other Campaigns

Other media campaigns have been targeted at a range of crime in different countries. Riley (1980; Riley and Mayhew, 1980) reports on a campaign to educate individuals about auto theft and vandalism in England. The attempt to deal with vandalism had no effect on parental attitudes or the crime rates in the target area. Auto thefts, on the other hand, declined in the experimental area relative to a control location. A media campaign aimed at auto theft in Australia using television, newspapers, magazines, and letters reached only 28 percent of the public but was able to increase the preventive behavior of those exposed to the campaign (Wortley et al., 1998).

A burglary awareness/education program in Jerusalem utilizing radio, public lectures, and various forms of literature was recalled by more than 50 percent of the surveyed public and 46 percent altered their behavior or took precautions in accordance with the campaign's suggestions (Geva and Israel, 1982). Participants also reported higher feelings of safety compared to non-participants or pre-exposure levels. The actual level of burglary dropped by 32 percent in the target area compared to a 22 percent increase in the rest of Jerusalem and a 6 percent rise in the control area (Geva and Israel, 1982).

Attempts to influence substance use and abuse are also common in the media. Elder et al. (2004) and Tay (2005) report that media campaigns to stem drunk driving have significantly reduced drunk driving and alcohol-related crashes. Conversely, an evaluation of the "Buzzed Driving is Drunk Driving" public service announcement campaign in the United States reveals minimal impact (Flexon and Guerette, 2009). The authors speculate the failure may be due to the belief by many that buzzed driving is *not* drunk driving, thus having little impact on attitudes or behavior.

The **National Youth Anti-Drug Media Campaign** sponsored by the White House Office of National Drug Control Policy does appear to be having success. Started in 1998, the effort has evolved into the Above the Influence program aimed at youths aged 12 to 17 and an Anti-Meth Campaign aimed at those aged 18 to 34. The Above the Influence campaign relies on digital media, including Facebook, YouTube, and Google, as well as more traditional media outlets (White House Office of National Drug Control Policy, 2012). Evaluation of the project reveals that more than 75 percent of teens are aware of the campaign, and teens who are aware report significantly stronger anti-drug beliefs than those unaware of the program (59 percent to 40 percent reporting anti-drug beliefs) (White House Office of National Drug Control Policy, 2012). Two independent evaluations (Carpenter and Pechmann, 2011; Slater et al., 2011) uncover similar strong impacts of the Above the Influence Campaign. These studies illustrate that media campaigns have the potential to change both behaviors and attitudes about crime and deviance.

> ┌─ **ON THE WEB** ─
> *More detail on the White House's media campaign against drug use and abuse can be accessed at http://www.whitehouse.gov/ondcp/anti-drug-media-campaign*

Inconsistent and weak results in some evaluations suggest that the programs may need to be better targeted. Sacco and Trotman (1990) note that the impact of a mass media crime prevention campaign is related to the saliency of the program for the viewer. Individuals who recognize crime as a problem are more likely to be influenced and report changes in attitude and behavior (see, for example, the Buzzed Driving is Drunk Driving results). While widespread exposure of a program is a plus, crime prevention campaigns need to reach the intended or most vulnerable audiences (see also O'Keefe at al., 1996). The generic nature of large-scale approaches may also hamper their effectiveness. Sacco and Trotman (1990) suggest that programs need to set modest, realistic goals that focus on specific attitudes and behaviors. Viewers are more likely to take precautions that are presented in the media than to strike out on their own to find the proper forms of crime prevention behavior (O'Keefe and Mendelsohn, 1984). More specific media campaigns, such as area newsletters and Crime Stoppers programs, may engender increased citizen participation in crime prevention activities.

Crime Newsletters

Providing more salient information to the public can be accomplished through the distribution of **crime newsletters**. Unlike widely distributed mass media campaigns,

---

TABLE 7.2 Newsletter Content Areas

Self-protection techniques
Ways to report crime
Locations of police or protection resources
Dangerous areas
Offender addresses
Area crime problems

Source: Compiled by the author from E. Barthe (2010) "Crime newsletters." In B.S. Fisher and S.P. Lab (eds.), *Encyclopedia of Victimology and Crime Prevention*. Thousand Oaks, CA: Sage.

---

which are limited in terms of their time frame and the level of specificity, newsletters can be targeted to a smaller audience and tailored to the needs of those individuals. Newsletters also can provide information on a wide range of related topics, including the level of crime in an area and prevention techniques for the public (see Table 7.2). In addition, they may provide detailed, in-depth discussions of both crime and potential crime prevention measures. Totally different newsletters need not be prepared for each neighborhood or targeted group. Instead, a single newsletter dealing with general crime and crime prevention information can be developed for wide distribution. Salience can be enhanced through the insertion of separate fact sheets and information sent to different areas and individuals.

Crime newsletters have been utilized in a large number of locations but have received extensive evaluation only in Evanston, Illinois (Lavrakas, 1986; Lavrakas et al., 1983), Houston (Brown and Wycoff, 1987; Lavrakas, 1986), and Newark (Lavrakas, 1986; Williams and Pate, 1987). Each newsletter included various articles on crime prevention and comments on crime problems, as well as crime information specific to different locations. The crime information included such items as the level and types of crime committed in the area, rough location of offenses, and relevant information about offenders and victims. This allowed the reader to assess the particulars about the crimes and apply that information to his own situation.

The newsletters had the potential to influence citizen behavior in a number of ways. First, the newsletters were an educational tool. They could present more realistic versions of the actual crime rate and, perhaps, bring down the fear of crime. The opposite effect, however, was also possible. Fear of crime could increase due to the distribution of crime news. This could restrict, rather than increase, citizen behavior. A second possibility was they could raise the level of concern about crime among the citizenry. Hopefully, any increase in concern will result in a third outcome—increased citizen crime prevention activities.

The evaluation of the newsletters in the three cities followed roughly the same procedures (Brown and Wycoff, 1987; Lavrakas, 1986; Williams and Pate, 1987). Each evaluation randomly assigned homes to one of three conditions. One set of homes received the newsletter containing crime-specific information. A second sample of homes received newsletters without the crime information. These subjects saw only the articles and crime prevention information. The remaining sample of homes acted as a control group and did not get any newsletter. Despite the similarity in content and evaluation design, the evaluation results differed across the three cities.

The most consistent finding was that individuals who reported receiving the newsletters held favorable assessments of them. This was true for both the newsletters with and without the specific crime information (Lavrakas, 1986). There was a slight tendency for those receiving the version containing crime data to view the letters as more interesting.

There was less consistency in the impact on fear of crime, concern for crime prevention, and precautions taken. In Evanston, the newsletters increased the recipient's knowledge of the crime problem but had no effect on the fear of crime (Lavrakas et al., 1983; Lavrakas, 1986). The Houston evaluation showed increased fear of property victimization among respondents receiving crime information (Brown and Wycoff, 1987; Lavrakas, 1986) and the Newark evaluation failed to uncover any changes in fear of crime or perceptions of change in the crime problem (Lavrakas, 1986; Williams and Pate, 1987). In terms of crime prevention activity, Evanston respondents who received letters containing crime information took more crime prevention precautions than those individuals not receiving the letters or those receiving letters without crime data (Lavrakas et al., 1983; Lavrakas, 1986). Houston respondents reported similar levels of crime prevention activity across all study groups, although those receiving the newsletter felt more competent to avoid victimization than did non-receivers (Lavrakas, 1986). Finally, Newark residents who did not receive the newsletter reported taking more crime prevention precautions than those who received either version of the newsletter. The newsletter did result in greater feelings of self-protection among those viewing the materials (Lavrakas, 1986).

The inconsistent findings in the evaluations may be attributable to differences in the study sites. Lavrakas (1986) points out that the more effective campaign in Evanston relied on hand distribution of the newsletter. Mailed newsletters may be relegated to the status of junk mail delivered by postal workers. A second difference between the cities concerns the educational level of the recipients. More Evanston respondents reported graduation from high school and participation in higher education than did those in either of the other locations (Lavrakas, 1986). This factor may influence the actual level of readership and impact of the newsletters. Third, Lavrakas (1986) notes that the Evanston evaluation relies on interviews with the head of the household while both the Houston and Newark studies interviewed any adult member of the household. It is reasonable to assume that the head of a household makes most decisions on household crime prevention activity. Failure to target the head of the house, therefore, may fail to uncover any precautions that are taken. One final problem may be the choice of information and format for the various newsletters. Both Houston and Newark borrowed the basic newsletter framework from Evanston. It is possible that the similarity of presentation, given the dissimilarity of cities, is partially at fault for the discrepant results.

Newsletters have the potential to affect fear of crime, perceptions of crime and victimization, and crime prevention behavior. The failure of the three newsletter evaluations presented here to uncover consistent impacts does not mean newsletters cannot work. The problems noted above suggest that more caution needs to be taken in the choice of format, presentation, and evaluation of a newsletter. The consistent findings of public interest and acceptance of the information should be enough to assure their continuation.

Information Lines

The idea behind **information lines** is twofold. First, and foremost, is the solicitation of information about specific crimes from the public. The second aspect is the public presentation of crime information involving citizens in crime prevention. Perhaps the most widely known program of this type is Crime Stoppers. **Crime Stoppers**, and variations on this program, generally operate by offering rewards to citizens for information about crimes. Often, unsolved offenses are presented to the public through the mass media along with a plea by law enforcement officials for information regarding the crime. The informant is usually guaranteed anonymity for the information through the use of code names or numbers and reward money comes from public donations. Crime Stoppers started in Albuquerque, New Mexico, in 1976 and as of 2012 there were almost 1,200 programs around the world (Crime Stoppers International, 2015). Programs are found in 24 countries, including the United States, Canada, the Caribbean, Europe, the United Kingdom, Australia, the Pacific, South Korea, India, South Africa, and other countries. While most programs are community based, there are chapters found at various schools and colleges. Programs typically offer rewards of up to $1,000 for information leading to the arrest of a suspect. Crime Stoppers programs are a tool to bring the public, media, and the criminal justice system into a cooperative crime prevention effort.

┌─ **ON THE WEB** ───────────┐
│ *You can explore more about Crime Stoppers* │
│ *at http://www.crimestoppersusa.com/ and* │
│ *http://www.csiworld.org/* │
└──────────────────────────┘

Crime Stoppers International (2015) claims that almost 1.6 million cases have been cleared since 1976 (see Table 7.3). More than 950,000 arrests have been made, with almost $117 million in rewards paid. In addition, the authorities have recovered $2.1 billion in stolen property and seized more than $10 billion in drugs as a result of the Crime Stoppers program (Crime Stoppers International, 2015). Money for the rewards is typically donated by businesses or solicited through fundraising, and the advertisements themselves are usually donated by the media.

Several evaluations of Crime Stoppers have been conducted. Rosenbaum et al. (1989) report on a national evaluation of Crime Stoppers in the United States. The

TABLE 7.3 Crime Stoppers Facts and Figures

	United States	International
Number of cases cleared	998,406	1,557,182
Number of arrests made	665,291	952,912
Amount of awards paid	$102M	$117M
Value of property recovered	$1.1B	$2.1B
Value of drugs seized	$3.0B	$8.3B
Total $ recovered	$4.2B	$10.3B

Source: Compiled by the author from www.csiworld.org/stats.php and www.crimestoppersusa.com

evaluation included a telephone survey of 602 Crime Stoppers programs and surveys of police coordinators, Crime Stoppers boards of directors, and mass media executives. The surveys show that programs typically share resources with one another and receive high praise from the administrators, media personnel, and police coordinators. Many media respondents indicate that, while they are not currently participating in the program, they would be happy to do so if they were approached. Unfortunately, these programs are difficult to evaluate in terms of any reduction in fear of crime or lower crime and victimization (Rosenbaum et al., 1989).

Gresham et al. (2001) report on an evaluation of Crime Stoppers in the United Kingdom. The researchers interviewed key stakeholders, conducted observations of program operations, tracked phone calls, and reviewed program documents. In 2000, more than 500,000 calls were received by Crime Stoppers, but only 12 percent of those provided usable information (i.e., actionable calls), and only 5,423 arrests were made (Gresham et al., 2001). The bulk of the actionable calls reflected drug and motor vehicle offenses. Interestingly, only one-fifth of the actionable calls were in direct response to specific media presentations. The rest of the calls dealt with offenses or crimes not presented in the media. Also of note, Gresham et al. (2001) found that most rewards went unclaimed. More than £3.7 million (over $7 million) worth of stolen property was recovered and more than £34 million (over $65 million) in drugs were seized (Gresham et al., 2001). As in the United States, there is strong support for Crime Stoppers from the police, media, and public.

The Crime Stoppers program in Australia has had similar success. Most of the targeted crimes presented on television are violent crimes (84 percent) and almost 140,000 calls were received in 2002 (Challinger, 2003). Unfortunately, less than 2 percent of the calls resulted in an arrest. Despite that fact, almost $600,000 (U.S.) worth of stolen property was recovered and over $5 million (U.S.) in drugs were seized (Challinger, 2003). Support for the program rivals that found in U.S. and U.K. assessments.

Social Media

The basic idea underlying Crime Stoppers has been expanded in recent years due to the growth of the Internet and **social media** sites. Police departments post crime videos and information on unsolved crimes on the organization web sites, YouTube, Facebook, and others asking for viewers to provide information on the crime and the offender (DiBlasio, 2012). Microblogs such as Twitter, blogs, Flickr, web chats, podcasts, and other emerging social outlets, can be used in a variety of ways by law enforcement and crime prevention (NNW, 2015; IACP, 2012). First, these outlets reach a wide array of people, particularly due to the ubiquitous nature of smart phones (NNW, 2015). Second, agencies can publicize events very quickly instead of being tied to news broadcasts or weekly show schedules. Third, more videos and events can be posted compared to broadcast media, and more information can be shared about each event. Fourth, agencies are using these forums to post prevention topics (IACP, 2012; LexisNexis Risk Solutions, 2014).

┌─ ON THE WEB ─────────────────────────┐
│ *The IACP Center for Social Media has a wealth of* │
│ *information. Visit http://www.iacpsocialmedia.org/* │
│ *GettingStarted.aspx and explore what it offers in* │
│ *relation to crime and crime prevention.* │
└──────────────────────────────────────┘

Unfortunately, there has been a lack of centralized information on these emerging programs and little information on their effectiveness. In 2010, the IACP and the Bureau of Justice Assistance initiated the IACP Center for Social Media. The Center is tasked with promoting the use of social media by law enforcement to solve and prevent crime. It is essentially a clearinghouse of information for preventive action (IACP, 2015). Included are links to law enforcement agencies, documents on social media, prevention information, and other useful materials.

Since 2010, the IACP Center for Social Media has conducted surveys of law enforcement agencies on the use of social media. The 2013 survey of 600 agencies across 46 states reveals that 95 percent of the agencies use social media (IACP, 2014). The respondents claim that social media has improved their ability to solve crimes and has enhanced their relationship with the community. Two-thirds use social media to solicit tips on crime, almost 80 percent use it to alert the public about crime and other issues, and 72 percent incorporate it in crime prevention initiatives (IACP, 2014).

There is no indication that programs like Crime Stoppers and social media efforts have reduced crime or the fear of crime. It is possible that fear could actually increase through the media presentation of unsolved, and often heinous, crimes. Reduced crime could only be affected through the greater risks of apprehension as a result of the programs. There also are concerns that publicity programs may engender negative results. Pretrial publicity from the presentations can bias cases in court, questions can be raised about the validity of paid testimony, and there may be problems with anonymous testimony and false accusations (Rosenbaum et al., 1989). Indeed, the U.S. national evaluation estimates that most tips come from criminals (25 percent) or fringe players

(41 percent) rather than from common citizens (35 percent) (Rosenbaum et al., 1989). Despite the potential problems, publicity and social media programs are valuable tools in the gathering of crime-related information and providing crime information to a wide range of citizens.

Crime-Time Television

One trend in the mass media since the mid-1980s has been the focus on previously unsolved crimes in prime-time network programming. Among the earliest of these programs were *America's Most Wanted*, *Unsolved Mysteries*, and *Top Cops* in the United States (Nelson, 1989) and *Crimewatch U.K.* in the United Kingdom (Dobash et al., 1998). More recent shows include *20/20*, *PrimeTime Live*, *48 Hours*, and *Dateline*. These shows typically re-enact serious crimes for which no offender has been apprehended. The dramatizations often use interviews with victims/witnesses and actual law enforcement personnel involved in the case. After the presentation of a case, viewers are prompted to call law enforcement or a toll free telephone number to report any information they may have about the case or the whereabouts of the suspect.

The impact of these shows has been the subject of debate. Kelley (1997) notes that of the 1,133 subjects showcased on *America's Most Wanted*, 441 have been found and taken into custody subsequent to the airing of the program. Leishman and Mason (2003) note that *CrimeWatch U.K.* claims there were 582 arrests of suspects between 1984 and 2000 as a result of the show. However, the degree to which the programs can be considered directly responsible for most of these apprehensions is uncertain. Nelson (1989) points out that these programs encourage citizen cooperation with the police. Donovan (1998) notes that *America's Most Wanted* received an average of 3,000 calls per show in 1994, but few contributed valuable information. A similar Dutch program claims a clearance rate of 25 to 30 percent for broadcast crimes (Brants, 1998). While most calls may not result in useful information, the fact that calls are being made can be considered a significant achievement of the programs. One producer views the program as the catalyst for a "nationwide neighborhood watch association" (Nelson, 1989).

On the other hand, these programs hold the potential for causing trouble. First, mass media presentations can potentially bias court cases and lead to appeals based on excessive pretrial publicity and the inability to seat an unbiased jury. Second, depictions of crimes where the offender has not been apprehended may lead other individuals to copy the offenses. Third, Winkel (1987) notes that viewers may generalize from the response being promoted in the program (such as simply calling for help) to other possible responses not featured in the program (such as carrying weapons and taking direct action). Such a **response generalization** would be an unintended consequence of the program. Vigilante behavior is one possible generalization of efforts to increase citizen involvement. While not all citizens will generalize beyond the message provided in the media, there is clear evidence that such actions do grow out of media presentations (Winkel, 1987). The popularity of "crime-time" programs will ensure that they continue to appear on television for the immediate future. The extent to which they will have an impact on crime, fear of crime, and citizen participation needs further examination.

Publicity and Prevention

While this chapter has focused primarily on large mass media efforts, smaller-scale and targeted publicity about prevention programs and initiatives can have an impact on the success of crime prevention efforts. That impact may actually occur prior to or separate from the actual prevention initiative. That is, the publicity may reduce crime in and of itself. The assumption underlying this possibility is that the publicity impacts the offender's perceptions of risk and payoff, rather than changing the behavior of victims (Johnson and Bowers, 2003).

Smith et al. (2002) suggest that changes in crime that predate the actual implementation of a crime prevention program are a form of **anticipatory benefit**. In one sense, this could be a form of diffusion of benefits that arises most probably from the fact that offenders, victims, and others know about a forthcoming prevention activity and begin to respond prior to the activation of the intervention. Publicity about an impending intervention may be the impetus for the anticipatory benefits. The publicity can be intentional, as in situations where public announcements are made about a project, or it may be more informal through networking that takes place during the planning and early implementation stages for an intervention.

Several studies reveal evidence of anticipatory benefits stemming from publicity. Barclay et al.'s (1996) analysis of activities aimed at reducing crimes in parking lots shows reductions in crime that began after publicity started but before the actual intervention took place. Similarly, both Brown's (1995) and Armitage et al.'s (1999) studies of CCTV present evidence of downward trends in crime prior to the actual installation of the cameras but after the program was announced. In an analysis of 21 Reducing Burglary Initiative sites, Johnson and Bowers (2003) assessed the timing of reductions in burglary against the initiation of publicity and the actual prevention activities. Their results show that there is a significant reduction in burglary preceding the actual program implementation. In addition the declines correspond to the advent of the publicity on the forthcoming efforts (Johnson and Bowers, 2003). Based on these results, the authors argue that publicity has an independent impact on crime and that programs could possibly bring down crime by publicizing a prevention program, even if the program never takes place (Bowers and Johnson, 2003; Johnson and Bowers, 2003)! Finally, Smith et al. (2002) present findings in support of the anticipatory benefit hypothesis based on an analysis of 52 studies in which there was evidence of pre-initiative crime reductions. At the very least, publicity should be considered as a part of any prevention initiative.

The Media's Responsibility for Crime Prevention

Throughout this chapter we have discussed the potential of the media for enhancing crime prevention activity. Lavrakas (1997) suggests that the media must assume some of the blame for the continued failure of policies to deal with crime. He argues that the media fails to critically assess claims regarding the efficacy of crime control policies. In particular, politicians are able to promote interventions and crime policy without being held accountable for their rhetorical arguments. The author argues that the media has a responsibility to do more than simply report what legislators say. Instead, the media should be critically questioning those positions and challenging politicians to provide proof for their arguments (Lavrakas, 1997).

Lavrakas (1997) demonstrates his argument through an analysis of 1994 anti-crime legislation. Analyzing stories in the *New York Times*, Lavrakas points out that the media often focuses on the disagreement between legislators about crime policy, but rarely examines the substantive merit of the various measures being debated. In essence, the media does a poor job at handling political posturing and tends to accept gross comments about value or lack of value in relation to programs without demanding that the source prove the claim.

Why does the media do such a poor job? First, Lavrakas (1997) suggests that the news media is typically not educated about criminal justice and crime policy. Few journalists receive any real education about the criminal justice system or crime prevention. Second, the media does not hold politicians accountable for their actions or rhetoric. Consequently, politicians will not change their posturing and the public will not receive the information it needs to make informed decisions. What the public receives is a sanitized version of what is taking place through "sound bites" or catchy phrases. Lavrakas (1997) calls for educating the media (and politicians) about crime prevention, as well as demanding that more research be conducted on prevention initiatives. He argues that crime prevention will continue to suffer until the media starts to hold policy makers accountable for their actions.

Summary

The use of the media is a relatively new approach in crime prevention. Research on the exposure of the public to media information and the findings that media portrayals of aggression may affect levels of viewer aggression suggest that the same tools could influence crime preventive behavior. Analysis of media crime prevention campaigns shows that media presentations can affect fear of crime, feelings of self-confidence in avoiding victimization, and the adoption of crime prevention precautions. Unfortunately, the level and extent of these changes is not uniform across the evaluations. It appears that the choice of presentation format and the modes of evaluation are key elements in uncovering positive effects. Any modification in actual crime is extremely difficult to uncover. This is primarily due to the focus on perceptions of fear and crime and not on crime itself. Changes in the level of actual crime must rely on the successful modification of these other factors. Once the fear of crime and the level of crime prevention efforts are changed, then the ultimate goal of reduced crime can start to appear.

KEY TERMS

- anticipatory benefit
- crime newsletters
- Crime Stoppers
- information lines
- McGruff
- National Youth Anti-Drug Media Campaign
- response generalization
- social media
- Take a Bite Out of Crime

CHAPTER 8 Developmental Crime Prevention

CHAPTER OUTLINE

LEARNING OBJECTIVES

After reading this chapter you should be able to:

- Define developmental crime prevention.
- Discuss the background of developmental prevention.
- List and discuss three theoretical models for developmental prevention.
- Discuss the role of risk factors in developmental prevention.
- Identify leading individual and family risk factors for delinquency/criminality.
- Demonstrate how skills training fits the developmental approach.
- List and discuss the effectiveness of two parenting training programs.
- Identify and explain the FRIENDS program.
- Outline the Perry Preschool program and discuss the impact of the program.
- Discuss mentoring programs, including Big Brothers/Big Sisters.
- Identify different multi-component programs.
- Discuss the Communities that Care program and relate how it can be applied in any setting.
- List and discuss different concerns or issues related to developmental crime prevention.

Thus far in this book, most of the ideas suggest that relatively simple efforts, such as making physical improvements in communities, organizing residents to combat crime, and convincing citizens to take precautions and participate in anti-crime measures can have a significant impact on crime and fear. Even the discussion on media crime prevention has a focus on protecting one's self, one's property, and the community. Research has shown that these primary prevention techniques can be, and are, effective. At the same time, there are numerous examples of programs that fail to affect crime or fear, and have an impact only in the short term. Primary prevention, however, is not restricted to those efforts. An important form of primary prevention entails actions that would alter the drive and motivation of potential offenders at a more basic level.

Developmental crime prevention targets the potential of individuals to become criminal. The basic assumption is that criminal and deviant activity is the result of early life experiences and learning (Tremblay and Craig, 1997). Societal failure to address those factors predisposes individuals, particularly youths, to crime. The focus of developmental prevention is not very different from core criminological theories about crime and deviance. The emphasis is on what causes individuals to commit deviant acts and what can be done about that activity. The major point of divergence is the focus on trying to address the causes early in the process, preferably prior to the initial act.

This chapter seeks to accomplish several things. First, it will outline the basic ideas and arguments underlying developmental prevention, including some of the theoretical underpinnings of the perspective. Second, the related issues of risk and protective factors will be discussed as they relate to developmental arguments and potential interventions. Finally, the chapter will discuss several major developmental prevention programs and initiatives that have been introduced. As in other chapters, the focus of the discussion on programs is on the success of the interventions to prevent crime.

Background

Developmental prevention has a solid foundation in the basic ideas of learning theory. The cornerstone of developmental approaches is that crime results from the behavior, beliefs, and attitudes that are learned, primarily, but not exclusively, as youths (Tremblay and Craig, 1997). This is not to suggest that classic learning theories, such as differential association or operant conditioning, are the sole basis for understanding the developmental approaches. While such learning theories provide insight on the development of behavior, they are simply too narrow to adequately explain criminality. The fact that early life experiences influence later behavior points out that a wealth of information and perspectives are important contributors.

In many respects, developmental prevention has benefited from the elaboration model that has become prominent in criminological theorizing. The **elaboration model** attempts to take components of various theories and build a single explanation that incorporates the best parts of the individual theories. These types of explanations can be both simple and complex. Several authors have attempted to combine social control and differential association theories to explain the development of delinquency (Massey and Krohn, 1986; Thornberry et al., 1994). Conger and Simons (1997) offer a more complex explanation. They start with biological factors that can play a role in cognitive development and abilities, which then impact on interactions between the individual, family, friends, and school. This interaction can impede success in school and can lead to pressures later in life. Moffit (1997) offers a sequence in which neuro-psychological deficits alter an individual's temperament, speech, learning ability, and other factors leading to withdrawal, rejection, poor self-concept, failure at school, and other problems. The underlying theme in these examples and many other attempts at elaborating theories is that there are a wide range of factors at work in dictating possible behaviors.

In their discussion of developmental prevention of delinquency, Tremblay and Craig (1997) offer three theoretical models. These models range from a simple, primarily single theoretical approach to a very complex model that incorporates many theoretical components. The simplest model is a linear explanation such as Gottfredson and Hirschi's (1990) **general theory of crime**. This explanation assumes that failures in early child rearing by parents lead to low self-control by the individual and a much greater chance that crime and deviance will be expressed. The second model assumes multiple possible pathways to adult offending (such as that offered by Loeber, 1990). These different pathways recognize that youthful misbehavior can take different forms, emerge at different times, and progress into different types of adult offending. The final model is not unlike the elaboration models discussed earlier in that it includes elements of strain theories (poverty), biological problems, poor parenting, cognitive deficits, and other factors, all interacting with each other and culminating in problem behavior (Tremblay and Craig, 1997). Farrington (2007) offers an elaboration model he refers to as the **Integrated Cognitive Antisocial Potential (ICAP) theory**. The ICAP model (see Figure 8.1) incorporates ideas from learning, social control, strain, and labeling theories, as well as rational choice theory. The individual components of the model work individually and in concert with one another to build the potential for criminality. Farrington (2007) does not argue that crime is inevitable, only that the odds are greater. It also indicates that there are many points at which interventions could be applied to try and halt the process. In every case, the goal of developmental prevention is to intervene early in the process in an attempt to mitigate those factors that make an individual more prone to commit later delinquency or crime.

Clearly, developmental crime prevention relies on ideas identifying the causes of crime and criminality that are related to an individual's disposition to commit crime. At its core, developmental prevention fits into the positivist school of criminology. According to **positivism** crime is caused by factors beyond the control of the individual.

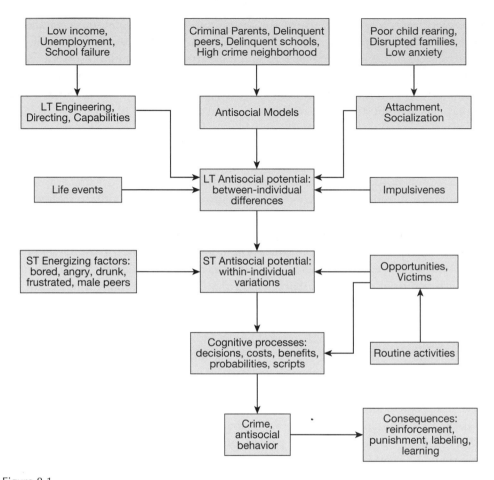

Figure 8.1

Integrated Cognitive Antisocial Potential (ICAP) Model

Source: D.P. Farrington (2007). "Childhood risk factors and risk-focused prevention." In M. Maguire, R. Morgan, and R. Reiner (eds.), *The Oxford Handbook of Criminology*, Fourth Edition. Oxford: Oxford University Press. Reprinted with permission from Oxford University Press.

Addressing and eliminating crime and deviance, therefore, require the identification and elimination of those factors causing individuals to act as they do. This is directly opposed to the ideas outlined in earlier chapters that assume individuals have the ability to respond to crime opportunities by either choosing to commit an act or choosing not to do so. Developmental approaches place a great deal of belief in the idea that individuals have little, if any, choice in their behavior. Rather, they are conditioned through past experiences and forced to act in certain ways. (This does not mean there is absolutely no choice, only that the ability to choose is severely limited.) The positivistic orientation to developmental prevention means that it has several goals (Crawford, 2007). First, it seeks to identify risk factors for future criminality. Second, it seeks to identify protective factors to reduce the chances for criminality. Finally, it seeks to identify ways that individuals can desist from further transgressions (Crawford, 2007). It is the issue of identifying risk and protective factors to which we now turn.

Risk Factors and Developmental Prevention

Any attempt to address crime through developmental factors is faced with a very broad spectrum of variables and issues that could be addressed. Virtually everything that occurs to individuals and around individuals as they grow and mature has a potential impact on later decision making and behavior. It is not feasible to try and address every possible factor. Indeed, attempts to do so would mean that an individual and his environment are subject to total control and regimen. The more reasonable approach is to identify and intervene in those factors that are most likely to influence an individual's choices and behaviors. In essence, this means identifying risk factors and implementing programs to mitigate their effect.

The list of potential risk factors that have been identified for later criminality is extensive and can be grouped into different categories. These categories include individual/psychological, family, peer, community, and school. It is the first two of these that receive the bulk of attention in the developmental prevention literature and the major ones to be focused on in this chapter (the remaining categories will be revisited in a later chapter). Farrington (2007) lists what he sees as the key individual and family risk factors (see Table 8.1). He claims that developmental prevention needs to design and implement programs to counteract these risk factors.

It is important to note that not all variables or factors that are related to criminality should be considered risk factors. First, many factors are strongly correlated with crime, such as age, sex, and race. Age, for example, is perhaps the most highly correlated with deviant behavior, with most crime being committed by persons in their late teens and early twenties. The problem is that these factors cannot be changed by a prevention program. Therefore, they are of no practical value for developmental prevention. Second, it is important to recognize the distinction between a simple correlate and a causal factor (Farrington, 2007). Just because something occurs at the same time as crime does not mean it is the cause of the crime. Farrington (2007) uses the example that just because a delinquent has delinquent friends does not mean that the friends cause the delinquency. Finally, it is important to recognize that the identification of risk factors is often based on finding a difference between two groups on some dimension. That dimension is then considered a risk factor. What is more important is to find out if a change in the

---

TABLE 8.1 Developmental Risk Factors

Individual Risk Factors	Family Risk Factors
Low intelligence and attainment	Family criminality
Low empathy	Large family size
Impulsiveness	Poor parental supervision
Poor social cognitive skills	Harsh punishment
	Poor/cold familial attachment
	Child abuse and neglect
	Broken home

Source: Compiled by author from D.P. Farrington (2007). "Childhood risk factors and risk-focused prevention." In M. Maguire et al. (eds.) *The Oxford Handbook of Criminology*, Fourth Edition. Oxford: Oxford University Press.

---

dimension for an individual is related to a change in the key behavior (Farrington, 2007). For example, if most offending is committed by those earning low income, income is considered a risk factor. What is more important to know is whether the commission of crime (or level of crime) is changed at the individual level when the individual's income goes up or down. It is this change that indicates a causal connection between the risk factor and the behavior (Farrington, 2007).

An important consideration in many developmental prevention programs is that they often address crime and delinquency indirectly. Since these programs are targeting risk factors, instead of measuring success in terms of reduced criminality, they look for changes in the risk factors and in intermediate outcomes that appear between the risk factor and later behavior. An example of this would be programs that address parental supervision. The underlying assumption is that better supervision and parenting methods will lead youths to avoid delinquency. In order to do that, the program analyzes change in the parenting and may focus on issues such as the child's coping mechanisms and skill sets that result from the program. Delinquency reduction may be the ultimate goal and is not fully addressed in evaluations. The following discussions of developmental crime prevention programs will look at behavioral changes when available, as well as other outcomes.

Programs

There are many different prevention programs that entail developmental interventions. It is impossible to cover all of the diverse approaches in this chapter. Instead, the following discussion will target some of the most promising and intriguing developmental prevention programs. The interventions chosen for inclusion are those that tend to have the following features: (1) they are aimed at young children (even infants) and their families, and (2) the youths are not those who have necessarily already exhibited anti-social behavior. This later criterion does not mean that delinquent youths are not handled in the program, only that the program addresses youths regardless of their current behavioral status. Included here are programs that address skills training, parental education, preschool preparation, and multi-component programs that work at a broad community level.

Skills Training

Many social skills training initiatives appear in school settings and appear under various titles, including life skills training. These programs seek to teach children how to recognize problem situations and react in an appropriate manner. This is done by attempting to teach self-control, anger management, how to recognize your feelings and emotions, building a positive self-image, identifying the needs and concerns of others, and how to solve problems. In essence, the skills to be learned are how to interact with others in your environment without resorting to aggressive or antisocial methods. To a large extent, the training seeks to provide youths with the skills to combat peer pressure and aggression from other youths.

The **Promoting Alternative Thinking Strategies (PATHS)** program has been recognized as model program. PATHS is taught in regular classrooms and, ideally, is a five-year-long curriculum offered in elementary schools (Greenberg and Kusche, 1998). The curriculum is intended to reduce both behavioral and emotional problems, while building self-control and problem-solving abilities. PATHS has undergone several evaluations utilizing experimental and control groups of regular students, as well as special needs students. The results reveal improved problem-solving ability, reduced hyperactivity, increased planning activity, reduced self-reported conduct problems, less peer aggression, and reduced teacher reports of conduct problems (Greenberg and Kusche, 1996, 1997; Greenberg et al., 1995). Greenberg and Kusche (1998) suggest that PATHS can be adopted for use with different populations and for implementation outside the school setting.

A second developmental training program in this venue is the FRIENDS program. FRIENDS is a cognitive therapy intervention targeting anxiety and stress in youths (FRIENDS, 2015). The focus on stress is due to its relation to school failure and academic problems, as well as later substance abuse and unemployment. The program has several age-graded versions that give training primarily in schools over 10 class sessions. FRIENDS stands for:

F   Feelings
R   Relax and feel good
I   I can do it
E   Explore solutions
N   Now reward yourself
D   Do it every day
S   Stay calm

These sessions focus on emotional resilience, problem solving, and self-confidence (FRIENDS, 2015). The program has been the subject of numerous evaluations in a variety of countries, including Australia, the United Kingdom, the United States, and others, and has been identified by the World Health Organization (2004) as an effective program. Results generally show significant reductions in anxiety and increases in self-esteem (Dadds et al., 1997; Lowrey-Webster et al., 2001; Rodgers and Dunsmuir, 2015; Stallard et al., 2005). The long-term impact of FRIENDS on crime and deviance has not been evaluated. At the same time, Maggin and Johnson (2014), in a meta-analysis, note that methodological problems in evaluations raise some qualifications about the program.

ON THE WEB

Visit the FRIENDS programs web site to see the variations in the program for different age groups, available resources, and other materials at http://friendsprograms.com/

Parent Training

Concern over the preparation and ability of parents to provide an appropriate environment for children is a major thrust in developmental prevention. These programs range from those targeting expectant mothers to those working with families of young children to those addressing families with school age children. Three recognized programs are examined below. These are the Elmira Prenatal/Early Infancy Project, the Syracuse Family Development program, and the Incredible Years project.

The **Elmira Prenatal/Early Infancy Project** targets the earliest stage of a child's development, specifically when the child is still in the womb. The center piece of the program is home visitation by nurses beginning during pregnancy and lasting through the child's second birthday (Olds et al., 1997, 1998). The target subjects are young, poor, first-time, and often unmarried mothers. Mothers were visited an average of nine times during pregnancy and 23 times after birth (Olds et al., 1998). The visiting nurses focus on three areas: health and health-related activities of the mother and child; learning how to provide appropriate care to the child; and social and personal skills development for the mothers. In addition, the nurses provide referrals and access to other assistance and the project provides transportation for the mothers to access assistance (Olds et al., 1997). Evaluation of the program revealed a number of positive outcomes. First, maternal abuse and neglect were significantly reduced. Second, in a 15-year follow-up, the children reported significantly less running away, arrests, and substance abuse. Third, there were also fewer arrests of the program mothers (Olds et al., 1997, 1998). The success of the project has led to its replication in other sites.

The **Syracuse Family Development Research Program** has many similar characteristics to the nurse home visitation program. Begun in 1969, the intervention targeted pregnant, young, single, African-American mothers and worked with the families from birth to age eight. The project included home visitation by child development trainers; parent training in health, nutrition, and child rearing; and individualized day care for the children (Lally et al., 1988). The key element of the project was weekly visits to the subjects' homes. Similar to the evaluations of the Elmira project, this program has proven to be effective. Children from the project have done better academically, demonstrate better self-control, and have fewer arrests than control youths (Honig et al., 1982; Lally et al., 1987, 1988).

Another program targeting parental training that has proven effective is the **Incredible Years program**. Whereas the first two programs discussed in this section selected expectant mothers, the Incredible Years initially identified families for intervention that had youths displaying early conduct problems from age four to eight (Webster-Stratton and Hammond, 1997). The current program works with families of youths from age two to age 12 (Incredible Years, 2012). The program includes strong parent and child training components, as well as a teaching training element for youths in school. Parents receive training in parenting skills, how to recognize and address their child's problem behaviors, how to set rules and use incentives, and other key components of child rearing. The child component focuses on helping them recognize emotions, how to deal with anger, appropriate responses to problem situations, and educational skills. The teacher training element deals with classroom management, providing skills to youths, handling problem youths and behaviors, and disciplinary practices (Incredible Years, 2012).

The Incredible Years program was established in 1987 and has since been implemented in hundreds of sites in throughout the United States and other countries (SAMHSA, 2012). Evaluations have examined the impact of the program on parental training methods, interaction between youths, child behavior problems, and antisocial

> ┌ **ON THE WEB**
> *A great deal of additional information on the Incredible Years program is available on the web, including specific program activities for parents, children, and teachers. Take a look at this material and see if you can find elements of the program in what you remember from school. http://www. incredibleyears.com/program/parent.asp*

behavior. These evaluations reveal consistent positive results. Participating parents display more positive parenting skills and less coercive and punitive punishments. Children display fewer antisocial behaviors, better interpersonal skills, and better preparation for school (SAMHSA, 2012; Webster-Stratton, 2001; Webster-Stratton and Hammond, 1997). The strength of the program, its wide adoption, and its consistent positive evaluations have led Substance Abuse and Mental Health Services Administration to list the Incredible Years on its National Registry of Evidence-based Programs and Practices.

Interest in and the growth of parent/child training interventions in recent years has prompted researchers to take a look at these programs as a group. In an attempt to summarize the state of the evidence on parent-child training programs, Piquero et al. (2009) conducted a meta-analysis of 55 studies that focused on disruptive behavior by the children. Based on data from self-reports of parents and teachers and some observational data, the authors found that these programs have a significant impact on youthful antisocial behavior and delinquency (Piquero et al., 2009).

Preschool Programs

One suggestion for addressing anti-social behavior involves early preparation of children for school. Preschool programs are viewed as a means of establishing a level of competence that avoids early placement into differential ability tracts, building a positive attitude toward school, and providing basic social skills to youths who are not prepared to enter school. The advent of preschool as a technique in fighting school problems and delinquency can be found in the 1967 President's Commission on Law Enforcement and the Administration of Justice. The expectation is that success in school will translate later to greater social success out of school and lower delinquency and criminality.

Perhaps the best-known preschool program is the Head Start program. **Head Start** proposes that disadvantaged youths are not prepared to enter school without some form of early intervention targeted at social and intellectual skills (Gottfredson, 1987). Advocates of preschool programs point out that early school failure typically persists into the later years (Schweinhart and Weikart, 1989). Head Start is meant to provide youths with positive early experiences and, in turn, successful long-term academic careers. The extent to which Head Start has succeeded in achieving its goals is questionable. Gottfredson (1987) notes that the program is typically not well-implemented and that any gains made in the program fade over a year or two. Head Start has not been evaluated in terms of its effect on later delinquency or criminality.

The most extensively studied preschool program is the **Perry Preschool program**. The program, begun in 1962, seeks to provide students with a positive introduction to education. This is accomplished by involving the children in the planning of activities, a low child–teacher ratio, and enhanced reinforcement of student achievement. Perhaps the most critical feature of the program is the frequent home visits with parents. Berrueta-Clement et al. (1984) claim that the program sets in progress a sequence of events that leads from program participation to higher academic performance to enhanced educational commitment and scholastic achievement to prosocial behavior. Unlike most preschool programs, the Perry program includes an evaluation component consisting of randomly assigning youths to either the program or a non-preschool control group. All study subjects are from low-income black families, typified by low parental education, unemployment, and single-parent households. All children were tracked throughout school and were periodically surveyed through age 19, with follow-up evaluations undertaken through age 40 (see Berrueta-Clement et al., 1984, for a more thorough discussion of the program methodology).

Evaluation of the Perry Preschool program presents some impressive claims. The program appears to significantly increase measures of academic performance, reduce the need for special education and remedial work, prompt more positive attitudes toward school, enhance the high school graduation rate, and result in lower unemployment after graduation from high school (Berrueta-Clement et al., 1984). The program also claims that fewer experimental students are arrested as either adults or juveniles than are control students. Schweinhart (1987) points out that the experimental group reports fewer serious offenses at both ages 15 and 19. Results through age 27 reveal that about one-half as many program participants are arrested compared to control group subjects. The frequency of their offenses is also about one-fourth of that for control youths (Schweinhart et al., 1993). Schweinhart and Xiang (2003), reporting on data through age 40, find significantly fewer lifetime and adult arrests among experimental subjects, with fewer arrests for violent crimes, property crimes, and drug offenses.

Other preschool projects also report positive effects on experimental subjects. The Consortium for Longitudinal Studies (Lazar et al., 1982) and reviews of various preschool programs (Berrueta-Clement et al., 1984; Gottfredson, 1987) present data showing improved academic performance and less need for special education in the future. Unfortunately, unlike the Perry Preschool program, these studies typically show that the results are short-term and fade within the first two years of elementary school. Most studies also either fail to address the program's impact on delinquency or fail to find any strong positive effects.

Many programs that suggest positive results typically focus on academic achievement rather than delinquency or criminality. The generalizability of the results is also limited due to the heavy study of lower-class, minority youths (Schweinhart and Weikart, 1989). No systematic study has been undertaken on more representative population groups.

Mentoring Programs

The idea of assisting in the development of youths is the cornerstone of mentoring initiatives. **Mentoring** involves pairing adult volunteers with youths in need of friendship, emotional support, guidance, and advice. Youths are typically aged 10 to 16 and from single-parent homes. Matching adults and youths is perhaps the most important part of the programs. The mentors and mentees are expected to meet two to four times per month for three to four hours each time. Both the adult volunteers and the youths undergo initial training that outlines expectations and requirements for the programs (Grossman and Tierney, 1998). Many programs also involve regular contact with the parents. Mentoring programs specifically target academic failure, dropping out of school, truancy, and delinquency, among other things.

Two prime examples of mentoring are **Big Brothers/Big Sisters (BB/BS)** and the **Juvenile Mentoring Program (JUMP)**. Big Brothers/Big Sisters is probably the most recognizable of the many mentoring programs, having begun in 1904 in New York City. It currently boasts 325 programs across all 50 U.S. states and 13 other countries, serving approximately 200,000 children (BB/BS, 2015). The JUMP program was initiated by the Office of Juvenile Justice and Delinquency Prevention (OJJDP) in 1996, which funded 164 programs in 41 states and the District of Columbia within three years of its start. A key component of the JUMP program is its partnership with educators and private-sector agencies (Novotney et al., 2000). In a 1998 reviews, JUMP enrolled almost 7,500 youths (Novotney et al., 2000). Beyond the BB/BS and JUMP programs, there are an estimated 5,000+ mentoring organizations in the United States (DuBois et al., 2011).

┌─ ON THE WEB ─────────────────┐
│ *Visit the BB/BS web site and explore more* │
│ *about the organization at http://www.bbbs.* │
│ *org/site/c.9iILI3NGKhK6F/b.5962335/k.* │
│ *BE16/Home.htm* │
└──────────────────────────────┘

Despite the longevity of BB/BS and mentoring programs, there has been relatively little quality research on them. The existing research, however, presents overwhelming positive results. Grossman and Tierney (1998) present an evaluation of BB/BS programs in eight locations. They use an experimental design with random assignment of roughly 1,000 youths to BB/BS and a non-mentoring control group. They report that mentored youths are 46 percent less likely to start illegal drug use, 27 percent less likely to start alcohol use, and 32 percent less likely to hit other youths. Grossman and Tierney (1998) also uncover positive impacts on academic performance and relationships with parents. There is also evidence of stronger results for minority youths.

Systematic review of the research also paints a positive picture of mentoring. DuBois et al. (2002) conducted a meta-analysis of 55 mentoring studies. The review shows favorable mentoring effects across different demographic groups of youths, especially disadvantaged youths. The greatest impact appears where the mentors and mentees establish strong relationships. The positive effects with disadvantaged mentees is reinforced in results showing mentoring is more effective with high-risk youths (DuBois et al., 2011). Finally, Tolan et al. (2014) report on a meta-analysis of 25 studies that include delinquency as a program outcome. The results reveal reductions in drug use, delinquency, and aggression, as well as improved academic performance. Mentoring has a greater impact on high-risk youths (Tolan et al., 2014).

The evidence on mentoring suggests it is an important developmental prevention approach. Additionally, the number of programs and youths involved demonstrate its level of acceptance in communities. The greatest obstacle in many communities is the inability to recruit enough adult mentors to meet the mentee demand.

Multi-Component Programs

The final group of programs to be considered can be generally listed as multi-component programs. These interventions often begin by targeting youths who have already displayed anti-social behavior and/or delinquency. In that sense it is possible to classify the programs as tertiary prevention since the targets have already exhibited the negative behavior and there is a goal of stemming further offending. At the core of the programs there is a recognition of a need to address the causal factors leading to the deviant behavior and keep the youths from developing more problematic activities. The programs also target youths as early as possible, thus stemming the problems in early adolescence. Multi-component programs also share the common feature of utilizing a range of interventions rather than only one or two approaches. While it is possible to find multiple inputs in the parent training programs discussed earlier, the programs below tend to be even more inclusive of different techniques.

The first program to examine is the **Seattle Social Development Project** started in 1981. The primary setting for the program is classrooms, although there is a strong home/family component to the project. The project was initiated to study social development of school-aged children and to identify the risk and protective factors for delinquency, substance abuse, and academic failure (Hawkins et al., 2007; Social Development Research Group (SDRG), 2012). The actual intervention can be divided into three parts targeting teachers, parents, and students. The teacher component involves training in appropriate classroom management techniques, establishment of rules and consequences, teaching positive social skills, and motivating students. Parents are trained to recognize problematic behavior, reward positive behavior, promote academic success, and build a strong family bond to help avoid antisocial activities. Finally, children learn to recognize and cope with peer pressure, build communication skills, appropriately respond to aggression by others, and avoid problematic situations and people (Hill et al., 2011; Hawkins et al., 2007; SDRG, 2012).

The Seattle project has been the subject of continuing evaluation since the late 1980s. Program participants (parents and children) have been interviewed on a regular basis to assess the impact of the project. The most recent data have been collected on the original youth cohort, at age 33 (SDRG, 2012). The results of the project have been overwhelmingly positive. Results indicate that youths who completed the program were more successful in school, had a higher graduation rate, committed

> **ON THE WEB**
>
> *The Seattle Social Development Research project has a long history and a great deal of research behind it. You can find much more information on the project at http://ssdp-tip.org/SSDP/index.html*

fewer delinquent and criminal offenses, and had lower levels of substance abuse (Hawkins et al., 2007). They also were less sexually promiscuous, and the females had a lower incidence of teenage pregnancy (Lonczak et al., 2002). Overall, the project was successful at identifying early risk factors, developing training and interventions to address those factors and build protective factors, and had a positive impact on youthful behavior.

A second program to consider is the **Families and Schools Together (FAST)** program. FAST is a developmental prevention program aimed at families of youths aged roughly four to eight (FAST, 2015). The program focuses on addressing risks of educational failure, substance abuse, violence, and delinquency. The program relies on parents, schools, teachers, the community, and professionals to build family bonds and target risk and protective factors. This involves multi-family groups that meet at the close of school days every week for eight weeks. Follow-up meetings occur monthly for two years afterward (Coote, 2000). The meetings include structured group activities and individual family interaction. A basic core curriculum comprises roughly 40 percent of the meetings, while the balance varies according to the needs of the groups (McDonald et al., 2012). Among the immediate goals is enhancing family functioning, building social cohesion, reducing social isolation, and generating social support among families (Coote, 2000; McDonald et al., 2012). FAST has been implemented in multiple countries, often targeting minority and disadvantaged groups.

Evaluations provide promising support for FAST. According to McDonald and Sayger (1999), parents report 32 percent lower child behavior scores than parents not involved in FAST, 30 percent lower attention problems, and 31 percent lower child anxiety. Similarly, teachers report 35 percent fewer conduct disorders, 42 percent fewer attention problems, and 24 percent less anxiety. Research also shows reductions in family conflicts, greater family cohesion, reduced aggression, and fewer in-school referrals to special education programs (Coote, 2000; Gamoran et al., 2012; Kratochwill et al., 2009; McDonald and Sayger, 1999). Differences emerge in evaluations based on different ethnic groups. Nevertheless, FAST is a promising developmental prevention program.

Finally, one of the most ambitious multi-component developmental prevention approaches is **Communities that Care (CTC)**. Compared to other programs, CTC is unique in that there is no single intervention or set of programs for addressing problems. Instead, the approach requires communities to undertake an analysis of the problems it is facing, identify the risk factors that are at work, and build an intervention that is tailored to the unique situation and needs of the community (Hawkins et al., 2008). Implementing the CTC model is a complicated task that requires the involvement of many individuals. The process of developing interventions has multiple stages (see Table 8.2). What is evident in the implementation plan is the need to

ON THE WEB

Communities that Care has been implemented in a number of different sites. An excellent discussion of the program and the efforts needed to implement the approach can be found at http://www.jrf.org. uk/sites/files/jrf/1859351840.pdf

TABLE 8.2 **Implementation of Communities that Care**

Phase 1	Community readiness	• Define the community • Assess community willingness to embark on CTC process • Identify possible participants
Phase 2	Organization and training	• Invite wide range of community participants • Form subgroups and committees on key topics • Educate participants in risk assessment and prevention
Phase 3	Assessment	• Undertake risk assessment • Include entire community • Compile list of available resources and needs in community
Phase 4	Development of comprehensive plan	• Create comprehensive plan • Define outcomes • Identify programs to implement • Develop evaluation plan • Implement programs
Phase 5	Implementation and evaluation	• Implement plan • Evaluate impact • Assess program operations • Identify needed modifications • Implement changes

Source: Constructed by author from J.D. Hawkins (1999). "Preventing crime and violence through Communities that Care." *European Journal on Criminal Policy and Research* 7: 443–458.

build a unique set of interventions from the ground up. A cornerstone of CTC is a social development strategy that focuses on identifying appropriate opportunities, teaching skills for success, building bonds between children and adults, and giving recognition for effort, improvement, and achievement (CTC, 2015). All of this means identifying risk factors and engendering protective factors.

Communities that Care has been implemented in many places both in the United States and abroad. There are a couple of things to note about the CTC process. First, it is looking to address multiple groups of risk factors, including family, school, community, and individual risk factors that need to be addressed (Flynn, 2008; Tilley, 2009). Second, a CTC project is a long-term endeavor. Changes in community-level risk factors will take anywhere from two to five years to emerge, and community-level changes in delinquency and substance abuse may take up to five to 10 years to appear (Blueprints for Healthy Youth Development, 2015). What this means is that patience and perseverance are necessary.

Evaluations of CTC uncover positive results. An early evaluation of CTC in 24 communities across seven states notes that CTC significantly reduces risk factors for 14- to 17-year-olds. Follow-up analyses through the twelfth grade reveal additional positive results on key outcome measures. Results from a randomized control group study of 4,407 students find that 32 percent of CTC youths are more likely to abstain from drug use, 31 percent are more likely to abstain from alcohol use, 18 percent are more likely to never commit a delinquent act, and 14 percent are less likely to commit a violent act (Hawkins et al., 2014). Oesterle et al. (2014) report that CTC appears to have slightly greater impact on male youths. Similar positive results are evident in an evaluation of CTC programs related to 41 school districts. CTC was able to reduce risk factors and lower delinquency and substance use among students in CTC schools (Feinberg et al., 2007). The results of these and other evaluations have led to CTC being classified as "promising" by both Blueprints and Crime Solutions.

Summary

This brief review of developmental prevention programs reveals primarily positive outcomes from the interventions. The programs range from those addressing prenatal issues to community-wide risk factors, and the positive results appear in evaluations conducted across many places. Some of the programs have defined interventions (such as in the Incredible Years program) while others (such as CTC) require extensive planning for tailor-made programming. In several cases the programs have been promoted by different organizations and governmental agencies as "blueprints" for prevention programming. It is important to note, however, there are many attempts at developmental prevention programming that are not as successful as those listed above, and not all attempts to implement the above programs bring about the same positive outcomes.

Developmental Concerns

The positive developmental prevention results do not mean there is universal acceptance of the developmental crime prevention approach. Indeed, several concerns can be noted with developmental prevention. Perhaps the first set of concerns revolves around the ability to adequately identify early risk factors that can be subjected to change. Despite the long list of risk factors that have been uncovered in past research, there remain issues with whether much can be done with them. As noted earlier, many of the risk factors, such as sex and race, are really not amenable to change. Others, like criminality of parents or community deprivation, require interventions where change may not be feasible, especially in any reasonable period of time.

A related concern with identifying risk factors is determining which ones need to be addressed and which are of secondary concern. In other words, what is the risk factor? Is there a combination of factors that require attention? What risk factors can be ignored? Unfortunately, there is no simple answer to these questions. It is evident that some developmental interventions have been effective when targeting specific risk factors. At the same time, those types of interventions have failed in other settings when targeting the same risk factors. It is unclear why this is the case. Perhaps the CTC approach of undertaking intensive study of the immediate situation is the most appropriate way of selecting risk factors for intervention.

Another issue for developmental prevention is that it does not clearly fit into primary prevention. Developmental programs that target an entire classroom or community for intervention clearly fit within primary prevention. Programs that address only those individuals or situations that are at high risk fit better in secondary prevention. Many developmental programs seek to intervene once individuals have broken the law and target reoffending. There is ample evidence that developmental pathways both emerge and change in later life. Individuals face new circumstances and opportunities over time that lead them to transition from one path to another throughout their lives (see, for example, the work of Sampson and Laub, 1993). Programs that address these changes are tertiary prevention. While the examples presented in this chapter are mainly primary in nature (and some lean into secondary), there are many developmental prevention interventions that are tertiary.

Developmental prevention programs also face several operational concerns. These programs typically need a relatively long time to have an impact. This is easy to understand since they are targeting risk factors that are not amenable to immediate change. An examination of the programs presented earlier shows that programs often require two to five years before an impact can be found, and even then they require longer time to make the changes permanent. While it is possible to dismiss this delay as inconsequential if the intervention makes real long-lasting changes to the individual, family, schools, or community, the ability to sustain such programming is not easy. Long-term programs require a great deal of funding that is often hard to sustain. A related problem is gaining the support of key participants for a lengthy intervention. Many individuals and groups (particularly funding agencies and politicians) ask for results in the short term (if not immediately) that are simply not possible when making basic changes under the developmental model. Consequently, implementing and sustaining a developmental approach is not easy. Communities facing crime and disorder are more prone to turn to interventions that have the potential for immediate results.

Summary

This brief discussion of developmental crime prevention offers a divergent view of how society should address crime from that found in most other discussions thus far in this book. What should also be evident is that many elements of developmental prevention emerge from more traditional criminological discussions of the causes and responses to antisocial behavior. The focus on risk factors and variables that may be deeply rooted in the family and community means that the interventions must be more involved and they will need a longer time to have an impact. The examples provided in this chapter demonstrate these facts very clearly. The long-term commitment required by developmental prevention, along with the typically large time gap between program initiation and outcome, is a tough sell for many who want something to be done now. Compared to developmental prevention programs, many of the other primary and secondary crime prevention initiatives covered in this book can make more timely changes. The potential advantage of developmental crime prevention is the hope that the solutions are more lasting since they attempt to address the root causes of crime and delinquency.

KEY TERMS

- Big Brothers/Big Sisters (BB/BS)
- Communities that Care (CTC)
- developmental crime prevention
- elaboration model
- Elmira Prenatal/Early Infancy Project
- Families and Schools Together (FAST)
- general theory of crime
- Head Start
- Incredible Years program
- Integrated Cognitive Antisocial Potential (ICAP) theory
- Juvenile Mentoring Program (JUMP)
- mentoring
- Perry Preschool program
- positivism
- Promoting Alternative Thinking Strategies (PATHS)
- Seattle Social Development Project
- Syracuse Family Development Research Program

CHAPTER 9 General Deterrence

CHAPTER OUTLINE

LEARNING OBJECTIVES

After reading this chapter you should be able to:

- Define deterrence.
- Identify and define the two types of deterrence.
- List and define the requirements for a deterrent effect.
- Discuss the findings of cross-sectional analyses of deterrence.
- Relate the results of longitudinal investigations of deterrence.
- Explain the brutalization effect of the death penalty.
- Demonstrate your knowledge of panel designs and results of research using them.
- Discuss the problems with making claims that executions reduce the homicide rate.
- Discuss the research on perceptions and deterrence.
- Define and discuss what is meant by the experiential effect.
- Provide a summary on the ability to deter people from committing crime.

Any discussion of primary prevention would not be complete without a look at the deterrent effects of punishment. Recall that primary prevention attempts to eliminate or reduce the level of deviant behavior prior to its occurrence. The bulk of the discussion so far has focused on the crime prevention activities of the general public. Most people today believe that official agencies of social control are, or should be, responsible for eliminating crime. Indeed, the actions of criminal justice agencies are aimed at the elimination of crime through deterrence.

One of the leading writers on the subject defines **deterrence** as "influencing by fear" (Andenaes, 1975). According to this writer, potential offenders decide to refrain from committing criminal acts due to a fear of apprehension and punishment. The likelihood of deterrence increases as the risk of punishment increases. An actual experience of punishment does not have to occur before an individual can be deterred. Instead, Andenaes (1975) assumes that the threat of punishment would be enough if the proper circumstances exist. The idea of "threat" and interest in diverting initial or future activity prompts Andenaes to refer to deterrence as "general prevention." It is prevention of the potential offense by use of fear. Deterrence is a major form of crime prevention and has served as a cornerstone of criminal justice. To ignore deterrence in a discussion of crime prevention would indicate a lack of understanding of the role of deterrence. On the other hand, deterrence has forged a place of its own in criminology. It is not necessary, therefore, to devote a large space to deterrence in this text. This chapter will present the underlying ideas of deterrence and briefly examine the research on one type of deterrence—general deterrence. More in-depth discussions of deterrence will be left for other writers.

Deterrence

Deterrence can be broken down into two distinct types—general and specific. **General deterrence** aims to have an impact on more than the single offender. The apprehension and punishment of one person hopefully serves as an example to other offenders and potential law violators. In this instance, the incarceration of a single burglar should deter other individuals from committing burglary. General deterrence fits primary prevention because of its focus on preventing an act before it occurs. It looks at the effect of punishing one individual on the future behavior of other persons. This means changing the behavior of societal members prior to their commission of criminal acts. General deterrence clearly fits the criteria of prevention before initial criminal action.

Specific deterrence refers to efforts that keep the individual offender from violating the law again in the future. The hope is that the experience of punishment will deter the individual who has been punished from future illegal activity. The offender who is incarcerated for burglary is expected to be deterred by the experience from committing any further acts of burglary once he is released from the institution. The punishment is

TABLE 9.1 **Types of Deterrence**	
General deterrence	Punishing offenders as an example to others with the express intent of having an impact on others who may contemplate breaking the law; others will not offend in order to avoid punishment
Specific deterrence	Focuses on the activity of an individual who has already violated the law and seeks to prevent such an individual from committing future criminal acts

not expected to affect anyone other than the targeted individual. Specific deterrence fits into tertiary prevention due to its focus on the activity of an individual who has already violated the law and seeking to prevent the individual from recidivating and committing future criminal acts. Specific deterrence (and the related issue of incapacitation) are taken up in Chapter 15.

Both types of deterrence assume a rational offender. Any deterrent effect rests upon the ability of an offender to make choices of whether or not to violate society's behavioral standards. Accordingly, the inability to make rational decisions would mitigate any effect of deterrence. Rationality also assumes that potential offenders are **hedonistic** (i.e., man seeks pleasure and avoids pain). Punishment is assumed to be painful to the individual and the outcome of criminal activity represents the pleasure component. Deterrence seeks to offset any pleasure received in the crime by introducing an equal or slightly higher level of pain. Such an action should result in an elimination of further law violation. General deterrence, resting heavily on the assumption of a rational individual, suggests that the pain experienced by one person will be seen as potential pain by persons contemplating a similar act.

Requirements for Deterrence

The deterrent effect of punishment relies on the existence of three factors. These are the severity, certainty, and celerity of the punishment. **Severity** involves making certain that punishments provide enough pain to offset the pleasure received from the criminal act. The basic assumption is that the individual chooses behavior after weighing the benefits of the crime against the potential costs incurred if he is caught. Crime is the result of an analysis that presents more pleasure from the illegal activity than pain. Severity seeks to eliminate the positive, pleasurable outcome of the activity and replace it with negative, unwanted pain.

Certainty deals with the chances of being caught and punished for one's behavior. The imposition of pain necessitates the identification, apprehension, conviction, and sentencing of the offender. For general deterrence, the absence of enforcement of a law suggests to other potential offenders that the system either does not care about the questionable behavior or that the system is incapable of imposing its will and the punishment.

The third component is celerity. **Celerity** refers to the swiftness of the societal response. The assumption underlying celerity is that a punishment that is temporally far removed from the action will not have the same impact as a punishment occurring soon after the action. The ability of the individual to equate delayed punishment (pain) with the earlier offense (pleasure) is greatly diminished over time. For example, a child who disobeys his mother at 10:00 a.m. and is told "Wait until your father gets home" will most likely fail to equate the discipline imposed by the father at 5:00 p.m. with the behavior occurring seven hours earlier. The time frame for adults might be greatly expanded beyond a single day or week, but the principle remains the same. The pleasure received from the deviant act has long since dissipated when the pain is applied long after the activity. The more closely the pain follows the pleasure, the greater the chance that the individual will equate the two events.

Deterrence relies on the existence of all three of these components. The absence of any one can seriously impede the deterrent effect of the punishment. Despite the close interrelationship between these factors, most research on deterrence has focused on only one factor at a time. The other two are taken as a given or ignored entirely. Research almost totally ignores celerity (perhaps because of the legal requirements placed on case scheduling) and deals mainly with severity and certainty. The following discussion of deterrence research is organized along two dimensions. The first part deals with studies of the deterrent effect of the law. Studies on the death penalty dominate this discussion due to its traditional place in deterrence research. Studies in this section will be further broken down into cross-sectional and longitudinal analyses. The second approach looks at studies based on the perceptual nature of deterrence. That is, what do individuals perceive about the possibilities for apprehension and punishment? Various researchers believe that the failure of deterrence is due to the lack of knowledge or misperceptions about the deterrent aspects of the law.

The Deterrent Effect of Legal Sanctions

Studies on deterrence take a variety of different forms. **Cross-sectional studies** compare differences between different individuals, groups, states, or other aggregate. **Longitudinal analyses** look for changes over time, primarily due to shifts in law or criminal justice system activity. **Panel designs** follow separate units (such as states or counties) over time. In many respects they are a combination of longitudinal and cross-sectional approaches. Finally, **meta-analysis** examines existing research by reanalyzing the data from numerous studies using a common measure to uncover results.

Cross-Sectional Analyses

One important source of deterrence research focuses on the impact of the death penalty across jurisdictions. The underlying assumption in this research is the belief that, given the severity of the penalty, the death sentence should have a great deterrent effect. While death penalty studies are well known, these studies deal only with an extreme form of punishment and generally ignore the issues of certainty and celerity. Consequently, it is important to look at a variety of punishments and actions.

Severity of Sanctions

Most cross-sectional studies of sentence severity focus on the death penalty. These studies examine the differences in homicide between states that have and those that do not have the death penalty. Homicide is typically the focus. The assumption is that, if the death penalty has a deterrent effect, the state with the penalty will have lower homicide rates.

In an early influential study, Ehrlich (1977), an economist, claimed a strong connection between the penalty and lower homicide rates. Comparing death penalty to non-death penalty states, Ehrlich reported that more than 20 homicides are deterred for every execution. The author noted that, not only does the death penalty deter, the length of imprisonment also lowers the homicide rate (Ehrlich, 1977).

The work of Ehrlich has been severely criticized on methodological grounds. Simply designating states as death penalty and non-death penalty does not reveal whether there are unknown differences other than the penalty between the states (McGahey, 1980). States are certainly not similar on all counts just because they do or do not use the death penalty. Other unknown factors may be the cause of the difference in homicide rates instead of the assumed effect of the death penalty. Another related criticism of cross-sectional studies (in general) is the use of states as the level of analysis. States are not necessarily homogeneous within themselves. That is, there may be a great deal of diversity within the state. In addition, jurisdictional boundaries of states do not totally eliminate the possible diffusion effect of the death penalty. Persons residing in one state may be influenced by the use or existence of the death sentence in a neighboring state. Clearly, the populace may not know about the law or may be affected by an execution regardless of where the penalty is imposed.

Archer et al. (1983) examine the deterrent effect of the death penalty across nations to minimize the likelihood of vicarious deterrence from one place to another. The authors look at "de jure," or the existence of death penalty statutes, instead of "de facto" death penalties, which refer to the actual use of the sentence. Archer et al. (1983) find the existence of the death penalty is related to lower homicide rates in some countries and higher levels of homicide in other countries. A major problem with this study is its failure to consider other confounding influences on the homicide rates. The inconsistent results may be due to other differences between the nations and not to a varying impact of death penalty laws. Another problem may involve the focus on severity to the exclusion of the other deterrent factors. The simple existence of a law says nothing about the actual use, or certainty, of that law being applied.

Certainty of Punishment

Studies examining the effect of certainty of punishment typically do not address the death penalty. Tittle and Rowe (1974), for example, look at the certainty of arrest and its effect on the overall crime rate. Using data for Florida, the authors note that certainty of arrest has no effect when the probability of arrest (the arrest rate) is very low. Certainty only plays a part when the arrest rate reaches and exceeds 30 percent. Geerken and Gove (1977) look at the certainty of arrest for other offenses. Property offenses, which have a higher likelihood of being planned and therefore should be deterred, are negatively related to the arrest rate. There is almost no relationship between more spontaneous personal crimes and arrest. Forst (1977) reports that states with higher conviction rates have lower levels of homicide. The relationship is confounded, however, by the influence of other variables such as the racial and economic make-up of the states. Finally, Yu and Liska (1993) report that arrest certainty is strongly related to deterrence, but the impact is race specific. That is, the black and white crime rates are related to the black and white arrest rates, respectively, and the relationship is stronger for blacks. These studies appear to show that while there is a connection between the certainty of arrest and punishment and lower crime rates, the nature of the relationship is not totally clear.

Combining Severity and Certainty

Various studies have combined the analysis of severity and certainty. Gibbs (1968), based on an analysis of differences between states in the number and length of prison sentences for homicide, reports that the homicide rate is negatively related to severity and certainty of punishment. Tittle (1969), conducting a similar analysis for Part I offenses and including controls for various demographic variables, finds a negative relationship between severity and homicide but not for the other offenses. The remaining Part I crimes are affected only by the certainty of the punishment. Passell (1975) reports finding an effect of both severity and certainty looking at legal and demographic variables for states. He finds that the conviction rate (certainty) and the prison sentence (severity) are both negatively associated with state homicide rates. Finally, Sampson (1986) assesses certainty through local arrest rates and severity by the risk of jail and imprisonment in 171 U.S. cities. Controlling for various demographic factors, both certainty and severity have an impact on robbery but have little effect on homicide (Sampson, 1986).

Summary

While not in full agreement, research has uncovered statistically significant impact of severity and certainty in the cross-sectional deterrence research. Logan (1972), however, suggests that the factors of severity and certainty act against one another. He notes that increases in the severity of punishment may lead criminal justice personnel to be more selective in who they subject to the punishment. Likewise, an increase in certainty could result in alteration of the charges or public outcries for changes in the law. Either way, certainty and severity are modified to accommodate alterations in the other factor.

Longitudinal Research

A common approach in deterrence research entails longitudinal analysis, which looks for a change in the outcome variable as a result of introducing a change in some condition. One example of this is the examination of homicide rates prior to and after the imposition of the death penalty. The advantages of the longitudinal approach are many. First, the same jurisdiction is being considered at both points in time, thereby negating the problem faced in cross-sectional studies of biased results due to differences between the areas under study. Second, with a single jurisdiction the researcher is able to isolate both the point in time that the intervention occurs and when changes in the dependent variable occur. A third advantage of longitudinal analysis is that the observer can see when the changes occur, evaluate the time lag between the intervention and the change, and examine whether the effect is short or long term. That is, do the changes in the dependent variable diminish over time and return to the pre-intervention level? These advantages, among others, make longitudinal analysis the preferred technique.

Severity of Sanctions

Ehrlich (1975), examining the relationship between homicide and probabilities of apprehension, conviction, and execution, claims that each execution deters seven to eight homicides. He argues that this result persists when controlling for a number of demographic variables, including age of the population and socioeconomic indicators. Ehrlich's results became the rallying cry for those in favor of the death penalty. It was also used as the basis of arguments in favor of the death penalty in front of the U.S. Supreme Court.

The results of this study came under immediate fire. Critics point to the choice of data and operationalization of the variables as problematic issues in Ehrlich's study. Passell and Taylor (1977) report that Ehrlich's deterrent finding holds true only for the years 1963 to 1969. Examination of 1933 to 1962 shows no significant deterrent effect. The inclusion of the 1960s is an important point of contention. It was during this time that the homicide rate was increasing, while use of the death penalty was decreasing or being removed from statutes. As a result, the finding of a deterrent relationship was inevitable. Passell and Taylor (1977) and Bowers and Pierce (1975) also demonstrate that altering the methodological technique eliminates much of the significance in Ehrlich's results.

The deterrent effect of the death penalty has received much subsequent attention. D.P. Phillips (1980), comparing the weeks immediately prior to executions to subsequent weeks, finds that the imposition of the death penalty results in a short-term reduction in homicide. The saving in life, however, is eliminated by an increase in homicides over time (D.P. Phillips, 1980). The executions appear to delay, instead of eliminate, homicide. Land et al. (2009, 2012) consider the effect of executions on homicide in Texas from 1994 to 2007. Texas was chosen due to its frequent use of executions. The authors find a small but significant reduction in homicide in the month after an execution. A small rebound in homicides occurs in subsequent months (Land et al., 2012).

Not all analyses report a deterrent effect for executions. Sorenson et al. (1999), examining the impact of executions over a 14-year period in Texas, report that monthly homicide rates are unrelated to the number of executions. Instead, various demographic measures are better predictors of the homicide rate (Sorenson et al., 1999). Katz et al. (2003), examining annual state-level data from 1950 to 1990, report that the death penalty has little, if any, impact on homicide rates. One strong explanation for the lack of a deterrent effect is the small number of executions that take place relative to the number of people convicted and those sentenced to death. There is also a great deal of variation over time in homicide rates, making it difficult to impart any changes in homicide to the rare executions (Donohue and Wolfers, 2005; Katz et al., 2003). Donohue and Wolfers (2005) note that the uncertainty of executions makes it difficult to assume that the death penalty would have much of an impact. With rare exceptions, the studies looking exclusively at the severity of the sanction fail to find a deterrent impact in the death penalty.

An alternative possible impact of executions is an increase in subsequent offending. Bowers and Pierce (1980) claim that there are two more homicides in the month immediately following an execution and one more in the second month after an execution than would be normally expected. It appears that the use of the death penalty causes an absolute increase of three homicides after the execution. They refer to this as the **brutalization effect** of the death penalty (Bowers and Pierce, 1980). Other researchers (Bailey, 1998; Cochran et al., 1994; Cochran and Chamlin, 2000) also report a brutalization effect as a result of executions.

Longitudinal studies of deterrence have not been confined to the death penalty. Ross (1982), reviewing the effects of drunk driving laws in different countries, finds increases in the severity of sanctions for drunk driving appear to have little, if any, impact on the level of drunk driving. West et al. (1989) analyzed changes in Arizona's drunk-driving laws in July 1982, mandating a 24-hour jail sentence, license suspension, and a minimum $250 fine for a first drunk-driving offense. Using monthly statistics from 1976 to 1984, West et al. (1989) note that there was a temporary decrease in fatalities and no impact on DWI citations. More importantly, the minor observed changes that did occur appear to be due to media coverage and not the legislated changes.

Studies on the impact of **three-strikes laws** also show qualified deterrent effects. These laws provide for lengthy prison terms for those who commit a third strikeable offense. Zimring et al. (2001) claim that the California three-strikes law was able to reduce felony offenses by roughly 2 percent, although it only impacted offenders with fewer than two strikes already. Helland and Tabarrok (2007) uncover a much greater impact. They report that arrests of offenders with two prior arrests fell by 20 percent after passage of the law. It is apparent that the increased punishment has a deterrent impact.

Certainty of Apprehension

Certainty of apprehension and punishment can be studied in a variety of ways. One method involves altering the law. For example, the British Road Safety Act established that a blood alcohol level above .08 percent constitutes an offense (Ross, 1982). There is no question of the guilt of an individual meeting this criteria. Ross (1982) reports that most alterations in the definition of legal drunkenness result in reduced levels of traffic casualties. The effect is short-lived, however, with the numbers of accidents returning to the pre-intervention levels. Phillips et al. (1984), reexamining the impact of the British Road Safety Act, find that the law has minimal impact on the number of traffic casualties. The number of miles driven and the incidence of rainfall are better explanatory variables. Interestingly, attempts to further increase the certainty of apprehension through the use of intensive police "blitzes" appear to have a positive deterrent effect (Ross, 1982). This holds true at least for the duration of the blitz.

The activity of the police may also provide a deterrent effect particularly as a result of police crackdowns on crime hot spots. Sherman and Weisburd (1995), reporting on intensive patrol at crime hot spots, find that patrol has a significant deterrent effect on calls for service and crime/disorder. Efforts to interrupt gang violence in Boston through intensive police and criminal justice system intervention also resulted in reduced offending (Kennedy, 2008). Cohen and Ludwig (2003) point out that redirecting police to areas experiencing high gang violence in Pittsburgh effectively reduced firearm assaults and reports of shots fired. In a recent review of problem-oriented policing projects, Weisburd et al. (2010) find that eight out of 10 studies show significant declines in area crime. The same type of impact is evident in analyses of police crackdowns in England (Tilley, 2004).

Panel Studies

Several recent analyses have relied on panel data as a means of avoiding problems with both cross-sectional and longitudinal approaches. A panel design follows a number of separate units (such as states, counties, or individuals) over a period of time. In many respects it is a combination of cross-sectional and longitudinal approaches in a single study. Shepherd (2005) notes that both cross-sectional and longitudinal designs suffer from serious problems. Simple longitudinal designs result in aggregating disparate observations into a single group. The results from one state, for example, may be offset by those from another state, thus masking the results from each individual state. Cross-sectional designs cannot account for changes over time and often miss key differences between study units within the same cross-section. Typical longitudinal and cross-sectional studies also have few observations, both across time and in terms of units (e.g., states) (Shepherd, 2005).

Various panel analyses claim strong support for a deterrent effect of the death penalty. Dezhbakhsh et al. (2003) investigate the deterrent effect of capital punishment using county-level data for 1977 to 1996. This data allows them to consider economic, demographic, and jurisdictional variations across the counties. Using a complex statistical model, the authors claim that each execution deters 18 homicides (Dezhbakhsh et al., 2003). Shepherd (2004) conducts a similar analysis using state-level panel data and considers both sentences to death row and actual executions as potential deterrents. The author claims that each death row sentence deters 4.5 murders, while each execution results in three fewer homicides. Shepherd (2004) also notes that death sentences that are carried out with greater celerity also reduce the number of homicides.

Interestingly, Shepherd (2005) uncovers important qualifiers on the deterrent impact of the death penalty. Undertaking a panel analysis using county-level data reports that each execution results in 4.5 fewer murders. The results, however, vary significantly across states. Indeed, the death penalty is a deterrent in six states, while it has a brutalization effect in 13 states. Attempting to identify the reason for this difference between states, Shepherd (2005) considers the number of executions carried out in the different states. She finds that there is a threshold number of executions that must be reached in order for the death penalty to have a deterrent impact. Specifically, her analysis shows that there need to be at least nine executions for capital punishment to be a deterrent to homicide (Shepherd, 2005). States conducting fewer executions will see an increase in homicides (the brutalization effect).

Unfortunately, several methodological concerns with deterrence research claiming a strong impact of the death penalty call the conclusions into question. First, the wide variation in year-to-year homicide rates along with few executions makes it difficult, if not impossible, to detect any impact of the executions (Donohue and Wolfers, 2005). Second, many of the measures of criminal justice system operations included in the analyses are subject to great variation and measurement error (Fagan et al., 2006), thus affecting the overall results (Tonry, 2008). Third, some studies (e.g., Dezhbakhsh et al., 2003) show increases in violent personal offenses (including rape and assault) at the same time that they present questionable changes in homicide (Donohue and Wolfers, 2005).

Finally, Kovandzic et al. (2009) point out that most of the studies claiming a strong deterrent effect of the death penalty focus on an economic model that ignores important social/criminological variables. When these factors are considered, research finds little deterrent impact of the death penalty. Many others (e.g., Kleck et al., 2005; Nagin and Pogarsky, 2004; Piquero and Rengert, 1999) point out that potential and actual violent offenders do not consider the consequences or make fully informed choices when contemplating or undertaking criminal behavior. In this case, an economic approach, which assumes a true cost–benefit analysis place without considering criminological influences, is ill-conceived. The general consensus is that executions have limited, if any, impact on homicide (see, for example, Donohue and Wolfers, 2005; Fagan et al., 2006; Katz et al., 2003; Kovandzic et al., 2009; Pratt et al., 2006).

Meta-Analyses

The conflicting evidence on the deterrent effect of executions and other sanctions has led some researchers to analyze published results in an attempt to provide some meaning to the state of knowledge. Pratt et al. (2006) applied meta-analysis to 40 deterrent studies looking at certainty, severity, and other factors. The authors arrive at several conclusions. First, deterrence measures have only a modest impact, at best, on crime. Perhaps more important is that other factors, especially non-legal factors, are more important. The impact of deterrence also varies across samples, with certainty having a greater impact than severity (Pratt et al., 2006).

Donohue (2009) reviews six studies of the impact of imprisonment on crime. He reports a statistically significant negative relationship between the level of imprisonment and area crime rates. Unfortunately, this result could be attributable to incapacitation, rather than deterrence (Donohue, 2009).

Yang and Lester (2008) examined 95 studies of the deterrent impact of executions. Of particular note, the authors divided the studies into five groups: time series, cross-sectional, panel, single execution, and publicity studies. Results of the meta-analysis show conflicting evidence. The 41 time series studies reveal 28 with a deterrent effect and 12 with a brutalization effect (Yang and Lester, 2008). This corresponds to a significant deterrent effect from combined studies. The panel studies show similar results with a statistically significant deterrent impact. Conversely, the cross-sectional, single execution and publicity studies provide no conclusive results. Yang and Lester (2008), combining all 95 studies, report an overall statistically significant deterrent effect.

Summary

This review points to a few general findings. First and foremost, research presents contradictory results on the deterrent effect of sentences, particularly the death penalty. There is little or no evidence that severity has an individual deterrent effect. Conversely, certainty of apprehension and punishment seems to have some impact on the level of offending. One problem with this latter statement is the fact that many of the studies that look at certainty also are dealing with crimes that have a fairly severe penalty attached. Clearly, increasing the certainty of apprehension and punishment for homicide is accompanied by either the death penalty or substantial lengths of imprisonment. The occurrence of one factor results in the second. Why, then, do studies that look at both severity and certainty only find an effect related to certainty? The answer may revolve around the perceived risk of apprehension and punishment.

Perceptions and Deterrence

The ability of punishment to deter offenders rests upon various assumptions about the knowledge held by potential violators regarding the law and the criminal justice system. The existence of a law or the actual imposition of a sanction will only affect individuals who perceive risks to themselves. Individuals ignorant of the law cannot be expected to refrain from the proscribed behavior simply due to the law's existence. The lack of knowledge about the chances for arrest and the penalty incurred for breaking the law also may result in a lack of deterrence. As noted earlier, deterrence also assumes that offenders consider the consequences of possible actions and make rational choices. While there is evidence that offenders make rational choices, there is also evidence that in interpersonal offenses and many violent crimes, the offenders do not undertake the cost–benefit analysis required for deterrence (Kovandzic et al., 2009).

Studies find that offenders, as well as the general population, often hold varied perceptions of legal codes and changes in the law. In one early study, Andenaes (1975) notes that the general public had little knowledge about penalties for offenses. More recently, Apel (2013) reviewed the empirical research and notes the individuals often have a general knowledge about legal sanctions, and those with experience in the legal system hold better perceptions of offenses and penalties. Of course, just knowing the legal statutes can only give information about possible sanctions. Statutes do not necessarily alter the chances of apprehension or the actual imposition of the maximum penalty possible. Indeed, research demonstrates that the criminal justice system adjusts to accommodate changes in the law through such means as charge and plea bargaining (Tonry, 2008). It is important to examine the role of perception in the study of general deterrence.

Perceived Certainty

The deterrence literature provides conflicting evidence that increased perception of risk is related to reduced deviant behavior. Erickson et al. (1977), surveying 1,700 high school students, find that the level of perceived certainty of arrest or incarceration is inversely related to the level of self-reported delinquency. That is, juveniles who envision higher chances of being arrested or incarcerated for a given offense are less likely to engage in that form of deviant behavior. Nagin (1998), reviewing the deterrence literature, claims that the research shows a clear impact of perceived risk on reduced chances for committing crime.

Other studies find little impact of perceptions. Jensen et al. (1978), studying 5,000 high school students, and Piliavin et al. (1986), examining 17- to 20-year-old dropouts, find little, if any, relationship between perceived certainty of apprehension and self-reported involvement. Indeed, Piliavin et al. (1986) report that the opportunity to commit a crime is more influential than the perception of risk or sanctions. Foglia (1997), testing the influence of perceptions on high school students from low-income, high-crime areas, shows that perceived certainty is not related to self-reported delinquency. The author suggests that the results may be attributable to income and residential status of the respondents.

One of the problems with research on perceived certainty of punishment is the time order of the perception and actual involvement with the criminal justice system. Researchers have questioned whether the perception of apprehension deters crime or whether the actual apprehension of an individual raises the perception of risk (Bishop, 1984a, 1984b; Jensen and Stitt, 1982; Paternoster et al., 1982, 1985; Saltzman et al., 1982). This latter possibility is termed the **experiential effect**. Research by Loughran et al. (2012) suggests that high-risk offenders perceive a lower risk while low-rate offenders have a higher perceived risk. A finding of low perceived risk along with past participation in criminal activity may indicate that the lack of past apprehension engenders the current view of low risk (an experiential effect). The perception comes (causally) after the behavior. There is a need to relate current perceptions to future deviant activity. This then would indicate a deterrent and not an experiential effect.

Bishop (1984a, 1984b) evaluates the impact of perceptions on future behavior (deterrence effect) and the impact of behavior on future perceptions (experiential effect). She finds that high levels of perceived risk of apprehension result in lower levels of future behavior. This supports the deterrence argument. The effect of past delinquent behavior, however, has a larger effect on subsequent perceptions than the perceptions have on the behavior. This means that the experiential effect is greater than the deterrent outcome (Bishop, 1984a). In a study based on self-reports of college freshmen, which also find that the experiential effect is stronger than the deterrent effect, Paternoster et al. (1985) note that inexperienced individuals who initially hold high perceptions of risk modify their perceptions after they begin to partake in the activity without being arrested. The experience with the behavior, devoid of apprehension, changes the perceptions. This is the experiential effect at work. A substantial number of other studies relate perceptions to past experience. Lochner (2007) notes that individuals with criminal experience hold more accurate perceptions of arrest probability and lower perceptions of risk of being arrested. Perceptions of risk of being arrested are strongly tied to prior experience (Carmichael and

Piquero, 2006; Pogarski and Piquero, 2003; Pogarski et al., 2005). Assessments of risk are also related to the experiences of one's acquaintances (Piquero and Pogarski, 2002; Stafford and Warr, 1993). Experiences are not separate from deterrence. Rather, they are a vital part of the deterrent effect (Jacobs, 1996; Paternoster and Piquero, 1995).

Experience is a key component of deterrence. Research reports a moderate deterrent effect from perceived risk of apprehension. The level of certainty of apprehension, however, is diluted by the absence of past apprehension. Although certainty appears to be the most important deterrent factor, based on the research reported earlier in this chapter, perceptions of severity and celerity, as individual factors and in relation to certainty, need to be investigated.

Perceived Severity

The perception of severity of punishment has not received as much attention as certainty of apprehension. In one study, Meier and Johnson (1977) look at self-reports of deviant behavior and reasons given for not offending. Focusing on adult marijuana use, they examine a variety of independent measures including legal variables (e.g., statutory knowledge, perceived severity), social support (i.e., friends' use), attitudes toward drug use, and various demographic factors. They find that as the perceived severity of the sanction increases the level of marijuana use decreases. Severity, along with the combined legal factors hold minimal influence compared to the contribution of social background characteristics and social support factors (Meier and Johnson, 1977). A replication of this study (Williams, 1983) reports the same basic findings, further questioning the importance of severity in deterrence.

Williams and Hawkins (1989) investigate the impact of arrest and perceived consequences of arrest for wife assault. Included in the study are measures of perceived legal sanctions, chances of going to jail, damage to interpersonal attachments, stigma from arrest, and putting conventional activities (such as one's job) at risk. Surveying married and cohabiting U.S. males, the authors report that the perception of stigma and social disapproval are the greatest concerns of the respondents. The possibility of going to jail and being sanctioned by the legal system are less of a deterrent than the social factors (Williams and Hawkins, 1989). Just as with the studies of perceived certainty, these studies may suffer from the competing issues of experiential and deterrent effects.

Combined Deterrence Factors

A few studies attempt to gauge perceptions of certainty, severity, and/or celerity within the same analysis. Hollinger and Clark (1983) find that perceived severity and certainty have a deterrent influence. The level of employee theft diminishes as perceptions of risk increase and the individual sees harsher sanctions as a possible outcome. Pestello

(1984) surveyed high school students about their school misbehavior and the perceptions of each of the deterrent elements as they relate to school discipline. The results show that perceived severity and celerity of punishment increase the fear of consequences for behavior that, in turn, reduces the possibility of misbehavior. This is one of the few studies that reports a significant effect of severity on behavior. Unfortunately, each of these studies suffers from the problem of time order in its analyses. The measures of perception are taken at the same time as the measures of behavior, which raises the possibility of the experiential effect.

Panel studies have attempted to isolate the deterrent effects from the possible confounding influences of experiences. Paternoster (1989a, 1989b), surveying high school students, notes that perceived severity and perceived certainty of punishment have only a minor influence on marijuana use, liquor use, petty theft, and vandalism. Decisions to offend or reoffend are based primarily on extralegal factors such as moral beliefs about the behavior, and peer associations and influences (Paternoster, 1989a). A minor deterrent effect appears only in relationship to perceived certainty of marijuana and liquor use among prior non-offenders (Paternoster, 1989b). Concentrating on drinking and driving behavior, Green (1989a, 1989b) also finds that perceived certainty and perceived severity have little impact. The most important influences on drunk-driving behavior are informal, extralegal factors such as moral commitment, social approval, and demographic differences (Green, 1989a, 1989b). Piquero and Paternoster (1998) similarly find that experience is more influential than deterrence in relation to drinking and driving. These studies add to the argument that perceptions of certainty and severity have little influence on actual behavior.

Klepper and Nagin (1989) provide one of the strongest arguments in favor of perceived certainty and severity as deterrents. The authors report that the perceived probability of detection and prosecution, as well as perceived severity of punishment, are strong deterrents for tax non-compliance. Klepper and Nagin (1989) argue that their findings are unique due to the fact that tax non-compliance is an affirmative action that must be consciously considered. That is, every individual must clearly choose to violate the tax law in light of both costs and incentives for the action. Additionally, they use a very homogeneous sample composed of 163 graduate students in business with a 100 percent response rate and they provide the respondents with very specific scenarios that alter the level of tax non-compliance.

Despite this last study, the overall research on perceptions reports similar findings to the results presented in earlier parts of this chapter. Perceptions of certainty of apprehension appears to hold the most potential for improving the possibility of deterrence. Perceptions of both severity and celerity tend to hold little or no impact in deterring behavior. It appears that experience plays a larger role in determining perceptions than perceptions have on future behavior. Perceptions seem to have some deterrent impact for individuals.

Summary

The deterrence literature fails to find any strong compelling arguments that the law and sanctions have any major impact on the level of offending. The most clear-cut finding seems to indicate that increased certainty of apprehension and punishment results in reduced offending. Severity appears to have little influence on behavior. The failure of severity to have much impact may be due to the lack of knowledge that individuals have about the actual sanctions and the chances of being caught and receiving the punishment. An analysis of the perceptual literature reveals that perceptions are based on past experiences much more than future activities are based on present perceptions. Again, certainty seems to hold the most power.

The finding that certainty of apprehension and punishment is the most important factor suggests that any deterrent effect must rest on efforts by the criminal justice system and society to increase the level of risk. At the same time, changes that increase perceptions of risk, whether through experience, avoidance or something else, also contribute to deterrence. This risk can come from the crime prevention techniques discussed in this book. Failure to increase the risk of apprehension and punishment does not mean that the crime rate will rise. Rather, it indicates that the sanctioning power of the criminal justice system alone is not enough to keep motivated individuals from offending.

KEY TERMS

- brutalization effect
- celerity
- certainty
- cross-sectional studies
- deterrence

- experiential effect
- general deterrence
- hedonistic
- longitudinal analyses
- meta-analysis

- panel designs
- severity
- specific deterrence
- three-strikes laws

PART II

Secondary Prevention

The orientation of secondary prevention focuses activity on individuals, places, and situations that have a high potential for deviance. Secondary prevention is concerned with intervening in those situations and with those persons who display a tendency toward criminal behavior. As in primary prevention, the emphasis is still on preventing crime prior to its initial occurrence. Once a criminal act has occurred, any intervention that takes place falls under the realm of tertiary prevention. Perhaps the core concern for secondary prevention, therefore, is the prediction of future criminal activity.

The problem of making predictions is taken up in Chapter 10. Typically, prediction is assumed to focus on the behavior of individuals. Two major methods for making predictions of future dangerousness are *clinical* and *actuarial*. These approaches generally fail to make adequate judgments and often result in large numbers of false predictions. Besides trying to make accurate predictions, it may be possible to identify risk factors for future behavior. In this case the idea is to uncover factors that are strongly related to later criminality. A third approach is to try to identify locations or situations where deviance is more likely. Consequently the focus shifts from people to places, times, and circumstances. Each of these approaches to prediction is considered.

The remaining chapters look at specific interventions. Chapter 11 focuses on situational crime prevention. Situational prevention techniques target specific problems, places, persons, or times. Problem identification and program planning are cornerstones of the situational approach. The impact of these interventions are more focused than typically found in primary prevention, although many of the same ideas will be used, particularly physical design changes. Chapter 12 shifts our focus to the role of the police and partnerships in crime prevention activity. Community policing and partnerships seek to build cooperative alliances among the police, other agencies, and citizens. Local problems and potential solutions are identified through the interaction among all interested parties. Similarly, the preventive actions will depend on a variety of people. The police act as "community managers" in the situational orientation and are key actors in any partnership.

Chapter 13 looks at the question of drug use and its relationship to crime. While drug use and trafficking have become major concerns again in recent years, we know little about the causal relationship between drug use and crime. What is known is that there is a strong correlation between drug use and deviant activity. Targeting drug users, therefore, is one method of identifying individuals at risk of committing other offenses. The chapter looks at the extent of drug use, the connection between drug use and crime, and the treatment/prevention programs aimed at curbing drug use.

Another possible source of intervention, aimed primarily at youths, is schools. Schools are in a prime position to identify and intervene with juveniles heading toward criminal activity. Chapter 14 examines the role schools play in engendering deviant life-styles as well as the secondary preventive efforts that schools can provide. The emphasis of secondary prevention on the future behavior of potential deviants leads to discussions of juveniles and delinquent activity. Most intervention with adults occurs after the commission of a criminal act and, thus, falls under tertiary prevention, which is discussed later.

CHAPTER 10 Prediction for Secondary Prevention

CHAPTER OUTLINE

LEARNING OBJECTIVES

After reading this chapter you should be able to:

- Identify key factors in making predictions about future behavior in criminal justice.
- Distinguish between false positive and false negative predictions.
- Compare and contrast clinical and actuarial prediction.
- Identify different categories of risk factors for crime and provide examples of factors within each category.
- Define life-course-persistent and adolescence-limited offending.
- Identify three pathways to delinquent behavior.
- Demonstrate your knowledge of hot spots, hot products, and prospective mapping.
- Define repeat victimization and discuss its extent.

- List and discuss different types of repeat victimization.
- Compare and contrast risk heterogeneity and event dependency explanations for repeat victimization.
- Provide arguments for why targeting repeat victimization makes sense for crime prevention.

Secondary prevention techniques rest heavily on the idea of identification and prediction. Rather than intervene with entire communities or neighborhoods, or establish programs to reach the general public, secondary prevention techniques rely on efforts to identify potential offenders, places, or situations that have a higher likelihood for criminal activity. One primary problem for secondary prevention, therefore, is proper identification and prediction. Predicting who will and who will not become deviant, where and when crime will occur, who will be a victim, what items will be targeted by offenders, and related topics is often a difficult or involved effort. This chapter briefly explores the problem of prediction and identification for prevention purposes. The discussion is divided into three general areas. These are predicting offending behavior, analysis of risk factors for deviance, and identifying places, times, and individual victimization.

Predicting Future Offending

Making predictions about future behavior, whether deviant or conventional, involves making a number of initial decisions. Perhaps the first issue is the determination of what is being predicted. In criminal justice, predicting recidivism is perhaps the most common endeavor. Impact evaluations of interventions, whether punitive or rehabilitative, typically look at various measures of subsequent offending. Rearrest, reconviction, reincarceration, seriousness of future activity, and revocation of probation or parole are common measures of recidivism. Prediction of recidivistic activity, however, does not address the central concern of secondary prevention, which would be predictions of initial deviant acts by individuals. This is often expressed in terms of predicting potential dangerousness. Potential dangerousness is an important consideration in the activity of criminal justice professionals and nowhere is this more evident than in the juvenile justice system, which is premised upon potential future involvement in adult criminal activity. Secondary prevention hopes to keep the potential offender from ever realizing that potential.

Prediction also requires choosing the proper variables for use in the analyses. Some variables or indicators will predict future behavior better than others. The challenge is to identify the best predictors. The choice of predictor variables often reflects the orientation of the researcher making the prediction. Psychologically trained evaluators typically rely on information gathered by means of clinical interviews and psychological tests covering an individual's personality, interpersonal relationships, and life experiences.

TABLE 10.1 **Potential Outcomes of Prediction**	
True positive prediction	Something is predicted to occur and it does (a successful prediction)
False positive prediction	Something is predicted to occur but it does not (a failed prediction)
True negative prediction	Something is predicted not to occur and it does not (a successful prediction)
False negative prediction	Something is predicted not to occur but it does occur (a failed prediction)

More sociologically oriented classifiers look to age, ethnicity, socioeconomic status, group affiliation, family background, and other demographic factors. Past deviant behavior and contact with formal systems of control are typically important for all researchers. Seldom are all of the variables used in the same study. It is the selective choice of variables that may invalidate or limit the applicability of the predictions.

A final important consideration in predicting future behavior is the degree of accuracy in the predictions. When we make a prediction and it proves to be accurate, we are not concerned. On the other hand, making wrong predictions can have dire consequences. Error in prediction takes two forms—false positive and false negative predictions. Each of these has a different impact on the individual being evaluated and/or society. In terms of criminal/deviant behavior, **false positive predictions** are those in which an individual is predicted to do something in the future (e.g., recidivate, offend, act dangerously) but is not found to act in that fashion after follow-up. Conversely, **false negative predictions** declare that the person is not a future threat but the individual does engage in the negative behavior at a later time. See Table 10.1.

The problems inherent in false predictions should be quite evident. "Potential" offenders or recidivists often are subjected to interventions or harsher and/or more prolonged treatment or punishment because of that potential. A false prediction means that the individual is unduly denied his freedom based on an inaccurate finding. On the other hand, false negative predictions may result in ignoring individuals, or granting early or outright release to individuals who will cause further harm to society. Mistakes of this kind subject society to unnecessary harm. Given the complexity of human behavior, it is unreasonable to suggest that prediction methods will ever be able to completely eliminate the incidence of false positive and false negative predictions. The issue, therefore, is limiting the number of false predictions.

Types of Prediction

Prediction generally falls into one of two categories—clinical prediction and actuarial prediction. Clinical predictions have predominated in criminal justice, particularly in terms of sentencing and treating individuals. Actuarial prediction has been a more recent choice given the availability of large amounts of data and problems with clinical techniques. Each of these is discussed below.

Clinical Prediction

Clinical predictions are based on a rater's evaluation of an individual, usually after interviews and direct examination of the subject and his records. The training and disposition of the individual rater often determines what variables and factors are important in arriving at a decision. The rater can use various psychological tests, demographic information about the individual, family and individual background information, or interviews of the subject in making a determination. There are no firm rules for which items must be used, when they should be used, which are the most important, or whether more than one type of information is used. In most cases, the individual rater has total discretion.

Research on the clinical prediction of violence reveals a great tendency for false determinations, both positive and negative. Monahan (1981), summarizing some of the more well-known clinical studies, finds remarkably consistent results, despite variation in what is being predicted, follow-up periods, and predictive items used in the studies. In all nine studies he reviews, the percentage of false positive predictions exceeds 50 percent and in six of the nine analyses it is more than 80 percent. These false positive predictions are disturbing, particularly in cases in which extended follow-up periods are considered. Longer follow-up should reduce the evidence of false positive predictions. For individuals predicted to commit an act of violence or aggression, few actually do so. Conversely, the false negative predictions are very small. Despite this, the combined level of false positives and false negatives is unacceptable. These results seriously damage any claim of predictive efficacy of clinical diagnosis.

A number of factors may explain the poor clinical predictions. First, the determination of subsequent offending or dangerousness may be too strict. Many analyses require actual injury to another person or reincarceration during the follow-up period. An offender, however, may not be severely sanctioned even though harm is committed by the individual. Second, the variables being used to determine future behavior may not be predictive of the type of behavior under consideration. This is a clear possibility given the level of disagreement found among individuals who normally conduct clinical evaluations. Ziskin (1970) notes that agreement between two psychiatrists cannot be found more than about 50 to 60 percent of the time. A final set of problems relates to the adequacy of the information on which evaluators make their judgments. Many clinical interviews are of short duration, which allow only minimal observation. Predictions based on limited observations may produce predictions relying on incomplete or distorted information. These factors, among others (see Ennis and Litwack, 1974; Pfohl, 1978; Scheff, 1966, 1967), may account for the great levels of false predictions found in clinical studies.

Actuarial Predictions

Actuarial prediction refers to making predictions based on known parameters in the data. The best example of actuarial prediction is the setting of rates by the insurance industry. The cost of life insurance is based on the known mortality rates for the population group to which the applicant belongs. Males have shorter life spans, on average, than females. This results in shorter periods in which to pay into the insurance account. In turn, the premiums for insurance are slightly higher for males. The prediction is based solely on known, statistical factors. Similarly, car insurance rates are determined by past accident levels and claims. Young males are involved in more accidents, which leads to higher insurance premiums for all young males.

The key to actuarial prediction is the identification of the appropriate predictive items. Factors typically used in criminal justice include age, race, sex, socioeconomic status, educational status, IQ, criminal history, the immediate offense, family background, and psychological test results. As in the clinical studies, actuarial evaluations greatly vary in their choice of items and techniques.

Burgess (1928) introduced a simple form of actuarial prediction in which individuals were scored as either 0 or 1 based on the presence or absence of certain predictive factors. The U.S. Parole Commission's Salient Factor Score was a prime example of this technique incorporating items addressing past convictions, past incarceration, age at first commitment, educational attainment, and employment history (Gottfredson et al., 1975). One point was awarded for each item characterizing an individual. Prisoners who accumulated higher numbers of points were viewed as better risks and subsequently awarded parole release. Greenwood (1982), using a Burgess-type method with self-report data from incarcerated adult offenders, claimed to be able to predict who was a high-rate and who was a low-rate offender (see Table 10.2). One point was added to a person's score for each of the items pertaining to the individual. A score of four or more indicated a high risk of offending. Neither the Salient Factor Scores nor the Selective Incapacitation system is in use today due to the questionable prediction ability of the techniques.

A wide variety of techniques have been used to construct actuarial prediction scales. The methods vary from the simple additive procedures of Burgess (1928) to more sophisticated techniques, including multiple regression, predictive attribute analysis, and association analysis. The results of these different approaches, however, do not uncover any single best method (Farrington, 1985; Gottfredson and Gottfredson, 1985; Wilbanks, 1985). Similar results emerge when using each and there is often little predictive power in any of the methods. Wilbanks (1985) reports between 25 and 33 percent false predictions for different methods. Similarly, Farrington (1985) finds that an average of 45 to 50 percent of the predictions are false positive predictions, regardless of the method used, with false negative predictions comprising about 10 to 15 percent of the predictors.

TABLE 10.2 Selective Incapacitation Items

1. Incarceration more than half of the two-year period preceding the most recent arrest.
2. Prior conviction for the crime type being predicted.
3. Juvenile conviction prior to age 16.
4. Commitment to state or federal juvenile facility.
5. Heroin or barbiturate use in the two-year period preceding the current arrest.
6. Heroin or barbiturate use as a juvenile.
7. Employed less than half of the two-year period preceding the current arrest.

Source: P.W. Greenwood (1982). *Selective Incapacitation*. Santa Monica, CA: RAND Corp.

A number of observations can be made about actuarial prediction based on the foregoing discussion. First, the level of error is smaller than that found in clinical studies (Meehl, 1954; Wilbanks, 1985). Second, the use of different predictive techniques does not appear to alter the results. The level of error remains about the same across methods, although different individuals are misclassified in the various approaches. Finally, on the negative side, actuarial prediction consistently attempts to predict individual behavior based on group data. This is a totally inappropriate use of the data and is referred to as the **ecological fallacy**. It is not possible (barring very specific circumstances) to impute the behavior of a single person from the activity of a larger group (Stouthamer-Loeber and Loeber, 1989). Instead, the results of an actuarial approach suggest that, given a group of people with certain characteristics, including a certain percentage of offending individuals, the same percentage of persons from an identical group would be expected to act in the same fashion. It is not possible, however, to identify which individuals will make up that offending percentage. Clearly, the inevitable result of both clinical and actuarial prediction is some degree of false prediction.

┌─ ON THE WEB ─────────────────────

Another approach to predicting criminal behavior is to look at criminal careers. Past research has focused on specialization, patterns in behavior, and desistance topics. A short discussion of this material can be found on the textbook web site.

└──────────────────────────────────

Prediction and Crime Prevention

Prediction remains an integral part of many activities in the criminal justice system. Decisions made at all levels of the system involve prediction, although rarely is "prediction" a conscious part of the decision. Choices by police officers to arrest, by prosecutors to press charges, by judges to sentence, and by parole commissions to release offenders all involve predicting the likelihood of future deviant behavior. Unfortunately, prediction is often inaccurate. The usefulness of traditional clinical and actuarial techniques for prediction in crime prevention is suspect.

Risk Factors and Prediction

A more recent trend in identifying who will commit offenses (i.e. prediction) involves the identification of risk factors related to deviant behavior. Most discussions of risk factors do not make the assumption that individuals who exhibit these traits will inevitably become criminal or act in some inappropriate fashion. Rather, the **risk factors** are indicators of who may become deviant in the future. There is usually no attempt to make predictions about specific individuals. The risk factors are only indicators or flags that can signal the need for increased attention or possible assistance for individuals.

The identification of potential risk factors is not a new idea. Indeed, the idea of working with youths at risk of becoming delinquents or later adult criminals is a cornerstone of the juvenile justice system. The very premise of the juvenile court is to work with troubled at-risk youths. Implicit in this task is the idea of identifying the factors underlying the juvenile's behavior and working to alter those conditions. Likewise, most criminological theory is based on the idea of identifying the best predictors of criminal activity in order to develop appropriate interventions. While not typically referred to as risk factors, the variables that are found to be related to delinquency and criminality are risk factors. A good deal of research is on identifying risk factors.

Risk factors can be broken down into various categories. Typical groupings found in the literature are family, peer, community, psychological/personality, and biological risk factors (see Table 10.3). While different authors may classify individual risk factors slightly differently, these categories are generally representative of those used in the literature. The information presented below is not intended as an exhaustive list of risk factors. Rather, the intent is to offer some insight into some of the more recognized variables that have been discussed in the literature.

Family Factors

A wide range of family situations and factors influence both the immediate care of an individual as well as later behavior. As noted in Chapter 8, poor parental supervision and inconsistent and harsh discipline are key early risk factors for later deviance. In one early study, McCord (1979) found a strong relationship between youthful offending and the type of parental discipline and supervision. Others (Capaldi and Patterson, 1996; Hawkins et al., 1995; Loeber and Stouthamer-Loeber, 1986; Wells and Rankin, 1988) report that violence and aggression are more prevalent for youths from homes exercising harsh and inconsistent discipline. One factor often promoted in the literature is the relation between parental criminality and the behavior of the offspring. Farrington (1989) claims that having a parent arrested is related to later offending by male offspring.

TABLE 10.3 Common Risk Factors Found in the Research

Family	School
Parental criminality	Suspension/expulsion
Poor parental supervision	Truancy
Harsh discipline	School attitude
Inconsistent discipline	Academic failure
Abuse/maltreatment	School quality
Family bonding/relationships	Dropping out
Broken homes	**Psychological/personality**
Family size	Hyperactivity
Socioeconomic status	Impulsivity
Family conflict	Inability to concentrate
Family functioning	Learning disabilities
Peers	Low IQ
Gang membership	Anxiety
Peer deviance/criminality	Aggressiveness
Sibling criminality	**Biological**
Community	Prenatal complications
Economic deprivation/poverty	Perinatal complications
Disorder/incivilities	Low birth weight
Availability of firearms/drugs	Drug use during pregnancy
Socioeconomic status	Poor nutrition
Gang activity	Neurotransmitter problems
Area crime/violence	Low at rest heart rate
Community disorganization	Neurological injuries

This relationship appears in a variety of other studies (e.g., Farrington, 1996; Farrington and Loeber, 1998; McCord, 1977; West and Farrington, 1973).

Exposure to violence and offending also appears in the form of abuse and maltreatment. In perhaps the most recognized study on this topic, Widom (1989) finds that both physical abuse and neglect predict later participation in criminal activity. Data from the Rochester Youth Study uncover similar findings (Smith and Thornberry, 1995). While these results support commonly held beliefs about the impact of abuse on later behavior, there is evidence in these same studies that the impact varies by type of abuse (such as between physical abuse and neglect) and inclusion of other factors (such as age, race, sex, etc.). These facts, however, do not eliminate the general finding that maltreatment is related to later deviance.

Other family factors that are considered in the literature include family relations or bonding (Catalano and Hawkins, 1996; Farrington and Loeber, 1998; Gorman-Smith et al., 1996; Hirschi, 1969), family size (Capaldi and Patterson, 1996; Farrington and Loeber, 1998), and broken homes (Farrington and Loeber, 1998). The most important observation to make based on this varied literature is that family functioning is an important contributor to the present and future behavior of youths. The identification of family risk factors offers an opportunity to develop appropriate interventions.

Peer Factors

The influence of peers is generally viewed as one of the most important factors involved in adolescent behavior (Elliott, 1994; Elliott and Menard, 1996; Lipsey and Derzon, 1998; Thornberry et al., 1995). Of particular importance to adolescence is the presence and/or participation in youth gangs. Participation in gangs is related to higher levels of offending (Esbensen and Huizinga, 1993; Thornberry et al., 1993; Thornberry, 1998) as well as initiation into deviant activity (Elliott and Menard, 1996). Data from the Cambridge Youth Study suggest that the antisocial behavior of siblings is also a potential predictor of delinquent activity (Farrington, 1989).

Community Influences on Behavior

Another potential source of risk is the community within which an individual is raised and resides. Studies of community influences are long-standing in criminology (see Shaw and McKay, 1942). Many analyses look to community problems, such as economic deprivation, disorder/incivility, poor neighborhood integration, and similar factors, as contributors to individual deviance (see, for example, Bursik and Grasmick, 1993; Sampson and Lauritsen, 1994; Shannon, 1991; Skogan, 1990). Other community influences related to levels of delinquency and criminality include the availability of firearms (Block and Block, 1993; Lizotte et al., 1994; Sheley and Wright, 1995), low socioeconomic status (Elliott et al., 1989; Farrington, 1989; Lipsey and Derzon, 1998; Smith and Jarjoura, 1988), and level of gang activity. Each of these community factors contributes to the level of risk.

School Factors

Another set of community factors that contribute to risk involves schools. While schools are a part of the community, they may contribute uniquely to risk. Poor academic performance and school failure are common factors related to current and later deviance. Hirschi (1969) points out that schools and academic participation are key factors in delinquent behavior. Various studies show that dropping out of school and low academic achievement are strong correlates of delinquency (Farrington, 1989; Gold and Mann, 1972; Maguin and Loeber, 1996; Thornberry et al., 1985; West and Farrington, 1973). While a relationship between school factors and delinquency clearly exists, the exact causal mechanism between the various factors is not as easily identified. This issue will receive more attention in Chapter 13.

Psychological/Personality Factors

An array of psychological and personality variables have been identified as risk factors for aggressive behavior. Brennan et al. (1993) note that hyperactivity among preteens is significantly related to violent behavior during the young adult years. Similar results appear in research comparing hyperactive boys with their non-hyperactive siblings (Loney et al., 1983). Impulsivity and problems with concentration also are related to higher levels of adolescent deviance (Farrington, 1989; Farrington and Loeber, 1998; Loney et al., 1983). Other factors often related to deviant behavior include learning disabilities, low IQ, and similar issues that may inhibit an individual's success in school and elsewhere (see, for example, Denno, 1990; Lipsey and Derzon, 1998; Loeber et al., 1993; Loeber et al., 1995; Maguin and Loeber, 1996).

Biological Risk Factors

Biological risk factors are identified in a number of studies, although they do not receive the same degree of attention as other factors. The major reason for this state of affairs is the fact that criminology is dominated by social scientists who focus their attention on other variables. Among the possible biologically based risk factors are prenatal and perinatal complications (Brewer et al., 1995; Farrington, 1996; Kandel and Mednick, 1991; Reiss and Roth, 1993). Included here are low birth weights, complications with pregnancy, drug use while pregnant, and poor nutrition. Neurotransmitters, such as serotonin, are other biological risk factors possibly related to deviant behavior (Moffitt et al., 1997). Neurotransmitters are bodily chemicals that transmit messages in the brain. Yet another biological factor related to violent delinquent behavior is a low resting heart rate (Farrington, 1997; Raine, 1993). The evidence for the impact of many of these factors on later behavior is relatively weak (see, for example, Denno, 1990), although there is some evidence of a relationship in various studies.

Using Risk Factors as Predictors

Many researchers attempt to use risk factors as predictors of later deviance. Lipsey and Derzon (1998) conducted a meta-analysis to specify risk factors from two different age groups—ages six to 11 and ages 12 to 14—on violent and serious behavior among individuals aged 15 to 25. They report that the key predictors from the six-to-11 age group are general offending and substance use, socioeconomic status of the family, and having antisocial parents, and being male. From the 12-to-14 age group, the best predictors are general offending, violence and aggression, and having antisocial peers. Overall, offending, substance use, and antisocial peers are the strongest risk factors for later deviant behavior (Lipsey and Derzon, 1998). A very important qualifier in their study, however, is the fact that there is a high level of false positive predictions using these risk factors. That is, use of the risk factors to predict behavior will err by predicting many individuals will be deviant when, in fact, they will not.

A second analysis attempts to show differences between risk factors for two types of offending. These are **life-course-persistent offending** and **adolescence-limited offending**. In simple terms, Howell and Hawkins (1998) are attempting to identify risks of continuing deviant behavior over the long term (i.e., life-course-persistent), as opposed to offending mainly in adolescence (i.e., adolescence-limited). Among the risk factors for life-course-persistent offending are poor social environments, social cognitive difficulties, poor academic abilities, poor family management, and neuropsychological problems. Conversely, adolescence-limited offending risk factors include prior antisocial behavior, poor parent-child relations, antisocial peers, and poor academic performance (Howell and Hawkins, 1998). Based on this information, the authors offer various suggestions for interventions aimed at the key risk factors.

Data from the Pittsburgh Youth Study also illuminate the use of risk factors to attack deviant behavior. Kelly et al. (1997) and Browning and Loeber (1999) identify three pathways to delinquent behavior. The first, **authority conflict**, reflects early stubbornness, which leads to later defiance and avoidance of authority. Related problems include running away, truancy, and ungovernability. **Covert behavior** typically begins with minor acts of lying and theft, moves on to property crimes (such as vandalism and property destruction), then moderately serious delinquency (such as joyriding and more serious theft), and eventually culminates in serious property delinquency, including burglary and auto theft. The final pathway of **overt behavior** commences with aggressive activity (bullying and teasing) and leads to fighting and violence (Kelly et al., 1997). It is important to note that these pathways are neither mutually exclusive nor exhaustive. That is, some youths will exhibit activity in all three and others may not be limited to these avenues. The authors show that many of the Pittsburgh youths fall into one of these patterns. The research also notes various risk factors, especially learning disorders, prior violence, problem behavior at home, and impulsivity (Browning and Loeber, 1999; Kelly et al., 1997).

These studies suggest that risk factors are useful tools in identifying potential problem individuals. Numerous jurisdictions have adopted risk assessments at various stages of criminal justice system intervention. Table 10.4 provides an example of one such risk instrument used by the state of Ohio to assess risk for those being considered for community supervision and the level of supervision needed. This is a Burgess-style instrument

TABLE 10.4 Ohio Risk Assessment Instrument: Community Supervision Tool

Criminal history

Most serious arrest under age 18

Number of prior adult felony convictions

Prior sentence as an adult to a jail or secure correctional facility

Received official misconduct while incarcerated as an adult

Prior sentence to probation as an adult

Community supervision ever been revoked for technical violation as an adult

Education, employment, and financial situation

Highest education

Ever suspended or expelled from school

Employed at the time of arrest

Currently employed

Better use of time

Current financial situation

Family and social support

Parents have criminal record

Currently satisfied with current marital or equivalent situation

Emotional and personal support available from family or others

Level of satisfaction with current level of support from family or others

Stability of residence

Neighborhood problems

High crime area

Drugs readily available in neighborhood

Substance use

Age first began regularly using alcohol

Longest period of abstinence from alcohol

Offender ever used illegal drugs

Drug use caused legal problems

Drug use caused problems with employment

Peer associations

Criminal friends

Contact with criminal peers

Gang membership

Criminal activities

Criminal attitudes and behavioral patterns

Criminal pride

Expresses concern about others' misfortunes

continued

TABLE 10.4 (continued)

Feels lack of control over events
Sees no problem in telling lies
Engages in risk-taking behavior
Walks away from a fight
Believes in "Do unto others before they do unto you"

Source: Adapted by author from E. Latessa et al. (2009). *Creation and Validation of the Ohio Risk Assessment System: Final Report.* Cincinnati, OH: University of Cincinnati.

with offenders receiving points based on each of the risk dimensions/questions. Latessa et al. (2009) have demonstrated the ability of the instrument to assess the risk level of different offenders. They have similarly developed risk assessments for other points in criminal justice processing.

Explicit attempts to assess accuracy of risk assessments do not always provide promising results (Lipsey and Derzon, 1998). Most analyses identify risk factors based on prior correlational analyses and fail to test the adequacy of any predictions based on those findings. Consequently, risk factors should be used as indicators of possible future problem behavior. They should not be viewed as perfect predictors of behavior. Indeed, many individuals, particularly youths, may exhibit multiple risk factors but fail to ever act in socially inappropriate ways. Because many risk factors are indicative of conditions or situations that are not optimal for normal functioning, they should be considered as a signal that some intervention is needed for the best interests of the individual. Should the interventions also reduce the level of subsequent offending, this would be an added bonus. Perhaps more appropriately for crime prevention, individuals who are already exhibiting antisocial behavior should be examined for signs of risk factors, and action should be taken to correct or ameliorate the problem.

ON THE WEB

The State of Ohio and the University of Cincinnati teamed up to create a risk assessment instrument. A brief introduction to that instrument can be found on the textbook web site along with the final report on its creation.

Predicting Places and Events

Prediction for secondary prevention does not have to be limited to predicting which individuals in which situations will turn to delinquency or criminality. It is also possible to consider predicting the where and when of offending/victimization. This activity is not a new or unique idea. Indeed, it is common for police agencies to distribute their resources differentially across their jurisdiction and at different times of the day. Today, researchers are employing new and developing technologies and data sources for identifying the "where" and "when" of offending. The following discussion will look at prediction in terms of hot spot analysis and hot products. The following section will examine repeat victimization and related topics.

Hot Spots for Crime

It has long been common practice for the police to identify locations and times that are more prone to criminal activity. Neighborhood bars, for example, experience more aggression and violence than lounges in nice restaurants. Similarly, assault is more prevalent in the evening than during the mid-morning. Knowing even these two basic facts shows that many problems cluster in both time and place. The challenge, therefore, is to identify these clusters and use that information as a starting point for implementing appropriate interventions.

Perhaps the most recognizable example of this activity involves "hot spot" research. Sherman (1995, p. 36) defines **hot spots** as "small places in which the occurrence of crime is so frequent that it is highly predictable, at least over a one-year period." Analyzing calls for police service in Minneapolis, Sherman et al. (1989) find that 50 percent of all calls for service came from only 3 percent of the locations. All domestic disturbance calls appear at the same 9 percent of the places, all assaults are at 7 percent of the locations, all burglaries occur at 11 percent of the places, and all robbery, sexual misconduct, and auto theft calls appear at 5 percent of the possible locations.

Other analyses reveal similar concentrations of crime in few locations. Spelman (1995) notes that 10 percent of the locations in Boston account for 30 percent of police calls for service. More recently, Braga et al. (2008) report that more than half of all fatal shootings occur in roughly 5 percent of the locations in town. Weisburd et al. (2004), examining data for Seattle, point out that roughly 50 percent of all crime occurs on less than 5 percent of the street segments. This result has remained stable over a 14-year period of time. There can be little doubt that crime clusters spatially.

Attempts to identify hot spots are also useful in pointing out what types of crimes and locations coincide. Block and Block (1995), using mapping techniques to examine crime data for three Chicago communities, report that hot spots often surround elevated transit stops and major intersections. These are locations where potential victims can be located and offenders have options for escape. Looking at auto theft in Philadelphia, Rengert (1997) identifies hot spots but notes that the locations of the hot spots change according to different times of the day and night. Tourist attractions and educational institutions may be hot spots for auto theft during the day, while entertainment venues, bars, and other adult night spots become greater target areas in the evenings and at night (Rengert, 1997). Clearly, hot spots can be anywhere—businesses, schools, abandoned buildings, vacant lots, housing complexes or intersections—or anytime—evenings, late night, weekends, holidays, or vacation months.

An important qualifier when considering hot spots should be stability over time. Is the identified crime concentration a temporary situation, or does the hot spot persist over a period of time? Townsley and Pease (2002) argue that relying on hot spots identified with limited temporal data may lead to targeting anomalous crime concentrations that will disappear as the crime settles back to its normal level (i.e., a regression artifact). Perhaps more importantly, Johnson et al. (2005, 2008) claim that the movement of crime, even over short periods, limits the value of identifying hot spots using traditional methods. The authors suggest the use of **prospective mapping**, or the creation of maps that predict future crime locations based on knowledge of recent events. This is based on findings that show a burglary at one location results in heightened chances of victimization at nearby locations (Johnson and Bowers, 2004). Prospective mapping alleviates the problem of targeting hot spots when they move around.

A finding that crime concentrates in certain locations or at certain times suggests that the targeting of hot spots may be an effective starting point for crime prevention. The identification of a hot spot should prompt analyses to uncover what factors make a location a good spot for crime (Spelman, 1995) and offer insight into preventive responses. One set of tools that is becoming a central component to police planning is computer mapping programs. Software, such as ArcGIS, MapInfo, the Spatial and Temporal Analysis of Crime program (STAC), and Drug Market Analysis Program (DMAP), are commonplace in policing (Rich, 1995). Mapping and hot spot research can supply information not only on crime but also on information about the neighborhood, site, or time at which an activity is taking place.

Hot Products

An interesting new approach to hot spots is the idea of **hot products**. Clarke (1999) discusses hot products as items that attract attention and are targeted by thieves. Further, such items may help explain the existence and distribution of hot spots. Hot products are those that fit Felson and Clarke's (1998) idea of **VIVA**: Value, Inertia, Visibility, and Accessibility. *Value* is determined by potential offenders and not necessarily the monetary cost of the item. What has value today may not be of interest tomorrow. This could be due to the maturation of the offender, the saturation of the item in society, changes in taste, or other factors. *Inertia* deals with the weight and portability of the item. Further, a target can only be at risk if it is *Visible* to potential offenders. Finally, the target must be *Accessible* to offenders (Felson and Clarke, 1998). The extent to which a target meets these criteria will have an impact on the chances of an offense occurring. Clarke (1999) expands on the idea of VIVA by proposing **CRAVED** (Concealable, Removable, Available, Enjoyable, and Disposable), which further explains the existence of hot spots.

Clarke argues that identifying and acknowledging the influence of "hot products" leads to a number of potential prevention measures. Physical design ideas, such as electronic tagging, location transmitters, barcoding, and similar methods of identifying property are prime examples of ways to address hot products. It is also possible to develop other actions specifically aimed at hot products.

Repeat Victimization

Yet another topic in the literature involves identifying repeat victimization and focusing efforts to prevent future transgressions. **Repeat victimization** can be considered in terms of either people or places being victimized at least a second time within some

TABLE 10.5 Typology of Repeat Victimization

Repeat type	Characteristics	Examples
Target	Crime against the same target	Crime against the same person, building, household, vehicle, or other target, however defined
Tactical (virtual)	Crimes requiring the same skill, or modus operandi, to commit. Often the same type of target	Particular type of locks picked (on different types of property); web sites with particular types of security are repeatedly targeted; theft of same model of car; burglary of property with same layout
Temporal	An offending spree—temporal proximity is the defining characteristic	Multiple burglaries of different properties in the same night; theft of car, then a robbery and getaway
Spatial (near)	Crime in nearby location due to proximity and characteristics	High-crime areas; hot spots
Crime type	The same target victimized by different types of crime	The same target is burglarized, assaulted, robbed at different times
Offender	Victimization of same target by different offenders	A property appears attractive to different offenders; any easy or rewarding target

Source: G. Farrell (2005). "Progress and prospects in the prevention of repeat victimization." In N. Tilley (ed.), *Handbook of Crime Prevention and Community Safety*. Portland, OR: Willan. Reprinted with permission.

period of time subsequent to an initial victimization event. Farrell (2005) offers six types of repeat victimization (see Table 10.5). These types are analogous to the variation found in forms of displacement offered in Chapter 6. For example, target repeat victimization considers the same person or place being victimized at least a second time. Target repeat is the one most commonly referenced in discussions of repeat victimization. No matter which type is being considered, the assumption is that evidence of recurring victimization can be used for directing preventive actions.

Repeat victimization is not an uncommon event. Polvi et al. (1990) are credited with introducing the idea of repeat victimization. In their analysis, the risk of being a repeat burglary victim is 12 times higher than expected by chance and this risk is more pronounced immediately after an initial burglary. This heightened risk persists for roughly three months and then levels off to normal expected levels. Victimization surveys are a major source of data on repeat victimization. Pease (1998) notes that 1 percent of people are victims of 59 percent of all personal crimes, and 2 percent of the households are the victims of 41 percent of all household crimes. Pease labels these victims as *supertargets* because of the high concentrations of crime they experience. Farrell and Pease (2014) argue that most crime is repeat offenses against the same victims.

British Crime Survey data from 1982 through 1992 reveals that roughly one-quarter to one-third of all property crime is committed against people victimized five or more times within a one-year period (Ellingworth et al., 1995). This means that almost two-thirds of victims are repeat victims, with roughly 50 percent of personal crimes appearing as repeat victimizations (Ellingworth et al., 1995). Using data from the 2000 International Crime Victims Survey (ICVS), Farrell et al. (2005) find that roughly 40 percent of all crimes, 43 percent of sexual crimes, and more than one-third of assaults and threats are repeats (Farrell et al., 2005).

Comparing repeat victimization in the NCVS, BCS, and other victim surveys relies on what is known as series victimizations. *Series victimizations* are instances where respondents report multiple acts of the same type over the reference period but cannot provide specifics on each event. Lauritsen et al. (2012) note that while there are problems with accurately assessing the exact level of repeat victimization, there is consistent evidence that the actual levels of victimization are much higher than found in annual victimization reports when series victimizations are included.

One problem with identifying repeat victimization involves the impact of short time frames within which repeats can occur. Ellingworth et al. (1995) note that most levels of repeat victimization are probably underreports because they rely on repeats only within a limited time frame, which minimizes the potential for repeats before or after the survey boundaries. The problem of short time frames for repeat victimization is very evident when considering the NCVS, which uses a six-month time frame. Compared to the 12-month time frame of the ICVS, the NCVS reveals significantly lower repeat victimization compared to the ICVS for every category of victimization, including sexual

TABLE 10.6 Time Frame for Repeat Victimization

Offense	Proportion of Repeats by Time Period	Where
Domestic violence	15% within 24 hours 25% within five weeks	Merseyside, England
Bank robbery	33% within three months	England
Residential burglary	25% within a week 51% within a month	Tallahassee, Florida
	11% within one week 33% within one month	Merseyside, England
Non-residential burglary	17% within one week 43% within one month	Merseyside, England
Property crime at schools	70% within a month	Merseyside, England

Source: D.L. Weisel (2005). *Analyzing Repeat Victimization. Problem Oriented Guides for Police.* Washington, DC: Office of Community-Oriented Policing Services.

offenses (51 percent repeats in the ICVS; 23 percent in the NCVS), assaults and threats (46 percent ICVS; 26 percent NCVS), and burglary (40 percent ICVS; 18 percent NCVS) (Farrell et al., 2005). Kleemans (2001) notes that 9 percent of repeat burglaries occur within one month, 30 percent occur within six months, and almost half occur within one year. Thus, the time frame under consideration makes a difference for the finding of repeat victimization.

Beyond documenting the extent of repeat victimization, research also provides information on the time frame of repeats. A great deal of revictimization tends to occur within a short period after the first victimization (Bowers et al., 1998; Johnson et al., 1997; Pease, 1998). Weisel (2005) demonstrates that the time frame for many repeats remains short for a range of offenses (see Table 10.6). For example, 15 percent of domestic violence repeats take place within one day and 35 percent occur within five weeks (Lloyd et al., 1994). Similarly, 25 percent of repeat burglaries occur within one week and 51 percent occur within one month (Robinson, 1998). The information on the time frame of repeats can be useful for the timing of prevention initiatives.

Explanations for Repeat Victimization

Explanations for repeat victimization can generally be divided into two categories—risk heterogeneity and state dependence (Farrell et al., 1995). Risk heterogeneity, or a flag explanation (Gill and Pease, 1998), suggests that the prior victimization or some other factor identifies the victim or location as an appropriate target for further victimization. As such, subsequent victimizations may be committed by different offenders who are attracted to the target by its apparent vulnerability or some other characteristic. Farrell et al. (1995) use the example of repeated fights at a bar as an indication of risk heterogeneity, where people looking for fights or interested in risky situations are attracted to establishments with a reputation for conflict. Those locations and/or the employees of those bars are then at a higher risk for repeat victimization.

Event dependency, or **boost explanations** (Gill and Pease, 1998), refers to situations in which (usually) the same offender commits another offense based on the past experiences with that victim or location. Successful past offending leads to another attempt against the same target. It is possible under this situation that a new offender commits a follow-up offense as a result of information shared between offenders. In this case, specific information about the target based on a past offense is the key to subsequent actions.

Farrell et al. (1995) point out that both risk heterogeneity and event dependency assume that potential offenders are rational (*rational choice theory*) and that their experiences (*routine activities*) offer information on the risk, effort, and payoff to be expected from different courses of action. Both arguments find support in Gill and Pease's (1998) study of incarcerated robbers. Their subjects indicate that repeat victimizations are related to information from past offenses (theirs or others) and planning. Bowers and Johnson (2004) uncover support for the event dependency explanation in a study of residential burglary.

Repeat Victimization and Crime Prevention

Targeting past victims and locations provides good information for preventing crime. Laycock and Farrell (2003) point out that targeting repeat victimization allows the police to better allocate manpower and resources where they have the greatest chance to have an impact. In a similar fashion, targeting repeat victimization often means targeting hot spots and hot products. A focus on repeat victimization also means implementing crime prevention in high-crime areas, thus having an impact on both the specific target and potential nearby targets (Laycock and Farrell, 2003). Ratcliffe and McCullagh (1999) note that the analysis of past offenses can provide information on the mode of entry, time of offending, property targeted, and other factors that can form the basis for preventive actions. Clarke et al. (2001) suggest that studies of repeat victimization can also provide insight into the decision-making process of the offenders. Evidence from an analysis of repeat burglary supports the idea that burglars repeat their offense after a period of time in order to steal the items that have been purchased to replace the goods taken in the first offense (Clarke et al., 2001). Importantly, there is greater similarity in repeats committed soon after the initial act, but the similarity declines over time (Ratcliff and McCullagh, 1999). Another advantage is that repeat victimization may involve more prolific and serious offenders; thus, prevention efforts have a greater potential impact (Laycock and Farrell, 2003). The authors also note that targeting repeat victimization should result in less displacement than initiatives that are more unfocused.

Research demonstrates that targeting repeat victimization can effectively reduce crime. The Kirkholt Burglary Prevention Program, for example, targeted repeat victimization and worked with current victims as a means of reducing further burglaries. This effort successfully reduced further offending (Pease, 1998). Farrell and Pease (2006), reviewing 11 studies from the United States, the United Kingdom, and Australia, note that both repeat burglary and overall burglary are reduced by focusing prevention efforts on repeat offending. In a review of 21 burglary studies, Grove and Farrell (2012) claim that targeting repeat victimization reduced burglary in 62 percent of the analyses. Chainey (2012) reports that targeting repeat burglaries in the Trafford borough of Greater Manchester reduced burglary by 27 percent in the first year of the project.

Issues with Repeat Victimization

Despite the increased interest in repeat victimization and evidence of the effectiveness of targeting repeat victimization, there are issues that require more attention. First, while evidence shows that there is a good deal of repeat victimization, not all criminal acts are followed by another one against the same location or individual. Identifying which acts will result in a repeat victimization prior to the subsequent act is an elusive task. The existing research offers an after-the-fact analysis of the extent of repeat victimization. It is possible, therefore, that targeting prevention activities at past victims may result in a great deal of unnecessary effort. On the other hand, such targeting should be more effective than interventions aimed at the general public, many of whom would never become a victim in the first place.

A second issue deals with **virtual repeats** (Pease, 1998). A virtual repeat involves a follow-up victimization of a similar person, place, or item. For example, a series of robberies at different locations of a single company (such as a fast-food store) or theft of the same brand of car could be considered repeat victimization if the subsequent offenses are committed due to the similarity in the situations (such as similar store layout or similar auto amenities). Pease (1998) suggests that these should be considered repeat victimizations. As such, they offer different issues for directing crime prevention activities. Johnson and Bowers (2002, 2004) illustrate this issue when they consider burglaries that take place at neighboring homes as a type of repeat victimization, which they call a **near repeat**. Their argument is that a local burglary elevates the risk of burglary, at least in the near term, for other proximate homes.

Other unanswered questions involve whether repeats should be considered in terms of people or places being victimized, how many victimizations are required before it is considered a repeat (especially in terms of common commercial thefts such as shoplifting),

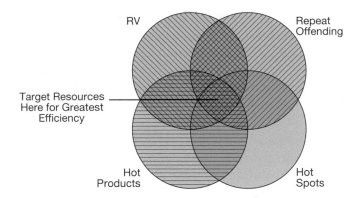

Figure 10.1

Intersection of Domains for Crime Prevention Efficiency

Source: G. Farrell (2005). "Progress and prospects in the prevention of repeat victimization." In N. Tilley (ed.), *Handbook of Crime Prevention and Community Safety*. Portland, OR: Willan. Reprinted with permission.

whether attempted offenses should be counted as repeats, and whether similar (but not identical) offenses should be used as a sign of repeat victimization (Pease, 1998). While no clear answers are available for these questions/issues, the potential for using repeat victimization within crime prevention remains strong.

Summary

Hot spot research, hot products, repeat victimization, and related topics represent innovative approaches to narrowing the individuals or situations that will be targeted by crime prevention activities. Farrell (2005) illustrates the overlap of several concepts found in this chapter and suggests that the effectiveness of preventive efforts will be most enhanced by targeting the intersection of the different domains (see Figure 10.1). Clearly, the idea of allocating resources by time and place is common in policing. It should be no more difficult to borrow that idea and apply it to general preventive efforts used by the criminal justice system or any other group or agency. Both hot spot and repeat victimization analyses, among others, offer insight into the "where" and "when" issues of instituting crime prevention.

Implications for Crime Prevention

Prediction is an important part of crime prevention—particularly secondary prevention. This is true especially for attempting to intervene with individuals and situations where a high propensity for criminal and deviant behavior exists. The identification of persons who are headed for future juvenile or adult criminality would allow the introduction of appropriate crime prevention techniques prior to the deviant activity. Unfortunately, the prediction of future behavior of individuals typically results in large numbers of false predictions. More recent research on risk factors uncovers a number of variables related to later deviant behavior. It may be possible to use identified risk factors as a basis for focused, preventive interventions.

Another approach to prediction is to turn attention away from predicting individual behavior and toward prediction of places, times, and targets of offending. This approach suggests that it may be fruitful to orient prevention activities from the perspective of the victim, rather than the potential offender. Any technique that assists in the delineation of potential victims or targets would offer insight into the "where" and "when" of prevention efforts. The geographic and temporal identification of hot spots, the identification of hot products, and the use of information on repeat victimization are approaches with potential use in secondary crime prevention. These approaches need to receive increased attention and continued refinement in order to make the information more useful for prevention.

KEY TERMS

- actuarial prediction
- adolescence-limited offending
- authority conflict
- boost explanations
- clinical predictions
- covert behavior
- CRAVED
- ecological fallacy
- event dependency
- false negative predictions
- false positive predictions
- flag explanation
- hot products
- hot spots
- life-course-persistent offending
- near repeat
- overt behavior
- prospective mapping
- repeat victimization
- risk factors
- risk heterogeneity
- virtual repeats
- VIVA

CHAPTER 11 Situational Crime Prevention

LEARNING OBJECTIVES

After reading this chapter you should be able to:

- Define situational prevention.
- Identify and discuss the theoretical bases for situational prevention.
- Explain the changes in the situational typology over time.
- Provide criticisms directed at situational prevention and give responses to those criticisms.
- Offer several examples of situational prevention in action, including the evaluation evidence on those techniques.
- Demonstrate how situational techniques can be used with personal crimes.

The targeting of crime prevention efforts is nowhere more evident than under the rubric of situational crime prevention. Many of the prevention techniques discussed under primary prevention form the basis of interventions discussed in this chapter. Instead of attempting to make sweeping changes in an entire community or neighborhood, situational prevention is aimed at specific problems, places, persons, or times. The situational approach assumes that a greater degree of problem identification and planning will take place prior to program implementation and that the impact will be more focused. The identification of places, individuals, and things at risk of victimization, especially focusing on repeat victimization, are central to a great deal of situational prevention. This chapter outlines the growth of situational crime prevention since the early 1980s, discusses the various traditional rationales upon which it is based, and provides examples of situational techniques in action.

The Growth of Situational Prevention

The root ideas for situational crime prevention can be traced largely to the crime prevention work of the British Home Office in the 1970s (Clarke, 1983). In pursuit of interventions that could successfully address different crime problems, the Home Office undertook a wide array of projects aimed at reducing factors specific to different crimes, places, and situations. Clarke (1995) points out that much of this work grew out of the recognition that crime often reflects the risk, effort, and payoff as assessed by the offender. In essence, offenders make choices about which opportunities are the most profitable, and act in accordance with that assessment.

Clarke (1983, p. 225) offers the following definition of **situational crime prevention**:

> situational crime prevention can be characterized as comprising measures (1) directed at highly specific forms of crime (2) that involve the management, design, or manipulation of the immediate environment in as systematic and permanent a way as possible (3) so as to reduce the opportunities for crime and increase the risks as perceived by a wide range of offenders.

Implicit in this definition are a number of assumptions about the offender and crime commission that appear in various theories and theoretical perspectives. The key part of the definition is the third caveat—"reduce the opportunities" and "increase the risks as perceived by offenders." Situational prevention rests on the idea that it is possible to make changes in the environment that will make offending less attractive to potential offenders. This assumes that offenders do not simply act on impulse, and they have control over whether they take action or not. There is a clear belief that offenders make choices. Cusson (1993) argues that crime is deterred because the offender perceives risk in a given situation. As a result, offenders seek out or respond to places, times, and potential victims that offer the least risk.

The Theoretical Basis

Rational choice, routine activities, the lifestyles perspectives, and crime pattern theory are important considerations for situational prevention. Each set of ideas provides insight into the ability of offenders to respond to crime opportunities. While it is common for discussions of these perspectives to focus on potential offenders, the potential victim is also an important part of the equation.

Rational Choice Theory

The cornerstone of situational crime prevention is the belief that offenders respond to opportunities and make choices in offending. **Rational choice theory** posits that individuals make decisions on whether to commit an offense based on an array of inputs, including the effort involved, the potential payoff, the degree of peer support for the action, the risk of apprehension and punishment, and the needs of the individual (Clarke and Cornish, 1985; Cornish and Clarke, 1986a, 1986b). This does not mean that individuals commit an offense every time an opportunity presents itself. Rather, potential offenders make a calculated decision about crime based on the available choices and the risk, effort, and payoff involved. Research on burglars serves as a good example of the issues involved in rational choice. Bennett (1986) and Wright and Decker (1994) point out that burglars often commit their crimes in order to fulfill other needs and desires. These may be immediate needs, such as cash for drug purchases or to meet expectations of one's peers, or longer-term desires for property or status. In attempting to satisfy these drives, the offender may consider a wide range of targets and methods. Among the physical and social factors that affect a burglar's decision may be the level of concealment, the amount of light, the presence of locks, evidence of valuable property, surveillability from other places, and the presence of other people (Bennett, 1986; Bennett and Wright, 1984; Cromwell et al., 1991; Nee and Taylor, 1988; Rengert and Wasilchick, 1985; Wright and Decker, 1994). It is important to note that throughout these discussions there is at least a tacit recognition of the limited nature of the offender's choices. Indeed, many of the choices may be made with little or no conscious decision making by the individual at the time of the offense (Wright and Decker, 1994). While it may appear that rational choice is not taking place, the decisions may have been fashioned through a variety of past experiences, activities, and inputs. This same process should not only apply to burglary, but also to other offenses.

The appearance that offenders' behavior is based on little conscious thought or choice may be due to the fact that individuals rely on **crime scripts** that drive their actions.

TABLE 11.1 Crime Script for Auto Theft

Script scene	Script action
Preparation	Gather tools
Entry	Enter lot
Pre-condition	Loiter unobtrusively
Instrumental pre-condition	Select vehicle
Instrumental initiation	Approach vehicle
Instrumental activation	Break into vehicle
Doing	Take vehicle
Post-condition	Reverse out of parking space
Exit	Leave lot

Cornish (1994, p. 159) notes that scripts are "a useful analytic tool for looking at behavioral routines in the service of rational, purposive, goal-oriented action." A crime script outlines the steps and actions required to commit a crime, including the responses that are needed to complete the act (Cornish and Clarke, 2008). A simple example of script steps and actions for auto theft is presented in Table 11.1. The script scene represents the steps and the script actions are the actual behaviors at each point in the scene. Different crimes will have different scripts. While scripts are typically developed over time through experience and practice, they can become second nature, requiring little, if any, conscious thought. A potential offender, therefore, happens across a situation offering all the elements outlined in a successful script and decides to act with little apparent decision making.

Routine Activities Theory

One source of the information upon which an offender builds scripts and bases decisions, whether consciously or subconsciously, is his daily routines. **Routine activities theory** argues that the daily activity of individuals results in the convergence of motivated offenders with suitable targets in the absence of guardians (Cohen and Felson, 1979). This convergence provides opportunities for crime to occur. Cohen and Felson (1979) demonstrate the importance of routine activities by showing that increases in the number of unoccupied homes during the day and the greater availability of portable valuables during the 1960s help to explain increases in residential burglary. Increasing mobility in society serves to bring targets and offenders together with greater frequency than ever before. Both the opportunity and choices for offending are enhanced.

Where routine activities deals with both the offender and the victim, the **lifestyle perspective** specifically focuses on the activity of the victim as a contributing factor in criminal acts. Hindelang et al. (1978) suggest that an individual's lifestyle and behavioral choices help determine whether he will be victimized. For example, frequenting a bar in which violent fights are common increases the risk you will be involved in such a confrontation. Similarly, working in a convenience store located in a high-crime neighborhood enhances the possibility of being a robbery victim. In both situations the individual's lifestyle has an impact on the potential of becoming a victim or a repeat victim.

It is possible to broaden the lifestyle ideas to consider both victimization risk and opportunity provision. That is, one's lifestyle has the potential to offer opportunities to commit crime, as well as become a victim. A lifestyle that offers little structure, such as a job where you are unsupervised and are greatly mobile, may place you in situations where targets are identifiable and guardians are absent. Consequently, the individual has the choice of either committing a crime or refraining from doing so. The combination of lifestyle and routine activities ideas is a natural extension of both perspectives and offers a broader view of potential choice parameters.

Crime Pattern Theory

The rational choice, routine activities, crime scripts, and lifestyles theories/perspectives fit nicely with **crime pattern theory**. This theory argues that criminal behavior fits patterns that can be understood in terms of when and where crime occurs (Brantingham and Brantingham, 1993b). It is through daily activities that individuals develop templates about the social and physical environment within which they operate. This information is important for identifying both targets as well as threats for potential offenders. Likewise, studying the behavior of offenders and analysis of past offending provides insight into the crimes and potential prevention mechanisms.

Summary

This brief review of rational choice, crime scripts, routine activities, lifestyle, and crime pattern theories/perspectives illustrates many of the issues underlying situational crime prevention ideas. In each case, deviant activity can be seen as a result of converging factors that influence opportunities for and the decision to commit crime. Actions that limit those choices, therefore, hold the potential to reduce crime and fear of crime.

Situational Typologies

The growth of situational crime prevention can be seen in the ongoing development of a situational typology. In one of the earliest presentations on situational prevention, Clarke (1983) provided a simple three-pronged approach to interventions:

- surveillance

- target hardening

- environmental management

Surveillance included many of the ideas discussed in earlier chapters, including the concepts of natural surveillance, formal surveillance, and surveillance by employees (see Clarke and Mayhew, 1980). Target hardening included interventions such as locks, unbreakable glass, safes, and other security devices. Environmental management referred to making changes that reduce the opportunity for crime.

As one would expect, the original three categories quickly became too simplistic and confining as the number of situational crime prevention interventions grew. In 1992, Clarke offered an expanded classification of situational techniques that reflected three very general orientations: "increasing the effort," "increasing the risk," and "reducing the rewards." Within each of these categories, Clarke (1992) outlined four subgroups of prevention approaches, yielding a total of 12 situational prevention techniques (see Table 11.2).

Many of the techniques are self-explanatory or rest on ideas introduced earlier in this book. Under "Increasing the Effort" are target hardening, access control, deflecting offenders, and controlling facilitators. "Deflecting offenders" involves actions that offer alternatives to undesirable behavior. Examples would include providing a board upon which graffiti can be painted, or a meeting place for youths away from open businesses or public thoroughfares (Clarke, 1992). The idea of "controlling facilitators" deals with limiting or eliminating situations or items that contribute to crime, such as guns, alcohol, or public phones (which may be used for drug sales). Methods for "Increasing the Risk" rest mainly on formal or informal surveillance efforts. "Entry/exit screening" is a form of surveillance that allows the detection of potential offenders. The screening of passengers at airports and placing electronic sensors in merchandise to prevent its theft

TABLE 11.2 Clarke's 1992 Situational Prevention Techniques

Increasing the Effort	Increasing the risk	Reducing the rewards
1. Target hardening	5. Entry/Exit screening	9. Target removal
2. Access control	6. Formal surveillance	10. Identifying property
3. Deflecting offenders	7. Surveillance by employees	11. Removing inducements
4. Controlling facilitators	8. Natural surveillance	12. Rule setting

Source: Adapted by author from R.V. Clarke (1992). *Situational Crime Prevention: Successful Case Studies*. Albany, NY: Harrow and Heston.

are two examples of entry/exit screening. The final category of "Reducing the Rewards" includes target removal, identifying property, removing inducements, and rule setting. "Target removal" reflects actions such as limiting the cash kept in the checkout register and requiring exact fare on buses. In both cases, the potential payoff from a robbery or theft is limited. Similarly, "removing inducements" means eliminating attractive targets such as a sports car parked on a public street or the wearing of popular sports team jackets to school. Finally, Clarke (1992) offers "rule setting" as a means of setting a standard of conduct for employees and the public, and placing people on notice that their behavior is being monitored for compliance.

Throughout these techniques, Clarke attempts to show the breadth of possibilities for crime prevention. He notes that relying on prevention activities that rest solely on making changes in hardware is too simplistic and short-sighted (Clarke, 1992). Instead, prevention needs to consider broader social bases for interventions, which situational prevention techniques offer. Any examination of Clarke's 12-stage typology can easily lead to interventions that are dominated by physical changes in the environment. Based on Clarke's (1983) definition, which proposes the "management, design, or manipulation of the immediate environment," a physical interpretation is not surprising. A closer look, however, that considers opportunity and the "choice" dimension of situational prevention, argues for a broader interpretation of situational interventions.

Expanding the Typology

Clarke and Homel (1997) responded to concerns and limitations in the original 12-cell typology by proposing an expanded list of 16 situational techniques. The expansion sought to address two key issues (Clarke and Homel, 1997). First, several of the original categories could be divided to enhance internal consistency of the ideas (Clarke and Homel, 1997). For example, "controlling facilitators" was divided into "controlling facilitators" (such as guns and other items that make crime easier) and "controlling disinhibitors" (factors that reduce the social and psychological barriers to crime commission, such as the use of alcohol and other drugs). Second, the original 12 categories failed to include techniques that focused on the social and psychological contexts of offending. Clarke and Homel (1997) added categories that addressed guilt, shame, and embarrassment. Guilt and similar feelings may emerge because of the incongruence individuals see between their actions and the moral code they hold or the view of significant others in their lives (Clarke and Homel, 1997).

This expanded typology shifted situational prevention away from the heavy emphasis on physical changes toward a greater reliance on psychological and social factors. For example, each of the original categories was relabeled to reflect the offender's perceptions—"Increasing *Perceived* Effort," "Increasing *Perceived* Risks," and "Reducing *Anticipated* Rewards." In each case the new categories recognized both an actual change

TABLE 11.3 Precipitators of Crime

Prompts	Events or situations that may support the opportunity for crime, such as open doors or others committing crime
Pressures	More direct stimuli that lead to action, such as deviant peers, going along with the crowd, or following orders to do something wrong
Permissibility	Situations or beliefs that place criminal behavior into an acceptable light, such as the belief that everyone breaks the law or that the victim had it coming
Provocation	Factors that make an individual uncomfortable, frustrated, irritable, or otherwise aroused to the point of taking some form of action

Source: Compiled by author from R. Wortley (2001). "A classification of techniques for controlling situational precipitators of crime." *Security Journal* 14:63–82.

in effort, risk, or reward *and* altered *perceptions* (Clarke and Homel, 1997). It is possible that a situational technique has little *physical* impact, but a major psychological impact.

Despite these changes, Wortley (2001) argued that the typology was still not complete. In particular, the area of "inducing guilt or shame" was not exhaustive. He posited that guilt and shame are not the same thing and that these concepts need to be separated. He also argued that the matrix of situational prevention overemphasized elements that can control or inhibit offending, while ignoring the factors that precipitate or lead to crime. He offered four categories of precipitators: **prompts, pressures, permissibility**, and **provocation** (see Table 11.3).

The addition of guilt, shame, and precipitating factors suggests that Clarke and Homel's (1997) social and psychological dimensions of both prevention and crime causation were under-developed. Clarke and Homel (1997), however, argued that Wortley's (1996) initial suggestions broaden situational prevention beyond a "situational" approach. They point out that a basic assumption underlying situational prevention is that there are always individuals who are willing to offend. A motivated offender is a given. Cornish and Clarke (2003) noted that Wortley's (1996, 2001) arguments take the opposite position that offenders are not always motivated. Instead, there are factors that will provide the needed motivation for criminal activity. Attempting to address Wortley's (2001) concerns, Cornish and Clarke (2003) offer a new situational typology that includes cues that may motivate individuals to offend.

The typology appearing in Table 11.4 attempts to incorporate elements of precipitation into the general situational crime prevention framework. The original ideas of taking actions to alter the real and perceived effort, risks, and rewards from criminal behaviors are maintained, with expanded techniques under each heading. Techniques addressing guilt and shame are maintained primarily under the heading of "Remove Excuses," as are

TABLE 11.4 Twenty-Five Techniques of Situational Prevention

Increase the effort	Increase the risks	Reduce the rewards	Reduce provocations	Remove excuses
1. Target harden: • Steering column locks and immobilizers • Anti-robbery screens • Tamper-proof packaging	6. Extend guardianship: • Take routine precautions: go out in groups at night, leave signs of occupancy, carry phone • "Cocoon" neighborhood watch	11. Conceal targets: • Off-street parking • Gender-neutral phone directories • Unmarked bullion trucks	16. Reduce frustrations and stress: • Efficient queues and police service • Expanded seating • Soothing music/ muted lights	21. Set rules: • Rental agreements • Harassment codes • Hotel registration
2. Control access to facilities: • Entry phones • Electronic card access • Baggage screening	7. Assist natural surveillance: • Improved street lighting • Defensible space design • Support whistleblowers	12. Remove targets: • Removable car radio • Women's refuges • Pre-paid cards for pay phones	17. Avoid disputes: • Separate enclosures for rival soccer fans • Reduce crowding in pubs • Fixed cab fares	22. Post instructions: • "No parking" • "Private property" • "Extinguish camp fires"
3. Screen exits: • Ticket needed for exit • Export documents • Electronic merchandise tags	8. Reduce anonymity: • Taxi driver IDs • "How's my driving?" decals • School uniforms	13. Identify property: • Property marking • Vehicle licensing and parts marking • Cattle branding	18. Reduce emotional arousal: • Controls on violent pornography • Enforce good behavior on soccer field • Prohibit racial slurs	23. Alert conscience: • Roadside speed display boards • Signatures for customs declarations • "Shoplifting is stealing"

continued

TABLE 11.4 (continued)

Increase the effort	Increase the risks	Reduce the rewards	Reduce provocations	Remove excuses
4. Deflect offenders: • Street closures • Separate bathrooms for women • Disperse pubs	9. Utilize place managers: • CCTV for double-decker buses • Two clerks for convenience stores • Reward vigilance	14. Disrupt markets: • Monitor pawn shops • Controls on classified ads • License street vendors	19. Neutralize peer pressure: • "Idiots drink and drive" • "It's OK to say no" • Disperse troublemakers at school	24. Assist compliance: • Easy library checkout • Public lavatories • Litter bins
5. Control tools/weapons: • "Smart" guns • Disabling stolen cell phones • Restrict spray paint sales to juveniles	10. Strengthen formal surveillance: • Red light cameras • Burglar alarms • Security guards	15. Deny benefits: • Ink merchandise tags • Graffiti cleaning • Speed bumps	20. Discourage imitation: • Rapid repair of vandalism • V-chips in TVs • Censor details of modus operandi	25. Control drugs and alcohol: • Breathalyzers in pubs • Server intervention • Alcohol-free events

Source: D.B. Cornish and R.V. Clarke (2003). "Opportunities, precipitators, and criminal decisions: A reply to Wortley's critique of situational crime prevention." In M.J. Smith and D.B. Cornish (eds.), *Theory for Practice in Situational Crime Prevention*. Monsey, NY: Criminal Justice Press. Reprinted with permission.

Wortley's (2001) ideas of reducing permissibility. Methods to address the precipitating factors of prompts, pressures, and provocations appear under the "Reducing Provocations" heading. Cornish and Clarke (2003) note that the addition of motivational factors to the more traditional opportunity factors in the matrix allows the techniques to address the behavior of various individuals with different levels of motivation to commit crime.

The situational typology serves various purposes. First, the typology places the great array of situational crime prevention activities and programs into a theoretical framework. Many specific interventions, such as the installation of locks and lights, take place with little understanding of the underlying rationale for why they should work. While there are implicit theoretical arguments in many of the programs, understanding why a program does or does not work requires more explicit recognition of the mechanisms at work. The situational typology helps to organize those discussions. Second, the cataloging of the diverse prevention efforts into a classification system helps to identify the potential causal factors at work. That is, the underlying theories gain support when it is possible to demonstrate their applicability and usefulness. The rational choice, routine activities, and lifestyle perspectives all contribute to the development of the situational techniques and benefit from the alignment of different studies into a coherent typology. The recent addition of techniques for addressing precipitating factors broadens the theoretical traditions and causal mechanisms under consideration in prevention initiatives. Finally, on a very practical note, a classification scheme such as this serves as a simple reference tool for those attempting to implement prevention programs.

> ┌─ **ON THE WEB** ─────────────────
> *Detail on each of the 25 techniques found in the Situational Crime Prevention model can be obtained by visiting the interactive table on the Center for Problem-Oriented Policing web site: http://www.popcenter.org/25techniques/*

Issues and Concerns with Situational Prevention

As with any topic, there are a number of concerns and unresolved issues. First, the general categorizations are not mutually exclusive. That is, various interventions may influence more than one factor (both objectively and subjectively). A technique that increases risk also may increase the effort. For example, the presence of security guards or CCTV increases the risk of being caught. These actions, however, also increase the effort needed to successfully complete an offense. At the same time, successfully completing a crime despite high risk and effort could lead to greater (psychic) rewards (or monetary gain if the presence of protection reflected greater value). The fact that the categories are not mutually exclusive does not negate the usefulness of the classification scheme. Rather, it suggests that the underlying mechanisms are more complex than they first appear in the typology.

Second, the typologies are incomplete and in need of further explication. Clarke and his colleagues view the typology as a dynamic undertaking that will require modification as research and theory emerge. The very fact that the typology evolved from 12 to 25 general techniques over roughly a 10-year period attests to the dynamic nature of the undertaking. Indeed, an attempt to finalize a typology could be viewed as limiting its usefulness.

Clarke (2005) addresses seven common misconceptions about situational crime prevention and offers rebuttals to each (see Table 11.5). Critics often note that situational prevention addresses symptoms rather than the causes of crime (Clarke, 1995; Crawford, 1998; Kleinig, 2000) and this may result in only temporary, short-lived solutions to immediate problems. They also argue that the situational interventions fail to consider more basic social and cultural problems, such as poor education, unemployment, and discrimination. Clarke (2005) counters that, despite this fact, situational crime prevention

---

TABLE 11.5 Seven Misconceptions of Situational Crime Prevention

Criticism	Rebuttal
1. It is simplistic and atheoretical	It is based on three crime opportunity theories: routine activities, crime pattern, and rational choice. It also draws on social psychology
2. It has not been shown to work; it displaces crime and often makes it worse	Many dozens of case studies show that it can reduce crime, usually with little displacement
3. It diverts attention from the root causes of crime	It benefits society by achieving immediate reductions in crime
4. It is a conservative, managerial approach to crime	It promises no more than it can deliver. It requires that solutions be economic and socially acceptable
5. It promotes a selfish, exclusionary society	It provides as much protection to the poor as to the rich
6. It promotes Big Brother and restricts personal freedoms	The democratic process protects society from these dangers. People are willing to endure inconvenience and small infringements of liberty when these protect them from crime
7. It blames the victim	It empowers victims by providing them with information about crime risks and how to avoid them

Source: R.V. Clarke (2005). "Seven misconceptions of situational crime prevention." In N. Tilley (ed.), *Handbook of Crime Prevention and Community Safety*. Portland, OR: Willan. Reprinted with permission.

provides clear benefits to society, and does not preclude simultaneous efforts to address other causes of crime. A second major criticism is that situational crime prevention is atheoretical. Such arguments fail to note the rich and developing theoretical arguments (e.g., routine activities and crime pattern) that direct a great deal of prevention activity.

Critics also argue that some situational techniques may be overly intrusive and border on "Big Brother" watching everyone's activities (Clarke, 1995; Crawford, 1998; von Hirsch, 2000). Indeed, the use of CCTV, electronic tagging, and other surveillance measures allows greater oversight of people. Interestingly, the use of technology (such as CCTV and x-ray technology at airports) for crime prevention has found widespread acceptance among the general public. Critics who argue that there is little evidence that situational prevention techniques are effective ignore the fact that many programs have successfully reduced crime. Arguments that situational interventions work against already marginalized groups and build barriers between citizens and the community (Crawford, 1998; von Hirsch, 2000) fail to note that situational techniques can be used to protect both the rich and the poor, and may include activities that bring citizens together in cooperative endeavors.

A last issue is the failure of situational crime prevention to address fear of crime. By focusing on the perceptions of potential offenders, situational techniques are geared mainly toward the reduction of criminal activity, and evaluations typically ignore the issue of fear. Any impact on fear would appear mainly to the extent that fear is directly related to the level of crime. This does not mean that some situational techniques would not affect fear. As interventions are implemented, particularly by residents and other legitimate users, fear may be reduced. Unfortunately, this possible outcome is rarely addressed.

Implementing Situational Prevention

Besides offering an extensive typology of potential interventions, situational prevention distinguishes itself by approaching problems in a very systematic fashion. Situational prevention has borrowed the SARA process from problem-oriented policing as the model for problem-solving. Proposed by Eck and Spelman (1989), **SARA** stands for **S**canning, **A**nalysis, **R**esponse, and **A**ssessment. Under scanning, situational prevention starts with a specific, identifiable crime problem. That problem is then subjected to analysis, drawing on as wide an array of information and perspectives as possible. This stage offers an important distinction from many other crime control efforts that rely on traditional police and criminal justice system responses to solve problems. Under situational prevention, formal social control agents are only one source of input. Based

> **ON THE WEB**
> *More information on the SARA model can be found on the Center for Problem-Oriented Policing web site at http://www.popcenter.org/about/?p=sara*

on the findings of the analysis, a response (intervention) is identified and implemented. At this point the prevention process continues with an assessment of the program's impact, with the intent of making changes in the response, if necessary. Situational prevention, therefore, is a dynamic process of problem identification, response identification, program implementation, and evaluation and adjustment.

While SARA is the most recognized approach, Ekblom (2002) proposed the 5Is as an alternative model for problem solving that is receiving increased attention in situational prevention. The **5Is** are **I**ntelligence, **I**ntervention, **I**mplementation, **I**nvolvement, and **I**mpact. The relationship between the 5Is and the more recognized SARA process is depicted in Figure 11.1. The greatest distinction to note is the greater detail introduced by breaking down the Response into Intervention, Implementation, and Involvement. Intervention represents the identification of actions and methods to "block, divert or weaken the causes, and attend to risk and protective factors, of *future* criminal events and careers or of wider community safety problems" (Ekblom, 2011a, p. 85). Once the crime prevention action is identified, Implementation represents the actual tasks of putting the plan into action. The third aspect, Involvement, focuses on marshalling the participation of other people and organizations in the intervention. Ekblom (2011a) argues that the greater emphasis on knowledge generation in the 5Is makes them useful for not only situational crime prevention, but also policy making and beyond.

Regardless of the differences and similarities between SARA and the 5Is, both models set a framework for situational crime prevention. They require clearly identifying the problem and appropriate responses. Once responses have been implemented, they are subjected to analysis and an evaluation of their impact. The outcome of this process is either sustaining the program due to its effectiveness or changing the program to address limitations or failures in the project.

More recently, Ekblom and Hirschfield (2014) suggest that, while the 25 situational crime prevention techniques offer a nice potpourri of potential interventions, they are too broad and not as easily applied as one may think. They argue there is a need for a design which is more applicable and action oriented for those who have to implement prevention and security interventions. The key is to identify what the perpetrator is trying to achieve, how that will be done, and how you can anticipate, recognize, and control the behavior (Ekblom and Hirschfield, 2014). In essence, it is necessary to think like the perpetrator. "The offender's behavior is both situationally *caused* … and *causing* of criminal … events" (Ekblom and Hirschfield, 2014, p. 6; emphasis in original). The authors propose the *11 Ds* (see Table 11.6). These are intervention principles that focus on the situation and the potential offenders, relying on the 25 situational crime prevention categories, SARA, the 5Is, and other approaches.

ON THE WEB

The Design Against Crime Research Center at the University of the Arts London is the home for the 5Is and its application. You can access more information at http://www.designagainstcrime. com/files/crimeframeworks/04_5i_framework.pdf

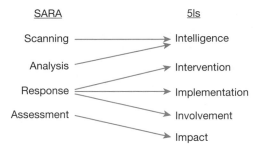

Figure 11.1

Relationship Between the 5Is and SARA

Source: Adapted by author from P. Ekblom (2011a). *Crime Prevention, Security and Community Safety using the 5Is Framework*. New York: Palgrave Macmillan.

TABLE 11.6 **The D Principles**	
Defeat	Physically block access and movement or block/obscure information that offenders want
Disable/Deny	Equipment helpful to offenders such as bugs or cameras
Direct/Deflect	Offenders towards/away from places or behavior
Deter-known	Offenders know the risk of exposure and abandon/abort the attempt
Deter-unknown	Offenders are uncertain what control methods they are up against, and judge the risk of exposure as unacceptable
Discourage	Offenders perceive the effort as too great and/or the reward as too little, relative to risk, so abandon/abort attempt
Demotivate	Awakening, within offenders, motives/emotions contrary to the mission (e.g., empathy with potential victims, removing excuses, coward image)
Deceive	Offenders act on wrong information concerning risk, effort, reward thus increasing chances of arrest or altering decision to act
Disconcert	Causing offenders to make overt involuntary movement or otherwise become startled
Detect	Passive and active exposure; offenders self-expose making legitimate presence/behavior distinctive; improving capacity of people to detect
Detain	Trace, catch, and/or hold identified offenders

Source: Adapted by author from P. Ekblom and A. Hirschfield (2014). "Developing an alternative formulation of SCP principles—the Ds (11 and counting)." *Crime Science* 3:2.

The 11 D principles fall within three basic, overlapping modes of action (depicted in Figure 11.2). These modes are: Practical (where the environment is altered to limit perpetrator action), Psychological (actions that impact the thought processes of the perpetrator), and Personal (involving identifying, tracking, and catching perpetrators) (Ekblom and Hirschfield, 2014). The overlap in the modes indicates that specific Ds/ interventions may impact the perpetrator/event in more than one way.

The D principles reflect a need to provide prevention and security professionals with steps for turning situational prevention techniques into action. These principles are mid-range between theory (such as rational choice and routine activities) and extended lists of potential interventions (such as the 25 situational techniques). Ekblom and Hirschfield (2014) suggest that this approach offers professionals a useful framework for identifying appropriate interventions for different situations. The 11 Ds can be viewed as a refinement of the broader situational crime prevention ideas.

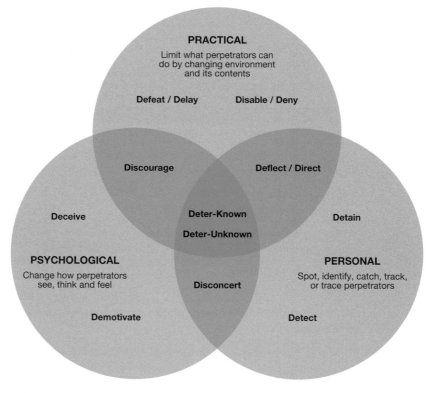

Figure 11.2

Modes of Action of the D Principles

Source: P. Ekblom and A. Hirschfield (2014). "Developing an alternative formulation of SCP principles—the Ds (11 and counting)." *Crime Science* 3:2.

Situational Prevention Studies

The balance of this chapter offers a brief overview of studies examining the implementation of various situational crime prevention techniques. For most of the discussion, the emphasis is on the impact of various prevention techniques. In some cases the examples highlight suggestions for situational prevention for specific crime problems. It is not possible to provide example studies for each of the 25 techniques offered by Cornish and Clarke (2003). Instead, the studies reviewed here should provide the reader with some insight into the types of initiatives/approaches that have been undertaken and the breadth of the problems to which situational techniques have been and could be applied. A broader array of studies can be found in other forums (see, for example, Clarke, 1992, 1993, 1996).

Fare Avoidance and Vandalism of Transit Systems

The failure to pay fares is a common problem on public transportation and a single response is not possible due to the diversity in types of transit system (bus, train, etc.) and the means by which offenders evade payments. An assessment of fare evasion on the British Columbia transit system identified various methods of fare evasion, which formed the basis for a redesign of ticket machines and passes, promotions encouraging the purchase of transit passes, and focused investigations of counterfeit fare media (DesChamps et al., 1991). An evaluation of the intervention revealed significant drops in the level of fare evasion. In an evaluation of the Dutch transit systems, van Andel (1989) found that fare evasion on buses often occurred due to the ability of riders to enter and exit the buses through a rear door, thus avoiding the driver. In response, the system introduced monitors on the buses and a change in procedure that required passengers to enter the bus near the driver and prove payment (van Andel, 1989). Fare evasion significantly fell from the pre-intervention levels.

Actions taken to address fare evasion in the London underground transit system and the New York subway system also have proven effective. The London system instituted a new ticketing system and installed automatic gates at select stations. Comparing post-intervention to pre-intervention ticket sales, Clarke (1993) reports reductions in fare evasion of almost two-thirds. The New York subway system introduced new ticketing systems, along with physical barriers and increased staff control of entrances (Weidner, 1996). Evaluating the impact by comparing the number of arrests and summonses after the changes to those before, Weidner (1996) reports a small but clear decline in the target station, with increases in neighboring stations.

Public transportation systems also suffer an undue level of vandalism. In one of the most widely cited studies, Sloan-Howitt and Kelling (1990) reported on the efforts to eliminate graffiti from New York subway trains. Numerous attempts to thwart graffiti artists, through such efforts as using graffiti-proof paint and securing rail yards, failed to have an impact. In a true situational approach, an assessment of why graffiti artists insisted on using the trains found that what was important to the artists was for their work to "get up" and for people to see it (Sloan-Howitt and Kelling, 1990). The logical solution to the problem, therefore, was to devise a means whereby no one would ever see the work, thus depriving the artist of his audience. Consequently, the subway system instituted a policy of cleaning up each train car. Once cleaned, the car was not allowed in service (and was immediately taken out of service) if it was ever vandalized by graffiti. This eliminated the ability of the artists to "get up" on the trains and eventually stopped further graffiti vandalism (Sloan-Howitt and Kelling, 1990).

Poyner (1988) reports on a different approach to curbing vandalism on double-decker buses in one area of England. An analysis of the problem found that offenders tended to be school-aged boys and vandalism occurred on buses with only a driver. The lack of surveillance was addressed by installing video cameras on several buses, although only two buses had functioning cameras. An important companion to the hardware introduction was heavy publicity and an educational program aimed at youths. The project resulted in a significant drop in repair costs (by roughly two-thirds) for the entire fleet of 80 buses (Poyner, 1988).

Motor Vehicle Theft

Motor vehicle theft is a continuing problem that has generated a variety of different proposed solutions. Mayhew et al. (1976) and Webb (1994) examined the impact of steering column locks on the level of motor vehicle theft in England, Wales, and West Germany. Both analyses show that increasing the difficulty of motor vehicle theft led to reductions in the level of theft. Since the mid-1990s, increased use of automobile immobilizers has been undertaken to avert auto theft. **Immobilizers** are electronic devices that, in the absence of the key, prevent the car from operating (Brown, 2004). These devices have been required in all new cars in the European Union since 1995. Analysis of immobilizers in the United Kingdom reveals clear reductions in auto theft (Brown, 2004). Efforts to address motorcycle theft have often involved legislating the use of helmets (Mayhew et al., 1989). The need for helmets

> **ON THE WEB**
>
> *Thefts of and from motor vehicles is not restricted to public parking lots or decks; it also occurs from homes. You can read more about this problem at http://www.popcenter. org/problems/residential_car_theft*

should reduce opportunistic theft because most offenders do not have a helmet available to them, thus making them easily recognizable to others. Evaluations in England, The Netherlands, and (the former) West Germany all find reduced motorcycle theft after the initiation of helmet laws (Mayhew et al., 1989).

Other efforts to limit auto theft have included changing the design of parking decks and parking areas, increasing use of security cameras, and introducing patrols. Poyner (1991) reports on prevention efforts in two different parking areas—a parking deck in town and a university parking lot. For the parking deck, it was determined that physical changes aimed at restricting access to the vehicles was the key to prevention, along with improved lighting and increased presence of legitimate users. The evaluation showed significant reductions in auto thefts after program implementation, as compared to two other area parking lots. The university project implemented improved lighting, closed-circuit television monitoring, and changes eliminating obstructions to observation. The lot receiving closed-circuit equipment showed the greatest drop in auto thefts, and there was some evidence that a nearby lot also benefited through decreased thefts (a possible diffusion effect) (Poyner, 1991). A study of the impact of bicycle patrols on auto theft in Vancouver uncovered a large drop in thefts during the month of patrol operation, as well as after the patrol was discontinued (Barclay et al., 1996).

There is evidence that interventions to reduce auto theft have caused some displacement. One form of displacement is to older cars that have not been outfitted with steering column locks or immobilizers (Brown, 2004; Mayhew et al., 1976; Webb, 1994). Brown (2004) also noted evidence of tactical displacement (movement to stealing keys) due to the introduction of immobilizers. Displacement has also appeared in increased thefts of motorcycles and mopeds (Mayhew et al., 1976; Webb, 1994). The bicycle patrol in Vancouver uncovered large increases in auto thefts for adjacent areas during the month of the intervention (Barclay et al, 1996). It would appear that displacement is evident in some evaluations of efforts to prevent auto theft.

Theft Offenses

Situational techniques have been used in relation to a wide array of theft offenses. The impact of electronic tagging of property has been demonstrated in a number of studies. In one study, Scherdin (1986) found that the tagging of books in a university library resulted in both a significant decrease in lost books and an increase in the number of items processed through circulation. Perhaps of greater impact was the simultaneous reduction in lost audiovisual materials that could not be tagged (Scherdin, 1986). This suggests a diffusion of benefits from the books to other library holdings. Farrington et al. (1993) report that electronic tagging significantly reduced the level of retail shoplifting. Similarly, Handford (1994) indicates that computer stores using electronic tagging experience low theft levels relative to national data for comparable stores.

The marketplace also offers targets other than the stores themselves. Poyner and Webb (1992) report on efforts to eliminate thefts from shopping bags in a crowded marketplace. An analysis of the problem suggested that an important contributing factor was the congestion caused by narrow aisles. The solution, therefore, was to widen the aisles, thereby relieving the congestion and increasing the surveillance opportunities. Their evaluation of the changes showed great reductions in the level of thefts after the redesign efforts (Poyner and Webb, 1992). Holt and Spencer (2005) report on efforts to reduce robberies at ATM locations. Based on interviews with convicted street robbers, the authors worked with banks to make ATMs safer by demarcating safe zones around the cash dispensers. This approach established a psychological barrier between potential victims and offenders. Holt and Spencer (2005) note a significant reduction in robberies at the marked ATMs compared to the control ATMs, which were unchanged.

Identity theft is a major problem in modern society, particularly given the Internet and other technologies that allow for impersonal commerce to take place. Berg (2008) demonstrates a variety of situational techniques that should be effective at combating identity theft. Among the suggestions are employing antivirus programs to block the theft of personal information from a computer, data encryption to make stolen information and computers useless, physical security of computers, banning the use of portable devices (e.g., memory sticks) that can capture data from computers, and stronger methods to validate the identification of an individual attempting to make a purchase (Berg, 2008). The impact of situational prevention techniques on identity theft and related fraud is evident in the analysis of changes to debit and credit card procedures. Levi (2008) reports huge reductions in losses after the introduction of computer chips to cards and the use of PINs (personal identification numbers). Other effective interventions are the use of fraud alerts (e.g., calls to card owners when unusual activity is noted on an account) and more in-depth identity checks when an individual applies for credit or forms of identity (e.g., passports) (Levi, 2008).

Product Design

One important aspect of situational crime prevention includes designing or redesigning at-risk products for crime prevention. It is possible to consider physically designing products in ways that protect them from theft or being used in other offenses. As Clarke and Newman (2005) point out, the targets of crime are everyday objects. It is possible to alter the design of objects to make them less amenable to crime.

Many products lend themselves to crime. These so-called *hot products* which are highly targeted by thieves may be characterized by being CRAVED—Concealable, Removable, Available, Valuable, Enjoyable and Disposable (Clarke, 1999). In essence, these are products desired by people because of their construction or makeup and are easily targeted by offenders. For example, electronic devices such as MP3 players and PDAs are easily concealed, expensive, small enough to carry away, and easily disposable. At the same time, automobiles are not easily concealable or even disposable, but they are a common theft target. It is also possible with modern technology to take seemingly low-risk items and make them more susceptible to theft. This can include making fraudulent credit cards, drugs, designer bags, and food (to name a few).

Ekblom (2008) points out several ways in which products play a role in crime beyond simply being a target for theft. Presented in terms of a **Misdeeds** and Security framework, products can be the target of an offense or used within offending behavior (see Table 11.7). In each case, the design of a product either makes the product a viable target for an offense, or the product facilitates some other offense. Following the CRAVED idea, many objects are targeted for their value. Other items may invite vandalism. Yet others can be used in the commission of other crimes, such as altering a document to allow an underage person to purchase alcohol. The key throughout these ideas is the need to recognize the potential problems with products and make appropriate design changes.

Ekblom (2005) outlines several methods for securing products through design. First, he suggests that it is possible to make products inherently secure. This can be done by making them less attractive or distinctive, and thus less likely to be targeted by offenders. A product can also be designed in such a way that it actually protects other property, such as chairs which can secure purses from theft. Second, product design may incorporate prevention/security devices within the product or its display. Ink tags on clothing or the use of cable locks are examples of this approach. The third approach is to restrict offender access to the target or tools used to target a product (Ekblom, 2005). Other ways of securing products against crime include adding security devices to products (such as security cables or alarms), securing the environment in which the product is located (such as by using safes or access control measures), and employing remote security interventions (such as restricting access to tools needed for crime or controlling the outlets for stolen goods) (Ekblom, 2008). The approach or mechanism

---

TABLE 11.7 Products and Misdeeds

	Examples
MISappropriated	Theft of the product itself
MIStreated	Vandalism or destruction of items
MIShandled	Returning of stolen goods, use of counterfeit currency, use of fake documents
MISused	Use of a product for illegal purposes such as prescription drugs or weapons
MISbehaved with	Contamination of products, the ability to set off false alarms without being observed

Source: Constructed by author from P. Ekblom (2008). "Designing products against crime." In R. Wortley and L. Mazerolle (eds.), *Environmental Criminology and Crime Analysis*. Cullompton, Devon, U.K.: Willan.

to use in protecting products is dictated by both the product itself and the situation in which the product is targeted.

Redesign of bicycle parking stands has received a great deal of attention in Europe due to the heavy use of bicycles for transportation. Thorpe et al. (2012) discuss seven different designs used in London to secure bicycles. Similarly, shopping carts incorporating a secure basket/safe and table clips have been designed to protect handbags from theft (Ekblom et al., 2012; Sidebottom et al., 2012). Other projects have introduced digital DNA (a unique non-sequential numerical code), holograms, watermarks, and bi-directional barcoding (which includes 10 to 30 times the information found in regular barcodes) affixed to products as means of deterring counterfeiting (Segato, 2012).

A wide range of products has been the subject of design changes for prevention purposes. The automobile is a prime example of redesign for crime prevention (see Table 11.8). A number of changes have been made in autos to prevent their theft or the theft of items from them (Clarke and Newman, 2005). Ignition locks and steering column locks are universal in new cars, and alarms and locator devices are common, particularly in more expensive autos. Removable radios or radio faces, stronger door locks, and the marking of auto parts with identification numbers all address theft from autos.

There are a number of other examples of product design for prevention purposes (Clarke and Newman, 2005). Theft of small items from stores can be made more difficult

TABLE 11.8 Changes Made at Manufacture to Cars and Crimes Prevented

Crime	Device or redesign
Unauthorized use and joy-riding	Ignition locks; improved door locks; steering column locks; alarms; immobilizers
Theft of cars or major body parts	As above but also: parts marking; GPS (global positioning system) locators; tamper-proof license plates; microdots
Theft from cars	Stronger door locks; alarms; lockable gas caps; redesigned emblems; security coded radios; removable radios; dispersed audio system
Vandalism	Retractable aerials
Assassination	Armor plating; ram bars
Illegal use of rental car	GPS locators to detect speeding

Source: R.V. Clarke and G.R. Newman (2005). "Modifying criminogenic products: What role for governments?" In Clarke, R.V. and G.R. Newman (eds.), *Designing Out Crime from Products and Systems*. Monsey, NY: Criminal Justice Press.

by putting the item in large packages that are more difficult to conceal. Purse snatching can be prevented by designing them with stronger straps that cannot be cut or broken. Computer hacking has been made more difficult with the introduction of special software. Caller ID has helped to stem telephone harassment (Clarke and Newman, 2005). The design of smart guns recognize the owner and will only discharge if used by that person (Lester, 2001). These and many other examples of product design changes are made for the purpose of preventing different types of crimes.

Cozens (2014) notes there is a crime life cycle for products that is tied to the market for each type of product. The first stage is Introduction of a new product. The product is relatively rare and has little market share or recognition; thus, it is not a high target for theft. This moves to the Growth stage where sales are increasing and knowledge and demand is on the up slope. The third stage is the Mature stage. Here the product is well known and desired. There are a lot of the items available for theft and the demand leads to theft for both use and sale to others. This is the peak period for crime. The final stage is Decline, where the product has either saturated the market or is being replaced with new products. Theft falls off in this stage. Some products go through this cycle quickly, some very slowly, and others may not fit the cycle at all (Cozens, 2014). It is not unusual that public pressure or government intervention is need to help interrupt this cycle and force project changes.

While the idea of product design for prevention purposes has been gaining attention, relatively few initiatives have been subjected to evaluation (Clarke and Newman, 2005). There are evaluations that often involve weak research designs with no control groups for comparison purposes. Evaluations that have been completed typically suggest that the design changes are effective at bringing about significant reductions in crime (Clarke and Newman, 2005). Stronger evaluation, however, needs to be undertaken.

A number of problems and issues face the movement toward product design for prevention. One primary concern is the fact that most designers are not trained with an eye toward crime prevention, thus making the design process difficult at the outset (Learmont, 2005). Second, the pre-

> **ON THE WEB**
>
> *Growth in interest in product design for prevention has been increasing in recent years. The Design Council in England offers a great deal of information on this topic. You can read more at its web site: http:// www.designcouncil.org.uk/knowledge-resources/ search/im_field_design_discipline/product-design-27*

vention features must be understood by the users/consumers and be simple enough to guarantee that they are employed (Ekblom, 2005; Lester, 2001). Basically, the features need to be user friendly. Third, any changes need to adhere to the aesthetic features of the product. Fourth, there may be both legal and ethical questions to be addressed. The incorporation of electronic tracking devices, for example, raises issues of privacy (Ekblom, 2008; Lester, 2001). Yet another concern with product design involves the issue of increased costs due to the extra features (Ekblom, 2008). It is possible that product redesign can result in costs that are prohibitive. Despite these (and other) concerns, product design for prevention is a growing area of interest that should receive increased attention, particularly for its impact on the level of crime.

Revictimization

Situational prevention has great potential in relation to targeting previous victims and offense sites. One place where this was undertaken was the Kirkholt housing estate near Manchester, England (Forrester et al., 1988, 1990). A major thrust of the program was to target burglary victims to prevent further offenses. Among the prevention actions were improved physical security of homes, property identification, and "cocoon" neighborhood watch (small numbers of homes per group). A key element of the project was the removal of pre-payment fuel meters in burglarized homes. Evaluations of these efforts revealed significant reductions in repeat burglaries after program implementation. The absence of the pre-payment meters may have been the most important of the prevention measures. Anderson and Pease (1997) report on another attempt at targeting repeat victimization in Huddersfield, England. Victims received a graduated response based on the number of prior victimizations. Possible responses included the installation of alarms, security surveys, consultation with police, and cocoon neighborhood watch. Inspection of offense figures over a 25-month period shows reduced repeat victimization in the target area and an overall burglary decline of 70 percent (Anderson and Pease, 1997). Other projects targeting repeat victimization (noted in the last chapter) have shown reductions due to targeting past victims (Chainey, 2012; Grove and Farrell, 2012).

> **ON THE WEB**
>
> *More information on repeat victimization and responses to it can be found in the Tool Guide from the Center for Problem-Oriented Policing at http:// www.popcenter.org/tools/repeat_victimization/*

Child Sexual Assault

Typical discussions of situational crime prevention involve property offenses and largely avoid interpersonal crimes. While it is possible to argue that personal crimes are more likely to be spontaneous and less likely to be planned than property crimes, this does not mean that situational techniques cannot be used with personal offenses. One example of situational crime prevention with personal crimes involves child sexual assault. Tremblay (2008) notes that the Internet has greatly enhanced the ability of pedophiles to interact, attract victims, and gain social support for their behavior. Wortley and Smallbone (2008) argue that it is possible to attack child sexual abuse by attacking the opportunity dimension of offending.

> **ON THE WEB**
>
> *Discussion of situational techniques for addressing organized crime and crowd violence can be found on the textbook web site.*

They suggest increasing the effort by making it difficult for offenders to enter areas where children are found or by enhancing the screening of potential employees in businesses that cater to youths. It is also possible to reduce facilitators by limiting access to pornography or contact with other offenders. Increasing risks and reducing permissibility are also avenues to explore with child sexual assault. Wortley and Smallbone's (2008) discussion of situational techniques with child sexual assault is illustrative of the possibilities for using situational prevention to combat personal offenses.

Other Crimes

The offense categories discussed above are just a sample of the many applications of situational techniques. The Center for Problem-Oriented Policing has produced guides addressing 80 types of offenses, ranging from check and card fraud to street racing to gun violence to elderly abuse. In each guide, situational techniques form a core of the discussion and recommendations for prevention.

> ┌─ ON THE WEB ─────────────
> *The Center for Problem-Oriented Policing has more*
> *information on situational approaches to crowd*
> *control, including Madensen and Eck's (2008) work.*
> *This can be accessed at http://www.popcenter.org/*
> *problems/spectator_violence*

Summary

Several observations can be drawn from studies of situational prevention. First, while there is an emphasis on property crimes, situational crime prevention is applicable to personal offenses. Second, a wide array of interventions appears in the literature and this diversity is evident both across different crime problems and within the same offenses. What this suggests is that the prevention initiatives truly are "situational" in nature and cannot simply be applied to the same crime that appears in different places at different times. Third, research successfully demonstrates the effectiveness of programs that target effort, risk, and reward, and there is emerging evidence on the use of guilt and shame. Fourth, in many analyses there is evidence of either displacement or diffusion, despite the fact that many of the research designs do not specifically test for them. It is important to note that displacement is never 100 percent. Finally, the focused nature of situational prevention efforts may help maximize the success of the programs. Programs that attempt to make modest changes in specific problems at specific times and places should be more successful than multifaceted programs aiming for large-scale changes.

Situational crime prevention offers an approach that seeks to target specific problems with individualized interventions. As such, these techniques epitomize the ideas of secondary prevention. This does not mean that we are looking at entirely new forms of interventions. Indeed, many of the actions discussed in the later part of this chapter are the same ideas we discussed under primary prevention. The success of situational approaches has moved these ideas into the forefront of many crime prevention discussions and will continue to receive a great deal of attention in the future. The next chapter addresses a topic that also seeks to identify specific problems and implement targeted interventions—partnerships.

KEY TERMS

- 5Is
- CRAVED
- crime life cycle
- crime pattern theory
- crime scripts
- digital DNA
- immobilizers
- lifestyle perspective
- Misdeeds
- permissibility
- pressures
- prompts
- provocations
- rational choice theory
- routine activities theory
- SARA
- situational crime prevention
- smart guns

CHAPTER 12 Partnerships for Crime Prevention

CHAPTER OUTLINE

LEARNING OBJECTIVES

After reading this chapter you should be able to:

- Debate the meaning of "community policing" by discussing different definitions and key features of it.
- List and define the features of community policing.
- Tell what SARA stands for and discuss its component parts.
- Provide examples of community policing programs and talk about their effectiveness.
- Discuss civil abatement and injunction approaches and their impact.
- Talk about hot spots policing and the evidence on its effectiveness.
- Demonstrate your knowledge of SACSI and PSN.
- Discuss Operation Ceasefire and its replications.
- Give an overview of Crime and Disorder partnerships in the United Kingdom.
- List and discuss the keys to successful partnerships.

The inability of the police to handle the crime problem alone and the recognition that crime and disorder cannot be dealt with solely through the arrest and prosecution of offenders has led to the development of alternative responses and methods. Partnership initiatives are at the forefront of these activities. While many of the ideas and interventions found in partnerships are similar to those found in general citizen crime prevention, the onus for action is on the police and social service agencies to work in cooperation with one another and the general public. These endeavors often seek to target specific problems. The underlying philosophy is to encourage interaction and cooperation between police officers, residents, community groups, and other agencies to solve problems. Rosenbaum (2002, p. 180) notes that:

> the value of partnerships in theory lies in their responsiveness to the etiology of complex problems, their ability to encourage interagency cooperation both inside and outside the criminal justice system, their ability to attack problems from multiple sources of influence and to target multiple causal mechanisms.

In many respects, partnerships mirror ideas found in situational prevention. A key assumption is that there are factors underlying the crime and disorder problems in the community. The typical police response to the problems, that being arrest and prosecution, does little to address the causes of the problems. Arrest and prosecution deal mainly with the overt symptoms. These new approaches seek to identify problems and potential solutions, as well as implement interventions. As such, partnerships fall squarely in the realm of secondary prevention. They target high-risk situations.

In the United States, the most recognized partnership effort is community policing (although community policing is not always called a partnership). Because of its high profile, community policing receives a great deal of attention in this chapter. After discussing the problems of defining community policing and identifying how community policing should work, the chapter turns to evaluating the effectiveness of community policing programs and partnership initiatives.

Community Policing

Understanding **community policing** requires some knowledge of the more traditional view of what the police are and what they should do. For most people, the formal police role is to answer calls about crime, undertake investigations, make arrests, and assist in the prosecution of offenders. Fighting crime (and crime prevention) is primarily the responsibility of the police. Consequently, the police are often judged by the level of crime in the community. Arrests are the benchmark by which the public judges police effectiveness.

The police also are called on to provide **order maintenance**, that is, functions that do not deal with an immediate criminal action. Order maintenance includes responding to disabled autos, escorting funerals and parades, dealing with barking dogs, responding to false alarms and noise complaints, and delivering messages. Various studies show that these activities consume the majority of police time, with the police spending roughly 20 percent of their time on actual law enforcement efforts (Kelling, 1978; Lab, 1984; Walker, 1983; Wilson, 1968). While critics argue that the police should not be involved in order-maintenance activities, Hoover (1992) argues that order maintenance is a key part of traditional policing and serves to keep society fun_____ fashion. As such, order maintenance enhances the law enforceme_____

Precursors to Community Policing

Trying to respond to all of the desires of the citizer_____ is one possible reason for the inability of the police to contro_____ of the police and the apparent failure of past police practice_____ have led to the introduction of different strategies. One app_____ patrol. Research shows that foot patrol has had a mixed impact on crime (Bowers ____ Hirsch, 1987; Esbensen, 1987; Police Foundation, 1981; Trojanowicz, 1983), although it appears to reduce the level of citizens' fear and improve attitudes toward the police (Brown and Wycoff, 1987; Police Foundation, 1981; Trojanowicz, 1983). The police are also a key ingredient of both the establishment and maintenance of neighborhood watch and citizen crime prevention initiatives. Underlying these activities has been the recognition that the police cannot solve crime on their own or address the increased calls for assistance by the public. The police need to build better relations with citizens and increase the involvement of citizens in crime prevention and crime policy.

Defining Community Policing

The fact that elements of community policing appear in past practices demonstrates that community policing is not a totally new idea, although the term "community policing" is a relatively new one. In addition, there has been a shift in the basic orientation of everyday police activity emerging under the rubric of "community policing." This shift is from the traditional view of "crime fighting" through arrests to a view that fighting crime involves a broader set of interventions.

Arriving at a single definition of community policing has proved to be an elusive goal. While a single definition has not emerged, the various definitions found in Table 12.1 tap the essential elements offered by most writers. Most of these definitions reflect the fact that community policing is more of a philosophy of policing, rather than a clearly definable method (see, for example, Greene and Mastrofski, 1988; Trojanowicz and

---

TABLE 12.1 Definitions of Community Policing

Weisel and Eck (1994, p. 51):
A diverse set of practices united by the general idea that the police and the public need to become better partners in order to control crime, disorder, and a host of other problems.

Wilkinson and Rosenbaum (1994, p. 110):
"Community Policing" represents a fundamental change in the basic role of the police officer, including changes in his or her *skills*, *motivations*, and *opportunity* to engage in problem-solving activities and to develop new partnerships with key elements of the community.

Oliver (1998, p. 51):
A systemic approach to policing with the paradigm of instilling and fostering a sense of community, within a geographical neighborhood, to improve the quality of life. It achieves this through the decentralization of the police and the implementation of a synthesis of three key components: (1) the redistribution of traditional police resources; (2) the interaction of police and all community members to reduce crime and the fear of crime through indigenous proactive programs; and (3) a concerted effort to resolve the cause of crime, rather than the symptoms.

Office of Community Oriented Policing Services (2006):
Community policing focuses on crime and social disorder through the delivery of police services that includes aspects of traditional law enforcement, as well as prevention, problem solving, community engagement, and partnerships. The community policing model balances reactive responses to calls for service with proactive problem solving centered on the causes of crime and disorder. Community policing requires police and citizens to join together as partners in the course of both identifying and effectively addressing these issues.

Bucqueroux, 1989; Walker, 1999). Beyond the fact of this philosophical shift, the various definitions of community policing generally include several essential features. These are community involvement, problem solving, a community base, and redefined goals for the police.

Community Involvement

First, community policing requires cooperation between the police and other members of the community. The community members may be individual citizens, citizen groups, business associations, legislative bodies, and other local agencies (such as health departments, building inspectors, and community development offices). Community involvement does not stop at the point of calling the police when something occurs. Instead, citizens must be involved in identifying and solving all sorts of community problems—not just criminal acts.

Problem Solving

The emphasis on **problem solving** is perhaps the most important element of community policing. Rather than simply dealing with the crime that occurs through investigation and arrest, community policing challenges officers to identify the underlying causes and contributors to the crime, and seek out solutions to those problems. Community policing, therefore, sees crime as a symptom of more basic concerns. The police can either deal with the symptom or try to address the ultimate cause. While law enforcement should do both, the community policing orientation shifts the primary attention to the underlying problems.

This orientation also appears under the name **problem-oriented policing**. Problem-oriented policing means approaching issues and problems differently based on the uniqueness of each situation. This is a drastic shift from the traditional view that the police should use the criminal code to respond to calls for service. If the code prohibits the activity, the police can (and should) make an arrest and set the criminal justice system in motion. At best, this response will eliminate further criminal behavior through either its deterrent or incapacitative effect. Events that are not proscribed in the criminal code can be ignored. The problem-oriented approach argues that invoking the criminal code is only one avenue for dealing with societal issues. Instead, different problems require alternative solutions or interventions. The police, therefore, need to identify and pursue solutions to the root problem.

The difference between problem-oriented policing and community policing is not always clear or great. One potential differentiating element is the explicit reliance on the community in community policing. This is not an absolute difference, because many "problem-oriented" approaches also rely on community involvement. At the same time, police sweeps and intensive patrol can be considered problem-oriented responses that do not need or require citizen participation. Second, Hoover (1992) suggests that problem-oriented and community policing differ in the duration of the police intervention. Problem-oriented policing involves sustained order maintenance focusing on specific problems and needs over a limited period. Conversely, community policing sets up the police as *community managers* who are involved in wide-ranging community issues over an extended period (Hoover, 1992). This distinction highlights the central role of the community in community policing.

Community Base

Critical to community policing is the decentralization of the police operation. Community policing typically means assigning officers to a specific neighborhood. This may be done in a variety of ways, including the establishment of neighborhood stations, storefront offices, foot patrol, and others. The assignments are long term, with the expectation that the officers will intimately get to know the community, its problems, and its citizens. Community policing assumes that the failure of the police to identify problems and relate to citizens, among others, is due to the distance that central stations and patrol cars place between officers and citizens. The daily interaction with the community should alert the officer to the problems and needs of the residents. The expected result is increased goodwill on the part of residents and an increased desire by citizens to assist and involve themselves with the police.

Redefined Goals

The fourth major element of community policing involves altering the goals of policing. In one sense, this is closely allied to the idea of identifying and attacking the root causes of problems. At the same time, however, this could mean a great shift in how the police are judged. Most departments are judged, both by themselves and the citizenry, in terms of the number of arrests made. Community policing initiatives, to the extent that they deal with underlying causes and involve officers in non-arrest activities, require that the department and officers be held to different standards. In addition to arrests, community policing programs can be judged by reduced crime, the elimination of problem properties, increased feelings of safety, less neighborhood disorder, community cohesion, and many other outcomes. It is important to note that community policing should emphasize the ends, rather than the means to the ends. That is, instead of focusing on how things get done, the primary concern is the elimination of the root problem.

Summary

Other key features of community policing offered in the literature include a less rigid organizational structure, a focus on disorder, different training for officers, collaboration, de-emphasizing calls for service or arrests, and recognizing the complexity of criminal behavior (Carter, 1995; Eck and Rosenbaum, 1994; Hope, 1994; Walker, 1999; Watson et al., 1998; Wilkinson and Rosenbaum, 1994). Many of these ideas are implicit in the four major themes listed above. It is important to note that all of these ideas must work in unison. Just having one component, such as community offices, is not enough. Community policing requires fundamental changes in philosophy, strategy, and programming (Cordner, 1995).

It is also possible to identify what community policing is not. Community policing is not police–community relations. While community policing should build better rapport and relations between the police and the public, that effort is not enough to qualify as community policing. Another common misconception is that moving police officers to foot patrol, storefront offices, or other methods of decentralization is the same as community policing. Unfortunately, unless there is a corresponding change in the other elements of community policing, these efforts only change the location of traditional policing. Community policing also is not simply targeting a problem or location using traditional police techniques. These efforts may be new for the police organization, but they do not involve other societal members in the problem solving. Indeed, many traditional police activities can masquerade as community policing by shifting officers and using new names. It is important, however, to make more fundamental changes in the organization's operations.

Problem Identification

Perhaps the central task of any partnership is the identification of problems and their solutions. Eck and Spelman (1989) offer a four-step process for problem solving. These steps are referred to as **SARA**: **S**canning, **A**nalysis, **R**esponse, and **A**ssessment. *Scanning* involves the identification of the problems, issues, and concerns in the community. This information may arise from the observations officers make as they work in the community, from residents or businesses who bring problems to the officers, from other agencies (such as schools or hospitals) in the community, or from the systematic study of data and information on the area. One primary method used in scanning involves computer-generated analyses of when and where crime occurs. The analysis of crime "hot spots" (Sherman, 1995) and the generation of crime maps represent two such attempts. Other efforts may involve the analysis of calls for service, systematic observation of the community, or surveying citizens or community groups. In every case, the police should be working in partnership with others to identify problems that need to be addressed.

The second stage is the *analysis* of the problem. It is particularly important that more than just the police are involved in this activity. An array of individuals and agencies should participate in the analysis. For example, if drug dealing is centered in a house, apartment, or public housing building, the police, landlords, housing authority personnel, the health department, and/or the city attorney need to be involved in the problem analysis. If the drug activity centers on youths, it may be advisable to include the schools, probation office, or youth groups in the process. The intent is to bring together a diversity of expertise and insight. This diversity will bring different information and viewpoints and assist in understanding what factors are involved in the problem.

It is from this cooperative interaction that different *responses* will emerge. Who is involved in implementing the response will vary greatly. In some cases the police may have little day-to-day involvement in the intervention because the identified response requires expertise and abilities that the police do not have. An example of this would be the use of civil litigation against owners of property where drug use is allowed to continue.

While the police can deliver summonses, much of the work will be conducted by lawyers for the jurisdiction and other departments that can help to shut down the building (such as a health department).

The final, but essential, step is *assessment*. Eck and Spelman (1989) note that this entire process can succeed only if the interventions are evaluated for their effectiveness. This evaluation, however, is not meant simply as a means of gauging success. Rather, its importance is found in the feedback it provides to the process and to improving (or altering) the intervention. A graphic depiction of the process can be seen in Figure 12.1.

Variations on the SARA process or other systematic problem-solving processes that involve the community are essential for community policing partnering. No matter what technique or approach is used, the effort revolves around dealing with the causes of the problems, not the symptoms. Consequently, assessment of the intervention requires looking at more than just reduced crime, increased arrests, or other outcomes typically relied on by the police.

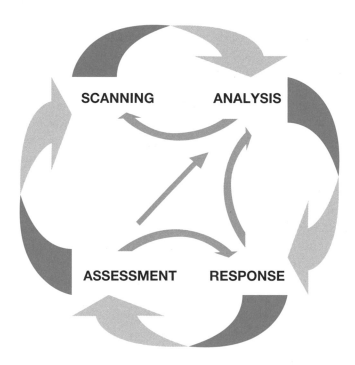

Figure 12.1

SARA Process

Source: R.V. Clarke and J.E. Eck (2005). *Crime Analysis for Problem Solvers in 60 Small Steps*. Washington, DC: Office of Community Oriented Policing Services.

Partnership Efforts and Assessment

Partnership programs have grown throughout the United States, Canada, the United Kingdom, and many other countries. Under the heading of community policing, Wycoff (1995) reports that approximately 800 law enforcement agencies in 1993 had implemented community policing in the United States. As of 2001, more than 10,000 law enforcement agencies report more than 113,000 community police officers on duty in the United States (Zhao et al., 2002). Partnerships, however, appear under a variety of headings and involve police in a wide range of capacities. These partnerships vary greatly, largely due to the emphasis on identifying interventions that address a specific problem. The following pages discuss various partnership initiatives.

Community Policing

The **Chicago Alternative Police Strategy (CAPS)** is perhaps the best example of successfully implementing a community-oriented policing approach. Chicago opted to move its entire police force into community policing. CAPS began in five of the city's 25 police beats in 1993 with the support of the police administration and the mayor (Hartnett and Skogan, 1999). Key aspects of the program include assigning officers to permanent neighborhood beats, the involvement of residents in the identification of problems and potential solutions, and reliance on other agencies (both public and private) to address identified issues. Citizen interaction is the cornerstone of the program and the police meet with neighborhood residents to engender meaningful interaction. These meetings identify a wide range of local problems, including gangs, drugs, graffiti, burglary, and physical and social disorder (Skogan and Hartnett, 1997).

As expected under community policing, CAPS responses vary from neighborhood to neighborhood. Improved police enforcement appears throughout the project and often focuses on drug problems. Efforts to clean up problem locations and generally improve the physical conditions of neighborhoods represent a major initiative in the program. The ability to improve the areas is directly related to the ability to mobilize other city services that are suited to those efforts. Mobilizing residents to provide surveillance, work with one another, call the police, and take other actions also appear throughout the project. These actions have successfully reduced the signs of physical decay, impacted the extent of visible gang and drug activity, reduced area crime rates, and improved resident's attitudes and assessments of the police and the city (Skogan and Hartnett, 1997). Unfortunately, CAPS is an exceptional case amid many others in which community policing is little more than a means to hire more officers and build good public relations.

One of the reasons for this state of affairs is the fact that community policing programs rarely undergo any form of rigorous impact evaluation. At best, evaluations tend to be process evaluations that look at the number of community policing officers hired and put on the street, or the assignment of officers to "community" or neighborhood offices or beats, thus making them community police officers. Most evaluations fail to assess the degree of problem solving taking place, the number and breadth of community members or agencies involved in the problem identification and problem solving, or the changes in crime, fear, or disorder related to the problem-solving efforts.

Evidence does exist that the police can build cooperative partnerships with citizens and other agencies, but when outcome evaluations are completed, the results are typically modest. Zhao et al. (2002, 2003), analyzing the impact of community policing, report that cities receiving community policing funds make a significantly greater number of arrests and experience significantly lower levels of violent and property crimes. What these analyses do not reveal is the actual community policing activities and the types of partnering efforts that bring about these changes. It does suggest, however, that community policing creates positive change.

Hot Spots Policing

The recognition that crimes often cluster in place and time has led to specific efforts to address that crime convergence, an approach called **hot spots policing**. Attacking hot spots requires analysis of the locale and the generation of interactions appropriate for the problem. This can include everything from traditional policing to problem-oriented policing to situational crime prevention techniques. As illustrated in Chapter 10, the confluence of crime by time and place means that prevention efforts have the potential to have a major impact.

Numerous evaluations report positive results of hot spots policing. Braga and Bond (2008) compare different problem-oriented policing activities at 17 hot spots in Lowell, Massachusetts. Most of the interventions rely on situational crime prevention techniques. Their analysis shows 20 percent fewer calls for service than in the control areas not receiving services. More importantly, robbery is down by 40 percent, with burglary and assault down by 33 percent (Braga and Bond, 2008). Taylor et al. (2011), investigating violent crime hot spots in Jacksonville, Florida, uncover mixed results. The authors compare three groups of hot spots: controls, those receiving saturation/directed police patrol, and those getting problem-oriented policing/situational crime prevention. Compared to the control areas, the problem-oriented policing hot spots experience a significant drop in violent crime. Interestingly, saturation/directed patrol hot spots show increased crime (Taylor et al., 2011).

Another recent evaluation reports on the impact of hot spots policing in Philadelphia. Groff et al. (2015) conducted a randomized field experiment. The authors looked at the impact of problem-oriented policing (using the SARA approach), foot patrols, and offender-focused policing (targeting repeat offenders) in 60 violent crime hot spots (with 20 hot spots randomly assigned to each condition) and 21 control hot spots. The offender-focused approach has the greatest impact, reducing crime by 42 percent. Neither the problem-oriented policing nor the foot patrols have a significant impact on crime (Groff et al., 2015). The authors claim the failure of the problem-oriented policing activities may be due to poor implementation. Telep et al. (2014), studying proactive policing in Sacramento, California hot spots, report significant reductions in both calls for service and Part I crime in experimental areas.

Two reviews provide support for hot spots policing. A National Research Council review notes that hot spots policing is effective at reducing crime (Skogan and Frydl, 2004). A more recent meta-analysis also reports positive results. Braga et al. (2014) identify 16 studies with data available for analysis. They report that 85 percent of the results show that hot spots policing is effective when compared to control settings. Pooling the individual study results, Braga et al. (2014) report a significant mean effect of hot spots policing. Problem-oriented policing approaches show twice the impact of traditional policing. The results of these reviews, along with individual study findings, show that hot spots policing is effective at reducing crime, although the extent of the impact varies by type of intervention and crime.

Civil Abatement and Injunctions

An interesting partnership for dealing with problems, particularly drug issues, involves the use of civil abatement and injunction procedures. **Civil abatement** uses mainly civil and administrative law and codes to control locations and behavior at locations. These activities may involve landlords, citizens, health departments, zoning boards, the police, and city/county attorneys. **Injunctions** involve court orders placing rules and/ or restrictions on the behavior of individuals. Civil gang injunctions may prohibit gang members from associating in public, marking territory, trespassing, loitering, or other similar activities (LA City Attorney's Office, 2009). The advent of these efforts can be traced to work in Portland, Oregon, in 1987 (Davis and Lurigio, 1998).

Two notable areas in which abatement has been used involve gang behavior and drug offenses. In terms of drug crimes, abatement efforts seek to eliminate the use of locations for drug sales or drug use. Property owners can be fined, buildings can be confiscated or boarded up, tenants can be evicted, or structures can be demolished as a result of abatement procedures (Mazerolle and Roehl, 1998). In terms of gang behavior, injunctions seek to ban gangs from congregating in public as a group, thus impacting offending behavior. Violating an injunction can result in arrest (O'Deane, 2012).

Oakland's **Specialized Multi-Agency Response Teams (SMART)** is a prime example of civil abatement. SMART relies on the cooperation of police, citizens, and other groups to solve neighborhood problems. Civil court remedies are a cornerstone of the project, although police enforcement and patrol are important components. In a series of reports, Mazerolle and her colleagues (Green, 1995b; Mazerolle and Roehl, 1999; Mazerolle et al., 1998) demonstrate the effectiveness of the program. One hundred target sites, divided evenly into experimental and control groups, formed the basis of the evaluation. At experimental sites, landlords were contacted by police and received assistance (from the police and other agencies) in dealing with problem tenants, including evicting intransigent individuals. Civil proceedings could be brought against both the landlords and the tenants. Data from calls for police service, interviews, and observations over more than three years reveal significant declines in signs of physical and social disorder, decreased drug sellers, and increased levels of civil behavior (Green, 1995b; Mazerolle and Roehl, 1999; Mazerolle et al., 1998). Control areas showed increased problems or little change in key outcomes.

Two other examples of civil abatement are San Diego's Drug Abatement Response Team (DART) and Project TOUGH (Taking Out Urban Gang Headquarters) in Los Angeles. The **Drug Abatement Response Team (DART)** works to compel landlords to take action against properties and tenants involved in drug offending (Eck, 1998; Eck and Wartell, 1998, 1999). **Project TOUGH (Taking Out Urban Gang Headquarters)** does the same in relation to gang headquarters and other gang hangouts. Both programs seek to force owners to take responsibility for their property. Cristall and Forman-Echols (2009) note that the use of civil suits is in some ways easier than invoking the criminal code because the burden of proof is "preponderance of evidence" rather than "beyond a reasonable doubt" and there is no right to jury trial. An evaluation of the DART program using a randomized control trial in problem neighborhoods showed greatest improvement at full DART intervention sites and the results persisted across a 30-month follow-up period. Evictions were more evident in the treatment group, as were lowered levels of crime and drug problems (Eck, 1998; Eck and Wartell, 1998, 1999).

Injunctions have been used extensively to address gang problems, particularly in California. Project TOUGH utilizes injunctions to keep gang members away from certain properties and locations (Cristall and Forman-Echols, 2009). O'Deane (2012) compared 25 gang injunctions to 25 matched controls using one year pre- and post-injunction data. Calls for service for Part I crimes fell almost 12 percent, and calls for service for Part II crimes fell almost 16 percent in the injunction areas (O'Deane, 2012). There was no decline in the control areas. Other research also reveals positive results in terms of reduced crime and fear in injunction target areas (Grogger, 2002; Maxson et al., 2004).

These results show that civil abatement projects and injunctions can be successful at building coalitions of citizens and agencies that are effective at curbing the target problem. At the same time, however, civil abatement can be a long, cumbersome process, particularly if the property owner opts to fight the procedures through the courts. Smith and Davis (1998) note that, while many landlords comply with abatement, there are significant costs associated with legal procedures, lost rental income, salaries for security guards, and other interventions. Consequently, landlords often oppose the programs and perceive themselves to be victims in the process. Injunctions require the identification of a specific problem, location, and remedy. In addition, the targets of the injunction must be notified in order to be held accountable (O'Deane, 2012). Each of these factors can pose problems for their use.

CCP, SACSI, and PSN

Three major U.S. initiatives for partnership building are the Comprehensive Communities Program (CCP), the Strategic Approaches to Community Safety Initiative (SACSI), and Project Safe Neighborhoods (PSN). Each of these projects has similar features. The **Comprehensive Communities Program (CCP)** was initiated in 1994 as a partnership-building initiative to fight crime and improve the quality of life in communities (Bureau of Justice Assistance, 2001). Fifteen communities have participated in the project. The major key to CCP is to use a problem-solving approach that includes a wide array of community individuals, agencies, and groups. Of particular interest is to bring the individuals and groups most affected by crime into the project. Materials available on the CCP spend a great deal of time describing the activities of the partnerships in each site, with special attention paid to the coalition-building activities (see Bureau of Justice Assistance, 2001; Kelling, 1998). Few of the sites provide outcome measures on changes in crime, and those that do generally fail to provide data for comparable control areas (Bureau of Justice Assistance, 2001). It is not possible, therefore, to know whether the results are due to the CCP initiative or some other cause.

The **Strategic Approaches to Community Safety Initiative (SACSI)** project was initiated in five sites in 1998 to fight primarily violent personal crimes. The lead agency in the SACSI sites is the local U.S. Attorney's Office, which attempts to build a partnership consisting mainly of other criminal justice agencies. In addition, each partnership includes a local research team whose task is to analyze the problem in the community, participate in selecting the appropriate response, and evaluate the operations of the SACSI team. Local, state, and federal law enforcement agencies, probation and parole offices, local, state, and federal attorneys, and social service agencies form the primary core of participants. Most material available on the SACSI project is restricted to process evaluations, which show that partnerships can be successfully established, although a concerted effort is often needed to sustain them. One analysis of SACSI in St. Louis (Decker et al., 2005) did look at reduction in the target behavior (gun crime) and notes that homicides decreased after the initiation of the project. An evaluation of the TimeZup SACSI program in New Haven uncovers decreased levels of violent gun crimes, calls for service, and numbers of guns seized. Other positive results included reduced fear of crime and increased confidence in the police (Hartstone and Richetelli, 2005). An impact evaluation of Chicago's PSN project presents significant reductions in homicide, gun-related homicides, and aggravated assaults, although no impact on gang-related homicides (Papachristos et al., 2007). Finally, Rosenbaum and Roehl's (2010) national evaluation of SACSI reveals decreases in homicide and violent crime in 10 program cities compared to all cities of 100,000 population or more.

The most recent federal effort at establishing partnerships to fight crime is the **Project Safe Neighborhoods (PSN)** project. Started in 2000, PSN can be considered an outgrowth of SACSI and it focuses primarily on reducing firearms violence (PSN, 2003). The project has five core components: partnerships, strategic plans, training, outreach, and accountability. Like SACSI, the project, led by the U.S. Attorney in each judicial district, attempts to bring together law enforcement and other criminal justice agencies in order to focus on identifying problems and initiating solutions. Each district is expected to have plans that fit the unique situation in the area. The public is involved mainly through an educational outreach plan. In an evaluation of violent crime trends in 82 PSN cities compared to 170 control cities, McGarrell et al. (2010) report a drop of 4.1 percent in PSN cities and a .9 percent drop in the controls. This represents a statistically significant impact for PSN, with the results being more striking in PSN sites receiving a greater dosage of the programmatic intervention.

> ┌─ ON THE WEB ─────────────────
> *The PSN project in Chicago maintains a web site that provides a great deal of information on its activities and impact. You can find out more about PSN on that site: http://psnchicago.org/*

Gun Violence

Several partnerships have addressed gun violence, particularly among juveniles and gang members. Perhaps the most well-known of these is Boston's **Operation Ceasefire**. Begun in 1996, the project had several key features. Perhaps the most important feature was the creation of an interagency working partnership. The task for the group was to assess the nature of the gun problem and the dynamics of youth violence in Boston, and to identify and implement an effective intervention (Kennedy et al., 2001). The outcome of the planning was a set of interventions aimed primarily at gangs and gang members. Utilizing the manpower and resources of the police, probation, parole, and district attorney's office, the project used a strict enforcement policy for all individuals and groups involved directly or indirectly in gun violence. Dubbed "**pulling levers**," the project would take any and all actions possible against violators. That meant that any gun violence would result in the immediate arrest and full prosecution of violators. Probation and parole violators were vigorously prosecuted for any violation of the conditions of their release. Gangs and gang members were notified of the project and the potential consequences of their actions (Kennedy et al., 2001). Social service agencies and federal agencies (such as Immigration and Naturalization, which was used to deport non-citizen offenders) were also included in the project.

An evaluation of Operation Ceasefire shows overwhelming positive results. Braga et al. (2001) report a 63 percent drop in monthly juvenile homicides after initiation of the project. Similarly, calls to the police about shots being fired decreased by 32 percent and there was a corresponding drop of 25 percent in assaults with guns (Braga et al., 2001). While it is not possible to claim that the drop in firearm offenses is due solely to Operation Ceasefire, there is reason to believe that the project was a major contributor to the declines.

Operation Ceasefire has been replicated in other cities. In Los Angeles, among the groups participating in the partnership were the local police departments, probation, parole, various prosecutors' offices, community centers, job training programs, churches, and school groups. Tita et al. (2005) note that violent crime fell as a result of the enforcement tactics, while a small change was found in gun and gang crime. Prevention measures had little impact. Replication in Indianapolis finds similar positive outcomes. Corsaro and McGarrell (2009, 2010) and McGarrell et al. (2006) report significant reductions in homicides, gang-related homicides, and homicides among 15- to 24-year-olds. Atlanta focused on juvenile firearms violence and relied on similar partners to those in the other programs. Both prevention and enforcement tactics appear in the project (Kellermann et al., 2006). The results, however, fail to show support for the program. Decreases in homicide cannot be attributed to the intervention (Kellermann et al., 2006). Despite the negative findings in Atlanta, it is evident that the "pulling levers" approach can be effective.

Crime and Disorder Partnerships

The passage of the U.K. Crime and Disorder Act in 1998 mandated the establishment of community partnerships to combat crime and related problems. These partnerships are meant to include the local police and a variety of community constituencies, including housing authorities, victims, health professionals, probation officers, and others. Newburn (2002) notes that the goal is to address "multi-dimensional problems with multi-dimensional responses." Crime is not the only problem to be tackled, thus the need for wide participation by varied groups other than law enforcement. More than £925 million were spent funding partnerships between 1999 and 2005 (Ellis et al., 2007).

A key component of the Crime and Disorder Act is that each partnership is to carry out a crime audit (data collected for planning and evaluation purposes) every three years, based on data for the prior three years. Information should come from a variety of sources, such as police statistics, victimization surveys, probation data, education, and environmental health. The police are required to consult with the partnership and use the data to form prevention strategies and evaluate those strategies (Walklate, 1999). Several authors point out that some attempts to form partnerships have met with less than full success, the police are often the major contributor to the process, and the exact role of the participants is often poorly outlined (see, for example, Hughes, 2002; Phillips, 2002;

Tierney, 2001). Hughes (2002) points out that many partnerships target crimes that are easier to address (such as burglary) while ignoring more difficult crimes and social problems that are harder to change. A good deal of the published work about the Crime and Disorder Act examines the politics surrounding the Act and the development of crime audits (see Crawford, 2001; Gilling, 2005; Hughes et al., 2002). The National Audit Office (2004) notes large reductions in reported crimes since the initiation of partnerships; however, it is not clear to what extent the partnerships caused the reductions. Consequently, it is unclear to what extent these new partnerships are having a significant impact on crime and disorder.

Gang Suppression Programs

In the mid-1990s, the Office of Juvenile Justice and Delinquency Prevention (OJJDP) initiated the *Community-Wide Approach to Gang Prevention, Intervention, and Suppression Program*. The program aimed to initiate a comprehensive set of strategies including suppression, opportunities provision, and social interventions. OJJDP funded program implementation and evaluation in five cities (Bloomington-Normal, IL; Mesa, AZ; Riverside, CA; Tucson, AZ; and San Antonio, TX). Each of the programs drew on the expertise of law enforcement, schools, employment organizations, and other social service agencies.

Several factors emerge across the evaluations. First, several cities struggled with building programs that included grassroots community organizations. Most of the participants remained official criminal justice agencies and other social service providers (Spergel et al., 2001, 2002, 2004a, 2004b). Second, suppression remains the primary response in at least three cities (Spergel et al., 2001, 2002, 2003, 2004b). Finally, the more successful programs offered a wider array of activities that could be considered opportunities provision and social interventions, such as counseling, referrals, and job training.

The program's impact on gang membership and crime is also mixed. The evaluations of the Bloomington-Normal, Mesa, and Riverside programs report reduced offending and reduced arrests among youths in the experimental neighborhoods (Spergel et al., 2001, 2002, 2003). While the Bloomington-Normal program appears to have reduced the level of gang participation (Spergel et al., 2001), there was no apparent impact in Riverside, Tucson, or San Antonio (Spergel et al., 2003, 2004a, 2004b). Despite the mixed results of the programs, the evidence suggests that a successfully implemented program that targets a wider array of interventions than just suppression activities has the ability to positively affect the level of gang crime and gang membership.

Another major gang suppression initiative is the **Comprehensive Anti-Gang Initiative (CAGI)**. This program was developed by the U.S. Department of Justice in response to the earlier "community-wide" program and PSN. As with the earlier initiative, CAGI seeks to build a coalition of agencies, including law enforcement, prosecutors, social services, governments, community groups, schools, and others. CAGI addresses enforcement, prevention, and reentry (McGarrell et al., 2012). A total of 12 cities received funding for program implementation.

Based on the partnership approach, different CAGI cities utilize varied interventions. Directed police patrol, enhanced probation/parole supervision, active contact with gang members, enhanced enforcement, new services for gang prevention, and educational programming are the most common activities (McGarrell et al., 2012). Evaluation of the program compared the CAGI sites to 249 comparable cities. Results show an 11.9 percent decline in gun homicides the year after CAGI was initiated, with greater impact emerging in cities with higher levels of enforcement (McGarrell et al., 2012). The authors note that the results vary by city, with some reductions not achieving statistical significance. McGarrell and colleagues call for continued funding of these efforts and the use of expanded planning for the programs.

Problems and Concerns

Many studies that show the potential positive impact of partnerships also demonstrate some stumbling blocks and weaknesses. Implementation is often a problem due to the change in philosophy being imposed on the police (Bennett, 1994; Eck and Rosenbaum, 1994; Rosenbaum, 2002; Sadd and Grinc, 1994) and other organizations. Crawford (2001) notes that clear power differentials often exist between participants, which makes cooperation difficult and the participants cautious about their roles. There are also differences in the level and type of resources that the various partners can contribute, thus raising the possibility that those with greater expertise and more resources have more input into the selection of problems and their solutions (Crawford, 2001; Tilley, 2005). Rosenbaum (2002) notes that some people are concerned that partnerships are dysfunctional and tend to act too slowly. Critics also claim that partnerships tend not to be truly representative of the community, thus defeating the intended purpose of having community input (Rosenbaum, 2002). At the same time, participants who are involved tend to develop a positive attitude toward partnership efforts (Rosenbaum, 2002; Skogan, 1995). While there remains a large number of evaluations questioning the efficacy of partnerships, the evidence appears to be turning in favor of partnership efforts. The key is to develop successful partnerships.

Successful Partnerships

The research on partnerships illuminates several keys to building successful partnerships (see Table 12.2). One of the most important factors is identifying and recruiting strong leaders and managers (Brown, 2006; Hedderman and Williams, 2001;

TABLE 12.2 Features of Successful Partnerships

1. Identify strong leaders and managers
2. Agree on the problem and intervention
3. Recruit qualified staff
4. Research the problem
5. Build grass roots support
6. Identify adequate funding and resources
7. Provide good oversight of project implementation
8. Evaluate the efforts

Homel et al., 2004; Scott, 2006). These individuals are essential for maintaining focus for the partnership and promoting enthusiasm over time. The failure to adequately identify the target problem and the appropriate intervention is a common problem. Building agreement is not an easy task (Homel et al., 2004; Kelling, 2005). Researching the problem to truly understand its extent and causes greatly assists in building agreement, as well as subsequent activities (Kelling, 2005; Scott, 2006). Once the problem and intervention are identified, it is necessary to recruit qualified staff for implementing the project (Homel et al., 2004; Hedderman and Williams, 2001; Scott, 2006). Training and education of the various participants in partnerships is essential to both the effectiveness of the efforts and their acceptance (Sadd and Grinc, 1996; Skogan, 1995; Skolnick and Bayley, 1988). Members of the partnership need to be educated about community outreach, coalition building, and problem identification.

Successfully proceeding with the intervention requires a number of other actions. Foremost among them is building grass roots support in the community (Scott, 2006). Interventions have a better chance of success if the public cooperates rather than fights the efforts. Many partnership initiatives become unilateral activities by the police, or are poorly coordinated and implemented (Buerger, 1994; Moore, 1994; Sadd and Grinc, 1994, 1996; Skogan, 1995, 1996). Community support also contributes to identifying and securing adequate resources and funding (Homel et al., 2004; Scott, 2006; Tilley, 2005). Without resources, projects cannot function. Once a project is operating there is a need for good project oversight (Brown, 2006; Hedderman and Williams, 2001; Homel et al., 2004). A final key to success is including a meaningful process and impact evaluation (Scott, 2006). This evaluation should be conducted by researchers or agencies not involved in the program delivery (Homel et al., 2004).

ON THE WEB

The Center for Problem-Oriented Policing has produced a guide specifically addressing business partnerships. You can access it at http://www.popcenter.org/tools/partnering/

Summary

A major argument underlying partnerships entails the fact that crime and community problems are beyond the ability of the criminal justice system to solve by itself. The police and other criminal justice agencies need to partner with social service agencies, community groups, and the citizenry if they are to have an impact on the underlying causes of crime. These collaborations have the potential to bring a wide array of new and innovative ways of looking at problems, as well as proposing solutions to those problems. They also bring different skills, abilities, and resources that can be used to implement the proposed solutions. Unfortunately, up to this point there have been relatively few good outcome evaluations conducted on community policing and partnership initiatives. What has been produced are extensive process evaluations that point out the issues and concerns with building and operating a coalition. The next step is to evaluate whether they have a significant impact on crime and fear.

KEY TERMS

- Chicago Alternative Police Strategy (CAPS)
- civil abatement
- community policing
- Comprehensive Anti-Gang Initiative (CAGI)
- Comprehensive Communities Program (CCP)
- Drug Abatement Response Team (DART)
- hot spots policing
- injunctions
- Operation Ceasefire
- order maintenance
- Project TOUGH (Taking Out Urban Gang Headquarters)
- problem solving
- Project Safe Neighborhoods (PSN)
- pulling levers
- SARA
- Specialized Multi-Agency Response Teams (SMART)
- Strategic Approaches to Community Safety Initiative (SACSI)

CHAPTER 13 **Drugs, Crime, and Crime Prevention**

CHAPTER OUTLINE

LEARNING OBJECTIVES

After reading this chapter you should be able to:

- Provide insight to the extent of drug use in society and among offending populations.
- Demonstrate your knowledge of key sources of data on drug use.
- Diagram the possible relationships between drug use and crime, and discuss the evidence on each.
- Tell what a psychopharmacological explanation of the drugs–crime relationship is.
- Identify different forms of drug treatment.
- Discuss NIDA's principles of effective treatment.
- Talk about maintenance programs and their impact on drug use.
- Explain what a therapeutic community is and the extent of its effect.
- Define "detoxification" and relate its ability to affect drug use.
- Discuss NIDA's principles of effective prevention.

- Discuss D.A.R.E. and its new version Keepin' It REAL: what it is and what impact it has had.
- Explain the purpose behind education/information/knowledge programs and their impact on drug use.

The relationship between drug use and crime is a persistent concern in society. Since the mid-1970s, violent crime stemming from the drug trade has been a regular feature on the evening news and in the print media. Graphic depictions of drug crimes pique the interest of both the public and the criminal justice system. The federal government responds to this concern by continuing its "war" on drugs. Efforts to reduce the supply of drugs are the primary means of attack in this war. This emphasis on supply reduction targets the drugs at various points—arrests of the street-level dealer, identifying and prosecuting the drug "kingpin," and drug interdiction at the borders to the country. Less emphasis is placed (at least at the federal level) on the treatment of substance abusers or the prevention of initial use.

The issue of drug use is best addressed within the framework of secondary prevention. For many individuals, drug use itself is not a concern. Those who use drugs do so voluntarily. They purchase the drug and use it themselves. At no point do they forcibly make another individual use drugs. In this respect, drug use is a victimless crime. Both the offender and the victim are the same individual. Most individuals do not know of anyone who uses illicit drugs on a daily basis, or at least are not aware that someone they know is a daily user. Consequently, actual drug use is not a concern. Societal concern arises from problems and issues related to drug use. For example, crimes committed to provide funds for drugs become a problem affecting more than the consensual user. There is now a clear victim. Similarly, society often bears the costs related to caring for a user's family or handling addicted individuals. There is also evidence of pressure on youths to participate in drug use. Such pressure may force an impressionable individual into use and other related problems. The drug problem, therefore, includes more than just the individual choice to use a drug.

Drug use is one means of predicting or identifying potential problems in society. Targeting those involved in drug use may serve to alleviate the problems (crime and otherwise) that stem from drug use. As with many interventions, those tied to drug issues do not fall exclusively in the realm of secondary prevention. Efforts to work with current users are themselves tertiary in nature. Other methods aimed at preventing initial use may be construed as primary prevention, especially if implemented on a broad scale. The fact that the actual concern in dealing with drugs lies with the related crime and societal problems, however, means that drug issues are most properly dealt with in terms of secondary prevention.

In discussions of the drug problem, there are a number of unresolved issues. The first deals with the actual level of drug use/abuse in society and changes in drug use over time. Second, implicit in the concern about drug use is the assumption of a clear drug–crime connection. The common belief is that drug use causes other criminal behavior. A third issue involves the effectiveness of different interventions. What impact do law enforcement, treatment, and other preventive approaches have on the level of drug use and related crime? Answers to this question may suggest the proper means of dealing with drug use in the future.

The Scope of Drug Use

The extent of drug use is somewhat difficult to gauge due to the difficulties of measuring private behavior. Unlike most other crimes, drug use has no victim independent of the offender—they are one and the same. Available data relies on self-reports of drug use in the general population or on information on known offenders. A discussion of both of these sources is presented below in order to gain some understanding about the drug problem.

Self-Reported Drug Use

Perhaps the most well-known survey of drug use is the **Monitoring the Future (MTF) project** carried out by Johnston and associates. This project consists of surveying representative high school students (eighth, tenth, and twelfth graders), college students, and young adults (Johnston et al., 2014). "Young adults" refers to high school graduates within 10 years of leaving school. While the survey probes a variety of factors, the most important set of information deals with the level and type of drug use. Table 13.1 presents information on lifetime, annual, and past-month drug use for high school seniors, college students, and young adults in 2013. It can be seen that drug use varies by type of drug.

Looking at the data for all age groups in 2013, the most prevalent drug is alcohol. This is true for all three time frames—lifetime, annual, and past month. Alcohol is used by roughly 70 percent or more of the individuals over their lifetime, with 40 percent of twelfth graders and two-thirds of college students and young adults claiming alcohol use during the past month. Marijuana is the next most prominent drug for all age groups over all time periods. The remainder of the drugs are used by very few respondents. This is particularly pronounced in the "past-month" category, where 5 percent or less of any age group admits to use of any drug besides alcohol or marijuana. While lifetime use is higher (as expected in light of the longer time frame) it is frequent use that should be of greatest interest, thus the focus on the past-month category.

Another source of information on drug use is the **National Survey on Drug Use and Health** which is conducted by the Substance Abuse and Mental Health Services Administration (SAMHSA). This survey covers a representative sample of U.S.

TABLE 13.1 **Lifetime, Past Year, and Last 30 Days Drug Use by 12th Graders, College Students and Young Adults, 2013 (percentages)**

Drug	Lifetime			Past Year			Last 30 Days		
	12th grader	College student	Young adult	12th grader	College student	Young adult	12th grader	College student	Young adult
Any illicit drug	50.4	51.0	60.5	40.3	38.9	36.3	25.5	22.5	21.8
Marijuana	45.5	47.7	57.1	36.4	35.5	32.2	22.7	20.6	19.0
LSD	3.9	4.4	6.3	2.2	2.6	2.0	0.8	0.4	0.4
Hallucinogens	6.4	6.8	11.4	4.5	4.5	3.9	1.4	1.0	1.0
Cocaine	4.5	5.1	12.2	2.6	2.7	3.9	1.1	0.9	1.5
Crack	1.8	0.7	1.6	0.6	0.3	0.6	0.3	0.2	0.3
Heroin	1.0	0.4	1.6	0.6	0.3	0.6	0.3	0.2	0.3
Amphetamines	12.4	15.3	18.7	8.7	10.6	7.8	4.1	5.3	3.2
Methamphetamine	1.5	0.9	3.1	0.9	0.4	0.6	0.4	0.0	0.2
Barbiturates	7.5	5.4	9.5	4.8	2.7	3.4	2.2	0.9	1.2
Alcohol	68.2	78.0	86.2	62.0	75.6	82.5	39.2	63.1	68.7

Source: Compiled by author from L.D. Johnston et al. (2C14). *Monitoring the Future National Survey Results on Drug Use, 1975–2013. Volume 2: College Students and Adults Ages 19–55.* Ann Arbor: Institute for Social Research, University of Michigan. Retrieved from http://monitoringthefuture.org/pubs.html

respondents aged 12 and older. Table 13.2 provides data for four adult age groups. As in the MTF, marijuana is the most commonly used illicit drug across all age groups and time frames. Hallucinogens and cocaine are the next most commonly used drugs, although the percentage claiming use drops significantly when considering the last-year or last-month time periods. For most drugs, few individuals report use in any time category.

> **ON THE WEB**
>
> *Data on drug use compiled by the Substance Abuse and Mental Health Services Administration can be examined at http://www.oas.samhsa.gov/NSDUH.HTM*

The figures in Tables 13.1 and 13.2 are interesting for several reasons. First, drugs that are of the most concern to society are used by very few individuals. Cocaine, crack, heroin, and the other drugs are not the most prevalent drugs in use. Alcohol, a legal drug for adults, is the most commonly used substance. Second, data based on drug use in the past year and last 30 days show the same depressed level of illicit drug use among all groups of respondents. Lifetime and past-year use should not be used as an indicator of a drug "problem" because such use may simply reflect ordinary experimentation (Stephens, 1987). The low figures in the tables suggest mainly experimental use of illicit drugs. Third, the use of most drugs has generally remained stable with some small increases and decreases over time (trend data not shown). These self-report data suggest that the drug problem (at least in terms of illicit drugs) is relatively minor, although the recent increases need to be carefully monitored.

The self-report figures must be considered cautiously due to some inherent deficiencies. With the MTF data there is a question of generalizability. The data are not representative of the entire population. The fact that the high school and college subjects are (or were) attending school ignores the fact that many youths drop out of high school or do not go to college. Dropping out is especially great among inner-city youths, where the drug trade appears to be most concentrated. Johnston et al. (1989) point out that roughly 15 to 20 percent of high school students drop out and are not included in the survey each year, and that dropouts tend to use drugs more often than non-dropouts. In a study of runaway/homeless youths, Fors and Rojek (1991) find that these individuals report two to seven times the level of substance use/abuse of school youths. These facts suggest that the MTF data underreport the level of drug use.

> **ON THE WEB**
>
> *A wealth of information on substance use is available from the Monitoring the Future project. You can explore this information at http://www.monitoringthefuture.org*

Self-report figures, such as those presented here, suggest that the drug problem is not as serious as usually presented. Clearly, the use of illicit drugs is not running rampant in society. Few individuals use illicit drugs with even the grossest measure of regularity (within 30 days). Figures for daily use fall to almost zero for illicit drugs. This is not to suggest that drugs are not a problem. Those who drop out appear to use drugs at a

TABLE 13.2 Drug Use by Different Adult Age Groups, 2013 (percentages)

Drug	Ever Used				Past Year				Past Month			
	18–20	21–25	26–34	35+	18–20	21–25	26–34	35+	18–20	21–25	26–34	35+
Any illicit drug	51.7	60.2	61.7	47.6	38.4	34.2	25.4	9.3	22.6	20.9	15.3	5.6
Marijuana	46.5	55.2	56.9	43.1	34.3	30.0	21.0	6.5	20.3	18.3	12.6	4.0
Cocaine	6.6	14.7	18.9	15.9	3.4	5.1	3.4	0.7	0.9	1.3	1.3	0.4
Crack	0.7	2.2	4.7	3.9	0.2	0.3	0.4	0.2	0.0	0.2	0.2	0.2
Heroin	1.0	2.3	3.1	1.8	0.4	0.9	0.7	0.1	0.2	0.3	0.3	0.0
Hallucinogens	13.2	20.3	23.5	14.6	7.0	6.5	2.5	0.4	2.1	1.6	0.6	0.2
Stimulants	6.7	11.1	12.9	7.9	3.5	1.0	2.9	0.5	1.1	1.4	1.1	0.2
Methamphetamine	1.7	3.8	6.8	5.2	0.8	0.4	0.8	0.3	0.3	0.4	0.4	0.2

Source: Compiled by author from SAMHSA (2014). Results from the 2013 National Survey on Drug Use and Health: Detailed Tables. Washington, DC: U.S. Department of Health and Human Services.

much higher rate than high school graduates. Similarly, criminal offenders may be more involved in drugs than non-offenders. The extent to which drugs are used by offenders can be examined through other sources of information.

Drug Use among Offending Populations

It is commonly assumed that many offenders are regular users of illicit drugs and that drug use is intricately related to the commission of crime. Support for such a contention comes from various studies of offenders. The **ADAM II (Arrestee Drug Abuse Monitoring) program** provides in-depth information on drug use by offenders in 10 cities. The original **ADAM** program was an expansion of the *Drug Use Forecasting* (DUF) program sponsored by the National Institute of Justice, which began in 1987. ADAM II is a scaled-down version of the original ADAM program, which gathered data in 35 cities.

Arrestees voluntarily agree to be interviewed and give a urine sample for testing. The urinalysis is tested for 10 different drugs (including cocaine, opiates, marijuana, methadone, benzodiazepine (Valium), phencyclidine (PCP), propoxyphene (Darvon), barbiturates, and amphetamines). All information is anonymous. The data provide information on the type of drug use, changes in use over time (data are collected quarterly), the age and race distribution of users, and arrest charges related to different drugs (Office of National Drug Control Policy, 2012). See Table 13.3.

TABLE 13.3 Percent of Arrestees Testing Positive for Select Drugs, 2011

	Marijuana	Cocaine	Opiates	Meth	Any
Atlanta	35.9	32.8	6.6	0.7	64.1
Charlotte	53.0	19.0	1.8	0.4	67.4
Chicago	54.9	25.2	18.6	1.0	80.5
Denver	44.3	24.8	12.1	5.9	68.7
Indianapolis	47.8	19.6	10.3	2.3	66.5
Minneapolis	50.8	20.6	7.7	2.8	69.6
New York	49.0	24.6	8.1	0.1	72.7
Portland	49.4	15.0	14.4	22.9	73.2
Sacramento	56.1	10.3	9.6	42.9	81.0
Washington, DC	44.5	17.5	11.3	0.4	67.7

Source: Office of National Drug Control Policy (2012). *ADAM II: 2011 Annual Report*. Washington, DC: The White House.

ADAM II results for 2011 show that drug use is very common among arrestees. Urinalysis reveals that better than 60 percent of all arrestees test positive for recent drug use of any type. In five cities, greater than 70 percent test positive for some drug type. Cocaine and marijuana are the most prevalent drugs according to test results. Drug use also varies from city to city. Data from the British ADAM program shows that 69 percent of arrestees test positive for drug use and 58 percent report alcohol use (Holloway and Bennett, 2004).

> ┌─ ON THE WEB ─────────────
> *Additional ADAM II data is available at*
> *https://www.whitehouse.gov/ondcp/*
> *arrestee-drug-abuse-monitoring-program*

Drug use figures are also available for inmates of correctional institutions and those in court. Mumola and Karberg (2006) note that over one-quarter of federal inmates and almost one-third of state prisoners report committing their offenses while using drugs. Additionally, over half of the prisoners report drug use in the month before offending Sickmund et al. (2013) report that roughly 7 percent of the youths in residential facilities are there due to drug-related offenses, while juvenile court statistics show roughly 165,000 youths entered court for drug law violations in 2010 (Puzzanchera and Hockenberry, 2013).

These figures, based on offending populations, provide a more serious picture of drug use than those from surveys of the general population. As with the other data, there are potential problems to keep in mind. First, this information reflects only the individuals who are caught by the system. It is possible that the use of drugs increases the risk of apprehension for these offenders. Those not apprehended may not use drugs, or at least not at the same level. Second, the ADAM II data reflect drug use in 10 major urban areas. Consequently, the results are only generalizable to other comparable large cities. Drug use probably differs between large and small communities, just as crime differs.

Summary

The data on drug use, both from self-reports of the general population and from offending groups, provide valuable information. The general population data suggest that illicit drug use is not as widespread as the media portrays. Most drug use appears to be experimental or occasional in nature. The data on offenders point out that drug use is common among those who are apprehended for crimes. While not necessarily representative of all offenders, those who are caught make up a large group of individuals. The results, therefore, should not be dismissed simply due to low clearance rates or lack of representativeness. Drug use may be considered a risk factor in other criminal behavior. That is, the use of drugs may be a predictor of other deviant activity. This fact receives further support when considering the relationship between drug use and crime, which is taken up next.

The Drugs–Crime Connection

The connection between drug use and crime has received a great deal of attention. A simple inspection of data reveals a strong correlation between drugs and crime. Situations in which many of the offenders test positive for drug use provide a strong basis for claiming a causal relationship. Simple correlations, however, are not enough to establish clear evidence of causation.

The relationship between drug use and crime has been hypothesized to take a variety of forms. White (1990) outlines four possible models for the relationship (see Figure 13.1). First, drug use causes criminal activity. Second, criminal activity causes drug use. Third, there is a reciprocal relationship in which both drug use and criminal activity cause one another. Finally, the relationship between the two is spurious with other factors (possibly the same ones) causing drug use and crime. Various studies have attempted to untangle which causal sequence is correct.

The first model attempts to show that drugs cause the user to commit other crimes. Crime may be the result of a psychopharmacological reaction, economic need, or simple participation in the drug trade (Goldstein, 1989). The **psychopharmacological explanation** suggests that various drugs have a direct impact on the user, both physically and psychologically, which impels the individual to act in such a way that society deems unacceptable. The intent of the individual may not be to commit a crime. The drug simply determines the action, which may or may not be criminal. The *economics* of drug use can also lead to deviance. The increasing need for money to secure drugs can lead to property crimes. Various studies show that drug users are often involved in property

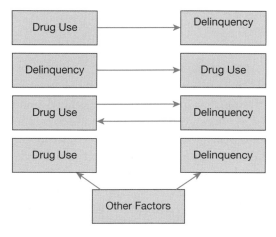

Figure 13.1

Possible Relationships Between Drug Use and Delinquency

offenses (Anglin and Speckart, 1988; Chaiken and Chaiken, 1982; Collins et al., 1985; Harrison and Gfroerer, 1992; Johnson et al., 1985, 1988; National Institute of Justice, 1990). Participation in drug use also may lead to systemic violence (Goldstein, 1989). **Systemic violence** refers to violence resulting from competition among drug dealers, retaliation for poor drug quality or high prices, robbery of drug dealers or users, and other factors related to the drug trade. Using New York City data, Goldstein et al. (1992) report that 74 percent of all drug-related homicides are due to systemic factors of the drug trade. To the extent that crime fits one of these categories, the first model finds qualified support. Of the three potential arguments, the psychopharmacological explanation is the most difficult to prove and has been criticized for ignoring evidence that much drug use actually reduces physical action and violent tendencies, and only appears in interaction with specific dispositions and social/cultural settings (McBride and Schwartz, 1990). The economic and systemic arguments require attention to the temporal order in the drugs–crime relationship.

Drug Use Causes Crime

Studies claiming support for drug use causing crime typically rely on studies of drug addicts or high-rate users of drugs. Ball et al. (1983), studying 354 heroin addicts, note that their crime rate is four to six times higher when they are actively using drugs. Similarly, Collins et al. (1985) report that daily heroin/cocaine users tend to commit property offenses at a substantially higher rate than weekly users or non-users. Drug use, especially involving expensive drugs and drug habits, necessitates the commission of "income-generating crimes" in order to maintain the pattern of use (Collins et al., 1985). Anglin and Hser (1987) and Anglin and Speckart (1988) note that arrests and self-reported crimes increase at the onset of first narcotics use and first daily use, and decrease at last daily use. Use also declines during treatment and increases when subjects leave treatment (Anglin and Hser, 1987; Anglin and Speckart, 1988). Huizinga et al. (1994) note that changes in substance abuse precede changes in the levels of other delinquent activity.

Crime Causes Drug Use

The second possibility is that involvement in crime causes drug use. Numerous studies suggest that involvement in criminal behavior precedes drug use. Using longitudinal data on almost 2,000 high school graduates in the Youth in Transition project, Johnston and associates (1978) report that general delinquency predates most drug use. The authors argue that youths turn to drug use as an extension of other deviant behavior. Data from the **National Youth Survey (NYS)**, an ongoing longitudinal panel study, reveal essentially the same result. Information on delinquency, drug use, and demographic factors for the first six waves of data collection (1976 to 1983) shows a general progression in behavior starting with minor delinquency and leading to alcohol use, index offenses, marijuana use, and polydrug use, in that order (Huizinga et al., 1989). Except for the early appearance of alcohol, illicit drug use temporally follows delinquent/criminal behavior. Indeed, the authors note that minor delinquency precedes polydrug use 99 to 100 percent of the time (Huizinga et al., 1989). Chaiken and Chaiken (1990), examining data from the NYS, a survey of prison inmates, and a sample of New York City drug addicts, note that delinquency predates drug use at least 50 percent of the time. The same pattern of drug use following delinquency is reported by Inciardi et al. (1993) in a study of serious inner-city delinquents. Other authors (Anglin and Hser, 1987; Anglin and Speckart, 1988; Elliott and Ageton, 1981; Elliott et al., 1989; Hunt, 1990; Johnson et al., 1985) also note that drug use follows crime. The typical explanation for this finding is that drug use is simply another form of deviant behavior, and involvement with delinquency/criminality provides resources and contacts necessary for entering into drug use.

Reciprocal Relationship

Given the studies reporting a different sequencing in the drugs–crime relationship, it is plausible to argue that the actual relationship is **reciprocal**. That is, criminal activity leads to drug use and drug use leads to criminal activity. Support for a reciprocal relationship can be found in many studies. Nurco et al. (1988) note that addiction increases crime by "previous offenders." Studies of drug addicts typically relate that arrests "increase" after drug use or intensified use, leading to the conclusion that the subjects committed offenses prior to that point in time (Anglin and Hser, 1987; Anglin and Speckart, 1988; Collins et al., 1985). Hunt (1990) points out that, while prostitution increases with drug use, a substantial number of female drug users participated in prostitution and other offenses prior to drug use. Finally, van Kammen and Loeber's (1994) analysis of data for Pittsburgh youths shows that property offending predicts the onset of drug use, although drug use escalates the commission of personal crime. It would appear that, regardless of which came first, drug use and crime may contribute to each other. Drug use leads to crime and crime leads to drug use.

Spurious Relationship

The argument that seems to be gaining the strongest support is the claim that the relationship between drug use and delinquency is **spurious**. This simply means that, while use and crime exist at the same time and vary in a similar fashion, neither is the ultimate cause of the other. Rather, they are caused by either the same common factors or by different factors. Huba and Bentler (1983) and Kandel et al. (1986) claim that there is no causal relationship between drug use and crime. Rather, these two sets of behavior are caused by other similar factors. White et al. (1987), using self-report data for almost

900 youths, point out that there are common causes of delinquency and drug use. Foremost among these factors are peer and school influences. The same analysis of the NYS data, which points out a sequence of behavior beginning with minor offending and ending with polydrug use (Huizinga et al., 1989), concludes that the actual cause of the behaviors probably lies with a common set of spurious influences. Other research leads to the same conclusion (Collins, 1989; Elliott et al., 1979, 1985; Fagan and Weis, 1990; Hawkins and Weis, 1985; Kandel et al., 1986; Loeber, 1988; White, 1990).

Summary

The fact that drug use is related to criminal activity cannot be disputed. The causal relationship, however, is unclear. The inability to definitively identify a causal sequencing does not render the relationship useless to crime prevention. A strong correlation between the two behaviors means that drug use can be used as a predictor of other criminal behavior (Elliott and Huizinga, 1984; Kandel et al., 1986; Newcomb and Bentler, 1988). The research cited above also suggests that each behavior contributes to the other, thereby providing insight for intervention and treatment. It may be possible to attack crime by attacking drug use. Certainly, targeting drug users for intervention means dealing with those who are at higher risk of participating in other criminal activities. Intervening with drug users will also reduce crime to the extent to which drug use does contribute to criminal activity.

Interventions and Prevention

Interventions aimed at limiting drug use and related crime take a variety of forms. Most of the approaches fall under three general areas—law enforcement, treatment, and prevention. The great number and diversity of possible responses to the drug–crime problem cannot be adequately discussed in the space available. Indeed, some of the proposed solutions do not fit in the present discussion. The following discussion, therefore, is somewhat selective. Among the topics not covered here (or covered in abbreviated fashion) are efforts at drug interdiction and foreign policy issues, targeting organized crime, drug testing, decriminalization, and legalization. While each of these topics is worthy of discussion, they are beyond the scope of the present work.

Law Enforcement Efforts

The current "drug war" is primarily an effort that uses law enforcement techniques as the primary weapon against drug use. This is evident in the federal government's budgetary priority favoring law enforcement over treatment or prevention programs. Underlying law enforcement actions is the assumption that drug use and related crime can be limited or eliminated by supply reduction. Taking drugs off the street will make it more difficult for users to locate the drugs and, if the drugs can be found, the price will be driven so high that many potential users will simply abstain. In essence, these approaches assume that the demand for drugs is a factor of the supply.

Police crackdowns on drug availability are common responses. New York City's Operation Pressure Point involved saturating the Alphabet City area on the Lower East Side of Manhattan with police officers and resources. Drug buyers could shop around different dealers, often in plain view, in order to secure the best price and quality in the area (Zimmer, 1987). The police operation was credited with thousands of arrests, the elimination of the drug supermarket, and significant reductions in robbery, burglary, and homicide (Kleiman, 1988). Unfortunately, the program led some dealers and buyers to find new means for doing business (i.e., displacement) and the program lasted only as long as the police maintained their heightened presence (Johnson et al., 1990; Kleiman and Smith, 1990). Similar results appeared in an evaluation of a police crackdown in Lynn, Massachusetts.

The fact that gangs are becoming more involved in drug use and sales (Fagan, 1989) has led various jurisdictions to jointly target gangs and drugs. Los Angeles's Community Resources Against Street Hoodlums (CRASH) program is a prime example of police targeting of gang behavior. These efforts, however, have yet to show an impact on the drug problem or other gang behavior, including gang homicides (Kleiman and Smith, 1990). As noted in the last chapter, the police also have been intimately involved in abatement programs that target drug locations.

The size and scope of the drug problem appear to be more than basic police enforcement can handle. Attacking the retail level of the drug chain may result in many arrests but will probably have little impact beyond overburdening the already overcrowded criminal justice system (Belenko, 1990). Similarly, assumptions that law enforcement efforts will significantly reduce the supply of drugs for any long period are ill-conceived. There is a need for an accompanying reduction in the demand for drugs.

Treatment of Drug Users

Drug treatment can take a wide variety of forms and may involve greatly divergent approaches. Research on treatment programs has provided some insights regarding what is most effective. The National Institute on Drug Abuse (NIDA) offers a list of 13 principles of effective treatment (see Table 13.4). These principles address the general issues that can be applied across different programs in ways that respond to the unique needs of the clients. The wide array of factors contributing to drug use/abuse means that treatment needs to comprehensively address the problems. Figure 13.2 provides a comprehensive model for drug abuse treatment.

TABLE 13.4 NIDA's 13 Principles of Effective Treatment for Drug Abuse

---

1. Addiction is a complex but treatable disease that affects brain function and behavior

2. No single program is appropriate for all individuals.

3. Treatment needs to be readily available.

4. Effective treatment attends to multiple needs of the individual.

5. Remaining in treatment for an adequate period of time is critical.

6. Behavioral therapies—including individual, family, or group counseling—are the most commonly used forms of drug abuse treatment.

7. Medications are an important element of treatment for many patients, especially combined with counseling and other behavioral therapies.

8. An individual's treatment and services plan must be addressed continually and modified as necessary to ensure it meets his changing needs. Addicted or drug-abusing individuals with coexisting mental disorders should have both disorders treated in an integrated way.

9. Many drug-addicted individuals also have other mental disorders.

10. Medically assisted detoxification is only the first stage of addiction treatment and by itself does little to change long-term drug abuse.

11. Treatment does not need to be voluntary to be effective.

12. Drug use during treatment must be monitored continuously, as lapses during treatment do occur.

13. Treatment programs should test patients for the presence of HIV/AIDS, hepatitis B and C, tuberculosis, and other infectious diseases, as well as provide targeted risk-reduction counseling, linking patients to treatment if necessary.

Source: NIDA (2012). *Principles of Drug Addiction Treatment: A Research-based Guide*, Third Edition. Washington, DC: National Institute on Drug Abuse. Retrieved from http://www.drugabuse. gov/publications/principles-drug-addiction-treatment-research-based-guide-third-edition/ frequently-asked-questions/what-drug-addiction-treatment

Most interventions can be grouped into one of four general types. These are maintenance programs, detoxification, therapeutic communities, and outpatient drug-free programs. While each of these groupings promotes a different major emphasis, many similarities and common features appear across the programs. For example, counseling and therapy of one sort or another appear in virtually all of the programs. A recent innovation has been the establishment of drug courts. Each of these will be briefly examined below.

Figure 13.2

Components of Comprehensive Drug Abuse Treatment

Source: NIDA (2012). *Principles of Drug Addiction Treatment: A Research-Based Guide*, Third Edition. Washington, DC: National Institute on Drug Abuse. Retrieved from http://www. drugabuse.gov/publications/principles-drug-addiction-treatment-research-based-guide-third-edition/frequently-asked-questions/what-drug-addiction-treatment

Maintenance Programs

Maintenance programs, a common intervention for addicted individuals, seek to establish a steady state in which the individual does not experience withdrawal symptoms when the drug begins to wear off. Consequently, the user will be able to function more normally and participate in everyday activities without the constant need for the drug (Stephens, 1987). The most common form of maintenance program is methadone maintenance. This involves the provision of methadone to heroin/opiate addicts. Methadone is an oral substitute for heroin, which needs to be taken only once in a 24-hour period. Over time, those on maintenance will no longer experience the highs and lows of addiction to other drugs. A primary assumption underlying these programs is that the patient is unable to function without some form of drug use and that methadone is an acceptable substitute for other, more damaging drugs.

Most methadone maintenance programs include a variety of components. Periodic urinalysis is used to check that patients are not using other drugs while receiving methadone. Counseling, both individual and group, along with guidelines for behavior and sanctions for violations, is common (Anglin and Hser, 1990). Some programs attempt to slowly detoxify their patients. That is, they attempt to reduce the methadone dosage and wean the subjects from the need for any drug use. The level of these various components, however, varies greatly from program to program (Ball et al., 1986).

> ── ON THE WEB ─────────────
> *The National Institute on Drug Abuse provides a great deal of information on drugs and drug treatment interventions. You can access this information at http://www.drugabuse.gov/ related-topics/treatment-research*

Evaluations of the effectiveness of methadone maintenance programs show generally positive results (NIDA, 2012). Various researchers (Anglin and McGlothlin, 1984; Ball et al., 1987; Hser et al., 1988) report that methadone patients use fewer illicit drugs, commit fewer crimes, and are arrested less often than when not on the program. Additionally, the termination of methadone maintenance shows a return to pre-program levels of drug use and criminal activity (Anglin et al., 1989; McGlothlin and Anglin, 1981). It would appear from these results that maintenance is a feasible approach to the drug–crime problem. The programs, however, are not without critics. Stephens (1987) points out that these programs are applicable only to narcotics and ignore the much larger numbers of other drug users. Additionally, the patients are often non-productive and on welfare. They do not necessarily re-enter the job market and become productive societal members. Anglin and Hser (1990) further point out that the research typically fails to use adequate control groups. The results, therefore, are subject to much criticism.

Detoxification

Closely related to maintenance programs is detoxification. **Detoxification** uses drugs in a short-term program of controlled withdrawal. The basic idea is to wean the client from the addiction with the minimal amount of discomfort and pain. These types of programs can be found in many hospitals and facilities throughout the country, and target a wide range of drugs from alcohol to heroin. Detoxification needs to be accompanied with counseling, referral, or other services to address the social, psychological, and related issues to the abuse (NIDA, 2012). Anglin and Hser (1990) point out that while short-term follow-up shows that detoxification is successful at eliminating drug use, detoxification has not been adequately evaluated over the long-term. Bellis (1981) notes that detoxification is used by some addicts to reduce the need for massive amounts of a drug in order to get high. The detoxification simply allows the addict to start the cycle of addiction over again by achieving a high with smaller amounts of the drug.

Therapeutic Communities

Therapeutic communities emphasize providing a supportive, highly structured atmosphere within which individuals can be helped to alter their personality and develop social relationships conducive to conforming behavior (Anglin and Hser, 1990). These residential programs operate as surrogate families for clients. In many cases, therapeutic communities are run by current or past clients. The daily routine is often very structured and includes intensive group sessions. Programs may also include education, vocational training, or mandatory employment (NIDA, 2012). Examples of therapeutic communities are Synanon, Daytop Village, and Phoenix House.

The research on therapeutic communities consistently show lowered drug use and criminal activity (Anglin and Hser, 1990; Coombs, 1981; DeLeon, 1984; DeLeon and Rosenthal, 1989).The Integrated Multi-Phasic Program Assessment and Comprehensive Treatment (IMPACT) program deals with single, unemployed, minority males with long criminal histories. The program results indicate that recidivism is tied to the length of treatment, with longer treatment resulting in lower recidivism (Swartz et al., 1996). Inciardi (1996) reports on the KEY program, which is a prison-based therapeutic community in Delaware. Both six- and 18-month follow-up data show that many more program clients remain drug- and arrest-free than do control group clients (Inciardi, 1996). These studies bolster the claims of program success.

Outpatient Drug-Free Programs

Outpatient programs often resemble therapeutic communities in most respects except for the residential component. Individual and group counseling is the cornerstone of these programs and may involve professionals or simply other group members. Social skills training, vocational programming, social interaction, referral to other sources of assistance, and possibly short-term drug maintenance are also common components (Anglin and Hser, 1990). Alcoholics Anonymous and Narcotics Anonymous are well-known examples of this type of program. The impact of these programs is highly questionable. The primary concern with most evaluations is the fact that clients can drop out at any time. These outpatient programs are more likely to suffer from client mortality than are other interventions (Anglin and Hser, 1990). Hubbard et al. (1984) note that the programs have a marginal impact on crime due to their open nature. Evaluations based only on those individuals who remain in treatment may result in artificially high success rates. The actual success based on all clients who enter the program, whether they complete or not, would be less impressive.

┌─ ON THE WEB ─────────────────────────┐
│ *Additional information and discussion of drug* │
│ *treatment can be found on the NIDA web site at* │
│ *http://www.drugabuse.gov/publications/princi-* │
│ *ples-drug-addiction-treatment-research-based-* │
│ *guide-third-edition/frequently-asked-questions/* │
│ *what-drug-addiction-treatment* │
└──────────────────────────────────────┘

Summary and Further Comments

It is generally accepted that most forms of treatment are effective at reducing the use of and need for drugs (Fareed et al., 2011; Visher, 1990). Indeed, Simpson and Sells (1982), studying data from the Drug Abuse Reporting Program (DARP), report that all four types of treatment (maintenance, therapeutic communities, out-patient, and detoxification) achieve lower drug use, lower criminal behavior, and improved employment status from four to six years after treatment. These results are significantly different than for a non-treatment control group. Research also suggests that, while forced treatment has less impact than voluntary treatment (Anglin, 1988; DeLong, 1972; Maddux, 1988), it does reduce the daily use of drugs and criminal activity (Anglin and McGlothlin, 1984). Thus, the new drug courts should be able to affect drug use and related criminal behavior. The impact of court-ordered programs may be attributable to the longer time spent in treatment which is typical of these programs (Visher, 1990). At the very least, the impact of enforced treatment provides further support to the claim that treatment has a positive impact on use and crime.

Prevention Programs

Prevention programs that aim to keep individuals from initially using drugs (primary prevention) usually target juveniles. It is during adolescence that most people experiment with and enter into patterns of drug use. Prevention modalities cover a range of issues and approaches, including the dissemination of factual information about drugs and their consequences, the building of self-esteem, taking responsibility for making choices, and learning how to handle peer pressure. Most often, prevention programs incorporate more than one approach. In a similar fashion

┌─ ON THE WEB ─────────────
As with treatment topics, the National Institute on Drug Abuse provides a great deal of information on prevention activities. You can access this information at http://www.drugabuse.gov/publications/ drugfacts/lessons-prevention-research
└──────────────────────────

to treatment programs, NIDA outlines 16 principles for effective prevention programs (see Table 13.5). The following discussion is divided into the two most prominently promoted and evaluated prevention techniques. These are the information/education/ knowledge programs and the resistance skills techniques.

Education/Information/Knowledge Programs

Education/information/knowledge programs focus their efforts on providing subjects with factual information about drugs, drug use, and the consequences of drug use. Such programs attempt to teach subjects about the different drugs, how they work, and

TABLE 13.5 NIDA's 16 Principles of Effective Prevention for Drug Abuse

1. Prevention programs should enhance protective factors and reverse or reduce risk factors.

2. Prevention programs should address all forms of drug abuse, alone or in combination, including underage use of legal drugs; the use of illegal drugs; and the inappropriate use of legally obtained substances, prescription medications, or over-the-counter drugs.

3. Prevention programs should address the type of drug abuse problem in the local community, target modifiable risk factors, and strengthen identified protective factors.

4. Prevention programs should be tailored to address risks specific to population or audience characteristics, such as age, gender, and ethnicity.

5. Family-based prevention programs should enhance family bonding and relationships and include parenting skills; practice in developing, discussing and enforcing family policies on substance abuse; and training in drug education and information.

6. Prevention programs can be designed to intervene as early as infancy to address risk factors for drug abuse, such as aggressive behavior, poor social skills and academic difficulties.

7. Prevention programs for elementary school children should target improving academic and social-emotional learning to address risk factors for drug abuse.

8. Prevention programs for middle or junior high and high school students should increase academic and social competence.

9. Prevention programs aimed at general populations at key transition points, such as the transition to middle school, can produce beneficial effects even among high-risk families and children.

10. Community prevention programs that combine two or more effective programs can be more effective than a single program alone.

11. Community prevention programs reaching populations in multiple settings are most effective when they present consistent, community-wide messages in each setting.

12. When communities adapt programs to match their needs, community norms, or differing cultural requirements, they should retain core elements of the original research-based intervention.

13. Prevention programs should be long-term with repeated interventions to reinforce the original prevention goals.

14. Prevention programs should include teacher training on good classroom management practices such as rewarding appropriate student behavior.

15. Prevention programs are most effective when they employ interactive techniques, such as peer discussion and parent role-playing, that allow for active involvement in learning about drug abuse and reinforcing skills.

16. Research-based prevention programs can be cost-effective.

Source: NIDA (2014). *Drug Facts: Lessons from Prevention Research*. Washington, DC: National Institute on Drug Abuse. Retrieved from http://www.drugabuse.gov/publications/drugfacts/lessons-prevention-research

their effects on the user. Information may also include data on the extent of drug use and what happens if an individual is caught and processed in the criminal justice system. The basic assumption is that such knowledge will allow the individual to make an informed choice about drug use. Proponents assume that, armed with these facts, most individuals will opt to avoid drugs.

Evaluations provide mixed results concerning these programs. Botvin (1990) points out that these programs are effective at increasing subjects' knowledge about drugs. Schaps et al. (1986) also claim that drug education reduces the use of alcohol and marijuana by females but has no impact on comparable males. The change in use, however, is short-lived and no effect is noted one year after the program ended. Tobler (1986), analyzing results from 143 drug prevention programs for youths, notes that information (knowledge) techniques have no impact on behavior. Other authors (Abadinsky, 1989; Botvin, 1990; Botvin and Dusenbury, 1989; Eiser and Eiser, 1988; Hanson, 1980; Kinder et al., 1980; Swadi and Zeitlin, 1987; Weisheit, 1983) report similar negative results and even suggest that the knowledge leads many youths to experiment with drugs in order to "find out for themselves" about drugs. The programs appear to pique the curiosity of some youths and prompt an increased, rather than decreased, use of drugs.

Resistance Skills Training

Resistance skills training comes under a variety of names with the most well-known being the "Just Say No" campaign and the D.A.R.E. (Drug Abuse Resistance Education) program. While many individuals view this as too simplistic an approach, resistance skills training involves a set of ideas dealing with recognizing problematic situations and issues, dealing with peer pressure, recognizing pressure from media presentations, knowing proper responses to temptations, building self-esteem and assertiveness, and knowing how and when to take a stand. The implicit assumption in this type of prevention is that drug use is largely a function of situation and peer involvement. Youths need to learn how to recognize peer pressure and how to make proper decisions in the face of that pressure. These programs may also provide factual information about drugs within the larger discussion of resisting temptations to participate in drug use. A key part of any information presented deals with the actual levels of use in society, emphasizing the fact that most individuals do not use illicit drugs. This provides youths with data that say they are in the majority if they resist drugs.

Research on the impact of resistance skills training is mixed. Botvin and associates have conducted a series of studies on the impact of Life Skills Training (LST) on subsequent tobacco, alcohol, and marijuana use (Botvin and Eng, 1980, 1982; Botvin et al., 1980; Botvin et al., 1983; Botvin et al., 1984). The reports show that the LST program is successful at reducing the number of youths who smoke, drink, and use marijuana. The program appears to be most effective at reducing the use of tobacco (Botvin and

Dusenbury, 1989). The longevity of the impact may be somewhat at issue with the longest follow-up being only two years. Other studies have reported similar positive results, especially for tobacco use (Botvin, 1990; Luepker et al., 1983; McAlister et al., 1980; Telch et al., 1982).

Perhaps the most recognized intervention is D.A.R.E. Begun in Los Angeles in 1983, D.A.R.E. targets elementary school youths through a police-officer-taught curriculum. In recent years D.A.R.E. has expanded to junior and senior high schools, as well as implementing a parent program. An estimated 22,000 police officers in 7,000 communities have taught D.A.R.E. to more than 25 million elementary school students since the program's inception (Bureau of Justice Assistance, 1995). Various methodologically rigorous evaluations of the original D.A.R.E. program fail to find any significant impact on drug use behavior. Ringwalt et al. (1991), Clayton et al. (1991), and Rosenbaum et al. (1994), looking at schools from different jurisdictions, all report no impact on substance use. In a recent evaluation, D.A.R.E. participants and control youths were tracked for more than a six-year period to assess the impact of the program. Rosenbaum and Hanson (1998) conducted surveys twice a year in order to consider the influence of D.A.R.E., other programs, dropping out, and other factors that could alter the results. The authors report that D.A.R.E. had little impact on attitudes, beliefs, or social skills directly addressed by the program. More importantly, D.A.R.E. had no significant impact on any measure of drug use. For suburban subjects, there was some evidence of *higher* drug use among D.A.R.E. participants (Rosenbaum and Hanson, 1998). Wysong et al. (1994) also found no impact in a similar longitudinal analysis.

ON THE WEB

Information on the new D.A.R.E. program—Keepin' It REAL can be found at http://www.kir.psu.edu

Due partly to these negative evaluations, D.A.R.E. has been reimaged as **Keepin' It REAL**. This 10-session curriculum is still taught to children and adolescents in schools by law enforcement officers. The focus of the program is on resistance skills. REAL stands for Refuse, Explain, Avoid, and Leave, and provides skills for youths to address situations, events, and people who promote or encourage them to use drugs or participate in other problem behaviors. The program is based on the NIDA prevention principles (refer to Table 13.5). At this point, the new program's effectiveness remains to be proven.

Given the lack of positive results, how do you explain the popularity and persistence of D.A.R.E.? There are several possible explanations. First, D.A.R.E. has a strong national organization behind it. Second, the program is minimally intrusive into the lives of the youths, primarily due to its presentation in schools. Third, the ability to bring police and juveniles together in a non-threatening situation has a great deal of appeal. Finally, the program may contribute to a more positive school environment.

Summary of Prevention Programs

The evidence on prevention programs suggests that the impact is often minimal. Resistance skills training presents mixed results. Programs that emphasize providing factual information about drugs fail to have much impact. In fact, these efforts may cause an increased curiosity on the part of adolescents and subsequent experimentation and use of illicit drugs. Other programs that stress self-esteem, self-awareness, and interpersonal growth in the absence of specific strategies for dealing with drugs (typically referred to as affective education programs) also demonstrate minimal influence on drug use (Botvin, 1990; Schaps et al., 1986; Tobler, 1986). While there appears to be hope for the prevention of drug use, most of the programs need to be evaluated with longer follow-up periods and better research designs, particularly using adequate comparison groups.

Drugs and Crime Prevention

The relationship between drug use and criminal activity is a complex one. The extent to which drug use causes crime or crime causes drug use is not clear. There is certainly a strong correlation between the two activities. This suggests that knowledge of one can be used to attack the other. From the standpoint of secondary crime prevention, drug use can be used as a predictor of individuals at a higher risk of committing other criminal acts. While not every user of drugs commits other offenses, the evidence shows that those who regularly use illicit drugs and/or use a large amount of drugs are more disposed to criminal behavior. At the very least, drug use can identify individuals for further intervention.

To the extent to which drug use is a cause or contributor to criminal activity, drug prevention and treatment programs may be effective at limiting or eliminating other crime. The treatment and prevention proposals and programs discussed in this chapter show that effective strategies do exist. Most need further analysis over longer periods in order to definitively outline their impact and potential. In a strict sense, the treatment programs outlined above are tertiary prevention programs—they deal with individuals who have already entered into drug use. Likewise, the prevention programs fall into the realm of primary prevention due to their implementation in schools and the targeting of all youths. If the emphasis is simply on targeting the drug use with no concern for related problems, these efforts belong under the headings of primary and tertiary prevention.

The emphasis of the present discussion, however, is on the role drug use plays in contributing to and/or causing other criminal acts. This brings the topic squarely into the realm of secondary crime prevention. Arguments about the victimless status of drug use, possession, and other drug crimes are automatically beyond the concerns of secondary prevention. The criminal status of drug use does not affect its place as a tool in secondary prevention. Consequently, other arguments, such as those over legalization and decriminalization, are not germane to the discussion. These topics are left for other authors to consider.

KEY TERMS

- ADAM (II) (Arrestee Drug Abuse Monitoring) program
- D.A.R.E. (Drug Abuse Resistance Education)
- detoxification
- Keepin' It REAL
- maintenance programs
- methadone maintenance
- Monitoring the Future (MTF) project
- National Survey on Drug Use and Health
- National Youth Survey (NYS)
- psychopharmacological explanation
- reciprocal
- resistance skills training
- spurious
- systemic violence
- therapeutic communities

CHAPTER 14 The School and Crime Prevention

LEARNING OBJECTIVES

After reading this chapter you should be able to:

- Provide insight into the role of schools and education in causing crime and delinquency.
- Define "tracking" and demonstrate how it relates to delinquency.
- Discuss the relationship between IQ and delinquency.
- Talk about the extent of victimization at school and responses to that problem.
- Demonstrate your knowledge of Project PATHE and its impact.
- Explain how altering the school atmosphere can change behavior.
- Identify at least four school programs that address conflict management/resolution.
- Talk about the G.R.E.A.T. program, including what it is and what evaluations of it show.
- Discuss bullying prevention programs and their impact.
- Explain what alternative schools are and related information on the degree to which they have an impact on delinquency.

The school has come to be seen as a prime actor in the development and prevention of delinquent behavior. This ascendance to prominence is reflected in a number of theories of deviant behavior, research focusing on the correlates and causes of behavior, government and private reports linking schools and education to delinquency, and the advent of delinquency intervention programs intimately tied to schools and education. Teachers and others in the schools have a great deal of contact with society's youths and are in a position to identify problems as they emerge. The ability to use school problems and concerns to predict possible problems later in life places school personnel in the midst of secondary prevention. Although not criminal, school problems are used as indicators of possible future delinquent or criminal activity both in and out of school. Schools are also prime locations for implementing secondary prevention programs. Many interventions often deal with predelinquent youths and youths having problems in school.

The relationship between school and delinquency is not always easy to understand. Many of the associations are indirect and must be understood within the context of the educational mission and the form of society. Consequently, prevention programs may not always seem to be aimed at delinquency. Rather, the interventions are geared toward the specific problematic factors found in the schools. The present chapter will attempt to develop the role of schools as an agent of secondary prevention through a three-step process. First, it is necessary to discuss the theoretical support for the role schools play in delinquency. Second, the specific aspects of the educational process that are important for discussing delinquency must be examined. Finally, the chapter will examine programs that have been established to intervene in the harmful aspects of school, with special attention paid to programs demonstrating an impact on subsequent delinquency and in-school misbehavior.

Theoretical Views

Many theorists emphasize the importance of schools in developing behavior. Cohen (1955), Cloward and Ohlin (1960), and Merton (1968) point to blocked attainment and feelings of failure as a source of deviant behavior. Each of these theorists claims that an individual faced with little or no chance of success in legitimate endeavors will turn to deviant avenues for sources of success and support. For juveniles who have not yet entered the adult world, the school becomes the setting for gauging success and failure. For example, a juvenile who is faced with failing grades while his friends are successful at their studies may be labeled as a failure by those same friends and/or teachers. The lack of success may push a youth to seek out others having the same difficulties. In an attempt to regain some feeling of status and success, failing youths may turn to deviance and acting-out behaviors.

The actual causal process relating schools and delinquency can take a variety of forms. Hirschi (1969) claims that diminished academic ability results in poor academic achievement. Failure in school can foster dislike for school attendance, a lack of concern for societally proscribed behavior, and eventual movement into delinquent behavior. An expanded, more detailed causal process (Gold, 1978) proposes that incompetence as a student leads to failed aspirations and success expectations that, in turn, results in being excluded from more successful students and student activities. This exclusion invariably lowers a youth's self-image and feelings of worth, resulting in associating with other marginal youths or deviant behavior as a means of salvaging a positive self-image. Gold (1978) refers to this choice of deviance as an *ego defense*, which acts to counterbalance the negative feedback experienced in the school setting. While only examples, these processes are indicative of how schools and the educational process can influence behavior.

These causal chains rest on the assumption that youths value scholastic achievement. Negative evaluations in the educational setting would then hold the potential for lowering the juvenile's self-esteem. Support for this proposition is found in many studies. One of the more influential studies of the educational system in the United States found that parents of all social classes are very interested in their children's scholastic success (Coleman, 1966). Vinter and Sarri (1965) report that this emphasis on educational success extends to the youths themselves. Two studies show that minority and poor students place a higher value on education than do other students (Coleman, 1966; Reiss and Rhodes, 1959). Despite this near-universal desire to achieve in school, lower-class and minority students invariably make up the group that most often fails. In addition, those who fail in school typically exhibit misbehavior and delinquency both in and out of school.

Any number of studies can be pointed to in support of the school failure–delinquency relationship. Polk and Hafferty (1966) note that students who do poorly in school and are not committed to scholastic achievement admit to higher levels of deviant behavior. Hirschi (1969), studying approximately 4,000 boys, finds that youths with low commitment to school and educational achievement display higher levels of self-reported delinquency. Thornberry et al. (1985) show that students who drop out of school exhibit higher levels of delinquency and adult criminal behavior than do high school graduates. Jarjoura (1993) specifies the dropout effect by demonstrating that the dropout–delinquency relationship only holds when the reason for dropping out is related to school problems. Studies by Gold and Mann (1972), West and Farrington (1973), and Jerse and Fakouri (1978) report that delinquents generally achieve lower grades than non-delinquents. A wide variety of other studies, using both self-report and official measures of deviance and various measures of academic achievement, support the academic achievement–delinquency relationship (Empey and Lubbeck, 1971; Kelly and Balch, 1971; Kelly and Pink, 1975; Phillips and Kelly, 1979; Polk and Schafer, 1972; Polk et al., 1974; President's Commission on Law Enforcement and the Administration of Justice, 1967).

Educational Factors and Delinquency

The relationship between educational achievement and delinquency is not a simple one. Various intervening variables enter into the formula. The basic causal processes outlined earlier provide reasonable starting points for identifying the specific aspects of school and education that lead a juvenile to deviant activity. Most of these explanations involve student success and achievement. The ability of a student to achieve can be affected by factors independent of the school. The ability of the student prior to entering school can affect academic success. One possible measure of ability is the IQ test. Another set of influences on achievement may be the format and workings of the school itself. Factors such as tracking, in-school indicators of success, and the quality of the teachers and resources can all affect student outcomes. An important additional factor may be the extent of victimization in the school. The victimization of an individual may drive the student away from school. Victimization problems in schools can result in a preoccupation with crime and safety, rather than obtaining a meaningful education. The following paragraphs attempt to outline the impact of various factors on student success.

IQ and Delinquency

The role of intelligence in the etiology of deviant behavior has been a matter of debate for many years. The early IQ tests were used to screen entrants to the United States in order to keep the mentally deficient out of the country. The so-called feeble-minded (those with low IQs) were viewed as a threat to the moral and intellectual life of the nation. It was assumed that these individuals would disproportionately contribute to the level of delinquency and criminal activity.

These early fears have found much support in later research. Hirschi and Hindelang (1977), in a review of the major research in the area, establish that IQ is an important correlate of delinquency. A variety of studies substantiate that low IQ is positively correlated to higher levels of official delinquency (Reiss and Rhodes, 1961; Short and Strodbeck, 1965; Wolfgang et al., 1972) and self-reported measures of delinquency (Hirschi and Hindelang, 1977; Weis, 1973; West, 1973). The major question unanswered in most of these analyses is whether IQ is a direct causal factor or simply lays the groundwork for other factors to intervene. Hirschi and Hindelang (1977) claim that IQ is not a direct causal factor. Instead, low IQ leads to a number of other events that, in turn, facilitate the acquisition of delinquent behavior. Among the intervening factors suggested by these authors is school achievement, academic performance, and attitude toward school. The introduction of these factors into the IQ–delinquency relationship as control variables tends to eliminate the relationship (Hirschi and Hindelang, 1977; West, 1973; Wolfgang et al., 1972). The influence of IQ, therefore, appears only in those instances when IQ affects other school variables.

School Practices and Delinquency

Achievement in school emerges as the key element in the relationship between school and delinquency. The failure to succeed in school leads to frustration, withdrawal from the institution, and an increased potential for deviant behavior. A variety of school practices can operate against success and school attachment and lead to delinquency. Among these practices is tracking, poor instruction, irrelevant instruction, and methods of evaluation.

Tracking refers to the process of assigning students to different classes or groups based on the perceived needs of the student. Some school districts, or groups of districts, have established magnet vocational high schools devoted to training and deemphasizing post-secondary education for some youths. This is an extension of the old placement of students into "college preparatory" or "vocational" groups. Schafer et al. (1971) show that students in the vocational track, regardless of their social class, prior grades, or IQ score, respond with lower grades. In addition, these students typically participate in fewer activities and are more likely to drop out of school, misbehave, and commit delinquent acts. The reasons for the lower achievement lay in the expectation, by both teachers and students, that lower-track students will not succeed, are not in the educational mainstream, and are not worth as much as college-bound students (Kelly and Pink, 1975; Schafer et al., 1971).

Many students also are faced with poor and/or irrelevant instruction. Views that lower-class and minority students are not college material often result in the assignment of less competent teachers to schools and classes serving these youths (Schafer and Polk, 1967; Schafer et al., 1971). In addition, these schools typically receive less financial support. As a result, the students develop a sense of failure, a lack of self-esteem, and may become dissatisfied and bitter toward the system. The practice of segregating some youths and implicitly labeling them as second class (particularly if they are in special classes within a larger school) can result in a self-fulfilling prophesy. They are expected to do worse and thus they live up (down?) to this expectation.

The irrelevance of instruction for some students grows out of the types of materials they are being taught, especially in the vocational education tracks (Wertleib, 1982). Schools are seldom able to keep up with the rapid changes and modifications in jobs and the workforce. The materials being taught in the school are outmoded before the youth has the opportunity to use the information. Vast changes in production and technology have established jobs for which many youths are unqualified and have eliminated jobs that previously employed hundreds or thousands of people. Instruction becomes more irrelevant when students cannot find employment upon leaving school. These factors make the instruction irrelevant and obsolete (Papagiannis et al., 1983). Students often are trained in very specific tasks that they cannot use outside of the school. At the same time, they are not prepared to enter college, undertake further instruction, or secure other jobs.

The emphasis on testing invariably leads to feelings of failure. For the "A" student, grades are a reward for hard work and indicate positive achievement. The movement toward proficiency tests (mandated for promotion and graduation in many states) often results in resentment on the part of those students who do not pass the tests. The failing student may be held back or placed into special classes that segregate and label him. Slow and failing youths may be excluded from many of the extracurricular activities that can help make school a fun, enjoyable experience. Failing students may be humiliated in front of other students, may not be expected to achieve, and are often considered second-class citizens within an institution they are forced to attend (Schafer and Polk, 1967).

Victimization in School

One result of these and other school practices is the attempt by some students to gain recognition and status through alternative, albeit unacceptable, behavior. School misbehavior leads to further alienation, exclusion from the mainstream of the student body, and further acting out. It also leads to an atmosphere in which education becomes secondary to security.

For the offending youth, school misbehavior can be seen as accomplishing three things (Gold, 1978). First, the behavior is aimed at the source of the problem—the school. Second, the youth's peers are present in school to view the activity and the offender is able to "show off" or bring attention to himself. Finally, the misbehavior is a declaration that the youth will not sit idly by while the school continuously belittles him. Continued sanctions and acting out may lead to delinquent behavior outside of the school setting.

Misbehavior also has an impact on others in the school, either directly as the target of an offense or indirectly through vicarious victimization and a shift in emphasis from learning to survival. The problem of crime in school has been described as "a serious national problem" (Gottfredson and Gottfredson, 1985). The U.S. Department of Justice routinely collects data on crime and victimization in schools. Figures from 2012 (Table 14.1) show that a total of 1,364,900 crimes were committed against students at school (Robers et al., 2014). This represents 52.4 offenses for every 1,000 students. Violent crimes are not uncommon, with more than half of the reported victimizations (almost 750,000). More than 52 students out of every 1,000 (5.2 percent) report being victimized. In light of media accounts of violent acts in schools (especially homicides), it is important to note that a good deal of in-school violence appears as threats and minor acts, including pushing and shoving (Anderson, 1998; Lockwood, 1997), rather than

TABLE 14.1 Student Victimization at School 2012[a]

Student Characteristics	Total	Theft	Violent[b]	Serious Violent[c]
Total N	1,364,900	615,600	749,200	89,000
Rate per 1,000 students	52.4	23.6	28.8	3.4

[a] Data for students aged 12 to 18.
[b] Violent crimes include rape, sexual assault, robbery, aggravated assault, and simple assault.
[c] Serious violent crimes include the violent crimes except for simple assault.
Source: Constructed by author from S. Robers et al. (2014). *Indicators of School Crime and Safety, 2013*. Washington, DC: National Center for Education Statistics, U.S. Department of Education, and Bureau of Justice Statistics, Office of Justice Programs, U.S. Department of Justice. Retrieved from http://nces.ed.gov/pubs2012/2012002.pdf

TABLE 14.2 Teacher Reports of Victimization at School, 2011 to 2012

	N	%
Threat of injury	352,900	9.2
Physically attacked	209,800	5.4

Source: Compiled by author from S. Robers et al. (2014). *Indicators of School Crime and Safety: 2013*. Washington, DC: National Center for Education Statistics, U.S. Department of Education, and Bureau of Justice Statistics, Office of Justice Programs, U.S. Department of Justice. Retrieved from http://nces.ed.gov/pubs2012/2012002.pdf

serious violence. Indeed, few homicides occur in school, with only 11 during the 2010 to 2011 school year (Robers et al., 2014).

Students are not the only individuals victimized at schools. Teachers and staff are also subject to crime and subsequent feelings of fear. During the 2011 to 2012 school year, over 350,000 teachers (9.2 percent) reported being threatened with injury by a student during school (Robers et al., 2014). Almost 210,000 teachers (5.4 percent) were actually the victim of physical attack by a student at school (see Table 14.2).

ON THE WEB

Extensive information on victimization at school is compiled each year by the Departments of Education and Justice. Detailed results can be found at http://www.nces.ed.gov/programs/crimeindicators

Bullying

A major topic of concern for many youths and their parents is the problem of bullying. The issue of bullying has received a great deal of attention over the past decade. This is partly due to the events at Columbine High School and other schools, where part of the blame/explanation for the behavior was attributed to past bullying. While most bullying does not lead to such levels of retaliatory violence, it clearly has an impact on the victim.

Bullying behavior can be classified into four types: verbal, physical, social, and cyberbullying. Too often it is assumed that bullying is primarily verbal, such as teasing and name calling. It is important to note that many forms of bullying involve physical confrontations that are actually forms of criminal victimization. Included here are hitting, shoving, and punching. Starting rumors about someone or ostracizing them from participating in events are examples of social bullying. The final major form, cyberbullying, involves the use of the Internet and other technologies to attack the victim. This can occur through posts on social media (such as Facebook, Myspace, and so on), texts, sexting, and unwanted Internet contacts.

Information on the extent of bullying generally comes from survey data. The 2011 NCVS provides a breakdown of types of bullying at school and cyberbullying in any setting as reported by youths aged 12 to 18 (see Table 14.3). Almost 40 percent of the students report being the victim of at least one form of bullying at school. The most common form of reported bullying is being made fun of, insulted, or called names (17.6 percent of respondents). Roughly one out of six is the subject of rumors, and almost 8 percent are physically bullied. Cyberbullying, which is not restricted to the school setting, is reported by 9 percent of the students.

Responses to In-School Victimization

Victimization has the potential of eliciting a variety of responses, many of which are debilitating or may lead the victim into criminal or delinquent behavior. One immediate response is fear. Robers et al. (2014) note that roughly 4 percent of students report being afraid at school. Lab and Clark (1996), studying junior and senior high schools in one large Midwestern county, found that more than 11 percent of the students fear being attacked at school. Additionally, 16 percent rate their school as "unsafe" or "very unsafe." This fear of school leads students to avoid school or take what they see as protective actions.

Table 14.4 presents data on the avoidance behaviors due to fear among students aged 12 to 18 over a six-month period (Robers et al., 2014). A total of 5.5 percent of students report avoiding school or places at school. Almost 5 percent avoid specific places in school due to fear, including hallways, restrooms, and the cafeteria. Other studies also show that a small but significant number of youth (10 percent or more) either stay home or avoid certain places/events at school due to fear of assault or theft (Kaufman et al., 1998; Lab

---

TABLE 14.3 Student Reports of Bullying, 2011

Bullying at school

Total	29.7%
Made fun of/called names/insulted	17.6
Subject of rumors	18.3
Threatened with harm	5.0
Pushed/shoved/tripped/spat on	7.9
Tried to make do things they did not want to do	3.3
Excluded from activities on purpose	5.6
Property destroyed on purpose	2.8

Cyberbullying anywhere

Total	9.0
Harmful info on Internet	3.6
Harassing instant messages	2.7
Harassing text messages	4.4
Harassing e-mails	1.9
Harassment while gaming	1.5

Source: Compiled by author from S. Robers et al. (2014). *Indicators of School Crime and Safety: 2013*. Washington, DC: National Center for Education Statistics, U.S. Department of Education, and Bureau of Justice Statistics, Office of Justice Programs, U.S. Department of Justice. Retrieved from http://nces.ed.gov/pubs2012/2012002.pdf

---

and Clark, 1996; Lab and Whitehead, 1994; Metropolitan Life, 1993, 1994; Ringwalt et al., 1992).

Another student response to crime and fear is to carry weapons to school for protection. Robers et al. (2014) report that almost 5.4 percent of youths carried a weapon in the past month at school. Lab and Clark (1996) report that 24 percent of junior and senior high school students have carried a weapon to school for protection at least once over a six-month period. Studies focusing on inner-city schools report even higher levels of weapons in school (Sheley et al., 1995).

For many youths, joining a gang is perceived as a way to garner protection and support in the face of threats. If a youth is victimized by gang members, either directly or by mistake, joining a gang further becomes a self-defense mechanism. It is natural for people to seek out support from those around them. Most victims will turn to family members for such assistance. Another source of support is close friends and peers. Joining gangs as a response to victimization, however, is a double-edged sword. While the gang may supply some sense of protection, it typically demands participation in illegal behavior and conflict with other gangs and individuals. These demands often result in further

TABLE 14.4 Students Avoiding School or Activities Due to Fear of Attack or Harm, 2011

	Percentage
Total	5.5
Stayed home from school	0.8
Avoided school activities	1.2
Avoided class	0.7
Avoided one or more places	4.7
Entrances to school	0.9
Hallways/stairways	2.5
Cafeterias	1.8
Restrooms	1.7
Other places	1.1

Source: Compiled by author from S. Robers et al. (2012). *Indicators of School Crime and Safety, 2011*. Washington, DC: Bureau of Justice Statistics. Retrieved from http://nces.ed.gov/pubs2012/2012002.pdf

victimization of the individual, rather than protection from victimization. At the same time that gang membership may alleviate victimization, joining a gang can also contribute to ongoing victimization, albeit as a member of a group and not just as an individual.

The level of misbehavior, victimization, fear, and safety responses by students in schools is a concern for various reasons. First, these concerns detract from the primary mission of educating youths. Time spent on crime and disruption means less time spent in getting an education. Similarly, avoiding school means the youths are missing out on important classroom time. Second, many of the responses to victimization and fear are more inappropriate than appropriate. Certainly, the presence of weapons offers the possibility of more serious confrontations and problems, not to mention the illegality of bringing weapons to school. The failure to address these problems will simply add to the other deleterious aspects of schools.

School Programs for Delinquency Prevention

A wide range of programs and educational strategies have emerged to address delinquency both in and outside of schools. Among the suggested educational changes are the provision of relevant instruction, the use of flexible groupings that allow movement in and out of ability levels, the development of meaningful and useful instruction, the use of teaching materials relevant for students of different backgrounds, the use of alternative grading strategies, and the institution of disciplinary measures that do not alienate or segregate students from the mainstream of the school (Schafer and Polk, 1967). Sadly, many of the suggested changes have not been instituted or have received only cursory attention in widely scattered locales. This indicates that the impact of such changes on education in general, and delinquency in particular, is still unknown. At the same time, several programs and strategies have received significant attention.

ON THE WEB

The National School Safety Center was established in 1984 by the federal government and is now an independent organization that provides services to make schools safe. It offers a great deal of information and expertise on prevention activities. You can investigate what it offers at http://www.schoolsafety.us/home

Elementary and High School Programs

Programs dealing with academic performance and school misbehavior can be found throughout the educational system. Unfortunately, most of these efforts fail to address the impact of the programs on subsequent delinquency and crime. Many researchers simply assume that changes in achievement, self-esteem, and other school-based outcomes will, in turn, affect delinquency (Gottfredson, 1987). Most programs that specifically address the question of delinquency are those that appear in junior and senior high schools. The reason for this is simple—in general, youths do not come to the attention of the juvenile justice system until they reach these grades. Prior to that time, misbehavior is handled in the home or is simply ignored.

School Atmosphere

Altering the general school environment is one suggestion for addressing misconduct in schools. Opening up participation in decision making (to both students and staff) allows everyone to take ownership of both the solutions and the successes of controlling problems. Gottfredson (1986a, 1986b) reports on the effectiveness of Project PATHE (Positive Action Through Holistic Education) in Charleston, South Carolina. This project takes a broad-based approach to the school environment by bringing teachers, administrators, students, parents, and agencies together in making decisions about education and the school. Underlying this approach is the idea that the various parties must see a stake in education and believe that education is important. The parties will care more about education if they have some say in the educational process. Project PATHE isolates a variety of factors including school pride, career-oriented programs, student team learning, and individual services as targets for change.

Project PATHE was initiated in five middle schools and two high schools from 1980 to 1983. Pre- and post-program measures, as well as data from two non-equivalent comparison schools were used in an evaluation of the program. The results offered mixed support. Experimental schools report higher test scores and graduation rates than the control schools (Gottfredson, 1986a). Attendance at school, however, did not seem to be affected by the program. Delinquency measures showed the greatest degree of disparity across and within schools. At the school level, there was some improvement in overall delinquency in the high school but no significant change for the middle schools. The control schools also showed no change over the study period. Changes in individual types of delinquency appeared in various schools. For example, drug use was reduced in one school but not in others. Some teachers reported lower levels of victimization in individual schools.

These results suggest that, while the program has no overall effect on the schools as a group, improvements can be found in individual schools (Gottfredson, 1986b). The qualified success of Project PATHE may be due to alterations in the school system and study design after the onset of the project. Changes in the school administration, the closing and consolidating of some schools, and the inability of some programs to be adequately implemented during the study suggest that the project would produce better results in a more stable setting (Gottfredson, 1986b).

ON THE WEB

More information on Project PATHE can be found at http://www.nationalgangcenter. gov/SPT/Programs/136

Lab and Clark (1996) also investigated the idea of altering the school environment through cooperative decision making. Evaluating 44 junior and senior high schools, the authors note that order and control in a school is engendered most effectively by bringing students, staff, and administrators together. The traditional methods of administratively imposing strict control and harsh discipline on students is not productive (Lab and Clark, 1996). The authors also find that schools with lower victimization and problem behaviors are those that work to develop a "normative" approach to discipline and control. This means that schools in which there is more agreement on discipline and control measures experience fewer problems than schools in which there is little agreement (Lab and Clark, 1996). Schools should strive, therefore, to build consensus through inclusion in the decision-making process.

The Charlotte School Safety Program attempts to address the issue of school safety by developing a cooperative problem-solving process that involves students, school staff, and police (Kenney and Watson, 1998). The program emphasizes changing the school environment using techniques similar to those found in community-oriented policing. Problem identification and problem solving are key elements of the intervention and an attempt is made to integrate these activities into the normal classroom curriculum. It is important to change the attitudes of the students and to turn the student body into an agent for positive change in the school (Kenney and Watson, 1998). The program was tested in the 11th grade social studies classes of a single Charlotte high school during the

1994 to 1995 school year. The problem-solving activities were addressed one to two days each week within small groups of six to 10 students.

An evaluation of the Charlotte program indicates positive changes in the target school compared to a matched control school. The evaluation used surveys of students at both schools, interviews with school staff, observations within the school, and inspections of student problem-solving worksheets. The first evidence of success is the ability of the students to identify and agree on problems in the school, and their ability to suggest and implement changes in school procedures. Kenney and Watson (1998) also note significant reductions in student's fear of crime at school, reduced fighting, fewer threats against teachers, lower numbers of suspensions for violence, and fewer calls for police assistance. Little change in these items was evident at the control school. Teachers also report fewer class disruptions and improved relations between students and faculty (Kenney and Watson, 1998). The greatest concern with the evaluation is its reliance on a single school and work with only those students in 11th grade social studies. In general, the results of research on changing the school environment suggest the efforts bring about positive changes in the schools.

Conflict Management/Resolution

Teaching students how to handle conflict and make proper choices when faced with difficult situations (such as peer pressure to use drugs or commit a crime) is a popular intervention that takes a variety of forms. Conflict management/resolution is a common program in schools. These programs appear under a variety of names, including dispute resolution, dispute mediation, conflict resolution, conflict management, and others. The basic goal of these programs is to avoid and/or resolve conflicts before they escalate into serious problems (such as physical confrontations). School programs typically include a strong teaching component in which kids learn that conflict is natural and that it can be managed through various processes (Ohio Commission on Dispute Resolution and Conflict Management, 1993). A key component in many programs is **peer mediation**, in which students are trained to assist one another in resolving disputes in such a way that all parties to the dispute accept the resolution. Many elements of school-based programs can be found in community mediation and dispute resolution programs (see Garofalo and Connelly, 1980 for a discussion of these programs). The growth of programs in the community and the generally positive evaluations of those programs (see, for example, Bridenback et al. 1980; Coates and Gehm, 1989; Reichel and Seyfrit, 1984; Roehl and Cook, 1982) have contributed to the establishment of school-based programs.

The **Resolving Conflict Creatively Program (RCCP)** in New York City included student mediation as a core component of the intervention. This program includes programming in the elementary, secondary, and special education curriculum, as well as a separate parent program (DeJong, 1993). The elementary curriculum consists of 12 lessons dealing with issues of communication, cooperation, feelings, diversity, peacemaking, and resolving conflicts. The entire curriculum (in primary and secondary schools) consists of 51 lessons and includes a heavy reliance on peer mediation and parental involvement. DeJong (1993) reports that students successfully learn the lessons, are involved in fewer fights, and believe that they can handle problems better as a result of the program. The impact of the program increases with the number of lessons and the quality of the teacher training (Samples and Aber, 1998).

Similarly, the **Responding in Peaceful and Positive Ways (RIPP)** program targets sixth graders and includes lessons on appropriate responses to conflict situations and how students can avoid violence (Farrell and Meyer, 1997). Evaluations of the program show fewer discipline problems, fewer suspensions from school, and less fighting by students participating in the program. The State of Ohio initiated a number of demonstration projects in schools aimed at providing students with problem-solving skills and instituting peer mediation programs in the schools. Based on the first three years of the program, participating schools report reduced suspensions and increased successful mediations. Students also report a greater willingness to stop fights and talk out disputes as a result of the program (Ohio Commission on Dispute Resolution and Conflict Management, 1993). Unfortunately, this program has not undergone a rigorous evaluation.

The growth of conflict management/resolution programs in schools remains an important effort in many places, despite that fact that many programs have not undergone rigorous evaluations and many studies suggest that the approach may not have a great impact (Bynum, 1996). The reason for this may be the fact that many programs do not reach a large enough portion of the student body and the programs are not very well integrated into other school activities. School-based conflict management programs are still relatively new and need to undergo further evaluation.

Peer Pressure

G.R.E.A.T. (Gang Resistance Education and Training) is a well-known program targeting peer pressure and the tendency for some youths to turn to gangs and gang behavior. Not unlike the Drug Abuse Resistance Education (D.A.R.E.) program, G.R.E.A.T. is taught by local police officers in middle schools. The original curriculum, consisting of nine lessons, was expanded to 13 one-hour lessons and is presented in middle schools (see Table 14.5). The goal of the program is to "prevent youth crime, violence and gang involvement"

┌─ ON THE WEB ─────────────────────────
│ *More details on G.R.E.A.T. and its individual compo-*
│ *nents can be found at http://www.great-online.org*
└──────────────────────────────────────

(Bureau of Justice Assistance, 2005). The thrust of the program is to provide youths with the necessary skills for identifying high-risk situations and resisting the pressure/allure of taking part in gangs and gang activity. Beyond targeting just ganging, program curricula

TABLE 14.5 G.R.E.A.T. Middle School Curriculum

1. Welcome to G.R.E.A.T.: A Gang and Violence Prevention Program
   - Lesson Goal: Students will identify the relationship among crime, violence, drug abuse, and gangs.

2. What's the Real Deal?: The Real Deal on Gangs and Violence
   - Lesson Goal: Students will analyze information sources and identify realistic, normative beliefs about gangs and violence.

3. It's About Us: Being Part of the Community
   - Lesson Goal: Students will define their roles and responsibilities in the family, school, and community.

4. Where Do We Go From Here?: How to Set Goals
   - Lesson Goal: Students will write realistic and achievable goals.

5. Decisions, Decisions, Decisions: Making the Right Choice
   - Lesson Goal: Students will practice decision-making skills.

6. Do You Hear What I Am Saying?: How to Communicate Effectively
   - Lesson Goal: Students will practice effective communication skills.

7. Walk in Someone Else's Shoes: Thinking of Others
   - Lesson Goal: Students will identify active-listening skills, how to recognize the emotional state of others, and how to demonstrate empathy toward victims of crime and violence.

8. Say It Like You Mean It: Some Ways of Refusing
   - Lesson Goal: Students will practice effective refusal skills.

9. Getting Along Without Going Along: Dealing With Peers
   - Lesson Goal: Students will practice effective refusal skills.

10. Keeping Your Cool: Managing Your Anger
    - Lesson Goal: Students will practice anger-management skills.
      - Practice Cooling Off

11. Keeping It Together: How to Calm Others
    - Lesson Goal: Students will identify how anger-management skills help prevent violence and conflicts.

12. Working It Out: How to Solve Conflicts
    - Lesson Goal: Students will practice conflict-resolution techniques.

13. G.R.E.A.T. Days Ahead: Applying Your G.R.E.A.T. Skills
    - Lesson Goal: Students will explain how their G.R.E.A.T. Project helped them develop a feeling of commitment and ownership of their school and their community.

Source: Bureau of Justice Assistance (2014). *Gang Resistance Education and Training*. http://great-online.org/Components/MiddleSchool.Aspx

are geared toward increasing self-esteem, changing attitudes, addressing peer pressure, and eliminating participation in violent behavior. A key component of G.R.E.A.T. is to teach non-violent conflict resolution techniques to the youths.

The G.R.E.A.T. program has undergone extensive evaluation. A longitudinal evaluation of the original G.R.E.A.T. programs showed positive outcomes. Esbensen et al. (2004), using data for four years following program participation, reported less victimization, less risk-taking behavior, improved attitudes toward the police, increased numbers of prosocial peers, and more negative views about gangs among those youths receiving the G.R.E.A.T. lessons. Unfortunately, the evaluation failed to find any impact on the more important target of the project—reduced gang participation. While this is disappointing, the promising results led the sponsors of the G.R.E.A.T. program to undertake a revision of the curriculum, which resulted in the current 13-lesson scheme.

The revised curriculum has been the subject of a rigorous national evaluation. A total of 195 classrooms in 31 schools in seven cities were included in the analysis, with a total of more than 3,800 students. One hundred thirty classrooms received the G.R.E.A.T. training, and 93 classrooms served as the controls. Data was gathered over a five-year period of time, including four years post-program participation (Esbensen et al., 2011). Preliminary results based on the first year of follow-up data reveal overall positive results. Results show that participants are more positive about the police, are less positive about gangs, more often use refusal skills they have been taught, are better able to resist peer pressure, and are less involved in gangs (Esbensen et al., 2011). Most importantly, the data reveal 39 percent less gang membership among G.R.E.A.T. participants (Esbensen et al., 2013). These positive results are also sustained at four years post-participation. G.R.E.A.T. participants are still 24 percent less likely to be gang members and they maintain positive attitudes toward police, use refusal skills, and hold more negative attitudes toward gangs (Esbensen et al., 2013). All of these results are significant.

Despite these positive results, the evaluation shows no impact on criminal and violent activity (Esbensen et al., 2013; Pyrooz, 2013). This may be a result of the fact that G.R.E.A.T. targets entire classrooms, which include youths at both low risk and high risk for gang membership. As a result, G.R.E.A.T. may influence a youth's self-identification as a gang member, but it may have little impact on the level of attachment to gangs and criminal gang activity among those who join (Pyrooz, 2013). While G.R.E.A.T. is a promising program, its full impact on behavior is not known.

Anti-Bullying Efforts

Bullying prevention is identified as an exemplary program for attacking violence by youths (Elliott, 2000). The most notable of these efforts is that of Olweus and his colleagues (Olweus 1994, 1995; Olweus and Limber, 2000). *Bullying* behavior includes both physical and verbal aggression that is repeated over time and is meant to intentionally harm the victim (Olweus and Limber, 2000). Studies in Norwegian, Swedish, and U.S. schools find that at least 15 percent of the students report being either bullied or being the offender (Melton et al., 1998, Olweus, 1993).

Developed in Norway, the model anti-bullying program is aimed at the entire school and relies on active student, teacher, and parent participation. The program attempts to raise awareness about the problem of bullying, establish rules and regulations governing the behavior and responses to offending, train staff on how to integrate discussions on bullying into the curriculum, require meetings between parents and teachers, and hold meetings between bullies and their victims. The program also works with the families of offenders to address the problems outside of school. Based on survey data gathered before the onset of the program and periodically over a two-year follow-up period, Olweus (1994, 1995) reports significant reductions in bullying, classroom disruption, and general delinquency. Replicating the program in England, Whitney et al.

┌─ ON THE WEB ─────────────────
│ *The Olweus Bullying Prevention Program has*
│ *been recognized as a blueprint for violence pre-*
│ *vention and has been adopted around the world*
│ *based on its proven impact. Read more details on*
│ *the program at http://www.colorado.edu/cspv/*
│ *blueprints/modelprograms/BPP.html*
└──────────────────────────────

(1994) report similar positive results, particularly for students in younger grades. This suggests that the intervention should be targeted at young students before bullying behavior becomes ingrained in individuals. Finally, Melton et al. (1998), testing the program in South Carolina grade schools, find significant reductions in bullying, as well as vandalism, general delinquency, and school misbehavior.

Based on these results, anti-bullying programs appear promising as a means to prevent both the initial aggression and subsequent offending and antisocial behavior. Olweus and Limber (2000), however, offer several cautions related to implementing the program. First, the program is better suited to elementary schools than junior or senior high schools. This suggests that earlier intervention is preferable over later projects. Second, the program requires significant time and effort on behalf of teachers and parents. Third, significant training of teachers and parents is required for the successful implementation of the program. Finally, schools need to actively include non-teaching staff, parents, and students in the daily operation of the intervention.

Alternative Schools

Many school programs are targeted at specific groups of youths, rather than at the entire school. Such programs may seek to remove those having problems from the school or may set up individual classrooms or programs within the school. **Alternative schools** represent a major attempt to dispel the negative experiences of many problem youths. The basic idea behind alternative schools is the provision of a positive learning atmosphere, which increases feelings of success within an atmosphere of warmth and acceptance

(Gold, 1978). The process involves recognizing the needs of the individual student and meeting those needs through interventions such as one-on-one instruction, unstructured grading practices, instruction tailored to the interests of the student, the development of close relationships between students and teachers, the involvement of the students in the instruction process, and advancement based on individual progress.

Although alternative education programs have become commonplace, few evaluations of these schools look at their effect on delinquent behavior, especially acts committed outside of the school. Gottfredson (1987) reports on the effectiveness of 17 school-based delinquency prevention programs in 15 high-crime communities. Most of the interventions entail alternative schools or classrooms within mainstream schools. The programming within the schools includes personalized instruction, student participation in decision making, the use of behavior modification techniques, informal control, and peer assistance. Overall, the results show reduced delinquency, improved school safety, reduced in-school victimizations, enhanced attachment to school, and reductions in interactions with delinquent peers (Gottfredson, 1987). While not all of the projects show the same degree of success, the pattern across the studies suggests that alternative educational practices can make a difference. The results must be tempered somewhat due to the lack of adequate comparison groups and the subsequent possibility of alternative factors that may be influencing the results. The consistency of the results, however, suggests that these problems may be minor.

Cox (1999) considers the impact of an alternative school program for middle school students (grades six to eight). Youths attend the program for one semester and then return to their regular school. While at the alternative school, students participate in activities aimed at improving their academic performance and self-esteem, as well as lowering their delinquent behavior. The program evaluation compared students randomly assigned to the alternative school and a control group. The results show an immediate impact on self-esteem and grades. Unfortunately, there is no change in self-reported delinquency, and the positive changes disappear after the subjects return to their regular school. Cox (1999) speculates that a one-semester program may not be long enough to ensure long-term change. Students may need prolonged exposure to the alternative school format.

One meta-analysis suggests that alternative schools have little, if any, impact on delinquency. In a **meta-analysis**, the data from different studies is reanalyzed in order to make direct comparisons between the results. Cox et al. (1995) analyzed the results from 57 studies conducted from 1966 to 1993. The authors uncover some evidence that alternative school programs increase school performance, improve attitudes toward school, and other similar outcomes. Unfortunately, they are unable to find any significant improvement in client delinquency. Compounding these results is the fact that the most methodologically rigorous studies show the least impact. Gold and Mann (1983) also caution that alternative school settings may isolate youths from the mainstream students and that this may cause other problems, particularly with later reintegration to regular schools. It would appear, therefore, that further study and experimentation with alternative schools is needed before making strong claims for its impact on subsequent delinquent behavior.

Police in Schools

The use of police officers in schools has grown considerably since the early 1990s. Violent crime, drug violations, weapons violations, and bullying, as well as highly publicized shootings, have aroused concern and calls for increased police officer presence in schools (Booth et al., 2011). Student surveys shows that more than 70 percent of students report that their school has either a security guard or an assigned police officer (Robers et al., 2014). See Table 14.6.

The presence of school resource officers (SROs) has become commonplace. A 2005 survey of almost 1,400 schools across the United States found that 48 percent had SROs and 76 percent relied on public law enforcement (Travis and Coon, 2005). James and McCallion (2013) report that there are more than 19,000 police officers and deputies employed as SROs in the United States. Most police in schools were involved in traditional police functions, including patrolling, making arrests, and providing security. At the same time, many police officers in schools, particularly those serving in an SRO capacity, provided mentoring and referrals, training to teachers and parents, taught programs such as Drug Abuse Resistance Education (D.A.R.E.), and chaperoned school events (Travis and Coon, 2005). Indeed, McDevitt and Finn (2005), in a survey of SROs,

---

TABLE 14.6 Activities of Law Enforcement in Schools

Law Enforcement	Advise/Mentor	Teaching
Patrol	Advise staff	D.A.R.E.
Operate metal detectors	Mediate disputes	Anti-gang classes
Conduct safety	Advise students	Anti-hate classes
inspections	Work with parent-teacher	Law-related education
Respond to crime/disorder	groups	Firearm safety
reports	Advise athletic teams	Crime awareness and
Make arrests	Mentor students	prevention
Write reports	Chaperone events	Conflict resolution
Perform drug sweeps	Present awards	Problem solving

Source: L.F. Travis and J.K. Coon (2005). *The Role of Law Enforcement in Public School Safety: A National Survey*. Washington, DC: National Institute of Justice.

uncover that two-thirds of the officers report performing law enforcement activities in the schools, with less than one-third reporting activities such as mentoring or counseling. May et al. (2014) note that most SRO activity involves monitoring the campus.

The introduction of police to schools has not been without controversy. Some observers argue that SROs try to balance their roles as law enforcers and mentors/instructors/problem solvers. Others contend that the widespread introduction of police into the school setting criminalizes school discipline.

At the same time as police have been introduced to school, there has been an introduction of zero tolerance policies whereby students are suspended or expelled for certain behaviors such as bringing a weapon to school. Critics contend that the introduction of police resource officers and zero tolerance policies are signs of criminalization in schools (Rich-Shea and Fox, 2014). In other words, instead of seeing discipline problems as requiring solutions by teachers and principals, these practices treat students as quasi-criminals and mandate quasi-criminal justice solutions and thereby label youths as criminals. Critics see this as part of a more general trend to ignore problems of poverty and deindustrialization. For example, "the transfer of disciplinary responsibilities from school professionals to the police also supports this purpose given that police are ill-equipped to recognize and address the psychological and social roots of school misconduct" (Hirschfield and Celinska, 2011, p. 7).

Evaluations of effective school–police partnerships indicate that more is needed than simply placing police officers in schools. First, police officers cannot address problems of overcrowding, low attendance, large minority populations, and low funding. Second, evaluations show that parent cooperation is essential and that any law enforcement presence needs to be accompanied "with intensive monitoring, counseling, and other related services that strengthen cooperation and collaboration with other community-based groups" (Brady et al., 2007).

Other Interventions

A wide range of other interventions are being used to alter youthful behavior, both in schools and in the community. The U.S. Department of Education has initiated two programs in recent years aimed at dealing with crime and other problem issues for youths. These are the Safe and Drug Free Schools program and the Safe Schools/Healthy Children initiative. While driven by legislative mandates, the two programs incorporate a wide range of different interventions. Much of the diversity rests on the decisions of the different school districts, who they include in the planning of programs (e.g., parents, police, etc.), and what programs they decide to implement. The programs have provided a great deal of funding and had a major impact on programming in schools. Along with other agencies (including the U.S. Office of Juvenile Justice and Delinquency Prevention), the Department of Education has undertaken various evaluations under these programs. Unfortunately, the research has been focused primarily in two areas—measuring the extent of victimization and fear in schools, and process evaluations of the implementation of programs. Relatively little comprehensive outcome evaluation has been conducted.

Truancy reduction programs have received increased attention in recent years in many jurisdictions. Many of these efforts involve a combination of picking up truant youths and returning them to school (or taking them into custody) and holding parents accountable for their truant children. Two underlying issues drive most of these efforts. First, removing truants from the street eliminates any offenses those youths might have committed while out of school. The school provides supervision, thereby reducing the level of crime during the school day. Second, reducing truancy should lead to increased educational attainment and higher graduation rates. This should lead to greater chances of (meaningful) employment and fewer chances of turning to crime in the future. Clearly, the arguments underlying such initiatives make sense and easily lead to anti-truancy initiatives. The impact of such programs on crime (both current and long-term), however, is unknown. Most truancy reduction programs rely on process evaluations, which count the number of youths handled and the methods used to dispose of the cases.

Another recent movement has been to establish after-school programs for youths. As with other programs, these efforts have multifaceted goals. Perhaps the most common argument underlying these initiatives is that keeping youths busy and supervised after school mitigates the possibility of them getting into trouble. Indeed, there is clear evidence that youthful offending peaks in the late afternoon and early evening, particularly on school days, with roughly 20 percent of all juvenile violent crime occurring on school days between 3:00 P.M. and 7:00 P.M. (OJJDP, 1999). Therefore, projects that can keep juveniles busy after school hold the potential of reducing the level of crime in the community. This same argument underlies the calls for midnight basketball leagues and other initiatives that occupy unsupervised free time. A secondary argument used to support many after-school programs reflects the belief that educationally based programs can increase the academic achievement of participating youths. Interestingly, despite the great interest in these kinds of interventions, almost no evaluation has been conducted. Most of the existing literature focuses on what these programs look like and how to initiate one, rather than on whether they are successful at achieving their intended mission. This holds true for both crime and educational outcomes.

A great deal of additional research is needed on these programs. While concerted efforts have gone into developing these interventions and implementing the projects, relatively little time and effort has gone into assessing the impact of the projects on delinquency and youthful misconduct. Most of the evaluations are simple process studies that tell how the program was initiated, who was involved, how many meetings took place, and how much money was spent. What is needed now is to know how much delinquency was averted and to what extent the schools are safer places.

The Future of School/Educational Programs in Crime Prevention

There is little doubt that schools hold a key position in the growth and development of youths. Schools deal with virtually every child for a major portion of his formative years. The trend in society has been to delay the entry of people into the societal mainstream and prolong the period known as adolescence. As a result, schools have had to assume more and more responsibility for the socialization of children. Increased responsibility for handling adolescents may prove to be a mixed blessing. Schools have so far failed to adequately respond to juvenile misbehavior displayed both in and out of school. To fault the schools, however, without considering the position that has been thrust upon them is not warranted. The schools have not expected or been prepared to lead the fight against delinquent activity. The criticism that they have failed in handling delinquency ignores this fact, and the additional fact that they have not been given the resources to adequately do their multifaceted job. Despite these facts, the school is a logical point for intervention.

The programs that have been initiated and evaluated provide some hope that future deviant behavior can be prevented. There are clear indications that some educational interventions are effective at reducing recidivism. Anti-bullying and dispute resolution are two that show positive results. Other promising approaches need to be subjected to thorough, long-term evaluations. Educational programs aimed at stemming misbehavior should be allowed sufficient time to operate prior to declaring them effective or ineffective. Just as society does not expect that an individual can be educated in a short time span, neither should it expect that short-term programs can reverse trends that have been growing for many decades. For example, the stigma of tracking cannot be overcome in the span of a single year in alternative classes. Positive outcomes from intervention programs should be used as a guide for expanding and altering the overall educational system. A companion problem is the fact that many educational programs and interventions have not undergone outcome evaluations. The Safe and Drug Free Schools program, the Safe Schools/Healthy Children initiatives, truancy reduction efforts, and most after-school programs have been the subject of process evaluations with little attention paid to their impact on crime and delinquency. A great deal of attention should be paid to evaluating these efforts.

The educational system should continue to serve as a focal point for modifying behavior and preventing deviant activity. Teachers and educators are in an ideal position to observe juvenile behavior, providing assistance, and alerting others to potential problems. The failure to incorporate the school and education system in crime prevention is to ignore a tool that has a great potential for success. The fact that schools and the criminal justice system can work together can be seen in various programs that have established cooperative arrangements between these institutions (Lindsey and Kurtz,

1987; Rubel, 1989). This does not mean that the solution to crime has been found. It does suggest that one of the most important ingredients in crime prevention has been underused.

KEY TERMS

- alternative schools
- bullying
- feeble-minded
- G.R.E.A.T. (Gang Resistance Education and Training)
- meta-analysis
- peer mediation
- Project PATHE (Positive Action Through Holistic Education)
- Resolving Conflict Creatively Program (RCCP)
- Responding in Peaceful and Positive Ways (RIPP)
- school resource officers (SROs)
- tracking

PART III

Tertiary Prevention

The following chapters are devoted to a brief overview of tertiary prevention methods. Tertiary crime prevention deals with the elimination of recidivistic behavior on the part of offenders. The emphasis is on actions taken to keep the confirmed offender from further harming society. Although the identification of individuals for insertion into prevention measures is straightforward (i.e., past deviant behavior), prediction is still an important component of many tertiary prevention approaches. Prediction at this stage of prevention focuses on predicting recidivism and not initial offending.

For the most part, tertiary prevention rests within the confines of the formal justice system. Chapter 15 explores the impact of specific deterrence and incapacitation on the level of crime and recidivism. Specific deterrence involves the imposition of sanctions upon the individual in the hopes that these actions will keep that specific individual from further engaging in crime once the punishment has ceased. Perhaps the clearest example of this approach is the setting of different imprisonment periods for different crimes and individuals with the aim of deterring offending once the individual is released. Incapacitation typically looks at the reduction in crime attributable to the confinement period itself. Physical control over a person's behavior makes the commission of criminal actions in larger society an impossibility. Incapacitation can also be accomplished using emerging technology through electronic monitoring. Specific deterrence and incapacitation are related features of imprisoning offenders. The effects of these actions on recidivism and the overall crime rate, as well as the costs of these approaches, are discussed.

Chapter 16 looks at the alternative goal of criminal justice intervention with offenders—rehabilitation. The rehabilitative ideal dominated the correctional end of the formal justice system throughout most of the twentieth century. This domination, however, has often been rhetorical and not in practice. Nevertheless, a wide array of rehabilitative practices has been introduced. The most common comment made about rehabilitation, however, is that "nothing works." This view has stirred controversy since its declaration in the mid-1970s and forms a basis for the chapter. Despite the discouraging results, rehabilitation continues to be a major focus of system effort. Numerous innovative approaches have emerged in recent years which advance the idea of rehabilitation. Two of these, restorative justice and specialty courts, are considered in this chapter.

Each of the following discussions is limited in scope and depth. The areas of deterrence, incapacitation, and rehabilitation each have voluminous literature devoted to them. It is not the aim of the chapters to explore the many nuances and issues raised in these areas. Instead, the chapters are intended to summarize the available materials as to their impact on crime and recidivism.

CHAPTER 15 Specific Deterrence and Incapacitation

CHAPTER OUTLINE

LEARNING OBJECTIVES

After reading this chapter you should be able to:

- Show the difference between specific deterrence and incapacitation.
- Discuss the effectiveness of imprisonment to have a specific deterrent effect.
- Outline the Minneapolis Domestic Violence Experiment, cite its findings, and discuss the results of its replication studies.
- Compare and contrast collective and selective incapacitation.
- List and define assumptions underlying incapacitation.
- Present information on the findings from studies of collective incapacitation of imprisonment.
- Discuss the costs of achieving a collective incapacitation effect.
- Outline findings on selective incapacitation or imprisonment.
- Point out problems with selective incapacitation.
- Compare and contrast active and passive electronic monitoring systems.
- List and discuss potential advantages of EM.
- Provide information on the effectiveness of EM to reduce recidivism and have other effects.
- Discuss problems and concerns with the use of EM.

Specific deterrence and incapacitation are two prominent methods for preventing convicted offenders from committing further crimes. Both methods seek to prevent crime through intervention with individuals who have already harmed society and shown a disposition toward deviant activity. The prevention of crime through these approaches revolves around punishment of the offender. The form of punishment most considered in evaluations of specific deterrence and incapacitation is incarceration. Despite the similarity in the punishment, the actual process by which specific deterrence and incapacitation brings about crime prevention is very different.

Specific deterrence is aimed at the individual offender and their future behavior. Chapter 9 discussed the general deterrent effect of punishment. At that time the emphasis was on the ability of the criminal law and its sanctions, whether de jure or de facto, to deter individuals who have not yet violated the criminal law but have the potential for so doing in the future. The emphasis shifts in specific deterrence from the non-offender to the criminal. Concern also shifts to the actual imposition of the law and its sanctions. Specific deterrence seeks to prevent the offender from further deviant actions through the imposition of punishments that will negate any pleasure or advantage gained by participation in criminal activity.

Incapacitation also seeks to prevent future crime on the part of the offender. The method by which this occurs is the simple control of the individual, which prohibits the physical possibility of future criminal activity. For example, if the person is locked up and under total physical control, it is a physical impossibility for the individual to commit a crime in society. The most commonly discussed form of incapacitation is incarceration. There is no assumption on the part of incapacitation that the individual will be deterred from committing further crimes once released from the institution. The only consideration is the number of offenses that can be prevented by keeping the offender locked up for a specified period. An alternative form of incapacitation is electronic monitoring of offenders.

The Specific Deterrent Effect of Criminal Sanctions

Relatively little research has been devoted to the study of specific deterrence. Interest in deterrence has focused on the impact of laws and sanctions on the general population and not just the individuals who are subjected to the actions of the criminal justice system. Intuitively, specific deterrence should be a logical outcome of system intervention. Among the goals of bringing an offender to justice is the prevention of future criminal activity by that individual. Punishments are different for different offenses due to the type of offense and the assumptions regarding the hedonistic value of the offense and the punishment. The sanction is meant to offset the amount of pleasure received through the crime. By so doing, the individual will see no advantage or gain in future transgressions. As in general deterrence, the individual is assumed to be a rational person making decisions based on a cost–benefit analysis.

Although many types of punishment are imposed by the criminal justice system, incarceration is assumed to have the greatest potential for deterring the individual from future criminal acts. This does not mean that fines, probation, community service orders, cease and desist orders, and other penalties have no deterrent value. These other forms of punishment, however, leave the individual their freedom and generally represent more lenient attitudes toward the behavior in question. The hope is that they will have some deterrent capability because they are reserved for more minor offenses. Incarceration is used in cases in which the offense is more heinous or the individual is a repeat offender for whom more mild punishments have not had the desired impact. The expected deterrent effect of punishment, regardless of the type, however, is not uniformly found in the research.

Studies of Imprisonment

Many evaluations of specific deterrence look to the effect of imprisonment on subsequent offending. The easiest form of evaluation considers the recidivism rate of individuals who have spent some time in an institution. This approach presents a bleak picture for specific deterrence. In one early analysis, Glaser (1964) reported that approximately one-third of prison releases are eventually reincarcerated. This figure represents subjects who were not deterred from further offending by their punishment. While this finding is somewhat disturbing, the specific deterrent effect of imprisonment is probably even worse. This is due to the fact that Glaser considers only reincarceration, and many offenses do not result in a prison sentence. Indeed, Langan and Levin (2002) note that two-thirds of offenders released from prison are rearrested within three years, almost half are reconvicted, and 25 percent are reincarcerated. Durose et al. (2014) find that two-thirds of state prison releasees are rearrested within three years and 77 percent are rearrested within five years.

The simple use of aggregate recidivism data can be misleading. One common mistake is the lumping together of serious with less serious offenders or offenders with differing offense careers. Recidivism is typically higher for individuals who have longer offense histories and those receiving harsher sentences (Gibbs, 1975). Consequently, the failure to randomly assign individuals to different punishments or to consider comparable groups of prisoners makes the interpretation of aggregate recidivism figures highly suspect. Such results, however, are commonly cited as representative of recidivism rates for institutionalized groups.

An alternative method for analyzing specific deterrence considers the effect of length of imprisonment on parole outcome. This approach usually compares the recidivism rate for parolees who serve differing amounts of time in an institution. One study of parole outcome looks at almost 15,000 burglars paroled in 1968 and 1969. Babst et al. (1972) examine the recidivism rate for 22 groups of burglars categorized by drug use, alcohol use, prior record, and age at release for the study subjects. Comparing similar groups of subjects with varying lengths of institutional stay reveals no consistent relationship between the time served and parole outcome after one year. The few instances in which a difference is accountable to length of stay appears in subgroups that contain few individuals (Babst et al., 1972).

Beck and Hoffman (1976) and Gottfredson et al. (1977) also examine the impact of sentence length on parole outcome. In the first study, the authors divide subjects into five groups based on their risk of recidivating while on parole. Using a two-year follow-up, the authors report that, in general, there is more recidivism as the length of time served in prison increases (Beck and Hoffman, 1976). Significantly, individuals who are given a fairly good prognosis for success on parole tend to do worse as the amount of time spent in prison increases. Gottfredson et al. (1977), dividing their subjects into nine separate categories based on various discriminating factors, reveal that the time served in prison has no impact on recidivism for four categories of parolees, while three groups of subjects show higher recidivism as the time served increases to 49 months. Conversely, time served has a positive impact for those who spend 50 months or more in prison (Gottfredson et al., 1977). The results of these studies strongly suggest that the length of imprisonment has a differential effect for different risk subjects.

One major problem with most studies is the inability to randomly assign parolees to varying lengths of time served and then compare the parole outcome figures. Berecochea and Jaman (1981), however, randomly varied the time served, with one group serving six additional months in prison. Looking at 12- and 24-month follow-up figures, the authors find no statistically significant differences in the likelihood of return or returns for new complaints. They conclude that the severity of punishment is unrelated to recidivism (Berecochea and Jaman, 1981). The major problem with this study is that the six-month difference in length of imprisonment may not be sufficient for a specific deterrent effect to become viable.

Finally, Weisburd et al. (1995) examine the specific deterrent effect of imprisonment on white-collar criminals. The authors use data from various jurisdictions and follow up incarcerated offenders over a 10-year period. Contrary to expectations, there is no evidence that imprisonment deters the subjects from further offending (Weisburd et al., 1995). Indeed, there is evidence that those in prison recidivate at a slightly higher rate than those in the control group. The authors speculate that, for white-collar criminals, the prison experience adds little to the impact of arrest, prosecution, and conviction. Thus, the non-prison controls have been equally deterred without the need for imprisonment.

These studies of length of imprisonment and deterrence suffer from various problems. First, Nagin et al. (2009) suggest that imprisonment may actually be more criminogenic than deterrent. Thus, the use of imprisonment for a specific deterrent effect may actually result in more offending post-release. Second, studies of the specific deterrent effect of imprisonment fail to consider the types of treatment received by the subjects. The failure to consider the rehabilitative programming that inmates receive may alter the study results. Villetaz et al. (2006) report that non-custodial sanctions have a greater deterrent effect than imprisonment.

Arrest for Domestic Violence

Several studies of specific deterrence examine the differential impact of police decisions on subsequent spouse abuse. The **Minneapolis Domestic Violence Experiment** (Sherman and Berk, 1984) investigates the deterrent effect of arrest, separation, and police counseling in misdemeanor spouse abuse situations. Officers were instructed to randomly apply the different responses (randomization determined by the researchers) in all cases of spouse abuse. The only exceptions to this process include cases in which the police officer is threatened, there is a demand for arrest by one party, or there is an injury as a result of the offense. Examining 314 cases over a 17-month period, the authors claim that arrests result in lower recidivism suggesting a strong specific deterrent effect (Sherman and Berk, 1984). Unfortunately, a number of problems are inherent in the study (Binder and Meeker, 1988). First, officers were not always able or willing to impose the sanction dictated by the experimental procedure. Second, few officers actually participated in the study. The officers were self-selected and a few of these provided the vast majority of the cases for study. Third, a self-report follow-up was completed on less than one-half of the cases. Finally, it is possible that many of the subjects chose not to file official reports or reply to self-reports concerning subsequent instances of spouse abuse.

Replications of the Minneapolis study fail to confirm the original results. Dunford (1990) reports that arrests in Omaha, Nebraska, have no greater impact on future activity than does separating or counseling the parties involved in the dispute. Interestingly, issuing warrants for suspects who left before the police arrived results in fewer subsequent arrests compared to those not arrested by warrant. Dunford (1990) suggests that this positive impact may be due to the fact that those who fled prior to the arrival of the police had more to lose from an arrest, thus an arrest or formal system involvement would be a deterrent. A second replication in Charlotte, North Carolina (Hirschel et al., 1991, 1992), uncovers results similar to those in Omaha. The researchers reveal that arrest is no better at deterring subsequent behavior than issuing citations or advising and separating the disputants. The results persist in both official and self-report data. Both of these evaluations pay particular attention to the shortcomings of the Sherman and Berk (1984) study and appear to have avoided the same problems. Consequently, the results of the original study need to be viewed with skepticism.

Where the prior studies considered the impact of arrest, other analyses consider the impact of prosecution on subsequent domestic violence. Thistlethwaite et al. (1998), studying misdemeanor domestic assault in Hamilton County, Ohio, report that offenders receiving more severe punishments tend to recidivate less often. Time on probation or in jail, however, is not related to future domestic violence (Thistlethwaite et al., 1998). Conversely, Davis et al. (1998) claim that the outcome of prosecution (i.e., cases declined, dismissed, or not convicted) is not related to recidivism in Milwaukee County data. Clearly, the factors related to deterring repeat domestic violence remain unknown.

Summary

Studies of specific deterrence are not confined to imprisonment and domestic violence. A number of studies on fines for drunk driving (e.g., Briscoe, 2004; Moffat and Poynton, 2007; Wagenarr et al., 2007; Weatherburn and Moffatt, 2011) find little or no specific deterrent impact of fines. Coupled with other analyses, there does not appear to be strong support for specific deterrence. As noted earlier, Nagin et al. (2009), reviewing imprisonment studies, find a more criminogenic impact than a deterrent effect.

Problems within study designs appear to be a major problem in the analyses. The inability to randomly assign punishments or choose subjects represents one stumbling block. A second failure involves the decision of researchers to ignore relevant factors such as the use or type of treatment applied to the subjects. Indeed, many studies of specific deterrence grew out of interest about the rehabilitative effect of imprisonment and various programs. Few evaluations address the possible confounding influence of any rehabilitative program that may have existed. The present state of knowledge does not provide strong support for the argument.

Incapacitation

While imprisonment may not deter an individual from committing deviant acts again in the future, it does keep the subject from committing crimes against society while in the institution. Simply put, incapacitation provides control over the individual, thus precluding behavior that is harmful to society. Incapacitation does not imply anything about the individual's behavior once released from incarceration or control. Incapacitation can take two different forms—collective and selective. Collective incapacitation refers to the imposition of sentences upon everyone exhibiting the same behavior with no concern for the potential of the individual. For example, all burglars receive the same sentence. No consideration is given to the potential of the different individuals who commit the offense. The end result is punishment aimed at all similar offenders with the intent of eliminating subsequent offenses. The basis of collective incapacitation is the legal finding of a past offense.

Under **selective incapacitation** the emphasis is on identifying high-risk offenders and subjecting only that group to intervention. All offenders found guilty of the same crime are not punished equally. Those who are judged to be greater threats to society may receive longer, harsher terms of imprisonment. Others judged to be of little threat are subjected to minimal time in prison or sentenced to an alternate punishment. The intent is to maximize the incapacitation effect without subjecting all offenders to long prison terms or control. A good example of selective incapacitation is **three-strikes laws** that mandate lengthy imprisonment for those convicted of a third offense.

The evaluation of incapacitation effects rests on a number of assumptions concerning criminal activity. The most basic assumption is that individuals commit some base rate of offenses every year. Using this figure, it is possible to estimate the number of offenses that are averted through the incapacitation of an individual. For example, if it is assumed that an individual commits 10 crimes per year, the incapacitative effect of a one-year prison sentence is a reduction of crime by 10 offenses for every person so incarcerated. This finding must be qualified, however, by other considerations.

It is also assumed that there is a constant rate of offending over time and an individual's criminal career is not simply put on hold while incapacitated. Instead, the number of years served in prison, for example, is subtracted from the overall number of years offending. The inability to make this assumption would result in no incapacitative effect because the time served would simply postpone and not eliminate the level of offending. A further assumption is that an incapacitated individual is not replaced by another offender. The simple replacement of one individual by another would again result in no net change in offending. Replacement could take two forms. First, the incapacitation of an individual who commits crimes as part of a group may result in the continuation of crime by the remaining group members. Second, crimes committed in the context of an ongoing business interest, such as organized crime, may result in the business finding a replacement for the incapacitated subject.

These assumptions have varying effects on the evaluation of collective and selective incapacitation. The following discussion focuses on the incapacitative effect of two interventions—imprisonment and electronic monitoring.

The Collective Incapacitation of Imprisonment

The evidence on collective incapacitation from imprisonment offers results ranging from small to large changes in the level of crime. Clarke (1974), using the Philadelphia cohort data (Wolfgang et al., 1972), estimates that incarcerating boys prior to age 18 reduces index offenses by 5 percent for white youths and 15 percent for non-whites. Adjusting the figures to reflect the contribution of juvenile activity to the overall crime rate, Clarke (1974) notes that incapacitating juveniles will only result in a modest 1 to 4 percent decrease in the index crime rate. Greenberg (1975), using official records to estimate the criminal careers of adult offenders, claims that doubling the amount of time spent in prison would only decrease crime by 0.6 percent to 4.0 percent. Conversely, reducing the prison population by 50 percent would only increase the number of crimes by 1.2 percent to 8.0 percent (Greenberg, 1975). Finally, Peterson and Braiker (1980), using self-report data on the level of offending prior to incarceration and estimates of the average individual crime rate, find that incarceration reduces the level of burglary by only 6 percent and auto theft by 7 percent (Peterson and Braiker, 1980). They claim a much larger incapacitation effect for armed robbery, where 22 percent of the offenses are averted through the imprisonment of offenders.

Each of the studies presented above assumes a constant crime rate across all offenders. The actual level of offending, however, probably varies greatly from individual to individual. Marsh and Singer (1972) consider individual differences in the level of offending by dividing their target population of robbers into six subgroups, each with different offense rates. Examination of the effect of a one-year increase in incarceration for each subgroup reveals an incapacitation effect ranging from 35 to 48 percent (Marsh and Singer, 1972). This is a great departure from the figures uncovered in the studies using constant, aggregate crime rates.

Differences in criminal justice system policies also may result in varying incapacitation effects. Petersilia and Greenwood (1978) estimate that a five-year mandatory sentence imposed on felony offenders would result in a 31 percent decrease in violent crimes and a 42 percent decrease in burglaries. Withholding the mandatory sentence until a second felony conviction would reduce the incapacitative effect to 16 percent for violent offenses and 15 percent for burglaries. Van Dine et al. (1979), looking at data for Columbus, Ohio, claim that a five-year mandatory sentence for a first felony offense would result in a 17.4 percent decrease in violent index crimes. Incarceration after a second offense would result in a 6 percent reduction. Cohen (1983) reports that five-year mandatory sentences for prisoners with prior records would reduce index crimes by Washington, D.C. arrestees by 13.7 percent.

The costs of incapacitation can be examined in terms of the number of people who need to be incarcerated. Cohen (1978) estimates the level of increased incarceration necessary to achieve a 10 percent reduction in index crime, a reduction of 100 index crimes, and a 10 percent reduction in violent crimes. Estimates for various states are found in Table 15.1. The table shows that small reductions in crime require large increases in the percentage of people sentenced to prison. For example, a 10 percent reduction in the California index crime rate requires a corresponding 157.2 percent increase in the prison population. The smallest change related to a decrease in index crimes appears in Mississippi, where it is still necessary to increase the incarcerated population by 33.7 percent. Using data from the Netherlands, Wermink et al. (2013) claim that, in order to avert 400 convictions,

TABLE 15.1 **Level of Change Needed in Imprisonment Necessary for Incapacitation**

State	Percentage Increase in Prison Population Needed to Achieve:		
	10% Decrease in Index Crimes	Reduction of 100 Index Crimes	10% Decrease in Violent Crime
California	157.2	36.1	22.8
New York	263.5	67.2	57.0
Massachusetts	310.5	103.4	26.6
Ohio	82.5	34.7	12.0
Kentucky	86.1	44.8	16.0
New Hampshire	118.0	98.9	8.4
Mississippi	33.7	39.1	13.0
North Dakota	122.0	144.2	19.6

Source: Adapted by author from J. Cohen (1978). "The incapacitative effect of imprisonment: a critical review of the literature." In A. Blumstein et al. (eds.), *Deterrence and Incapacitation: Estimating the Effects of Criminal Sanctions on Crime Rates*. Washington, DC: National Academy Press.

it is necessary to incarcerate an additional 5,707 offenders. It is clear that incapacitation exacts a high cost in terms of the number of offenders who need to be incarcerated.

Incapacitation also involves an increased monetary burden for society. Walker (1985) presents a number of estimates related to an incapacitation strategy. Using conservative figures related to the number of people who must be incarcerated (based on Van Dine et al., 1979), Walker (1985) notes that, nationally, a 25 percent incapacitation effect necessitates the incarceration of 1,200,000 new prisoners. Each of these new prisoners will require bed space and upkeep, and these costs can be considerable. Henrichson and Delaney (2012) compute the yearly costs of imprisonment at $31,286 per inmate for states. Based on Walker's projected increase in needed beds, the increased costs to the states would exceed $375 billion! This does not include the costs of constructing the space.

It would appear that the costs, both in terms of numbers of persons in prison and the dollars needed to accomplish this feat, outweigh the benefits accrued from the effort. A possible solution to this would be the incapacitation of only the individuals who are a clear threat to society. Such selective incapacitation may eliminate the need to increase the prison population in order to bring about lower levels of crime.

The Selective Incapacitation of Imprisonment

Selective incapacitation differs from collective efforts by imposing punishment on a select few individuals. The emphasis is on the identification of offenders who are high risk. The individuals who are more likely to display antisocial behavior in the future, and thus pose a risk to society, are subjected to longer periods of incarceration. Advocates of selective incapacitation point to the lower cost of incarcerating only a portion of all offenders along with presumed savings in the number of future offenses.

The idea of selective incapacitation received its greatest boost from a Rand Corporation report written by Greenwood (1982). In an attempt to identify a group of individuals who should be incapacitated, Greenwood surveyed almost 2,200 prison inmates in California, Texas, and Michigan who were serving time for burglary or robbery. Examining self-report records and official documents concerning past behavior, arrests, convictions, and incarcerations, the author composed a seven-item scale that purportedly distinguishes between high-, medium-, and low-rate offenders (see Table 15.2). Greenwood (1982) applied this scale to the Texas and California prisoners to test for the incapacitative effect of the scale.

Greenwood (1982) suggests that by reducing the time served by low- and medium-risk inmates and increasing the terms for high-risk offenders, it is possible to reduce robbery by 15 percent while lowering the California prison population by 5 percent. He compares this to a collective incapacitation approach that would require a 25 percent increase in the prison population to achieve the same 15 percent reduction in robberies. On the other hand, a 15 percent decrease in burglary requires a 7 percent increase in the number of prisoners in California, even using a selective incapacitation approach (Greenwood, 1982).

TABLE 15.2 Greenwood's Selective Incapacitation Prediction Scale

1. Prior conviction for the same offense

2. Incarcerated for more than 50 percent of the preceding two years

3. Conviction before the age of 16

4. Served time in a juvenile facility

5. Drug use in the preceding two years

6. Drug use as a juvenile

7. Employed less than 50 percent of the preceding two years

Source: P.W. Greenwood (1982). *Selective Incapacitation*. Santa Monica, CA: RAND Corp.

Figures for Texas are not as encouraging, with a 10 percent decrease in robbery requiring a 30 percent increase in the prison roles. A similar reduction in burglary requires a 15 percent rise in the prison population. The differences between California and Texas are due to the much lower offense rates in Texas, which affect the estimates. Despite the contradictory results, advocates of selective incapacitation often point to the 15 percent robbery reduction accomplished through an overall decrease of 5 percent in the prison population (Greenwood, 1982).

Greenwood's (1982) figures have been severely criticized by other researchers. Visher (1986, 1987) points out that there are serious problems with the data, including the inability of some inmates to accurately recall past events and time periods, and problems with estimating the level of offending prior to incarceration. Large differences between California, Texas, and Michigan offense rates complicate the analysis (Visher, 1986). Reanalyzing the data, Visher (1987) reports lower estimates of the number of crimes committed and subsequently lower estimates of incapacitation. She finds a selective incapacitative effect of only 5 to 10 percent in California and increased crime in both Texas and Michigan. These new estimates seriously question the efficacy of selective incapacitation.

A number of other problems permeate the issue of selective incapacitation. The foremost concern rests on the ability to predict future behavior. As discussed in Chapter 10, the ability to predict behavior is poor at best. Second, incapacitation assumes that the rate of offending remains constant over time. If an offender's career would end during the time served in prison, the value of incarceration is lost. Third, estimates of incapacitation typically assume constant levels of arrest, conviction, and incarceration. This assumption is very questionable. High-rate offenders face a greater chance of detection and subsequent system action, simply because of their increased level of behavior. Fourth, prison inmates may not be representative of the entire criminal population and results based on studies of inmates have questionable generalizability. Finally, there is a serious question concerning society's right to punish an individual for potential dangerousness and not just actual behavior. Implicit in selective incapacitation is the imposition of a longer sentence in order to avoid what might happen if an individual is released. Given the poor ability to accurately predict future behavior, this approach subjects many individuals to unnecessary punishment. In summary, although selective incapacitation holds much intuitive appeal, there does not seem to be a solid empirical basis for invoking the process at this time.

Electronic Monitoring

Incapacitation can also be achieved without the use of incarceration. The advent of electronic monitoring (EM) introduced a new avenue to incapacitation. Home confinement using EM has prospered largely due to two things: (1) the growth and problems encountered by the prison system in the United States, and (2) the great developments in technology over the past 40 years. Many jurisdictions are under court orders to reduce the size of their jail or prison populations. The initial response to these challenges has been the call for additional prisons. The public, however, is reluctant to pay the costs for new bed space, despite their calls for getting tough on offenders.

The response to overcrowding, legal challenges, rising crime, and public sentiment has been the development of various alternatives to incarceration. Electronic monitoring is one possible solution to the call for increased supervision and protection of society when offenders are released into the community. The idea of keeping track of individuals using an electronic device dates back to Schwitzgebel et al. (1964), who described an EM system and discussed its potential uses. Jack Love, a New Mexico judge, took the idea of monitoring offenders from a 1977 comic strip in which Spiderman was tracked by means of a wrist transmitter and commissioned the development of a tracking device. The device, often called a "GOSSlink" after its inventor Michael Goss, was first used in 1983 on a small group of offenders in New Mexico (Niederberger and Wagner, 1985). The primary aim of the EM system was to monitor compliance with curfews and home confinement (Vaughn, 1989). Interest in this novel technique quickly prompted the development of similar devices by various companies and the adoption or testing of the technology in jurisdictions across the country.

The initial forms of EM involved the use of **radio frequency (RF) transmitters**. These transmitters fall into one of two primary systems or types—active or passive. **Active**, or **continuous signaling**, **systems** keep track of the offender on a continuous basis. This system consists of a transmitter, receiver, and a central computer. The transmitter is a small, tamper-proof device, often smaller than a package of cigarettes, which is typically strapped to the offender's ankle. A constant signal is emitted by the transmitter and is picked up by a receiver. Early receivers were attached to the home phone. Today, the receiver can be at a remote location and contacted via wireless systems. The receiver notifies the central computer of a violation if the offender moves out of a specified range. A probation officer or other individual typically checks on the violation in order to confirm the information and take appropriate action. The computer system can be programmed to allow the offender to go to work, attend school, or participate in other activities. The system simply logs the times the offender leaves and returns home. A continuous computer printout of the offender's activity can be evaluated at any time.

The **passive system** consists of similar equipment, but requires periodic activation of the system. This system is also referred to as a **programmed contact system**. A passive system may randomly call the offender's home to certify the presence of the individual. When called, the offender must place the transmitter/encoder into a verifier/receiver. The individual may also be required to answer questions that are used in a voice verification. The system can also be activated by a mobile (drive-by) monitor. Passive systems are often set up with a graduated schedule of contacts in which the system checks on offenders more often in the early weeks and gradually reduces the number of contacts as time passes without violations (Gable, 1986; Maxfield and Baumer, 1990).

The most recent innovation has been a coupling of these systems with global positioning system (GPS) technology (Lilly, 2006). GPS technology uses satellites to locate a person or monitor their movements. This can be done on either a continuous basis or intermittently. One major advantage of this technology is there is no need for a home monitoring device or the use of any telephone lines. GPS technology has been used for many years for locating stolen vehicles. Adding GPS to EM programs makes it more difficult for offenders to abscond.

> ── **ON THE WEB** ──
>
> *An extensive discussion of electronic monitoring is offer by DeMichele and Payne in their 2009 work* Offender Supervision with Electronic Technology: Community Corrections Resources. ***Second Edition.*** *Washington, DC: Bureau of Justice Assistance, found on the textbook web site.*

Proponents of electronic monitoring point to a variety of advantages stemming from its use. First, EM can possibly alleviate the overcrowding of correctional institutions. Second, the use of electronic monitors enhances the ability to supervise offenders in the community and can incapacitate offenders better than simple probation or parole. Third, the system reduces the costs of monitoring offenders in the community. Fourth, EM provides an "intermediate" level of punishment for offenders who do not need to be sentenced to an institution, yet may need more than simple probation. Fifth, advocates see EM as a more humane method for dealing with offenders as compared to incarceration. Finally, electronic monitors assist reintegration into society by allowing offenders to remain in the community, maintain family and friendship ties, and support the family. The discussion that follows focuses primarily on issues of recidivism.

Extent of EM Use

The adoption of EM has steadily increased since its initial use in New Mexico in 1983. In 1986, there were 10 known manufacturers of EM equipment and only 10 jurisdictions in the United States using the technology (Friel et al., 1987; Schmidt, 1986). The number of EM programs has increased greatly since that time. The use of EM technology has spread beyond the United States to more than 17 countries, including Canada, the United Kingdom, Australia, New Zealand, Germany, Argentina, Israel, and Taiwan (Stacey, 2006). In the United States, a 2009 estimate placed EMS use at almost 110,000 offenders on RF systems and another 91,000 under GPS tracking (DeMichele and Payne, 2009). Haverkamp et al. (2004) provide estimates for yearly caseloads on EM for various European countries (see Table 15.3), with approximately 20,000 in England and 3,000 in Sweden.

EM is not intended to be used with all offenders. The fact that the beginnings of EM and home confinement are rooted in the problem of jail and prison overcrowding

TABLE 15.3 Estimates of EM Use in Europe, 2004

Country	Yearly EM Number
England	20,000
Sweden	3,000
Belgium	2,100
The Netherlands	390
France	255
Portugal	39

Source: Adapted by author from R. Haverkamp et al. (2004). "Electronic monitoring in Europe." *European Journal of Crime, Criminal Law and Criminal Justice* 12:36–45.

points to the idea that these alternatives are meant for offenders who would normally be confined in an institution. Most programs require that potential clients come from pools of offenders ordered to jail, prison, pretrial detention, or those who cannot raise bail (Charles, 1989; Ford and Schmidt, 1985; Maxfield and Baumer, 1990; Vaughn, 1989). Excluding offenders from EM who would normally be set free with minimal or no supervision avoids the problem of using the new program as a means of intervening with an entire new set of clients. EM programs do not wish to be seen as a form of **net-widening** (i.e., bringing more people under the umbrella of social control). Programs also tend to target less serious offenders or offenders deemed inappropriate for incarceration (such as DUI offenders), although serious offenders (such as sex offenders and violent gang members) are targeted by some programs (Friel et al., 1987; Gies et al., 2013; Maxfield and Baumer, 1990; Padgett et al., 2006).

Impact on Offending and Technical Violations

Interestingly, despite the growth in EM forms and the number of individuals under EM, relatively little research has been conducted on its impact. The evaluations that have been done on EM generally show favorable results in terms of both technical violations and further offending. Evaluation of one post-conviction program in Kenton County, Kentucky, reveals that roughly 8 percent of the offenders placed on EM commit some technical violation resulting in their removal from the program (Ball et al., 1988; Lilly et al., 1987). More importantly, slightly more than 5 percent of the offenders commit new crimes. This recidivistic behavior, however, is significantly less than that of a pre-program control group of offenders (20 percent recidivism). Evaluation of a Palm Beach

County, Florida, program reveals similar positive results with less than 10 percent recidivism (Ball et al., 1988; Palm Beach County Sheriff's Department, 1987). Unfortunately, the Palm Beach program provides no figures for comparable offenders handled under alternative or traditional methods. This lack of a control group leaves in doubt the actual impact of the program.

Two evaluations in Florida provide strong support for EM. Padgett et al. (2006) examining data for 1998 to 2002, note that those on EM commit fewer technical violations and have lower recidivism levels, despite the fact that those on EM are higher-risk clients. The second evaluation (Bales et al., 2010), considering EM use from 2001 to 2007, finds that EM usage reduces offender failure by 31 percent compared to those not on EM. The impact is significant for all types of offenders (violent, property, or drug). In addition, the use of GPA systems is more effective than RF equipment (Bales et al., 2010).

Electronic monitoring is also used as a form of pretrial supervision for individuals who cannot post bond or who would otherwise be released. Cooprider and Kerby (1990), reporting on a pretrial program in Lake County, Illinois, note that those released on EM have a higher violation rate than those released on recognizance (19 per cent compared to 13 percent), although the violations are for technical problems and not new offenses. A second evaluation of EM reports a higher violation rate for pretrial releasees than post-conviction offenders (27 per cent compared to 19 percent) (Maxfield and Baumer, 1990). Violations could include new charges, absconding, and technical violations. Maxfield and Baumer (1990) and Baumer et al. (1993) suggest that greater violations by pretrial subjects may be due to the fact that a wider array of clients and problems are involved at pretrial than at post-conviction. Those on post-conviction release also have a greater degree of certainty concerning the future, whereas pretrial subjects are awaiting word of the future. In general, studies dealing with pretrial use of EM present generally favorable results with relatively low levels of violations.

An interesting variation in the use of EM involves the enforcement of domestic violence protection orders. Erez et al. (2004) report on a program in which defendants are ordered to wear the ankle bracelet but the base monitoring unit is placed in the home of the victim. When a defendant nears the victim's home, the EM system registers the defendant's presence and an alert is sent to the authorities and the victim. Victims can also carry a monitor when away from home to protect against the defendant (Erez et al., 2004). An analysis of more than 600 cases in which the EM was used shows few violations, with most involving simple "drivebys" and no attempt to actually contact the victim (Erez et al., 2004).

Electronic monitoring with GPS monitoring is also used with sex offenders in New Jersey and California. The New Jersey State Parole Board (NJPB, 2007) notes that the technology has been employed with 225 dangerous sex offenders. The California Department of Correction and Rehabilitation reports using GPS monitoring with almost 7,000 sex offenders in 2011 (Gies et al., 2013). The use of GPS offers a variety of advantages, most notably the ability to place an offender at an offense location during the commission of a crime. This enhances the ability to clear a case and greatly improves the odds of getting a conviction. Based on data for the first year of operation, only one of 225 New Jersey parolees under GPS surveillance committed a new sex crime, with an additional 19 committing a technical violation (NJPB, 2007). This is significantly lower that the U.S. recidivism rate for sex offenders.

Impact on Overcrowding

The goal of reducing overcrowding also has not been realized. The fact that most programs deal with a relatively small number of individuals at any point in time means that there is little if any relief for overcrowded jails and prisons. The continued growth of the prison/jail population, despite the growth of EM, is adequate evidence showing that EM has had no impact on overcrowding. Changing the analysis to an examination of the number of days spent outside of an institution, however, provides more positive results. Offenders in Kenton County spent 1,712 days of incarceration at home. The Palm Beach County offenders completed 10,716 incarceration days in the community (Ball et al., 1988). Where the number of offenders is not large, each day outside the institution represents an improvement in the crowding situation.

Issues and Concerns

Despite the great growth and support for EM, a number of problem areas and concerns are advanced by various writers. One area of concern relates to operational issues faced by agencies using the technology. Vaughn (1989) notes that EM is a labor-intensive system that operates 24 hours a day. This round-the-clock monitoring increases the personnel costs to the administrative agency, especially if the agency is traditionally oriented to daytime operations (Friel and Vaughn, 1986). In addition, many offenders spend only a short time on the system before being granted outright release or moving on to other programs. This great turnover means that the screening process, data entry, program hook-up, and other tasks must be undertaken on a continuing basis with new clients (Vaughn, 1989).

Second, critics of electronic monitoring point out the potential of the technology to simply extend the reach of the criminal justice system. They note that most innovations aimed at reducing the size and scope of intervention actually result in more persons under some form of social control (i.e., net-widening). Because electronic monitoring does not eliminate or limit the existing institutional space, it is possible that the technology will increase the number of individuals under daily supervision of the criminal or juvenile justice systems. While few studies attempt to evaluate the degree of net-widening that may be taking place, Ball et al. (1988), Lilly et al. (1987), and Maxfield and Baumer (1990) provide preliminary evidence that net-widening is not occurring to any great degree.

Another concern is that the use of EM may place the public at greater risk. EM programs cannot guarantee that the offenders will not or cannot commit additional offenses while in the community. There is nothing to physically keep an offender from offending or absconding. There are times, such as when an offender is supposed to be at school or work, when he is not being monitored. Any mistake by the equipment at detecting a violation also leaves society at risk.

Finally, EM is viewed by many as an Orwellian means of controlling the population. The government is taking on the image of Big Brother—always watching us in order to correct our behavior whenever we step out of line. The extent of that ability is apparent in the fact that there are offenders under 24-hour surveillance using GPS technology. Electronic monitoring can extend state intervention into our homes and daily activities. The fact that EM requires the compliance of the entire family exacerbates this feeling of control. Many individuals object to such interventions on the basis of the sanctity of the home and the fear of an overreaching government. While the technology and monitoring may be legal, there is the larger social question of where to draw the line of governmental intervention in the community.

Summary

The use of electronic devices to monitor offenders has quickly found a place in the daily operations of the criminal justice system. Since the early 1980s, EM has grown from the plot of a comic strip to programs in every state and other countries. The growth can be attributed to the overcrowding of prisons, the development of the technology, the desire to do something with offenders, and the acceptance of the idea by criminal justice system personnel and the public. This review suggests that EM is a viable method for handling both adults and juveniles at post-conviction and pretrial stages of intervention. The low violation rates and the dominance of technical violations favor the use of EM. Despite concerns and shortcomings, EM appears to be a permanent component of criminal justice supervision.

Future Implications

The research on specific deterrence and incapacitation presents a mixed picture. Studies of specific deterrence present contradictory results concerning the deterrent effects of punishment. While society calls for stronger sanctions, it may be that these interventions play an aggravating role in deviant behavior. The offender may view harsh punishment as a breaking point with conventional society and an opportunity to turn to further deviant activity. The act of putting an individual behind bars may be more criminogenic than deterrent. The uncertain knowledge about individual hedonistic values makes the selection and imposition of punishment for deterrence a difficult, if not impossible, task. The lack of attention paid to specific deterrence and the inability to separate rehabilitation from punishment in research impedes the evaluation of this approach.

Incapacitation, whether collective or selective, has great intuitive appeal for society. The idea of punishing an individual for the harm he caused is an accepted method for dealing with deviant behavior. Extending that period of punishment in order to keep an individual from committing another offense is an easily acceptable modification. The costs of such a policy, however, may be high. The number of persons who must be housed in order to achieve even a small decrease in crime is staggering even using the most conservative figures. Translating these bodies into dollars leads to budgets that the public has not been willing to accept. As with specific deterrence, the research literature holds little promise for an acceptable incapacitation strategy at this time.

Another possible alternative is incapacitating offenders in the community through the use of EM. Electronic monitoring offers a cost-effective means for releasing offenders into the community while providing a degree of control over them. The evaluation research suggests that the level of both technical violations and new offending is relatively low. Despite problems and concerns with EM programs, they appear to be a viable alternative to incapacitation through incarceration.

KEY TERMS

- active (continuous signaling) system
- Big Brother
- collective incapacitation
- electronic monitoring (EM)
- global positioning system (GPS) technology
- incapacitation
- Minneapolis Domestic Violence Experiment
- net-widening
- passive system
- programmed contact system
- radio frequency (RF) transmitters
- selective incapacitation
- specific deterrence
- three-strikes laws

CHAPTER 16 Rehabilitation

CHAPTER OUTLINE

LEARNING OBJECTIVES

After reading this chapter you should be able to:

- Give arguments on both sides of the "nothing works" controversy.
- List and discuss different outcome measures used in treatment research.
- Compare and contrast aggregate and individual-level evaluation.
- Provide examples of cognitive behavioral interventions, relate their approach, and tell how effective they are.
- Explain what ISP programs are and what impact they have had.
- Define restorative justice and name three different types.
- Outline victim–offender mediation.
- Explain how family group conferencing works.
- Discuss circle sentencing.
- Relate the impact of restorative justice in terms of participant satisfaction and recidivism.
- Explain how drug courts are expected to influence their clients.
- Briefly discuss the common elements of drug court programs.
- List advantages of drug courts.
- Identify problems/issues with drug court programs.

Throughout most of the twentieth century, the major method of achieving tertiary prevention was the rehabilitation of offenders. Various forms of rehabilitation dominated the handling of criminals, and a complete listing and brief explanation of all of the various treatment programs set up to deal with deviant behavior would fill many volumes. Despite the move toward increased punitiveness since the 1970s, rehabilitation has remained a driving interest in the correctional field. Given this, one would assume that there is clear evidence of successful intervention. The state of the evidence, however, is not as clear. This chapter examines the debate on the rehabilitation controversy, discusses the problems inherent in the research and debate, and considers a few promising rehabilitation approaches. Space and time constraints prohibit all but a brief examination of specific intervention approaches. Many other texts have been written and devoted exclusively to the examination of rehabilitation.

The "What Works?" Argument

No one truly interested in the study of rehabilitation can be unaware of the eulogy placed on treatment that "with few and isolated exceptions, the rehabilitative efforts that have been reported so far have had no appreciable effect on recidivism" (Martinson, 1974). With this single statement, the very basis of correctional intervention was shaken. The foundation for this assessment was an examination of literature on rehabilitation appearing between 1945 and 1967 (Lipton et al., 1975). The authors considered 231 studies in which there was a treatment evaluation with a control group, an outcome measure attributable to the treatment, sufficient information about the intervention and evaluation for making a judgment, a sufficiently large sample size to make inferences, and, in general, a sound research methodology. The authors examined a wide range of intervention techniques, including counseling, educational and vocational training, medical treatment, psychological therapy, probation, parole, and community programs. As already noted, the effect of these various programs on recidivism was negligible (Martinson, 1974). Other outcome variables, such as adjustment to prison, attitude adjustment, and educational improvement, show some positive effects on offenders. These changes, however, are relatively unimportant given the major goal of preventing further criminal behavior.

Subsequent Analyses

The finding of little or no effect of rehabilitation on recidivism appears in a variety of other reports since the work of Martinson (1974) and Lipton et al. (1975). Wright and Dixon (1977), reviewing 96 studies from 1965 to 1974, report that treatment has little impact on recidivism. The authors further note that most of the evaluations employ poor research design, fail to use random assignment, and do not present adequate information for subsequent analysis. Another examination of 18 rehabilitation programs in New York City, comparing both pre- and post-program levels of deviance and program participants with a control group, arrives at the same conclusion (Fishman, 1977). Fishman reports higher recidivism for participants under age 18, no difference for those ages 19 and 20, lower recidivism for young adult participants (ages 21 to 39), and no difference for subjects aged 40 and over. Comparison of recidivism rates for the various projects does not uncover any significant differences among the rehabilitative techniques.

A reanalysis of the Lipton et al. (1975) findings undertaken by the National Academy of Sciences concludes that the original authors "were reasonably accurate and fair in their appraisal of the rehabilitation literature" (Sechrest et al., 1979). The only major point of departure in the reanalysis involves the feeling that the earlier analysis *overstates the effectiveness* of the reviewed programs. Sechrest et al. (1979) claim that the earlier report falls short in its criticism of the studies. The original review appears to have overlooked a variety of critical problems within the research reports, particularly concerning the methodological shortcomings and the results of the evaluations. Other reviews of the literature also fail to find strong support for rehabilitation. Gensheimer et al. (1986) report that, of 44 studies spanning 1967 to 1983, there is no evidence of a rehabilitative effect accruing from the interventions. Finally, Lab and Whitehead (1988), presenting data from 55 research reports from 1975 to 1984, reveal 33 comparisons with no difference or worse recidivism by experimentals and only 15 with positive results. Based on these literature reviews, which span a variety of decades and rehabilitative strategies, it is possible to conclude that rehabilitation is not very effective at reducing recidivism.

Not all researchers, however, are ready to sound the death knell for rehabilitation. One leading proponent of rehabilitation (Palmer, 1975), claims that Martinson (1974) ignores a variety of positive findings in his analysis. Palmer (1975) notes that certain programs have positive effects on certain individuals under certain conditions. The emphasis should not be on finding a single cure-all for the entire range of offenders (Palmer, 1975). Indeed, Martinson (1979) agrees that there are instances in which rehabilitation does have a positive impact on an individual's behavior. Nevertheless, the overall finding that most programs report little or no success with the majority of subjects still holds true (Martinson, 1979). Support for the belief that some programs work with some select individuals also can be found in reviews by Graziano and Mooney (1984), Garrett (1985), and Mayer et al. (1986). While the evidence shows some reduced recidivism, the greatest changes appear in other outcome measures (e.g., psychological adjustment, academic improvement, institutional adjustment). The data also suggest that more rigorous studies find less of an impact on recidivism than evaluations that are not as concerned with the research methodology.

Andrews et al. (1990) argue that treatment has a definite positive impact on recidivism. The authors suggest that treatment that pays attention to the principles of **risk,**

need, and responsivity (basically matching the correct subjects with the correct intervention) can have a significant impact on recidivism (Andrews et al., 1990). They purportedly prove their point through a reanalysis of the Whitehead and Lab (1989) data and an analysis of adult data. Lab and Whitehead (1990), however, argue that Andrews and associates fail to define their terms in such a way that their argument can be tested, and they fail to follow their own criteria in classifying subjects and studies. More importantly, their presentation is **tautological**. That is, they use a circular argument in which they use the existing literature to identify risk, need, and responsivity and then use that same literature as data to prove the correctness of their position (Lab and Whitehead, 1990; Logan and Gaes, 1993). Anyone can prove something that already exists.

In a series of papers, Lipsey (1990, 1999; Lipsey and Wilson, 1993, 1998) reports on perhaps the most extensive evaluations of the rehabilitation literature. Throughout the analyses, the author finds positive effects from rehabilitative treatment. For example, Lipsey and Wilson (1998) report an overall 6 percent difference in recidivism between experimental and control subjects across 200 studies. It is important to note, however, that there is a great deal of heterogeneity across the studies, with different types of treatment having different effects. Treatments that focus on interpersonal skills, cognitive-behavioral interventions, multimodal approaches, and community-based programs typically have a greater impact than other interventions (Lipsey and Wilson, 1998; Lösel, 1995). Lipsey (1990) argues that research on the impact of rehabilitation needs to consider the type of treatment, the setting in which it is delivered, the method of evaluation, and other factors when assessing the evidence. Lowenkamp et al. (2006) note that interventions with stronger program integrity (that is, strong program implementation, good offender assessment, etc.) are more effective at reducing recidivism than those that have weak integrity.

There is no uniform opinion regarding the effectiveness of rehabilitation. This state of disarray can be attributed to underlying conceptual differences between the opponents in the debate. Major points of divergence are the choice of outcome measure and the level of evaluation. Each of these factors can alter the results of evaluations and reviews.

Outcome Measures

The traditional measure of success in rehabilitation has been the elimination of deviant behavior. Usually this means lowering recidivism. Measuring recidivism, however, can be very difficult. Recidivism has been defined in many ways—ranging from reincarceration (a very strict criterion) to simple referral of the individual to any source of help (a very lax definition). Each of the definitions is problematic. For example, reincarceration is a relatively rare event for some types of offenders and, therefore, the levels of recidivism may be quite low. Alternatively, recidivism measured as simple contact with the police can greatly inflate the outcome. The varied choice of recidivism measure is a major problem in attempts to review and consolidate the results of different reports.

Perhaps the most common outcome measures in the rehabilitation literature are those that do *not* look to recidivism or deviant behavior. These measures include educational and vocational achievement, changes in self-esteem, attitudinal shifts, psychological adjustment, community adjustment, and costs of intervention. Many proponents of rehabilitative efficacy point to improvements in these dimensions as proof of program effectiveness. Unfortunately, while many of these outcomes are found in the literature, changes in these dimensions often appear during the in-program period and fail to persist long after release from the program. The alternative outcome measures, however, should remain secondary concerns to the prevention of criminal activity. The major problem for rehabilitation is future deviant behavior. Unless a clear connection can be found between the alternative outcomes and lower recidivism, these outcomes should remain secondary in the evaluation of rehabilitation programs. Indeed, the emphasis of tertiary crime prevention is on subsequent levels of recidivism.

Levels of Evaluation

The debate between critics and proponents of rehabilitation often rests on the appropriate level of evaluation to be employed in the analysis. Studies that report negative findings for rehabilitation usually rely on aggregate evaluation. **Aggregate-level evaluation** looks for changes across large groups of subjects. Changes in rates of offending or recidivism are the common metric by which programs are to be judged. A small or nonexistent change in the overall rate of crime is indicative of a failed intervention. In essence, aggregate evaluation searches for quantitative changes in behavior. The reviews cited earlier, which indicated minimal impact (e.g., Gensheimer et al., 1986; Lab and Whitehead, 1988; Lipton et al., 1975; Martinson, 1974; Sechrest et al., 1979; Whitehead and Lab, 1989; Wright and Dixon, 1977) all rely heavily on the failure of rehabilitation to shift recidivism rates.

Proponents of rehabilitation favor **individual-level evaluations**. The individual level focuses on qualitative changes rather than quantitative shifts in offending. These qualitative movements may appear as simple adjustments in the type of offending. For example, an offender may shift from robbery, which involves a physical confrontation, to property offenses, such as burglary or larceny. This would affect the rate for specific offenses but do little for the overall crime rate. Individual-level analysis also is able to focus on other, non-crime-related measures of change. Attitudinal shifts, psychological adjustment, ability to relate to others, and increased life skills are examples of alternate outcomes that can be found when looking at individual progress. Virtually any program can point to at least a few successes when the criteria for success is movement along one of these qualitative dimensions. It is this individual level of evaluation that prompts Palmer (1975, 1983), Martinson (1979), Garrett (1985), and others to claim that some rehabilitation works for some clients.

Summary

There is still a great deal of debate on the impact of rehabilitation on recidivism, although most reviews claim to find at least some positive support for rehabilitation. Strong claims of success typically rely on alternative outcome measures. Evaluations that do not use random assignment of study subjects or follow strict methodological techniques tend to show better results (Garrett, 1985; Mayer et al., 1986), as do evaluations of demonstration projects where there is a great deal of control over the intervention and its implementation (see, for example, Lipsey et al., 2001). Perhaps the key to developing effective interventions is matching the appropriate subjects to the proper treatment. Andrews et al. (1990) incorporate this in their discussion of risk, need, and responsivity. Unfortunately, as we have seen elsewhere in this book, correctly identifying risk is an elusive problem. The majority of programs do not know which clients are best served by their treatment, nor do they know how to identify the proper subjects once they are aware of differential program impact. As a result, tertiary crime prevention can be achieved only in a limited way.

Evaluations of Rehabilitation Programs

Rehabilitation efforts persist despite the many criticisms of rehabilitation. A variety of intervention programs continue to be tried and some present encouraging results. Several programs attempt to adhere to the basic premises of risk, need, and responsivity as proposed by Andrews et al. (1990). Other programs are the outgrowth of existing correctional programs, such as **intensive supervision probation (ISP)** (an enhanced form of probation). The following presentations are not meant to be all-inclusive nor representative of all types of intervention. It should briefly acquaint the reader with a few interesting approaches of the recent past.

Cognitive-Behavioral Interventions

The results of meta-analyses of treatment programs and the debate about the effectiveness of correctional treatment have led to several suggestions about appropriate treatment. Cullen and Gendreau (2000) outline several general principles that appear to underlie effective programs. First, interventions should target known predictors of deviant behavior and recidivism. Second, interventions should be behavioral and address the cognitive processes that lead to antisocial activity. Such interventions would seek to alter the decision-making processes of individuals, help offenders to identify prosocial responses to challenges, and develop skills and techniques for avoiding problem behavior. Third, successful programs will target high-risk offenders in community settings using well-trained staff and interventions matched to the needs of offenders. These programs generally fall under the heading of **cognitive-behavioral therapy (CBT)**. Cullen and Gendreau (2000) claim that interventions that follow these guidelines will achieve positive results.

Various programs appear under the CBT heading. Multi-Systemic Therapy and the Cognitive Thinking Skills Program are two examples. The idea that behavior is affected by a wide array of social and environmental factors underlies **Multi-Systemic Therapy (MST)** (Cullen and Gendreau, 2000). Multi-Systemic Therapy is a community-based intervention that attempts to address family, peer, school, community, and other influences that may prompt or lead to deviant behavior. The actual intervention will vary based on the needs of the individual, and it is dynamic and changes according to the needs and progress of the client. Each client receives intensive services, in the community, from a team of therapists who are held accountable for the successes or failures of the program (Cullen and Gendreau, 2000). Evaluations of MST reveal reduced delinquency and improvements in risk-related behaviors (Borduin et al., 1995; Brown et al., 1999).

The **Cognitive Thinking Skills Program (CTSP)** is also a multi-modal intervention that utilizes a range of techniques targeting cognitive-behavioral problems (Gaes et al., 1999). The CTSP focuses on identifying cognitive deficits and inappropriate decision making by individuals. Typical problems are impulsive behavior, egocentric activity, selfishness, and an inability to express oneself (Gaes et al., 1999). Highly trained program staff offer 70 hours of skills training to clients. CTSP has been adopted across Canada, as well as in several U.S. states and the United Kingdom. Gaes et al. (1999), reviewing evidence on CTSP, report that fewer treatment subjects recidivate than non-treatment control clients. While the differences tend to be statistically significant, many of the differences are small. The most positive findings emerge from CTSP implementation in community settings (Gaes et al., 1999).

The increased use of cognitive-behavioral interventions has prompted several meta-analytic reviews. Lipsey et al. (2001) considered only 14 evaluations that included experimental or quasi-experimental designs with a focus on recidivism. The results show that all but one project reports lower recidivism among experimental youths, although in only three of the 13 positive findings are the results statistically significant (Lipsey et al., 2001). Despite this fact, the authors point out that the global mean difference (i.e., the results across all studies) is statistically significant, indicating that the results are greatly influenced by a minority of the evaluations. The strongest results appear in demonstration projects in which the intervention is set up specifically for testing and evaluation, and there is reason to believe that the program is better implemented and delivered (Lipsey, 1999; Lipsey et al., 2001). The better results also appear in studies of juveniles treated in the community.

Lipton et al. (2002) examined 44 studies of programs from around the globe. Overall, CBI significantly reduced recidivism, although there is a great deal of variability in impact among the studies. In a final analysis of 14 studies from the United States and Canada, Lipsey and Landenburger (2006) report the combined result was statistically significant and in favor of CBI. Unfortunately, while all 14 studies reported positive results, only four were statistically significant from zero, indicating that the overall results were driven by only a few projects.

Intensive Supervision

Many proponents of rehabilitation point to the intensive supervision of probationers and parolees as a tool in reducing subsequent deviant activity. *Intensive supervision (ISP) programs* exist in every state. Typical features of ISP are team supervision, a high number of contacts between the client and officer, curfew and/or house arrest, restitution, employment or school attendance, drug testing, community service, counseling, and treatment (Byrne, 1990; Petersilia and Turner, 1993).

The New Jersey ISP program is a good example of such interventions. The program deals with relatively low-risk, non-violent offenders who have spent a short time in prison. The average caseload for the probation officer is 16, with the expectation that the officer will have almost daily contact with each client (either in person or by phone) (Pearson, 1985). The number of contacts is lessened as the client is found to be reliable and no infractions are detected. Evaluation of the New Jersey program shows that ISP clients have a lower recidivism rate (measured as new arrests) than individuals who remain in prison (Pearson, 1988; Pearson and Harper, 1990). The lower recidivism rate, however, may be due to the fact that ISP clients are not randomly selected and may be at lower risk for recidivism at the outset (Pearson, 1988). Indeed, the fact that ISP deals with less serious offenders can artificially inflate the success of the program (Clear and Hardyman, 1990).

Evaluations of other ISP programs present varying results. Erwin (1990), using data on 2,322 clients in Georgia, notes that the ISP clients commit less serious subsequent offenses. Unfortunately, there is no difference in reincarceration rates in three and five year follow-ups for ISP clients and individuals who served their time in prison (Erwin, 1990). These results are even more discouraging in light of the fact that the program actually targets low-risk offenders (Morris and Tonry, 1990). Three California ISP programs report no difference in subsequent arrests or incarceration for randomly assigned subjects (Petersilia and Turner, 1990). At the same time, the study reports more violence by ISP clients, possibly due to the random assignment used in conjunction with serious offenders. Evaluations across sites in the United States also fail to find any strong impact on recidivism (see Gowdy, 1993; Petersilia and Turner, 1993; Turner et al., 1992). As expected from intensive monitoring, most studies report relatively high rates of technical violations (Erwin, 1990; Gowdy, 1993; Pearson, 1988; Pearson and Harper, 1990; Petersilia and Turner, 1990, 1993; Turner et al., 1992). Latessa and Allen (2003), reviewing ISP evaluations, report that ISP clients recidivate less than control subjects (i.e., at least 5 percent lower recidivism) in four studies, recidivate more in six analyses, and perform comparably to controls in six other evaluations.

Research on intensive supervision suggests varied effects. Results differ somewhat by type of offender and measures of recidivism. There appears to be limited evidence of a positive effect of intensive supervision. The fact that the public accepts ISP as a viable program, perhaps due to the perceived safety from increased surveillance, may explain the continued interest in the program.

Restorative Justice

An emerging and growing approach for addressing criminal acts is restorative justice. As opposed to retributive justice, which focuses on the lawbreaker and the imposition of sanctions for the purposes of deterrence, vengeance and/or punishment, **restorative justice** seeks to repair the harm that was done to both the victim and the community. At the same time, there is an underlying assumption that the offender can benefit or be "repaired" by participating in the restorative process. This is accomplished by bringing together a range of interested parties in a non-confrontational setting, including the victim and the offender, as well as family members or friends, criminal justice system personnel, and members of the general community. The participants, as a group, seek to understand the actions that led to the criminal or antisocial behavior, reveal the feelings and concerns of all parties, negotiate or mediate a solution agreeable to everyone, and assist in implementing that solution (Bazemore and Maloney, 1994). Kurki (2000, p. 266) notes that "restorative justice is about relationships—how relationships are harmed by crime and how they can be rebuilt to promote recovery and healing for people affected by crime."

While the term "restorative justice" is relatively new, elements of restorative justice have been around for a long time. Braithwaite (1999, p. 2) notes that "[r]estorative justice has been the dominant model of criminal justice throughout most of human history for all the world's peoples." Weitekamp (1999) points out that many of the restorative justice practices being used today can be traced directly to historical traditions that have survived in indigenous cultures. Of particular note are the practices of Aboriginal tribes, Inuits, and Native American and Native Canadian Indian tribes.

Restorative justice takes a variety of different forms, although they all attend to the same basic tenets. Indeed, "restorative justice" is often referred to as "transformative justice," "social justice," "balanced and restorative justice," "peacemaking," or other terms. Braithwaite (2002) notes that many of these terms and programs have been incorporated into the more general idea of restorative justice. Most discussions of restorative justice outline

┌─ **ON THE WEB** ─────────────────────
Various organizations offer information on different forms of restorative justice and the operations of the programs. Two such sources of information are the International Institute for Restorative Practices (http://www.iirp.edu) and the Restorative Justice Online Blog (http://restorativejustice.org).

four primary types of programs—victim–offender mediation, family group conferencing, neighborhood reparative boards, and peacemaking/sentencing circles.

Victim–Offender Mediation

Victim–Offender Mediation, also referred to as Victim–Offender Reconciliation Programs (VORP), is a direct outgrowth of the dispute resolution/dispute mediation programs of the early 1970s (Umbreit, 1999). **Victim–offender mediation (VOM)** is typically a post-conviction process (although pre-conviction programs exist) in which the victim and the offender are brought together to discuss a wide range of issues. A trained mediator also attends these meetings. Participation in VOM is voluntary for the victim, but the offender may be required by the court to participate as a part of the court process (Umbreit, 1999). Victim–Offender Mediation programs may be a part of the formal criminal justice system, or may be run by other agencies that are not directly connected to the system.

The most important concern addressed in the VOM meetings is to identify for the offender the types and level of harm suffered by the victim as a result of the crime. At the same time, the offender is given the chance to explain why he committed the act and the circumstances that may underlie his behavior. The focus of the meetings is on repairing the harm done to the victim, helping the victim heal (both physically and emotionally), restoring the community to the pre-crime state, and reintegrating the offender into society (Umbreit et al., 2003). Both parties are considered equal participants in the process and given time to express themselves and their feelings about the crime. The outcome of these meetings should be a mutually agreeable resolution. Among the potential tangible outcomes for the victim may be the offender making monetary restitution or providing service to repair the harm done. Perhaps of equal importance are changes in understanding by both parties about each other, and changes in behavior and attitude on the part of the offender.

Family Group Conferencing

Family group conferencing (FGC) is based on practices of the Maori in New Zealand. The greatest difference between FGC and VOM is the inclusion of family members, close friends, and other support groups of the victim and offender in the conferences. There is also the possibility of including criminal justice system personnel, including social workers, police officers, and an offender's attorney (Van Ness and Strong, 2015). This expansion of participants is very important, in that the families and support persons are expected to take some responsibility in monitoring the offender and making certain that any agreements are carried out after the conference (Kurki, 2000).

Family group conferencing first appeared in 1989 in New Zealand with an exclusive focus on juveniles aged 14 to 17 (Kurki, 2000). While most conferences deal with minor juvenile misbehavior, they can include serious offenses and repeat offenders. Similar to VOM, the emphasis in FGC is on engendering discussion among the parties about what took place, why it occurred, and the most appropriate steps to take to address the harm. Unlike VOM, the conferences do not include a formal mediator. Rather, FGC includes a facilitator who attempts to keep the discussions moving in a positive direction until an agreement can be reached among all parties. Conferences can be held either pre-trial or post-trial, and have become a part of police and pre-trial diversion programs in both the United States (McGarrell et al., 2000) and Australia (Moore and O'Connell, 1994).

Neighborhood Reparative Boards

Neighborhood reparative boards (NRBs), or neighborhood accountability boards, have existed since the mid-1990s and typically deal with non-violent youthful offenders. Not unlike other restorative practices, NRBs seek to restore the victims and community to pre-offense states, require the offender to make amends, and aid the offender in understanding the impact of his actions on the victim and community. Cases are referred to the boards by the court, most often prior to formal adjudication.

Despite the philosophical similarities between NRBs and other types of restorative conferencing, there are several key differences in how this approach operates. First, victims are not required to participate. Indeed, many early boards frowned on victim participation (Strickland, 2004), although victim participation is becoming more common. Second, while the conferences are often open to the public, actual participation is limited by the board and who they wish to interview. The board questions the offenders and examines statements made by members of the offender's family and others knowledgeable about the event (Bazemore and Umbreit, 2001). Third, the boards are composed of a small group of citizens who have been specially trained in conducting hearings and constructing appropriate sanctions.

At the conclusion of the hearing, the board undertakes private deliberations and outlines a suggested set of actions to be followed by the offender. If the offender agrees with the plan, the board oversees the offender's compliance with the terms and reports to the court about the success or failure of the offender (Bazemore and Umbreit, 2001). Typical conditions of agreements include restitution, apologies, and community service (Karp, 2001).

Peacemaking/Sentencing Circles

Peacemaking/sentencing circles are based on North American Indian processes, which invite all interested parties to participate in determining the appropriate sanctions for offenders (Van Ness and Strong, 2015). Included in the circles are all of those typically found in FGCs, as well as other community members who wish to be included. Most cases handled by sentencing circles involve minor offenses, although some programs will consider more serious crimes (Stuart, 1996). A major difference between circle sentencing and the other forms of restorative justice is that this approach is regularly used with both adults and juveniles (Kurki, 2000).

Every participant in the sentencing circle is given the opportunity to speak, express his feelings about the crime, and offer opinions and rationales about the outcome of the discussion. The fact that the circles include (potentially) a wide array of participants means that a great deal of planning and preparation is needed before the actual meeting (Kurki, 2000). The intended outcome of the circle is consensus on a plan of action, which may include explicit sentencing recommendations (potentially jail or prison) to the trial judge and/or a range of community-based interventions (Van Ness and Strong, 2015). The decision of the circle is often binding on the offender and a failure to adhere to the decision may result in further criminal justice system processing or being returned to the circle (Van Ness and Strong, 2015).

The Impact of Restorative Justice

Restorative justice programs are intended to have a number of different possible outcomes, including repairing the harm done to the victim and rehabilitating the offender. Many evaluations focus on victim and offender satisfaction with the process, and the level of compliance or completion of the agreed-upon settlement. With very few exceptions, both victims and offenders express satisfaction with the restorative process in which they have participated (Braithwaite, 1999). Evaluations of VOM typically reveal that between 75 and 100 percent of the participants express satisfaction with the mediation (Kurki, 2000). Similarly high levels of satisfaction arise from FGCs (Bazemore and Umbreit, 2001; Moore and O'Connell, 1994; Umbreit et al., 2003). The level of satisfaction is also reflected in feelings by participants that the process is fair (McGarrell et al., 2000; Umbreit, 1999; Umbreit and Coates, 1993; Umbreit et al., 2003).

A companion to satisfaction is the ability of the meetings to achieve consensus on a solution and whether the parties carry through with the agreement. Again, there is evidence that most meetings culminate in an agreement and most parties comply with the settlement (Braithwaite, 1999; Kurki, 2000; Schiff, 1999; Umbreit and Coates, 1993). Restitution is a common component of many agreements and evaluations reveal that 90 percent or more of the offenders in FGC comply with the ordered restitution (Wachtel, 1995). McGarrell et al. (2000) note that participants in a conferencing program completed the program at a significantly higher rate than normal diversion clients.

This information on satisfaction and compliance must be tempered somewhat by the fact that participation in the programs is voluntary. This is especially true for victims, although offenders can also opt out of the process in many places. The fact that the program is voluntary may mean that only individuals who are more amenable to the process to begin with are included in the programs. There may be a built-in bias in favor of positive results. Umbreit et al. (2003), for example, point out that only 40 to 60 percent of the victims and offenders who are asked to participate in VOM agree to do so. Similarly, McCold and Wachtel (1998) report that almost six out of 10 FGC cases never materialize due to a refusal to participate.

While reductions in the level of subsequent offending is the crime prevention goal one would desire from restorative justice, there is relatively little research on offender recidivism in the restorative justice literature. Umbreit and Coates (1993), comparing youths who participated in VOM to those undergoing typical juvenile justice processing in three states, report significantly less recidivism on behalf of the VOM sample. In their analysis of restorative justice conferences for youths in Indianapolis, McGarrell et al. (2000) report a 40 percent reduction in recidivism for the program youth when compared to those undergoing normal system processing. Umbreit et al. (2001) provide evidence that youths completing VOM projects in two Oregon counties reduce their offending by at least 68 percent in the year after program participation compared to the year before the intervention. Calhoun and Pelech (2010) note the conferencing in Calgary (Canada) led offenders to assume greater responsibility and repaired the victim–offender relationship. Other research (Hayes and Daley, 2004; Rodriguez, 2005) reveals reduced recidivism after conferencing, although the impact varies across types of offences and offenders. Finally, Latimer et al. (2005), conducting a meta-analysis, reported that restorative justice is more effective at reducing recidivism than traditional criminal justice programs. There also remains a need to identify and understand the conditions under which different restorative justice programs work and do not work (Braithwaite, 2002).

Summary

The increasing interest in restorative justice in recent years has led to the growth of programs around the world. Despite the growing popularity with restorative justice approaches, a great deal of additional research is needed on its impact, especially in relation to sentencing circles. There is still a lack of good evaluation of the preventive efficacy of the interventions. A lingering concern is that there is an underlying level of coercion in most programs and many programs do not allow (or at least frown upon) the presence of defense attorneys, thus raising the issue of an accused's constitutional rights and procedural safeguards (Feld, 1999; Levrant et al., 1999). Feld (1999) notes that there is a distinct imbalance of power in most restorative justice programs. This is especially problematic when juvenile offenders must face not only the victim but also the victim's support groups, members of the criminal justice system, and potentially strangers from the general community.

Specialized Courts

Specialized courts for addressing specific forms of offenders and offenses are becoming common throughout the United States. Three specialized courts are considered here: drug courts, teen courts, and mental health courts.

Drug Courts

Drug courts are perhaps the most recognizable and widespread (although it can be argued that the juvenile court system is itself a specialized court). The tremendous increase in drug crimes in the late 1980s and early 1990s, coupled with the get-tough approach to crime and mandatory sentencing laws, helped contribute to overcrowded court dockets and overcrowding in the correctional system. In an attempt to address these problems in 1989, Dade County, Florida, established the first separate court for processing drug offenders. The underlying philosophy for **drug courts** is to use the court's authority to prompt participation in and successful completion of treatment aimed at reducing drug use and related criminal behavior. The courts represent a coalition of prosecutors, police, probation officers, judges, treatment professionals, social service agencies, and other community groups working together to get the offenders off drugs and keep them off drugs (Drug Courts Program Office, 2000). The court can use its coercive powers to force offenders into the program and to maintain abstinence from drugs by dismissing criminal charges or withholding sentencing of offenders if they agree to enter and complete the drug court program. Drug courts operate both at the pre-adjudication and post-adjudication stage of criminal justice processing.

There is a set of common core elements that are found throughout most drug court programs. Among the common elements are frequent appearances before the court, regular drug testing, treatment assessment, participation in at least one treatment program, and aftercare. The court appearances typically follow a graduated pattern with more appearances in the early weeks of the program and fewer appearances as the client demonstrates progress. Initial appearances could be as often as twice a week or as seldom as two to three times a month. These appearances serve as a time for the judge to offer praise and support, warn the offender to do better, or threaten the offender with sanctions if his behavior and progress do not improve (Gottfredson et al., 2003). Regular drug testing is a critical second component of drug court intervention. The knowledge that they will be tested on a regular basis for an extended period provides an added level of accountability to the entire process.

The third common element, treatment assessment, serves to identify the needs of the individual offender and to match up the offender with the appropriate interventions. Common treatment programs may include detoxification, methadone maintenance, support groups, counseling, and other activities directly related to the drug problem. Treatment can also take the form of educational programming, vocational training, employment assistance, housing assistance, and similar help with everyday living experiences (Drug Courts Program Office, 1998). The mandated treatment typically lasts for at least one year, although the specifics of the treatment regimen may change over that period. The final major component is an aftercare plan for the individual. Rather than simply releasing the individual from the drug court and treatment program, most programs offer some form of follow-up assistance ranging from further treatment to support groups.

> ┌─ **ON THE WEB**
> *More information on drug courts can be found on the National Institute of Justice web site at http://www.nij.gov/topics/courts/drug-court/Pages/welcome.aspx and the National Association of Drug Court Professionals at http://www.nadcp.org*

The National Institute of Justice (2015) reports that there are more than 3,400 drug courts in operation and one found in every state. Over 1,500 are adult courts, 433 are for juveniles, 300 are focused on families, and the rest target other groups (National Institute of Justice, 2015). The great growth in drug courts is partly attributable to the passage of the Violent Crime Control and Law Enforcement Act of 1994, which authorized federal funding for drug court programs.

Evaluations of the effectiveness of drug court programs present a mixed picture. Most analyses report that drug court participants recidivate at a significantly lower level than comparison groups (Brewster, 2001; Goldkamp and Weiland, 1993; Gottfredson et al., 2003; Harrell, 1998; Henggeler et al., 2006; Listwan et al., 2003; MacKenzie, 2006; Marlowe, 2010; Spohn et al., 2001). A five-year longitudinal analysis of adult drug courts across the United States reports that participants are significantly more likely (by 17 percent) to remain drug-free, as well as commit 12 percent fewer crimes (Rossman and Zweig, 2012). One major issue in many analyses is that the evaluations fail to consider those who do not complete the treatment or use those who do not complete as the control group. It should not be surprising to find that those who complete the program recidivate less because they are successes to begin with, while those who did not complete are failures at the outset of the evaluation and would be expected to also commit more offenses. A second concern is that many evaluations only measure recidivism during program participation (GAO, 1997).

The number of drug courts is growing every year and the idea is expanding to specialized drug courts for DWI, veterans, reentry, and other topics/groups. The driving forces behind the movement are a combination of federal and state funding, vociferous support from drug court advocates, savings over incarcerating offenders, and an acceptance that combining treatment with the sanctioning power of the court is the best way to proceed.

Teen Courts

Teen courts (sometimes called youth courts) are an emerging alternative to processing youths in a traditional juvenile court setting. The teen court philosophy is based on restorative justice, and youths act as judge (about half the time), attorney (prosecutor and defense attorney), and jury in cases involving status offenses, misdemeanors, and occasionally a low-level felony. The most common penalty is community service. Other sentences include serving as a teen court jury member, writing essays and apologies, community service, and monetary restitution. It is estimated that there are more than 1,050 teen court programs operating in 49 states and the District of Columbia handling over 110,000 cases per year, making them a primary diversion option (National Association of Youth Courts, 2015).

┌─ ON THE WEB ──────────

The National Association of Youth Courts has a wealth of information on teen courts at http://www.youthcourt.net

Research on the impact of teen courts provides promising, but not conclusive, results. A recent study of an Illinois teen court found that recidivism was only 12 percent after one year and 19 percent after two years (Rasmussen, 2004). A multi-site study of teen courts in Alaska, Arizona, Maryland, and Missouri found statistically less recidivism for teen court youths in two of the four sites. In Alaska, 6 percent of teen court youths recidivated, compared to 23 percent of non-teen court youths; in Missouri, 9 percent of teen court youths recidivated, compared to 28 percent of non-teen court youths. The authors of the study concluded that "teen courts represent a promising alternative for the juvenile justice system" (Butts et al., 2002, p. 34). Two studies using random assignment found no significant effect (Patrick and Marsh, 2005; Stickle et al., 2008). Finally, a study of the Xenia, Ohio, teen court program found no impact on recidivism, and the authors concluded that their finding of no impact and previous systematic research suggests that teen courts are "equivalent to or only slightly better than traditional diversion" (Norris et al., 2011, p. 215).

Teen court is not intended to deal with serious delinquency. Most of the offenses handled are low-level infractions such as shoplifting, curfew violation, possession of marijuana, and disorderly conduct, although two-thirds of the courts accept cases involving assaults (National Association of Youth Courts, 2015). It is also noteworthy that the use of volunteer staff and low budgets mean that teen courts are inexpensive. As one author put it, teen court may be a "partial solution to the juvenile justice system's failure to give anything more than a 'slap on the wrist' to first-time offenders" (Rasmussen, 2004, p. 615).

Mental Health Courts

The final specialized court to be addressed is mental health courts. As with the prior specialized courts, **mental health courts** seek to address the specialized needs and circumstances of mentally ill individuals brought to the criminal courts for processing. The major deinstitutionalization of the mentally ill over the past 30 years has resulted in an increasing number of mentally ill individuals being arrested and processed in the criminal justice system. This is largely due to the lack of an alternative intervention that is more suited to the needs and problems of individuals and families faced with mentally ill individuals. While there were few mental health courts in 1990, today there are more than 250 (Rossman et al., 2012), including specialized juvenile mental health courts (Cocozza and Shufelt, 2006).

The primary goal of mental health courts is to reduce the number of mentally ill individuals suffering from being handled in the criminal courts and subsequently being sent to the correctional system (MHA, 2009). Other goals are to enhance community safety, improve the living conditions of the clients, coordinate services and resources needed by the mentally ill, and provide needed treatment for those in need. These goals are accomplished by establishing a specialized court docket that marshals the expertise of mental

> **ON THE WEB**
>
> *Mental Health America (MHA) provides a great deal of useful information about mental health needs and interventions, including mental health courts on its web site at http://www.nmha.org/*

health professionals, social service providers, and criminal justice system personnel. The court provides screening and assessment, followed by treatment that is overseen by the court (Council of State Governments Justice Center, 2008). Many of those requiring help suffer from severe mental illness and have co-occurring problems, especially substance abuse (Council of State Governments Justice Center, 2008; MHA, 2009).

Evaluations of mental health courts, while few in number, present promising results. An assessment of court operations and outcomes by the Council of State Governments Justice Center (2008) finds that individuals processed through the courts have few repeat bookings, few new charges, and spend fewer days in jail. This is accompanied with greater independent functioning on the part of the clients. An analysis of courts in the Bronx and Brooklyn, New York, reports similar positive results. In a three-year evaluation, Rossman et al.

> **ON THE WEB**
>
> *You can get more detailed information on the evaluation of mental health courts in New York by downloading the document at http://www.ncjrs.gov/ pdffiles1/NIJ/grants/238264.pdf*

(2012) uncover lower recidivism (in terms of both rearrest and reconviction) for mental health court clients in comparison to matched cases processed in regular court. The differences between the courts are statistically significant. These results suggest that mental health courts are effective at assisting those with specialized needs.

Summary

The growth of specialty courts offers new avenues for intervening with problem individuals and situations. The flexibility inherent in these courts allows them to address the unique situations and individual needs of those handled. The great growth and success of drug courts has set the stage for the development of both teen and mental health courts. Across the various types of courts, the evidence on their effectiveness is largely positive.

Assessing Rehabilitation and Crime Prevention

The results of the various summaries and programs presented here raise both hopes and concerns over the effectiveness of rehabilitation as a tool of crime prevention. Even though many specific rehabilitation programs are, by necessity, omitted from the present discussion, the array of reviews and programs that are discussed show a mixed bag on recidivism. This results in many researchers giving up on rehabilitation as a viable form of crime prevention. It is important to note, however, that some interventions show promising results. Among those promising programs are cognitive-behavioral therapies and multi-dimensional interventions, both of which match offenders and treatments in intensive programming, particularly in the community.

The greatest support for rehabilitation programs can be found in studies that use alternate outcome measures. There is clear evidence that rehabilitation can improve an individual's outlook and self-esteem. Various programs have been successful at increasing the educational and vocational achievement of clients. Psychological adjustment has been improved by some interventions. These and other outcomes, however, do not address the central concern of tertiary crime prevention. Tertiary prevention is focused on the elimination or lowering of subsequent levels of delinquent/criminal behavior. It is here that evaluations of rehabilitation have had limited success.

Proponents of rehabilitation point to these alternate forms of success along with the great cost savings of many programs as a rationale for continued work with offenders. Indeed, few studies show a deleterious impact from rehabilitation. The clients simply do no better than if they had been handled through conventional processing and incarceration. Any cost savings of rehabilitation over traditional handling without any risk to society may be reason enough to continue experimenting with various interventions. Also, the failure of past programs should inform us about possible effective programs. Evidence that this is occurring can be seen in the many attempts to match the proper client to the proper intervention.

Interestingly, many of the most recent rehabilitation efforts, such as ISP, restorative justice, and specialty courts, rely on the community as either the source of or setting for interventions. Intensive supervision works with clients outside the residential setting. Restorative justice includes a wide array of community members and groups in the interventions. Specialized courts seek rehabilitation and treatment in the community setting. The reason for this is the recognition and belief that the community influence and atmosphere are important aspects of rehabilitation and crime prevention. The ideas of identifying and using community resources are no different from that found in both primary and secondary crime prevention. While these rehabilitative efforts have not always engendered great reductions in recidivism, the positive results that are available suggest that these are fruitful directions for tertiary prevention to pursue.

KEY TERMS

- aggregate-level evaluation
- circle sentencing
- cognitive-behavioral therapy (CBI)
- Cognitive Thinking Skills Program (CTSP)
- drug courts
- family group conferencing (FGC)
- individual-level evaluation
- intensive supervision probation (ISP)
- mental health courts
- Multi-Systemic Therapy (MST)
- neighborhood reparative boards (NRBs)
- peacemaking/sentencing circles
- restorative justice
- risk, need, and responsivity
- tautological
- teen courts
- victim–offender mediation (VOM)

CHAPTER 17 Some Closing Thoughts on Crime Prevention and the Future

LEARNING OBJECTIVES

After reading this chapter you should be able to:

- Provide an overview of the evidence on crime prevention.
- Identify problems of evaluation that need to be addressed in future analyses.

Crime prevention encompasses a wide diversity of ideas and approaches. Indeed, no two individuals will necessarily see or define crime prevention in exactly the same way. It is not unlike the old parable where several blind men are led to an elephant and asked to explain what it is in front of them. The individual touching the trunk will define it differently than those persons touching a leg or the tail. While it may be easier for sighted people to provide a more complete description, it is still probable that each individual will emphasize or concentrate on different aspects of the elephant. Discussions of crime prevention often provide that same type of variation in explanations. Both the person relating the information and the individual hearing it may be envisioning slightly different things. While neither is inherently right or wrong, they are not exactly the same.

Throughout this book, an attempt has been made to offer a variety of perspectives on crime prevention. In essence, I have tried to touch the elephant at a variety of different places and relate the important facts about each. At the same time, there has been a conscious effort to relate the varied parts to one another in order to try to show how the parts can make up a more meaningful whole. Each of the individual chapters can, for the most part, stand on its own. Each relates some facet of crime prevention. Taking them together, however, should offer a more complete view of crime prevention in its many possible incarnations. I am equally convinced that I have missed a leg or an ear, here or there. In the balance of this brief concluding chapter, I will attempt to offer some summary comments about crime prevention, and point out areas or ideas that I have omitted or given only cursory attention.

The State of the Evidence

There should be no doubt that crime prevention works. Effective interventions have been offered throughout the chapters. The extent of crime prevention's impact, however, varies across time and place, as well as from one approach to another. Indeed, not every program has the same impact in every situation. Crime may be reduced in one place while there is no impact on the fear of crime. Transplanting that same program to another location may result in the opposite outcome—crime stays the same but fear is reduced. No single approach to crime prevention has proven to be applicable in all situations. Indeed, most interventions appear to work in limited settings with different types of offenders and problems. The greatest challenge, therefore, is to identify the causal mechanisms at work so that effective programs can be replicated in other places and other times.

Traditionally, actions that fall under primary prevention have been the ones most people think of when they hear of crime prevention. Physical security devices and neighborhood prevention programs dominate many discussions. There is little doubt that changes in the physical design of a building or an area can alter the form and extent of crime. At the very least, these actions make crime more difficult for the potential offender to successfully complete. Citizens also report feeling safer as a result of such design changes. Neighborhood watch and other cooperative citizen programs also show promise at changing crime and citizens' perceptions. The major stumbling block is getting fearful citizens out of their homes and into these prevention groups. Programs and initiatives still struggle with engendering citizen participation after more than 30 years of concentrated efforts to build such grassroots organizations.

Even when primary prevention efforts do take hold, there are many unanswered questions that need to be addressed. Foremost among those questions is how much of the impact on crime is the result of overall reductions and how much is simply displaced?

While not all crime is displaced, there is ample evidence to suggest that displacement is a real possibility in most analyses. One important challenge, therefore, is to further investigate the mechanisms that cause displacement and identify measures that can mitigate the extent of its occurrence.

The shift toward situational prevention is evidence of an admission that prevention initiatives need to be targeted at smaller, more well-defined problems and that the interventions need to be cooperative ventures between different individuals and groups. Many times the activities under situational prevention are the same as those found in primary prevention programs. Situational prevention and community policing are perhaps the most recognizable ideas under what constitutes secondary prevention. At the same time, other efforts and interventions, such as those taking place in schools to deal with problem youths, also qualify as secondary techniques. What draws these diverse ideas together is the explicit attempt to deal with individuals, groups, or places that have a high potential to cause later trouble. There is clear evidence that careful consideration of a problem can lead to effective solutions. Among the key problems here are the difficulties in predicting the future, problems with engendering support from other individuals and groups, and convincing people that the criminal justice system cannot do the job by itself. While much secondary prevention relies on the police and the system to initiate activities, the solutions often fall outside the training and abilities of system personnel. The community must be involved.

Despite the growth of prevention activities that focus on citizen and community involvement, the formal system of justice remains an important player in the prevention of crime. No one has yet called for eliminating the criminal justice system in favor of informal community action. Indeed, the criminal justice system is important in dealing with the people and situations in which a crime has already occurred. Specific deterrence, incapacitation, and rehabilitation are functions for which the system retains primary responsibility. At the same time that society turns these activities over to formal social control agencies, it is clear that the community has a role to play in tertiary prevention. The move to keep offenders in the community, whether through intensive supervision, electronic surveillance, or drug courts, is growing. Efforts to punish and rehabilitate offenders are also including the community more and more. Where tertiary prevention remains a part of the formal system of justice, there is evidence that a broader base for interventions is emerging.

In general, crime prevention encompasses a broad range of ideas and activities. More importantly, many of the efforts have been successful at reducing crime and fear of crime. Unfortunately, uncovering the exact mechanism at work is not always evident and continuing work is needed in these areas.

Improving Our Knowledge

While there is clear evidence that many crime prevention initiatives successfully reduce crime and fear, there is parallel data that show minimal impact of the same efforts at other places or times. The key issue, therefore, becomes unraveling the mechanism at work in the differing assessments. In general, more attention needs to be paid to the evaluation component of the prevention programs. First, many programs have not been subjected to any evaluation beyond simple description of the process used in establishing the intervention and the success of that process in terms of the number of meetings held and the level of attendance. This type of evaluation tells nothing about the impact on crime and fear of crime, although the programs are often touted as successful because of the organizing efforts. A second evaluation problem is the lack of appropriate control or comparison groups in the research. Where reductions in criminal behavior do appear, the studies often fail to adequately assess the changes in relation to an area or group which is not the subject of the intervention. Thus, it is difficult, if not impossible, to make an informed judgment on the success or failure of the project. The reason for this failure is often tied to the fact that many evaluations are afterthoughts to the project. The evaluation is added after the project is initiated, thus making it more difficult to undertake a strong research design. It is impossible at that point to undertake an experimental design, and difficult to set up a strong quasi-experimental design.

The problem of evaluation is further complicated by the introduction of many actions at the same time. For example, physical design changes, neighborhood watch, citizen patrols, Operation Identification, and media campaigns often overlap. It becomes impossible to evaluate which, if any, intervention has a positive (or negative) impact on crime. The default assumed by most observers when positive results emerge (i.e., reduced crime and reduced fear) is that the entire package is a success. Unfortunately, it may be that a single component is driving the results and there is no need to implement the large-scale, perhaps costly, package of initiatives. Knowing what aspect of the project worked best is an important piece of information. Conversely, finding that a package of initiatives has little or no impact may lead the evaluators to conclude overall failure when the more appropriate assessment might be that the individual efforts are working against one another. For example, the installation of home security devices may serve to drive people into their fortress at the same time that block watch is trying to bring the residents together. An evaluation may show no impact on crime and suggest that the project is a failure. An assessment that can disentangle the two initiatives, however, may show that the block watch organizing has a positive impact, while the physical security impedes positive change. Research needs to focus on disentangling the impact of simultaneous prevention efforts.

A fourth evaluation issue is to recognize that every crime prevention technique cannot be expected to have an equal or positive impact in all possible situations. Some techniques are better suited for certain problems and places than others. This is one of the central tenets of situational prevention and community policing efforts. Evaluations need to carefully assess the match between techniques and the location and timing of their implementation. This concern is not only evident in primary and secondary prevention efforts, but is also pivotal for tertiary crime prevention, particularly in relation to rehabilitation and treatment efforts. Research shows that certain programs have a positive impact on certain individuals, given the proper conditions. The major problem is in predicting potential offenders and identifying those who are amenable to different interventions. Many positive results of crime prevention interventions may be directly attributable to utilizing the proper approach in individual circumstances.

A final concern for evaluation deals with the time frame in which a technique is expected to make a difference. Many interventions are evaluated shortly after implementation. The expectation is that the program should have an immediate impact of crime, fear, and other factors. In reality, however, many changes take time to appear. This may be due to several factors. First, an intervention that appears to be in full operation may require a longer period to make changes in long-standing community or individual behaviors. Second, change may be gradual and the initiation of positive outcomes may not be identifiable in an evaluation undertaken immediately after the project. A third possibility is that a short-term evaluation finds a significant change in crime and/or fear. Unfortunately, long-term evaluation may uncover a diminishing impact, perhaps back to pre-program levels. In each of these cases, the evaluation must be cognizant of the potential confounding introduced by short follow-up periods.

Recognizing the Diversity in Crime Prevention

One goal of the book has been to demonstrate the diversity of crime prevention techniques. At the same time, it is important to recognize that the topics and literature covered in the chapters is somewhat selective. There are many topics that have not been addressed, and most of those that do appear in these pages could receive a great deal more attention. There is simply no way to comprehensively cover all the different permutations that make up crime prevention in a single book. The following paragraphs are meant to alert the reader to some of the other topics that fall under the rubric of crime prevention.

One key topic that has not been addressed is the politics of crime prevention. Crawford (1998) and Gilling (1997) both address the political forces that have directed crime prevention initiatives, particularly in the United Kingdom. They argue that many prevention programs follow the prevailing political sentiment in the countries. Thus, neighborhood watch will be promoted at one point, physical design will dominate at another time, and an emphasis on working with offenders may emerge at yet a different point. Large societal changes, such as social prevention, will require the right political climate to emerge before any significant alterations appear. These arguments may be more salient in the United Kingdom and other countries where the national government has more influence over policy than in the United States, but this perspective is somewhat applicable in the United States when one considers that the federal government does set funding and research priorities. A clear example of this is the fact that community policing is a "favored child" in Washington, D.C. at this point. Another example may be that most communities have some area that serves, in Barr and Pease's (1990) words, as a "crime fuse." The choice of that area, whether conscious or unconscious, is tied to political considerations. Perhaps the most important issue to remember is that crime prevention, in whatever form, does not exist in a vacuum. The political nature of crime prevention is one area that could receive more attention.

A wide range of other topics has received minimal or no attention in this book. Some of those include possible discussions of juvenile diversion, gun control, interventions with gangs, three-strikes laws, shaming of offenders, and private police and private security. The book has also avoided technical discussions of security devices, such as the relative value of different locks, doors, or alarms. These topics, along with many others, could be included in discussions of crime prevention. Indeed, there are other materials that focus on many of these areas. Many topics are emerging at a rate faster than most people can keep up with the information. Improved technology is a prime example of these changes. These issues are fodder for other discussions.

Summary

The ideas and topics addressed in this book are among the many possible prevention approaches that are used and are emerging to address the persistent problems of crime and fear in society. Such efforts will continue to grow. The effectiveness of these ideas rests on quality evaluation and a willingness to adapt and change. Only through research and modifications can the programs evolve into effective interventions. Evaluation of crime prevention techniques will remain a pivotal issue in dealing with crime and fear of crime throughout the future.

GLOSSARY

5Is: an alternative model for problem solving that is receiving increased attention in situational prevention; the *5Is* are intelligence, intervention, implementation, involvement, and impact

Access control: the idea of only allowing people who have legitimate business in an area to enter; reduces the opportunity for crime by increasing the effort needed to enter and exit a building or area for the purpose of committing crime

Action (in cognitive mapping): the behavior determined to be appropriate based on the information gained in the first three steps of cognitive mapping (i.e., recognition, prediction, and evaluation)

Active (continuous signaling) system: a form of electronic monitoring of offenders that keeps track of the offender on a continuous basis; system consists of a transmitter, receiver, and a central computer

Activity space: the term for a location where it is deemed through cognitive mapping or experience as a place to take action

Activity support: actions taken to build a community atmosphere; efforts that enhance the ability to recognize neighbors and identify needs of the community; efforts that enhance social cohesion among residents and contribute to a communal atmosphere, which works to eliminate crime and other common problems; includes efforts such as street fairs, community days, and other social events

Actuarial prediction: estimate based on known parameters in the data; an example is the setting of life or auto insurance rates

ADAM (Arrestee Drug Abuse Monitoring) program: a means of ascertaining the extent of drug use by arrested subjects; arrestees voluntarily agree to be interviewed and give a urine sample for testing

ADAM II (Arrestee Drug Abuse Monitoring) program: the most recent scaled-down version of the original ADAM program

Adolescence-limited offending: offending that takes place mainly in adolescence

Aggregate-level evaluation: looking for changes across large groups of subjects; changes in rates of offending or recidivism

Alley gating: erecting gates on alleys that run behind homes and businesses, thereby restricting access to residents or other legitimate users

Alternative schools: individual classrooms or programs within a school set up to dispel the negative experiences of many problem youths; the provision of a positive learning atmosphere that increases feelings of success within an atmosphere of warmth and acceptance

Anticipatory benefit: changes in crime that predate the actual implementation of a crime prevention program; most probably due to the fact that offenders, victims, and others know about a forthcoming prevention activity and begin to respond prior to activation of the intervention

Assize of arms: obligation for men to have weapons available for use when called on to protect the community

Authority conflict: offending pathway that begins with early stubbornness and leads to later defiance and avoidance of authority; running away, truancy, and ungovernability

Available guardians: guardians who are present but are not actively paying attention to what is happening in the area

Awareness space: nodes and paths with which an individual has gained knowledge that can be used for determining whether to act

Benign displacement: the argument that changes due to displacement may benefit society

Big Brother: term used to refer to the ability of the government to monitor the behavior of the citizenry

Big Brothers/Big Sisters (BB/BS): youth mentoring program boasting 325 programs across all 50 U.S. states and 13 other countries

Boost explanations: also known as *event dependency*; situations in which (usually) the same offender commits another offense based on the past experiences with that victim or location

Brutalization effect: the argument that the use of the death penalty causes an increase in subsequent homicides

Bullying: behavior that includes both physical and verbal aggression that is repeated over time and is meant to intentionally harm the victim

Capable guardians: guardians who are visible and actively observing/monitoring

Celerity: requirement for deterrence; refers to the swiftness of societal response to an offense

Certainty: requirement for deterrence; deals with the chances of being caught and punished for one's behavior

Chicago Alternative Police Strategy (CAPS): program that includes assigning officers to permanent neighborhood beats, the involvement of residents in the identification of problems and potential solutions, and reliance on other agencies (both public and private) to address identified issues

Chicago Area Project: founded in 1931, sought to work with the residents to build a sense of pride and community, thereby prompting people to stay and exert control over the actions of people in the area

Circle sentencing: also referred to as *peacemaking circles*; all interested parties are invited to participate in determining the appropriate sanctions for offenders; includes families, friends, agency representatives, and members of the general community; intended outcome of the circle is consensus on a plan of action that may include explicit sentencing recommendations to the trial judge and/or a range of community-based interventions

Citizen patrols: often a key element of neighborhood watch; its purpose is to put more eyes on the street in order to increase the chances of detecting strangers in the area and discovering crimes in progress; residents are discouraged from physically intervening into any suspicious activity

Civil abatement: the use of civil codes to attack crime problems; most notable is the involvement of landlords, citizens, health departments, zoning boards, and city/county attorneys in addressing drug problems

Clinical predictions: predictions based on a rater's evaluation of an individual, usually after interviews and direct examination of the subject and his records

Closed-circuit television (CCTV): systems that allow the active or passive surveillance of activity

Cognitive maps: mental images of the environment

Cognitive Thinking Skills Program (CTSP): a multi-modal intervention that utilizes a range of techniques targeting cognitive-behavioral problems; focuses on identifying cognitive deficits and inappropriate decision making by individuals

Cognitive-behavioral therapy (CBT): short-term, goal-oriented psychotherapy treatment that takes a hands-on, practical approach to problem-solving

Collective incapacitation: the imposition of sentences on everyone exhibiting the same behavior with no concern for the potential of the individual

Communities that Care (CTC): approach that requires a community to undertake an analysis of the problems it is facing, identify the risk factors that are at work, and build an intervention tailored to the unique situation and needs of the community

Community anti-drug (CAD) programs: residents banding together with each other, the police, and various agencies and organizations to attack drug use, drug sales, and related problems

Community policing: a newer philosophy of policing rather than a clearly definable method; generally includes community involvement, problem solving, a community base, and redefined goals for the police

Comprehensive Anti-Gang Initiative (CAGI): a gang suppression initiative developed by the U.S. Department of Justice that seeks to build a coalition of agencies, including law enforcement, prosecutors, social services, governments, community groups, schools, and others

Comprehensive Communities Program (CCP): a partnership-building initiative designed to fight crime and improve the quality of life in communities by using a problem-solving approach that includes a wide array of community individuals, agencies, and groups

Constable: an unpaid position responsible for coordinating the watch and ward system and overseeing other aspects of the law

Context: the idea that "the relationship between causal mechanisms and their effects is not fixed, but contingent" (Pawson and Tilley, 1997, p. 69); the impact of prevention efforts is contingent on the context in which they operate, and subsequently will affect whether the program has a similar impact in different settings

Cost–benefit evaluation: also known as *cost–benefit analysis*; seeks to assess whether the costs of an intervention are justified by the benefits or outcomes that accrue from it

Covert behavior: offending pathway that typically begins with minor acts of lying and theft, moves on to property crimes, and then moderately serious delinquency, and eventually culminates in serious property delinquency

CRAVED: Concealable, Removable, Available, Valuable, Enjoyable, and Disposable

Crime and Disorder Act (CDA): U.K. legislation that mandated the cooperation of many agencies in addressing crime problems

Crime attractors: areas to which potential offenders and others are drawn, such as drug markets, sites of street prostitution, or adult clubs and bars

Crime control: maintenance of a given or existing level of crime and management of that amount of behavior; fails to adequately address the problem of fear of crime

Crime displacement: the shift of crime due to the preventive actions of the individual or society; six types: territorial, temporal, tactical, target, functional, and perpetrator

Crime fuses: places where society allows crime to run relatively unchecked as a safety valve for the rest of society

Crime generators: locations that draw potential victims to the area

Crime life cycle: the notion that products go through a cycle of stages where they are at varying levels of risk for crime

Crime newsletters: printed materials targeted to a limited audience and tailored to the needs of those individuals;

provide detailed, in-depth discussions of both crime and potential crime prevention measures

Crime pattern theory: theory proposing that crime and criminal behavior fit patterns that can be identified and understood when viewed in terms of where and when they occur; crime patterns can be understood because of similarities that emerge when you consider "the specific criminal event, the site, the situation, the activity backcloth, the probable crime templates, the triggering events, and the general factors influencing the readiness or willingness of individuals to commit crimes" (Brantingham and Brantingham, 1993b, pp. 284–285)

Crime prevention: any action designed to reduce the actual level of crime and/or the perceived fear of crime

Crime Prevention Through Environmental Design (CPTED): in general, efforts to alter physical design to affect crime

Crime science: a new discipline, or at the very least a new paradigm, for addressing crime by coupling efforts to prevent crime with the detection of and intervention with offenders; "the application of the methods of science to crime and disorder" (Laycock, 2005)

Crime scripts: outlines of the steps and actions required to commit a crime, including the responses that are necessary to complete the act

Crime spillover: the shift of crime from one place to another

Crime Stoppers: the most widely known information-line program; generally operates by offering rewards to citizens for information about crimes

Cross-sectional studies: studies that compare differences among different individuals, groups, states, or other aggregates

D.A.R.E. (Drug Abuse Resistance Education): in-school program taught by law enforcement officers, emphasizing resistance skills training

Defensible space: proposes "a model which inhibits crime by creating a physical expression of a social fabric which defends itself" (Newman, 1972)

Deterrence: "influencing by fear" (Andenaes, 1975)

Detoxification: the use of drugs in an effort to remove an individual from an addiction to another illicit drug; the basic idea is to wean the client from the addiction with a minimal amount of discomfort and pain

Developmental crime prevention: an approach that targets the potential of individuals to become criminal

Developmental prevention: focuses on at-risk factors that may lead individuals to deviant behavior

Diffusion of benefits: "the spread of the beneficial influence of an intervention beyond the places which are directly targeted, the individuals who are the subject of control, the crimes which are the focus of intervention or the time periods in which an intervention is brought" (Clarke and Weisburd, 1994, p. 169)

Digital DNA: a unique non-sequential numerical code

Distance decay: the commission of crime decreases as the distance from the offender's home increases

Drug Abatement Response Team (DART): a team that works to compel landlords to take action against properties and tenants involved in drug offending

Drug courts: represent a coalition of prosecutors, police, probation officers, judges, treatment professionals, social service agencies, and other community groups working together to get the offenders off drugs and keep them off drugs

Ecological fallacy: the attempt to predict individual behavior based on group data; imputing the behavior of a single person from the activity of a larger group

Edges: areas on the periphery of nodes and paths that are prime spots for deviant behavior; edges, both physical and perceptual, experience greater diversity in people and activity

Elaboration model: an approach that attempts to take components of various theories and build a single explanation that incorporates the best parts of the individual theories

Electronic monitoring (EM): a form of home confinement in which individuals can be tracked by placing an electronic device on them

Elmira Prenatal/Early Infancy Project: a project that targets the earliest stage of a child's development, specifically when the child is still in the womb; home visitation by nurses begins during pregnancy and continues through the child's second birthday

Environmental backcloth: the social, economic, cultural, and physical conditions within which people operate

Escape: the ability of both offenders and victims to escape from an area before or after an offense

Euclidean distance: measures in a straight line from the start to the end point

Experiential effect: the idea that the actual apprehension of an individual raises the perception of risk

Evaluation: refers to investigating the usefulness of some exercise or phenomena; evaluation of crime prevention refers to investigating the impact of a prevention technique or intervention on the level of subsequent crime, fear, or other intended outcome

Evaluation (in cognitive mapping): the process by which the individual uses the information gathered in the earlier stages of cognitive mapping and determines which options are acceptable modes of behavior

Event dependency: also known as a *boost explanations*; situations in which (usually) the same offender commits another offense based on past experiences with that victim or location; successful past offending leads to another attempt against the same target

False negative predictions: predictions that declare that the person is not a future threat but the individual does engage in the negative behavior at a later time

False positive predictions: predictions in which an individual is predicted to do something in the future (e.g., recidivate, offend, act dangerously) but is not found to act in that fashion after follow-up

Families and Schools Together (FAST): a developmental prevention program aimed at families of youths aged roughly four to eight

Family group conferencing (FGC): similar to victim–offender mediation, but includes family members, close friends, and other support groups of the victim and offender in the conferences; may also include criminal justice system personnel (e.g., social workers, police officers, offender's attorney)

Fear: "an emotional response of dread or anxiety to crime or symbols that a person associates with crime. This definition of fear implies that some recognition of potential danger, what we may call perceived risk, is necessary to evoke fear" (Ferraro, 1995, p. 8)

Fearing subject: someone who becomes responsible for the safety of himself and his property

Feeble-minded: term used in the early 1900s to denote those with low IQs

Flag explanation: also called *risk heterogeneity*; a prior victimization or some other factor identifies the victim or location as an appropriate target for further victimization

Formal or organized surveillance: the use of guards or employees specifically tasked with watching for offending

Functional displacement: when offenders change to a new type of offense, such as shifting from larceny to burglary or burglary to robbery

Functional fear: fear as a good thing, when the individual uses it as motivation to take precautions

General deterrence: aims to have an impact on more than the single offender; the apprehension and punishment of a single individual serves as an example to other offenders and potential law violators

General theory of crime: an explanation that assumes that failures in early child rearing by parents lead to low self-control by the individual and a much greater chance that crime and deviance will be expressed

Generalizability: a measure of whether results would be applicable in other places, settings, and times

Global positioning system (GPS) technology: technology that uses satellites to locate a person or monitor his movements

Gold standard: term that has come to be used to refer to true experimental design in evaluation

Google Streetview: an application that allows the user to look at an address from the main street, take a 360-degree look around where the observer is positioned, move up and down the street, and zoom in to look at details

G.R.E.A.T. (Gang Resistance Education and Training): taught by local police officers in middle schools; goal of the program is to "prevent youth crime, violence and gang involvement" (Bureau of Justice Assistance, 2005); provides youths with the necessary skills for identifying high-risk situations and resisting the pressure or allure of taking part in gangs and gang activity; program curricula are geared toward increasing self-esteem, changing attitudes, and eliminating participation in violent behavior

Guardian Angels: one example of citizen patrolling that has gained international attention; mainly found in large urban areas and consisting primarily of young individuals

Head Start: best-known preschool program; proposes that disadvantaged youths are not prepared to enter school without some form of early intervention targeted at social and intellectual skills

Hedonistic: attribute of humans to seek pleasure and avoid pain

Hot products: items that attract attention and are targeted by thieves

Hot spots: "small places in which the occurrence of crime is so frequent that it is highly predictable, at least over a one-year period" (Sherman, 1995, p. 36)

Hot spots policing: specific efforts by police to address crime convergence in "hot spots"; requires analysis of the locale and the generation of interactions appropriate for the problem

Hue and cry: alarm and call for help raised by those watching over the town when threats were identified

Hunting ground: nodes where offenders recognize that potential victims frequent the area, there is a lack of guardians, and, consequently, the offender follows victims to that place

Image: refers to building a neighborhood or community that does not appear vulnerable to crime and is not isolated from the surrounding community

Immobilizers: electronic devices that, in the absence of the key, prevent a car from operating

Impact evaluations: evaluations that focus on what changes (e.g., to the crime rate) occur after introduction of a policy, intervention, or program

Incapacitation: method to prevent future crime on the part of the offender by imposing control over the individual that prohibits the physical possibility of future criminal activity

Incivility: various factors involved in disorder and community decline; two general categories of incivility outlined in the literature are physical (e.g., deterioration of buildings, litter, graffiti, vandalism, abandoned buildings and cars) and social (e.g., public drunkenness, vagrancy, groups of loitering youths, harassment such as begging or panhandling, visible drug sales and use)

Incredible Years program: program that identifies families for intervention that have youths displaying early conduct problems from ages four to eight; program includes strong parent and child training components, as well as a teaching training element for youths in school

Individual-level evaluation: an evaluation that focuses on qualitative changes rather than quantitative shifts; may appear as simple adjustments in the type of offending

Inelastic: term used to describe crime in which offenders are driven to commit a certain number of offenses over a given period of time

Information lines: programs with a dedicated telephone line for the solicitation of information about specific crimes from the public; involving citizens in crime prevention

Injunctions: court orders placing rules and/or restrictions on the behavior of individuals

Integrated Cognitive Antisocial Potential (ICAP) theory: theory that incorporates ideas from learning, social control, strain, and labeling theories, as well as rational choice theory

Intensive supervision probation (ISP): probation using team supervision, a high number of contacts between the client and officer, curfew and/or house arrest, restitution, employment or school

attendance, drug testing, community service, counseling, and treatment

Intervening guardians: guardians who are visible, monitoring the area, and take action when something occurs

Invisible guardians: guardians who are not evident or visible in the area

Journey to crime: the fact that offenders will travel to commit crimes

Juvenile Mentoring Program (JUMP): a program initiated by the Office of Juvenile Justice and Delinquency Prevention (OJJDP) in 1996; its key component is partnership with educators and private-sector agencies

Keepin' It REAL: a new version of D.A.R.E. that includes a 10-session curriculum taught to children and adolescents in schools by law enforcement officers, with a focus on resistance skills; REAL stands for Refuse, Explain, Avoid, and Leave

Kirkholt Burglary Prevention Project: major anti-burglary initiative in the United Kingdom that relied on partnership

Lex talionis: the principle of "an eye for an eye"; retribution

Life-course-persistent offending: offending that continues over the long term, including as a juvenile and as an adult

Lifestyle perspective: grows out of research on victimization and specifically focuses on the activity of the victim as a contributing factor in criminal acts; an individual's lifestyle and behavioral choices help determine whether he will be victimized

Longitudinal analyses: look for changes over time, primarily due to shifts in law or criminal justice system activity

Macro-level crime prevention: looks at large communities, society as a whole, or other very large collectives

Maintenance programs: programs that seek to establish a steady state in which the individual does not experience withdrawal symptoms when the drug begins to wear off

Malign displacement: the idea that efforts aimed at reducing crime may prompt an increase in offending or more serious crime

Manhattan distance: distance measured in terms of roadways, walkways, and other paths that avoid obstruction and reduce both distance and travel time

Maryland Scale of Scientific Methods: rating method for determining how closely a study adheres to the standards of a true experimental design

McGruff: part of the Take a Bite Out of Crime campaign; a cartoon dog in a trench coat who presents simulated crimes and depicts the proper actions viewers should take when confronted with similar situations

Mechanical surveillance: surveillance that utilizes cameras or other devices to observe activities, or lights to simply increase the ability of people to see what is taking place

Mechanism: "what it is about a program which makes it work" (Pawson and Tilley, 1997, p. 66)

Mental health courts: special courts that seek to address the specialized needs and circumstances of mentally ill individuals brought to the criminal courts for processing; specialized court docket that marshals the expertise of mental health professionals, social service providers, and criminal justice system personnel; provides screening and assessment, followed by treatment that is overseen by the court

Mentoring: an approach that involves pairing adult volunteers with youths in need of friendship, emotional support, guidance, and advice

Meso-level crime prevention: prevention techniques that target larger communities or neighborhoods, or larger groups of individuals or businesses, for intervention

Meta-analysis: the reanalysis of data from various studies in order to make direct comparisons between the results

Methadone maintenance: outpatient programs that involve the provision of methadone to heroin/opiate addicts; the primary assumption is that the patient is unable to function without some form of drug use and that methadone is an acceptable substitute for other, more damaging drugs

Micro-level crime prevention: prevention techniques that target individuals, small groups, small areas, or small businesses for intervention

Milieu: idea that placement of a community within a larger, low-crime, high-surveillance area will inhibit criminal activity

Minneapolis Domestic Violence Experiment: project to investigate the deterrent effect of arrest, separation, and police counseling in misdemeanor spouse abuse situations

Misdeeds: per Ekblom's Misdeeds and Security framework, products can be MISappropriated, MIStreated, MIShandled, MISused, or MISbehaved with

Monitoring the Future (MTF) project: annual survey of representative high school students (eighth, 10th, and 12th graders), college students, and young adults; probes a variety of factors; the most important set of information deals with the level and type of drug use

Motivation reinforcement: actions taken to build a community atmosphere; efforts that enhance the ability to recognize neighbors and identify needs of the community; efforts that enhance social cohesion among residents and contribute to a communal atmosphere, which works to eliminate crime and other common problems; includes efforts such as street fairs, community days, and other social events

Multi-Systemic Therapy (MST): a community-based intervention that attempts to address family, peer, school, community, and other influences that may prompt or lead to deviant behavior; involves parental and family interventions, social-cognitive strategies, and academic skills services to address a range of related risk factors and behavioral problems

National Crime Victimization Survey (NCVS): the best known of the victimization surveys, an annual data collection conducted by the U.S. Census Bureau for the Bureau of Justice Statistics (BJS)

National Neighborhood Watch (NNW): a division of the National Sheriffs' Association (NSA) that empowers citizens to become active in community efforts through participation in Neighborhood Watch groups

National Night Out: program coordinated by local police agencies; consists of educational programs, neighborhood organizing, social events, and anti-drug and anti-crime activities

National Survey on Drug Use and Health: a survey conducted by the Substance Abuse and Mental Health Services Administration (SAMHSA) that measures drug use by a representative sample of U.S. respondents aged 12 and older

National Youth Anti-Drug Media Campaign: media effort to combat drug use and abuse that relies on the heavy use of digital media, including Facebook, YouTube, and Google

National Youth Survey (NYS): an ongoing, longitudinal panel study of youths; collects information on delinquency, drug use, and demographic factors

Natural surveillance: designing an area that allows legitimate users to observe the daily activities of both friends and strangers; permits residents to observe criminal activity and take action (also called *informal surveillance*)

Near repeat: offenses that take place at neighboring locations; a type of repeat victimization

Neighborhood reparative boards (NRBs): also known as *accountability boards*, boards that seek to restore victims and community to pre-offense states, require the offender to make amends, and aid the offender in understanding the impact of his actions on the victim and community

Neighborhood watch: bringing together neighbors and residents of an area in order to promote crime prevention activity

Net-widening: bringing more people under the umbrella of social control

New parochialism: an approach that argues that struggling neighborhoods can bring about change if they are provided outside assistance by a combination of parochial and public control

Nodes: locations of activity, such as home, work, school, and shopping

Obligatory policing: a form of citizen policing in which male citizens were required to band together into groups for the purpose of policing each other

Operation Ceasefire: partnership in Boston to address gun violence, particularly among juveniles and gang members; creation of an interagency working partnership to assess the nature of the gun problem and the dynamics of youth violence and to identify and implement an effective intervention

Operation Identification: marking property to increase the difficulty for offenders to dispose of marked items

Order maintenance: police functions that do not deal with an immediate criminal action; includes responding to disabled autos, escorting funerals and parades, dealing with barking dogs, responding to false alarms and noise complaints, and delivering messages

OTREP (Opportunity is the result of Target, Risk, Effort, and Payoff): assumption that offenses can be avoided when there is a high risk of apprehension with little potential payoff

Outcome evaluations: See Impact evaluations

Overt behavior: offending pathway that commences with aggressive activity (bullying and teasing) and leads to fighting and violent activity

Panel designs: research designs that follow a number of separate units (such as states, counties, or individuals) over a given period

Panel survey: survey in which a group of subjects is surveyed repeatedly over a specified period; the NCVS surveys the same households every six months over a three-year period

Parens patriae: philosophy underlying

the juvenile court that argues that youths need help rather than processing in adult court, which is geared toward punishment rather than prevention

Parochial control: sources of control from neighborhood networks and institutions, such as schools, churches, or businesses

Parochial police: police hired by the wealthy to protect their homes and businesses

Part I crimes: part of the Uniform Crime Reports and also known as *index crimes*; includes the violent crimes of murder, rape, robbery, and assault, as well as the property crimes of burglary, larceny, auto theft, and arson

Part II crimes: part of the Uniform Crime Reports; includes all offenses not included in the Part I category

Passive system: a form of electronic monitoring that requires periodic activation of the system; the system randomly calls the offender's home to certify the presence of the individual; also referred to as *Programmed contact system*

Paths: transit routes between nodes

Peacemaking (sentencing) circles: based on North American Indian processes, groups that invite all interested parties to participate in determining the appropriate sanctions for offenders

Peer mediation: a program in which students are trained to assist one another in resolving disputes in such a way that all parties to the dispute accept the resolution

Permeability: access and egress to an area

Permissibility: situations or beliefs that place criminal behavior into an acceptable light; for example, the belief that everyone breaks the law or that the victim had it coming

Perpetrator displacement: occurs when one offender ceases his deviant behavior, only to be replaced by another offender

Perry Preschool program: also known as *High/Scope*; most extensively studied preschool program; seeks to provide students with a positive introduction to education by involving the children in the planning of activities, with a low child-to-teacher ratio, and enhanced reinforcement of student achievement

Positivism: a belief that crime is caused by factors beyond the control of the individual

Prediction (in cognitive mapping): making connections between the identifiable objects in the area and possible lines of behavior

Pressures: direct stimuli that lead to action; deviant peers, going along with the crowd, or following orders to do something wrong

Primary prevention: "identifies conditions of the physical and social environment that provide opportunities for or precipitate criminal acts" (Brantingham and Faust, 1976)

Private control: control based on interpersonal relationships among family members, friends, and close associates

Problem-oriented policing: approaching

issues and problems differently based on the uniqueness of each situation

Problem solving: perhaps the most important element of community policing; deals with crime by identifying the underlying causes and contributors to crime and seeking out solutions to those problems

Process evaluations: evaluations that consider the implementation of a program or initiative and involve determining the procedures used to implement a specific program

Programmed contact system: See Passive system

Project PATHE (Positive Action Through Holistic Education): a broad-based approach to the school environment that brings teachers, administrators, students, parents, and agencies together to make decisions about education and the school

Project Safe Neighborhoods (PSN): an outgrowth of SACSI that focuses primarily on reducing firearms violence through partnerships, strategic plans, training, outreach, and accountability

Project TOUGH (Taking Out Urban Gang Headquarters): a program that works to compel landlords to take action against properties and tenants used as gang headquarters and other gang hangouts

Promoting Alternative Thinking Strategies (PATHS®): a five-year-long curriculum offered in elementary schools focusing on self-control, understanding emotions, building a positive self-image, relationships, and interpersonal problem solving; intended to reduce both behavioral and emotional problems while building self-control and problem-solving abilities

Prompts: events or situations that may support the opportunity for crime, such as doors that are open or others who are committing crime

Prospect: the ability of individuals to see an area; areas that offer greater prospect should engender less fear and victimization than locations that limit sight lines

Prospective mapping: the creation of maps that predict future crime locations based on knowledge of recent events

Provocations: factors that make an individual uncomfortable, frustrated, irritable, or otherwise aroused to the point of taking some form of action, of which crime is one possibility

Psychopharmacological explanation: an approach suggesting that various drugs have a direct impact on the user, both physically and psychologically, which impels the individual to act in a way that society deems unacceptable

Public control: the ability to marshal input, support, and resources from public agencies

Public health model: an approach that classifies prevention as primary, secondary, or tertiary

Pulling levers: a term used to signify a strict enforcement policy for all individuals and groups involved directly or indirectly in a crime problem; coined in Operation Ceasefire

Radio frequency (RF) transmitters: used in electronic monitoring, a set of equipment used to generate and transmit electromagnetic waves carrying messages or signals; one of two primary systems or types—active or passive

Rational choice theory: an approach that assumes that potential offenders make choices based on various factors in the physical and social environment; offenders respond to payoff, effort, peer support, risks, and similar factors in making decisions to commit a crime

Real territoriality: engendered by walls, fences, gates, or other items that place a physical barrier in front of people

Realistic evaluation: evaluation that considers the phenomenon in its entirety rather than relying exclusively on experimental approaches; two key ideas central to realistic evaluation are mechanism and context

Reciprocal: in relation to crime, the idea that criminal activity leads to drug use and drug use leads to criminal activity

Recognition (in cognitive mapping): being able to identify your location and various features in the area

Reducing Burglary Initiative (RBI): program in the United Kingdom that relies on local communities to identify the causes of the burglary problems in their area and to develop appropriate interventions; includes a wide range of interventions, many of which are

physical design changes, such as target hardening, the installation of alley gates, lighting improvements, fencing, and property marking

Refuge: the presence or absence of concealment in which offenders could hide from potential victims; provides both hiding places and protection for potential offenders

Repeat victimization: people or places being victimized at least a second time within a certain period of time subsequent to an initial victimization event

Resistance skills training: a set of ideas that address recognizing problematic situations and issues, dealing with peer pressure, recognizing pressure from media presentations, knowing proper responses to temptations, building self-esteem and assertiveness, and knowing how and when to take a stand

Resolving Conflict Creatively Program (RCCP): a school program including student mediation as a core component; elementary curriculum consists of 12 lessons dealing with issues of communication, cooperation, feelings, diversity, peacemaking, and resolving conflicts

Responding in Peaceful and Positive Ways (RIPP): a program that targets sixth graders and includes lessons on appropriate responses to conflict situations and how students can avoid violence

Response generalization: the act of generalizing from the response being promoted in a program (such as simply calling for help) to other possible responses not featured in the program (such as carrying weapons and taking direct action)

Restorative justice: an approach that seeks to repair the harm done to both the victim and the community and to "repair" the offender; accomplished by bringing together a range of interested parties in a non-confrontational setting, including the victim and the offender, as well as family members or friends, criminal justice system personnel, and members of the general community

Risk factors: individual or environmental conditions that have been found to be associated with an increased likelihood of antisocial behavior, such as crime or violence

Risk heterogeneity: also called a *flag explanation*, a prior victimization or some other factor identifies the victim or location as an appropriate target for further victimization

Risk, need, and responsivity: according to advocates of rehabilitation, the three factors that are essential to meet for successful interventions; basically involves matching the correct subjects with the correct intervention

Routine activities theory: argues that the normal movement and activities of both potential offenders and victims play a role in the occurrence of crime; crime requires (1) a suitable target, (2) a motivated offender, and (3) an absence of guardians

Safer Cities program: a program under which the British government provided funds for local initiatives aimed at reducing crime and the fear of crime, and the creation of safer cities; key was building multi-agency partnerships for fighting social, physical, and economic problems in urban areas

SARA: problem-solving approach that includes Scanning, Analysis, Response, and Assessment

School resource officers (SROs): police officers assigned to schools who are involved in mentoring and referrals, training teachers and parents, teaching programs, and performing traditional police functions

Seattle Social Development Project: a comprehensive developmental crime prevention strategy; program creates a template for communities and researchers to work together to evaluate particular risk factors in a specific context and match interventions that have been successful at addressing those risk factors while strengthening protective factors

Second-generation CPTED: an approach to crime prevention that focuses on the four components of: (1) social cohesion between residents, businesses, and others; (2) connectivity of the local area to government agencies, businesses, and others that can contribute to area improvement; (3) community cultural initiatives that can bring people together; and (4) threshold capacity that builds cohesion among residents and serves to enhance the community and support the needs and efforts of the residents

Secondary prevention: "engages in early identification of potential offenders and seeks to intervene" (Brantingham and Faust, 1976, p. 288)

Secured By Design (SBD): an ongoing program in England that emphasizes and promotes the inclusion of safety and security measures in new and existing buildings

Selective incapacitation: emphasizes identifying high-risk offenders and subjecting only that group to intervention

Severity: requirement for deterrence; involves making certain that punishments provide enough pain to offset the pleasure received from the criminal act

Situational crime prevention: "characterized as comprising measures (1) directed at highly specific forms of crime (2) that involve the management, design, or manipulation of the immediate environment in as systematic and permanent a way as possible (3) so as to reduce the opportunities for crime and increase the risks as perceived by a wide range of offenders seeks to identify existing problems at the micro level and institute interventions which are developed specifically for the given problem" (Clarke, 1983, p. 225)

Smart guns: guns that recognize the owner and will only discharge if used by that person

Social media: tools that allow people, including police organizations, to create, share or exchange information, ideas, and pictures/videos in virtual communities

Social prevention: activities typically aimed at alleviating unemployment, poor education, poverty, and similar social ills that may reduce crime and fear by attending to the root causes underlying deviant behavior

Social/crime template: the idea that people have templates that outline expectations of what will happen at certain times and places given certain behavior by the individual; a template tells an offender what should occur in a certain place, time, or situation

Soft determinism: individuals make choices but only within the realm of available alternatives presented to them

Specialized Multi-Agency Response Teams (SMART): a civil abatement strategy that relies on the cooperation of police, citizens, and other groups to solve neighborhood problems

Specific deterrence: efforts that keep an individual offender from violating the law again in the future

Spurious: when neither factor is the ultimate cause of the other; rather, both are caused by either the same common factors or by different factors

Status offenses: offenses that are only illegal if committed by individuals of a certain status; typically used with juveniles and outlines behavior such as curfew violation, smoking, playing in the street, and incorrigibility

Strategic Approaches to Community Safety Initiative (SACSI): a partnership program initiated in five sites in 1998 to fight primarily violent personal crimes

Street Angels: a U.K. citizen patrol group boasting 120 patrols

Street Pastors: a U.K. citizen patrol group that operates in 250 locations and claims more than 9,000 volunteers

Streetblock: area containing the homes on either side of a single block (that is, between two cross-streets)

Super controllers: "the people, organizations and institutions that create incentives for controllers to prevent … crime" (Sampson et al., 2010)

Surveillance: any action that increases the chance that offenders will be observed by residents

Symbolic territoriality: things such as signs, landscaping, or other items that signal a change in ownership or area

Syracuse Family Development Research Program: a program with characteristics similar to those of nurse home visitation programs; targeted pregnant, young, single, African-American mothers and worked with the families from birth to age eight; project included home visitation by child development trainers, parent training (health, nutrition, and child rearing), and individualized daycare for the children

Systemic violence: violence resulting from competition between drug dealers, retaliation for poor drug quality or high prices, robbery of drug dealers or users, and other factors related to the drug trade

Tactical displacement: utilizing new means to commit the same offense

Take a Bite Out of Crime: a public information media campaign; objectives include altering the public's feelings about crime and the criminal justice system, generating feelings of citizen responsibility and cooperation with the criminal justice system, and enhancing already existing crime prevention efforts

Target displacement: choosing different victims within the same area

Target hardening: efforts that make potential criminal targets more difficult to victimize, such as the installation of locks, bars on windows, unbreakable glass, intruder alarms, fences, safes, and other devices

Tautological: the nature of a circular argument

Teen courts: sometimes called *youth courts*; an emerging alternative to processing youths in a traditional juvenile court setting; youths act as judge (about half the time), attorney (prosecutor and defense attorney), and jury in cases involving status offenses, misdemeanors, and occasionally a low-level felony

Temporal displacement: the movement of offending to another time period while remaining in the same area; may manifest itself through a shift in larcenies from the late evening to the early morning

Territorial (spatial) displacement: movement of crime from one location to another

Territoriality: the ability and desire of legitimate users of an area to lay claim to the area

Tertiary prevention: "deals with actual offenders and involves intervention in such a fashion that they will not commit further offenses" (Brantingham and Faust, 1976, p. 288)

Therapeutic communities: residential communities that emphasize providing a supportive, highly structured atmosphere within which individuals can be helped to alter their personality and develop social relationships conducive to conforming behavior; operate as surrogate families for clients

Thief takers: voluntary bounty hunters; organized under the leadership of English magistrates; typically, reformed criminals "paid" to protect the public by being able to keep a portion of all recovered property

Third-generation CPTED: an approach to crime prevention that uses green sustainable design to improve communities and reduce crime (and other social) problems, including four major components: (1) places, (2) people, (3) technology, and (4) networks

Threats to external validity: factors that would limit the generalizability of the results to other places, settings, and times

Threats to internal validity: factors that could cause the results other than the measures that were implemented

Three-strikes laws: laws that mandate lengthy imprisonment for those convicted of a third offense

Tracking: the process of assigning students to different classes or groups based on the perceived needs of the student; common forms of tracking appear in high school, where students find themselves placed into "college preparatory" or "vocational" groups

True negative prediction: when something is predicted not to occur and it does not (a successful prediction)

True positive prediction: when something is predicted to occur and it does so (a successful prediction)

Uniform Crime Reports (UCR): the most widely used and cited official measures of crime in the United States; collected by the Federal Bureau of Investigation; reflects the number of criminal offenses known to the police

Vicarious victimization: a sympathetic reaction or empathetic fear of crime due to knowing someone who has been the victim of a crime or simply being told of a harmful act against a third party

Victim–offender mediation (VOM): typically a post-conviction process in which the victim and the offender are brought together with a mediator to discuss a wide range of issues; the most important concern addressed in the meetings is to identify for the offender the types and level of harm suffered by the victim as a result of the crime; focus of the meeting is on repairing the harm done to the victim, helping the victim heal (both physically and emotionally), restoring the community to the pre-crime state, and reintegrating the offender into society

Victimization surveys: surveys of the population carried out to measure the level of criminal victimization in society

Vigilante movement: an approach that mirrored early ideas of "hue and cry"; a major component of enforcing law and order in the growing frontier of the young country in which posses of citizens were formed when an offender needed to be apprehended and punished

Virtual repeats: follow-up victimizations of a similar person, place, or item after the initial action; for example, a series of robberies at different locations of a single company (such as a fast-food store) or theft of the same brand of car

VIVA: the risk of a target is directly related to Value, Inertia, Visibility, and Access

Watch and ward: a system whereby the responsibility for keeping watch over the town or area, particularly at night, was rotated among the male citizens

Whistle Stop: residents blow a whistle if they see something happening out of the ordinary as they are shopping, working, or simply walking out of doors

REFERENCES

Abadinsky, H. (1989). *Drug Abuse: An Introduction*. Chicago: Nelson Hall.

Akers, R.L., A.J. LaGreca, C. Sellers, and J. Cochran (1987). "Fear of crime and victimization among the elderly in different types of communities." *Criminology* 25:487–506.

Allatt, P. (1984). "Residential security: Containment and displacement of burglary." *Howard Journal* 23:99–116.

Amir, M. (1971). *Patterns of Forcible Rape*. Chicago: University of Chicago Press.

Andenaes, J. (1975). "General prevention revisited: Research and policy implications." *Journal of Criminal Law and Criminology* 66:338–365.

Anderson, D. and K. Pease (1997). "Biting back: Preventing repeat burglary and car crime in Huddersfield." In Clarke, R.V. (ed.), *Situational Crime Prevention: Successful Case-Studies*, Second Edition. Guilderland, NY: Harrow and Heston.

Anderson, D.C. (1998). "Curriculum, culture, and community: The challenge of school violence." In Tonry, M. and M.H. Moore (eds.), *Youth Violence*. Chicago: University of Chicago Press.

Anderson, K.B. (2013) *Consumer Fraud in the United States, 2011: The Third FTC Survey*. Washington, DC: Federal Trade Commission. Retrieved from http://www.ftc.gov/os/2013/04/130419fraudsurvey.pdf

Anderton, K.J. (1985). *The Effectiveness of Home Watch Schemes in Cheshire*. Chester, U.K.: Cheshire Constabulary.

Andison, F.S. (1977). "TV violence and viewer aggression: A culmination of study results, 1956–1976." *Public Opinion Quarterly* 41:314–331.

Andresen, M. (2010). "Displacement." In Fisher, B.S. and S.P. Lab (eds.), *Encyclopedia of Victimology and Crime Prevention*. Thousand Oaks, CA: Sage.

Andresen, M.A. (2014). *Environmental Criminology: Evolution, Theory and Practice*. New York: Routledge.

Andrews, D.A., I. Zinger, R.D. Hoge, J. Bonta, P. Gendreau, and F.T. Cullen (1990). "Does correctional treatment work? A clinically relevant and psychologically informed meta-analysis." *Criminology* 28:369–404.

Anglin, M.D. (1988). "The efficacy of civil commitment in treating narcotics addiction." *Journal of Drug Issues* 18:527–546.

Anglin, M.D. (1990). "Treatment of drug abuse." In Tonry, M. and J.Q. Wilson (eds.), *Drugs and Crime*. Chicago: University of Chicago Press.

Anglin, M.D. and Y. Hser (1987). "Addicted women and crime." *Criminology* 25:359–397.

Anglin, M.D. and Y. Hser (1990). "Treatment of drug abuse." In Tonry, M. and J.Q. Wilson (eds.), *Drugs and Crime*. Chicago, IL: University of Chicago Press.

Anglin, M.D. and W.H. McGlothlin (1984). "Outcome of narcotic addict treatment in California." In Times, F.M. and J.P. Ludford (eds.), *Drug Abuse Treatment Evaluation: Strategies, Progress and Prospects*. Washington, DC: National Institute on Drug Abuse.

Anglin, M.D. and G. Speckart (1988). "Narcotics use and crime: A multisample, multimethod analysis." *Criminology* 26:197–233.

Anglin, M.D., G.R. Speckart, M.W. Booth and T.M. Ryan (1989). "Consequences and costs of shutting off methadone." *Addictive Behaviors* 14:307–326.

Aos, S. (2003a). "Cost and benefits of criminal justice and prevention programs." In Kury, H, and J. Obergfell-Fuchs (eds.), *Crime Prevention: New Approaches*. Mainz, Germany: Weisser Ring.

Aos, S. (2003b). *The Criminal Justice System in Washington State: Incarceration Rates, Taxpayer Costs, Crime Rates, and Prison Economics*. Olympia: Washington State Institute for Public Policy.

Apel, R. (2013) Sanctions, perceptions, and crime: Implications for criminal deterrence. *Journal of Quantitative Criminology* 29:67–101.

Archer, D., R. Gartner and M. Beittel (1983). "Homicide and the death penalty: A cross-sectional test of a deterrence hypothesis." *Journal of Criminal Law and Criminology* 74:991–1013.

Armitage, R. (2000). *An Evaluation of Secured By Design Housing within West Yorkshire*. Briefing Note 7/00. London: Home Office.

Armitage, R. (2007). "Sustainability versus safety: Confusion, conflict and contradiction in designing out crime." In Farrell, G., K.J. Bowers, S.D. Johnson, and M. Townsley (eds.), *Imagination for Crime Prevention: Essays in Honour of Ken Pease*. Cullompton, Devon, U.K.: Willan.

Armitage, R., G. Smythe, and K. Pease (1999). "Burnley CCTV evaluation." In Painter, K. and N. Tilley (eds.), *Surveillance of Public Space: CCTV, Street Lighting and Crime Prevention*. Monsey, NY: Criminal Justice Press.

Armitage, R., I. Colquhoun, P. Ekblom, L. Monchuk, K. Pease, and M. Rogerson (2010) *Residential Design and Crime: Final Report*. London: CABE and Home Office.

Armitage, R. and L. Monchuk (2011). "Sustaining the crime reduction impact of designing out crime: Re-evaluating the Secured by Design scheme 10 years on." *Security Journal* 24:320–343.

Armitage, R., L. Monchuk, and M. Rogerson (2011). "It looks good, but what is it like to live there?: Exploring the impact of innovative housing design on crime." *European Journal of Criminal Police and Research* 17:29–54.

Arthur Young and Co. (1978). *Second Year Report for the Cabrini–Green High Impact Project*. Chicago: Chicago City Department of Development and Housing.

Association of Chief Police Officers (ACPO) (2009). *Secured By Design*. http://www.securedbydesign.com

Association of Chief Police Officers (ACPO) (2015). *Design Guides*. http://www.securedbydesign.com

Atkins, S., S. Husain, and A. Storey (1991). *The Influence of Street Lighting on Crime and the Fear of Crime*. London: Home Office.

Babst, D.V., M. Koval, and M.G. Neithercutt (1972). "Relationship of time served to parole outcome for different classifications of burglars based on males paroled in fifty jurisdictions in 1968 and 1969." *Journal of Research in Crime and Delinquency* 9:99–116.

Bachman, R., A. Randolph, and B.L. Brown (2011). "Predicting perceptions of fear at school and going to and from school for African American and White students: The effects of school security measures." *Youth & Society* 43:705–726.

Bailey, W.C. (1998). "Deterrence, brutalization, and the death penalty: Another examination of Oklahoma's return to capital punishment." *Criminology* 36:711–734.

Baker, G. and A. Gray (2005) *Research on the Effectiveness of Police Practice in Reducing Residential Burglary, Report 8: Victims of Burglary.* New Zealand: Ministry of Justice.

Bales, W., K. Mann, T. Blomberg, G. Gaes, K. Barrick, K. Dhungang, and B. McManus (2010). *A Quantitative and Qualitative Assessment of Electronic Monitoring.* Washington, DC: National Institute of Justice.

Ball, J.C., E. Corty, R. Bond, and A. Tommasello (1987). "The reduction of intravenous heroin use, non-opiate abuse and crime during methadone maintenance treatment: Further findings." Paper presented at the Annual Meeting of the Committee on Problems on Drug Dependency, Philadelphia.

Ball, J.C., E. Corty, S.P. Petroski, H. Bond, and A. Tommasello (1986). "Medical services provided to 2,394 patients at methadone programs in three states." *Journal of Substance Abuse Treatment* 3:203–209.

Ball, J.C., J.W. Shaffer, and D.N. Nurco (1983). "The day-to-day criminality of heroin addicts in Baltimore: A study in the continuity of offense rates." *Drug and Alcohol Dependence* 12:119–142.

Ball, R.A., C.R. Huff, and J.R. Lilly (1988). *House Arrest and Correctional Policy: Doing Time at Home.* Newbury Park, CA: Sage.

Barclay, P., J. Buckley, P.J. Brantingham, P.L. Brantingham, and T. Whinn-Yates (1996). "Preventing auto theft in suburban Vancouver commuter lots: Effects of a bike patrol." In Clarke, R.V. (ed.), *Preventing Mass Transit Crime.* Monsey, NY: Criminal Justice Press.

Barr, R. and K. Pease (1990). "Crime placement, displacement, and deflection." In Tonry, M. and N. Morris (eds.), *Crime and Justice*, vol. 12. Chicago: University of Chicago Press.

Barrile, L.G. (1980). "Television and attitudes about crime." Ph.D. dissertation, Boston College.

Barthe, E. (2010). "Crime newsletters." In Fisher, B.S. and S.P. Lab (eds.), *Encyclopedia of Victimology and Crime Prevention.* Thousand Oaks, CA: Sage.

Baum, K. (2007). *Identity Theft, 2005.* Washington, DC: Bureau of Justice Statistics.

Baumer, T.L. (1985). "Testing a general model of fear of crime: Data from a national survey." *Journal of Research in Crime and Delinquency* 22:239–255.

Baumer, T.L. and F. DuBow (1977). "Fear of crime in the polls: What they do and do not tell us." Paper presented at the American Association of Public Opinion Research Meeting.

Baumer, T.L., M.G. Maxfield, and R.I. Mendelsohn (1993). "A comparative analysis of three electronically monitored home detention programs." *Justice Quarterly* 10:121–142.

Bazemore, G. and D. Maloney (1994). "Rehabilitating community service: Toward restorative service in a balanced justice system." *Federal Probation* 58:24–35.

Bazemore, G. and M.S. Umbreit (2001). "A comparison of four restorative conferencing models." *Juvenile Justice Bulletin.* Washington, DC: Office of Juvenile Justice and Delinquency Prevention.

Beck, A. and A. Willis (1999). "Context-specific measures of CCTV effectiveness in the retail sector." In Painter, K. and N. Tilley (eds.), *Surveillance of Public Space: CCTV, Street Lighting and Crime Prevention.* Monsey, NY: Criminal Justice Press.

Beck, J.L. and P.B. Hoffman (1976). "Time served and release performance: A research note." *Journal of Research in Crime and Delinquency* 13:127–132.

Belenko, S. (1990). "The impact of drug offenders on the criminal justice system." In Weisheit, R. (ed.), *Drugs, Crime and the Criminal Justice System.* Cincinnati, OH: Anderson Publishing Co.

Bellis, D.J. (1981). *Heroin and Politicians: The Failure of Public Policy to Control Addiction in America.* Westport, CT: Greenwood.

Belson, W.A. (1978). *Television Violence and the Adolescent Boy.* Westmead, U.K.: Saxon House.

Bennett, R.R. and J.M. Flavin (1994). "Determinants of fear of crime: The effect of cultural setting." *Justice Quarterly* 11:357–382.

Bennett, S.F. and P.J. Lavrakas (1989). "Community-based crime prevention: An assessment of the Eisenhower Foundation's neighborhood program." *Crime and Delinquency* 35:345–364.

Bennett, T. (1986). "Situational crime prevention from the offender's perspective." In Heal, K. and G. Laycock (eds.), *Situational Crime Prevention: From Theory into Practice.* London: Her Majesty's Stationery Office.

Bennett, T. (1987). *An Evaluation of Two Neighborhood Watch Schemes in London.* Cambridge: Institute of Criminology.

Bennett, T. (1989). "Factors related to participation in neighbourhood watch schemes." *British Journal of Criminology* 29:207–218.

Bennett, T. (1990). *Evaluating Neighborhood Watch.* Aldershot: Gower.

Bennett, T. (1994). "Community policing on the ground: Developments in Britain." In Rosenbaum, D.P. (ed.), *The Challenge of Community Policing: Testing the Promises.* Thousand Oaks, CA: Sage.

Bennett, T. and R. Wright (1984). *Burglars on Burglary.* Brookfield, VT: Gower.

Berecochea, J.E. and D.R. Jaman (1981). *Time Served in Prison and Parole Outcome: An Experimental Study. Report No. 2.* Sacramento: California Department of Corrections.

Berg, A. (2008). "Preventing identity theft through information technology." In McNally, M.M. and G.R. Newman (eds.), *Perspectives on Identity Theft.* Monsey, NY: Criminal Justice Press.

Berk, R.A. and P.H. Rossi (1999). *Thinking About Program Evaluation,* Second Edition. Thousand Oaks, CA: Sage.

Bernasco, W. (2010). "A sentimental journey to crime: Effects of residential history on crime location choice." *Criminology* 48:389–416.

Berrueta-Clement, J.R., L.J. Schweinhart, W.S. Barnett, A.S. Epstein, and D.P. Weikart (1984). *Changed Lives: The Effects of the Perry Preschool Program on Youths Through Age 19.* Ypsilanti, MI: High/Scope Press.

Bevis, C. and J.B. Nutter (1977). *Changing Street Layouts to Reduce Residential Burglary.* St. Paul, MN: Governor's Commission on Crime Prevention and Control.

Bicheler, G., C.A. Orosco, and J.A. Schwartz (2012). "Take the car keys away: Metropolitan structure and the long road to delinquency." *Journal of Criminal Justice* 40:83–93.

Biderman, A.D., L.A. Johnson, J. McIntyre, and A.W. Weir (1967). *Report on Victimization and Attitudes Toward Law Enforcement.* Washington, DC: U.S. Government Printing Office.

Big Brothers/Big Sisters of America (BB/BS) (2015). http://www.bbbs.org/site/c.9iILI3NGKhK6F/b.5962335/k.BE16/Home.htm

Binder, A. and J.W. Meeker (1988). "Experiments as reforms." *Journal of Criminal Justice* 16:347–358.

Bishop, D.M. (1984a). "Deterrence: A panel analysis." *Justice Quarterly* 1:311–328.

Bishop, D.M. (1984b). "Legal and extralegal barriers to delinquency: a panel analysis." *Criminology* 22:403–319.

Bjørgo, T. (2013) *Strategies for Preventing Terrorism.* New York: Palgrave.

Blevins, K., J. Kuhns, and S. Lee (2012) *Understanding Decisions to Burglarize from the Offender's Perspective.* Charlotte: University of North Carolina at Charlotte, Department of Criminal Justice and Criminology. Retrieved from http://airef.org/wp-content/uploads/2014/06/BurglarSurveyStudyFinalReport.pdf

Block, R.L. and C.R. Block (1993). "Street Gang Crime in Chicago." *Research in Brief.* Washington, DC: National Institute of Justice.

Block, R.L. and C.R. Block (1995). "Space, place and crime: Hot spot areas and hot places of liquor-related crime." In Eck, J.E. and D. Weisburd (eds.), *Crime and Place.* Monsey, NY: Criminal Justice Press.

Blueprints for Healthy Youth Development (2015). *Communities that Care.* http://www.blueprintsprograms. com/evaluationAbstracts.php?pid=9a3e61b6bcc8abec08f195526c3132d5a4a98cc0

Boda, Z. and G. Szabó (2011). "The media and attitudes towards crime and the justice system: A qualitative approach." *European Journal of Criminology* 8:329–342.

Boggs, S.L. (1971). "Formal and informal crime control: An exploratory study of urban, suburban and rural orientations." *Sociological Quarterly* 12:319–327.

Bolkcom, C.A. (1981). *Rock Island Anti-Crime Block Club Organizing.* Washington, DC: National Criminal Justice Reference Service.

Booth, B., V.B. Van Hasselt, and G.M. Vecchi (2011). "Addressing school violence." *FBI Law Enforcement Bulletin* 80(5):1–9.

Borduin, C.M., B.J. Mann, L.T. Cone, S.W. Henggeler, B.R. Fucci, D.M. Blaske, and R.A. Williams (1995). "Multi-systemic treatment of serious juvenile offenders: Long-term prevention of criminality and violence." *Journal of Consulting and Clinical Psychology* 63:569–578.

Botvin, G.J. (1990). "Substance abuse prevention: Theory, practice and effectiveness." In Tonry, M. and J.Q. Wilson (eds.), *Drugs and Crime.* Chicago: University of Chicago Press.

Botvin, G.J., E. Baker, N. Renick, A.D. Filazzola, and E.M. Botvin (1984). "A cognitive-behavioral approach to substance abuse prevention." *Addictive Behaviors* 9:137–147.

Botvin, G.J. and L. Dusenbury (1989). "Substance abuse prevention and the promotion of competence." In Bond, L.A. and B.E. Compas (eds.), *Primary Prevention and Promotion in the Schools.* Newbury Park, CA: Sage.

Botvin, G.J. and A. Eng (1980). "A comprehensive school-based smoking prevention program." *Journal of School Health* 50:209–213.

Botvin, G.J. and A. Eng (1982). "The efficacy of a multicomponent approach to the prevention of cigarette smoking." *Preventive Medicine* 11:199–211.

Botvin, G.J., N. Renick, and E. Baker (1983). "The effects of scheduling format and booster sessions on a broad spectrum psychological approach to smoking prevention." *Journal of Behavioral Medicine* 6:359–379.

Bowers, K.J., A. Hirschfield, and S.D. Johnson (1998). "Victimization revisited: A case study of non-residential repeat burglary on Merseyside." *British Journal of Criminology* 38:429–452.

Bowers, K.J. and S.D. Johnson (2003). "Measuring the geographical displacement and diffusion of benefit effects of crime prevention activity." *Journal of Quantitative Criminology* 19:275–301.

Bowers, K.J. and S.D. Johnson (2004). "Who commits near repeats? A test of the boost explanation." *Western Criminology Review* 5(3):12–24.

Bowers, K.J. and S.D. Johnson (2005). "Using publicity for preventive purposes." In Tilley, N. (ed.), *Handbook of Crime Prevention and Community Safety.* Portland, OR: Willan.

Bowers, K.J., S.D. Johnson, and A.F.G. Hirschfield (2003). *Pushing Back the Boundaries: New Techniques for Assessing the Impact of Burglary Schemes.* Home Office Online Report 24/03. London: Home Office.

Bowers, W.J. and J.H. Hirsch (1987). "The impact of foot patrol staffing on crime and disorder in Boston: An unmet promise." *American Journal of Police* 6:17–44.

Bowers, W.J. and G.L. Pierce (1975). "The illusion of deterrence in Isaac Ehrlich's research on capital punishment." *Yale Law Journal* 85:187–208.

Bowers, W.J. and G.L. Pierce (1980). "The illusion of deterrence in Isaac Ehrlich's research on capital punishment." *Yale Law Journal* 85:187–208.

Brady, K.P., S. Balmer, and D. Phenix (2007). "School-police partnership effectiveness in urban schools: An analysis of New York City's impact schools initiative." *Education and Urban Society* 39:455–478.

Braga, A.A. and B.J. Bond (2008). "Policing crime and disorder hot spots: A randomized controlled trial." *Criminology* 46:577–607.

Braga, A.A., D. Hureau, and C. Winship (2008). "Losing faith? Police, black churches, and the resurgence of youth violence in Boston." *Ohio State Journal of Criminal Law* 6:141–172.

Braga, A.A., D.M. Kennedy, A.M. Piehl, and E.J. Waring (2001). "Measuring the impact of Operation Ceasefire." In National Institute of Justice, *Reducing Gun Violence: The Boston Gun Project's Operation Ceasefire.* Washington, DC: National Institute of Justice.

Braga, A.A., A.W. Papachristos and D.M. Hureau (2014). "The effects of hot spots policing on crime: An updated systematic review and meta-analysis." *Justice Quarterly* 31:633–663.

Braga, A.A., D.L. Weisburd, E.J. Waring, L.G. Mazerolle, W. Spelman, and F. Gajewski (1999). "Problem-oriented policing in violent crime places: A randomized controlled experiment." *Criminology* 37:541–580.

Braithwaite, J. (1999). "Restorative justice: Assessing optimistic and pessimistic accounts." In Tonry, M. (ed.), *Crime and Justice: A Review of Research*, vol. 25. Chicago: University of Chicago Press.

Braithwaite, J. (2002). *Restorative Justice and Responsive Regulation.* New York: Oxford University Press.

Brantingham, P.L. (2010). "Crime pattern theory." In Fisher, B.S. and S.P. Lab (eds.), *Encyclopedia of Victimology and Crime Prevention.* Thousand Oaks, CA: Sage.

Brantingham, P.L. and P.J. Brantingham (1981). "Notes on the geometry of crime." In Brantingham, P.J. and P.L. Brantingham (eds.), *Environmental Criminology.* Beverly Hills, CA: Sage.

Brantingham, P.L. and P.J. Brantingham (1984). "Burglar mobility and crime prevention planning." In Clarke, R. and T. Hope (eds.), *Coping with Burglary.* Boston: Kluwer-Nijhoff.

Brantingham, P.L. and P.J. Brantingham (1993a). "Nodes, paths and edges: Considerations on the complexity of crime and the physical environment." *Journal of Environmental Psychology* 13:3–28.

Brantingham, P.L. and P.J. Brantingham (1993b). "Environment, routine, and situation: Toward a pattern theory of crime." In Clarke, R.V. and M. Felson (eds.), *Routine Activities and Rational Choice.* New Brunswick, NJ: Transaction.

Brantingham, P.L. and P.J. Brantingham (1996). "Environmental criminology and violent choices." Paper presented at the American Society of Criminology Annual Meeting, Chicago.

Brantingham, P.L. and P.J. Brantingham (2003). "Anticipating the displacement of crime using the principles of environmental criminology." In Smith, M.J. and D.B. Cornish (eds.), *Theory for Practice in Situational Crime Prevention.* Monsey, NY: Criminal Justice Press.

Brantingham, P.J. and F.L. Faust (1976). "A conceptual model of crime prevention." *Crime & Delinquency* 22:284–296.

Brants, C. (1998). "Crime fighting by television in The Netherlands." In Fishman, M. and G. Cavender (eds.), *Entertaining Crime: Reality Television Programs*. New York: Aldine de Gruyter.

Brennan, P.A., B.R. Mednick, and S.A. Mednick (1993). "Parental psychopathology, congenital factors, and violence." In Hodgins, S. (ed.), *Mental Disorder and Crime*. Newbury Park, CA: Sage.

Brewer, D.D., J.D. Hawkins, R.F. Catalano, and H.J. Neckerman (1995). "Preventing serious, violent, and chronic offending: A review of evaluations of selected strategies in childhood, adolescence, and the community." In Howell, J.C., B. Krisberg, J.D. Hawkins, and J. Wilson (eds.), *Sourcebook on Serious, Violent, and Chronic Juvenile Offenders*. Thousand Oaks, CA: Sage.

Brewster, M.P. (2001). "An evaluation of the Chester County (PA) drug court program." *Journal of Drug Issues* 31:171–206.

Bridenback, M.L., P.L. Imhoff, and J.P. Blanchard (1980). *The Use of Mediation/Arbitration in the Juvenile Justice Process: A Study of Three Programs*. Tallahassee, FL: Office of the State Courts Administrator.

Briscoe, S. (2004). *The Impact of Increased Drink-driving Penalties on Recidivism Rates in NSW*. Alcohol Studies Bulletin 5. Sydney: NSW Bureau of Crime Statistics and Research.

Brodie, D.Q. and D.I. Sheppard (1977). "Neighbors Against Crime Together: A project evaluation." Paper presented at the National Conference on Criminal Justice Evaluation.

Brown, B. (1995). *CCTV in Town Centres: Three Case Studies*. London: Home Office Police Research Group.

Brown, E.J., T.J. Flanagan, and M. McLeod (1984). *Sourcebook of Criminal Justice Statistics*. Washington, DC: U.S. Government Printing Office.

Brown, L.P. and M.A. Wycoff (1987). "Policing Houston: Reducing fear and improving service." *Crime & Delinquency* 33:71–89.

Brown, R. (2004). "The effectiveness of electronic immobilization: Changing patterns of temporary and permanent vehicle theft." In Maxfield, M.G. and R.V. Clarke (eds.), *Understanding and Preventing Car Theft*. Monsey, NY: Criminal Justice Press.

Brown, R. (2006). "The role of project management in implementing community safety initiatives." In Knutsson, J. and R.V. Clarke (eds.), *Putting Theory to Work: Implementing Situational Prevention and Problem-Oriented Policing*. Monsey, NY: Criminal Justice Press.

Brown, T.L., S.W. Henggeler, S.K. Schoenwald, M.J. Brondino, and S.G. Pickerel (1999). "Multisystemic treatment of substance abusing and dependent juvenile delinquents: Effects on school attendance at posttreatment and 6-month follow-up." *Children's Services: Social Policy, Research and Practice* 2:81–93.

Browning, K. and R. Loeber (1999). "Highlights of findings from the Pittsburgh Youth Study." *OJJDP Fact Sheet, No. 95*. Washington, DC: Office of Juvenile Justice and Delinquency Prevention.

Buck, A.J., S. Hakim, and G.F. Rengert (1993). "Burglar alarms and the choice behavior of burglars: A suburban phenomenon." *Journal of Criminal Justice* 21:497–508.

Buerger, M.E. (1994). "The limits of community." In Rosenbaum, D.P. (ed.), *The Challenge of Community Policing: Testing the Promises*. Thousand Oaks, CA: Sage.

Bullock, H.A. (1955). "Urban homicide in theory and fact." *Journal of Criminal Law, Criminology and Police Science* 45:565–575.

Bullock, K. (2014). *Citizens, Community and Crime Control*. New York: Palgrave.

Bureau of Justice Assistance (1995). *Drug Abuse Resistance Education (DARE)*. Washington, DC: U.S. Department of Justice.

Bureau of Justice Assistance (1997). *Comprehensive Communities Program: Promising Approaches*. Washington, DC: Bureau of Justice Assistance.

Bureau of Justice Assistance (1998). *The Watch Your Car Program*. Washington, DC: U.S. Department of Justice.

Bureau of Justice Assistance (2001). *Comprehensive Communities Program: Program Account*. Washington, DC: U.S. Department of Justice.

Bureau of Justice Assistance (2005). *Gang Resistance Education and Training*. Washington, DC: Bureau of Justice Assistance. Retrieved from http://www.great-online.org

Bureau of Justice Assistance (2014). *Gang Resistance Education and Training*. http://great-online.org/Components/MiddleSchool.Aspx

Bureau of Justice Assistance (2015). *Neighborhood Watch Logic Model*. https://www.bja.gov/evaluation/program-crime-prevention/cbcp6.htm

Bureau of Justice Statistics. (2010). *Criminal Victimization in the United States, 2007, Statistical Tables*. Washington, DC: Bureau of Justice Statistics.

Burgess, E.W. (1928). "Factors influencing success or failure on parole." In Bruce, A.A., A.J. Harno, E.W. Burgess, and L. Landesco (eds.), *The Workings of the Indeterminate-sentence Law and the Parole System in Illinois*. Springfield, IL: Illinois State Board of Parole.

Bursik, R.J. and H.G. Grasmick (1993). *Neighborhoods and Crime: The Dimensions of Effective Community Control*. New York: Lexington.

Butts, J.A., J. Buck, and M.B. Coggershall (2002). *The Impact of Teen Court on Young Offenders*. Washington, DC: Urban Institute Press.

Bynum, T. (1996). "Reducing school violence in Detroit." Paper presented at the National Institute of Justice Crime Prevention Conference, Washington, DC.

Byrne, J.M. (1990). "The future of intensive supervision and the new intermediate sanctions." *Crime & Delinquency* 36:6–41.

Calhoun, A. and W. Pelech (2010). "Responding to young people responsible for harm: A comparative study of restorative and conventional approaches." *Contemporary Justice Review* 13:287–306.

Callanan, V.J. (2012). "Media consumption, perceptions of crime risk and fear of crime: Examining race/ethnic differences." *Sociological Perspectives* 55:93–115.

Capaldi, D.M. and G.R. Patterson (1996). "Can violent offenders be distinguished from frequent offenders? Prediction from childhood to adolescence." *Journal of Research in Crime and Delinquency* 33:206–231.

Caplan, G. (1964). *Principles of Preventive Psychiatry*. New York: Basic Books.

Carmichael, S.E. and A.R. Piquero (2006). "Deterrence and arrest ratios." *International Journal of Offender Therapy and Comparative Criminology* 50:71–87.

Carpenter, C.S. and C. Pechmann (2011). "Exposure to the Above the Influence antidrug advertisements and adolescent marijuana use in the United States, 2006–2008." *American Journal of Public Health* 101:948–954.

Carter, D.L. (1995). "Community policing and D.A.R.E.: A practitioner's perspective." *BJA Bulletin* (June). Washington, DC: U.S. Department of Justice.

Catalano, R.F. and J.D. Hawkins (1996). "The social development model: A theory of antisocial behavior." In Hawkins, J.D. (ed.), *Delinquency and Crime: Current Theories*. New York: Cambridge University Press.

Cedar Rapids Police Department (1975). *Installation, Testing, and Evaluation of a Large-scale Burglar Alarm System for a Municipal Police Department—A Second Phase Completion Report*. Cedar Rapids, IA: Cedar Rapids Police Department.

Chaiken, J.M. and M.R. Chaiken (1982). *Varieties of Criminal Behavior*. Santa Monica, CA: RAND.

Chaiken, J.M. and M.R. Chaiken (1990). "Drugs and predatory crime." In Tonry, M. and J.Q. Wilson (eds.), *Drugs and Crime*. Chicago: University of Chicago Press.

Chainey, S. (2012). "Repeat victimization: Summary (1 of 5)." Available at http://www.jdibrief.com

Challinger, D. (2003). *Crime Stoppers: Evaluating Victoria's Program*. Canberra, Australia: Australian Institute of Criminology.

Charles, M.T. (1989). "The development of a juvenile electronic monitoring program." *Federal Probation* 53(2):3–12.

Chermak, S.M. (1994). "Body count news: How crime is presented in the news media." *Justice Quarterly* 11:561–582.

Chermak, S.M. (1998). "Predicting crime story salience: The effects of crime, victim, and defendant characteristics." *Journal of Criminal Justice* 26:61–70.

Chermak, S.M. and N. Chapman (2007). "Predicting crime story salience: A replication." *Journal of Criminal Justice* 35:351–363.

Chiricos, T.G., S. Eschholz, and M. Gertz (1996). "Crime news and fear: Toward an identification of audience effects." Paper presented at the American Society of Criminology Annual Meeting.

Chiricos, T.G., M. Hogan, and M. Gertz (1997). "Racial composition of neighborhood and fear of crime." *Criminology* 35:301–324.

Cirel, P., P. Evans, D. McGillis, and D. Whitcomb (1977). *Community Crime Prevention Program, Seattle, Washington: An Exemplary Project*. Washington, DC: National Institute of Justice.

Cirino, R. (1972). *Don't Blame the People*. New York: Vantage Books.

Clarke, R.V. (1983). "Situational crime prevention: Its theoretical basis and practical scope." In Tonry, M. and N. Morris (eds.), *Crime and Justice*, vol. 4. Chicago: University of Chicago Press.

Clarke, R.V. (1992). *Situational Crime Prevention: Successful Case Studies*. Albany, NY: Harrow and Heston.

Clarke, R.V. (1993). "Fare evasion and automatic ticket collection on the London underground." In Clarke, R.V. (ed.), *Crime Prevention Studies*, vol. 1. Monsey, NY: Criminal Justice Press.

Clarke, R.V. (1995). "Situational crime prevention." In Tonry, M. and D.P. Farrington (eds.), *Building a Safer Society: Strategic Approaches to Crime Prevention*. Chicago: University of Chicago Press.

Clarke, R.V. (1996). *Preventing Mass Transit Crime*. Monsey, NY: Criminal Justice Press.

Clarke, R.V. (1999). *Hot Products: Understanding, Anticipating and Reducing Demand for Stolen Goods*. London: Home Office Policing and Reducing Crime Unit.

Clarke, R.V. (2005). "Seven misconceptions of situational crime prevention." In Tilley, N. (ed.), *Handbook of Crime Prevention and Community Safety*. Portland, OR: Willan.

Clarke, R.V. and D. Cornish (1985). "Modeling offenders' decisions: A framework for policy and research." In Tonry, M. and N. Morris (eds.), *Crime and Justice*, vol. 4. Chicago: University of Chicago Press.

Clarke, R.V. and J.E. Eck (2005). *Crime Analysis for Problem Solvers in 60 Small Steps.* Washington, DC: Office of Community Oriented Policing Services

Clarke, R.V. and R. Homel (1997). "A revised classification of situational crime prevention techniques." In Lab, S.P. (ed.), *Crime Prevention at a Crossroads*. Cincinnati, OH: Anderson Publishing Co.

Clarke, R.V. and P.M. Mayhew (1980). *Designing Out Crime*. London: Her Majesty's Stationery Office.

Clarke, R.V. and G.R. Newman (2005). "Modifying criminogenic products: What role for governments?" In Clarke, R.V. and G.R. Newman (eds.), *Designing Out Crime from Products and Systems*. Monsey, NY: Criminal Justice Press.

Clarke, R.V., E. Perkins, and D.J. Smith, Jr. (2001). "Explaining repeat residential burglaries: An analysis of property stolen." In G. Farrell and K. Pease (eds.), *Repeat Victimization*. Monsey, NY: Criminal Justice Press.

Clarke, R.V. and D. Weisburd (1994). "Diffusion of crime control benefits: Observations on the reverse of displacement." In Clarke, R.V. (ed.), *Crime Prevention Studies*, vol. 2. Monsey, NY: Criminal Justice Press.

Clarke, S. (1974). "Getting em out of circulation: Does incarceration of juvenile offenders reduce crime?" *Journal of Criminal Law and Criminology* 65:528–535.

Clayton, R.R., A. Cattarello, and K.P. Walden (1991). "Sensation seeking as a potential mediating variable for school-based prevention interventions: A two-year follow-up of DARE." *Journal of Health Communications* 3:229–239.

Clear, T.R. and P.L. Hardyman (1990). "The new intensive supervision movement." *Crime & Delinquency* 36:42–60.

Cloward, R. and L. Ohlin (1960). *Delinquency and Opportunity: A Theory of Delinquent Gangs*. New York, NY: The Free Press.

Coates, R.B. and J. Gehm (1989). "An empirical assessment." In Wright, M. and B. Galaway (eds.), *Mediation and Criminal Justice: Victims, Offenders and Community*. Newbury Park, CA: Sage.

Cochran, J.K. and M.B. Chamlin (2000). "Deterrence and brutalization: The dual effects of executions." *Justice Quarterly* 17:685–706.

Cochran, J.K., M.B. Chamlin, and M. Seth (1994). "Deterrence or brutalization?: An impact assessment of Oklahoma's return to capital punishment." *Criminology* 32:107–134.

Cocozza, J.J. and J.L. Shufelt (2006). *Juvenile Mental Health Courts: An Emerging Strategy.* Delmar, NY: The National Center for Mental Health and Juvenile Justice.

Cohen, A.L. (1955). *Delinquent Boys: The Culture of the Gang*. Glencoe, IL: The Free Press.

Cohen, J. (1978). "The incapacitative effect of imprisonment: a critical review of the literature." In Blumstein, A., J. Cohen, and D. Nagin (eds.), *Deterrence and Incapacitation: Estimating the Effects of Criminal Sanctions on Crime Rates*. Washington, DC: National Academy Press.

Cohen, J. (1983). "Incapacitation as a strategy for crime control: possibilities and pitfalls." In Tonry, M. and N. Morris (eds.), *Crime and Justice*, vol. 5. Chicago: University of Chicago Press.

Cohen, J. and J. Ludwig (2003). "Policing crime guns." In Ludwig, J. and P.J. Cook (eds.), *Evaluating Gun Policy: Effects on Crime and Violence*. Washington, DC: Brookings Institution Press.

Cohen, L.E. and M. Felson (1979). "Social change and crime rate trends: A routine activities approach." *American Sociological Review* 44:588–608.

Cohen, S. (1975). "The evidence so far." *Journal of Communication* 25:14–24.

Cohn, E.S., L. Kidder, and J. Harvey (1978). "Crime prevention vs. victimization: The psychology of two different reactions." *Victimology* 3:285–296.

Coleman, J.S. (1966). *Equality of Educational Opportunity*. Washington, DC: U.S. Government Printing Office.

Collins, J.J. (1989). "Alcohol and interpersonal violence: Less than meets the eye." In Weiner, N.A. and M.E. Wolfgang (eds.), *Pathways to Criminal Violence*. Newbury Park, CA: Sage.

Collins, J.J., R.L. Hubbard, and J.V. Rachal (1985). "Expensive drug use and illegal income: A test of explanatory hypotheses." *Criminology* 23:743–764.

Communities that Care (CTC) (2015). http://www.communitiesthatcare.net/how-ctc-works/social-development-strategy/

Conger, R.D. and R.L. Simons (1997). "Life-course contingencies in the development of adolescent antisocial behavior: A matching law approach." In T.P. Thornberry (ed.) *Advances in Criminological Theory*. New York: Aldine.

Conklin, J.E. (1975). *The Impact of Crime*. New York: Macmillan.

Conklin, J.E. (2003). *Why Crime Rates Fell*. Boston: Allyn & Bacon.

Coombs, R.H. (1981). "Back on the streets: Therapeutic communities' impact upon drug abusers." *American Journal of Alcohol Abuse* 8:185–201.

Cook, R.F. and J.A. Roehl (1983). *Preventing Crime and Arson: A Review of Community-based Strategies*. Reston, VA: Institute for Social Analysis.

Cook, T.D. and D.T. Campbell (1979). *Quasi-experimentation: Design and Analysis Issues for Field Settings*. Chicago: Rand McNally College.

Cooprider, K.W. and J. Kerby (1990). "A practical application of electronic monitoring at the pretrial stage." *Federal Probation* 54:28–35.

Coote, S. (2000) "Families and Schools Together (FAST)." Paper presented at the Reducing Criminality Conference, Perth, Australia.

Cordner, G.W. (1995). "Community policing: Elements and effects." *Police Forum* 5(3):1–8.

Cornish, D. (1994). "The procedural analysis of offending and its relevance for situational prevention." In Clarke R.V. (ed.), *Crime Prevention Studies*, vol. 3. Monsey, NY: Criminal Justice Press.

Cornish, D.B. and R.V. Clarke (1986a). *The Reasoning Criminal*. New York: Springer-Verlag.

Cornish, D.B. and R.V. Clarke (1986b). "Situational prevention, crime displacement and rational choice theory." In Heal, K. and G. Laycock (eds.), *Situational Crime Prevention: From Theory into Practice*. London: Her Majesty's Stationery Office.

Cornish, D.B. and R.V. Clarke (2003). "Opportunities, precipitators and criminal decisions: A reply to Wortley's critique of situational crime prevention." In Smith, M.J. and D.B. Cornish (eds.), *Theory for Practice in Situational Crime Prevention*. Monsey, NY: Criminal Justice Press.

Cornish, D.B. and R.V. Clarke (2008). "The rational choice perspective." In Wortley, R. and L. Mazerolle (eds.) *Environmental Criminology and Crime Analysis*. Cullompton, Devon, U.K.: Willan.

Corsaro, N. and E. McGarrell (2009). "Testing a promising homicide reduction strategy: Rassessing the impact of Indianapolis' 'pulling levers' intervention." *Journal of Experimental Criminology* 5:63–82.

Corsaro, N. and E. McGarrell (2010). "Reducing homicide risk in Indianapolis between 1997 and 2000." *Journal of Urban Health* 87:851–864.

Council of State Governments Justice Center (2008). *Mental Health Courts: A Primer for Policymakers and Practitioners.* Washington, DC: Bureau of Justice Assistance. Retrieved from http://www.bja.gov/publications/mhc_primer.pdf

Covington, J. and R.B. Taylor (1991). "Fear of crime in urban residential neighborhoods: Implications of between- and within-neighborhood sources for current models." *Sociological Quarterly* 32:231–249.

Cox, S.M. (1999). "An assessment of an alternative education program for at-risk delinquent youth." *Journal of Research in Crime and Delinquency* 36:323–336.

Cox, S.M., W.S. Davidson, and T.S. Bynum (1995). "A meta-analytic assessment of delinquency-related outcomes of alternative education programs." *Crime & Delinquency* 41:219–234.

Coyne, S.M. (2007). "Does media violence cause violent crime?" *European Journal of Criminal Policy and Research* 13:205–211.

Cozens, P.M. (2014) *Think Crime! Using Evidence, Theory and Crime Prevention Through Environmental Design (CPTED) for Planning Safer Cities.* Quinns Rocks, Australia: Praxis Education.

Cozens, P.M. and T. Davies (2013). "Crime and residential security shutters in an Australian suburb: Exploring perceptions of 'eyes on the street,' social interaction and personal safety." *Crime Prevention and Community Safety* 15:175–191.

Cozens, P.M., G. Saville and D. Hillier (2005). "Crime prevention through environmental design (CPTED): A review and modern bibliography." *Property Management* 23:328–356.

Crawford, A. (1998). *Crime Prevention and Community Safety: Politics, Policies and Practices.* London: Longman.

Crawford, A. (2001). "Joined-up but fragmented: Contradiction, ambiguity and ambivalence at the heart of New Labour's 'Third Way'." In Matthews, R. and J. Pitts (eds.), *Crime, Disorder and Community Safety.* New York: Routledge.

Crawford, A. (2007). "Crime prevention and community safety." In Maguire, M., R. Morgan, and R. Reiner (eds.) *The Oxford Handbook of Criminology*, Fourth Edition. Oxford: Oxford University Press

Crime Stoppers International (2015). http://csiworld.org/

Cristall, J., and Forman-Echols, L. (2009). *Property Abatements—The Other Gang Injunction: Project T.O.U.G.H.* Washington, DC: Bureau of Justice Assistance. National Gang Center Bulletin 2.

Cromwell, P.F., J.N. Olson, and D.W. Avary (1991). *Breaking and Entering: An Ethnographic Analysis of Burglary.* Newbury Park, CA: Sage.

Cullen, F.T. and P. Gendreau (2000). "Assessing correctional rehabilitation: Policy, practice and prospects." In Horney, J. (ed.), *Policies, Processes, and Decisions of the Criminal Justice System. Criminal Justice 2000.* Washington, DC: National Institute of Justice.

Cusson, M. (1993). "A strategic analysis of crime: Criminal tactics as responses to precriminal situations." In Clarke, R.V. and M. Felson (eds.), *Routine Activity and Rational Choice.* New Brunswick, NJ: Transaction.

Dadds, M.R., S.H. Spence, D.E. Holland, P.M. Barrett, and K.R. Laurens (1997). "Prevention and early intervention for anxiety disorders: A controlled trial." *Journal of Consulting and Clinical Psychology* 65:627–635.

Dallas Area Criminal Justice Council (1975). *Geographic Crime Displacement in the Dallas Area.* Dallas, TX: Dallas Area Criminal Justice Council.

Davis, R.C. and A.J. Lurigio (1996). *Fighting Back: Neighborhood Antidrug Strategies.* Thousand Oaks, CA: Sage.

Davis, R.C. and A.J. Lurigio (1998). "Civil abatement as a tool for controlling drug dealing in rental properties." *Security Journal* 11:45–50.

Davis, R.C., A.J. Lurigio, and D.P. Rosenbaum (1993). *Drugs and the Community: Involving Community Residents in Combating the Sale of Illegal Drugs.* Springfield, IL: Charles C Thomas.

Davis, R.C., B.E. Smith, A.J. Lurigio, and W.G. Skogan (1991). *Community Response to Crack: Grassroots Anti-Drug Programs.* Washington, DC: National Institute of Justice.

Davis, R.C., B.E. Smith, and L.B. Nickles (1998). "The deterrent effect of prosecuting domestic violence misdemeanors." *Crime & Delinquency* 44:434–442.

Decker, S.H., G.D. Curry, S. Catalano, A. Watkins, and L. Green (2005). *Strategic Approaches to Community Safety Initiative (SACSI) in St. Louis.* Washington, DC: National Institute of Justice.

DeJong, W. (1993). "Building the peace: The resolving conflict creatively program (RCCP)." *NIJ Program Focus.* Washington, DC: Department of Justice.

DeLeon, G. (1984). "Program-based evaluation research in therapeutic communities." In Tims, F.M. and J.P. Ludford (eds.), *Drug Abuse Treatment Evaluation: Strategies, Progress and Prospects.* Washington, DC: National Institute on Drug Abuse.

DeLeon, G. and M.S. Rosenthal (1989). "Treatment in residential therapeutic communities." In Kleber, H. (ed.), *Treatment of Psychiatric Disorders: A Task Force Report of the American Psychiatric Association,* vol. 2. Washington, DC: American Psychiatric Association.

del Frate, A.A. (1998). *Preventing Crime: Citizens' Experiences Across the World.* UNICRI Issues and Reports No. 9. New York: United Nations.

DeLong, J.V. (1972). "Treatment and rehabilitation." *Dealing with Drug Abuse: A Report to the Ford Foundation.* New York: Praeger.

DeMichele, M. and B. Payne (2009). *Offender Supervision with Electronic Technology: Community Corrections Resources,* Second Edition. Washington, DC: Bureau of Justice Assistance. Retrieved from http://www.appa-net.org/eweb/docs/APPA/pubs/OSET_2.pdf

Denno, D.W. (1990). *Biology and Violence: From Birth to Adulthood.* Cambridge: Cambridge University Press.

DesChamps, S., P.L. Brantingham, and P.J. Brantingham (1991). "The British Columbia transit fare evasion audit: A description of a situational prevention process." *Security Journal* 2:211–218.

Deutshmann, P.J. (1959). *News-page Content of Twelve Metropolitan Dailies.* Cincinnati, OH: Scripps-Howard Research Center.

Dezhbakhsh, H., P.H. Rubin, and J.M. Shepherd (2003). "Does capital punishment have a deterrent effect?: New evidence from postmoratorium panel data." *American Law and Economics Review* 52:344–376.

DiBlasio, N. (2012). "YouTube: The latest crime solver." *USA Today* July 5:A1.

Ditton, J. and J. Duffy (1983). "Bias in the newspaper reporting of crime news." *British Journal of Criminology* 23:159–165.

Ditton, J. and E. Short (1999). "Yes, it works, no, it doesn't: Comparing the effects of open-street CCTV in two adjacent Scottish town centres." In Painter, K. and N. Tilley (eds.), *Surveillance of Public Space: CCTV, Street Lighting and Crime Prevention.* Monsey, NY: Criminal Justice Press.

Dobash, R.E., P. Schlesinger, R. Dobash, and C.K. Weaver (1998). " 'Crimewatch UK': Women's interpretation of televised violence." In Fishman, M. and G. Cavender (eds.), *Entertaining Crime: Television Reality Programs.* New York: Aldine de Gruyter.

Dominick, J.R. (1978). "Crime and law enforcement in the mass media." In Winick, C. (ed.), *Deviance and Mass Media.* Beverly Hills, CA: Sage.

Donnelly, P. and C. Kimble (1997). "Community organizing, environmental change, and neighborhood crime." *Crime & Delinquency* 43:493–511.

Donohue, J.J. (2009). "Assessing the relative benefits of incarceration: The overall change over the previous decades and the benefits on the margin." In Raphael, S. and M.A. Stoll (eds.), *Do Prisons Make Us Safer?: The Benefits and Costs of the Prison Boom.* New York: Sage.

Donohue, J.J. and J. Wolfers (2005). "Uses and abuses of empirical evidence in the death penalty debate." *Stanford Law Review* 58:791–846.

Donovan, P. (1998). "Armed with the power of television: Reality crime programming and the reconstruction of law and order in the United States." In Fishman, M. and G. Cavender (eds.), *Entertaining Crime: Reality Television Programs.* New York: Aldine de Gruyter.

Doob, A.N. and G.E. Macdonald (1979). "Television viewing and fear of victimization: Is the relationship causal?" *Journal of Personality and Social Psychology* 37:170–179.

Doran, B.J. and M.B. Burgess (2012). *Putting Fear of Crime on the Map: Investigating Perceptions of Crime Using Geographic Information Systems.* New York: Springer.

Drug Courts Program Office (1998). *Looking at a Decade of Drug Courts.* Washington, DC: U.S. Department of Justice.

Drug Courts Program Office (2000). *About the Drug Courts Program Office.* Washington, DC: U.S. Department of Justice.

DuBois, D.L., N. Portillo, J.E. Rhodes, N. Silverthorn, and J.C. Valentine (2011). "How effective are mentoring programs for youth?: A systematic assessment of the evidence." *Psychological Science in the Public Interest* 12:57–91.

DuBois, D.L., B.E. Holloway, J.C. Valentine, and H. Cooper (2002). "Effectiveness of mentoring programs for youth: A meta-analytic review." *American Journal of Community Psychology* 30:157–197.

Dunford, F.W. (1990). "System initiated warrants for suspects of misdemeanor domestic assault: A pilot study." *Justice Quarterly* 7:631–654.

Durose, M.R., A.D. Cooper, and H.N. Snyder (2014). *Recidivism of Prisoners Released in 30 States in 2005: Patterns from 2005 to 2010.* Washington, DC: Bureau of Justice Statistics. Retrieved from http://www.bjs.gov/content/pub/pdf/rprts05p0510.pdf

Eck, J.E. (1993). "The threat of crime displacement." *Criminal Justice Abstracts* 25:527–546.

Eck, J.E. (1994). "Drug Markets and Drug Places: A Case-control Study of the Spatial Structure of Illicit Drug Dealing." Ph.D. dissertation, College Park, MD: University of Maryland.

Eck, J.E. (1998). "Preventing crime by controlling drug dealing on private rental property." *Security Journal* 11:37–43.

Eck, J.E. (2002). "Learning from experience in problem-oriented policing and situational prevention: The positive functions of weak evaluations and the negative functions of strong ones." In N. Tilley (ed.), *Analysis for Crime Prevention.* Monsey, NY: Criminal Justice Press.

Eck, J.E. and D.P. Rosenbaum (1994). "The new police order: Effectiveness, equity, and efficiency in community policing." In Rosenbaum, D.P. (ed.), *The Challenge of Community Policing: Testing the Promises.* Thousand Oaks, CA: Sage.

Eck, J.E. and W. Spelman (1989). "A problem-oriented approach to police service delivery." In Kenney, D. (ed.), *Police and Policing: Contemporary Issues.* New York: Praeger.

Eck, J.E. and J. Wartell (1998). "Improving the management of rental properties with drug problems: A randomized experiment." In Mazerolle, L.G. and J. Roehl (eds.), *Civil Remedies and Crime Prevention.* Monsey, NY: Criminal Justice Press.

Eck, J.E. and J. Wartell (1999). "Reducing crime and drug dealing by improving place management: A randomized experiment." *NIJ Research Preview.* Washington, DC: National Institute of Justice.

Ehrlich, I. (1975). "The deterrent effects of capital punishment: A question of life and death." *American Economic Review* 65:397–417.

Ehrlich, I. (1977). "Capital punishment and deterrence: Some further thoughts and additional evidence." *Journal of Political Economy* 85:741–788.

Eiser, C. and J.R. Eiser (1988). *Drug Education in Schools.* New York: Springer-Verlag.

Ekblom, P. (1993). "Scoping and scoring: Linking measures of action to measures of outcome in a multi-scheme, multi-site crime prevention programme." In Zahm, D. and P. Cromwell (eds.), *Proceedings of the International Seminar on Environmental Criminology and Crime Analysis.* Coral Gables, FL: Florida Criminal Justice Executive Institute.

Ekblom, P. (2002). "From the source to the mainstream is uphill: The challenge of transferring knowledge of crime prevention through replication, innovation and anticipation". In N. Tilley (ed.), *Analysis for Crime Prevention.* Monsey, NY: Criminal Justice Press.

Ekblom, P. (2005). "Designing products against crime." In Tilley, N. (ed.), *Handbook of Crime Prevention and Community Safety.* Portland, OR: Willan.

Ekblom, P. (2008). "Designing products against crime." In Wortley, R. and L. Mazerolle (eds.), *Environmental Criminology and Crime Analysis.* Cullompton, Devon, U.K.: Willan.

Ekblom, P. (2011a). *Crime Prevention, Security and Community Safety using the 5Is Framework.* New York: Palgrave Macmillan.

Ekblom, P. (2011b). "Deconstructing CPTED … and reconstructing it for practice, knowledge management and research." *European Journal of Criminal Policy and Research* 17:7–28.

Ekblom, P., K. Bowers, L. Gamman, A. Sidebottom, C. Thomas, A. Thorpe, and M. Willcocks (2012). "Reducing handbag theft." In Ekblom, P. (ed.), *Design Against Crime: Crime Proofing Everyday Products.* Boulder, CO: Lynne Rienner.

Ekblom, P. and A. Hirschfield (2014). "Developing an alternative formulation of SCP principles—the Ds (11 and counting)." *Crime Science* 3:2.

Ekblom, P., H. Law, and M. Sutton (1996a). *Safer Cities and Domestic Burglary.* London: Home Office Research and Statistics Directorate.

Ekblom, P., H. Law, and M. Sutton (1996b). *Domestic Burglary Schemes in the Safer Cities Programme. Research Findings No. 42.* London: Home Office Research and Statistics Directorate.

Ekblom, P. and K. Pease (1995). "Evaluating crime prevention." In Tonry, M. and N. Morris (eds.), *Crime and Justice: A Review of Research*, vol. 19. Chicago: University of Chicago Press.

Elder, R., R. Shults, D. Sleet, J.L. Nichols, R.S. Thompson, and W. Rajab (2004). "Effectiveness of mass media campaigns for reducing drinking and driving and alcohol-involved crashes: A systematic review." *American Journal of Preventive Medicine* 27:57–65.

Elfers, H., D. Reynald, M. Averdijk, W. Bernasco, and R. Block (2008). "Modelling crime flow between neighbourhoods in terms of distance and of intervening opportunities." *Crime Prevention and Community Safety* 10:85–96.

Ellingworth, D., G. Farrell, and K. Pease (1995). "A victim is a victim is a victim? Chronic victimization in four sweeps of the British Crime Survey." *British Journal of Criminology* 35:360–365.

Elliott, D.S. (1994). "Serious, violent offenders: Onset, developmental course, and termination." *Criminology* 32:1–21.

Elliott, D.S. (2000). "Editor's introduction." In Olweus, D. and S. Limber (eds.), *Bullying Prevention Program: Blueprints for Violence Prevention*. Boulder, CO: Institute of Behavioral Science.

Elliott, D.S. and S.S. Ageton (1981). *The Epidemiology of Delinquent Behavior and Drug Use Among American Adolescents, 1976–1978*. Boulder, CO: Behavioral Research Institute.

Elliott, D.S., S.S. Ageton, and R.J. Canter (1979). "An integrated theoretical perspective on delinquent behavior." *Journal of Research in Crime and Delinquency* 16:3–27.

Elliott, D.S. and D.H. Huizinga. (1984). *The Relationship Between Delinquent Behavior and ADM Problems*. Boulder, CO: Behavioral Research Institute.

Elliott, D.S., D.H. Huizinga, and S.S. Ageton (1985). *Explaining Delinquency and Drug Use*. Beverly Hills, CA: Sage.

Elliott, D.S., D.H. Huizinga, and S. Menard (1989). *Multiple Problem Youth: Delinquency, Substance Use and Mental Health Problems*. New York: Springer-Verlag.

Elliott, D.S. and S. Menard (1996). "Delinquent friends and delinquent behavior: Temporal and developmental patterns." In Hawkins, J.D. (ed.), *Delinquency and Crime: Current Theories*. Cambridge: Cambridge University Press.

Ellis, E., J. Fortune and G. Peters (2007). "Partnership problems: Analysis and re-design." *Crime Prevention and Community Safety* 9:34–51.

Empey, L.T. and S.G. Lubbeck (1971). *Explaining Delinquency*. Lexington, MA: Lexington Books.

Ennis, B.J. and T.R. Litwack (1974). "Psychiatry and the presumption of expertise: Flipping coins in the courtroom." *California Law Review* 62:693–752.

Ennis, P.H. (1967). *Criminal Victimization in the U.S.: A Report of a National Survey. President's Commission on Law Enforcement and the Administration of Justice. Field Surveys II*. Washington, DC: U.S. Government Printing Office.

Erez, E., P. Ibarra, and N.A. Lurie (2004). "Electronic monitoring of domestic violence cases: A study of two bilateral programs." *Federal Probation* 68(1). Retrieved from http://www.uscourts.gov/fedprob/June_2004/monitoring.html

Erickson, M.L., J.P. Gibbs, and G.F. Jensen (1977). "The deterrence doctrine and the perceived certainty of legal punishments." *American Sociological Review* 42:305–317.

Erwin, B.E. (1990). "Old and new tools for the modern probation officer." *Crime & Delinquency* 36:61–74.

Esbensen, F. (1987). "Foot patrols: Of what value?" *American Journal of Police* 6:45–65.

Esbensen, F. and D. Huizinga (1993). "Gangs, drugs and delinquency in a survey of urban youth." *Criminology* 31:565–589.

Esbensen, F., D.W. Osgood, D. Peterson, T.T. Taylor, and D.C. Carson (2013). "Short- and long-term outcome results from a multisite evaluation of the G.R.E.A.T. program." *Criminology and Public Policy* 12, 375–412.

Esbensen, F., D. Peterson, T.J. Taylor, A. Freng, and D.W. Osgood (2004). "Gang prevention: A case study of a primary prevention program." In F. Esbensen, S.G. Tibbetts and L. Gaines (eds.), *American Youth Gangs at the Millennium*. Long Grove, IL: Waveland Press.

Esbensen, F., D. Peterson, T.J. Taylor, A. Freng, D.W. Osgood, D.C. Carson, and K.N. Matsuda (2011). "Evaluation and evolution of the gang resistance education and training (G.R.E.A.T.) program." *Journal of School Violence* 10:53–70.

Everson, S. and P.F. Woodhouse (2007). "Designing out crime: Has section 17 of the UK's Crime and Disorder Act 1998 been effective?" In Farrell, G., K.J. Bowers, S.D. Johnson and M. Townsley (eds.), *Imagination for Crime Prevention: Essays in Honour of Ken Pease*. Cullompton, Devon, U.K.: Willan.

Fabricant, R. (1979). "The distribution of criminal offenses in an urban environment: A spatial analysis of criminal spillovers and of juvenile offenders." *American Journal of Economics and Society* 38:31–47.

Fagan, J. (1989). "The social organization of drug use and drug dealing among urban gangs." *Criminology* 27:633–670.

Fagan, J., and J.G. Weis (1990). *Drug Use and Delinquency Among Inner City Youth*. New York: Springer-Verlag.

Fagan, J., F.E. Zimring, and A. Geller (2006). "Capital punishment and capital market: Market share and the deterrent effects of the death penalty." *Texas Law Review* 84:1803–1867.

Families and Schools Together (FAST) (2015). http://www.familiesandschools.org/

Fareed, A., Vayalapalli, S., Stout, S., Casarella, J., Drexler, K., and Bailey, S. P. (2011). "Effect of methadone maintenance treatment on heroin craving: A literature review." *Journal of Addictive Diseases* 30:27–38.

Farrell, A.D. and A.L. Meyer (1997). "The effectiveness of a school-based curriculum for reducing violence among urban sixth-grade students." *American Journal of Public Health* 87:979–988.

Farrell, G. (2005). "Progress and prospects in the prevention of repeat victimization." In Tilley, N. (ed.), *Handbook of Crime Prevention and Community Safety*. Portland, OR: Willan.

Farrell, G. and K. Pease (2006). "Preventing repeat residential burglary victimization." In Welsh, B.C. and D.P. Farrington (eds.), *Preventing Crime: What Works for Children, Offenders, Victims and Places*. New York: Springer.

Farrell, G. and K. Pease (2014). "Repeat victimization." In Bruinsma, G. and D. Weisburd (eds.), *Encyclopedia of Criminology and Criminal Justice*. New York: Springer.

Farrell, G., C. Phillips, and K. Pease (1995). "Like taking candy: Why does repeat victimization occur?" *British Journal of Criminology* 33:384–399.

Farrell, G., A. Tseloni, and K. Pease (2005). "Repeat victimization in the ICVS and the NCVS." *Crime Prevention and Community Safety* 7(3):7–18.

Farrington, D.P. (1985). "Predicting self-reported and official delinquency." In Farrington, D.P. and R. Tarling (eds.), *Prediction in Criminology*. Albany, NY: SUNY Press.

Farrington, D.P. (1989). "Early predictors of adolescent aggression and adult violence." *Violence and Victims* 4:79–100.

Farrington, D.P. (1996). "The explanation and prevention of youthful offending." In Hawkins, J.D. (ed.), *Delinquency and Crime: Current Theories*. Cambridge: Cambridge University Press.

Farrington, D.P. (1997). "The relationship between low resting heart rate and violence." In Raine, A., P.A. Brennan, D.P. Farrington and S.A. Mednick (eds.), *Biosocial Bases of Violence*. New York: Plenum.

Farrington, D.P. (2007). "Childhood risk factors and risk-focused prevention." In Maguire, M., R. Morgan and R. Reiner (eds.) *The Oxford Handbook of Criminology*, Fourth Edition. Oxford: Oxford University Press.

Farrington, D.P., T.H. Bennett, and B.C. Welsh (2007). "The Cambridge evaluation of the effects of CCTV on crime." In Farrell, G., K.J. Bowers, S.D. Johnson, and M. Townsley (eds.), *Imagination for Crime Prevention: Essays in Honour of Ken Pease*. Cullompton, Devon, U.K.: Willan.

Farrington, D.P., S. Bowen, A. Buckle, T. Burns-Howell, J. Burrows, and M. Speed (1993). "An experiment on the prevention of shoplifting." In Clarke, R.V. (ed.), *Crime Prevention Studies*, vol. 1. Monsey, NY: Criminal Justice Press.

Farrington, D.P. and R. Loeber (1998). "Transatlantic replicability of risk factors in the development of delinquency." In Cohen, P., C. Slomkowski, and L.N. Robbins (eds.), *Where and When: Geographic and Generational Influences on Psychopathology*. Mahwah, NJ: Erlbaum.

Farrington, D.P. and K.A. Painter (2003). "How to evaluate the impact of CCTV on crime." *Crime Prevention and Community Safety* 5(3):7–16.

Federal Bureau of Investigation (FBI) (2014). *Crime in the United States, 2013.* https://www.fbi.gov/about-us/cjis/ucr/crime-in-the-u.s/2013/crime-in-the-u.s.-2013

Feeney, F. (1986). "Robbers as decision makers." In Cornish, D.B. and R.V. Clarke (eds.), *The Reasoning Criminal: Rational Choice Perspectives on Offending*. New York: Springer Verlag.

Feinberg, M.E., M.T. Greenberg, D.W. Osgood, J. Sartorius, and D. Bontempo (2007). "Effects of the Communities that Care model in Pennsylvania on youth risk and problem behaviors." *Prevention Science* 8:261–270.

Feld, B.C. (1999). "Rehabilitation, retribution and restorative justice: Alternative conceptions of juvenile justice." In G. Bazemore and L. Walgrave (eds.), *Restorative Juvenile Justice: Repairing the Harm of Youth Crime*. Monsey, NY: Criminal Justice Press.

Felson, M., M.E. Belanger, G.M. Bichler, C.D. Bruzinske, G.S. Campbell, C.L. Fried, K.C. Grofik, I.S. Mazur, A.B. O'Regan, P.J. Sweeney, A.L. Ullman, and L.M. Williams (1996). "Redesigning hell: Preventing crime and disorder at the port authority bus terminal." In Clarke, R.V. (ed.), *Preventing Mass Transit Crime*. Monsey, NY: Criminal Justice Press.

Felson, M. and R.V. Clarke (1998). *Opportunity Makes the Thief: Practical Theory for Crime Prevention*. London: Home Office Police and Reducing Crime Unit.

Ferguson, C.J. (2013). *Adolescents, Crime and the Media: A Critical Analysis*. New York: Springer.

Ferguson, K.M. and C.H. Mindel (2007). "Modeling fear of crime in Dallas neighborhoods: A test of social capital theory." *Crime & Delinquency* 53:322–349.

Ferraro, K.F. (1995). *Fear of Crime: Interpreting Victimization Risk*. Albany, NY: SUNY Press.

Ferraro, K.F. and R.L. LaGrange (1987). "The measurement of fear of crime." *Sociological Inquiry* 57:70–101.

Ferraro, K.F. and R.L. LaGrange (1988). "Are older people afraid of crime?" *Journal of Aging Studies* 2:277–287.

Figgie International (1983). *The Figgie Report, Part IV: Reducing Crime in America, Successful Community Efforts*. Willoughby, OH: Figgie International.

Finch, E. (2011). "Strategies of adaptation and diversification: The impact of chip and PIN technology on the activities of fraudsters." *Security Journal* 24:251–268.

Fisher, B.S. (1989). "The 'community hypothesis' revisited: The effects of participation after controlling for self-selection bias." Paper presented at the American Society of Criminology Annual Meeting, Washington, DC.

Fisher, B.S. and J.L. Nasar (1992). "Fear of crime in relation to three exterior site features: Prospect, refuge, and escape." *Environment and Behavior* 24:35–65.

Fishman, R. (1977). "An evaluation of criminal recidivism in projects providing rehabilitation and diversion services in New York City." *Journal of Criminal Law and Criminology* 68:283–305.

Fleming, Z., P. Brantingham, and P. Brantingham (1994). "Exploring auto theft in British Columbia." In Clarke, R.V. (ed.), *Crime Prevention Studies*, vol. 3. Monsey, NY: Criminal Justice Press.

Flexon, J.L. and R.T. Guerette (2009). "Differential effects of an offender-focuses crime prevention media campaign." *Journal of Criminal Justice* 37:608–616.

Flynn, R.J. (2008). "Communities that Care: A comprehensive system for youth prevention and promotion, and Canadian applications to date." *IPC Review* 2:83–106.

Foglia, W.D. (1997). "Perceptual deterrence and the mediating effect of internalized norms among inner-city teenagers." *Journal of Research in Crime and Delinquency* 34:414–442.

Ford, D. and A. Schmidt (1985). *Electronic Monitored Home Confinement. National Institute of Justice Research in Action*. Washington, DC: National Institute of Justice.

Forrester, D.H., M.R. Chatterton, and K. Pease (1988). "The Kirkholt Burglary Prevention Demonstration Project." *Home Office Crime Prevention Paper No. 13*. London: Her Majesty's Stationery Office.

Forrester, D.H., S. Frenz, M. O'Connell, and K. Pease (1990). *The Kirkholt Burglary Prevention Project: Phase II*. London: Home Office.

Fors, S.W. and D.G. Rojek (1991). "A comparison of drug involvement between runaways and school youths." *Journal of Drug Education* 21:13–25.

Forst, B.E. (1977). "The deterrent effect of capital punishment: A cross-state analysis of the 1960s." *Minnesota Law Review* 61:743–767.

Fowler, F. and T.W. Mangione (1982). *Neighborhood Crime, Fear and Social Control: A Second Look at the Hartford Program*. Washington, DC: National Institute of Justice.

Fowler, F., M.E. McCalla, and T.W. Mangione (1979). *Reducing Residential Crime and Fear: The Hartford Neighborhood Crime Prevention Program*. Washington, DC: National Institute of Law Enforcement and Criminal Justice.

Friel, C.M. and J.B. Vaughn (1986). "A consumer's guide to the electronic monitoring of probationers." *Federal Probation* 50(3):3–14.

Friel, C.M., J.B. Vaughn, and R. del Carmen (1987). *Electronic Monitoring and Correctional Policy: The Technology and its Application*. Washington, DC: National Institute of Justice.

FRIENDS (2015). *The FRIENDS Program*. http://friendsprograms.com/

Furstenburg, F.F. (1972). "Fear of crime and its effects on citizen behavior." In A. Biderman (ed.), *Crime and Justice: A Symposium*. New York: Nailburg.

Gable, R.K. (1986). "Application of personal telemonitoring to current problems in corrections." *Journal of Criminal Justice* 14:167–176.

Gabor, T. (1981). "The crime displacement hypothesis: An empirical examination." *Crime & Delinquency* 27:390–404.

Gabor, T. (1990). "Crime displacement and situational prevention: Toward the development of some principles." *Canadian Journal of Criminology* 32:41–73.

Gaes, G.G., T.J. Flanagan, L.T. Motiuk, and L. Stewart (1999). "Adult correctional treatment." In Tonry, M. and J. Petersilia (eds.), *Prisons*. Chicago: University of Chicago Press.

Gamoran, A., R.N. López Turley, A. Turner, and R. Fish (2012). "Differences between Hispanic and non-Hispanic families in social capital and child development: First-year findings from an experimental study." *Research in Social Stratification and Mobility* 30:97–112.

Garofalo, J. (1979). "Victimization and the fear of crime." *Journal of Research in Crime and Delinquency* 16:80–97.

Garofalo, J. (1981). "Crime and the mass media: A selective review of research." *Journal of Research in Crime and Delinquency* 18:319–350.

Garofalo, J. and K.J. Connelly (1980). "Dispute resolution centers, part I: major features and processes." *Criminal Justice Abstracts* 12:416–436.

Garofalo, J. and M. McLeod (1988). "Improving the use and effectiveness of neighborhood watch programs." *NIJ Research in Action*. Washington, DC: National Institute of Justice.

Garrett, C.J. (1985). "Effects of residential treatment on adjudicated delinquents: A meta-analysis." *Journal of Research in Crime and Delinquency* 22:287–308.

Gates, L.B. and W.M. Rohe (1987). "Fear and reactions to crime: A revised model." *Urban Affairs Quarterly* 22:425–453.

Geen, R.G. and S.L. Thomas (1986). "The immediate effects of media violence on behavior." *Journal of Social Issues* 42:7–27.

Geerken, M.R. and W.R. Gove (1977). "Deterrence, overload, and incapacitation: An empirical evaluation." *Social Forces* 56:424–447.

General Accounting Office (GAO) (1997). *Drug Courts: Overview of Growth, Characteristics, and Results*. Washington, DC: U.S. Government Printing Office.

Gensheimer, L.K., J.P. Mayer, R. Gottschalk, and W.S. Davidson (1986). "Diverting youth from the juvenile justice system: A meta-analysis of intervention efficacy." In Apter, S.J. and A.P. Goldstein (eds.), *Youth Violence: Programs and Prospects*. New York: Pergamon.

Gerbner, G., L. Gross, M.F. Eleey, M. Jackson-Beeck, S. Jeffries-Fox, and N. Signorielle (1977). "TV violence no. 8: The highlights." *Journal of Communication* 27:171–180.

Gerbner, G., L. Gross, M. Jackson-Beeck, S. Jeffries-Fox, and N. Signorielle (1978). "Cultural indicators: Violence profile no. 9." *Journal of Communication* 28:176–207.

Gerbner, G., L. Gross, N. Signorielle, and M. Morgan (1980). "Television violence, victimization, and power." *American Behavioral Scientist* 23:705–716.

Gerbner, G., L. Gross, N. Signorielle, M. Morgan, and M. Jackson-Beeck (1979). "The demonstration of power: Violence profile no. 10." *Journal of Communication* 29:177–196.

Geva, R. and I. Israel (1982). "Anti-burglary campaign in Jerusalem: Pilot project update." *Police Chief* 49:44–46.

Gibbs, J.P. (1968). "Crime, punishment, and deterrence." *Social Science Quarterly* 48:515–530.

Gibbs, J.P. (1975). *Crime, Punishment and Deterrence*. New York: Elsevier.

Gies, S.V., R. Gainey, M.I. Cohen, E. Healy, M. Yeide, A. Bekelman and A. Bobnis (2013). *Monitoring High-risk Gang Offenders with GPS Technology: An Evaluation of the California Supervision Program Final Report*. Washington, DC: Department of Justice.

Gill, M. and R. Matthews (1994). "Robbers on robbery: Offenders' perspectives." In Gill, M. (ed.), *Crime at Work: Studies in Security and Crime Prevention*. Leicester, U.K.: Perpetuity Press.

Gill, M. and K. Pease (1998). "Repeat robbers: Are they different?" In Gill, M. (ed.), *Crime at Work: Increasing the Risk for Offenders*. Leicester, U.K.: Perpetuity Press.

Gill, M. and A. Spriggs (2005). *Assessing the Impact of CCTV*. London: Home Office.

Gilling, D. (1997). *Crime Prevention: Theory, Policy and Politics*. London: UCL Press.

Gilling, D. (2005). "Partnerships and crime prevention." In Tilley, N. (ed.), *Handbook of Crime Prevention and Community Safety*. Portland, OR: Willan.

Glaser, D. (1964). *The Effectiveness of a Prison and Parole System*. Indianapolis, IN: Bobbs-Merrill.

Gold, M. (1978). "Scholastic experiences, self-esteem, and delinquent behavior: A theory for alternative schools." *Crime & Delinquency* 24:290–308.

Gold, M. and D. Mann (1972). "Delinquency as defense." *American Journal of Orthopsychiatry* 42:463–477.

Gold, M. and D. Mann (1983). "Alternative schools for troublesome youths." *Urban Review* 14:305–316.

Goldkamp, J.S. and D. Weiland (1993). "Assessing the impact of Dade County's felony drug court." *NIJ Research in Brief*. Washington, DC: U.S. Department of Justice.

Goldstein, P.J. (1989). "Drugs and violent crime." In Weiner, N.A. and M.E. Wolfgang (eds.), *Pathways to Criminal Violence*. Newbury Park, CA: Sage.

Goldstein, P.J., H.H. Brownstein, and P.J. Ryan (1992). "Drug-related homicide in New York: 1984 and 1988." *Crime & Delinquency* 38:459–476.

Gomme, I.M. (1986). "Fear of crime among Canadians: A multi-variate analysis." *Journal of Criminal Justice* 14:249–258.

Gomme, I.M. (1988). "The role of experience in the production of fear of crime: A text of a causal model." *Canadian Journal of Criminology* 30:67–76.

Gordon, M.T., J. Reiss, and T. Taylor (1979). *Crime in the Newspapers and Fear in the Neighborhoods: Some Unintended Consequences*. Evanston, IL: Center for Urban Affairs, Northwestern University.

Gorman-Smith, D., P.H. Tolan, A. Zelli, and L.R. Huesmann (1996). "The relation of family functioning to violence among inner-city minority youths." *Journal of Family Psychology* 10:115–129.

Gottfredson, D.C. (1986a). "An empirical test of school-based environmental and individual interventions to reduce the risk of delinquent behavior." *Criminology* 24:705–731.

Gottfredson, D.C. (1986b). *An Assessment of a Delinquency Prevention Demonstration with both Individual and Environmental Interventions*. Baltimore: Johns Hopkins University.

Gottfredson, D.C. (1987). "Examining the potential of delinquency prevention through alternative education." *Today's Delinquent* 6:87–100.

Gottfredson, D.M., M.R. Gottfredson, and J. Garofalo (1977). "Time served in prison and parole outcomes among parolee risk categories." *Journal of Criminal Justice* 5:1–12.

Gottfredson, D.M., P.B. Hoffman, M.H. Sigler, and L.T. Wilkins (1975). "Making paroling policy explicit." *Crime & Delinquency* 21:34–44.

Gottfredson, D.M., S.S. Najaka, and B. Kearley (2003). "Effectiveness of drug treatment courts: Evidence from a randomized trial." *Criminology and Public Policy* 2:171–198.

Gottfredson, G.D. and D.C. Gottfredson (1985). *Victimization in Schools.* New York: Plenum.

Gottfredson, M.R. and T. Hirschi (1990). *A General Theory of Crime.* Stanford, CA: Stanford University Press.

Gowdy, V.B. (1993). "Intermediate sanctions." *NIJ Research in Brief.* Washington, DC: U.S. Department of Justice.

Graber, D. (1977). "Ideological components in the perceptions of crime and crime news." Paper presented at the Meeting of the Society for the Study of Social Problems.

Graber, D. (1980). *Crime News and the Public.* New York, NY: Praeger.

Graziano, A.M. and K. Mooney (1984). *Children and Behavior Therapy.* New York: Aldine.

Green, D.E. (1989a). "Past behavior as a measure of actual future behavior: An unresolved issue in perceptual deterrence research." *Journal of Criminal Law and Criminology* 80:781–804.

Green, D.E. (1989b). "Measures of illegal behavior in individual-level deterrence research." *Journal of Research in Crime and Delinquency* 26:253–275.

Green, L. (1995a). "Cleaning up drug hot spots in Oakland, California: The displacement and diffusion effect." *Justice Quarterly* 12:737–754.

Green, L. (1995b). "Policing places with drug problems: The multi-agency response team approach." In Eck, J.E. and D. Weisburd (eds.), *Crime and Place.* Monsey, NY: Criminal Justice Press.

Greenberg, D. (1975). "The incapacitative effect of imprisonment: some estimates." *Law and Society Review* 9:541–580.

Greenberg, M.T. and C. Kusche (1996). *The PATHS Project: Preventive Intervention for Children: Final Report.* Washington, DC: National Institute of Mental Health.

Greenberg, M.T. and C. Kusche (1997). "Improving children's emotion regulation and social competence: The effects of the PATHS curriculum." Paper presented at the Society for Research in Child Development Meeting, Washington, DC.

Greenberg, M.T. and C. Kusche (1998). *Promoting Alternative Thinking Strategies (PATHS): Blueprints for Violence Prevention.* Boulder, CO: Institute of Behavioral Science.

Greenberg, M.T., C. Kusche, E.T. Cook, and J.P. Quamma (1995). "Promoting emotional competence in school-aged children: The effects of the PATHS curriculum." *Development and Psychopathology* 7:117–136.

Greenberg, S.W., W.M. Rohe, and J.R. Williams (1982). *Safe and Secure Neighborhoods: Physical Characteristics and Informal Territorial Control in High and Low Crime Neighborhoods.* Washington, DC: National Institute of Justice.

Greenberg, S.W., W.M. Rohe, and J.R. Williams (1985). *Informal Citizen Action and Crime Prevention at the Neighborhood Level: Synthesis and Assessment of the Research.* Washington, DC: National Institute of Justice.

Greene, J.R. and S.D. Mastrofski (1988). *Community Policing: Rhetoric or Reality?* New York: Praeger.

Greenwood, P.W. (1982). *Selective Incapacitation*. Santa Monica, CA: RAND Corp.

Greer, C. and R. Reiner (2012). "Mediated mayhem: Media, crime, criminal justice." In Maguire, M., R. Morgan, and R. Reiner (eds.), *The Oxford Handbook of Criminology*. Oxford: Oxford University Press.

Gresham, P., J. Stockdael, I. Bartholomew, and K. Bullock (2001). *An Evaluation of the Impact of Crimestoppers*. Briefing Note 10/01. London: Home Office.

Groff, E.R., J.H., Ratcliffe, C.P. Haberman, E.T. Sorg, N.M. Joyce, and R.B. Taylor (2015). "Does what police do at hot spots matter? The Philadelphia policing tactics experiment." *Criminology* 53:23–53.

Grogger, J. (2002). "The effects of civil gang injunctions on reported violent crime: Evidence from Los Angeles County." *Journal of Law and Economics 4,* 69–90.

Grohe, B., M. DeValve, and E. Quinn (2012). "Is perception reality?: The comparison of citizens' levels of fear of crime versus perception of crime problems in communities." *Crime Prevention and Community Safety* 14:196–211.

Grossman, J.B. and J.P. Tierney (1998). "Does mentoring work?: An impact study of the Big Brothers Big Sisters program." *Evaluation Review* 22:403–426.

Grove, L. and G. Farrell (2012). "Once bitten, twice shy: Repeat victimization and its prevention." In B.C. Welsh and D.P. Farrington (eds.), *The Oxford Handbook of Crime Prevention*. Oxford: Oxford University Press.

Guerette, R.T (2009). *Analyzing Crime Displacement and Diffusion*, Tool Guide No. 10. Centre for Problem-Oriented Policing. Available at http://www.popcenter.org/tools/pdfs/displacement.pdf

Guerette, R.T. and K.J. Bowers (2009). "Assessing the extent of crime displacement and diffusion of benefits: A review of situational crime prevention evaluations." *Criminology* 47:1331–1368.

Gunter, B. (1987). *Television and the Fear of Crime*. London: Libby.

Hamilton-Smith, N. (2002). "Anticipated consequences: Developing a strategy for the targeted measurement of displacement and diffusion of benefits." In Tilley, N. (ed.), *Evaluation for Crime Prevention*. Monsey, NY: Criminal Justice Press.

Handford, M. (1994). "Electronic tagging in action: A case study in retailing." In Gill, M. (ed.), *Crime at Work: Studies in Security and Crime Prevention*. Leicester, U.K.: Perpetuity Press.

Hanson, D.J. (1980). "Drug education: Does it work?" In Scarpitti, F.S. and S.K. Datesman (eds.), *Drugs and the Youth Culture*. Beverly Hills, CA: Sage.

Harrell, A. (1998). "Drug courts and the role of graduated sanctions." *NIJ Research Preview*. Washington, DC: National Institute of Justice.

Harrell, E. and L. Langton (2013). *Victims of Identity Theft, 2012*. Washington, DC: Bureau of Justice Statistics.

Harrison, L. and J. Gfroerer (1992). "The intersection of drug use and criminal behavior: Results from the national household survey on drug abuse." *Crime and Delinquency* 38:422–443.

Hartnagel, T.F., T.J. Teevan, and J.J. McIntyre (1975). "Television violence and violent behavior." *Social Forces* 54:341–351.

Hartnett, S.M. and W.G. Skogan (1999). "Community policing: Chicago's experience." *National Institute of Justice Journal* (April):3–11.

Hartstone, E.C. and D.M. Richetelli (2005). *Final Assessment of the Strategic Approaches to Community Safety Initiative in New Haven.* Washington, DC: National Institute of Justice.

Haverkamp, R., M. Mayer and R. Levy (2004). "Electronic monitoring in Europe." *European Journal of Crime, Criminal Law and Criminal Justice* 12:36–45.

Hawkins, J.D. (1999). "Preventing crime and violence through Communities that Care." *European Journal on Criminal Policy and Research* 7: 443–458.

Hawkins, J.D., M.W. Arthur, and R.F. Catalano (1995). "Preventing substance abuse." In Tonry, M. and D.P. Farrington (eds.), *Building a Safer Society: Strategic Approaches to Crime Prevention.* Chicago: University of Chicago Press.

Hawkins, J.D., E.C. Brown, S. Oesterle, M.W. Arthur, R.D. Abbott, and R.F. Catalano (2008). "Early effects of Communities that Care on targeted risks and initiation of delinquent behavior and substance use." *Journal of Adolescent Health* 43:15–22.

Hawkins, J.D., S. Oesterle, E.C. Brown, R.D. Abbott, and R.F. Catalano (2014). "Youth problem behaviors 8 years after implementing the Communities that Care prevention system: A community-randomized trial." *JAMA Pediatrician* 168:122–129.

Hawkins, J.D., B.H. Smith, K.G. Kosterman, and R.F. Catalano (2007). "Promoting social developments and preventing health and behavior problems during the elementary grades: Results from the Seattle Social Development Project." *Violence and Offenders* 2:161–181.

Hawkins, J. D., and J.G. Weis (1985). "The social development model: An integrated approach to delinquency prevention." *Journal of Primary Prevention* 6:73–97.

Hayes, H. and K. Daly (2004). "Conferencing and reoffending in Queensland." *Australian and New Zealand Journal of Criminology* 37:167–191.

Hayes, J.G. (1982). *The Impact of Citizen Involvement in Preventing Crime in Public Housing.* Charlotte, NC: Charlotte Housing Authority.

Hayes, R. and D.M. Downs (2011). "Controlling retail theft with CCTV domes, CCTV public view monitors, and protective containers: A randomized controlled trial." *Security Journal* 24:237–250.

Haywood, J., P. Kautt, and A. Whitaker (2009). "The effects of 'alley-gating' in an English town." *European Journal of Criminology* 6:361–381.

Hearnden, I. and C. Magill (2004) *Decision-making by House Burglars: Offenders' Perspectives.* London: Home Office.

Heath, L. (1984). "Impact of newspaper crime reports on fear of crime: Multimethodological investigations." *Journal of Personal and Social Psychology* 47:263–276.

Hedderman, A. and C. Williams (2001). *Making Partnerships Work: Emerging Findings from the Reducing Burglary Initiative.* Briefing Note 1/01. London: Home Office.

Helland, E. and A. Tabarrok (2007). "Does three strikes deter? A nonparametric estimation." *Journal of Human Resources* 42:309–330.

Heller, N.B., W.W. Stenzel, A.D. Gill, R.A. Kolde, and S.R. Shimerman (1975). *Operation Identification Projects: Assessment of Effectiveness.* Washington, DC: Law Enforcement Assistance Administration.

Henggeler, S.W., C.A. Halliday-Boykins, P.B. Cunningham, J. Randall, S.B. Shapiro, and J.E. Chapman (2006). "Juvenile drug court: Enhancing outcomes by integrating evidence-based treatments." *Journal of Consulting and Clinical Psychology* 74:42–54.

Henig, J.R. (1984). *Citizens against crime: An assessment of the neighborhood watch program in Washington, D.C.* Washington, DC: George Washington University, Center for Washington Area Studies.

Henrichson, C. and R. Delaney (2012). *The Price of Prisons: What Incarceration Costs Taxpayers.* New York: Vera Institute of Justice. Retrieved from http://www.pewstates.org/uploadedFiles/PCS_Assets/2012/http___www.vera.org_download_file=3495_the-price-of-prisons-updated.pdf

Hesseling, R.B.P. (1994). "Displacement: A review of the empirical literature." In Clarke, R.V. (ed.), *Crime Prevention Studies*, vol. 3. Monsey, NY: Criminal Justice Press.

Hesseling, R.B.P. (1995a). "Theft from cars: Reduced or displaced?" *European Journal on Criminal Policy and Research* 3:79–92.

Hesseling, R.B.P. (1995b). "Functional surveillance in The Netherlands: Exemplary projects." *Security Journal* 6:21–25.

Higgins, P.B. and M.W. Ray (1978). *Television's Action Arsenal: Weapon Use in Prime Time.* Washington, DC: U.S. Conference of Mayors.

Hill, P.L., B.W. Roberts, J.T. Grogger, J. Guryan, and K. Sixkiller (2011). "Decreasing delinquency, criminal behavior, and recidivism by intervening on psychological factors other than cognitive ability: A review of the intervention literature." In Cook, P.J., J. Ludwig, and J. McCrary (eds.) *Controlling Crime: Strategies and Tradeoffs.* Chicago: University of Chicago Press.

Hindelang, M. (1975). *Public Opinion Regarding Crime, Criminal Justice, and Related Topics.* Washington, DC: Department of Justice.

Hindelang, M., M.R. Gottfredson, and J. Garofalo (1978). *Victims of Personal Crime: An Empirical Foundation for a Theory of Personal Victimization.* Cambridge, MA: Ballinger.

Hirschel, J.D., I.W. Hutchinson, C.W. Dean, J.J. Kelly, and C.E. Pesackis (1991). *Charlotte Spouse Assault Replication Project: Final Report.* Charlotte, NC: University of North Carolina at Charlotte.

Hirschel, J.D., I.W. Hutchinson, and C.W. Dean (1992). "The failure of arrest to deter spouse abuse." *Journal of Research in Crime and Delinquency* 29:7–33.

Hirschfield, P.J. and K. Celinska (2011). "Beyond fear: Sociological perspectives on the criminalization of school discipline." *Sociological Compass* 5:1–12.

Hirschi, T. (1969). *Causes of Delinquency.* Berkeley: University of California Press.

Hirschi, T. and M. Hindelang (1977). "Intelligence and delinquency: A revisionist review." *American Sociological Review* 42:571–587.

Hofstetter, C.R. (1976). *Bias in the News.* Columbus, OH: Ohio State University Press.

Holcomb, J.E. and S.P. Lab (2003). "Evaluation: Building knowledge for crime prevention." In Kury, H. and J. Obergfell-Fuchs (eds.), *Crime Prevention: New Approaches.* Mainz, GER: Weisser Ring.

Holden, R.N. (1992). *Law Enforcement: An Introduction.* Englewood Cliffs, NJ: Prentice Hall.

Hollinger, R.C. and J.P. Clark (1983). "Deterrence in the workplace: perceived certainty, perceived severity of employee theft." *Social Forces* 62:398–419.

Hollis-Peel, M.E., D.M. Reynald, M. van Bavel, H. Elffers, and B.C. Welsh (2011). "Guardianship for crime prevention: A critical review of the literature." *Crime, Law and Social Change* 56:53–70.

Holloway, K. and T. Bennett (2004). "The results of the first two years of the NEW-ADAM Programme". *Home Office Online Report 19/04.* London: Home Office.

Holloway, K., T. Bennett, and D.P. Farrington (2008). *Crime Prevention Research Review No. 3: Does*

Neighborhood Watch Reduce Crime? Washington, DC: U.S. Department of Justice Office of Community Oriented Policing Services.

Holt, T. and J. Spencer (2005). "A little yellow box: The targeting of automatic teller machines as a strategy in reducing street robbery." *Crime Prevention and Community Safety* 7(2):15–28.

Home Office (2001). *Installing Alley-gates: Practical Lessons from Burglary Prevention Projects.* Briefing Note 2/01. London: Home Office.

Home Office (2003a). *Reducing Burglary Initiative Project Summary—Fordbridge, Solihull.* Supplement 2 to Findings #204. London: Home Office.

Home Office (2003b). *Reducing Burglary Initiative Project Summary—Stirchley, Birmingham.* Supplement 4 to Findings #204. London: Home Office.

Home Office (2003c). *Reducing Burglary Initiative Project Summary—Rochdale.* Supplement 1 to Findings #204. London: Home Office.

Home Office (2003d). *Reducing Burglary Initiative Project Summary—Yew Tree, Sandwell.* Supplement 3 to Findings #204. London: Home Office.

Home Office (2004). *Safer Places: The Planning System and Crime Prevention.* London: Home Office.

Homel, P., S. Nutley, B. Webb, and N. Tilley (2004). *Investing to Deliver: Reviewing the Implementation of the UK Crime Reduction Program.* London: Home Office.

Honig, A.S., J.R. Lally, and D.H. Mathieson (1982). "Personal and social adjustment of school children after five years in the Family Development Research Program." *Child Care Quarterly,* 11:136–146.

Hoover, L.T. (1992). "Police mission: An era of debate." In Hoover, L.T. (ed.), *Police Management: Issues and Perspectives.* Washington, DC: Police Executive Research Forum.

Hope, T. (1994). "Problem-oriented policing and drug market locations: Three case studies." In Clarke, R.V. (ed.), *Crime Prevention Studies,* vol. 2. Monsey, NY: Criminal Justice Press.

Hope, T. and S.P. Lab (2001). "Variation in crime prevention participation: Evidence from the British Crime Survey." *Crime Prevention and Community Safety: An International Journal* 3(1):7–22.

Hough, M. (1995). *Anxiety about Crime: Findings from the 1994 British Crime Survey.* London: Home Office.

Howell, J.C. and J.D. Hawkins (1998). "Prevention of youth violence." In Tonry, M. and M.H. Moore (eds.), *Youth Violence.* Chicago: University of Chicago Press.

Hser, Y., M.D. Anglin, and C. Chou (1988). "Evaluation of drug abuse treatment: A repeated measure design assessing methadone maintenance." *Evaluation Review* 12:547–570.

Huba, G.J. and P.M. Bentler (1983). "Causal models of the development of law abidance and its relationship to psycho-social factors and drug use." In Laufer, W.S. and J.M. Day (eds.), *Personality Theory, Moral Development and Criminal Behavior.* Lexington: D.C. Heath.

Hubbard, R.L., J.V. Rachal, S.G. Craddock, and E.R. Cavanaugh (1984). "Treatment outcome prospective study (TOPS): Client characteristics and behaviors before, during and after treatment." In Tims, F.M. and J.P. Ludford (eds.), *Drug Abuse Treatment Evaluation: Strategies, Progress and Prospects.* Washington, DC: National Institute on Drug Abuse.

Huesmann, L.R. and N.M. Malamuth (1986). "Media violence and antisocial behavior: An overview." *Journal of Social Issues* 42:1–6.

Huizinga, D.H., R. Loeber, and T. Thornberry (1994). *Urban Delinquency and Substance Abuse:*

Initial Findings: Research Summary. Washington, DC: Office of Juvenile Justice and Delinquency Prevention.

Huizinga, D.H., S. Menard, and D.S. Elliott (1989). "Delinquency and drug use: Temporal and developmental patterns." *Justice Quarterly* 6:419–456.

Hughes, G. (2002). "Crime and disorder reduction partnerships: The future of community safety?" In Hughes, G., E. McLaughlin, and J. Muncie (eds.), *Crime Prevention and Community Safety: New Directions*. Thousand Oaks, CA: Sage.

Hughes, G., E. McLaughlin, and J. Muncie (2002). *Crime Prevention and Community Safety: New Directions*. Thousand Oaks, CA: Sage.

Hunt, D.E. (1990). "Drugs and consensual crimes: Drug dealing and prostitution." In Tonry, M. and J.Q. Wilson (eds.), *Drugs and Crime*. Chicago: University of Chicago Press.

Hunter, A. (1978). "Symbols of incivility: Social disorder and fear of crime in urban neighborhoods." Paper presented at the American Society of Criminology Annual Meeting, Dallas.

Hunter, A. (1985). "Private, parochial and public school orders: The problem of crime and incivility in urban communities." In Suttles, G.D. and M.N. Zald (eds.), *The Challenge of Social Control: Citizenship and Institution Building in Modern Society*. Norwood, NJ: Ablex Pub.

Hunter, R. (2010). "Crime prevention: Micro, meso, and macro levels." In Fisher, B.S. and S.P. Lab (eds.), *Encyclopedia of Victimology and Crime Prevention*. Thousand Oaks, CA: Sage.

Inciardi, J.A. (1996). "A corrections-based continuum of effective drug abuse treatment." *NIJ Research Preview*. Washington, DC: U.S. Department of Justice.

Inciardi, J.A., R. Horowitz, and A.E. Pottieger (1993). *Street Kids, Street Drugs, Street Crime: An Examination of Drug Use and Serious Delinquency in Miami*. Belmont, CA: Wadsworth.

Incredible Years (2012). *Incredible Years: Parents, Teachers and Children's Training Series*. Retrieved from http://www.incredibleyears.com/program/Incredible-Years_factsheet.pdf

International Association of Chiefs of Police (IACP) (2012). *Social Media and Crime Prevention, Fact Sheet*. Retrieved from https://www.google.com/url?q=http://www.iacpsocialmedia.org/Portals/1/documents/Fact%2520Sheets/Crime%2520Prevention%2520Fact%2520Sheet.pdf&sa=U&ei=eGuNVYnkOZSXoQTCxJToAg&ved=0CAYQFjAB&client=internal-uds-cse&usg=AFQjCNEf_SiggsW9zNhzXQowtBDD7C9kgw

International Association of Chiefs of Police (IACP) (2014). *2013 Social Media Survey Results*. Retrieved from http://www.iacpsocialmedia.org/Portals/1/documents/2013SurveyResults.pdf

International Association of Chiefs of Police (IACP) (2015). *IACP Center for Social Media*. http://www.iacpsocialmedia.org/

Internet Crime Complaint Center (2013). *2012 Internet Crime Report*. Retrieved from http://*www.ic3.gov/media/annualreport/2012_ic3report.pdf*

Jackson, J. and E. Gray (2009). "Functional fear and public insecurities about crime." *British Journal of Criminology* 49:1–22.

Jackson, J. and E. Gray (2010). "Functional fear and public insecurities about crime." *British Journal of Criminology* 50:1–22.

Jacobs, B.A. (1996). "Crack dealers and restrictive deterrence: Identifying narcs." *Criminology* 34:409–432.

Jacobs, J. (1961). *The Death and Life of Great American Cities*. New York: Random House.

James, N. and G. McCallion (2013). *School Resource Officers: Law Enforcement Officers in Schools.* Washington, DC: Congressional Research Service

Jarjoura, G.R. (1993). "Does dropping out of school enhance delinquent involvement?: Results from a large-scale national probability sample." *Criminology* 31:149–172.

Jeffery, C.R. (1971). *Crime Prevention Through Environmental Design.* Beverly Hills, CA: Sage.

Jenkins, A.D. and I. Latimer (1987). *Evaluation of Merseyside Home Watch.* Liverpool: Merseyside Police.

Jensen, G.F., M.L. Erickson, and J.P. Gibbs (1978). "Perceived risk of punishment and self-reported delinquency." *Social Forces* 57:57–78.

Jensen, G.F. and B.G. Stitt (1982). "Words and misdeeds: Hypothetical choices versus past behavior as measures of deviance." In Hagan, J. (ed.), *Deterrence Reconsidered: Methodological Innovations.* Beverly Hills, CA: Sage.

Jerse, F.W. and M.E. Fakouri (1978). "Juvenile delinquency and academic deficiency." *Contemporary Education* 49:108–109.

Jewkes, Y. (2011). *Media and Crime*, Second Edition. Los Angeles: Sage.

Johnson, B.D., K. Anderson, and E.D. Wish (1988). "A day in the life of 105 drug addicts and abusers: Crimes committed and how the money was spent." *Sociology and Social Research* 72:185–191.

Johnson, B.D., P.J. Goldstein, E. Prebel, J. Schmeidler, D.S. Lipton, B. Sprunt, and T. Miller (1985). *Taking Care of Business: The Economics of Crime by Heroin Abusers.* Lexington, MA: Lexington Books.

Johnson, B.D., T. Williams, K.A. Dei, and H. Sanabria (1990). "Drug abuse in the inner city: Impact on hard-drug users and the community." In Tonry, M. and J.Q. Wilson (eds.), *Drugs and Crime.* Chicago: University of Chicago Press.

Johnson, D., V. Gibson and M. McCabe (2014). "Designing *in* crime prevention, designing *out* ambiguity: Practice issues with the CPTED knowledge framework available to professionals in the field and its potentially ambiguous nature." *Crime Prevention and Community Safety* 16:147–168.

Johnson, S.D. and K.J. Bowers (2002). "Domestic burglary repeats and space-time clusters: The dimensions of risk." *European Journal of Criminology* (forthcoming).

Johnson, S.D. and K.J. Bowers (2003). "Opportunity is in the eye of the beholder: The role of publicity in crime prevention." *Criminology and Public Policy* 2:497–524.

Johnson, S.D. and K.J. Bowers (2004). "The burglary as a clue to the future: The beginnings of prospective hot-spotting." *The European Journal of Criminology* 1:237–255.

Johnson, S.D. and K.J. Bowers (2010). "Permeability and burglary risk: Are cul-de-sacs safer?" *Journal of Quantitative Criminology* 26:89–111.

Johnson, S.D., K. Bowers, and A. Hirschfield (1997). "New insight into the spatial and temporal distribution of repeat victimization." *British Journal of Criminology* 37:224–241.

Johnson, S.D., K.J. Bowers, and K. Pease (2005). "Predicting the future or summarizing the past? Crime mapping as anticipation." In Smith, M.J. and N. Tilley (eds.), *Crime Science: New Approaches to Preventing and Detecting Crime.* Portland, OR: Willan.

Johnson, S.D., S.P. Lab, and K.J. Bowers (2008). "Stable and fluid hotspots of crime: Differentiation and identification." *Built Environment* 34:32–45.

Johnston, L.D., P.M. O'Malley, and J.G. Bachman (1989). *Drug Use, Drinking, and Smoking: National Survey Results from High School, College, and Young Adult Populations.* Washington, DC: U.S. Government Printing Office.

Johnston, L.D., P.M. O'Malley, J.G. Bachman, J.E. Schulenberg, and R.A. Miech (2014). *Monitoring the Future National Survey Results on Drug Use, 1975–2013. Volume 2: College Students and Adults Ages 19–55*. Ann Arbor: Institute for Social Research, University of Michigan. Retrieved from http://monitoringthefuture.org/pubs.html

Johnston, L.D., P.M. O'Malley, and L.K. Eveland (1978). "Drugs and delinquency: A search for causal connections." In Kandel, D.B. (ed.), *Longitudinal Research on Drug Use: Empirical Findings and Methodological Issues*. Washington, DC: Hemisphere Pub.

Jones, J. (2010). "Americans still perceive crime as on the rise." *Gallup Politics*. Retrieved from http://www.gallup.com/pool/144827/americans-perceive-crime-rise.aspx

Kandel, D.B., O. Smicha-Fagan, and M. Davies (1986). "Risk factors for delinquency and illicit drug use from adolescence to young adulthood." *Journal of Drug Issues* 16:67–90.

Kandel, E. and S.A. Mednick (1991). "Perinatal complications predict violent offending." *Criminology* 29:519–529.

Kaplan, H.M., K.C. O'Kane, P.J. Lavrakas, and E.J. Pesce (1978). *Crime Prevention Through Environmental Design: Final Report on Commercial Demonstration; Portland, Oregon*. Arlington, VA: Westinghouse Electric Corp.

Karp, D.R. (2001). "The offender/community encounter: Stakeholder involvement in the Vermont reparative boards." In Karp, D.R. and T. Clear (eds.), *What Is Community Justice? Case Studies of Restorative Justice and Community Supervision*. Thousand Oaks, CA: Sage.

Katz, L., S.D. Levitt, and W. Shustorovich (2003). "Prison conditions, capital punishment, and deterrence." *American Law and Economics Review* 5:318–343.

Kaufman, P., X. Chen, S.P. Choy, K.A. Chandler, C.D. Chapman, M.R. Rand, and C. Ringel (1998). *Indicators of School Crime and Safety, 1998*. Washington, DC: Office of Educational Research and Improvement and Office of Justice Programs.

Keane, C. (1995). "Victimization and fear: Assessing the role of offender and offence." *Canadian Journal of Criminology* 37:431–455.

Kellermann, A.L., D. Fuqua-Whitley, and C.S. Parramore (2006). *Reducing Gun Violence: Community Problem Solving in Atlanta*. Washington, DC: National Institute of Justice.

Kelley, J. (1997). "Police lines often clogged with false, unreliable clues." *USA Today* Jan. 31:1–2.

Kelling, G.L. (1978). "Police field services and crime: The presumed effects of a capacity." *Crime & Delinquency* 24:173–184.

Kelling, G.L. (1998). *Columbia's Comprehensive Communities Program: A Case Study*. Washington, DC: BOTEC Analysis Corporation.

Kelling, G.L. (2005). "Community crime reduction: Activating formal and informal control." In Tilley, N. (ed.), *Handbook of Crime Prevention and Community Safety*. Portland, OR: Willan.

Kelly, B.T., R. Loeber, K. Keenan, and M. DeLamatre (1997). "Developmental pathways in boys' disruptive and delinquent behavior." *Juvenile Justice Bulletin*. Washington, DC: Office of Juvenile Justice and Delinquency Prevention.

Kelly, D.H. and R. Balch (1971). "Social origins and school failure: A re-examination of Cohen's theory of working class delinquency." *Pacific Sociological Review* 14:413–430.

Kelly, D.H. and W.T. Pink (1975). "Status origins, youth rebellion, and delinquency: A reexamination of the class issue." *Journal of Youth and Adolescence* 4:339–347.

Kennedy, D. (2008). *Deterrence and Crime Prevention*. London: Routledge.

Kennedy, D.M., A.A. Braga, and A.M. Piehl (2001). "Developing and implementing operation ceasefire." In National Institute of Justice, *Reducing Gun Violence: The Boston Gun Project's Operation Ceasefire*. Washington, DC: National Institute of Justice.

Kennedy, L.W. and H. Krahn (1984). "Rural–urban origin and fear of crime: The case for rural baggage." *Rural Sociology* 49:247–260.

Kennedy, L.W. and R.A. Silverman (1985). "Perception of social diversity and fear of crime." *Environment and Behavior* 17:275–295.

Kenney, D.J. (1986). "Crime on the subways: Measuring the effectiveness of the Guardian Angels." *Justice Quarterly* 3:481–498.

Kenney, D.J. and T.S. Watson (1998). *Crime in the Schools: Reducing Fear and Disorder with Student Problem Solving*. Washington, DC: Police Executive Research Forum.

Kinder, B.N., N.E. Pape, and S. Walfish (1980). "Drug and alcohol education programs: A review of outcome studies." *International Journal of the Addictions* 15:1035–1054.

Kleck, G., B. Sever, S. Li, and M. Gertz (2005). "The missing link in general deterrence research." *Criminology* 43:623–659.

Kleemans, E.R. (2001). "Repeat burglary victimisation: Results of empirical research in the Netherlands." In G. Farrell and K. Pease (eds.), *Repeat Victimization*. Monsey, NY: Criminal Justice Press.

Kleiman, M.A.R. (1988). "Crackdowns: The effects of intensive enforcement on retail heroin dealing." In Chaiken, M. (ed.), *Street Level Drug Enforcement: Examining the Issues*. Washington, DC: National Institute of Justice.

Kleiman, M.A.R. and K.D. Smith (1990). "State and local drug enforcement: In search of a strategy." In Tonry, M. and J.Q. Wilson (eds.), *Drugs and Crime*. Chicago: University of Chicago Press.

Kleinig, J. (2000). "The burdens of situational crime prevention: An ethical commentary." In von Hirsch, A., D. Garland, and A. Wakefield (eds.), *Ethical and Social Perspectives on Situational Crime Prevention*. Oxford: Hart.

Klepper, S. and D.S. Nagin (1989). "The deterrent effect of perceived certainty and severity of punishment revisited." *Criminology* 27:721–746.

Klockars, C.B. (1985). *The Idea of Police*. Beverly Hills, CA: Sage.

Kodz, J. and K. Pease (2003). *Reducing Burglary Initiative: Early Findings on Burglary Reduction*. Findings #204. London: Home Office.

Kohfeld, C.W., B. Salert, and S. Schoenberg (1981). "Neighborhood associations and urban crime." *Community Action* (Nov/Dec):37–44.

Kovandzic, T.V., L.M. Vieraitis, and D.P. Boots (2009). "Does the death penalty save lives? New evidence from state panel data, 1977–2006." *Criminology and Public Policy* 8:803–844.

Kratochwill, T.R., L. McDonald, J.R. Levin, P.A. Scalia, and G. Coover (2009). "Families and schools together: An experimental study of multi-family support groups for children at risk." *Journal of School Psychology* 47:245–265.

Kurki, L. (2000). "Restorative and community justice in the United States." In Tonry, M. (ed.), *Crime and Justice: A Review of Research*, vol. 27. Chicago: University of Chicago Press.

Kushmuk, J. and S.L. Whittemore (1981). *A Reevaluation of the Crime Prevention Through Environmental Design Program in Portland, Oregon*. Washington, DC: National Institute of Justice.

Lab, S.P. (1984). "Police productivity: The other eighty percent." *Journal of Police Science and Administration* 12:297–302.

Lab, S.P. (1987). "Pornography and aggression: A response to the U.S. Attorney General's commission." *Criminal Justice Abstracts* 19:301–321.

Lab, S.P. (1990). "Citizen crime prevention: Domains and participation." *Justice Quarterly* 7:467–492.

Lab, S.P. and R.D. Clark (1996). *Discipline, Control and School Crime: Identifying Effective Intervention Strategies. Final Report.* Washington, DC: National Institute of Justice.

Lab, S.P. and T. Hope (1998). "Assessing the impact of area context on crime prevention behavior." Paper presented to the Environmental Criminology and Crime Analysis Conference, Barcelona, Spain.

Lab, S.P. and J.T. Whitehead (1988). "An analysis of juvenile correctional treatment." *Crime & Delinquency* 34:60–85.

Lab, S.P. and J.T. Whitehead (1990). "From 'nothing works' to 'the appropriate works': The latest stop on the search for the secular grail." *Criminology* 28:405–418.

Lab, S.P. and J.T. Whitehead (1994). "Avoidance behavior as a response to in-school victimization." *Journal of Security Administration* 17(2):32–45.

Lacoste, J. and P. Tremblay (2003). "Crime and innovation: A script analysis of patterns in check forgery." In Smith, M.J. and D.B. Cornish (eds.), *Theory for Practice in Situational Crime Prevention*. Monsey, NY: Criminal Justice Press.

LaGrange, R.L. (1993). *Policing American Society*. Chicago: Nelson-Hall.

Lally, J.R., P.L. Mangione, and A.S. Honig (1987). *The Syracuse University Family Development Research Program: Long-range Impact of an Early Intervention with Low-income Children and Their Families*. New York: W.T. Grant Foundation.

Lally, J.R., P.L. Mangione, and A.S. Honig (1988). "The Syracuse University Family Development Research Program: Long-range impact on an early intervention with low-income children and their families," in Powell, D. R. and I. E. Sigel (eds.), *Parent Education as Early Childhood Intervention: Emerging Direction in Theory, Research, and Practice. Annual Advances in Applied Developmental Psychology.* Norwood, NJ: Ablex.

Land, K.C., R.H.C. Teske, and H. Zheng (2009). "The short-term effects of executions on homicides: Deterrence, displacement, or both?" *Criminology* 47:1009–1044.

Land, K.C., R.H.C. Teske, and H. Zheng (2012). "The differential short-term impacts of executions on felony and non-felony homicides." *Criminology and Public Policy* 11:541–564.

Lane, J. (2002). "Fear of gang crime: A qualitative examination of the four perspectives." *Journal of Research in Crime and Delinquency* 39:437–471.

Lane, J. and K. Fox (2012). "Fear of crime among gang and non-gang offenders: Comparing the effects of perpetration, victimization, and neighborhood factors." *Justice Quarterly* 29:491–523.

Lane, J. and J.W. Meeker (2000). "Subcultural diversity and the fear of crime and gangs." *Crime & Delinquency* 46:497–521.

Lane, J. and J.W. Meeker (2003a). "Fear of gang crime: A look at three theoretical models." *Law and Society Review* 37:425–456.

Lane, J. and J.W. Meeker (2003b). "Ethnicity, information, sources and fear of crime." *Deviant Behavior* 24:1–26.

Lane, J. and J.W. Meeker (2005). "Theories and fear of gang crime among whites and Latinos: A replication and extension of prior research." *Journal of Criminal Justice* 33:627–641.

Lane, J. and J.W. Meeker (2011). "Combining theoretical models of perceived risk and fear of gang crime among whites and Latinos." *Victims and Offenders* 6:64–92.

Langan, P.A. and D.J. Levin (2002). *Recidivism of Prisoners Released in 1994.* Washington, DC: Bureau of Justice Statistics.

Langworthy, R.H. and L.F. Travis III (1994). *Policing in America: A Balance of Forces.* New York, NY: Macmillan.

Lasley, J. (1998). " 'Designing out' gang homicides and street assaults." *NIJ Research in Brief.* Washington, DC: National Institute of Justice.

Latessa, E., P. Smith, R. Lemke, M. Makarios, and C. Lowenkamp (2009). *Creation and Validation of the Ohio Risk Assessment System: Final Report.* Cincinnati, OH: University of Cincinnati.

Latessa, E.J. and H.E. Allen (1980). "Using citizens to prevent crime: An example of deterrence and community involvement." *Journal of Police Science and Administration* 8:69–74.

Latessa, E.J. and H.E. Allen (2003). *Corrections in the Community,* Third Edition. Cincinnati, OH: Anderson.

Latessa, E.J. and L.F. Travis (1987). "Citizen crime prevention: Problems and perspectives in reducing crime." *Journal of Security Administration* 10:38–50.

Latimer, J., C. Dowden, and D. Muise (2005). "The effectiveness of restorative justice practices: A meta-analysis." Ottawa, Canada: Canada Department of Justice. Cited in Rodriguez, N. (2007). "Restorative Justice at Work: Examining the impact of restorative justice resolutions on juvenile recidivism." *Crime & Delinquency* 53:355–379.

Lauritsen, J.L., J.G. Owens, M. Planty, M.R. Rand, and J.L. Truman (2012). *Methods for Counting High-frequency Repeat Victimizations in the National Crime Victimization Survey.* Washington: Bureau of Justice Statistics.

LaVigne, N.G., S.S. Lowry, J.A. Marksman and A.M. Dwyer (2011) *Evaluating the Use of Public Surveillance Cameras for Crime Control and Prevention—A Summary.* Washington, DC: Urban Institute.

Lavrakas, P.J. (1986). "Evaluating police-community anticrime newsletters: The Evanston, Houston, and Newark field studies." In Rosenbaum, D.P. (ed.), *Community Crime Prevention: Does It Work?* Beverly Hills, CA: Sage.

Lavrakas, P.J. (1997). "Politicians, journalists, and the rhetoric of the 'crime prevention' public policy debate." In Lab, S.P. (ed.), *Crime Prevention at a Crossroads.* Cincinnati, OH: Anderson Publishing Co.

Lavrakas, P.J. and E.J. Herz (1982). "Citizen participation in neighborhood crime prevention." *Criminology* 20:479–498.

Lavrakas, P.J. and D.A. Lewis (1980). "The conceptualization and measurement of citizens' crime prevention behaviors." *Journal of Research in Crime and Delinquency* 17:254–272.

Lavrakas, P.J., J. Normoyle, W.G. Skogan, E.J. Herz, G. Salem, and D. Lewis (1981). *Factors Related to Citizen Involvement in Personal, Household, and Neighborhood Anti-Crime Measures: Executive Summary.* Washington, DC: National Institute of Justice.

Lavrakas, P.J., D.P. Rosenbaum, and F. Kaminski (1983). "Transmitting information about crime and crime prevention to citizens: The Evanston newsletter quasi-experiment." *Journal of Police Science and Administration* 11:463–473.

Lawton, B.A., R.B. Taylor, and A.J. Loungo (2005). "Police officers on drug corners in Philadelphia, drug crime, and violent crime: Intended, diffusion and displacement impacts." *Justice Quarterly* 22:427–451.

Laycock, G. (1984). *Reducing Burglary: A Study of Chemist's Shops*. London: Home Office.

Laycock, G. (1985). *Property Marking: A Deterrent to Domestic Burglary? Crime Prevention Planning Unit: Paper 3*. London: Home Office.

Laycock, G. (1990). "Operation identification: How much of a solution?" Paper presented at the American Society of Criminology Annual Meeting, Baltimore.

Laycock, G. (2002). "Methodological issues in working with policy advisers and practitioners." In Tilley, N. (ed.), *Analysis for Crime Prevention*. Monsey, NY: Criminal Justice Press.

Laycock, G. (2005). "Defining crime science." In Smith, M.J. and N. Tilley (eds.), *Crime Science: New Approaches to Preventing and Detecting Crime*. Portland, OR: Willan.

Laycock, G. and G. Farrell (2003). "Repeat victimization: Lessons for implementing problem-oriented policing." In Knutsson, J. (ed.), *Problem-oriented Policing: From Innovation to Mainstream*. Monsey, NY: Criminal Justice Press.

Laycock, G. and N. Tilley (1995a). "Implementing crime prevention." In Tonry, M. and D.P. Farrington (eds.), *Building a Safer Society: Strategic Approaches to Crime Prevention*. Chicago: University of Chicago Press.

Laycock, G. and N. Tilley (1995b). *Policing and Neighbourhood Watch: Strategic Issues*. London: Home Office Police Research Group.

Lazar, I., R. Darlington, H. Murray, J. Royce, and A. Snipper (1982). "Lasting effects of early education: A report from the Consortium for Longitudinal Studies." *Monographs of the Society for Research in Child Development,* no. 47.

Learmont, S. (2005). "Promoting design against crime." In Clarke, R.V. and G.R. Newman (eds.), *Designing Out Crime from Products and Systems*. Monsey, NY: Criminal Justice Press.

Leavell, H.R. and E.G. Clarke (1965). *Preventive Medicine for the Doctor in His Community: An Epidemiological Approach,* Third Edition. New York, NY: McGraw-Hill.

Lee, M. (2007). *Inventing Fear of Crime: Criminology and the Politics of Anxiety*. Cullompton, Devon, U.K.: Willan.

Leishman, F. and P. Mason (2003). *Policing and the Media: Facts, Fictions and Factions*. Cullompton, Devon, U.K.: Willan.

Lester, A. (2001). *Crime Reduction through Product Design*. Canberra, Australia: Australian Institute of Criminology.

Letkemann, P. (1973). *Crime as Work*. Englewood Cliffs, NJ: Prentice Hall.

Levi, M. (2008). "Combating identity and other forms of payment fraud in the UK: An analytical history." In McNally, M.M. and G.R. Newman (eds.), *Perspectives on Identity Theft*. Monsey, NY: Criminal Justice Press.

Levrant, S., F.T. Cullen, B. Fulton, and J.F. Wozniak (1999). "Reconsidering restorative justice: The corruption of benevolence revisited?" *Crime & Delinquency* 45:3–27.

Lewis, D.A., J.A. Grant, and D.P. Rosenbaum (1988). *The Social Construction of Reform*. Evanston, IL: Northwestern University Press.

Lewis, D.A. and G. Salem (1986). *Fear of Crime: Incivility and the Production of a Social Problem*. New Brunswick, NJ: Transaction.

LexisNexis Risk Solutions (2014). *Survey of Law Enforcement Personnel and Their Use of Social Media.* http://www.lexisnexis.com/investigations

Lichter, S.R., L.S. Lichter, and S. Rothman (1994). *Prime Time: How TV Portrays American Culture.* Washington, DC: Regnery.

Lilly, J.R. (2006). "Issues beyond empirical EM reports." *Criminology and Public Policy* 5:93–102.

Lilly, J.R., R.A. Ball, and J. Wright (1987). "Home incarceration with electronic monitoring in Kenton County, Kentucky: An evaluation." In McCarthy, B.R. (ed.), *Intermediate Punishments: Intensive Supervision, Home Confinement and Electronic Surveillance.* Monsey, NY: Criminal Justice Press.

Lindsey, E.W. and P.D. Kurtz (1987). "Evaluation of a school-juvenile court team approach to delinquency prevention." *Children and Youth Services Review* 9:101–115.

Lipsey, M.W. (1990). "Juvenile delinquency treatment: A meta-analytic inquiry into the variability of effects." Paper presented at the American Society of Criminology Annual Meeting, Denver.

Lipsey, M.W. (1999). "Can rehabilitative programs reduce the recidivism of juvenile offenders? An inquiry into the effectiveness of practical programs." *Virginia Journal of Social Policy and Law* 6:611–641.

Lipsey, M.W., G.L. Chapman, and N.A. Landenberger (2001). "Cognitive-behavioral programs for offenders." *Annals of the American Academy of Political and Social Sciences* 578:144–157.

Lipsey, M.W. and J.H. Derzon (1998). "Predictors of violent or serious delinquency in adolescence and early adulthood: A synthesis of longitudinal research." In Loeber, R. and D.P. Farrington (eds.), *Serious and Violent Juvenile Offenders: Risk Factors and Successful Interventions.* Thousand Oaks, CA: Sage.

Lipsey, M.W. and N.A. Landenberger (2006). "Cognitive-behavioral interventions." In Welsh, B.C. and D.P. Farrington (eds.), *Preventing Crime: What Works for Children, Offenders, Victims, and Places.* New York: Springer.

Lipsey, M.W. and D.B. Wilson (1993). "The efficacy of psychological, educational, and behavioral treatment." *American Psychologist* 48:1181–1209.

Lipsey, M.W. and D.B. Wilson (1998). "Effective interventions for serious juvenile offenders: A synthesis of research." In Loeber, R. and D.P. Farrington (eds.), *Serious and Violent Juvenile Offenders: Risk Factors and Successful Interventions.* Thousand Oaks, CA: Sage.

Lipton, D., R. Martinson, and J. Wilks (1975). *The Effectiveness of Correctional Treatment: A Survey of Treatment Evaluation Studies.* New York: Praeger.

Lipton, D., F.S. Pearson, C.M. Cleland, and D. Yee (2002). "The effectiveness of cognitive-behavioural treatment methods on recidivism." In McGuire, J. (ed.), *Offender Rehabilitation and Treatment: Effective Programmes and Policies to Reduce Re-offending.* Chichester, West Sussex, U.K.: John Wiley & Sons.

Liska, A.E. and W. Baccaglini (1990). "Feeling safe by comparison: Crime in the newspapers." *Social Problems* 37:360–374.

Liska, A.E., J.L. Lawrence, and A. Sanchirico (1982). "Fear of crime as a social fact." *Social Forces* 60:760–770.

Listwan, S.J., J.L. Sundt, A.M. Holsinger, and E.J. Latessa (2003). "The effects of drug court programming on recidivism: The Cincinnati experience." *Crime & Delinquency* 49:389–411.

Lizotte, A.J., J.M. Tesoriero, T.P. Thornberry, and M.D. Krohn (1994). "Patterns of adolescent firearms ownership and use." *Justice Quarterly* 11:51–73.

Lloyd, S., G. Farrell, and K. Pease (1994) *Preventing Repeated Domestic Violence: A Demonstration Project on Merseyside.* London: Home Office.

Lochner, L. (2007). "Individual perceptions of the criminal justice system." *American Economic Review* 97:444–460.

Lockwood, D. (1997). "Violence among middle school and high school students: Analysis and implications for prevention". *NIJ Research in Brief*. Washington, DC: National Institute of Justice.

Loeber, R. (1988). "Natural histories of conduct problems, delinquency and related substance abuse." In Lahey, B.B. and A.E. Kazdin (eds.), *Advances in Clinical Child Psychology*, vol. 11. New York: Plenum Press.

Loeber, R. (1990). "Development and risk factors of juvenile antisocial behavior and delinquency." *Clinical Psychology Review* 10:1–41.

Loeber, R., S.M. Green, K. Keenan, and B.B. Lahey (1995). "Which boys will fare worse? Early predictors or the onset of conduct disorder in a six-year longitudinal study." *Journal of the American Academy of Child and Adolescent Psychiatry* 34:499–509.

Loeber, R. and M. Stouthamer-Loeber (1986). "Family factors as correlates and predictors of juvenile conduct problems and delinquency." In Tonry, M. and N. Morris (eds.), *Crime and Justice: An Annual Review of Research*, vol. 7. Chicago: University of Chicago Press.

Loeber, R., P. Wung, K. Keenan, B. Giroux, M. Stouthamer-Loeber, W.B. VanKammen, and B. Maughan (1993). "Developmental pathways in disruptive child behavior." *Development and Psychopathology* 5:103–133.

Logan, C.H. (1972). "General deterrence effects of imprisonment." *Social Forces* 51:63–72.

Logan, C.H. and G.G. Gaes (1993). "Meta-analysis and the rehabilitation of punishment." *Justice Quarterly* 10:245–264.

Lonczak, H.S., R.D. Abbott, J.D. Hawkins, R. Kosterman, and R.F. Catalano (2002). "Effects of the Seattle Social Development Project on sexual behavior, pregnancy, birth, and STD outcomes by age 21." *Archives of Pediatrics and Adolescent Medicine* 156:438–447.

Loney, J., M.A. Whaley-Klahn, T. Kosier, and J. Conboy (1983). "Hyperactive boys and their brothers at 21: Predictors of aggressive and antisocial outcomes." In Van Dusen, K.T. and S.A. Mednick (eds.), *Prospective Studies of Crime and Delinquency*. Boston: Kluwer-Nijhof.

Lösel, F. (1995). "The efficacy of correctional treatment: A review and synthesis of meta-evaluations." In McGuire, J. (ed.), *What Works: Reducing Reoffending*. Chichester, West Sussex, U.K.: John Wiley & Sons.

Loughran, T.A., A.R. Piquero, J. Fagan, and E.P. Mulvery (2012). "Differential deterrence: Studying heterogeneity and changes among serious youthful offenders." *Crime & Delinquency* 58:3–27.

Lowenkamp, C.T., E.J. Latessa, and P. Smith (2006). "Does correctional program quality really matter?: The impact of adhering to the principles of effective intervention." *Criminology and Public Policy* 5:575–594.

Lowrey-Webster, H.M., P.M. Barrett, and M.R. Dadds (2001). "A universal prevention trial of anxiety and depressive symptomatology in childhood: Preliminary data from an Australian study." *Behavior Change* 18:36–50.

Lowry, D. (1971). "Greshaw's law and network TV news selection." *Journal of Broadcasting* 15:397–408.

Luepker, R.V., C.A. Johnson, D.M. Murray, and T.F. Pechacek (1983). "Prevention of cigarette smoking: Three year follow-up of educational programs for youth." *Journal of Behavioral Medicine* 6:53–61.

Lumb, R.C., R.D. Hunter, and D.J. McLain (1993). "Fear reduction in the Charlotte Housing Authority." In Zahm, D. and P. Cromwell (eds.), *Proceedings of the International Seminar on Environmental Criminology and Crime Analysis*. Coral Gables, FL: Florida Criminal Justice Executive Institute.

Lurigio, A.J. and R.C. Davis (1992). "Taking the war on drugs to the streets: The perceptual impact of four neighborhood drug programs." *Crime & Delinquency* 38:522–538.

Luxenburg, J., F.T. Cullen, R.H. Langworthy, and R. Kopache (1994). "Firearms and Fido: Ownership of injurious means of protection." *Journal of Criminal Justice* 22:159–170.

Lynch, J. and D. Cantor (1992). "Ecological and behavioral influences on property victimization at home: Implications for opportunity theory." *Journal of Research in Crime and Delinquency* 29:335–362.

MacKenzie, D.L. (2006). *What Works in Corrections: Reducing the Criminal Activities of Offenders and Delinquents.* New York: Cambridge University Press.

Maddux, J.F. (1988). "Clinical experience with civil commitment." In Leukefeld, C.G. and F.M. Tims (eds.), *Compulsory Treatment of Drug Abuse: Research and Clinical Practice.* Washington, DC: National Institute on Drug Abuse.

Madensen, T.D. and J.E. Eck (2008). *Spectator Violence in Stadiums.* Problem-specific Guide Series #54. Washington, DC: Office of Community Oriented Policing.

Maggin, D.M. and A.H. Johnson (2014). "A meta-analytic evaluation of the FRIENDS program for preventing anxiety in student populations." *Education and Treatment of Children* 37:277–306.

Maguin, E. and R. Loeber (1996). "Academic performance and delinquency." In Tonry, M. and N. Morris (eds.), *Crime and Justice*, vol. 20. Chicago: University of Chicago Press.

Maguire, K. (2011). *Sourcebook of Criminal Justice Statistics.* Washington, DC: Bureau of Justice Statistics. Retrieved from http://www.albany.edu/sourcebook

Maguire, K. and A.L. Pastore (1995). *Sourcebook of Criminal Justice Statistics, 1994.* Washington, DC: Bureau of Justice Statistics.

Marlowe, D.B. (2010). *The Facts on Juvenile Drug Treatment Courts.* Alexandria, VA: National Association of Drug Court Professionals. Retrieved from http://www.ndrc.org

Marsh, H.L. (1991). "A comparative analysis of crime coverage in newspapers in the United States and other countries from 1960–1989: A review of the literature." *Journal of Criminal Justice* 19:67–80.

Marsh, M. and M. Singer (1972). *Soft Statistics and Hard Questions.* Croton-on-Hudson, NY: Hudson Institute.

Martinson, R. (1974). "What works? Questions and answers about prison reform." *The Public Interest* 35:22–54.

Martinson, R. (1979). "New findings; new views: A note of citation regarding sentencing reform." *Hofstra Law Review* 7:243–258.

Massey, J.L. and M.D. Krohn (1986). "A longitudinal examination of an integrated social process model of deviant behavior." *Social Forces* 65:106–134.

Mawby, R.I. (2001). *Burglary.* Portland, OR: Willan.

Maxfield, M.G. and T.L. Baumer (1990). "Home detention with electronic monitoring: Comparing pretrial and postconviction programs." *Crime & Delinquency* 36:521–536.

Maxson, C.L., K.M. Hennigan, D.C. Sloane, and K.A. Kolnick (2004). *Can Civil Gang Injunctions Change Communities?: A Community Assessment of the Impact of Civil Gang Injunctions.* Washington, DC: National Institute of Justice.

May, D.C., B. Wright, G. Cordner, and S. Fessel (2014). "School resource officers: Effective tools when used properly?" In D.C. May (ed.) *School Safety in the United States: A Reasoned Look at the Rhetoric.* Durham, NC: Carolina Academic Press.

Mayer, J.P., L.K. Gensheimer, W.S. Davidson, and R. Gottschalk (1986). "Social learning treatment within juvenile justice: a meta-analysis of impact in the natural environment." In Apter, S.J. and A.P. Goldstein (eds.), *Youth and Violence: Problems and Prospects*. New York: Pergamon.

Mayhew, P., R.V. Clarke, and D. Elliot (1989). "Motorcycle theft, helmet legislation and displacement." *Howard Journal* 28:1–8.

Mayhew, P., R.V. Clarke, A. Sturman, and J.M. Hough (1976). *Crime as Opportunity*. London: Her Majesty's Stationery Office.

Mazerolle, L.G. and J.A. Roehl (1998). "Civil remedies and crime prevention: An introduction." In Mazerolle, L.G. and R. Roehl (eds.), *Civil Remedies and Crime Prevention*. Monsey, NY: Criminal Justice Press.

Mazerolle, L.G. and J.A. Roehl (1999). "Controlling drug and disorder problems: Oakland's Beat Health Program." *NIJ Research in Brief*. Washington, DC: National Institute of Justice.

Mazerolle, L.G., J. Roehl, and C. Kadleck (1998). "Controlling social disorder using civil remedies: Results from a randomized field experiment in Oakland, California." In Mazerolle, L.G. and J. Roehl (eds.), *Civil Remedies and Crime Prevention*. Monsey, NY: Criminal Justice Press.

McAlister, A., C.L. Perry, J. Killen, L.A. Slinkard, and N. Macoby (1980). "Pilot study of smoking, alcohol, and drug abuse prevention." *American Journal of Public Health* 70:719–721.

McBride, D.C. and J.A. Schwartz (1990). "Drugs and violence in the age of crack cocaine." In Weisheit, R. (ed.), *Drugs, Crime and the Criminal Justice System*. Cincinnati, OH: Anderson Publishing Co.

McCleary, R., B.C. Nienstedt, and J.M. Erven (1982). "Uniform crime reports as organizational outcomes: Three time series experiments." *Social Problems* 29:361–371.

McCold, P. and B. Wachtel (1998). *Restorative Policing Experiment: The Bethlehem, Pennsylvania, Police Family Group Conferencing Project*. Pipersville, PA: Community Service Foundation.

McCollister, K.E., M.T. French and H. Fang (2010). "The cost of crime to society: New crime-specific estimates for policy and program evaluation." *Drug and Alcohol Dependence* 108:98–109.

McCord, J. (1977). "A comparative study of two generations of native Americans." In Meier, R.F. (ed.), *Theory in Criminology: Contemporary Views*. Beverly Hills, CA: Sage.

McCord, J. (1979). "Some child-rearing antecedents of criminal behavior in adult men." *Journal of Personality and Social Psychology* 37:1477–1486.

McCoy, H.V., J.D. Wooldredge, F.T. Cullen, P.J. Dubeck, and S.L. Browning (1996). "Lifestyles of the old and not so fearful: Life situation and older persons' fear of crime." *Journal of Criminal Justice* 24:191–205.

McDevitt, J. and P. Finn (2005). *National Assessment of School Resource Offers Programs: Survey of Students in Three Large New SRO Programs*. Washington, DC: National Institute of Justice.

McDonald, L., S. FitzRoy, I. Fuches, I. Fooken, and H. Klasen (2012). "Strategies for high retention rates of low-income families in FAST (Families and Schools Together): An evidence-based parenting programme in the USA, UK, Holland, and Germany." *European Journal of Developmental Psychology* 9:75–88.

McDonald, L. and T.V. Sayger (1999). "Impact of family and school based prevention program on protective factors for high risk youth." *Drugs and Society* 12:61–85.

McGahey, R.M. (1980). "Dr. Ehrlich's magic bullet: Economic theory, econometrics, and the death penalty." *Crime & Delinquency* 26:485–502.

McGarrell, E.F., S. Chermak, J. Wilson and N. Corsaro (2006). "Reducing homicide through a 'level-pulling' strategy." *Justice Quarterly* 23:214–231.

McGarrell, E.F., N. Corsaro, N.K. Hipple, and T.S. Bynum (2010). "Project safe neighborhoods and violent crime trends in US cities: Assessing violent crime impact." *Journal of Quantitative Criminology* 26:165–190.

McGarrell, E.F., N. Corsaro, C. Melde, N.K. Hipple, J. Cobbina, T.S. Bynum, and H. Perez (2012). *An Assessment of the Comprehensive Anti-gang Initiative: Final Project Report.* Washington, DC: National Institute of Justice.

McGarrell, E.F., A.L. Giacomazzi, and Q.C. Thurman (1997). "Neighborhood disorder, integration, and the fear of crime." *Justice Quarterly* 14:479–500.

McGarrell, E.F., K. Olivares, K. Crawford, and N. Kroovand (2000). *Returning Justice to the Community: The Indianapolis Juvenile Restorative Justice Experiment.* Indianapolis, IN: Hudson Institute.

McGlothlin, W.H. and M.D. Anglin (1981). "Shutting off methadone: Costs and benefits." *Archives of General Psychiatry* 38:885–892.

McLean, S.J., R.E. Worden and M. Kim (2013). "Here's looking at you: An evaluation of public CCTV cameras and their effects on crime and disorder." *Criminal Justice Review* 38:303–334.

McLennan, D. and A. Whitworth (2008). *Displacement of Crime or Diffusion of Benefits: Evidence from the New Deal for Communities Programme.* Wetherby, West Yorkshire, U.K.: Communities and Local Government Publications. Retrieved from http://www.communities.gov.uk/documents/communities/pdf/737988.pdf

Meehl, P.E. (1954). *Clinical vs. Actuarial Prediction.* Minneapolis: University of Minnesota Press.

Meier, R.F. and W.T. Johnson (1977). "Deterrence as social control: The legal and extralegal production of conformity." *American Sociological Review* 42:292–304.

Melton, G.B., S.P. Limber, P. Cunningham, D.W. Osgood, J. Chambers, V. Flerx, S. Henggeler, and M. Nation (1998). *Violence Among Rural Youth: Final Report.* Washington, DC: Office of Juvenile Justice and Delinquency Prevention.

Menard, S. and H.C. Covey (1987). "Patterns of victimization, fear of crime, and crime precautions in nonmetropolitan New Mexico." *Journal of Crime and Justice* 10:71–100.

Mental Health America (MHA) (2009). *Position Statement #53: Mental Health Courts.* Retrieved from http://www.nmha.org/go/position-statements/53

Merry, S.E. (1981). "Defensible space undefended: Social factors in crime control through environmental design." *Urban Affairs Quarterly* 16:397–422.

Merton, R.K. (1968). *Social Theory and Social Structure.* New York: Macmillan.

Metropolitan Life (1993). *Violence in America's Public Schools.* New York: Louis Harris and Assoc.

Metropolitan Life (1994). *Violence in America's Public Schools: The Family Perspective.* New York: Louis Harris and Assoc.

Miethe, T.D. (1991). "Citizen-based crime control activity and victimization risks: An examination of displacement and free-rider effects." *Criminology* 29:419–440.

Millie, A. and M. Hough (2004). "Assessing the impact of the reducing burglary initiative in southern England and Wales." *Home Office Online Report 42/04.* London: Home Office.

Miller, T.R., M.A. Cohen and B. Wiersma (1996). *Victim Costs and Consequences: A New Look.* Washington, DC: National Institute of Justice. Retrieved from https://www.ncjrs.gov/pdffiles/victcost.pdf

Ministry of Justice (2005). *Crime Prevention Through Environmental Design Principles*. New Zealand Ministry of Justice. http://www.justice.govt.nz/policy/crime-prevention/environmental-design

Moffat, S. and S. Poynton (2007) "The deterrent effect of higher fines on recidivism: Driving offences." *Crime and Justice Bulletin 106*. Sydney: NSW Bureau of Crime Statistics and Research.

Moffitt, T.E. (1997). "Adolescence-limited and life-course-persistent offending: A complementary pair of developmental theories." In Thornberry, T.P. (ed.), *Developmental Theories of Crime and Delinquency*. New Brunswick, NJ: Transaction.

Moffitt, T.E., A. Caspi, P. Fawcett, G.L. Brammer, M. Raleigh, A. Yuwiler, and P.A. Silva (1997). "Whole blood serotonin and family background relate to male violence." In Raine, A., P.A. Brennan, D.P. Farrington, and S.A. Mednick (eds.), *Biosocial Bases of Violence*. New York: Plenum.

Monahan, J. (1981). *The Clinical Prediction of Violent Behavior*. Washington, DC: U.S. Department of Health and Human Services.

Moore, D. and T. O'Connell (1994). "Family conferencing in Wagga Wagga: A communitarian model of justice." In C. Adler and J. Wundersitz (eds.), *Family Conferencing and Juvenile Justice: The Way Forward or Misplaced Optimism?* Canberra, Australia: Australian Institute of Criminology.

Moore, M.H. (1994). "Research synthesis and policy implications." In Rosenbaum, D.P. (ed.), *The Challenge of Community Policing: Testing the Promises*. Thousand Oaks, CA: Sage.

Morris, N. and M. Tonry (1990). *Between Prison and Probation: Intermediate Punishments in a Rational Sentencing System*. New York: Oxford University Press.

Morrison, S.A. and I. O'Donnell (1996). "An analysis of the decision-making practices of armed robbers." In Homel, R. (ed.), *The Politics and Practice of Situational Crime Prevention*. Monsey, NY: Criminal Justice Press.

Morselli, C. and M.N. Royer (2008). "Criminal mobility and criminal achievement." *Journal of Research in Crime and Delinquency* 45:4–21.

Mumola, C. and J. Karberg (2006). *Drug Use and Dependence, State and Federal Prisoners, 2004*. Washington, DC: U.S. Department of Justice, Office of Justice Programs.

Mustaine, E.E. and R. Tewksbury (1998). "Predicting risks of larceny theft victimization: A routine activity analysis using refined lifestyle measures." *Criminology* 36:829–858.

Nagin, D.S. (1998). "Criminal deterrence research at the outset of the twenty-first century." *Crime and Justice* 23:1–42.

Nagin, D.S., F.T. Cullen, and C.L. Jonson (2009). "Imprisonment and reoffending." In Tonry, M. (ed.) *Crime and Justice: A Review of Research*, vol. 38. Chicago: University of Chicago Press.

Nagin, D.S. and G. Pogarsky (2004). "Time and punishment: Delayed consequences and criminal behavior." *Journal of Quantitative Criminology* 20:295–317.

Nasar, J.L. and B.S. Fisher (1993). " 'Hot spots' of fear and crime: A multi-method investigation." *Journal of Environmental Psychology* 13:187–206.

National Association of Town Watch (2015). *About*. https://natw.org/about

National Association of Youth Courts (2015). *Facts and Stats*. http://www.youthcourt.net/?page_id=24

National Audit Office. (2004). *Reducing Crime*. London: Her Majesty's Stationery Office.

National Crime Prevention Council (NCPC) (2015). http://www.ncpc.org

National Institute of Justice (1990). *Drugs and Crime: 1989 Drug Use Forecasting Report*. Washington, DC: National Institute of Justice.

National Institute of Justice (2015). *Drug Courts*. http://www.nij.gov/topics/courts/drug-courts/Pages/welcome.aspx

National Institute on Drug Abuse (NIDA) (2012). *Principles of Drug Addiction Treatment: A Research-based Guide*, Third Edition. Washington, DC: National Institute on Drug Abuse. Retrieved from http://www.drugabuse.gov/publications/principles-drug-addiction-treatment-research-based-guide-third-edition/frequently-asked-questions/what-drug-addiction-treatment

National Institute on Drug Abuse (NIDA) (2014). *Drug Facts: Lessons from Prevention Research*. Washington, DC: National Institute on Drug Abuse. Retrieved from http://www.drugabuse.gov/publications/drugfacts/lessons-prevention-research

National Neighborhood Watch (NNW) (2015) *USAonWatch*. http://nnw.org/

Nee, C. and M. Taylor (1988). "Residential burglary in the Republic of Ireland: A situational perspective." *Howard Journal of Criminal Justice* 27:105–116.

Neighborhood and Home Watch Network (2015). *The History of Neighborhood and Home Watch*. http://www.ourwatch.org.uk/about_us/our_history/

Nelson, S. (1989). "Crime-time television." *FBI Law Enforcement Bulletin* 58:1–9.

New Jersey State Parole Board (NJPB) (2007). *Report on New Jersey's GPS Monitoring of Sex Offenders*. Trenton, NJ: New Jersey State Parole Board.

New South Wales (2015). *Safer By Design*. http://www.police.nsw.gov.au/community_issues/crime_prevention/safer_by_design

Newburn, T. (2002). "Community safety and policing: Some implications of the Crime and Disorder Act 1998." In Hughes, G., E. McLaughlin, and J. Muncie (eds.), *Crime Prevention and Community Safety: New Directions*. Thousand Oaks, CA: Sage.

Newcomb, M.D. and P.M. Bentler (1988). *Consequences of Adolescent Drug Use*. Newbury Park, CA: Sage.

Newman, O. (1972). *Defensible Space: People and Design in the Violent City*. New York: Macmillan.

Newman, O. (1996). *Creating Defensible Space*. Washington, DC: Department of Housing and Urban Development.

Newman, O. and K.A. Franck (1980). *Factors Influencing Crime and Instability in Urban Housing Developments*. Washington, DC: National Institute of Justice.

Newman, O. and F. Wayne (1974). *The Private Street System in St. Louis*. New York, NY: Institute for Community Design Analysis.

Nichols, W.W. (1980). "Mental maps, social characteristics, and criminal mobility." In Georges-Abeyie, D.E. and K.D. Harries (eds.), *Crime: A Spatial Perspective*. New York: Columbia University Press.

Niederberger, W.V. and W.F. Wagner (1985). *Electronic Monitoring of Convicted Offenders: A Field Test Report*. Washington, DC: National Institute of Justice.

Norris, C. and M. McCahill (2006). "CCTV: Beyond penal modernism?" *British Journal of Criminology* 46(1):97–118.

Norris, M., S. Twill, and C. Kim (2011). "Smells like teen spirit: Evaluating a midwestern teen court." *Crime & Delinquency* 57:199–221.

Novotney, L.C., E. Mertinko, J. Lange, and T.K. Baker (2000). *Juvenile Mentoring Program: A Progress Review*. Washington, DC: Office of Juvenile Justice and Delinquency Prevention.

Nubani, L. and J. Wineman (2009). "The role of space syntax in identifying the relationship between space and crime." Paper presented at the 5th Space Syntax Symposium, Delft, Holland.

Nurco, D.N., T.W. Kinlock, T.E. Hanlon, and J.C. Ball (1988). "Nonnarcotic drug use over an addiction career: A study of heroin addicts in Baltimore and New York City." *Comprehensive Psychiatry* 29:450–459.

O'Brien, R.M. (1985). *Crime and Victimization Data*. Beverly Hills, CA: Sage.

O'Deane, M.D. (2012) *Gang Injunctions and Abatement: Using Civil Remedies to Curb Gang-related Crimes*. Boca Raton, FL: CRC Press.

Oesterle, S., J.D. Hawkins, A.A. Fagan, R.D. Abbott, and R.F. Catalano (2014). "Variation in the sustained effects of the Communities that Care prevention system on adolescent smoking, delinquency, and violence." *Prevention Science* 15:138–145.

Office of Community Oriented Policing Services (2006). http://www.cops.usdoj.gov

Office of Juvenile Justice and Delinquency Prevention (OJJDP) (1999). *Violence after School*. Washington, DC: Office of Juvenile Justice and Delinquency Prevention.

Office of National Drug Control Policy (2012). *ADAM II: 2011 Annual Report*. Washington, DC: The White House.

Ohio Commission on Dispute Resolution and Conflict Management (1993). *Conflict Management in Schools: Sowing Seeds for a Safer Society*. Columbus, OH: Ohio Commission on Dispute Resolution and Conflict Management.

O'Keefe, G.J. and H. Mendelsohn (1984). *"Taking a Bite Out of Crime": The Impact of a Mass Media Crime Prevention Campaign*. Washington, DC: National Institute of Justice.

O'Keefe, G.J., D.P. Rosenbaum, P.J. Lavrakas, K. Reid, and R.A. Botta (1996). *Taking a Bite Out of Crime: The Impact of the National Citizens' Crime Prevention Media Campaign*. Thousand Oaks, CA: Sage.

Olds, D., J. Eckenrode, C.R. Henderson, H. Kizman, J. Powers, R. Cole, K. Sidora, P. Morris, L.M. Pettitt, and D.W. Luckey (1997). "Long-term effects of nurse home visitation on maternal life course and child abuse and neglect: 15 year follow-up of a randomized controlled trial." *JAMA* 278:637–643.

Olds, D., C.R. Henderson, R. Cole, J. Eckenrode, H. Kitzman, D. Luckey, L. Pettitt, K. Sidora, P. Morris, and J. Powers. (1998). "Long-term effects of nurse home visitation on children's criminal and antisocial behavior: 15 year follow-up of a randomized controlled trial." *JAMA* 280:1238–1244.

Oliver, M.B. (1994). "Portrayals of crime, race, and aggression in 'reality-based' police shows: A content analysis." *Journal of Broadcasting and Electronic Media* 38:179–192.

Oliver, M.B. and G.B. Armstrong (1998). "The color of crime: Perceptions of caucasians' and African-Americans' involvement in crime." In Fishman, M. and G. Cavender (eds.), *Entertaining Crime: Television Reality Programs*. New York: Aldine de Gruyter.

Oliver, W.M. (1998). *Community-Oriented Policing: A Systemic Approach to Policing*. Upper Saddle River, NJ: Prentice Hall.

Olweus, D. (1993). "Victimization by peers: Antecedents and long-term outcomes." In K.H. Rubin and J.B. Asendorf (eds.), *Social Withdrawal, Inhibition, and Shyness*. Hillsdale, NJ: Erlbaum.

Olweus, D. (1994). "Bullying at school: Basic facts and effects of a school-based intervention program." *Journal of Child Psychology and Psychiatry and Allied Disciplines* 35:1171–1190.

Olweus, D. (1995). "Bullying or peer abuse at school: Facts and intervention." *Current Directions in Psychological Science* 4:196–200.

Olweus, D. and S. Limber (2000). *Bullying Prevention Program. Blueprints for Violence Prevention*. Boulder, CO: Institute of Behavioral Science.

Ortega, S.T. and J.L. Myles (1987). "Race and gender effects on fear of crime: An interactive model with age." *Criminology* 25:133–152.

Otto, H.A. (1962). "Sex and violence on the American newsstand." *Journalism Quarterly* 40:19–26.

Padgett, K.G., W.D. Bailes, and T.G. Blomberg (2006). "Under surveillance: An empirical test of the effectiveness and consequences of electronic monitoring." *Criminology and Public Policy* 5:61–92.

Painter, K. and D.P. Farrington (1997). "The crime reducing effect of improved street lighting: The Dudley project." In Clarke, R.V. (ed.), *Situational Crime Prevention: Successful Case Studies*, Second Edition. Gulderland, NY: Harrow and Heston.

Painter, K. and D.P. Farrington (1999a). "Improved street lighting: Crime reducing effects and cost-benefit analysis." *Security Journal* 12:17–32.

Painter, D. and D.P. Farrington (1999b). "Street lighting and crime: Diffusion of benefits in the Stoke-on-Trent project." In Painter, K. and N. Tilley (eds.), *Surveillance of Public Space: CCTV, Street Lighting and Crime Prevention*. Monsey, NY: Criminal Justice Press.

Palm Beach County Sheriff's Department (1987). "Palm Beach County's in-house arrest work release program." In McCarthy, B.R. (ed.), *Intermediate Punishments: Intensive Supervision, Home Confinement and Electronic Surveillance*. Monsey, NY: Criminal Justice Press.

Palmer, T. (1975). "Martinson revisited." *Journal of Research in Crime and Delinquency* 12:133–152.

Palmer, T. (1983). "The effectiveness issue today: An overview." *Federal Probation* 46:3–10.

Papachristos, A.V., T.L. Meares, and J. Fagan (2007). "Attention felons: Evaluating Project Safe Neighborhoods in Chicago." *Journal of Empirical Legal Studies* 4:223–272.

Papachristos, A.V., C.M. Smith, M.L. Scherer, and M.A Fugiero (2011). "More coffee, less crime?: The relationship between gentrification and neighborhood crime rates in Chicago, 1991 to 2005." *City and Community* 10:215–240.

Papagiannis, G.J., R.N. Bickel, and R.H. Fuller (1983). "The social creation of school dropouts: Accomplishing the reproduction of an underclass." *Youth and Society* 14:363–392.

Parker, K.D. (1988). "Black–white differences in perceptions of fear of crime." *Journal of Social Psychology* 128:487–494.

Parker, K.D. and M.C. Ray (1990). "Fear of crime: An assessment of related factors." *Sociological Spectrum* 10:29–40.

Passell, P. (1975). "The deterrent effect of the death penalty: A statistical test." *Stanford Law Review* 28:61–80.

Passell, P. and J.B. Taylor (1977). "The deterrent effect of capital punishment: Another view." *American Economic Review* 65:445–451.

Pate, A., M. McPherson, and G. Silloway (1987). *The Minneapolis Community Crime Prevention Experiment*. Washington, DC: Police Foundation.

Paternoster, R. (1989a). "Decisions to participate in and desist from four types of common delinquency: Deterrence and the rational choice perspective." *Law and Society Review* 23:7–40.

Paternoster, R. (1989b). "Absolute and restrictive deterrence in a panel of youth: Explaining the onset, persistence/desistance, and frequency of delinquent offending." *Social Problems* 36:289–309.

Paternoster, R. and A. Piquero (1995). "Reconceptualizing deterrence: An empirical test of personal and vicarious experiences." *Journal of Research in Crime and Delinquency* 32:251–286.

Paternoster, R., L.E. Saltzman, G.P. Waldo, and T.G. Chiricos (1982). "Causal ordering in deterrence research: An examination of the perceptions-behavior relationship." In Hagan, J. (ed.), *Deterrence Reconsidered: Methodological Innovations*. Beverly Hills, CA: Sage.

Paternoster, R., L.E. Saltzman, G.P. Waldo, and T.G. Chiricos (1985). "Assessments of risk and behavioral experience: An exploratory study of change." *Criminology* 23:417–436.

Patrick, S. and R. Marsh (2005). "Juvenile diversion: Results of a 3-year experimental study." *Criminal Justice Policy Review* 16:59–73.

Pawson, R. and N. Tilley (1997). *Realistic Evaluation*. London: Sage.

Pearson, F.S. (1985). "New Jersey's intensive supervision program: A progress report." *Crime & Delinquency* 31:393–410.

Pearson, F.S. (1988). "Evaluation of New Jersey's intensive supervision program." *Crime & Delinquency* 34:437–448.

Pearson, F.S. and A.G. Harper (1990). "Contingent intermediate sentences: New Jersey's intensive supervision program." *Crime & Delinquency* 36:75–86.

Pease, K. (1998). *Repeat Victimization: Taking Stock*. London: Home Office Police Research Group.

Pease, K. (1999). "A review of street lighting evaluations: Crime reduction effects." In Painter, K. and N. Tilley (eds.), *Surveillance of Public Space: CCTV, Street Lighting and Crime Prevention*. Monsey, NY: Criminal Justice Press.

Pennell, F.E. (1978). "Private vs. collective strategies for coping with crime: The consequences for citizen perceptions of crime, attitudes the police and neighborhood activity." *Journal of Voluntary Action Research* 7:59–74.

Pennell, S., C. Curtis, and J. Henderson (1986). *Guardian Angels: An Assessment of Citizen Response to Crime*. Washington, DC: National Institute of Justice.

Perkins, D.G. and R.B. Taylor (1996). "Ecological assessments of community disorder: Their relationship to fear of crime and theoretical implications." *American Journal of Community Psychology* 24:63–107.

Perry, K. (1984). "Measuring the effectiveness of neighborhood crime watch in Lakewood, Colorado." *Police Journal* 57:221–233.

Pestello, H.F. (1984). "Deterrence: A reconceptualization." *Crime & Delinquency* 30:593–609.

Petersilia, J. and P.W. Greenwood (1978). "Mandatory prison sentences: Their projected effects on crime and prison populations." *Journal of Criminal Law and Criminology* 69:604–615.

Petersilia, J. and S. Turner (1990). "Comparing intensive and regular supervision for high-risk probationers: Early results from an experiment in California." *Crime & Delinquency* 36:87–111.

Petersilia, J. and S. Turner (1993). "Intensive probation and parole." In Tonry, M. (ed.), *Crime and Justice*, vol. 17. Chicago: University of Chicago Press.

Peterson, M.A. and H.B. Braiker (1980). *Doing Crime: A Survey of California Prison Inmates*. Santa Monica, CA: RAND Corp.

Petrosino, A.J. and D. Brensilber (2003). "The motives, methods and decision making of convenience store robbers: Interviews with 28 incarcerated offenders in Massachusetts." In Smith, M.J. and D.B. Cornish (eds.), *Theory for Practice in Situational Crime Prevention*. Monsey, NY: Criminal Justice Press.

Pfohl, S.J. (1978). *Predicting Dangerousness*. Lexington, MA: Lexington Books.

Phillips, C. (2002). "From voluntary to statutory status: Reflecting on the experience of three partnerships established under the Crime and Disorder Act 1998." In Hughes, G., E. McLaughlin and J. Muncie (eds.), *Crime Prevention and Community Safety: New Directions*. Thousand Oaks, CA: Sage.

Phillips, D.P. (1980). "The deterrent effect of capital punishment." *American Journal of Sociology* 86:139–148.

Phillips, D.P. (1982). "The impact of fictional television stories on US adult fatalities: New evidence on the effect of the mass media on violence." *American Journal of Sociology* 87:1340–1359.

Phillips, D.P. (1983). "The impact of mass media violence on US homicides." *American Sociological Review* 48:560–568.

Phillips, J.C. and D.H. Kelly (1979). "School failure and delinquency: Which causes which?" *Criminology* 17:194–207.

Phillips, L., S. Ray, and H.L. Votey (1984). "Forecasting highway casualties: The British Road Safety Act and a sense of deja vu." *Journal of Criminal Justice* 12:101–114.

Phillips, P.P. (1980). "Characteristics and typology of the journey to crime." In Georges-Abeyie, D.E. and K.D. Harries (eds.), *Crime: A Spatial Perspective*. New York: Columbia University Press.

Piliavin, I., C. Thornton, R. Garten, and R.L. Matsueda (1986). "Crime, deterrence, and rational choice." *American Sociological Review* 51:101–119.

Piquero, A. and R. Paternoster (1998). "An application of Stafford and Warr's reconceptualization of deterrence to drunk driving." *Journal of Research in Crime and Delinquency* 35:3–39.

Piquero, A. and G.F. Rengert (1999). "Studying deterrence with active residential burglars: A research note." *Justice Quarterly* 16:451–472.

Piquero, A.R., D.P. Farrington, B.C. Welsh, R. Tremblay, and W.G. Jennings (2009). "Effect of early family/parent training programs on antisocial behavior and delinquency." *Journal of Experimental Criminology* 5:83–120.

Piquero, A.R. and G. Pogarski (2002). "Beyond Stafford and Warr's reconceptualization of deterrence: Personal and vicarious experiences, impulsivity, and offending behavior." *Journal of Research in Crime and Delinquency* 39:153–186.

Podolefsky, A. and F. DuBow (1980). *The Reactions to Crime Papers, Vol. II: Strategies for Community Crime Prevention*. Evanston, IL: Northwestern University.

Pogarski, G., K. Kim, and R. Paternoster (2005). "Perceptual change in the national youth survey: Lessons for deterrence theory and offender decision-making." *Justice Quarterly* 22:1–29.

Pogarski, G. and A.R. Piquero (2003). "Can punishment encourage offending? Investigating the 'resetting' effect." *Journal of Research in Crime and Delinquency* 40:95–120.

Police Foundation (1981). *The Newark Foot Patrol Experiment*. Washington, DC: Police Foundation.

Polk, K., D. Frease, and L. Richmond (1974). "Social class, school experience, and delinquency." *Criminology* 12:84–96.

Polk, K. and D. Hafferty (1966). "School culture, adolescent commitments, and delinquency." *Journal of Research in Crime and Delinquency* 4:82–96.

Polk, K. and W.E. Schafer (1972). *Schools and Delinquency*. Englewood Cliffs, NJ: Prentice Hall.

Polvi, N., T. Looman, C. Humphries, and K. Pease (1990). "Repeat break and enter victimization: Time course and crime prevention opportunity." *Journal of Police Science and Administration* 17:8–11.

Popkin, S.J., V.E. Gwiasda, D.P. Rosenbaum, J.M. Amendolia, W.A. Johnson, and L.M. Olson (1999). "Combating crime in public housing: A qualitative and quantitative longitudinal analysis of the Chicago Housing Authority's anti-drug initiative." *Justice Quarterly* 16:519–558.

Popkin, S.J., L.M. Olson, A.J. Lurigio, V.E. Gwiasda, and R.G. Carter (1995). "Sweeping out drugs and crime: Residents' views of the Chicago Housing Authority's Public Housing drug elimination program." *Crime & Delinquency* 41:54–72.

Poyner, B. (1988). "Video cameras and bus vandalism." *Security Administration* 11:44–51.

Poyner, B. (1991). "Situational crime prevention in two parking facilities." *Security Journal* 2:96–101.

Poyner, B. (1994). "Lessons from Lisson Green: An evaluation of walkway demolition on a British housing estate." In Clarke, R.V. (ed.), *Crime Prevention Studies*, vol. 4. Monsey, NY: Criminal Justice Press.

Poyner, B. and B. Webb (1992). "Reducing theft from shopping bags in city center markets." In Clarke, R.V. (ed.), *Situational Crime Prevention: Successful Case Studies*. Albany, NY: Harrow and Heston.

Pratt, T.C., F.T. Cullen, K.R. Blevins, L.E. Daigle, and T.D. Madensen (2006). "The empirical states of deterrence theory: A meta-analysis." In Cullen, F.T., J.P. Wright, and K.R. Blevins (eds.), *Take Stock: The Status of Criminological Theory*. New Brunswick, NJ: Transaction.

President's Commission on Law Enforcement and the Administration of Justice (1967). *Task Force Report: Juvenile Delinquency and Youth Crime*. Washington, DC: U.S. Government Printing Office.

Project Safe Neighborhoods (PSN) (2003). *Fact Sheet, Project Safe Neighborhoods: America's Network Against Gun Violence*. Retrieved from http://psn.gov/crime.asp

Puzzanchera, M. and S. Hockenberry (2013). *Juvenile Court Statistics 2010*. Pittsburgh, PA: National Center for Juvenile Justice.

Pyle, G.F. (1974). *The Spatial Dynamics of Crime*. Chicago: University of Chicago, Department of Geography Research Paper #159.

Pyrooz, D.C. (2013). "Gangs, criminal offending, and an inconvenient truth: Considerations for gang prevention and intervention in the lives of youth." *Criminology and Public Policy* 12:427–436.

Raine, A. (1993). *The Psychopathology of Crime: Criminal Behavior as a Clinical Disorder*. San Diego, CA: Academic Press.

Ramey, D.M. (2013). "Immigrant revitalization and neighborhood violent crime in established and new destination cities." *Social Forces* 92:597–629.

Ramey, D.M. and E.A. Shrider (2014). "New parochialism, sources of community involvement, and the control of street crime." *Criminology and Public Policy* 13:193–216.

Rand, M.R. (2009). *Criminal Victimization, 2008*. Washington, DC: Bureau of Justice Statistics.

Rand, M.R., J.P. Lynch, and D. Cantor (1997). *Criminal Victimization, 1973–1995*. Washington, DC: Bureau of Justice Statistics.

Rasmussen, A. (2004). "Teen Court referral, sentencing, and subsequent recidivism: Two proportional hazards models and a little speculation." *Crime & Delinquency* 50:615–635.

Rasmussen, M., W. Muggli, and C.M. Crabill (1979). *Evaluation of the Minneapolis Community Crime Prevention Demonstration*. St. Paul, MN: Crime Control Planning Board.

Ratcliffe, J. and M. McCullagh (1999). "Burglary, victimization and social deprivation." *Crime Prevention and Community Safety: An International Journal* 1:37–46.

Ratcliffe, J.H., T. Taniguchi and R.B. Taylor (2009). "The crime reduction effects of public CCTV cameras: A multi-method spatial approach." *Justice Quarterly* 26:746–770.

Reichel, P. and C. Seyfrit (1984). "A peer jury in the juvenile court." *Crime & Delinquency* 30:423–438.

Reid, A.A. and M.A. Andresen (2012). "The impact of closed-circuit television in a car park on the fear of crime: Evidence from a victimization survey." *Crime Prevention and Community Safety* 14:293–316.

Reiner, R., S. Livingstone, and J. Allen (2000). "No more happy endings? The media and popular concern about crime since the Second World War." In Hope, T. and R. Sparks (eds.), *Crime, Risk and Insecurity*. New York: Routledge.

Reiss, A.J. and A.L. Rhodes (1959). *A Sociopsychological Study of Adolescent Conformity and Deviation*. Washington, DC: U.S. Office of Education.

Reiss, A.J. and A.L. Rhodes (1961). "The distribution of juvenile delinquency in the social class structure." *American Sociological Review* 26:720–732.

Reiss, A.J. and J.A. Roth (1993). *Understanding and Preventing Violence*. Washington, DC: National Academy Press.

Rengert, G.F. (1997). "Auto theft in central Philadelphia." In Homel, R. (ed.), *Policing for Prevention: Reducing Crime, Public Intoxication and Injury*. Monsey, NY: Criminal Justice Press.

Rengert, G.F. and J. Wasilchick (1985). *Suburban Burglary: A Time and a Place for Everything*. Springfield, IL: Thomas.

Rennison, C.M. and M.R. Rand (2003). *Criminal Victimization, 2002*. Washington, DC: Bureau of Justice Statistics.

Reppetto, T.A. (1974). *Residential Crime*. Cambridge, MA: Ballinger

Reppetto, T.A. (1976). "Crime prevention and the displacement phenomenon." *Crime & Delinquency* 22:166–177.

Reynald, D.M. (2011). *Guarding Against Crime: Measuring Guardianship within Routine Activities Theory*. Burlington, VT: Ashgate.

Rhodes, W., J. Norman, and R. Kling (1997). *An Evaluation of the Effectiveness of Automobile Parts Marking on Preventing Theft*. Washington, DC: Abt Assoc.

Rhodes, W.M. and C. Conley (1981). "Crime and mobility: An empirical study." In Brantingham, P.J. and P.L. Brantingham (eds.), *Environmental Criminology*. Beverly Hills, CA: Sage.

Rich, T.F. (1995). "The use of computerized mapping in crime control and prevention programs." *NIJ Research in Action*. Washington, DC: U.S. Department of Justice.

Rich-Shea, A.M. and J.A. Fox (2014). "Zero-tolerance policies." In Muschert, G.W., S. Henry, N.L. Bracy, and A.A. Peguero (eds.), *Responding to School Violence: Confronting the Columbine Effect*. Boulder, CO: Lynne Rienner.

Rifai, M.Y. (1982). "Methods of measuring the impact of criminal victimization through victimization surveys." In H.J. Schneider (ed.), *The Victim in International Perspective*. New York: de Gruyter.

Riger, S., M.T. Gordon, and R. LeBailly (1978). "Women's fear of crime: From blaming to restricting the victim." *Victimology* 3:274–284.

Riley, D. (1980). "An evaluation of a campaign to reduce car thefts." In Clarke, R.V.G. and P. Mayhew (eds.), *Designing Out Crime*. London: Her Majesty's Stationery Office.

Riley, D. and P. Mayhew (1980). *Crime Prevention Publicity: An Assessment*. London: Home Office.

Ringwalt, C.L., S.T. Ennett, and K.D. Holt (1991). "An outcome evaluation of project D.A.R.E." *Health Education Research: Theory and Practice* 6:327–337.

Ringwalt, C.L., P. Messerschmidt, L. Graham, and J. Collins (1992). *Youth's Victimization Experiences, Fear of Attack or Harm, and School Avoidance Behaviors. Final Report*. Washington, DC: National Institute of Justice.

Robers, S., Kemp, J., Rathbun, A., and Morgan, R. (2014). *Indicators of School Crime and Safety: 2013*. Washington, DC: National Center for Education Statistics, U.S. Department of Education, and Bureau of Justice Statistics, Office of Justice Programs, U.S. Department of Justice. Retrieved from http://nces.ed.gov/pubs2012/2012002.pdf

Robers, S., J. Zhang, J. Truman, and T.D. Snyder (2012). *Indicators of School Crime and Safety, 2011*. Washington, DC: Bureau of Justice Statistics. Retrieved from http://nces.ed.gov/pubs2012/2012002.pdf

Robinson, M. (1998). "Burglary revictimization: The time period of heightened risk." *British Journal of Criminology* 38:78–87.

Robinson, M.B. (2011). *Media Coverage of Crime and Criminal Justice*. Durham, NC: Carolina Academic Press.

Rodgers, A. and S. Dunsmuir (2015). "A controlled evaluation of the 'FRIENDS for Life' emotional resiliency programme on overall anxiety levels, anxiety subtype levels and school adjustment." *Child and Adolescent Mental Health* 20:13–19.

Rodriguez, N. (2005). "Restorative justice, communities, and delinquency: Whom do we reintegrate?" *Criminology & Public Policy* 4:103–130.

Roehl, J.A. and R.F. Cook (1982). "The neighborhood justice centers field test." In Tomasic, R. and M.M. Feeley (eds.), *Neighborhood Justice: Assessment of an Emerging Idea*. New York: Longman.

Roehl, J.A. and R.F. Cook (1984). *Evaluation of the Urban Crime Prevention Program: Executive Summary*. Washington, DC: National Institute of Justice.

Roehl, J.A., H. Wong, R. Huitt, and G.E. Capowich (1995). *A National Assessment of Community-based Anti-drug Initiatives: Final Report*. Pacific Grove, CA: Institute for Social Analysis.

Rogers, C. (2013). "Alley-gates in urban South Wales: Six years down the road. *Crime Prevention and Community Safety* 15:106–126.

Rosenbaum, D.P. (1987). "The theory and research behind neighborhood watch: Is it sound fear and crime reduction strategy?" *Crime & Delinquency* 33:103–134.

Rosenbaum, D.P (1988). "Community crime prevention: Review and synthesis of the literature." *Justice Quarterly* 5:323–396.

Rosenbaum, D.P (2002). "Evaluating multi-agency anti-crime partnerships: Theory, design and measurement issues." In Tilley, N. (ed.), *Evaluation for Crime Prevention*. Monsey, NY: Criminal Justice Press.

Rosenbaum, D.P, R.L. Flewelling, S.L. Bailey, C.L. Ringwalt, and D.L. Wilkinson (1994). "Cops in the classroom: A longitudinal evaluation of Drug Abuse Resistance Education (DARE)." *Journal of Research in Crime and Delinquency* 31:3–31.

Rosenbaum, D.P. and G.S. Hanson (1998). "Assessing the effects of school-based drug education: A six-year multilevel analysis of project D.A.R.E." *Journal of Research in Crime and Delinquency* 35:381–412.

Rosenbaum, D.P. and S.L. Kaminska-Costello (1998). *Salt Lake City's Comprehensive Communities Program: A Case Study*. Washington, DC: BOTEK Analysis Corporation.

Rosenbaum, D.P., P.J. Lavrakas, D.L. Wilkinson, and D. Faggiani (1997). *Community Responses to Drug Abuse National Demonstration Program: An Impact Evaluation*. Washington, DC: National Institute of Justice.

Rosenbaum, D.P., D.A. Lewis, and J.A. Grant (1985). *The Impact of Community Crime Prevention Programs in Chicago: Can Neighborhood Organizations Make a Difference?* Evanston, IL: Northwestern University.

Rosenbaum, D.P., D.A. Lewis, and J.A. Grant (1986). "Neighborhood-based crime prevention: Assessing the efficacy of community organizing in Chicago." In Rosenbaum, D.P. (ed.), *Community Crime Prevention: Does It Work?* Beverly Hills, CA: Sage.

Rosenbaum, D.P., A.J. Lurigio, and P.J. Lavrakas (1989). "Enhancing citizen participation and solving serious crime: A national evaluation of Crime Stoppers programs." *Crime & Delinquency* 35:401–420.

Rosenbaum, D.P. and J. Roehl (2010). "Building successful anti-violence partnerships: Lessons from the strategic approaches to community safety initiative (SACSI)." In Klofas, J.M., N.K Hipple, and E.F. McGarrell (eds.), *The New Criminal Justice: American Communities and the Changing World of Crime Control*. New York: Routledge.

Ross, H.L. (1982). "Interrupted time series studies of deterrence of drinking and driving." In Hagan, J. (ed.), *Deterrence Reconsidered: Methodological Innovations*. Beverly Hills, CA: Sage.

Rossman, S.B., J.B. Willison, D. Mallik-Kane, K. Kim, S. Debus-Sherrill, and P.M. Downey (2012). *Criminal Justice Interventions for Offenders with Mental Illness: Evaluation of Mental Health Courts in Bronx and Brooklyn, New York*. Retrieved from https://www.ncjrs.gov/pdffiles1/nij/grants/238264.pdf

Rossman, S.B. and J.M. Zweig (2012). *The Multisite Adult Drug Court Evaluation*. National Association of Drug Court Professionals. Retrieved from http://nadcp.org/sites/default/files/nadcp/Multisite%20 Adult%20Drug%20Court%20Evaluation%20-%20NADCP.pdf

Roundtree, P.W. (1998). "A reexamination of the crime fear linkage." *Journal of Research in Crime and Delinquency* 35:341–372.

Rubel, R.J. (1989). "Cooperative school system and police responses to high risk and disruptive youth." *Violence, Aggression and Terrorism* 3:295–325.

Rubenstein, H., C. Murray, T. Motoyama, and W.V. Wourse (1980). *The Link Between Crime and the Built Environment: The Current State of Knowledge*. Washington, DC: National Institute of Justice.

Sacco, V.F. and M. Trotman (1990). "Public information programming and family violence: Lessons from the mass media crime prevention experience." *Canadian Journal of Criminology* 32:91–105.

Sadd, S. and R. Grinc (1994). "Innovative neighborhood oriented policing: An evaluation of community policing programs in eight cities." In Rosenbaum, D.P. (ed.), *The Challenge of Community Policing: Testing the Promises*. Thousand Oaks, CA: Sage.

Sadd, S. and R. Grinc (1996). "Implementation challenges in community policing: Innovative neighborhood-oriented policing in eight cities." *NIJ Research in Brief*. Washington, DC: U.S. Department of Justice.

Saltzman, L., R. Paternoster, G.P. Waldo, and T.G. Chiricos (1982). "Deterrent and experiential effects: The problem of causal order in perceptual deterrence research." *Journal of Research in Crime and Delinquency* 19:172–189.

SAMHSA (2012). *Incredible Years*. http://www.nrepp.samhsa.gov/ViewIntervention.aspx?id=93#std174

SAMHSA (2014). *Results from the 2013 National Survey on Drug Use and Health: Detailed Tables.* Washington, DC: U.S. Department of Health and Human Services.

Samples, F. and L. Aber (1998). "Evaluations of school-based violence prevention programs." In Elliott, D.S., D.P. Farrington, and K.R. Williams (eds.), *Violence in American Schools.* Cambridge: Cambridge University Press.

Sampson, R. and J.E. Eck (2008). "Super controllers: Can I be your superman?" Paper presented at the POP Conference. Retrieved from http://www.popcenter.org/conference/conferencepapers/2008/supercontrollers.pdf

Sampson, R., J.E. Eck, and J. Dunham (2010). "Super controllers and crime prevention: A routine activity explanation of crime prevention success and failure." *Security Journal* 23:37–51.

Sampson, R.J. (1986). "Crime in cities: the effects of formal and informal social control." In Reiss, A.J. and M. Tonry (eds.), *Communities and Crime. Crime and Justice*, vol. 8. Chicago: University of Chicago Press.

Sampson, R.J. and J.H. Laub (1993). "Crime in the making: Pathways and turning points through life." Cambridge: Harvard University Press.

Sampson, R.J. and J. Lauritsen (1994). "Violent victimization and offending: Individual-, situational-, and community-level risk factors." In Reiss, A.J. and J.A. Roth (eds.), *Understanding and Preventing Violence, Vol. 3: Social Influences.* Washington, DC: National Academy Press.

Saville, G. and G. Cleveland (2003). "An introduction to 2nd generation CPTED: Parts 1 and 2." *CPTED Perspectives* 6(1):7–9; 6(2):4–8.

Schafer, W.E., C. Olexa, and K. Polk (1971). "Programmed for social class: Tracking in high school." In Polk, K. and W.E. Schafer (eds.), *Schools and Delinquency.* Englewood Cliffs, NJ: Prentice Hall.

Schafer, W.E. and K. Polk (1967). "Delinquency and the schools." In *President's Commission on Law Enforcement and the Administration of Justice. Task Force Report: Juvenile Delinquency and Youth Crime.* Washington, DC: U.S. Government Printing Office.

Schaps, E., J.M. Moskowitz, J.H. Malvin, and G.A. Schaeffer (1986). "Evaluation of seven school-based prevention programs: A final report of the Napa project." *International Journal of the Addictions* 21:1081–1112.

Scheff, T.J. (1966). *Being Mentally Ill: A Sociological Theory.* Chicago: Aldine Press.

Scheff, T.J. (1967). *Mental Illness and the Social Processes.* New York: Harper and Row.

Scherdin, M.J. (1986). "The halo effect: Psychological deterrence of electronic security systems." *Information Technology and Libraries* (Sept.):232–235.

Schiff, A. (1999). "The impact of restorative interventions on juvenile offenders." In Bazemore, G. and L. Walgrave (eds.), *Restorative Juvenile Justice: Repairing the Harm of Youth Crime.* Monsey, NY: Criminal Justice Press.

Schlossman, S. and M. Sedlak (1983). *The Chicago Area Project Revisited.* Santa Monica, CA: RAND.

Schmidt, A. (1986). "Electronic monitors." *Federal Probation* 50(2):56–59.

Schweinhart, L.J. (1987). "Can preschool programs help prevent delinquency?" In Wilson, J.Q. and G.C. Lowrey (eds.), *From Children to Citizens, Vol. 3: Families, Schools and Delinquency Prevention.* New York: Springer-Verlag.

Schweinhart, L.J., H.V. Barnes, and D.P. Weikart (1993). *Significant Benefits.* Ypsilanti, MI: High/Scope Press.

Schweinhart, L.J. and D.P. Weikart (1989). "Early childhood experience and its effects." In Bond, L.A. and B.E. Compas (eds.), *Primary Prevention and Promotion in the Schools*. Newbury Park, CA: Sage.

Schweinhart, L.J. and Z. Xiang (2003). "Evidence that the High/Scope Perry Preschool program prevents adult crime." Paper presented at the American Society of Criminology Annual Meeting, Denver, CO.

Schwitzgebel, R.K., R.L. Schwitzgebel, W.N. Pahnke, and W.S. Hurd (1964). "A program of research in behavioral electronics." *Behavioral Science* 9:233–238.

Scott, M.S. (2006). "Implementing crime prevention: Lessons learned from problem-oriented policing projects." In Knutsson, J. and R.V. Clarke (eds.), *Putting Theory to Work: Implementing Situational Prevention and Problem-Oriented Policing*. Monsey, NY: Criminal Justice Press.

Seattle Law and Justice Planning Office (1975). *Evaluation Report: Target Hardening*. Washington, DC: Law Enforcement Assistance Administration.

Sechrest, L., S.O. White, and E.D. Brown (1979). *The Rehabilitation of Criminal Offenders: Problems and Prospects*. Washington, DC: National Academy Press.

Segato, L. (2012). "Packaging against counterfeiting." In Ekblom, P. (ed.), *Design Against Crime: Crime Proofing Everyday Products*. Boulder, CO: Lynne Rienner.

Shadish, W., T. Cook and D. Campbell (2002). *Experimental and Quasi-experimental Designs for Generalized Causal Inference*. Boston: Houghton Mifflin.

Shah, S.A. and L.H. Roth (1974). "Biological and psychophysiological factors in criminality." In Glaser, D., (ed.), *Handbook of Criminology*. Chicago: Rand-McNally.

Shannon, L.W. (1991). *Changing Patterns of Delinquency and Crime: A Longitudinal Study in Racine*. Boulder, CO: Westview.

Shapland, J. (1988). "Policing with the public?" In Hope, T. and M. Shaw (eds.), *Communities and Crime Reduction*. London: Her Majesty's Stationery Office.

Shaw, C.R. and H.D. McKay (1931). *Social Factors in Juvenile Delinquency*, vol. 2, no. 13. Washington, DC: U.S. Government Printing Office.

Shaw, C.R. and H.D. McKay (1942). *Juvenile Delinquency in Urban Areas*. Chicago: University of Chicago Press.

Sheley, J.F., Z.T. McGee, and J.D. Wright (1995). *Weapon-related Victimization in Selected Inner-city High School Samples*. Washington, DC: National Institute of Justice.

Sheley, J.F. and J.D. Wright (1995). *In the Line of Fire: Youth, Guns and Violence in Urban America*. New York: Aldine de Gruyter.

Shepherd, J.M. (2004). "Murders of passion, execution delays and the deterrence of capital punishment." *Journal of Legal Studies* 33:283–322.

Shepherd, J.M. (2005). "Deterrence versus brutalization: Capital punishment's differing impacts among states." *Michigan Law Review* 104:203–255.

Sherizan, S. (1978). "Social creation of crime news: All the news fitted to print." In Winick, C. (ed.), *Deviance and Mass Media*. Beverly Hills, CA: Sage.

Sherman, L.W. (1990). "Police crackdowns: Initial and residual deterrence." In Tonry, M. and N. Morris (eds.), *Crime and Justice*, vol. 12. Chicago: University of Chicago Press.

Sherman, L.W. (1995). "Hot spots of crime and criminal careers of places." In Eck, J.E. and D. Weisburd (eds.), *Crime and Place*. Monsey, NY: Criminal Justice Press.

Sherman, L.W. and R.A. Berk (1984). "The specific deterrent effect of arrest for domestic assault." *American Sociological Review* 49:261–272.

Sherman, L.W., D.P. Farrington, B.C. Welsh, and D.L. MacKenzie (2002). *Evidence-based Crime Prevention.* New York: Routledge.

Sherman, L.W., P.R. Garten, and M.E. Buerger (1989). "Hot spots of predatory crime: Routine activities and the criminology of place." *Criminology* 27:27–56.

Sherman, L.W., D.C. Gottfredson, D.L. MacKenzie, J. Eck, P. Reuter, and S.D. Bushway (1997). *Preventing Crime: What Works, What Doesn't, What's Promising.* Washington, DC: National Institute of Justice.

Sherman, L.W., D.C. Gottfredson, D.L. MacKenzie, J. Eck, P. Reuter, and S.D. Bushway (1998). "Preventing crime: What works, what doesn't, what's promising." *Research in Brief.* Washington, DC: National Institute of Justice.

Sherman, L.W. and D.P. Rogan (1995). "Effects of gun seizures on gun violence: 'Hot spots' patrol in Kansas City." *Justice Quarterly* 12:673–694.

Sherman, L.W. and D. Weisburd (1995). "General deterrent effects of police patrol in crime 'hot spots': A randomized, controlled trial." *Justice Quarterly* 12:625–648.

Shernock, S.K. (1986). "A profile of the citizen crime prevention activist." *Journal of Criminal Justice* 14:211–228.

Short, J.F. and F.L. Strodbeck (1965). *Group Process and Gang Delinquency.* Chicago: University of Chicago Press.

Shover, N. (1991). "Burglary." In Tonry, M. (ed.), *Crime and Justice: A Review of Research*, vol. 14. Chicago: University of Chicago Press.

Sickmund, M., T.J. Sladky, W. Kang, and C. Puzzanchera (2013). "Easy access to the census of juveniles in residential placement." Retrieved from http://www.ojjdp.gov/ojstatbb/ezacjrp/

Sidebottom, A., P. Guillaume, and T. Archer (2012). "Supermarket carts to reduce handbag theft." In Ekblom, P. (ed.), *Design Against Crime: Crime Proofing Everyday Products.* Boulder, CO: Lynne Rienner.

Silloway, G., and M. McPherson (1985). "The limits to citizen participation in a government-sponsored crime prevention program." Paper presented at the American Society of Criminology Annual Meeting.

Simpson, D.D. and S.B. Sells (1982). *Highlights of the DARP Follow-up Research on the Evaluation of Drug Abuse Treatment Effectiveness.* Washington, DC: National Institute on Drug Abuse.

Skogan, W.G. (1981). "On attitudes and behaviors." In Lewis, D.P. (ed.), *Reactions to crime.* Beverly Hills, CA: Sage.

Skogan, W.G. (1987). "The impact of victimization on fear." *Crime & Delinquency* 33:135–154.

Skogan, W.G. (1988). "Community organizations and crime." In Tonry, M. and N. Morris (eds.), *Crime and Justice*, vol. 10. Chicago: University of Chicago Press.

Skogan, W.G. (1989). "Communities, crime, and neighborhood organization." *Crime & Delinquency* 35:437–357.

Skogan, W.G. (1990). *Disorder and Decline: Crime and the Spiral of Decay in American Neighborhoods.* New York: Free Press.

Skogan, W.G. (1995). "Community policing in Chicago: Year two." *NIJ Research Preview.* Washington, DC: U.S. Department of Justice.

Skogan, W.G. (1996). "The community's role in community policing." *NIJ Journal* 231:31–34.

Skogan. W.G. and K. Frydl (eds.), Committee on Law and Justice, Division of Behavioral and Social Sciences and Education, National Research Council (2004). *Fairness and Effectiveness in Policing: The Evidence.* Washington, DC: National Academies Press.

Skogan. W.G. and S.M. Hartnett (1997). *Community Policing: Chicago Style.* New York: Oxford University Press.

Skogan, W.G. and A.J. Lurigio (1992). "The correlates of community antidrug activism." *Crime & Delinquency* 38:510–521.

Skogan, W.G. and M.G. Maxfield (1981). *Coping with Crime: Individual and Neighborhood Reactions.* Beverly Hills, CA: Sage.

Skogan, W.G. and M.A. Wycoff (1986). "Storefront police offices: The Houston field test." In Rosenbaum, D.P. (ed.), *Community Crime Prevention: Does It Work?* Beverly Hills, CA: Sage.

Skolnick, J.H. and D.H. Bayley (1988). "Theme and variation in community policing." In Tonry, M. and M. Morris (eds.), *Crime and Justice,* vol. 10. Chicago: University of Chicago Press.

Slater, M.D., K.J. Kelly, F.R. Lawrence, L.R. Stanley, and M.L.G. Comello (2011). "Assessing media campaigns linking marijuana non-use with autonomy and aspirations: 'Be Under Your own Influence' and ODNCP's 'Above the Influence'." *Prevention Science* 12:12–22.

Sloan-Howitt, M. and G. Kelling (1990). "Subway graffiti in New York City: 'getting' up' vs. 'meaning it and cleaning it'." *Security Journal* 1:131–136.

Smith, B.E. and R.C. Davis (1998). "What do landlords think about drug abatement laws?" In Mazerolle, L.G. and J. Roehl (eds.), *Civil Remedies and Crime Prevention.* Monsey, NY: Criminal Justice Press.

Smith, C. and T.P. Thornberry (1995). "The relationship between childhood maltreatment and adolescent involvement in delinquency." *Criminology* 33:451–481.

Smith, C.J. and G.E. Patterson (1980). "Cognitive mapping and the subjective geography of crime." In Georges-Abeyie, D.E. and K.D. Harries (eds.), *Crime: A Spatial Perspective.* New York: Columbia University Press.

Smith, D.R. and G.R. Jarjoura (1988). "Social structure and criminal victimization." *Journal of Research in Crime and Delinquency* 25:27–52.

Smith, G.B and S.P. Lab (1991). "Urban and rural attitudes toward participating in an auxiliary policing crime prevention program." *Criminal Justice and Behavior* 18:202–216.

Smith, M.J., R.V. Clarke, and K. Pease (2002). "Anticipatory benefits in crime prevention." In N. Tilley (ed.), *Analysis for Crime Prevention.* Monsey, NY: Criminal Justice Press.

Smith, W.R. and M. Torstensson (1997). "Gender differences in risk perception and neutralizing fear of crime: Toward resolving the paradoxes." *British Journal of Criminology* 37:608–634.

Snook, B. (2004). "Individual differences in distance travelled by serial burglars." *Journal of Investigative Psychology and Offender Profiling* 1:53–66.

Social Development Research Group (SDRG) (2012). http://www.sdrg.org

Sorenson, J., R. Wrinkle, V. Brewer, and J. Marquart (1999). "Capital punishment and deterrence: Examining the effect of executions on murder in Texas." *Crime & Delinquency* 45:481–493.

Sorenson, S.L. (1998). "Empowering capable guardians in high crime and low income settings." *Security Journal* 11:29–35.

Spelman, W. (1993). "Abandoned buildings: Magnets for crime?" *Journal of Criminal Justice* 21:481–296.

Spelman, W. (1995). "Criminal careers of public places." In Eck, J.E. and D. Weisburd (eds.), *Crime and Place*. Monsey, NY: Criminal Justice Press.

Spergel, I.A., K.M. Wa, and R.V. Sosa (2001). *Evaluation of the Bloomington-Normal Comprehensive Gang Program. Final Report*. Washington, DC: Office of Juvenile Justice and Delinquency Prevention.

Spergel, I.A., K.M. Wa, and R.V. Sosa (2002). *Evaluation of the Mesa Gang Intervention Program (MGIP). Final Report*. Washington, DC: Office of Juvenile Justice and Delinquency Prevention.

Spergel, I.A., K.M. Wa, and R.V. Sosa (2003). *Evaluation of the Riverside Comprehensive Community-wide Approach to Gang Prevention, Intervention and Suppression. Final Report*. Washington, DC: Office of Juvenile Justice and Delinquency Prevention.

Spergel, I.A., K.M. Wa, and R.V. Sosa (2004a). *Evaluation of the Tucson Comprehensive Community-wide Approach to Gang Prevention, Intervention and Suppression. Final Report*. Washington, DC: Office of Juvenile Justice and Delinquency Prevention.

Spergel, I.A., K.M. Wa, and R.V. Sosa (2004b). *Evaluation of the San Antonio Comprehensive Community-wide Approach to Gang Prevention, Intervention and Suppression. Final Report*. Washington, DC: Office of Juvenile Justice and Delinquency Prevention.

Spohn, C., R.K. Piper, T. Martin, and E.D. Frenzel (2001). "Drug courts and recidivism: The results of an evaluation using two comparison groups and multiple indicators of recidivism." *Journal of Drug Issues* 31:149–176.

Stacey, T. (2006). "Electronic tagging of offenders: A global view." *International Review of Law Computers and Technology* 20:117–121.

Stafford, M. and M. Warr (1993). "A reconceptualization of general and specific deterrence." *Journal of Research in Crime and Delinquency* 30:123–135.

Stallard, P., N. Simpson, S. Anderson, T. Carter, C. Osborn, and S. Bush (2005). "An evaluation of the FRIENDS programme: A cognitive behavior therapy intervention to promote emotional resilience." *Archives of Disease in Childhood* 90:1016–1019.

State of Victoria Department of Sustainability and Environment (2005). *Safe Design Guidelines for Victoria*. East Melbourne: Department of Sustainability and Environment.

Stead, P.J. (1983). *The Police of France*. New York, NY: Macmillan.

Stempl, G. (1962). "Content patterns of small metropolitan dailies." *Public Opinion Quarterly* 39:88–90.

Stephens, R.C. (1987). *Mind-Altering Drugs: Use, Abuse, and Treatment*. Newbury Park, CA: Sage.

Stickle, W.P., N.M. Connell, D.M. Wilson, and D. Gottfredson (2008). "An experimental evaluation of teen courts." *Journal of Experimental Criminology* 4:137–163.

Stott, M. (1967). "A content comparison of two evening network television programs with four morning Ohio daily newspapers". Master's thesis, The Ohio State University.

Stouthamer-Loeber, M. and R. Loeber (1989). "The use of prediction data in understanding delinquency." In Bond, L.A. and B.E. Compas (eds.), *Primary Prevention and Promotion in the Schools*. Newbury Park, CA: Sage.

Strickland, R.A. (2004). *Restorative Justice*. New York: Peter Lang.

Stuart, B. (1996). "Circle sentencing: Turning swords into ploughshares." In B. Galaway and J. Hudson (eds.), *Restorative Justice: International Perspectives*. Monsey, NY: Criminal Justice Press.

Surette, R. (1992). *Media, Crime and Criminal Justice: Images and Realities*. Pacific Grove, CA: Brooks/Cole.

Surette, R. (1998). *Media, Crime and Criminal Justice: Images and Realities*, Second Edition. Pacific Grove, CA: Brooks/Cole.

Sutton, M. (1996). *Implementing Crime Prevention Schemes in a Multi-agency Setting: Aspects of Process in the Safer Cities Programme*. London: Home Office Research and Statistics Directorate.

Swadi, H. and H. Zeitlin (1987). "Drug education to school children: Does it really work?" *British Journal of Addiction* 82:741–746.

Swartz, J.A., A.J. Lurigio, and S.A. Slomka (1996). "The impact of IMPACT: An assessment of the effectiveness of a jail-based treatment program." *Crime & Delinquency* 42:553–573.

Synovate (2007). *Federal Trade Commission: 2006 Identity Theft Survey Report*. McLean, VA: Synovate.

Tay, R. (2005). "The effectiveness of enforcement and publicity campaigns on serious crashes involving young male drivers: Are drink driving and speeding similar?" *Accident Analysis and Prevention* 37:922–929.

Taylor, B., C.S. Koper, and D.J. Woods (2011). "A randomized controlled trial of different policing strategies at hot spots of violent crime." *Journal of Experimental Criminology* 7:149–181.

Taylor, D.G., R.P. Taub, and B.L. Peterson (1987). "Crime, community organization, and causes of neighborhood decline." In Figlio, R.M., S. Hakim, and G.F. Rengert (eds.), *Metropolitan Crime Patterns*. Monsey, NY: Criminal Justice Press.

Taylor, M. and C. Nee (1988). "The role of cues in simulated residential burglary." *British Journal of Criminology* 28:396–407.

Taylor, R.B. (1988). *Human Territorial Functioning*. New York: Cambridge University Press.

Taylor, R.B. (1997). "Crime, grime and responses to crime: Relative impacts of neighborhood structure, crime, and physical deterioration on residents and business personnel in the twin cities." In Lab, S.P. (ed.), *Crime Prevention at a Crossroads*. Cincinnati, OH: Anderson Publishing Co.

Taylor, R.B. and S. Gottfredson (1986). "Environmental design, crime, and prevention: An examination of community dynamics." In Reiss, A.J. and M. Tonry (eds.), *Communities and Crime*. Chicago: University of Chicago Press.

Taylor, R.B., B.A. Koons, E.M. Kurtz, J.R. Greene, and D.D. Perkins (1995). "Street blocks with more nonresidential land use have more physical deterioration: Evidence from Baltimore and Philadelphia." *Urban Affairs Review* 31:120–136.

Teedon, P., T. Reid, P. Griffiths, K. Lindsay, S. Glen, A. McFadyen, and P. Cruz (2009) *Secured By Design Impact Evaluation: Key Findings*. Glasgow: Caledonian Environment Centre.

Teedon, P., T. Ried, P. Griffiths, and A. McFayden (2010). "Evaluating Secured by Design door and window installations." *Crime Prevention and Community Safety* 12:246–262.

Telch, M.J., J.D. Killen, A.L. McAlister, C.L. Perry, and N. Macoby (1982). "Long-term follow-up of a pilot project on smoking prevention with adolescents." *Journal of Behavioral Medicine* 5:1–8.

Telep, C.W., R.J. Mitchell, and D. Weisburd (2014). "How much time should the police spend at crime hot spots?: Answers from a police agency directed randomized field trial in Sacramento, California." *Justice Quarterly* 31:905–933.

Thistlethwaite, A., J. Wooldredge, and D. Gibbs (1998). "Severity of dispositions and domestic violence recidivism." *Crime & Delinquency* 44:388–398.

Thornberry, T.P. (1998). "Membership in youth gangs and involvement in serious and violent offending." In Loeber, R. and D.P. Farrington (eds.), *Serious and Violent Juvenile Offenders: Risk Factors and Successful Interventions*. Thousand Oaks, CA: Sage.

Thornberry, T.P., D. Huizinga, and R. Loeber (1995). "The prevention of serious delinquency and violence: Implications from the program of research on the causes and correlates of delinquency." In Howell, J.C., B. Krisberg, J.D. Hawkins, and J.J. Wilson (eds.), *Sourcebook on Serious, Violent, and Chronic Juvenile Offenders.* Thousand Oaks, CA: Sage.

Thornberry, T.P., M.D. Krohn, A.J. Lizotte, and D. Chard-Wierschem (1993). "The role of juvenile gangs in facilitating delinquent behavior." *Journal of Research in Crime and Delinquency* 30:55–87.

Thornberry, T.P., A.J. Lizotte, M.D. Krohn, M. Farnsworth, and S.J. Jang (1994). "Delinquent peers, beliefs, and delinquent behavior: A longitudinal test of interactional theory." *Criminology* 32:47–84.

Thornberry, T.P., M. Moore, and R.L. Christiansen (1985). "The effect of dropping out of high school on subsequent criminal behavior." *Criminology* 23:3–18.

Thorpe, A., S.D. Johnson, and A. Sidebottom (2012). "Designing against bicycle theft." In Ekblom, P. (ed.) *Design Against Crime: Crime Proofing Everyday Products.* Boulder, CO: Lynne Rienner.

Tien, J.M., V.F. O'Donnell, A.I. Barnett, and P.B. Mirchondani (1977). *Street Lighting Projects: National Evaluation Program, Phase I Summary Report.* Washington, DC: National Institute of Law Enforcement and Criminal Justice.

Tierney, J. (2001). "Audits of crime and disorder: Some lessons from research." *Crime Prevention and Community Safety: An International Journal* 3(2):7–18.

Tilley, N. (1992). "Safer cities and community safety strategies." *Crime Prevention Unit Paper 38.* London: Home Office.

Tilley, N. (1993). *Understanding Car Parks, Crime and CCTV: Evaluation Lessons from Safer Cities.* London: Home Office Police Research Group.

Tilley, N. (2002). "Introduction: Evaluation for crime prevention." In Tilley, N. (ed.), *Analysis for Crime Prevention.* Monsey, NY: Criminal Justice Press.

Tilley, N. (2004). "Using crackdowns constructively." In Hopkins Burke, R. (ed.), *Hard Cop, Soft Cop.* Cullompton, Devon, U.K.: Willan.

Tilley, N. (2005). "Introduction: Thinking realistically about crime prevention." In Tilley, N. (ed.), *Handbook of Crime Prevention and Community Safety.* Portland, OR: Willan.

Tilley, N. (2009). *Crime Prevention.* Cullompton, Devon, U.K.: Willan.

Tilley, N. and J. Webb (1994). *Burglary Reduction: Findings from Safer Cities Schemes.* London: Home Office Police Research Group.

Tita, G.E., K. J. Riley, G. Ridgeway, and P.W. Greenwood (2005). *Reducing Gun Violence: Operation Ceasefire in Los Angeles.* Washington, DC: National Institute of Justice.

Tittle, C.R. (1969). "Crime rates and legal sanctions." *Social Problems* 16:408–423.

Tittle, C.R. and A.R. Rowe (1974). "Certainty of arrest and crime rates: A further test of the deterrence hypothesis." *Social Forces* 52:455–462.

Titus, R.M. (1984). "Residential burglary and the community response." In Clarke, R. and T. Hope (eds.), *Coping with Burglary: Research Perspectives on Policy.* Boston: Kluwer-Nijhoff.

Tobler, N.S. (1986). "Meta-analysis of 143 adolescent drug prevention programs: Quantitative outcome results of program participants compared to a control or comparison group." *Journal of Drug Issues* 16:537–567.

Tolan, P.H., D.B Henry, M.S. Schoeny, P. Lovegrove, and E. Nichols (2014). "Mentoring programs to affect delinquency and associated outcomes of youth at risk: A comprehensive meta-analytic review." *Journal Experimental Criminology* 10:179–206.

Tonry, M. (2008). "Learning from the limitations of deterrence research." In Tonry, M. (ed.), *Crime and Justice: A Review of Research*. Chicago: University of Chicago Press.

Tonry, M. and D.P. Farrington (1995). "Strategic approaches to crime prevention." In Tonry, M. and D.P. Farrington (eds.), *Building a Safer Society: Strategic Approaches to Crime Prevention*. Chicago: University of Chicago Press.

Toseland, R.W. (1982). "Fear of crime: Who is most vulnerable?" *Journal of Criminal Justice* 10:199–210.

Townsley, M. and K. Pease (2002). "Hot spots and cold comfort: The importance of having a working thermometer." In Tilley, N. (ed.), *Analysis for Crime Prevention*. Monsey, NY: Criminal Justice Press.

Travis, L.F. and J.K. Coon (2005). *The Role of Law Enforcement in Public School Safety: A National Survey*. Washington, DC: National Institute of Justice.

Tremblay, P. (2008). "Convergence settings for non-predatory 'boy lovers'." In Wortley, R. and S. Smallbone (eds.), *Situational Prevention of Child Sexual Abuse*. Monsey, NY: Criminal Justice Press.

Tremblay, R.E. and W.M. Craig (1997). "Developmental juvenile delinquency prevention." *European Journal on Criminal Policy and Research* 5(2):33–49.

Trojanowicz, R. (1983). *An Evaluation of the Neighborhood Foot Patrol Program in Flint, Michigan*. East Lansing: Michigan State University.

Trojanowicz, R. and B. Bucqueroux (1989). *Community Policing: A Contemporary Perspective*. Cincinnati, OH: Anderson Publishing Co.

Troyer, R.J. and R.D. Wright (1985). "Community response to crime: Two middle-class anti-crime patrols." *Journal of Criminal Justice* 13:227–242.

Truman, J.L. and L. Langton (2014). *Criminal Victimization, 2013*. Washington, DC: Bureau of Justice Statistics.

Tunnell, K.D. (1992). *Choosing Crime: The Criminal Calculus of Property Offenders*. Chicago: Nelson-Hall.

Turner, S., J. Petersilia, and E.P. Deschenes (1992). "Evaluating intensive supervision probation/parole (ISP) for drug offenders." *Crime & Delinquency* 38:539–556.

U.K. Office of Fair Trading (2006). *Research on Impact of Mass Marketed Scams: A Summary of Research into the Impact of Scams on UK Consumers*. London: Office of Fair Trading.

Umbreit, M.S. (1999). "Avoiding the marginalization and 'McDonaldization' of victim–offender mediation: A case study of moving toward the mainstream." In Bazemore, G. and L. Walgrave (eds.), *Restorative Juvenile Justice: Repairing the Harm of Youth Crime*. Monsey, NY: Criminal Justice Press.

Umbreit, M.S. and R.B. Coates (1993). "Cross-site analysis of victim offender mediation in four states." *Crime & Delinquency* 39:565–585.

Umbreit, M.S., R.B. Coates, and B. Vos (2001). *Juvenile Victim Offender Mediation in Six Oregon Counties*. Salem: Oregon Dispute Resolution Commission.

Umbreit, M.S., B. Vos, R.B. Coates, and K.A. Brown (2003). *Facing Violence: The Path of Restorative Justice and Dialogue*. Monsey, NY: Criminal Justice Press.

United Nations Interregional Crime and Justice Research Institute (UNICRI) (2011). *Improving Urban Security Through Green Environmental Design*. Retrieved from http://www.unicri.it/news/files/2011-04-01_110414_CRA_Urban_Security_sm.pdf

U.S. Attorney General's Commission on Pornography (1986). *Final Report*. Washington, DC: U.S. Government Printing Office.

van Andel, H. (1989). "Crime prevention that works: The care of public transport in the Netherlands." *British Journal of Criminology* 29:47–56.

Van Daele, S. and T. Vander Beken (2011). "Outbound offending: The journey to crime and crime sprees." *Journal of Environmental Psychology* 31:70–78.

van Dijk, J.M. (1978). "Public attitudes toward crime in the Netherlands." *Victimology* 3:265–273.

van Dijk, J.M. and J. deWaard (1991). "A two-dimensional typology of crime prevention projects." *Criminal Justice Abstracts* 23:483–503.

Van Dine, S., J.P. Conrad, and S. Dinitz (1979). *Restraining the Wicked: The Dangerous Offender Project*. Lexington, MA: Lexington Books.

van Kammen, W.B. and R. Loeber (1994). "Are fluctuations in delinquent activities related to the onset and offset in juvenile illegal drug use and drug dealing?" *Journal of Drug Issues* 24:9–24.

Van Ness, D.W. and K.H. Strong (2015). *Restoring Justice: An Introduction to Restorative Justice*, Fifth Edition. New York: Routledge (Anderson).

van Steden, R., B. van Caem, and H. Boutellier (2011). "The 'hidden strength' of active citizenships: The involvement of local residents in public safety projects." *Criminology and Criminal Justice* 11:433–450.

Vandeviver, C., S. Van Daele, and T. Vander Beken (2015). "What makes long crime trips worth undertaking?: Balancing costs and benefits in burglars' journey to crime." *British Journal of Criminology* 55:399–420.

Vaughn, J.B. (1989). "A survey of juvenile electronic monitoring and home confinement programs." *Juvenile and Family Court Journal* 40:1–36

Velez, M.B. and K. Richardson (2012). "The political economy of neighborhood homicide in Chicago." *British Journal of Criminology* 52:490–513.

Villetaz, P., M. Killias, and I. Zoder (2006). *The Effects of Custodial vs. Noncustodial Sentences on Re-offending: A Systematic Review of the State of the Evidence*. Retrieved from http://campbellcollaboration.org/lib/project/22/

Vinter, R.D. and R.S. Sarri (1965). "Malperformance in the public school: A group work approach." *Social Work* 10:3–13.

Visher, C.A. (1986). "Incapacitation and crime control: Does a 'lock 'em up' strategy reduce crime?" *Justice Quarterly* 4:513–544.

Visher, C.A. (1987). "The Rand inmate survey: A reanalysis." In Blumstein, A., J. Cohen, J.A. Roth, and C.A. Visher (eds.), *Criminal Careers and "Career Criminals."* Washington, DC: National Academy Press.

Visher, C.A. (1990). "Incorporating drug treatment in criminal sanctions." *NIJ Reports No. 221*. Washington, DC: National Institute of Justice.

von Hirsch, A. (2000). "The ethics of public television surveillance." In A. von Hirsch, D. Garland, and A. Wakefield (eds.), *Ethical and Social Perspectives on Situational Crime Prevention*. Oxford: Hart.

Wachtel, T. (1995). "Family group conferencing: Restorative justice in practice." *Juvenile Justice Update* 1(4):1–2, 13–14.

Wagenarr, C., M. Maldonado-Molina, D.J. Ericson, L. Ma, A.L. Tobeler, and K.A. Konro (2007). "General deterrence effects of U.S. statutory DUI fine and jail penalties: Long-term follow-up in 32 states." *Accident Analysis and Prevention* 39:982–994.

Walker, S. (1983). *The Police in America: An Introduction*. New York: McGraw-Hill.

Walker, S. (1985). *Sense and Nonsense About Crime: A Policy Guide*. Monterey, CA: Brooks/Cole.

Walker, S. (1999). *The Police in America: An Introduction*, Third Edition. Boston: McGraw-Hill.

Walklate, S. (1999). "Some questions for and about community safety partnerships and crime." *Crime Prevention and Community Safety: An International Journal* 1(3):7–16.

Waples, S. and M. Gill (2006). "The effectiveness of redeployable CCTV." *Crime Prevention and Community Safety* 8(1):1–16.

Warr, M. (1984). "Fear of victimization: Why are some women and the elderly more afraid?" *Social Science Quarterly* 65:681–702.

Watson, E.M., A.R. Stone, and S.M. DeLuca (1998). *Strategies for Community Policing*. Upper Saddle River, NJ: Prentice Hall.

Weatherburn, D. and S. Moffatt (2011). "The specific deterrent effect of higher fines on drink-driving offenders." *British Journal of Criminology* 51:789–803.

Webb, B. (1994). "Steering column locks and motor vehicle theft: Evaluations from three countries." In Clarke, R.V. (ed.), *Crime Prevention Studies*, vol. 3. Monsey, NY: Criminal Justice Press.

Webster-Stratton, C. (2001). "The Incredible Years: Parent, teacher and child training series." *Blueprints for Violence Prevention*. Boulder: University of Colorado.

Webster-Stratton, C. and M. Hammond (1997). "Treating children with early-onset conduct problems: A comparison of child and parent training interventions." *Journal of Consulting and Clinical Psychology* 65:93–109.

Weidner, R.R. (1996). "Target hardening at a New York City subway station: Decreased fare evasion—at what price?" In Clarke, R.V. (ed.), *Preventing Mass Transit Crime*. Monsey, NY: Criminal Justice Press.

Weis, J.G. (1973). "Delinquency Among the Well-to-do." Ph.D. dissertation. University of California at Berkeley

Weisburd, D., S. Bushway, C. Lum, and S. Yang (2004). "Trajectories of crime at places: A longitudinal study of street segments in the city of Seattle." *Criminology* 42:283–322.

Weisburd, D. and L. Green (1995). "Measuring immediate spatial displacement: Methodological issues and problems." In Eck, J.E. and D. Weisburd (eds.), *Crime and Place*. Monsey, NY: Criminal Justice Press.

Weisburd, D., E.R. Groff, and S. Yang (2012). *The Criminology of Place: Street Segments and Our Understanding of the Crime Problem*. Oxford: Oxford Univ. Press.

Weisburd, D., C. Telep, J. Hinkle, and J. Eck (2010). "Is problem-oriented policing effective in reducing crime and disorder? Findings from a Campbell systematic review." *Criminology and Public Policy* 9:139–172.

Weisburd, D., E. Waring, and E. Chayet (1995). "Specific deterrence in a sample of offenders convicted of white-collar crime." *Criminology* 33:587–607.

Weisburd, D., L.A. Wyckoff, J. Ready, J.E. Eck, J.C. Hinkle, and F. Gajewski (2006). "Does crime just move around the corner? A controlled study of spatial displacement and diffusion of crime control benefits." *Criminology* 44:549–592.

Weisel, D.L. (2005). *Analyzing Repeat Victimization. Problem Oriented Guides for Police*. Washington, DC: Office of Community-Oriented Policing Services.

Weisel, D.L. and J.E. Eck (1994). "Toward a practical approach to organizational change: Community polic-ing initiatives in six cities." In Rosenbaum, D.P. (ed.), *The Challenge of Community Policing: Testing the Promises*. Thousand Oaks, CA: Sage.

Weisheit, R.A. (1983). "The social context of alcohol and drug education: Implications for program evalua-tions." *Journal of Alcohol and Drug Education* 29:72–81.

Weitekamp, E.G.M. (1999). "The history of restorative justice." In Bazemore, G. and L. Walgrave (eds.), *Restorative Juvenile Justice: Repairing the Harm of Youth Crime*. Monsey, NY: Criminal Justice Press.

Weitzer, R. and C.E. Kubrin (2004). "Breaking news: How local TV news and real-world conditions affect fear of crime." *Justice Quarterly* 21:497–520.

Wells, L.E. and J.H. Rankin (1988). "Direct parental controls and delinquency." *Criminology* 26:263–285.

Welsh, B.C. and D.P. Farrington (2009). *Making Public Places Safer: Surveillance and Crime Prevention*. New York: Oxford University Press.

Wermink, H., R. Apel, R. Nieuwbeerta, and A.A.J. Blokland (2013). "The incapacitation effect of first-time imprisonment: A matched samples comparison." *Journal of Quantitative Criminology* 29:579–600.

Wertleib, E.L. (1982). "Juvenile delinquency and the schools: A review of the literature." *Juvenile and Family Court Journal* 33:15–24.

West, D.J. (1973). *Who Becomes Delinquent?* London: Heinemann.

West, D.J. and D.P. Farrington (1973). *The Delinquent Way of Life*. New York: Crane Russack.

West, S.G., J.T. Hepworth, M.A. McCall, and J.W. Reich (1989). "An evaluation of Arizona's July 1982 drunk driving law: Effects on the city of Phoenix." *Journal of Applied Social Psychology* 19:1212–1237.

White, H.R. (1990). "The drug use-delinquency connection in adolescence." In Weisheit, R. (ed.), *Drugs, Crime and the Criminal Justice System*. Cincinnati, OH: Anderson Publishing Co.

White, H.R., R.J. Pandina, and R.L. LaGrange (1987). "Longitudinal predictors of serious substance use and delinquency." *Criminology* 25:715–740.

White, R.C. (1932). "The relation of felonies to environmental factors in Indianapolis." *Social Forces* 10:498–509.

Whitehead, J.T. and S.P. Lab (1989). "A meta-analysis of juvenile correctional treatment." *Journal of Research in Crime and Delinquency* 26:276–295.

White House Office of National Drug Control Policy (2012). *Drug Free Communities Support Program*. http://www.whitehouse.gov/ondcp/Drug-Free-Communities-Support-Program

White House Office of National Drug Control Policy (2015). *Drug Free Communities Support Program*. http://www.whitehouse.gov/ondcp/Drug-Free-Communities-Support-Program

Whitney, I., I. Rivers, P. Smith, and S. Sharp (1994). "The Sheffield project: Methodology and findings." In Smith, P. and S. Sharp (eds.), *School Bullying: Insights and Perspectives*. London: Routledge.

Widom, C.S. (1989). "The cycle of violence." *Science* 244:160–166.

Wilbanks, W.L. (1985). "Predicting failure on parole." In Farrington, D.P. and R. Tarling (eds.), *Prediction in Criminology*. Albany, NY: SUNY Press.

Wilkinson, D.L. and D.P. Rosenbaum (1994). "The effects of organizational structure on community policing: A comparison of two cities." In Rosenbaum, D.P. (ed.), *The Challenge of Community Policing: Testing the Promises*. Thousand Oaks, CA: Sage.

Will, J.A. and J.H. McGrath (1995). "Crime, neighborhood perceptions, and the underclass: The relationship between fear of crime and class position." *Journal of Criminal Justice* 23:163–176.

Williams, F.P. (1983). "Deterrence and social control: Rethinking the relationship." *Journal of Criminal Justice* 13:141–151.

Williams, H. and A.M. Pate (1987). "Returning to first principles: Reducing fear of crime in Newark." *Crime & Delinquency* 33:53–70.

Williams, K.R. and R. Hawkins (1986). "Perceptual research on general deterrence: A critical review." *Law and Society Review* 20:545–572.

Williams, P. and J. Dickinson (1993). "Fear of crime: Read all about it?" *British Journal of Criminology* 33:33–56.

Wilson, J.Q. (1968). *Varieties of Police Behavior.* New York: Harvard University Press.

Wilson, J.Q. and G. Kelling (1982). "Broken windows." *Atlantic Monthly* (March):29–38.

Winge, S. and J. Knutsson (2003). "An evaluation of the CCTV scheme at Oslo central railway station." *Crime Prevention and Community Safety* 5(3):49–59.

Winkel, F.W. (1987). "Response generalization in crime prevention campaigns." *British Journal of Criminology* 27:155–173.

Wolfer, L. (2001). "Strengthening communities: Neighborhood watch and the elderly in a Pennsylvania town." *Crime Prevention and Community Safety: An International Journal* 3(3):31–40.

Wolfgang, M.E., R.M. Figlio, and T. Sellin (1972). *Delinquency in a Birth Cohort.* Chicago: University of Chicago Press.

Wood, E. (1961). *Housing Design, A Social Theory.* New York: Citizens' Housing and Planning Counsel of New York.

World Health Organization (2004). *Prevention of Mental Disorders: Effective Interventions and Policy Options.* Geneva: WHO.

Wortley, R. (1996). "Guilt, shame and situational crime prevention." In Homel, R. (ed.), *The Politics and Practice of Situational Crime Prevention.* Monsey, NY: Criminal Justice Press.

Wortley, R. (2001). "A classification of techniques for controlling situational precipitators of crime." *Security Journal* 14:63–82.

Wortley, R., R. Kane, and F. Gant (1998). "Public awareness and auto-theft prevention: Getting it right for the wrong reason." *Security Journal* 10:59–64.

Wortley, R. and S. Smallbone (2008). "Applying situational principles to sexual offenses against children." In Wortley, R. and S. Smallbone (eds.), *Situational Prevention of Child Sexual Abuse.* Monsey, NY: Criminal Justice Press.

Wright, R., M. Heilweil, P. Pelletier, and K. Dickinson (1974). "The impact of street lighting on street crime." Ann Arbor, MI: University of Michigan.

Wright, R.T. and S.H. Decker (1994). *Burglars on the Job: Streetlife and Residential Break-ins.* Boston: Northeastern University Press.

Wright, W.E. and M.C. Dixon (1977). "Community prevention and treatment of juvenile delinquency." *Journal of Research in Crime and Delinquency* 14:35–67.

Wycoff, M.A. (1995). "Community policing strategies." *NIJ Research Preview.* Washington, DC: U.S. Department of Justice.

Wysong, E., R. Aniskiewicz, and D. Wright (1994). "Truth and DARE: Tracking drug education to graduation and as symbolic politics." *Social Problems* 41:448–472.

Yagerlener, W.G. (1980). *Crime Prevention Project of the Walter P. Reuther Senior Centers.* Washington, DC: National Criminal Justice Reference Service.

Yang, B. and D. Lester (2008). "The deterrent effect of executions: A meta-analysis thirty years after Ehrlich." *Journal of Criminal Justice* 36:453–460.

Yin, R.K., M.E. Vogel, J.M. Chaiken, and D.R. Both (1977). *Citizen Patrol Projects, National Evaluation Program, Phase I Summary Report.* Washington, DC: National Institute of Law Enforcement and Criminal Justice.

Yu, J. and A.E. Liska (1993). "The certainty of punishment: A reference group effect and its functional form." *Criminology* 31:447–464.

Zhao, J.S., B. Lawton, and D. Longmire (2015). "An examination of the micro-level crime-fear of crime link." *Crime & Delinquency* 61:19–44.

Zhao, J.S., M.C. Scheider, and Q. Thurman (2002). "Funding community policing to reduce crime: Have COPS grants made a difference?" *Criminology and Public Policy* 2:7–32.

Zhao, J.S., M.C. Scheider, and Q. Thurman (2003). "A national evaluation of the effect of COPS grants on police productivity (arrests). 1995–1999." *Police Quarterly* 6:387–409.

Zimmer, L. (1987). "Operation Pressure Point: The disruption of street-level drug trade on New York's lower east side." Occasional paper. New York: New York University School of Law.

Zimring, F.E., G. Hawkins, and S. Kamin (2001). *Punishment and Democracy: Three Strikes and You're Out in California.* New York: Oxford University Press.

Ziskin, J. (1970). *Coping with Psychiatric and Psychological Testimony.* Beverly Hills, CA: Sage.

NAME INDEX

SUBJECT INDEX

Note: page numbers in italic type refer to Figures; those in bold type refer to Tables